THREE PAGODAS

THAILAND & BORDERING COUNTRIES

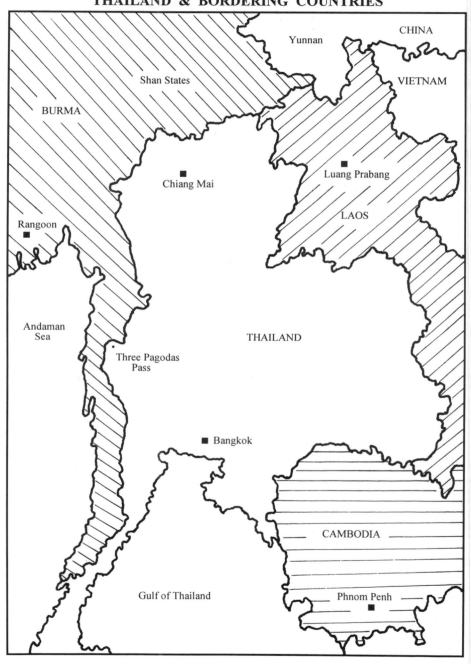

About the author

Christian Goodden, 1949 vintage, grew up in the English county of Suffolk. After completing a modern languages degree at the University of East Anglia (Norwich), he went on to do research at Gonville & Caius College, Cambridge, where he was awarded a Ph.D. in 1977 for a thesis on Austrian literature and thought at the turn of the 19th/20th centuries. In the following eleven years, Dr Goodden lectured in English and translation at the Universities of Cologne, Trier and Basel, publishing at the same time a variety of articles on German and English culture in journals and newspapers. In 1988 he returned to Britain to work as a freelance translator, editor and proofreader, specializing in art, art history, photography and travel. At the same time he started travelling in South-East Asia. A keen photographer and travel writer, he currently divides his time between England and northern Thailand. The author of four books about Thailand, he is currently working on a motorcycle trekking guide and on a volume of photos taken during his travels. He has one daughter.

Also by Christian Goodden

Around Lan-Na: A Guide to Thailand's Northern Border Region from Chiang Mai to Nan

Trek It Yourself in Northern Thailand: Twenty-Five Solo Jungle Treks on Foot & by Motorcycle

Hinterlands: Sixteen New Do-It-Yourself Jungle Treks in Thailand's Nan & Mae Hong Son Provinces

(details – see end of book)

DEDICATION

For the border Karen people in their time of need

In memoriam

WNA Major Kong Mong
Telakhon cultist Toom Yai of Lae Tong Ku
KNLA commander Mor Thaing Chor of Kui Le Toeng

△
△ △

THREE PAGODAS

CHRISTIAN GOODDEN

A JOURNEY DOWN THE THAI-BURMESE BORDER

JUNGLE BOOKS
"BY TRAVELLERS FOR TRAVELLERS"

Published by
JUNGLE BOOKS (HALESWORTH)
England

e-mail: junglebooks2000@hotmail.com

ISBN 0-9527383-4-1

First published in 1996

This second revised & expanded edition issued in 2002

Text and maps © Christian Goodden
Photos © Christian Goodden and Nittaya Tananchai

Printed in Thailand by Darnsutha Press Co. Ltd., Bangkok

Distribution: see page 448

Front cover photo: Journeying south by longtail boat down the River Moei, which here forms the border – Burma and Dawna range (L) & Thailand (R)
Back cover photo: Riding in the Toyota pick-up truck of Baptist Karen Joi-ih through the Burmese jungle between Ti Po Mo and Ti Lai Pa

CONTENTS

LIST OF MAPS

MAP 1: OVERVIEW of JOURNEY

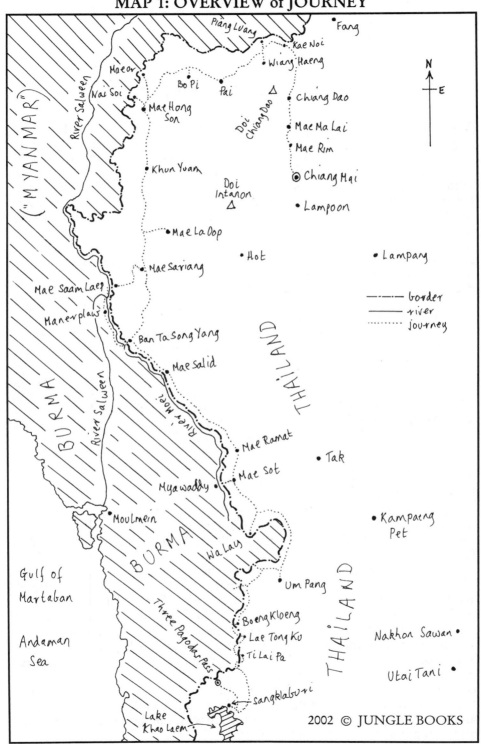

Piang Luang
Fang
Kae Noi
Maeor
Wiang Haeng
Nai Soi
Bo Pi
Pai
Chiang Dao
Mae Hong Son
Doi Chiang Dao △
Chiang Dao
Mae Ma Lai
Mae Rim
Khun Yuam
◎ Chiang Mai
Doi Intanon △
Lampoon
Mae La Oop
Hot
Lampang
Mae Sariang
Mae Saam Laep
----- border
Manerplaw
——— river
Ban Ta Song Yang
········· journey
Mae Salid

THAILAND

River Moei

BURMA

River Salween

Mae Ramat

Tak
Mae Sot
Myawaddy
Moulmein
BURMA
Kampaeng Pet
Wa Lay
THAILAND
Gulf of Martaban
Um Pang
Andaman Sea
Three Pagodas Pass
Boeng Kloeng
Lae Tong Ku
Nakhon Sawan •
Ti Lai Pa
Utai Tani •
Sangklaburi
Lake Khao Laem

("MYANMAR")

River Salween

N
E

2002 © JUNGLE BOOKS

11

ACKNOWLEDGEMENTS

This book would never have been possible without the help of Nittaya 'Daeng' Tananchai, who, when the volume was originally being researched, asked countless questions and facilitated the journey at every turn. I must also mark the forebearance of our Eurasian daughter, Tanya, whom we took with us on some sections of the trip, when the bulk of it was being researched first time round in 1994, even though she was just three years old at the time. She will grow to understand the not insignificant role she played. An infant can slow one down when travelling, but in Thailand can also unlock many doors, and quite especially so in remote and hill-tribe areas. The generous assistance of Doug Boynton and Andrew Wolton, who helped me re-research the journey in the winter of 2000/2001, is acknowledged below, in the preface to the second revised edition of *Three Pagodas*.

Too many people (notably headmen, villagers, forestry personnel and wildlife sanctuary staff) have helped us all in the detailed execution of the travelling both from 1989 to 1994 and 2000/2001 for me to be able to acknowledge them all individually. My sincere gratitude is expressed to them collectively. However, for showing us particular kindness I would like to single out for especial thanks the following: Somsak Suriyamongkol and his staff at Wiang Haeng district office; Pastor Somkiet of Wiang Haeng; Witit Terkae of Chong, Wiang Haeng; WNA Major Ta Kong Mong and his kindly wife Chang Soe of Mae Or; WNO Chairman Maha San and his wife Janoo of Mae Or; Karenni Army commander Jo Lae of Pang Yon; headman Boonyeuan Promsermsook of Mae La Oop; Gen. Bo Mya and Minister Saw Shwi Ya Hae of KNLA GHQ Manerplaw, Burma; Sombat Singharaj of Um Pang; KNLA commander Saw Tae Tu and Than Oo of Sa Kaang Thit, Burma; Thai army commander Kaet Tai Wongsuwan of Nu Po refugee camp; 'Mr Fixit' Sampan and Sooksi of Boeng Kloeng; KNLA commander Saw Kyi Shwi of Mae Ta Ro Ta, Burma; Oh Sae Tae, Toom Yai and the BPP teachers of Lae Tong Ku; KNLA commander Mor Thaing Chor of Kui Le Toeng, Burma; and the incomparable Joi-ih of Ti Po Mo.

The following travellers met with on the trail also deserve a warm *khop khun kap* and *chok dii*: Thorben of Denmark; Mike Batley of London; Peter and Lidya Scheurenberg of Düsseldorf; Béatrice and Didier Dumaine-Chereau of France; and Soeren and Wanida 'Aeao' Skibsted of Denmark. I would further like to thank Stephen and Liz Brough for their help, encouragement and advice during the long realization of the original edition of this book; Sylvia Samms and Richard Gibbens for their patient unstinting efforts printing up the black-and-white photographs for respectively the first and second editions of *Three Pagodas*; and Wichai 'Berm' Tananchai and his wife Jariya 'Poom' both for often looking after daughter Tanya while we were travelling and researching, and for helping us interface with the 'Long-Neck' Padaung and 'Long-Ear' Kayaw people.

Finally, I must record my indebtedness to several authors, on whose works I have drawn extensively – more perhaps than I should have done – in penning the ethnographical, cultural and historical accounts in this volume. Some information is so hard to get that one cannot help but rely on certain key pieces of literature. I refer here to the historian Martin Smith, from whose masterly and compendious *Burma: Insurgency and the Politics of Ethnicity* I have learned a great deal, particularly about the history and politics of the Shan State and of the Karen rebellion; to Col. Kanchana Pragadwootisan, from whose *History of Doi Mae Salong – Ban Santikiri* and *The 93rd Regiment of the Former Nationalist Army in Doi Pa Taang* (both unfortunately still in Thai) I have gleaned much valuable information about the history and movements of the KMT; to Richard K. Diran, whose magnificent and informative *The Vanishing Tribes of Burma* I have raided for data especially on the Padaung, Kayaw, Wa and Mon peoples; and to Joachim Schliesinger, whose *Ethnic Groups of Thailand: Non-Tai-Speaking Peoples* I have also leaned on in describing some of Thailand's and Burma's ethnic minority groups.

PREFACE
TO THE FIRST EDITION

In his books *A Dragon Apparent* (1951) and *Golden Earth* (1952) Norman Lewis wrote that he was visiting Cambodia, Laos, Vietnam and Burma because he wanted to see traditional life there before it changed forever. Also, he foresaw that the incoming repressive xenophobic regimes in the region, embracing Chinese-inspired policies of self-isolation, would soon put these countries beyond the reach of the ordinary traveller. The reasons for visiting Thailand in the 1990s are on the first count not dissimilar, while on the second they could hardly be more different. Traditional life in the kingdom, as elsewhere in South-East Asia, is changing fast and irrevocably, but not because the bamboo curtain is coming down, rather because it is all too rapidly going up. Ancient oriental traditions and lifestyles are being overwhelmed by Western influences, and access, expanding in line with a flourishing tourist industry and comprehensive roadbuilding programme, grows daily easier. Nowhere is this more the case than in Thailand's rural and isolated border areas. One of the aims of *Three Pagodas: A Journey Down the Thai-Burmese Border* is to record something of the impact of these far-reaching changes on the peoples and cultures along the margins, to provide a snapshot of an existence in convulsive transition.

Based on the author's extensive travels in northern Thailand over a period of six years (1989-95), the book is an account of his explorations and adventures in the mountains and jungle of the country's western border with Burma in a 1500-km-long section running from Chiang Dao in the north to the Three Pagodas Pass in the south. *Three Pagodas* is the story of a journey made by motorbike, truck, bus, boat, elephant, and on foot through a swathe of remote volatile border territory, which is home to migrant hill tribes, diverse rare and obscure minority peoples, jungle sects, insurgent guerrilla groups, warlords and heroin traffickers. The book also sets out to show what it is like to make one's way through this remarkable terrain and what life is like for the people living there.

The book grew out of the encouragement of the many friendly travellers the author met 'on the road' who remarked: "if only we had all your information – you should write it up in book form so that others would then be better informed about where to go, what to see, and what it all means". But *Three Pagodas* is not a thoroughgoing guidebook. It is an anecdotal account of people, places and incidents off the beaten track, supplemented where appropriate with background cultural and historical information. Outline route detail and personally researched maps have been included, but they are diagrammatic only and not to scale, intended to illuminate the text. Intrepid independent travellers who choose to use the book and maps as a resource in an attempt to retrace part or all of the journey described do so entirely at their own risk. The author cannot be held liable for anything that may happen to them and hereby explicitly disclaims all responsibility.

In the matter of the transliteration of Thai, Karen and other names, placenames and words in the book, a somewhat simplified spelling has generally been adopted which might most easily lead an English-speaker to correctly pronounce the original word (i.e. a lot of redundant "h's" have been dropped, hence *pratat* instead of the perhaps more correct but rather misleading *phrathat*). The exception to this is with well-established words (e.g. 'Mekhong' whisky, or the Karen HQ of 'Manerplaw'), where it would be churlish to transliterate otherwise.

C. G.
Suffolk, England
1996

PREFACE

TO THE

SECOND REVISED & EXPANDED EDITION

When the first edition of *Three Pagodas* began to sell out in 2000 and a new issue became due, it seemed a good idea not merely to reprint the book unchanged, but to revise and update it while reprinting. The result is the present volume, which is a second revised and expanded edition of my first Thailand travel title. As things have turned out, it is a major new edition of *Three Pagodas*. If I had known prior to the revision just how much the situation had meanwhile changed down the Thai-Burmese border and just how much time and effort would be involved in revising my account of that situation, I am not sure that I would have had the energy to undertake the task. But a revised edition was required. The material on which the original edition was based was only as recent as 1995, when the book was first written, and bits and pieces of it dated back to 1989, when some legs and aspects of the journey were first researched. Yet Thailand is famously a fast-developing and changing country, and nowhere is this more the case than in the western frontier area. Much of the material, particularly on the politico-military front and in that it related to the Burmese side of the border, had been overtaken by events and was significantly out of date.

Between December 2000 and February 2001, I redid the journey as far as I was able, re-researching the route and rechecking details. I was accompanied in this both by my American friend Doug Boynton, veteran of many an expedition with me, who patiently stood by my side throughout, and also a young English acquaintance of mine, Andrew Wolton, who came with us in the second half of the journey, from Mae Hong Son to Boeng Kloeng. To Doug: I am most grateful for all your help, understanding and solidarity; and to Andrew: I hope that you got the adventure and experiences that you were looking for, and sincere thanks also for your assistance.

Despite our best efforts, we were only able to retravel a large part of the journey, but not all of it, and hence I am not able completely to revise the original text. Thus we could not revisit rebel GHQ at Manerplaw in Burma or redo the associated leg from Mae Saam Laep to Ban Ta Song Yang. Nor could we revisit the Telakhon rishi jungle cultist village of Lae Tong Ku or retrek the final expedition from Lae Tong Ku to the Three Pagodas Pass. Accordingly, I have only been able to revise the journey, broadly speaking, from Chiang Mai and Chiang Dao to Boeng Kloeng, with the 'tail' of the revised travelogue lopped off.

This is because of swingeing changes all down the western frontier between 1995 and 2001, especially on the Burmese side. In 2002, the Thai-Burmese border from the latitude of Chiang Dao to the Three Pagodas is a very different place from what it was in the early and mid-1990s. Correspondingly, a journey down it is also quite different. Although in 2001 much had changed little (e.g. places such as Kae Noi, Muang Noi, Mae Hong Son town, Khun Yuam, Mae Sariang, Mae La Oop and Kui Le Tor), some features of the itinerary had altered dramatically, astonishing me. Thus, for example, Wiang Haeng had developed considerably, and places such as Mae Saam Laep, Rim Moei/Myawaddy (near Mae Sot) and Boeng Kloeng were so transformed that I hardly recognized them. Some of these changes were due to infrastructural developments in a modernizing Thailand. The roadbuilding programme had been advanced, dirt roads or tracks had been upgraded or paved, dirt roads had been forged where there used to be footpaths, bridges had been built, and health centres, schools and shops had sprung up.

But the greatest changes concerned the frontier itself, the villages on it, and the territory just across the border, on the Burmese side. Here, in 2001, the ethno-politico-military complexion was utterly and unforeseeably different from what it had been in the early 1990s. Where in essence opium warlord Khun Sa and his Mong Tai Army had once controlled the border territory in the Shan State, including 'our' stretch from opposite Chiang Dao to Mae Or, now the Burmese but mainly their henchmen the Wa with their United Wa State Army basically did so. And where the Karenni (Karenni Army) and very largely the Karen (Karen National Liberation Army/Karen National Union) had once controlled the Burmese side of the border from Mae Or all the way south to the Three Pagodas Pass, now the Burmese and to a limited extent the Democratic Kayin (Karen) Buddhist Army (DKBA) basically did so. For the first time ever, the Burmese essentially controlled the whole of their eastern border with Thailand, where previously it had been dominated by ethnic rebel groups and warlords. In early 1996, Khun Sa surrendered his army and territory to Rangoon, as a result of which the Burma army stepped into some of his former strongholds, while the 'Red' Wa UWSA filled out the rest of the vacuum left by him. In early 1995, the Burma army with its infamous protégé the DKBA captured ethnic rebel GHQ Manerplaw and also another key Karen stronghold, Kawmoorah, to oust the KNU Karen from and seize the border areas of KNU 7th Brigade district (Papun-Pa'an). And, in early 1997, the Burmese followed this up by ousting the Karen from and seizing the border areas of KNU 6th Brigade district (Duplaya), all the way down to the Three Pagodas Pass.

This is why we were unable to revisit Manerplaw, which in 2001 was still in the hands of the DKBA and Burma army, or to redo the thrilling boat ride from Mae Saam Laep to Ban Ta Song Yang (see front cover photo). It also explains why in 2001 we were unable to revisit the KNU stronghold and black market village of Sa Kaang Thit, which was overrun by the Burmese in 1997 and destroyed. And it says why, even if we had been able to reach the rishi cultist village of Lae Tong Ku, we would not have been able to repeat the great adventure from there to the Three Pagodas – at least not in the form described in the first edition of *Three Pagodas*, where we often went south on the Burmese side of the border. The Burmese had interdicted that route.

So, at the time of writing in 2002, rebel 'Burmese' Karen no longer control the Burmese side of the border all the way south from Mae Saam Laep to the Three Pagodas, and there is no more flitting across the frontier to visit positions held by them, to travel down through territory controlled by them, or to gain assistance from them. Altogether, the situation of the Karen of the Karen State, Burma, has become dire. Another radical change that Doug, Andrew and I discovered during our updating trip was that where the Burmese and DKBA now held most of the territory formerly dominated by the KNU (a few pockets were still in KNU hands), thousands upon thousands of Karen had been forced to flee across the border into Thailand, where they now languished in a number of vast refugee camps. Their situation could not be more different from that of the early 1990s. A further concomitant of these politico-military developments is that where the border between the Karen State and Thailand used to be relatively quiescent, even benign, now it is 'hot', troubled and even dangerous again. This is especially true of territory 'con-trolled' by the DKBA and of the border stretch between Mae Saam Laep and Mae Sot. In recent years, the DKBA has torched and half destroyed Mae Saam Laep (another change), and attacked numerous refugee camps, villages, Thai soldiers and policemen, and vehicles in Thailand roughly down the H105 Mae Sariang/Mae Sot road. Rather the reverse is the case up on the Shan State/Thai border. Here, things used to be 'hot' and it used to be dangerous to travel close to Khun Sa territory, but now, with the Burmese in charge, the area is quieter and relatively benign, even if the dubious UWSA also lurks and looms in it.

Of course, even if I have been unable to revisit places such as Manerplaw or Sa Kaang Thit, this does not mean that I have been prevented from revising my account of the position across the border, and I have tried to update the picture of the MTA, UWSA, Burma army, Karenni Army and KNU/KNLA as well as of the Shan, Wa, Karenni, Padaung, Karen and Mon peoples in Burma. However, my update of these ethno-politico-military developments makes no pretension to completeness. I am not a professional historian, but only a traveller interested in border life, and most of my information pertaining to recent developments has been gleaned in a non-systematic way from news-paper cuttings collected during my winter visits to Thailand and from people quizzed here and there while on the road during these visits.

A problem that exercised me when I came to update *Three Pagodas* was just how to make the revision. At first, I thought I would modify the original text, substituting new material for old and creating a travelogue valid for 2001. But many people objected to this idea, saying that it would disturb the cast of the original book, would destroy the flow, would devalue the appeal and interest of the original, and would make it less of 'a good read'. Then I had the idea to integrate the new updated material along with the old. But that would have been to upset the sense of time (even more than it is already disturbed in the original!), with the new composite text hopping too much from one older time level to another more recent one. An intention of the original version of the book had been to provide a snapshot of border life in the mid-1990s. But to represent the original version by updating and rewriting it would have been to destroy that snapshot.

18

In the end, it seemed to me best largely to leave the original text as it was, preserving the mid-1990s snapshot (not least for historical reasons), and to add new, updated and supplementary material relating to how things had changed meanwhile in a series of postscripts. My only problem ultimately was whether to introduce these postscripts all together, in a single block at the end of the book, which would have had the virtue of representing the original text in a single unbroken block at the beginning, or whether to introduce them chapter-by-chapter, with the updating postscripts immediately following the chapter they refer to. On balance, I though that this latter option was preferable. The pieces of text that relate to each other are all together, and the reader does not need to read a chapter and then hunt for its postscript at the end of the book. The downside of this arrangement, of course, is that the overall text is now even more fragmented and less flowing than it already was. But I have discovered that many readers do not read the whole text from cover to cover anyway, but instead dip into what interests them, e.g. Lawa culture or the Karen rebellion, and such readers will prefer to have all the elements of their topic together. Other readers, wanting only to follow the story, can skip the post-scripts, just as they can the more formal factual cultural and historical accounts of, say, the Lawa or Karen.

I indicated that I am aware that the sense of time in the original text is sometimes upset. Some readers have pointed this out to me, much to my chagrin and embarrassment, as I had tried to suppress such disruptions and discontinuities. They said that they occasionally felt chronologically queasy when reading *Three Pagodas*. The years did not always fit together (the description of Mae Or was true for perhaps 1990, while the account of Manerplaw was valid for 1994), and the seasons did not properly sequence (in Wiang Haeng at Christmas it was cool, while a couple of days later in Mae Hong Son town I describe a sultry heat in the *Sanguan Sin Hotel* that is appropriate to May). Now that the book has proved its worth and enjoyed success, I am less defensive about all this and can own up to what is going on. Of course, to create the original text, I could not possibly have done and researched the whole journey and story in a single pass lasting a few weeks in one particular year. In truth, the travelogue was cobbled together from research trips to all the places and peoples visited in different winters/years and at different times of those winters – hence the anachronisms. In the revised text, I have tried to be more specific and honest about what was visited when.

From readers I have discovered not just that some like to dip into particular topics covered by *Three Pagodas*, while others suffer from a chrono-logical queasiness, but that quite a few have been using the adventure travel-ogue in the book as a kind of guide. To help such readers, I have now included in the postscripts in the new revised edition of the book some practical information about where to stay and eat at places en route, about prices, about motorcycle hire, about the possibility of getting from A to B variously by motorbike and public transport, about the conditions of roads and tracks, and so on. I hope that this supplementary material will satisfy the many people who have asked me over the years to provide such data. In supplying it, I have made the revised version of *Three Pagodas* more of a narrative guide than an adventure travelogue, at the same time bringing it more into line with my second Thailand travel book, *Around Lan-Na*, which forms a companion volume to the present book. Although I give this route detail, I am not suggesting that you use it, cannot be held responsible for anything that might happen to you if you use it, and hereby explicitly disclaim any liability for any harm or injury that you might sustain as a result of using it (see also the boxed warning below).

In the second edition of *Three Pagodas*, besides updating the story in the postscripts and besides supplying travel information and much more precise route detail, I have also added a fair amount of new material, on e.g. the 'Long-Ear' Kayaw tribe, the Mon people, 'Spirit Cave' near Soppong, the Japanese army in Thailand during the Second World War, and the Karenni people and state as well as the two Karenni organizations the KNPP and KNLP. Further, I have added to and rigorized the accounts of the ethnic minority groups and their histories as well as cultures. For better or worse, this turns some of these accounts into regular essays, which will perhaps impede the armchair-traveller type of reader or the reader on the ground in Thailand's western border region, but which I hope will please my many scholarly readers. The maps have also been added to and increased in number, from just 13 in the first edition to 30 in the second. Wherever possible, I have tried to update them in line with changes in the interim. I have not reproduced the old maps. It seemed point-less to preserve out-of-date maps valid for the early 1990s, and so I simply replaced the old ones with the new, which are now authoritative. All this additional material has substantially increased – nearly doubled – the size of the book.

C. G.
Suffolk, England
January 2002

WARNING

For many years, parts of the Thai-Burmese border area have been dangerous or potentially dangerous. Both flitting out of Thailand and flitting into Burma are illegal, and travellers who cross into either the Shan State or the Karenni (Kayah) State or the Karen State – easy and tempting as this might be to do – could be playing with their lives. At the time of writing, the Pang Ma Pa border area west of Piang Luang and stretches of the Moei river south of Mae Saam Laep were highly dangerous. In 2001, Lae Tong Ku was off-limits because of fighting and a fluid situation locally. The wilderness south of Boeng Kloeng in Tung Yai Naresuan Wildlife Sanctuary, especially close to the border, could be hazardous at present. Sections of 'Death Highway' (route 1090) are always potentially lethal, not because of any fighting or cross-border attacks and banditry, but because the road is difficult and the traffic dangerous. And in recent years, the northern half of the H105 Mae Sariang/Mae Sot road has been dodgy and sometimes closed because of DKBA attacks on or near it. By contrast, in 2001 places such as Kae Noi, Wiang Haeng and Piang Luang had become relatively safe, while Pai, Mae Hong Son, Mae Or, Mae Sot, Um Pang and the Three Pagodas Pass were safe, already figuring to a greater or lesser extent on the well-trodden tourist trail. But the western border is a troubled area which changes from year to year. What was safe last year might not be so this, and vice versa. Anyone intending to poke about in northern Thailand's remoter corners, especially near the border, should either speak some Thai, and/or take along a Thai companion, or first ascertain from locals if it is safe to proceed. In practice, the Thai military should stop you before you enter a hazardous area and put yourself at risk, but do not rely on this.

1

MR DONUT COMING SOON

THE KMT

Chiang Mai – Chiang Dao – Muang Ngai – Muang Na – Kae Noi – Chong – Wiang Haeng

C hiang Mai, Thailand's northerly second city, is where adventures are mooted and plans laid. It is the base from which travellers explore the mountainous north of the country, both the western flank towards Burma, and the eastern reaches towards Laos. Later, after rough dusty tours, this one-time capital of the ancient Lan-Na kingdom is a welcome place in which to clean up and become reacquainted with Western food. But for us, for the moment, it was a convenient spot in which to acclimatize and overcome jet lag following the 12-hour long-haul flight from Europe. After the gloom of an English winter, the intense Lan-Na light pricked our eyes.

'The Rose of the North', as Chiang Mai is sometimes known, used to detain us longer, but on recent stopovers we have been increasingly dismayed by developments there. During the late 1980s and early 90s, the town had its share of changes – the northern capital is no more proof to the transformation sweeping the country than any other part. But whereas previously the alterations had always seemed modest, piecemeal, assimilable, cumulative, now suddenly the city was convulsed. In the space of twelve months, a watershed had been reached, and unfortunately Chiang Mai's legendary balance of traditional charm and modernity, of easy living and commerce, had tipped decisively in favour of the latter.

The 'northerly rose' had lost her bloom. 'Condomania' had struck along the banks of the city's leisurely River Ping. High-rise hotels in the vicinity of the modest *Suriwong Hotel* were falling all over each other. Estates of fancy, gleaming white houses, built in 'wedding-cake' architectural style, were mushrooming everywhere. The Nawarat Bridge across the Ping river, the Tapae Road, the Chang Klan Road through the heart of the Night Bazaar, the Charoen Pratet Road, and the Moon Muang as well as Kotchasan Roads each side of a spur of the old city moat were choked with traffic. In a short time our throats were rasping from the exhaust fumes of innumerable motorized three-wheeler *tuk tuks*, motorbikes, share-taxi *silor*, pick-ups and tourist coaches. The air was loud with the noise of engines revving, vehicles tooting and security men blowing shrill whistles. Chiang Mai was becoming more like Bangkok by the hour.

MR DONUT COMING SOON

Our guest house, which had once been a haven of tranquillity in a leafy lane on the banks of the Ping, was suddenly a dilapidated block on a busy connecting road, overshadowed by a giant condominium and passed nearby by a brand-new river bridge, which roared day and night with traffic. The old Vieng Ping Bazaar on the Chang Klan Road, which had once been such an intriguing place to browse among hill-tribe artifacts, had been relegated to a dismal corner of the Anusarn Market. Some brash shopping mall was all set to take its former place. The Anusarn Market, where we had so often supped inexpensively on *pat thai* and noodle soup, where, Mekhong whisky in hand, we had enjoyed watching the nightly proceedings of the market, was in the throes of an unfathomable transformation. It looked as if a pizza parlour was taking shape in the middle of a car park.

Only 15 years earlier, *farang* (foreigners, Westerners) were such an unusual sight in Chiang Mai that schoolchildren used to tail them down the quiet dusty streets out of curiosity, keeping a safe distance for fear of the unknown. Now luxury coaches blocked up the Night Bazaar, disgorging groups of elderly French package tourists, who tried to haggle in French over the price of a pair of fake Lacoste socks. Where once ladies in conical straw hats had sold fruit and other foods from panniers at the side of the Chang Klan Road, now a spanking new shopping plaza was waiting to be opened. In the plate glass windows huge signs proclaimed: KENTUCKY FRIED CHICKEN OPENING SOON, BURGER KING OPENING HERE SOON and MISTER DONUT COMING SOON.

✲

Sooner than expected we were riding out of town. It was a relief to be on our way, heading for the hills. The Chang Puak (White Elephant) Road led into the Chotana Road, which crossed the Superhighway and proceeded north in the direction of Chiang Dao (Map 2). The literature speaks of Chiang Mai as a town of 200,000 inhabitants. But a trip through the Chang Puak and Chotana suburbs tells a different story. If these teeming bustling quarters are taken into account, the true total population of the city must easily exceed one million. From a rental shop in town, we had hired a Honda Wing motorcycle. Although getting rather long in the tooth, these 125-cc air-cooled 4-stroke workhorses had one great advantage over the other bikes available (the finicky MTX trails machine or the strong but lightweight Dream town bike): a large petrol tank. The roadsters could manage more than 300 kms on one tankful – an important consideration when making a long flit through the mountains or jungle. We drew into a petrol station to fill up and make ready for the ride. On the station forecourt, in the shade of a giant ESSO sign, we strapped one of our two rucksacks onto the Wing's tank with expanders, and pulled on a pair of those maroon acrylic bobble-hats seen everywhere in Thailand, useful for keeping the dust, bugs and diesel flecks of the highway out of one's hair. Preparations were completed with a liberal smearing on our faces of factor-35 sun cream – essential protection in the hills against the fierce oriental sun.

THREE PAGODAS

Our plan was to ride north 70 kms to Chiang Dao and then north and west up a side road towards the mountainous Burmese border. We had heard intriguing things about a remote place up there called Wiang Haeng. Our enquiries had revealed that there were apparently two ways to reach this outpost (see overview Map 3). One was via a new dirt road which skirted round the back of Thailand's third-highest mountain, Doi Chiang Dao, before it climbed 55 kms up to Wiang Haeng (Map 9). Evidently this was the new dirt track that had only recently connected the village to the outside world. The other way was via a closed road which went up to the forbidden multi-ethnic village of Kae Noi (Maps 3, 4 and 5). To the best of our knowledge, no travellers had reached this volatile settlement. The writers of one German guidebook spoke of being unceremoniously repulsed by the Thai military at the first checkpoint along the route. Evidently the track continued after Kae Noi over the border to Namaklwe and Mong Hang, two places in an area of the Shan State (Burma) controlled by opium warlord Khun Sa. However, we figured that there might be a track which looped back after Kae Noi, but before the border, west and south to Wiang Haeng (Maps 3, 6 & 7). Certainly it would have been odd if two villages which on the map seemed quite close together were not linked by some way. Thus, for the first leg of our journey down the Thai-Burmese border, we thought we would try to negotiate this alternative indirect roundabout route to Wiang Haeng, before cutting through the mountains from there to Pai (Maps 3, 8, 10 & 11).

With the promise of adventure programmed into our journey from the start, our adrenalin was up. But we were elated for other reasons. The open road and the narrowing trail beckoned again – always the occasion for an upwelling of anticipation. What lay ahead? What experiences, surprises and mishaps might befall us? Who would we meet? What would we learn? Where would we end up? Where would we stay, and what would we eat? The answers to these questions could not be imagined in advance. But one thing was certain, that when we did reach our journey's end, memorable things would have happened and we would have met some remarkable people. And this, surely, is the mainspring of travelling. In what at the time often seems hard, dispiriting, bewildering, even senseless, there is the promise of a cache of rewarding experiences and enriching memories.

A succession of sights unfolded beside Highway 107 out of Chiang Mai: the Tribal Museum, Lanna Golf Course, Chiang Mai Hospital, Chiang Mai City Hall, Pack Squadron barracks, the Nong Haw horse-racing course, and some fields with hundreds of horses and donkeys grazing on dessicated grass. At first sight these meagre animals seemed part of a sanctuary or awaiting shipment to the knacker's yard. But in fact they were 'cavalry' horses, belonging to the barracks. The better ones, apparently, were even raced at Nong Haw. Thais like a flutter on the horses, and racing took place, so the hoardings announced, every Sunday morning. Other facets of Thai life revealed themselves. Clapped-out mopeds puttered north with bamboo cages, one suspended each side, containing piglets. A troop of hundreds of boy scouts and girl guides snaked its way single file along the side of the road to a camp somewhere. A raucous merit-making band of villagers proceeded to their local temple, bearing money and gifts. A sombre funeral cortège moved slowly out of a village to a cremation site, where the body would be burnt on a pyre. A pick-up among the black-clad mourners bore the gaudy coffin.

Fourteen kms out from the centre of Chiang Mai, the chaotic little town of **Mae Rim** greeted us (Map 2). Fortunately, we lost here most of the numerous coaches and minibuses which had thundered dangerously past us on the highway. Just after Mae Rim, they turned left into the H1096 side road towards the Mae Sa valley. Their goal was the plethora of 'attractions' developed in this picturesque valley to entertain the package tourists making their three-day stopover in Chiang Mai. The forest of signs at the mouth of the road indicated the diversions that awaited them: elephant 'training' camps, 'scenic' resorts, restaurants offering 'traditional' food served by waitresses in 'authentic' costume, mini waterfalls, and orchid, butterfly and snake farms.

Our route continued north, passing the hilltop monastery-temple of Wat Pratat Doi Chom Chaeng. The *wat* stood out because of a long flight of steps leading up to it, which was flanked by two enormous wavy-backed snakelike *naga*. A few kms more brought us to **Mae Ma Lai** (35 kms out from Chiang Mai). The market and shops of this busy little trading place seemed interesting enough to warrant a quick look round. Shopkeepers told us that Thais and especially hill-tribe people came down here from the westerly mountains to buy and sell. Of significance for us was the key turn-off left (west) plumb in the middle of the market onto Highway 1095. This was the beginning of the exciting northerly route to Mae Hong Son, some 200 kms distant. Pai, a station on our way, lay up this mountain road, almost exactly half way to Mae Hong Son. The road invited and Pai called, but we were able to resist the temptation. Our rendezvous with Pai would come later, after a more circuitous journey. First there was the little matter of our assignation with Kae Noi and Wiang Haeng.

For the moment, therefore, we carried on in a northerly direction, through the village of **Mae Taeng**, past a turning left/west for the valley of the Mae Taeng river[1], and on towards Chiang Dao. With the sphere of

---

[1] Passing this turning, we were reminded of words written by the 19th-century British surveyor-explorer Holt Hallett in his *A Thousand Miles on an Elephant in the Shan States* (1890). His words, which relate to his passage in 1884 from Chiang Mai via Chiang Dao to Fang (part of a larger overall journey), shed atmospheric light on the history of not only the Mae Taeng valley, but also Wiang Haeng, Chiang Dao, Muang Ngai and Kae Noi, all places on our route. As he passed Mae Taeng village and crossed the River Taeng, Hallett says that he noticed a great valley extending westwards as far as the eye could see. In this valley of the Mae Taeng "lie many ruined cities: Ken Noi [Kae Noi], Muang Hâng [Wiang Haeng], Muang Kong [Muang Khong], Muang Keut [Muang Kut], and others whose names are now forgotten". "Two ancient cities, Muang Hâng and Muang Teung [possibly Piang Luang], and several villages are situated [up there in an] old lake basin, which forms part of the British Shan States; it is solely occupied by Burmese Shans, and was included in the Burmese Shan States under the name of Muang Hâng." These *muang* or 'cities' (just villages by today's standards) west of Chiang Dao – in the 19th century seemingly part of British Burma or at least claimed as such – were a territory inhabited at the time by aggressive Shan chiefs, who frequently raided and destroyed Chiang Dao and other nearby lowland towns, coming into conflict with the local northern Tai or Lan-Na Tai. In 1869, for example, *chao paya* Roi Saam, a Shan chieftain from Muang Wiang Haeng burnt down Muang Ngai (not far from Chiang Dao), driving out the local Tai, while in the late 1860s and early 1870s

THREE PAGODAS

influence of greater Chiang Mai receding, and with Mae Ma Lai and its
strategic H1095 turn-off behind us, the traffic thinned noticeably now. The
route began to shadow the River Ping, passing through luxuriant wooded
mountain country. A sinuous road cut through steep hillsides of lovely green,
golden and brown trees with outsize leaves. Lychee orchards appeared, and
we saw piles of orange maize at the side of the road. On the descending run-
in to Chiang Dao, we were presented on the western side with an impressive
view of the massive grey block of Doi Chiang Dao, Thailand's third-highest
peak (2180 m or 7150 ft). Indistinct in the haze and against the sun, the
mountain's summit was shrouded, as it often is, in cloud.

The district town of **Chiang Dao**, strung out along the main road 70
kms north of Chiang Mai, seemed a good place to stop for an early *kao soi*
lunch and soft drinks. We figured that it might be the last opportunity to eat
regular food for a few days, perhaps until distant Pai. Although an attractive
place, there is not a great deal to detain the traveller in Chiang Dao. Its long
narrow main street is lined with many colourful stores, some in old wooden
buildings. Local people, including costumed tribals, come from round about
to shop in the market town, negotiating the traffic passing through – the 107
highway goes slap-bang through the centre, up the main street. Nor is there
anywhere in Chiang Dao very suitable for travellers to stay. The principal
appeal of the place is its magnificent location near the base of Mount Chiang
Dao (or Doi Luang, as the monolith is also known), which can be climbed
from the town (for an account of how to do this, see my guidebook *Trek It
Yourself in Northern Thailand*, Chapter 4). Two other compelling reasons to
come here are to visit celebrated Chiang Dao Cave at nearby Ban Tam (Cave
village) and explore or walk in close-at-hand Chiang Dao Wildlife Sanctuary,
which is renowned for its bird life and birdwatching. The mountain, cave and
sanctuary are all respectively climbed, visited and explored from a few kms
up the side road that strikes left/west from the top/northern end of the
town's main street (Map 2).

Ampoe Chiang Dao sometimes hits the headlines because of fighting to
the north-west between the private army of Shan opium warlord Khun Sa
and the Wa. For years Sa's Mong Tai Army and various Wa factions have
been battling it out along this stretch of the Thai-Burmese border for control
of territory, certain strategic hills and narcotics-trafficking routes. It might be
thought that during such fighting traffic on the Chiang Dao road would be
stopped. However, down on the H107 there is little hint of the deadly
skirmishing up there – perhaps only some additional troop movements of
the Thai army. The exception to this is when the warring factions bring their
wounded down to be treated at their own expense in the local Thai hospitals.
A bizarre consequence is that the Thai authorities then have the task of

Shan from the same area twice invaded nearby Prao district, razing some eight villages. And in
1869 or 1870, Chiang Dao itself was apparently "destroyed by *chao paya* Kolon, a Burmese Shan
chief [from Mawkmai, a state west of the Salween river]", to be at once reoccupied upon his
withdrawal. For a while there was general downward pressure from the Shan into the Ping valley,
displacement of the Tai, and disputes between British Shan and the Siamese as to who
possessed the upper parts of the valleys of the Rivers Ping, Taeng, Pai and Fang.

keeping the wounded from the two sides apart, directing, for example, the Shan MTA casualties to Chiang Dao hospital and the Wa wounded to nearby Fang. Sometimes, ironically, this cannot be managed, and casualties who are mortal enemies in the field have to recuperate in the same hospital in beds side by side.

✣

Five kms beyond Chiang Dao town (75 kms north of Chiang Mai) we found our turn-off. With Highway 107 continuing NNE to Fang and Taton, our side road, the H1178, headed left (just W of N) off the beaten track up towards Kae Noi and Wiang Haeng (Maps 2 & 3). Neither of our destinations was signposted. For a short distance, we rode on a speedy metalled surface (now see Map 4 – odometer readings start again at km 0.0 at the junction of the H107 and the H1178). The villages of Lai Tung, Mae Khon and Muang Ngai came and went. The protracted community of **Muang Ngai** (km 4) was distinguished by a monument and fort commemorating the exploits of King Naresuan of Ayuttaya. We briefly visited the complex, which we found to the left/south of the road and village centre, but it was hardly worth the effort, as the monument was a modern affair and the fortress just an impressionistic reconstruction. History relates that in the mid-1580s Thai national hero Naresuan set up a large military encampment in Muang Ngai as part of his crusade of liberation against the Burmese, Thailand's traditional enemy, who had basically occupied both Lan-Na and Siam since 1558. For us, passing through this pleasant rural backwater on a sunny December afternoon, it was difficult to conceive of armies of thousands of foot soldiers and war elephants tramping this way 400 years earlier.[2]

Not far beyond Muang Ngai, we came to a second junction (km 9.5). Here, a turning left/west was the start of the new H1322 dirt road through the mountains to Wiang Haeng. The way was the short direct route (a further 55 kms – see Maps 3 & 9) to that place of former marauding Shan chieftains up

---

[2] In Muang Ngai, we were again reminded of the English fact-finder Holt Hallett, who in 1884 visited and stayed at Muang Ngai. In his *Thousand Miles on an Elephant in the Shan States* (1890), he writes: "...passing through the city, we camped for the night at two *sala* outside the north gate. The city of Muang Ngai is surrounded, like Chiang Dao, with a strong stockade, and contains 100 houses... I visited the remains of the ancient city of Muang Ngai, which lies ¾ of a mile to the north-west, and is said to have been built by the Lawas, under a chief named A-Koop-Norp, who is still worshipped as the guardian spirit of the district." Hallett called on the 'governor' of Muang Ngai, an old man who had been in the 'city' ever since the age of 25, when there had been only two houses in it. It was from the governor that Hallett learned, as mentioned earlier in Footnote 1, that 15 years before his visit, in 1869, *chao paya* Roi Saam, a Shan chief from Muang Wiang Haeng had burned down Muang Ngai, driving the Lan-Na Tai occupants out of the 'province'. The 'province' had then been repopulated and now, in 1884, had 2000 inhabitants. These people were chiefly 'witches' (people considered to be possessed of evil spirits) who had been turned out of Chiang Mai. As a result of Muang Ngai being populated by witches, other people were reluctant to settle there, fearing that the witches might work harm on them. As we flitted through the village, it occurred to us that the people at the side of the road might well be the descendants of these witches!

on the Shan plateau. Straight on (north) at the junction continued up the
H1178 to Muang Na and then the closed track to Kae Noi. It was the parting
of the ways. Steeling ourselves, we pushed on for Muang Na. We calculated
that if we were turned back somewhere, we could always return to this junction
and get up to Wiang Haeng the 'quick' way. At worst we would sacrifice Kae
Noi and the backdoor approach to Wiang Haeng. Almost immediately came
Mae Ja Nuea or northern Mae Ja (with its turning north-east back down to
Ping Kong and the junction for Prao on the H107), followed by a string of
other small places: Huai Tin Tang (= chair leg stream), Tungkao Puang, Huai
Pao, Huai Sai and La Po Han.

We had already passed a first checkpoint, positioned near the start of the
H1322 road for Wiang Haeng. It was hardly a serious one – there was no
barrier across the road, and the guard, who was watching TV, did not even
glance up as we passed. However, riding through **Na Wai**, we spotted trouble
ahead. A more menacing-looking checkpoint (km 24.5) lay at the wayside with
a barrier across the road, slightly raised. This was it, we thought. Here our jolly
jaunt would be terminated even as it started. We slowed down, wondering
whether to stop or whether to duck our heads and scoot through. As we
approached, something remarkable happened. The soldier on guard stepped
out of his hut and, without looking, went round to the back to relieve himself.
As he stood there, back turned, we cruised under the red-and-white-painted
barrier and accelerated away. Our burst of speed was short-lived, for immediately the paved road gave out, and we plunged onto a bumpy dirt surface.

The dirt road, continuing almost due north, headed uphill and down dale,
along a broad valley, between low hills, and with fields of rice and other crops
each side of the way. Then we passed cliffs on our right side and entered
forest, to reach next the small village of **Rin Luang** (also known as Kasemrat).
It was distinguished by a pink-painted school and a kindergarten (both left), as
well as by a modest Christian church. But the main feature of the backwoods
place was another junction (km 31), at which a significant dirt road struck
right/NNE 6 kms for Nong Ook, a large Kuomintang Chinese village, also
known officially as Aroonothai. Beyond Nong Ook, this route continued to
other KMT settlements and up an exciting new border dirt road all the way to
Doi Ang Karng (for an account of interesting Nong Ook and the border road
beyond it, see my cultural guide *Around Lan-Na: A Guide to Thailand's Northern
Border Region*, Chapters 3 & 4).

After Rin Luang, the stony, bumpy, boneshaker dirt road veered NW and
then W, mitigating the way it infuriated us on our rattling Honda Wing by
providing entrancing views NE of the wavy-backed snakelike Kiu Pa Wok
ridge. Now we passed the Lahu hill-tribe settlement of **Nong Kiao**, just a
collection of straw-roofed huts, (km 34) and a track right to Muang Na Nuea
Cave, before arriving at Muang Na village (42 kms from the H107).

Muang Na turned out to be the last place of any consequence before
Kae Noi. If we had known both the state of the 'road' between the two places,
and the paucity of facilities and food that we were to find in Kae Noi, we
would certainly have stopped at Muang Na for chow and refreshments, and
might even have spent the night there. We saw noodle shops and other

amenities in the place. But, by definition, one cannot know what lies ahead until one has encountered it, and also, with the day advancing, we wanted to press on. Muang Na was a relatively large village, with its main street ascending or, conversely, spilling down the side of a hill, rather in the manner of Doi Mae Salong, with which it had certain affinities. Its inhabitants were a mixture of KMT Nationalist Chinese (such as lived at Mae Salong), local Shan people, local Thais, and Lahu tribals, but predominantly KMT. Evidence of the presence of Shans was a Shan or Burmese-style *wat* on the left/south side of the ascending main street. The monastery-temple's principal building was a big old wooden construction on stilts, similar to the *wat* that we later found in Wiang Haeng. Evidence of Chinese occupancy was a kind of Chinese temple building, also situated left off the main street, single-storey Chinese-style homesteads around square courtyards (especially in the alleyways on the right side of the village), a couple of simple eating places in the main street serving Chinese noodle soups, and banners and signs with Chinese characters. At the top end of town, on the left side of the road, there was a big school, and elsewhere a military camp. The Thai army had the place staked out on account of the close proximity of the border and of Khun Sa MTA militiamen and drug traffickers just across the frontier. Muang Na struck us as a nice undiscovered little place with a Yunnanese aspect. Funny to be in Yunnan in northern Thailand!

Mid-afternoon, we continued from Muang Na towards Kae Noi (see now Map 5). At the top end of town, where the trail passed the school, flattened out and headed off into the countryside, we ran into a third checkpoint. Our fear here was that not only would we be intercepted in the ordinary way, but that the guard at the earlier Na Wai checkpoint would have radioed through, so that now all eyes would be peeled for us. With trepidation, we glided towards the barrier. There was no point in trying to sneak past this thoroughgoing wayside military post, so with a show of innocence we rode straight up to it and searched the open window. We saw inside two or three soldiers – but also, on the table, empty Mekhong whisky bottles... The guards were either dozing or drunk or both. Again, we ducked our heads, passed under the barrier, and free-wheeled on far enough for nobody to be able to hear us, when we once again wound up the 125-cc engine. Between Muang Na and Kae Noi, there were no more checkpoints. By good fortune and almost without trying, we had entered the closed zone. Our elation at slipping through the net turned out to be very misplaced. What we did not know was that the stretch ahead was one of the most dangerous in all Thailand. Ironically, that first leg of our journey down the Thai-Burmese border could so easily have been the last.

Not far beyond Muang Na came the small Lahu hill-tribe village of **Jia Chan**. Now that we were putting more and more distance between us and the end of the paved road (already 20 kms behind us, back at Na Wai), we were becoming increasing anxious for information about the route ahead. But clearly, for fear of betraying our intentions, we could not ask at Muang Na, let alone at the checkpoint. At Jia Chan, we found a roadbuilders' camp. Although it was only a modest one, this was good news because, as we had often found travelling elsewhere in Thailand, roadbuilders were naturally in possession of reliable route information and also did not tend to put a superfluous obfuscatory gloss on everything, as the military liked to do. We found two men fiddling with a vehicle. There was a route through to Kae Noi, one confirmed, although it was not easy. You had to cross two ridges on the way. The main problem, the other man said, was that nobody went up there. He did not elaborate, and the two merely looked at us and our backpacks as if we were not in possession of all our marbles. We asked how far it was now to Kae Noi? About another 25 kms, they thought. Were there any villages between Muang Na/Jia Chan and Kae Noi? There were a couple of Lahu settlements on and off the track. Was Jia Chan a Lahu place? Yes, it was. And then, in a matter-of-fact manner, the men went on to tell us an interesting but disquieting story about Jia Chan. It had been relocated to here from higher up because a number of villagers had been killed by warlord Khun Sa's men in a conflict over heroin.

Heartened by the fact that Kae Noi now seemed to be within our grasp, but discouraged by the thought of another 25 kms of bad road, we set off again. The lingering look the men gave us as we rode away hardly inspired confidence either. In fact, the rest of the trip was one of the roughest, loneliest and most frightening stretches we encountered anywhere on our journey – a baptism of fire. The mountain track threw everything at the poor Honda, and we passed not a single vehicle or person until Kae Noi. First, after Muang Na and Jia Chan, the way passed some dramatic karstic limestone outcroppings that shouldered up on the left/south side. Covered with a hair of bushes and trailing creepers, these ominous monoliths reared up above the surrounding jungle canopy like weed-bedecked monsters out of some primaeval seabed. Then the dirt road climbed a fair way up a shoulder, zigzagging to the top of the first ridge. After this, it went steeply down through several corkscrew bends to a bridge and river. On the rubble surface of the headlong downgrade, the tyres of the Wing shuddered and slipped, bringing a sweat to our brow and a prickle of fear to our entrails. But we made it safely to the bottom. Following the bridge, the way narrowed on the river valley floor into a 4WD track. Now it passed through defiles that had us scanning the features ahead and glancing nervously over our shoulders. The vegetation closed in oppressively on all sides. Suddenly we realized we were in deep jungle. Far too slowly, the trail made its way up the river and its damp thin valley, crossing more bridges, all wooden and broken-down like the first. Little footpaths went off to the sides, perhaps to one of the Lahu settlements. At the end of the valley, where the way began to ascend again, we passed the Lahu settlement of **Ho Kiang**, somewhat offroad.

After Ho Kiang came the second and more challenging of the two ridges that had to be crossed between Muang Na and Kae Noi. Aggressively, the track zigzagged up another steep mountainside. As we were grinding up the corkscrew bends, we had a crisis. The motorbike gave up the uneven contest, coming to a halt on the steepest, most boulder-strewn incline. With two up, it was overwhelmed, even in first gear. Of course, the machine would not hold on the precipitous loose surface, slipped back and toppled over. We, too, came to rest on the dirty stones. Picking ourselves up and dusting ourselves down, we checked that nothing was broken, either on the bike or ourselves. After the screaming of the engine and the noise of our curses, the dark green foliage all around fell uncannily silent. So here we were, stuck with a stalled, underpowered, overheated bike on a dangerous jungle mountainside – already seriously compromised on our first day out!

What to do? If the rest of the leg to Kae Noi continued in the same way, the bike would not be up to it. The nightmare of a series of crashes ahead flickered through our minds. But the thought of going back was equally appalling, not least in terms of hurt pride. We looked at the bike's tripmeter. Apparently, if the roadbuilders were right, we were almost exactly half way between Muang Na and Kae Noi. So the way back was as far as the way forward. In fact, counting from Chiang Dao or even from the end of the paved road at Na Wai, we had the lion's share of the leg behind us. There should be only another 12 or 13 kms to go. So we decided to go on.

It would have been very awkward to try to start the Honda on the screelike hill, so we eased it back to the last twist in the corkscrew and kicked it to life on the flatter outer edge. Then, while one of us scrambled the bike up the rubble to higher, more level ground, the other toiled up behind on foot with a backpack. Fortunately, not too far above, the crest of the second ridge appeared. Thereafter, the track levelled off, skirted round hilltops, proceeded along a high spine through upland conifer woods, and reached a kind of pass, near where there were some grand views north to the Thai-Burmese border ridge as well as west and north-west down onto the Shan *moeng* or broad valley of Kae Noi. What goes up must come down, and now the elevated way began to descend. It did so partly on an awful stretch of fist-sized stones and bulldust. We passed a turning left/south for Na Si Ri, probably a Lahu village, which according to a sign lay 4.5 kms away. Another very poor stretch taxed us, after which we came to a fork with a *sala* or open-sided waiting hut. A welcome reassuring sign pointed left to the Red Lahu village of Pa Bong Mai as well as some Royal Project, and right to Kae Noi school. Where the school was, so also, we surmised, was the village. A final downgrade on another mediocre surface brought us to the floor of the valley, or, rather, to the highland plateau area of Kae Noi. And, indeed, riding through the Lahu satellite settlement of **Huai Loek**, we finally coasted, a couple of kms further and to our great relief, into Kae Noi, its centre being marked by a large school on the right/north side of the main street (69 kms from the H107, and some 144 kms from Chiang Mai).

Kae Noi was a mixed Chinese, Shan, Lahu and Lisu village. With a predominantly Chinese nucleus of about 200 families, it was surrounded by a number of Red and Black Lahu as well as Lisu satellite settlements, comprising a further 100 families. Mixed into the ethnic hotchpotch were an additional 20 or so Shan families. The Chinese in Kae Noi, like the many other Chinese refugees along this stretch of the Thai-Burmese border, were so-called 'KMT' or Kuo-Min Tang (Kuomintang) people. With KMT villages such as Kae Noi and Muang Na figuring so prominently especially in the early parts of our journey, it is appropriate to sketch in who these Chinese refugee people are and

31

how they came to be here. Readers anxious to press on with the travelogue may like to pass over the following excursion into recent Chinese and Thai history, as well as into the rise of the 'Golden Triangle' drugs trade.

❖

Brief history of the KMT in Burma and Thailand

KMT people take their name from a Chinese political party, the Kuo-Min Tang or National People's Party (Nationalist Party). Dating back to the early 20th century, the KMT movement was bound up for most of its history with its leading figure, Chiang Kai-shek. The success of the Nationalists was to curb the power and autonomy of China's many regional warlords as well as to play a major role in repelling the Japanese during their 1931-45 invasion of the mainland. But they were ultimately no match for Mao Tse-tung's Communists. Civil war between Chiang Kai-shek's virulently anti-communist KMT and Chairman Mao's revolutionaries ended in 1949 with the defeat of the Nationalists.

The bulk of the KMT, some two million people, including dictatorial Generalissimo Chiang Kai-shek himself, escaped to Formosa (now Taiwan), an island off the coast of mainland China. Here they formed the Republic of China (Nationalist China), nursing plans to retake the communist mainland. However, many Kuomintang were cut off during the escape in the southern Chinese province of Yunnan, unable to reach Taiwan. These elements were then forced to flee from Mao's People's Liberation Army (PLA) in their thousands across the Sino-Burmese border into the Wa sub-state, Kokang, and the Shan State. They included parts of the 93rd Regiment (or Division) and of the 26th, 8th and 13th Armies, along with their families, as well as other volunteers and irregulars, and many Wa and Shan sympathizers, although overall leader Gen. Li Mi of the 8th Army was not among them. Hundreds of 93rd Regiment[3] troops went south to settle near Takilek (Tachilek), opposite Thailand's northernmost town of Mae Sai. At the same time, thousands of 26th Army soldiers and others headed south-west to settle at Muang Saat (Mong

---

[3] Thailand's KMT refugees are often collectively referred to as 93rd Regiment people, which is erroneous for more than one reason. Only some of these refugees stemmed from the famous 93rd Regiment, the rest deriving either from other regiments or from Chinese, Wa and Shan civilians and volunteers sympathetic to the Nationalist cause, who moved with the 93rd Regiment and also 26th Army. Further, post-1949 the 93rd Regiment, along with the 26th Army, was split up, transformed into new units, and renamed. In spite of this, in Thailand in general and in Mae Salong in particular the description '93rd' has stuck, although most of the KMT refugees and their descendants deny any real connection with the 93rd Regiment.

Prior to the watershed year of 1949, the 93rd Regiment, a division of Gen. Li Mi's 8th Army, operated in Yunnan and also Burma. In Burma during the Second World War, the regiment fought alongside British and US troops against the Japanese and also Thais. Based on Chiang Tung (Kengtung), Li Mi's force battled from 1941 on, when the Japanese and Thais went north into Burma and China, against the Imperial Army in Chiang Tung and also Sipsong Pan-Na, Yunnan province. In 1945, following the Japanese capitulation, the 93rd Regiment went to Laos to accept their surrender, after which in 1946 it withdrew to Yunnan, joining up with the 26th Army and staying there until 1949.

Hsat), about 50 kms north-west of Thailand's Taton, up the Kok river. Troops from the 8th and 13th Armies stationed themselves west of Muang Saat. At that time, Mae Sai/Takilek was the only regular Thai-Burmese border crossing point in northern Thailand and as such was valued by Rangoon. Not willing to tolerate the KMT at Takilek, the Burma army in June 1950 attacked and dispersed the 93rd Regiment group, some of whom fled to Laos, while the rest went west to join up with the 26th Army group at Muang Saat.

In the early years, the KMT quickly developed from being a refugee force in the Wa sub-state, Kokang and the Shan State that was temporarily poised to retake the homeland into something like an army of occupation. They were strong, heavily armed and relatively well organized, while the Wa and Shan were fragmented, poorly armed and weak. The Nationalist interlopers won over some local leaders and warlords, subdued others, and recruited or pressganged Wa, Shan and Lahu men to swell the ranks of their force. It has been said that the KMT were indisciplined and that marauding bands of the Chinese intruders, who were much loathed, caused considerable death and destruction in large tracts of the trans-Salween region, not least infuriating a young Khun Sa, who would never forget their behaviour and vowed that he would one day repay the KMT for their actions, which he indeed went on to do.

At this point Gen. Li Mi re-enters the story. This famous commander of the Nationalist 8th Army had escaped from the Communists by fleeing with the main body of KMT to Taiwan via Chiang Hai and Hong Kong. But in 1950 he was sent by the Taiwanese government to Muang Saat to set up a headquarters there, establish posts up in the Wa sub-state from which intelligence could be gathered about Yunnan, from which the province could be infiltrated, and from which cross-border sabotage missions could be conducted, and coordinate KMT resistance to Mao's Communists with a view to retaking Yunnan and China. To a certain extent he was successful. He wound up the 93rd Regiment and 26th Army and divided up their troops as well as the other volunteers and sympathizers to form four new groups: the 3rd, 5th, 7th and 9th Armies. He appointed Duan Shi-wen and Li Wen-fan (= Lao Li) as generals, giving Duan command of the new 5th Army and Li command of the new 3rd Army. Beyond this, Gen. Duan had overall command of the new forces with special responsibility for the KMT officers, while Gen. Li had deputy command with special responsibility for the NCOs. The two set up a military training school south of Muang Saat at Pong Pa Kaem village, opposite Nong Ook (Aroonothai), enrolling and training new recruits. In the early 1950s, the Muang Saat force burgeoned to number some 20,000 troops. It grew strong not least because of substantial aid from the US. Almost daily parachute drops were made from C-46 and C-47 transport aircraft, an old Second World War landing strip was reopened at Muang Saat, and CIA and Taiwanese advisers were in evidence. The force grew so strong that between May 1951 and June 1953 it went back up to Yunnan to battle the communists with a view to retaking the province. The KMT managed to recapture three towns there, but ultimately each of their three forays into Yunnan was unsuccessful, and they were beaten back into Burma.

THREE PAGODAS

The Burmese became unhappy about the size and expansion of KMT Muang Saat on their soil. They were worried that the Chinese might think that the Burmese were harbouring and aiding the KMT, and feared an attack by the PLA not just on the ebullient KMT, but also on themselves. So they did two things. In 1953, they appealed to the UN, complaining about the KMT presence and about the American support, and at the same time, in conjunction with the Chinese PLA, they attacked Muang Saat. The attack caused the KMT to fragment and disperse mostly along the Thai-Burmese border and throughout the Shan State. But some 5000, especially from the 7th and 9th Armies, fled into Laos and thence into Vietnam, where they were disarmed and sent for internment on the Vietnamese island of Phu Quoc, from where they were deported to Taiwan. The UN charged the US, Taiwan, Thailand and Burma with dealing with the KMT problem, and in 1953 a first evacuation from Burma to Taiwan was organized. Most of the 7th and 9th Armies went, but the 3rd and 5th Armies (the ones that interest us) did not want to go. Those KMT wishing to leave emerged from the jungle near Takilek and Huai Sa La (on the H1089 road, 13 kms north-east of Taton) as pre-arranged, laying down their weapons. They were taken to airports at Chiang Rai, Chiang Mai and Lampang, and between November 1953 and March 1954 7785 people were flown in four stages to Taiwan. The Burmese complained that the evacuation was a sham and that only hill tribals, women, children and old people went, not soldiers.

The period 1953-1955 saw Gen. Li Mi quit the scene, the remaining KMT regroup at Chiang Laap (Mong Pa Liao), and further involvement of both the Taiwanese and the US. Li Mi returned to Taiwan ostensibly for health reasons and recuperation, but in reality because of disagreements with the UN about evacuating KMT troops to Taiwan. He was replaced by Gen. Liu Yen-ling. After Muang Saat, Gen. Lao Li and his 3rd Army went for a while up to the Wa sub-state (opposite Yunnan), while Gen. Duan and his 5th Army went to Doi Larng (on the Thai-Burmese border opposite Mae Ai). A third officer from Muang Saat, Gen. Ma Joong-gua, set up a KMT propaganda radio station by the River Salween up in the Wa sub-state. Lao Li and Duan sent troops to guard it. Then the 3rd and 5th Armies, and those others who had not been evacuated, reunited at Chiang Laap, a place north-east of Mae Sai in Burma on the Mae Khong (Mekong river), which forms the border here between Burma and Laos. Taiwan sent a battalion of 800 men, led by Col. Sia Siao, to Chiang Laap, and all the troops there were reorganized into the 1st-5th Armies. As the Korean War ended, the US increasingly switched its support from South Korea to the anti-communist KMT in Burma, helping with the Taiwanese to build airstrips at Chiang Laap and flying in more supplies and advisers. By 1955, all these moves were complete, and the KMT with all their friends were regularly ensconced there until the end of the decade. Lying east of Chiang Tung and opposite Luang Nam Ta in Laos, Chiang Laap was defensively ideal for the KMT and boasted not only its own runway, but also access to an airstrip in Laos. Despite the earlier evacuations, the KMT had some 10-20,000 troops at their new HQ.

MR DONUT COMING SOON

The menace of the KMT was such that the PLA mobilized 400,000 troops along the Sino-Burmese border to prevent any fresh Nationalist incursions into Yunnan. The Chinese also entered into a secret agreement with the Burmese, whereby each country's army could enter the other's territory up to a distance of 80 kms. The main upshot of their cooperation was Operation Mae Khong, which effectively spelled the demise of the KMT in Burma. In the winter of 1960-61, between the end of November and January, 6,000 Burma army troops joined 20,000 PLA troops, by all accounts wearing Burmese military uniform, to mount an offensive against the KMT at Chiang Laap. They took several villages, seized five tons of US weapons, and defeated the Nationalists, causing a second dispersal and a second evacuation of the KMT.

In January 1961, many KMT (especially the 1st, 2nd and 4th Armies) went east, crossed the Mae Khong (Mekong), entered Laos, and traversed a spur of Laos to reach Huai Sai, from where they recrossed the Mae Khong river to enter Thailand at Chiang Khong (opposite Huai Sai). Others, primarily the 3rd and 5th Armies, went south-west, following the west bank of the Mae Khong and then skirting the Thai-Burmese border until they reached the vicinity of Mae Salong. As in 1953, at the time of its attack on Muang Saat, Burma linked its offensive with an appeal and protest to the UN, which in February 1961 led to the second evacuation of the KMT. Now a further 4,349 people, mainly from the 1st, 2nd and 4th Armies, were flown to Taiwan, being taken from Chiang Khong and Mae Sai to the airport at Chiang Rai, and from Fang district to Chiang Mai airport.

The troops of the 3rd and 5th Armies under Generals Li and Duan refused as always to be evacuated to Taiwan, claiming that they were not regular soldiers from China's former 93rd Regiment and 26th Army, but civilian volunteers who in 1949 had merely tagged along with the Nationalist forces fleeing Communist Yunnan. They were, therefore, more akin to refugees, displaced from their homeland and with nowhere to go in Burma, who now wanted to enter Thailand. And so we come to the second watershed year for the KMT, 1961, when under Duan and Lao Li the 5th and 3rd Armies entered Thailand. As they did so, refusing to be evacuated to Taiwan, the Taiwanese said that henceforth they would disclaim all responsibility for these Duan and Li followers. The 5th and 3rd Army troops would get no aid and would have to earn their own living. But as these men were no longer free to roam around Burma, but were confined to Thailand's border ridges, income was a problem, and so they took to making money primarily through drugs, extortion and arms dealing. In large part, the rapid growth of narcotics production and trafficking in the 'Golden Triangle' dates back to 1961 and the settlement of the KMT just inside Thailand. To put it another way, it was basically the KMT on the Thai-Burmese border who launched the 'Golden Triangle' as the massive source of opium and heroin for worldwide consumption that it has since become.

It was not the first time, as we have seen, that the KMT had stayed on the Thai-Burmese border, nor even the first time that they had crossed the frontier. They had already had unofficial back-door access to Thailand. In 1953, parts of Duan's 5th Army and of Li's 3rd were not at Chiang Laap, but camping out on the border from Doi Larng east via Doi Tung and Takilek to the Mae Khong. They took control of the border, trading with the Thais as well as with other groups on the Burmese side. Occasionally, the Burmese cleared the KMT from the frontier, whereupon they retreated into Thailand. After this had happened a few times, the Thai authorities set up refugee camps at Ban Tam (on the H110 road, just south of Mae Sai) and other places, where the Nationalists received US aid. But now the KMT entered the kingdom much more 'formally' and grandly. In early 1961, Lao Li had centralized his 3rd Army troops on the Thai border at Muang Pong, where they were joined by KMT soldiers under Liu Sao-tang. Numbering together 3,000 troops, they moved west to link up with Duan's 5th Army at Lao Lor opposite Doi Tung, the whole force now grown to some 6,500 men. A report details that they were in possession of 742 small arms, 101 machine guns and anti-aircraft guns, 82,646 rounds of ammunition and grenades, 20 communications stations, 39 portable field radio sets, and 1,000 horses. From Lao Lor there is a route across the border to the Thai villages of Tam and Pla, where some KMT dependants were already living. Leaving Lao Lor, Duan crossed with his 5th Army into Thailand and originally settled at Hua Muang Ngam (Sukluthai on the H1089 Mae Ai/Mae Chan road), five kms from the Kok river, but finding it not to his liking down in the valley, soon moved his HQ up to Doi Mae Salong.

Lao Li and Liu Sao-tang meanwhile proceeded from Lao Lor to enter Thailand between Hin Taek and Mae Salong, struck east and then south, passed through Huai Shom Pu and the Wawi mountain range, headed south-east into Pan district (some 50 kms south of Chiang Rai), swung east through Toeng, and then marched north-east up the Doi Yao ridge, finally to arrive at Doi Pa Mon (the Lao border ridge on which the present-day KMT village of Pa Taang is situated), where he set up his HQ – an incredible journey unchallenged smack through the middle of modern northern Thailand of the year 1961! Another part of Lao Li's 3rd Army entered Thailand at Doi Ang Karng and Taton, spreading out to settle mainly at Ban Luang, Sui Tang and Pa Daeng. Some Ma Joong-gua troops (the ones manning the KMT propaganda radio station up in the Wa sub-state) also came to Doi Ang Karng, settling there and setting up a military training school at Mae Ngon, Fang district (down in the valley just east of Xing Shoon or Mai Nong Bua). Altogether, more than 8,000 KMT entered northern Thailand, 4,570 coming to Chiang Mai province and 3,560 into Chiang Rai province. Lao Li settled on the Doi Pa Mon and Doi Yao ridges over by the Lao border (south of Chiang Khong) with 900 troops. But he did not stay there long, for in 1963 he and about half of his men were moved by the Thai authorities to Tam Ngop (back over on the Burmese border, north of Chiang Dao and close to Muang Na), where they set up a new and permanent 3rd Army HQ, which, although now effectively defunct, has survived to this day. The other half did not want to go and hid at nearby Huai Ku, Huai Haan and Seng Meng, today all Hmong villages near Pa Taang, as well as at Doi Pa Ji further south. The reason why Lao Li was moved to Tam Ngop was that the anti-communist KMT came into conflict at Doi Pa Mon and Doi Yao with the Communist Party of Thailand (CPT) insurgents who at that time were infiltrating the region. By 1967, all the remaining 500 3rd Army KMT had been cleared out of the area and likewise sent to Tam Ngop. And with that we come to the era of the communist insurgency in Thailand.[4]

I do not propose to detail here the KMT's involvement in the war against the CPT, which would take us too far astray from the KMT and their presence in villages such as Muang Na, Kae Noi, Piang Luang and Mae Or, but for continuity's sake will outline the main points (for more detailed coverage of the communist insurgency in Thailand, the CPT, and KMT involvement in suppressing both, see my narrative guide *Around Lan-Na*, Chapter 12). After Li's 3rd Army left the Doi Pa Mon area, the CPT spread all over it. The communists became so strong that Bangkok decided to move against them, and the war against the CPT in and around Pa Taang dates from 1967. The Thai authorities suggested to the KMT that as a quid pro quo for being allowed to settle in Thailand they might like to help combat the CPT, a task for which, as Gen. Lao Li stressed, they volunteered. Accordingly, in December 1970 some many hundreds of 3rd and 5th Army troops, including numerous Wa, but without Generals Li or Duan, were trucked over to join Thai army units to secure the Doi Luang, Doi Yao and Doi Pa Mon ridges (in that order). In a number of actions that went on until 1974, sometimes with heavy fighting, control of the mountainous border area between Chiang Khong and Chiang Kham was regained, although the KMT (and Wa) suffered losses of about 100 killed and 300 wounded. To permanently secure the area, bases and villages were set up in 1973 at Pa Taang (3rd Army) and Mae Aeb (5th Army), which were settled by KMT and Wa soldiers and then their families as a reward for their efforts.

The KMT were involved in other security work. Thus, in 1980, 200 3rd Army troops (including many Wa) from Tam Ngop and Pa Taang volunteered as a way of earning money to go and guard stretches of the H1148 Chiang Kham/Ta Wang Pa road currently under construction against CPT sabotage,

---

[4] It might be wondered why the Thai authorities, knowing the freewheeling nature of the KMT militias and their involvement in the narcotics trade, should allow them to enter Thailand, set up bases at Mae Salong, Tam Ngop and elsewhere, establish rear communities for their families up and down the border, and not repulse the Chinese encroachers on Thai soil. The curious welcome extended by the Siamese to the KMT had exactly to do with the growing communist threat both within and especially outside the country's borders. To understand the logic of the welcome, one has to remember the politics of the period. Almost all of Thailand's neighbours had either gone or threatened to go communist or revolutionary 'socialist' – China, Korea, Laos, Cambodia... In Burma, the Communist Party of Burma (CPB) was enjoying considerable success, while, more alarmingly, in the kingdom itself the CPT was making serious advances in the mountainous jungle areas of the north-west and north-east. There was a very real danger that the CPB and the CPT would soon link up, with Thailand falling as the next domino in South-East Asia to the communists. In these circumstances, and with American approval, the Thai authorities embraced the dubious KMT. The staunchly anti-communist Chinese Nationalists would form a crucial link in the security cordon of friendly rebel armies and ethnic insurgent buffer states that the Thais were trying to encourage around their borders to counter the red menace (these armies and states included at different times the KMT 3rd and 5th Armies, Khun Sa's SUA, Mo Heng's SURA, the Wa WNA and WNC, and various Shan outfits in the Shan State, the Karenni KA in the Karenni State, and the Karen KNLA as well as the Mon NMSP in the Karen State).

THREE PAGODAS

and 300 5th Army troops (including many Wa) from Mae Salong and Mae Aeb likewise went to guard sections of the H1155 road (the easternmost way from Chiang Khong to Toeng). Further scores of KMT and Wa were killed in these dangerous operations. In 1981, 200 3rd Army and 200 5th Army troops went to fight the CPT at Khao Kor and Khao Ja. And in the late 1970s and early 1980s, KMT soldiers went to guard road construction and roadbuilders against CPT attack and sabotage during the engineering of the H1090 Mae Sot/Um Pang road ('Death Highway'), in the course of which some 30 workers were massacred by the communists, as we will see later, in Chapter 11. A proof of the success of the Thai strategy of accepting the KMT and of using it both to attack and deter the communists was that in areas where the Chinese Nationalists operated, the CPT had, broadly speaking, minimal impact.

However, the Siamese cosying up to and utilization of the KMT came with a price. For at the same time as the Chinese Nationalists were aiding the Thais in their security dirty work, the KMT continued to be involved in dirty work of their own – in the narcotics business. Soon after 1961, extensive poppy fields suddenly sprang up around places such as Mae Salong and Kae Noi, and refineries for producing heroin began operating in Mae Salong and Piang Luang (just west of Kae Noi). But most of the opium was produced in and came down from the north. It had long been grown in the Chinese provinces of Yunnan and Sichuan, from where, to avoid Chinese taxation, it had been transported to Burma, Thailand and Indo-China for onward shipment. Post-1949, growing switched to the 'Golden Triangle', through which caravans of up to 400-500 mules, each carrying up to 50 kgs of raw opium, moved down to the Thai-Burmese and Thai-Lao borders. The KMT, already present in Burma in the 1950s and camped out along the Thai border, became involved. Their pre-eminence as a large armed militia in the 'Golden Triangle' meant that they were soon able to dominate other groups involved in the trade and the trade itself. The two evacuations of KMT people did not mean an end to this predominance, nor did the move to Thailand in 1961. Post-1961, the 3rd and 5th Armies still had some troops in the Shan State. The KMT was less involved in growing opium and more in trafficking it, and especially in taxing other groups' caravans passing through KMT-controlled areas and gateways. Lao Li's and Duan's men were also involved in arms and jade trading. In the 1960s, the KMT essentially controlled the Shan State, some of the Wa sub-state, Kokang and a bit of the northerly Kachin State. To put an end to arguments between the 3rd and 5th Armies, Li and Duan agreed to split control of the opium area, so that west of the River Salween fell to Lao Li, and east to Duan. At this time, the KMT's main income was from these dubious activities, and some of the money it spent on weapons to further strengthen itself.

The years from about 1961 to 1967 were the heyday of the KMT in the region. Arriving on the Siamese doorstep in 1961 depleted and dispirited after being routed by combined Burma army and Chinese PLA forces and after the second evacuation of their people, they were now safely ensconced just inside Thailand in a series of strongholds and villages, and enjoyed the blessing both of Bangkok and the CIA. Even if now militarily thinner on the ground across the border in the Shan State, they nevertheless had men and agents there, had free rein of the area, were unchallenged drugswise, and controlled key sections of the frontier and hence cross-border trafficking routes.

The KMT's pre-eminence was seriously challenged in 1967. Caravanners and their accompanying pocket warlord armies objected to having to pay extortionate taxes to the Chinese interlopers, and in July of that year Khun Sa, himself by now a big trafficking fish, sought to avoid payment of a 5-million-baht levy (Chapter 3 contains an account of Khun Sa). Coming south from Saen Wi with 200 troops minding a particularly large caravan carrying 16 tons of opium destined for Huai Tang in Laos, he varied his route to evade a KMT taxation checkpoint. The result was the (in)famous Opium War of 1967 between Khun Sa and the KMT, which also spelled the beginning of the end of KMT pre-eminence. Instead of chasing after Sa's caravan, the KMT allowed it to deliver its load to Huai Tang and then ambushed it at Ban Kwan (in Laos, opposite Sob Ruak, just north of Chiang Saen) as it returned. During the last four days of the month, fighting raged, with many casualties on both sides. Finally, the Lao army ended it by bombing all the participants from the air.

The KMT retreated across the Mae Khong river to enter Thailand in Chiang Saen district, openly continuing to the Mae Chan area. The Thai government was so outraged that it sent troops to the Thai-Burmese border area in Chiang Rai province to bridle the KMT. Because of this, and because Khun Sa claimed far and wide that he had won the Kwan battle and the Opium War, the KMT lost influence and prestige in the Shan State, and began to be eclipsed as the leading player there by Khun Sa. In October 1970, the Thai government officially agreed to allow the KMT to stay and settle in Thailand as refugees, but on condition that they abandoned their involvement in the drugs business. This further emasculated the KMT in respect of their role in Burma and the narcotics business. In 1972, perhaps making a token compliance with the strictures of their Siamese hosts, Duan and Li ostentatiously handed over to the Thai authorities respectively 32 and 8 tons of raw KMT opium, which was burned. The US government gave $240 per kg of the opium, which made Gen. Duan at least a rich man. Thus KMT involvement in drugs trafficking waned during the 1970s, although did not completely end, continuing to some extent in the 1980s (as it undoubtedly still continues today) in places like Nong Ook, Kae Noi, Piang Luang, Mae Or and Pa Taang.

During the 1980s, the fortunes of the KMT declined further. By then, the CPT insurgency in Thailand had largely petered out, while the CPB threat across the border in Burma had also receded (and ended in 1989). There was little need anymore for the Nationalist veterans to act as a proxy security corps. Rewarded in some cases with Thai identity and with fresh border villages to settle, the KMT had served their purpose as far as the Thais were concerned. But, beyond this, they had become an anachronism. Mao's victory of 1949 was history, and any idea of the Nationalists reinvading mainland China 35 years on was just wishful thinking. Most troubling from the Thai point of view was the fact that the once highly-valued anti-communist bulwark was still dabbling in the narcotics trade and had now virtually degenerated into little more than armed merchant militias, which continued to make entrepreneurial forays into neighbouring Burma from Thai soil. World opinion was beginning to tut-tut. All in all, the Thai patrons realized that there was hardly further justification for harbouring a corrupt and embarrassing alien army in their land, and in 1984 they moved against the Kuomintang, ordering them to disband, subjecting KMT villages to a 'pacification' programme, and encouraging the 15,000 Chinese dependants to integrate into regular Thai society.

However, the ageing KMT warriors were not entirely played out. In 1973, following the takeover of the Wa sub-state by the CPB People's Army, Wa groups fleeing the communists and led notably by Maha San and Ai Siao-su started appearing along the Shan-Thai border. The Wa were also involved in narcotics trafficking, and before long they tangled with opium king Khun Sa just as the KMT had done, even replacing the KMT as Sa's arch-rival. In the late 1980s and early 90s, the grumbling Opium War along Thailand's north-western border flared up anew, this time between the Wa and Khun Sa. With a common enemy in Khun Sa, it was logical that the KMT should side with the Wa newcomers, and all the more so because there had been connections with them since 1949. During the 1980s, the KMT commenced fresh machinations along the border, using their experience and financial clout to build up various Wa factions with a view to challenging Sa and securing cross-border trafficking routes. The new KMT strategy was not without its success. More details of the relationships both between the KMT and the Wa, and between the KMT and Khun Sa, as well as of the vying for supremacy of the three groups in the 'Golden Triangle' drugs trade are given respectively in Chapter 6 under 'Maha San and recent Wa history' and 'The Wa and recent politico-military developments in the "Golden Triangle"' and in Chapter 3 under 'Warlord Khun Sa and the "Golden Triangle"'.

The Nationalists' informal alliance with the Wa brings the story of the Kuomintang Chinese in the north-west of Thailand up to date. Today the KMT can be found continuing to live along the frontier in some ten principal outposts and in around two dozen settlements altogether. Undoubtedly, they are still engaged to some extent in narcotics-trafficking activities. But otherwise the Thai pacification and development programmes aimed at the KMT are paying off, and now the descendants of the Nationalist refugees are engaged in farming and normal trading. Places like Mae Salong, which is – as it were – the 'capital' of the KMT communities and the largest KMT enclave in the world outside Taiwan, and to a lesser extent Mae Or nowadays make a lot of their money from tea growing and tourism. Recently KMT families in Thailand have profited from a 'bounty' paid to them by the 'home country' of Taiwan, which has also financed a series of infrastructural improvements in Thailand's KMT villages (roadbuilding, TV satellite dishes etc.). By 1979, the number of KMT in the kingdom had grown to 10,500, and by 1984 to 12,690. Today it must surely easily exceed 20,000. The KMT often share their villages with other peoples, e.g. the Shan (as in Kae Noi, Piang Luang, Wiang Haeng and Nong Ook), the Akha (as in Mae Salong) and the Wa. We were to stumble on a joint KMT/Wa community later in our journey.

For the sake of completeness, I include here a few words about recent events in **Mae Salong**, Thailand's principal KMT village, which well illustrate

MR DONUT COMING SOON

the thrust of the Thai authorities' programme for pacifying and integrating the Chinese Nationalist refugees (for a more anecdotal description of Mae Salong, see my *Around Lan-Na*, Chapter 7). In the early years of 5th Army settlement on Doi Mae Salong, the KMT were quite cut off. There was no road to their village, and when they wanted supplies, they used to go down to the valley with their mules, causing fear among the lowland Thai. The Thai authorities, too, were apprehensive about such a powerful unchecked militia lodged up in the border mountains. Following the KMT's formal acceptance as refugees in Thailand in 1970, the slow process of their integration into Siamese society began. The military established checkpoints in an attempt to control the Mae Salong area as well as the drugs and arms trading in it. Various groups of officials trekked up there on fact-finding missions, and in 1973 the local authorities came to help build the main street and clear the surrounding area for tea growing. In 1974, a water system was installed, using US Vietnam-War pipes from Khorat. The poppy fields on the hillsides all around Mae Salong were cut down to be replaced from 1975 on by other, temperate cash crops. Instead of opium, the KMT began growing apricots, plums, peaches, lychees, prunes, coffee, Chinese chestnuts, rice, peanuts, maize and, as said, tea. Overproduction led to the making of fruits pickled in vinegar and preserved in sugar, and to the making of fruit 'wines' and liqueurs.

The Thai paramilitary BPP brought teachers with them to Mae Salong, who started running the schools in Thai along Thai lines, and the 800 children (in 1975) now took their Chinese lessons either before or after Thai school. A key figure in the integration of the KMT was Thai army man (later prime minister) Kriang Saak Chamanan, who acted as an intermediary between the KMT, the US, Taiwan and Bangkok. He arranged for the KMT to be able to stay in Thailand, for them to have some land, and to start getting Thai citizenship. Each Nationalist family was given 15 *rai* of land to help it and allow it to support itself, although soon the arrangement was abused, with the Chinese selling off, buying and developing the plots. And, by 1994, some 3,000 KMT had acquired Thai ID – actually a laughably low figure, considering all the intervening years since 1970 (let alone since 1961), which can be put down to bureaucratic heel-dragging. Kriang Saak made himself popular at Mae Salong and Tam Ngop, and the KMT rewarded him with a splendid villa in Mae Salong. From the mid-1970s until 1989, Bangkok pump-primed Mae Salong, Tam Ngop, Pa Taang and Mae Aeb with 250,000 baht each per year, later rising to 1.9 million baht per annum. During the 70s, control of Mae Salong gradually transferred from the Thai military to the civilian authorities, and in 1984 it came under the jurisdiction of the Ministry of the Interior, although to this day the army retains a residual interest. Finally, a road was built up to the mountaintop village, taking five years to construct and costing some 33 million baht, or about one million baht per km, and in 1980 Mae Salong was opened as a tourist attraction. In the late 1980s, when I first went to Mae Salong, I climbed on a motorcycle up the steep new road from Pasang and passed no fewer than ten 'tourist security checkpoints' on the way, all of which have now fallen into disuse.

41

Finally, also for the sake of the completeness of our KMT account, I include two thumbnail sketches of Generals Lao Li and Duan. **Gen. Li Wen-fan** (or Li Woen-huan), commonly known as **Lao Li** (not to be confused with Gen. Li Mi), was born in 1919 and said in a speech given in 1975 upon his retirement that he was a Yunnanese farmer living on China's border with Burma until Mao's Communists confiscated his land, causing him to leave China and link up with Gen. Li Mi and the 93rd Regiment Nationalists to combat the Communists. Even though he was appointed a general by Li Mi and at Muang Saat was made commander of the 3rd Army, he has always maintained that he was never a career military man, but a farmer forced by circumstances to become involved in army life. Because of this, he and other farming-minded Nationalists (the 3rd and 5th Armies and their dependants) did not want to join either of the two evacuations of 1953 and 1961 to Taiwan, when the real military men went to the island. Being farmers, they were not drawn to life on a small island, but preferred to stay put in Burma and then Thailand, hoping to return to farming in either Yunnan or Burma or Thailand. For many years, Lao Li divided his time between his KMT 3rd Army HQ at Tam Ngop and a residence he had in Chiang Mai, on the banks of the River Ping, in the Charoenrat Road, Fah Ham district. During the 1960s and 70s, this villa and extensive compound almost amounted to a rear base for the KMT, which is perhaps why around 1983/84 a Khun Sa SUA hit squad blew it up. Lao Li gained Thai citizenship in 1970, acquiring the name Chai Chaisiri. In 2001, he was still alive as an old man with senile dementia in his Chiang Mai residence, hardly ever leaving his sickroom, to which only one or two trusted people were admitted, and guarded in the compound by a motley crew of Chinese, Wa and Akha men as well as ferocious dogs.

Gen. Duan Shi-wen (or Tuan Si-wan) was born in Yi Liang district, Yunnan province, and went to military school. He married a Chinese-Shan lady and had four children, two boys and two girls. Duan's father went to Taiwan, where he became a senator. It is said that all Duan's children were educated abroad, and in 1991 one of the sons became *kamnaan* (mayor) of Mae Salong, running one of the town's resorts. It was Duan who once famously commented, justifying the KMT's involvement in the opium trade: "We have to continue to fight the evil of communism; to fight, you must have an army, and an army must have guns; and to buy guns, you must have money. In these mountains the only money is opium." By all accounts Duan was a relaxed, gentlemanly, much-respected man, and a clever and effective leader both of the 5th Army and Mae Salong. He became very rich from the 1972 opium-for-dollars exchange and had a house in Bangkok. But he preferred not to live there or in Taiwan, but in Mae Salong, liking to exist simply and mostly alone with his people. He was popularly known as *si gong* or 'Grandfather General'. On gaining Thai citizenship, he acquired the name Chawan Kamlu. In May 1980, Duan suffered a stroke and was helicoptered to Chiang Rai hospital. Against doctors' orders, he had himself flown to his personal physician at Payatai Hospital in Bangkok, where he died on 23 May. A month later, his body was helicoptered back to Mae Salong. When he was still alive, Duan himself chose the hillside site of his tomb, which is above his former house and facing east, overlooking the town. Today Duan's splendid tomb is much visited especially by ageing surviving KMT warriors, who like to sit there reminiscing about *si gong* and the old times.

✳

Kae Noi

Our first impression of Kae Noi was of a desultory and in some way sinister aggregation of mean houses, spread out in a wide featureless basin. An incongruous paved road ran for two or three kms through the Chinese core, after which it terminated in some fields. We scooted up and down this drawn-out main street a couple of times, trying to interpret what we saw. The Chinese influence was palpable. Around the doorframes of the low mudbrick dwellings were various banners, gold Chinese characters on red paper. In the wooden panels of the doors were diamond-shaped pictures of Samurai-like warriors or dragons. One or two richer families had built cement-rendered houses, washed over in characteristic Chinese style with pale green or pink. Mules were tethered in yards, and ox-carts lay around. We tried to find some kind of centre. But there was none, just a snake of dispersed dwellings. Finally, we spotted a couple of low wooden shops side by side. Finding no eating place anywhere, we dismounted at these rudimentary stores and surveyed their minimal provisions. There was the usual assortment of goods one finds in all such village shops – tinned sardines, washing powder, loose tobacco and noodles – but also a selection of tinned produce which had made its way down through the Shan State from China. The Jiin owners eyed us coolly, suspiciously. One woman seemed to have been selling noodle soup, but although it was not late, she refused to serve us. From another lady, we bought a rusty tin of chicken curry, years past its sell-by date. To this meagre acquisition, we added a bar of peanut crunch and some other titbits to see us through the long evening ahead.

 Word of our arrival must have spread round Kae Noi like wildfire, for we had hardly been in the village 15 minutes when a Border Patrol Police (BPP) truck came scorching along the main street, clearly aiming for us. Four paramilitary *dorchodor*, as they are called in Thai, got out and bore down on us ominously. They demanded our passports, scrutinized the pages (even though none of them could read English), and asked us what we were doing in Kae Noi, making it abundantly clear that we had no business there. We thought trouble was brewing, but actually there was little this officious squad could do. They could not send us deeper into the closed area, but equally they could hardly send us back. If they did send us on – well, that was just what we wanted. Finally, finding no solution to the problem, the *dorchodor* retreated, threatening that they would think about the matter and would return later.

 Our next concern was to find somewhere to stay the night. Obviously, there were no guest houses in such a place, but we had discovered that Kae Noi boasted no fewer than three schools. There is a tradition in Thailand that if you cannot find anywhere to stay in a village, you can fall back on the local temple or, sometimes, the school. We approached the obvious school in the middle of the village. It was a long low wooden affair with an uneven tin roof. Classes were out, but some of the teachers were playing takraw near their accommodation block. They were very surprised to see us and could not understand how we had got past all the roadblocks. We said we could not find anywhere to stay in Kae Noi and asked if we might possibly spend the night in the school. There was nowhere to stay in the school, they said, and they had no spare space in their block.

Once we had stayed in a school sickroom, and we put it to them that we could perhaps do the same here. After some discussion, they supposed that this would be alright. Presently they brought mats and blankets, and even tried unsuccessfully to rig up an electric light. But apart from that, disappointingly, they took little notice of us. Other teachers we have stayed with in other far-flung parts of the kingdom have proved remarkably friendly and hospitable, offering food, inviting us to sit with them around their evening fire, showing us their village, and so on. But this group, when they had eaten their evening meal, withdrew into their slummy block, shut the doors, switched on the TV, and left us out in the gathering mist and cold. We begged some leftover rice from one of the wives and ate our curry out of the tin. The curry seemed to consist mostly of rabbit or turkey bones. We nibbled at the peanut crunch, which was brittle and sugary. The reception from the teachers was almost as cool as that from the soldiers, and we felt most unwelcome in Kae Noi, even disconsolate. That first night of our journey was one of the least successful ones.

The next morning, finding nowhere to wash, we unplugged a hosepipe serving a sprinkler in front of the school, and washed from the tap. The headmaster was at hand, and in an unexpected access of hospitality he brought coffee, tea and biscuits for the three of us to eat at a trestle table in the emerging sun. Over this breakfast, the *kru yai* informed us of some details about the village. The bamboo *wat* we had noticed the evening before was inhabited by one solitary Shan monk. The monk had built the *wat* himself just a month or two before. There were at least two Christian churches in the village. One was nine years old and run by an Akha hill-tribe man. The churches were used separately by converted Chinese and Lahu Christians. Of the three schools in Kae Noi, this one in the middle was an ordinary school run by ordinary teachers. It was a Buddhist place, and most of the children were Chinese. Another school, run by BPP teachers, was attended by Christian pupils – mainly converted Lahu. What the third school was we never discovered – perhaps a kindergarten. The reason why there were so many schools in such a small place was that there was antagonism between the religious and ethnic groupings, so that the schoolchildren had to be kept apart. The headteacher was of the opinion that the Shan children were the brightest, while the Chinese were difficult and unmotivated. The authorities, he said, had many problems with the KMT. This had not stopped them, however, from exploiting the Third Army veterans, for the Kae Noi KMT had been used by the Thai government in security work (guarding road construction) and in suppressing the Thai communists. In exchange some had been given Thai identity.

With Chinese youngsters milling around our breakfast table, the conversation turned to us and our project. When the headteacher learned that we had come up from Muang Na, his eyebrows rose in disbelief. He was so scandalized that he called over some of the other teachers. They shook their heads, tut-tutting. Generously, the *kru yai* explained that he thought we had been very brave (read: foolhardy). He would certainly not have made the journey alone. The route was scarcely used at the best of times, but in the winter months, when people had to go down that way, they went in a convoy of several trucks and motorbikes, if possible with armed soldiers. The reason was that the track was preyed upon by cross-border bandits, particularly from December to February. At the treacherous corkscrew where we had stalled the motorbike, a pick-up driver had been shot and killed just two days earlier. After the rice harvest, people were flush with money and were out buying goods. The bandits knew this and so were especially active at this time of year.

The winter months were also the season of the opium poppy harvest. There were heroin refineries, processing at that very moment, only two kilometres behind Kae Noi. The refined drugs found their way down the local footpaths and tracks, bound for Chiang Mai. The traffickers could be jumpy and very dangerous if encountered. Naturally, they did not like being observed going about their business. Especially *farang* might easily be mistaken for agents of the drug-suppression authorities and took their lives into their own hands. And then there were the battles between Khun Sa's guerrillas and the Wa Daeng or Red Wa. These raged periodically around Kae Noi for control of the poppy fields and trafficking routes. When that happened, the headteacher said, people did not leave the village, but stayed in their houses for weeks on end, eating all their provisions until there was nothing left but salted fish. The *tahaan praan*, Thailand's élite black-uniformed army rangers, were sitting along the border behind Kae Noi, but they were unable to fully secure the area. Unchallenged, Khun Sa's people infiltrated Kae Noi itself, coming down to buy things from the shops. The authorities and villagers could never recognize them because they were indistinguishable from the local Shan. These were some of the reasons why the Kae Noi area was firmly closed.

Seeing the headteacher's evident concern for our safety, we reassured him that we had no intention of returning to Muang Na, but wanted if possible to go on to Wiang Haeng. He was relieved when he heard this, but worried anew about our fresh proposal. He discussed the matter with the other teachers, but none of them was sure about the possibility of getting on to Wiang Haeng. One thought a way existed, another not. One thought that a border track was under construction, another that it was far too dangerous to venture into those remotest of valleys. Finally, a forestry boy was called, who said that there was a way through, which could be managed by motorbike. Our worry was that we would not have enough petrol for the trip – there was no fuel in Kae Noi. But the *anuraak* lad said that it was only about 35 kms round to the *ampoe*. Just go to the end of the paved street, he said airily, and carry on down the track.

It was time for school to start. The teachers got up, and we took our leave of them, thanking in particular the headmaster for his kindness. Before quitting Kae Noi, we wanted briefly to investigate the Royal Project. Accordingly, we went back to the division of the ways at the run-in to the village and followed a track through the fields to the south-east side of the wide valley. Here we found, slightly elevated, the Red Lahu village of Pa Bong Mai and beyond it the Royal Project. There was little sign of traditional costume among the Lahu, and the Project buildings were deserted. But from the reluctant headman of Pa Bong Mai and a large circle of searching onlookers, we gleaned that the project, initiated by the Thai royal family, was an old one, some 20 years old, and sought to encourage the local people to grow (instead of opium) temperate fruit trees, kidney beans and certain vegetables. But the best thing about the early morning excursion was the view north-west across the shallow misty *moeng* to Kae Noi proper. The straggling houses, smoke drifting silently through their *ka*-grass roofs, crouched at the foot of the sinister border hills. Almost more than any other village we visited, Kae Noi looked a place with a dark secret.

✳

Back at the school, we readied the Honda and set off (now see Map 6). We exactly followed the instructions of the *anuraak* youth. Beyond Kae Noi's central school, the paved street gave over to a dirt road, and the end of the village was marked by a BPP camp, complete with sandbag fortifications and machine-gun posts. Outside Kae Noi, the sun was completing its job of burning off the overnight mist from the harvested rice fields and luxuriant valleys. The ride was stony and bumpy, making progress slow, but by way of compensation the track was flatter than we had feared. As the teachers had warned us, it passed through some very isolated territory indeed, twisting and turning around the forested hillsides, affording long views into Burma over untouched uninhabited mountain scenery. What we did not know, for better or for worse, was that this stretch along the border after Kae Noi was every bit as dangerous as the stretch up to the village. The truth of this was borne in on us by local Karen friends we were shortly to meet in Wiang Haeng. With typical Karen understatement, they said that it was "not a road to stop on". A woman in her car had been ambushed and shot at just recently as she drove along the stretch – it was not known by whom, but probably by Lahu bandits.

Fortunately, we were oblivious to all this and enjoyed a sunny ride for a long hour round to the village of Chong. Ten kms out from Kae Noi, we came across the Black Lahu settlement of **Pa** (km 77.5), which we stopped to look at. Excited people immediately gathered round. A man ushered us up a ladder and into a house. All the others followed, sitting down on the bamboo floor in a circle around us. The man was the village headman and priest, and the room he had brought us into was some kind of church. Handsome pictures of a long-haired hippie-style Christ adorned the walls. The settlement was ten years old, the pious *pu yai baan* explained. There were 19 houses, of which seven were Christian. He himself had moved up here from the Mae La Na area, while the people had moved down from Kae Noi. But the real point of interest for us was an impromptu fashion show. Two girls suddenly appeared through the door, having hastily put on festive Red and Black Lahu costumes, beautifully made in Burma. The people wanted nothing more than to show them to us. The Red Lahu (Lahu Nyi) costume consisted of a black tube skirt with a lot of red banding, and of a blue bolero trimmed with red and blue. The Black Lahu (Lahu Na) costume was a mainly black skirt with some red wiggly detailed trimming around the hem, and a short black jacket with long frontal tails, trimmed with intricate small red panels and small silver baubles.

Another 10 kms and a slow, stony, bike-rattling descent took us past the scenically positioned Lisu village of **Huai Loek** (km 80.5) to bring us to a succession of low-lying settlements: the new KMT habitation of Pang Kae and the communities of Huai Krai and Muang Krua. Finally, the track, now a dirt road, emerged at a T-junction in the village of **Chong** (km 92.5). Right (north) went to Piang Luang, and left (approximately south) to Wiang Haeng. Chong was a relatively large place, and we stopped to walk around. People were surprised to see us. After all, we were still in the forbidden zone. The word *chong* in Shan means *wat*, and near the junction stood a substantial monastery-temple in the Shan style, called Wat Mak Gai Yon. A square wooden structure raised high above the ground on piles, it had a complicated roof consisting of no fewer than seven tiers. In the temple grounds, there was a whitewashed stone pagoda with several Buddha figures looking out of niches. They were encircled by a group of praying figures looking in.

The remaining 11 kms of dirt road south to Wiang Haeng was a wider, well-beaten way (Map 7). We soon discovered why. It was a route taken by log transporters. Laden, they ground past us from behind, and, empty, they came rattling towards us. Each time they left clouds of blinding dust in their wake. Otherwise it was very pleasant along here. The flattish road followed a fertile high-level valley with hills on each side. In the fields, people were busy cutting rice and laying it on its side to dry. And there was a string of small self-protection villages both on and off the road. Onroad, we passed through the communities of **Muang Pok** and **Mahatat** before we spotted trouble ahead. A barrier firmly blocked the road, guarded by two soldiers. It was the checkpoint at **Pang Po** village. The checkpoint lay on the edge of the closed area, at the end of it if you were coming from Kae Noi or Piang Luang, and at the start of it if you were coming from Wiang Haeng, which lay just seven more kms beyond Pang Po. Our problem now, having got into the forbidden zone, was how to get out of it without a lot of unpleasantness. We saw a pick-up coming the other way and slowed down until it reached the post. The barrier went up and the soldiers questioned the people in the cab. They looked like Chinese from Piang Luang. While the guards were thus diverted, we slowly rode through. Of course, they saw us, but they made no attempt to stop us. Their mouths fell open, and they stood there speechless. Imagine their puzzlement at seeing a *farang* ride out of a closed area who had not ridden in! They must have thought we had come straight out of warlord Khun Sa's fiefdom in the Shan State.

After the Pang Po checkpoint came the village of **Kong Lom** (km 100), which marked the start of the cross-country way down to Pai, which we would later take. Kong Lom was followed by an extensive 'godown' or logging customs camp. Thousands of logs lay strewn around, lorries were being loaded up and others sat idle in various states of disrepair. At the rear of the compound were some shacks, where the drivers and camp workers lived.

Finally, we passed the satellite settlement of **Pa Pai** as well as one more checkpoint, after which, 35 kms out from Kae Noi and just as the forestry boy had said (104 kms from the H107, or 180 kms from Chiang Mai, coming the roundabout way), we entered the first principal objective of our journey – Wiang Haeng.

* *

Postscript 2002

Chiang Mai

By the mid-1990s, Mr Donut had indeed, as the posters proclaimed, arrived in Chiang Mai, in the company of Col. "finger-lickin' good" Sanders and the Burger King. A great deal else also turned up or began to be installed. But the great boom of the time in Chiang Mai, as everywhere else in Thailand, was followed by bust. The Asian economic crash of 1997-98, which started in Thailand, put paid to the hand-over-fist building spree. Numerous construction projects were abandoned half-finished, to be slowly reclaimed by the vegetation and allowed to rust and discolour in the tropical rain and sun, millions lost their jobs, and hundreds of thousands of shophouses, homes and cars were seized by the banks from borrowers defaulting on their credit repayments. These buildings, too, stood empty, while the cars cluttered second-hand vehicle sales lots. It is only now, 2001-02, that the situation is starting to normalize and that some building work is being resumed. For an account of the economic implosion, as well as of the history both of Chiang Mai and of the Lan-Na kingdom, the reader is referred to my *Around Lan-Na: A Guide to Thailand's Northern Border Region* (Chapter 1).

The food section of Chiang Mai's Anusarn Market must now vie with the Galare Foodcentre (the voucher place) in the heart of the Night Bazaar (east side of Chang Klan Road) in an unequal contest, for the latter is an attractive venue in which to sit and eat out under the stars, as much used by Thais as foreign tourists, with a wide selection of inexpensive dishes, and with a free nightly show of traditional Thai and hill-tribe dancing.

There are hundreds of places to stay in Chiang Mai of all types and price, and everyone has their favourite. Some old favourites of ours include *Eagle House 1* and *2*, *Chiang Mai Inn*, and the guest houses in the *soi* or side lanes off Moon Muang Road, behind the Sompet Market, e.g in Soi 7 and 9.

On the subject of motorcycles and of hiring one in Chiang Mai, the Honda Wing that we used when originally researching this book is now defunct. A main advantage of the Wing – its big fuel tank – has become irrelevant because petrol is now widely available in Thailand, even in obscure off-the-beaten-track villages. Assuming that you always start a journey or leg with a full tank, and fill up judiciously as and when, it is pretty difficult to run dry these days. Chiang Mai has an oversupply of bikes for rent, meaning competitive rental prices. At the time of writing, the machines for rent are all semi-automatic clutchless 'stepthru' 100-cc Honda Dreams and 110-cc Honda Waves, both excellent little bikes. Opt for a new or newish Wave, with its useful extra 10% of power. There are many motorcycle rental shops along the Moon Muang and Kotchasan Roads. In recent years, we have found *Jaguar* and *Mr Kom* on Moon Muang reliable and good value places (avoid the troublesome *Mr Beer*), where you can get a newish Wave for about 150 baht per day (discounted to 130 baht/day if you hire for a longer time, say, 10 days).

MR DONUT COMING SOON

When you take a bike from a rental shop, acquire from it also a crash helmet – they will have some. Following a change in Thai law, motorcyclists are now obliged – sensibly – to wear helmets, and failure to do so could land you a police fine. You are most likely to be caught and fined in cities and perhaps sometimes at checks on the highways. But the further you get away from the cities and into the countryside, the less likely you are to be troubled. Many Thais flout the law, as they scoff at all laws, and some *farang* think it is cool to 'ride free', reckoning that they are unlikely to be hassled by a police force instructed to be tourist-friendly. But at least in the chaotic traffic of Thai cities and on the kingdom's dangerous larger roads, it makes complete sense to wear a helmet. So the era of wearing bobble hats on bikes on the H107 is basically over. Offroad, away from the highways and on dirt roads and tracks, the situation is different, and here you can still ride free with impunity. Thus, in Chapters 1-4 of this book, you could easily ride from Muang Na all the way to Pai without anyone objecting and without running the risk of incurring a fine. Nevertheless, I personally favour wearing a helmet even offroad – it protects me if I take a tumble and also helps shade my face from the burning sun.

Chiang Mai – Chiang Dao

As you exit the centre of Chiang Mai and proceed north up the Chang Puak Road, you pass *Rimping Superstore* (left, just offroad, near a *Novotel* hotel), which has a fine offering of Thai and Western foods and is a good place for stocking up with provisions for touring and trekking.

In 1997, we discovered a nice place to stay in the accommodation desert of **Chiang Dao**. This is *Malee's Nature Lovers' Bungalows*, a guest house that is not actually in the town itself, but 6.5 kms west of Chiang Dao. At the time of writing, it was still flourishing and looks set to continue to do so. The guest house makes a convenient, pleasant and recommendable base from which to explore the whole local area, including both places on our itinerary, such as Kae Noi, Wiang Haeng and Piang Luang, and other features of interest, such as Doi Chiang Dao mountain, Doi Chiang Dao Wildlife Sanctuary, Chiang Dao Cave and the KMT village of Nong Ook. In 2002, prices at *Malee's* were 300 baht for a bungalow (for 2 or 3 people, with own bathroom and hot shower) and 100 baht for a dormitory bed. For 50 baht, you can put up a tent in the garden as I once did. To reach the guest house, turn left/west into the side road at the top/northern end of Chiang Dao's main street, as if you were going to Chiang Dao Cave, which is signed. The turning lies diagonally opposite a restaurant and small petrol station. On this side road, you head straight towards Mount Chiang Dao, proceeding through a wood of tall trees and the village of Tam. Go past the cave complex, situated on the left (km 5.2), ignore a right turn for a monastery and a second right turn leading to another monastery and also Muang Khong, and proceed past a bizarre-looking Hindu meditation building (left) until you reach the guest house (km 6.5), located right, set back from the road. *Malee's* has a reputation for birdwatching, and several birders have left logs there of what they have seen in the vicinity. *Malee's* provides food.

Chiang Dao – Muang Na – Kae Noi – Wiang Haeng

Since the early 1990s, the whole road system connecting Muang Na, Kae Noi, Wiang Haeng and Piang Luang has changed dramatically, both in terms of security and access, and in terms of the nature and construction of the roads. Now, in 2002, you can go to any of these places, even all the way to dubious Piang Luang on the border, by whatever route, without being stopped or even scrutinized at checkpoints. The checkpoints at Na Wai and Muang Na, and at Pang Po and the entrance to Piang Luang are all gone. How times have changed since we had to evade the first two checkpoints to reach no-go Kae Noi and acquire special written official permission to get past the latter two to visit forbidden Piang Luang – a sign of the normalization, pacification and transformation of northern Thailand's border areas! You can imagine how we, remembering all that hassle, were stunned in early 1998 to see a small bus bowling along the H107, marked 'Chiang Mai – Wiang Haeng – Piang Luang – Chiang Mai'. The bus, which still runs daily to those places, probably starts in Chiang Mai's Chang Puak bus station. Not only can you now get to these places unimpeded, but you can access them by public transport! And you can do so with two types of public transport: bus and *silor* or *songtaew*. Thus, you can take the bus from Chiang Mai or Chiang Dao to Wiang Haeng (direct route via H1322) and Piang Luang, or you can take a *silor* several times a day from Chiang Dao to the same two places (same direct route). And you can even now take a yellow *silor* from Chiang Dao to Muang Na and Kae Noi (in 2001 I saw *silor* in these places with my own eyes) – unthinkable just a few years ago! All this means that some of the adventure has gone out of poking around in these corners, but that, on the other hand, they can be fairly easily and conveniently visited by all travellers.

The picture is a similar from the point of view of road condition. The 'new' direct-access dirt road to Wiang Haeng of the early 1990s is now, in 2002, no longer new, and no longer a dirt trail either, but has meanwhile been upgraded and asphalted throughout, all the way to Piang Luang, becoming the H1322. This route, especially from the H1178 to Wiang Haeng (Map 9), is now a great unproblematic scenic ride. At the time of writing, the other indirect route to Wiang Haeng via Kae Noi has also been improved, but remains problematic in places. Thus, as far as Muang Na, the road is good, has been upgraded, and is largely paved. Between Muang Na and Kae Noi, roadbuilders were in 2001 in the process of blasting a huge new highway, parts of which had already been tarred. Certain sections remained in a lamentable condition and difficult to ride. Beyond Kae Noi, and as far as Chong, the way in 2001 had been widened and somewhat upgraded, but was still largely a mixture of dirt and bulldust, in places moderately taxing to ride. However, by the time you read this, the whole way from the H107 to Kae Noi will probably have been upgraded and asphalted throughout, and the remaining stretch to Chong will probably be the same upgraded dirt road, although ultimately this leg too will, I suspect, be tarred over. In 2001, there was a steady trickle of traffic proceeding from Kae Noi to Chong and vice versa, trundling along the mainly dirt stretch in clouds of bulldust. And in the same year, we learned that the occasional *farang* or group of *farang* had taken to visiting Kae Noi and Wiang Haeng, as well as Piang Luang, both by motorcycle and jeep.

A factor in the relaxation of security on the Muang Na – Kae Noi – Chong stretch is the political demise in early 1996 of warlord Khun Sa and the dissolution or reallocation of his MTA militia to other factions (more below and under Chapter 3). With this change, fighting between the MTA and the Wa UWSA, but also between the MTA and the Burma army, largely ended, as did raids by Khun Sa men on the Kae Noi road and Kae Noi itself. By the same token, the flow of MTA and Wa casualties down to the hospitals of Chiang Dao and Fang ceased. However, to a limited extent the situation across the border, opposite Kae Noi, Wiang Haeng and Piang Luang, has not changed, or has only changed outwardly, because now there are sporadic clashes between the Shan State Army and the UWSA and/or the Burmese *tatmadaw*, and the Wa are no less given to cross-border raiding and drug trafficking than were the MTA.

Route detail: H107 – Muang Ngai – Muang Na – Kae Noi
km 0   Junction H107/H1178 (see Map 4)
          Lai Tung village
          Mae Khon village

MR DONUT COMING SOON

km 4.2   **Muang Ngai** centre, with eating places
        Naresuan monument and reconstructed fort offroad L
km 9.5   Turning L (west) for Wiang Haeng on H1322 (+55 kms)
        Opposite junction: a little eating place with good food
        Mae Ja village
        At Huai Tin Tang village: strange maroon-coloured pagoda structure (L)
        Villages of Tungkao Puang, Huai Pao, Huai Sai and La Po Han
km 24.5 **Na Wai** police box/checkpoint. A pretty good paved road thus far
        At Na Wai: a way L to a waterfall and into Chiang Dao Wildlife Sanctuary
        Paved road passes low cliffs (R) and through forest
km 30.8 In **Rin Luang**: turning R onto paved road for Nong Ook (Aroonothai)
        (+6.4 kms). Exciting new border road continues beyond the KMT village a
        long way to Doi Larng, Palaung Nor Lae, and even (if open) round the
        back of Doi Pahom Pok to Doi Larng and ultimately Taton
        Pink school (L) and kindergarten (L)
        Road still paved thus far
km 33.8 Lahu hill-tribe village of Nong Kiao, with simple huts
        Views R of lumpy Kiu Pa Wok ridge
        In 2001, improvements being made to an intervening dirt section of road
        Way R to Muang Na Nuea Cave
km 41.9 **Muang Na** centre, with Burmese/Shan-style *wat* (L)
        In 2001, this mixed-population village with a strong Chinese KMT element
        was still a nice undiscovered little place. Take a 15-baht noodle soup at one
        of the eating places (R). The steady trickle of yellow *silor* you can see
        continue to Kae Noi. At Muang Na, if you look 340° or just W of N, you
        can see a mountaintop Burma army position on the border, which has
        probably been taken over from Khun Sa's MTA. In 2001, the Thai military
        were still in Muang Na, now not because of Khun Sa, but because of the
        UWSA.

        At top of Muang Na main street: school and phone box (L). After the
        village (now see Map 5), a good paved road continues
km 43.2 Not far beyond Muang Na: small Lahu village of **Jia Chan**
        Scenic fairy-tale karstic outcroppings (L)
        Where the houses of Jia Chan end: roadbuilders' compound (L)
km 43.9 Chiang Dao National Park branch office (L)
        Brand-new (in 2001) road climbs a long way up a spur to cross a ridge
        Road descends very steeply through several corkscrew bends to:
km 48.6 Bridge and river
        Cross many more bridges, following river upstream
        Early 2001: a very bad section of road being remade
        Flattish bad dirt surface for a way, then tarred surface again
        Road ascends to:
km 52.4 Thai army camp, checkpoint, barrier and Lahu settlement of **Ho Kiang**
        Up steep again on asphalt through more corkscrew bends
        Then new dirt highway under construction (2001)
        Into upland conifers and along elevated spine
km 55.3 Over a 'pass' and along and down on old dirt road
        Intermittent asphalt, then (in 2001) a bad stretch of fist-sized stones and
        bulldust. Some great views c. kms 55-57

THREE PAGODAS

km 56.7 View N to mountaintop Burmese military position on border with pagoda and flagpole (near roadside km-marker 57) – it's the same post that you can see from Muang Na

km 62.6 Turning L for Na Si Ri village (Lahu) (+4.5 kms)
Another very poor stretch

km 65.5 Junction with *sala*: L to Pa Bong Mai village (Red Lahu) and Royal Project, R to Kae Noi
Steep down a final very mediocre stretch on a broad brown dirt road

km 66.1 Edge of Kae Noi agglomeration and *grom pamai* forestry conservation office (R) on a bend, by a bridge

km 66.4 **Huai Loek**: Lahu satellite settlement before Kae Noi proper

km 66.7 Kae Noi health centre (L)
Highways Department office (R) on a corner, with an A-frame chalet

km 68.7 **Kae Noi** centre with shops and noodle places each side of main street, and school (R)

In early 2001, **Kae Noi** was – to our surprise – not much changed from what we had found almost ten years earlier. Here was the same squat lugubrious place surrounded by extensive denuded countryside, some of which, however, had meanwhile been given over to neat orchard growing. The KMT Chinese and Shan were still in residence in Kae Noi itself, with the Lahu and Lisu distributed among the satellite and outlying settlements. The place still seemed relatively backward, impoverished and down at heel, and the frontier-town atmosphere of yore remained palpable. But the school had been given a facelift, as had some houses in the centre, official buildings had sprung up (health centre, forestry conservation compound, Highways Department office), there were more shops and eating places, you could now buy petrol from a booth, and public-transport *silor* reached the village from Chiang Dao. By contrast, Kae Noi's long main drag had reverted to awful dust, its metalled surface having long since broken up and gone. Staying a couple of days in 'town', we found that the inhabitants had become much more friendly, with 50% of them now having Thai ID cards. Behind Kae Noi, across the border, the political situation had changed, as said. Khun Sa and the MTA were no longer in control, but apparently the Burma army and in places the UWSA or even sometimes the SSA.

If readers want to stay overnight in Kae Noi, they can easily do so now – informally – in one of three places. You could camp on a corner of the main school's foreground, as *farang* occasionally do, so we learned, when they pass through. Or you could stay at a nearby Doi Chiang Dao National Park branch office, situated 6.4 kms beyond Kae Noi on the way to Chong, near km-marker 76, left side of road (see Map 6). Or you could camp at the *grom pamai* (forest conservation) office at the edge of Kae Noi, by a bridge, east side of road as you enter the village from Muang Na (km 66.1 or 2.6 kms before Kae Noi school/centre). At New Year 2000/01, Doug and I stopped here, putting up our tents in a beautiful garden before the office, amid numerous red Christmas plants (poinsettias) in flower. Two or three forestry men welcomed us, made no fuss of us or of our wanting to camp, showed us their washroom (freezing water), allowed us to stay free of charge, and let us get on with things. You might also be able to put up or camp at the health centre. We ate at one of the three or four noodle soup places in the village. One lies on a corner of the school grounds, another opposite the school. Eat early – they all give up by 6 or 7pm. In December and January, it can often be downright cold in the night up on the Shan plateau in Kae Noi, so if you do camp locally, make sure you have a reasonable sleeping bag with you.

MR DONUT COMING SOON

Route detail: Kae Noi – Chong – Pang Po – Kong Lom – Wiang Haeng

km 68.7   Kae Noi centre and school (R). See Map 6
           Towards end of village, at a fork, go R/straight and up, not L and down
km 70.3   Army camp (L) and checkpoint
           Flattish stony dirt road winds through low hills, with asphalt interlude
km 75.1   Chiang Dao National Park branch office up L (near roadside km-marker
           76). You can stay here if you want
km 77.6   Black Lahu settlement of **Pa** (R)
           If you look roughly W: fine views of mountains, including border ridge
km 80.5   Lisu village of **Huai Loek** both R and also up L. In L part, at entrance,
           nice views W through poinsettia plants
           Long stony downgrade to:
km 88.2   Bridge
           Fields
km 89.8   KMT houses, some with mud walls. Community used to be known as Pang
           Kae, but has now merged with Huai Krai. Pick up tarred road. Chinese
           Christian church (R)
km 90.9   **Huai Krai** village
           Shan-style *wat* (R) and school (R)
           Muang Krua settlement now merged with Huai Krai
km 92.4   T-junction at **Chong** village: go L/south 11.3 kms for Wiang Haeng and
           R/north 5.3 kms for Piang Luang. In Chong: fuel booths, eating places and
           Shan-style Wat Mak Gai Yon with seven-tiered roof and pagoda

km 92.4   Go L/south for Wiang Haeng on road now asphalted throughout (Map 7)
km 94.6   Village of **Muang Pok** with school (R) and health centre (L)
km 95.6   Wat Pratat Saen Hai with golden pagoda (up L)
           Mahatat village
km 96.9   Centre of **Pang Po** village. Old checkpoint now gone
           Khum Wiang Haeng (R), a kind of upmarket guest house with six A-frame
           bungalows in nice gardens (details: Postscript to Chapter 2)
km 100.3   On a corner of road: way (R) to Karen villages of Mae Haat and Na Mon,
           as well as to Mae Haat Waterfall
km 100.6   Centre of **Kong Lom** village and start of way R/west for Muang Noi and
           Pai (Map 10). Turning lies by a shop and phone box, almost opposite Kong
           Lom school
           Log godown after Kong Lom now disappeared
           Pa Pai, a satellite of Wiang Haeng. In Pa Pai, way L for Karen village of
           Mae Paem
           Wiang Haeng hospital (L)
km 103.7   Centre of **Wiang Haeng** with petrol station and store (L) and noodle place
           with row of shops (R). 200 m further:
km 103.9   Turning R into original main street of Wiang Haeng. Down here: more
           shops and Wat Wiang Haeng with pagoda.

2

THE WIANG HAENG HILTON

Wiang Haeng

At first Wiang Haeng disappointed us. This old Shan village seemed exactly like Kae Noi, only bigger. Here was the same god-forsaken featureless place, spread out on a broad valley floor. What on earth had induced us to spend so much effort reaching it? Perhaps it was just the magic of the name. 'Wiang Haeng' had always seemed to conjure up a picture of some wild dusty mountaintop settlement, inhabited by a shifting mixture of dubious peoples, eyeing the visitor suspiciously. But here was the reality, altogether more prosaic. A dismal conglomeration of low buildings was traversed by a dirt road, broad and dusty at this point, which continued on north out of the village with a purposefulness which seemed to suggest that even it had no desire to linger here.

We struck off down a side alley. Paved in cement sections, and lined on each side by single-storey wooden dwellings with tin or leaf roofs, this turned out to be the main street. There were a couple of simple shops and a modest noodle restaurant. Taking a noodle soup lunch, we asked the lady owner whether she served food in the evenings and whether she knew of any accommodation in 'town'. No, she answered simply.

We continued to scout round the village. The centre was a grid of unpaved alleyways and tracks. Wandering among the lowly houses, with their sacks of rice and their chickens scratching around, we caught a glimpse of old-world rural Thailand. In a lane, we met three Karen men with their *yaam* or sling-bags. In fact, the population of Wiang Haeng district consisted not just of Thais, but also of numerous hill-tribe people. Apart from Shan or *Tai Yai* (= 'Big Tai') and Siamese Thais or *Tai Noi* (= 'Small Tai' – actually the Thai of Wiang Haeng are probably Lan-Na Tai or Tai Yuan, i.e. the Thai of northern Thailand, not Siamese Tai), there were also Karen, Lahu, Lisu and Kachin folk, with an admixture of KMT Chinese.

At the bottom end of town, in a rather decrepit compound surrounded by white walls and overarched by tall leafy trees, we found the Buddhist Wat Wiang Haeng. A ramshackle wooden building in the Shan-style, it was raised on 6-ft stilts and had acres of corrugated iron roofing. Inside we discovered numerous red-painted pillars and a singular collection of some 25 Buddha figures. An emerald green enclosure on the right of the group housed a pair of life-size bronze images, swathed in saffron and gold cloth. Sitting before them were two or three miniature figures, one of them – 50 years old – of solid gold. In the centre of the collection was the main Buddha, resplendent in yellow apparel and made of polished bronze. Facing him from the left were a remarkable group of 18 merit figures of varying sizes, some quite large, all dressed in saffron robes. They looked like giant wooden Chinese dolls, although the monks told us that they were made of painted cement. Their faces were alabaster with features depicted in fine black lines, with very large elongated ears, and yellow headbands (see colour photo). They were typical Shan Buddha figures. Many sprays of brightly coloured plastic flowers set off the collection, votive *tung* or banners hung from the ceiling, and instead of the East German grandfather clock that somehow found its way into so many Thai monasteries, there was a surprising cuckoo clock.

A short distance from the temple, in the shade of a large tree, we found a splendid old Shan-style pagoda in an enclosure. The *chedi* was surrounded by half a dozen two-metre-high stupas, and outside the enclosure were a number of other, much smaller, urn-like stupas. The pagoda, little gold bells tinkling from the top of its tapering spire, enjoyed a commanding view over the Mae Taeng river valley. We thought that the pagoda might be a memorial to the founder of Wiang Haeng. But, in fact, this lay elsewhere. We later found it east of the main road, behind the electricity office. Here, under a young bodhi tree, was an old stupa and spirit house. The stupa, whitewashed and in danger of keeling over, contained the ashes of *chao pu* Haeng Sao Wa, an important former Shan ruler of Wiang Haeng.

Also on the south side of the village, between the *wat* and the primary school, we stumbled across the remains of some extensive earthworks. At some time, great ditches had been dug here, with the earth piled up at the sides. The ditches were full of water, forming a moat. Trees and plants had grown up around the earthworks, and in the misty early mornings or evenings they made a peaceful idyll. Apparently, Wiang Haeng was on King Naresuan's path during his crusades against the Burmese in the 16th century. Perhaps he proceeded up here from his encampment down at Muang Ngai, or maybe on another occasion he came up the valley of the Mae Taeng. This would make it possible that the earthworks had been built by his soldiers, perhaps as a defensive system around a forward camp. Or perhaps he made use of ramparts already constructed by *chao pu* Haeng Sao Wa or some other Shan leader to defend the frontier village. Or maybe he utilized ramparts originally built by the ancient indigenous Lawa people, subsequently also used by the Shan. Everything is obscure, and a great deal remains to be done researchwise in respect of the history of places like Wiang Haeng. Whatever the case, the name 'Wiang Haeng' seems to derive from these earthworks. In old northern Thai, *wiang* means 'town fortified with ramparts and a moat'.

The explanation sometimes given for the origin of 'Haeng' is altogether less plausible. A story from Buddhist literature tells of a wandering monk who came up here to teach the people Buddhism. Resting at nearby Doi Huai Pak Gu mountain, he was approached by a Karen, who offered him some melon to eat. While the holy man was eating this, he cracked or broke a tooth. In old Thai, *haeng* means 'cracked' or 'broken', and the idea of the crack or broken-ness was added to the 'wiang' to make 'Wiang Haeng' – 'cracked/broken moated town'. But the story does not end there. For the monk threw the melon skin into the river running past Wiang Haeng, thus also giving the local river its name – Mae Taeng means 'River Melon'.

Back at the top end of the 'main street', where it joined the main through road, we found a store run by an ample Chinese woman. Her son, fat and with a crew cut, was scooting around at the front in the dirt on a broken child's bicycle. The woman had just finished butchering some animal on a wooden block, and there was a mess of blood and unwanted bits lying around. We asked her if there was anywhere to stay in the village. She motioned with her bloody knife to a building right next to where she was standing. We had not even noticed this wooden shack, which stood absolutely on the corner of the road. Some wag had chalked on the front of it 'Vieng Haeng Hilton Hotel'. Whether this was an ironic allusion to the chain of luxury hotels or to Lom Jao prison in Bangkok, known colloquially as the 'Bangkok Hilton', was not clear. But, sure enough, one could stay there.

Inside were four walls, full of cracks through which the light filtered, and a crude pallet bed covered with dust. There was nothing else. Seeing the horror on our faces, the woman said that she could bring some things to make up the bed. We asked her how much the room was. One hundred baht, she said with an expressionless face. This was a staggering amount for an unlit, unfurnished shack between the butcher's block and the log transporters. Thirty baht maximum would have been enough. We reminded her that this was Wiang Haeng and that for 100 baht you would normally get a proper room with furnishings, a hot shower and toilet, even in Chiang Mai. Could she not discount a little? No, she could not, came back the answer. It was the only place to stay in town and, moreover, other *farang* paid this price when they came to the village. Poor deluded other *farang*! As politely as we could, we told her where she could put her room. We would find somewhere else to sleep. With a knowing sickening smile, she watched us trudge off aimlessly up the dusty main road in the flattening afternoon heat. It seemed to us that even the awful pampered son was grinning.

A short distance up the through road in the direction of Piang Luang, we made some useful discoveries. A turn to the right led up to the *ampoe* building (district office) and a small post office. On one side of the junction there was a fuel kiosk, where it was possible to buy petrol siphoned out of a drum. On the other was a country hospital. Opposite was a low tin-roofed building with the name *Sayan*, meaning 'dusk', which looked like a rudimentary restaurant. And, indeed, it was. We lost no time in asking if they were open in the evening and what time they closed. They closed, the pleasant lady owner said, when the customers went. We asked her about accommodation, and she suggested the Chinese lady's room, which was the only place in town. We walked back along the dirt road, kicking up the dust and cursing every time a vehicle went past, enveloping us in beige moon powder. We were still resolved not to go to the rapacious Jiin butcheress and looked the other way as we passed her shack. But our options were running out, and it seemed increasingly likely that in the end we would have to swallow our pride and pay up to stay in her slummy 'Hilton'. But suddenly we spied a sign pointing to the primary school, and we had the idea to try there, just as we had asked at Kae Noi school.

THE WIANG HAENG HILTON

Tuition for the little ones was just finishing, and the teachers and their charges were all hurrying away. However, we found a janitor locking up the classrooms of the low wooden school building. His name was Rak-kiet. We asked this young foxy-faced man with Mongoloid eyes if there was anywhere to stay at the school. He said that there was no guest room, but why did we not stay with the Chinese lady? Every visitor to Wiang Haeng stayed there. We explained that the room was dismal and that the woman had tried to overcharge us. Perhaps because he himself was on a modest income, the janitor sympathized with us. He went off to consult with the headteacher. After a while Rak-kiet returned with a bunch of keys, some mats and a couple of blankets, and said it would be alright for us to sleep in the sickroom, although we would have to be up and out before the children arrived the next morning.

The sickroom was little better than the 'Hilton'. It was a cubicle, nominally partitioned from the most junior classroom, with nothing in it except a narrow child's pallet bed, too short to sleep on. There was no lighting, and the softboard partition had been punched through everywhere with holes about the size of an infant's fist. We laid out our things on the floor and strung up our mosquito net. At intervals along the front of the building, there were taps. Later, when it was getting dark and the mist was forming, we washed off the caked sweat and dust of the day, looking out over the playing field.

Remote mountain villages have a habit of shutting down very early, and we were concerned about not getting to *Sayan* in time for supper. But we need not have worried. Three of the half dozen tables were occupied by eaters and drinkers. The restaurant was well placed to catch state employees coming out of work from the district office or hospital. There was no menu – food depended on what was available in the kitchen. The idea was to tell the cook what you wanted, and she told you whether you could have it or not.

While we were eating stir-fried pork and vegetables, a group of moustachioed bobble-hatted Chinese men came in, evidently from Piang Luang. They brought in with them three one-kilo plastic bags containing some white substance. It looked like pure N°. 4 heroin. Strangely, two of the bags went into the cold drinks fridge, and the other went out to the kitchen. The men ordered Mekhong whisky, soda and ice and sat waiting, rubbing their hands and licking their lips. Not believing that the men should want to chill their heroin, I went over to the fridge to inspect the bags. They contained a mass of white two-inch-long worms, each with a tiny black head. The grubs had been gathered from rotten wood and were considered a delicacy by Thai and Chinese alike. Sometimes they were cooked in an omelette, but on this occasion they were being deep fried as a snack to accompany the whisky.

Outside, the beginning of the night's convoy of log-transporters started to go past. Old battered vehicles, festooned with lights of every colour, ground past at walking speed, engines screaming. All told, some 45 lorries plied the route between the Shan State and Highway 107, passing down from Wiang Haeng the 'direct' way. A typical convoy consisted of 6-10 transporters. Each lorry carried a dozen tree trunks. The number of tons of teak and other precious hardwoods coming this way alone day after day was frightening. But multiply it by the innumerable cross-border logging points all down the 2000-km frontier with Burma (not to mention the crossings along the Cambodian border), and one could get some idea of the environmental rape that was going on in Burma's virgin forests now that there was little left to plunder in Thailand. Much of the wood, apparently, went to Japan, while some ended up as furniture in the houses of Thailand's new rich. The logging at Wiang Haeng, which came from Khun Sa territory and beyond through Piang Luang, was one of the most substantial operations in Thailand. When we commented to people at *Sayan* on the size of the convoys, they laughed, saying that the ten or so lorries we would see tonight were as nothing compared to what happened in November, after the rainy season. Then, to make up for time lost when the road down to Chiang Dao was impassable and to reduce the vast stockpile that had accumulated, convoys of more than 30 transporters went past nightly. At a dozen trunks per vehicle, that was nearly 400 teak trees a day.

The vehicles travelled at night, partly so as not to inconvenience other road users, partly to remain as inconspicuous as possible to ecologically concerned onlookers, but also because it was cooler at night and the engines did not overheat so easily. It was a wonder how these lorries, negotiating first gear gradients and hairpin bends, groaning under their loads, the trees audibly cracking, ever got down the mountains at all. Often, of course, they did not, or not at once. It was common to see them broken down or crashed, usually in the most problematic places, with chocks under their wheels or the load spilled all over the roadside. Frequently the families of the drivers travelled along too, so that when one did come across a breakdown, it was not uncommon to light upon a little domestic scene – food being cooked over a roadside fire, people eating or sleeping in the shade of the lorry, and even a lineful of washing strung up between a cab mirror and a jungle branch.

At about 9.30pm, most people had gone from *Sayan*, and the owner began shuttering the front. Once again we walked up the dusty main road, more groping our way this time. There was electricity in Wiang Haeng, but no street lighting. The moon helped, otherwise it was pitch black. In few places have the stars seemed so bright and tangibly near. Outside the teachers' block, we found the janitor, his wife and some of the teachers sitting round a crackling wood fire, well wrapped up in anoraks, scarves and hats. As in many other mountain villages down the Thai-Burmese border, it was downright cold at night during the winter months especially of December and January – not something you would normally associate with tropical Thailand. In many places, too, as we had already seen in Kae Noi, there was a thick mist, which the sun often did not burn off until mid-morning. Wiang Haeng was no exception, and as we sat with the teachers, wedges of fog visibly shifted around the corners of the buildings in the light from the windows.

A TV was on in the porch of Rak-kiet's billet, and everybody was watching an interminable Thai soap opera. A villager and a BPP man came and joined in the gentle fun. Seeing us arrive, they became interested in our story, and so against a background of sentimental soap we told them about Kae Noi. Most of the group had never even heard of the place, let alone been there. We took the opportunity to quiz them about local routes. But the result was not satisfactory. It was the same vagueness and confusion, even from people who should have known better, that one found all over Thailand and which could so infuriate the Western mind, with its demand for order and clarity. Thus no one knew if there was a way down to Pai, although someone thought there was a trail up through the Huai Nam Dang National Park to Wiang Haeng from somewhere along the Mae Ma Lai – Pai road (this was true: it went via Muang Khong). We asked about visiting Piang Luang, but the fogbound gathering around the wood fire were clear about one thing. The road to Piang Luang was closed to all outsiders after Pang Po, putting the border village firmly out of bounds.

With a torch lent to us by the janitor, we picked our way over to the school building and cleaned our teeth over the railing of the veranda. It could not have been often that the flowers in the bed below got a dowsing of 'Darkie' toothpaste and bottled water. Then we retired into the sickroom, only fractionally more salubrious than the 'Vieng Haeng Hilton'. We got into our sleeping bags on the hard wooden floor, pulled down the mosquito net and settled down to a cold sleep, surrounded by bottles of Stomachic Mixture, Thimerosal Mixture, Rubbing Alcohol and Scabicide Emulsion. The beam of the torch picked out a wall diagram showing how to insert a coil into a woman's vagina – rather out of place in a primary school. The night was punctuated by terrifying crashes, as large fruits from some overhanging tree fell onto the tin roof of the building.

*

After what seemed like only a couple of hours – actually it was 7.30am – the janitor threw open all the classroom doors of the school. Children began arriving, even though school did not start until 9am. Several eager curious faces peered at us in our sleeping bags through the holes in the partition. We got up, dressed and washed, watched by a group of po-faced bobble-hatted infants. Outside, the mist was so thick that it was impossible to see even halfway across the playing field. Later, at 9.30, when the whole school was lined up for outside assembly by age, size, sex and class, the smallest at the front and the tallest at the rear, the mist was still so thick that the children at the back of the files tailed off into obscurity. The janitor's wife had set up a stall at the side of the field and was selling sweeties, biscuits and grilled meatballs. She was doing a brisk trade, the children eating their titbits in a ring around a blazing wood fire.

Sayan was already open, and we took coffee for breakfast there. This was one of those accommodating places where, in addition to the coffee, they automatically served unlimited China tea free of charge. Foregoing a Thai breakfast of rice soup or pork with garlic and pepper, we filled up on coconut cake. While we were contemplating how to spend the day, a gang of youths in nondescript clothing rode up on MTXs and other motorbikes, parked and hung around. They were bristling with guns, and one, wearing a white headscarf and dark glasses, had a walkie-talkie, which he used all the while (see photo section). They eyed us as they spoke, and for a moment we wondered if they were not Khun Sa or Red Wa bandits. But on one of the motorbikes was painted in small letters *grom pamai*, meaning that they were forestry-protection boys. Their guns were US-made, Mossburg, 3-shot, large bore, warning rifles. They had an unenviable and dangerous job, patrolling the forest trails and seeking to apprehend anyone involved in illegal logging.

It seemed a good idea to call in at the *ampoe* office to see if we could glean any interesting information about Wiang Haeng district. In true bureaucratic fashion, we were handed with a succession of *wai* from one official to another until finally we were sitting in the office of the district chief himself. He was a laid-back young man with a Chinese-looking face and the name of Somsak Suriyamongkol. He came from Khorat and confessed that he had only been in Wiang Haeng a month. Thai civil servants in the fast track are moved around fairly speedily, but what this raw remote district must have seemed like after worldly Khorat could only be imagined – probably like Siberian exile. Nevertheless, Somsak was committed and knowledgeable, and proved to be one of the most helpful officials we ever came across on our journey.

Wiang Haeng, he thought, could be as old as 700 or 800 years – at all events it was quite old. He was of the opinion that the Shan were probably the first to settle the area, and they were followed by the Karen, Lahu, Lisu, Thais and KMT Chinese. I feel pretty sure myself that Wiang Haeng was originally settled by the ancient Lawa tribe, who are widely considered to be Thailand's aboriginals (a few Lawa still live in the mountains north-east of Mae Sariang – see Chapter 8). Many centuries ago, the Lawa lived all over northern Thailand. They claim to have founded Chiang Mai, and other cities in modern-day Thailand seem to have Lawa origins (Chiang Saen, Chiang Khong, Mae Sariang etc.). Lawa pipes, pots and other artefacts have been dug up in the Wiang Haeng area. Conceivably, as indicated earlier, the Lawa built the fortifications at Wiang Haeng. They inhabited northern Thailand until they were gradually supplanted first by the Mon and then by the Tai. In Wiang Haeng, they were undoubtedly replaced by the Shan or Tai Yai sub-group of the Tai peoples. For many centuries, the Shan lived and continue to live up in the Wiang Haeng area, as we know, and also in other parts of northern Thailand (e.g. Pai, Mae Hong Son and Khun Yuam districts) as well as in Burma's Shan State. It was from the *muang* of Wiang Haeng that in the 19th century, as Hallett reports (see Footnotes 1 & 2 in Chapter 1), marauding Shan chieftains came down into the Ping valley. In 1869, for example, *chao paya* Roi Saam descended from the *muang* to burn down Muang Ngai, temporarily driving out the Lan-Na Tai inhabitants. Hallett claims that at the time the Wiang Haeng area was part of British colonial Burma, included in the British Shan States under the name of 'Muang Hâng', before becoming part of Siam.

Our informant Somsak continued with further *ampoe* information. Out of a total district population of some 9,000 people (2,250 families), a good third of these, he said, were hill-tribe and minority people, the Chinese of Piang Luang accounting for the lion's share of the latter. There were some 20 villages in the *ampoe* (excluding Wiang Haeng itself), with about half of these based on Wiang Haeng, and half on Piang Luang.

Wiang Haeng district lay at roughly 2,500 ft above sea level, and more than 90% of its total surface area of 700 sq. kms consisted of mountains and national park. That left only 50 sq. kms for villages and fields. There was a severe shortage of agricultural land – something typical of these border settlements – which meant that many people kept livestock as a way of earning a living. Some hill-tribe people cultivated opium poppies, and others were still involved in logging, which was unfortunate because the area was a watershed of the River Ping. One of the priorities of the *ampoe* was to try to provide more crop land and more water for irrigation.

Until recently, Wiang Haeng had been no more than a self-protection village. Administratively, the area had consisted of two far-flung precincts or *tambon* within the ambit of *ampoe* Chiang Dao: *tambon* Wiang Haeng itself and *tambon* Piang Luang. It still consisted of these two precincts, but in May 1981 Wiang Haeng was given branch or sub-district status of its own, and in October 1993 accorded full district status. The reason for the promotions was that the area was too remote from Chiang Dao. Prior to the construction of the access dirt road in 1982, Wiang Haeng and the surrounding villages had been completely cut off from the outside world. It had taken officials three days to walk from Chiang Dao to Wiang Haeng and four days to walk from Chiang Dao to Piang Luang, making communication, administration and development understandably difficult. But there were other reasons too for the upgrading of administrative status. Wiang Haeng was a mountainous area, sharing a 35-km border with the Shan State. This meant that there were (and still are) numerous problems connected with illegal logging, opium-growing and heroin-trafficking, subterfuge immigration, contraband, and communist insurgency. The border area was also a haven for fugitive criminals. It was thought that all these things could be better dealt with by an independent authority on the spot.

However, the situation remained problematic because during the long rainy season (May to October) the road became virtually impassable, leaving the district isolated for weeks on end. To illustrate the point, the chief produced some photographs, which showed a mixed convoy of vehicles hopelessly bogged down in a 2-ft-deep quagmire of rutted slimy mud. It was common for people to use snow chains in these conditions – a practice frowned upon by the Highways Department because the chains churned up the mud even more, completely destroying the road. When people tried to make the journey in the rainy season, they took meals with them to eat on the way because no one ever knew how long the trip would take.

In the photo album, we noticed some other pictures showing an intriguing-looking temple, and we asked what it was. It was the famous Shan *wat pratat* at Piang Luang, Somsak said. The pictures had been taken during the *poi sang long* festival, which the Shan held there every year, just as they did in Mae Hong Son town. This was a wild colourful festival, staged when local Shan boys went to become novice monks. Unfortunately, it was not possible to visit the *wat* because the area was closed off for security reasons. Just a few days before, two French travellers had tried to go there, but had been rejected at the Pang Po checkpoint.

It seemed as if the interview was at an end. We thanked Somsak for his time, and he escorted us down to the entrance. Shaking hands with him there, we asked if it was really impossible for us to go to Piang Luang and view the forbidden monastery and pagoda. Now that we had seen the photos of them, our appetite had been whetted. And, of course, the fact that the *wat pratat* was out of bounds merely made it all the more alluring. But Somsak held out little hope. The matter did not rest with him, he regretted, but was in the hands of the military. However, he volunteered to see what he could do.

This set in train a process quite out of proportion to a visit to a border village and monastery. Back in the chief's office again, we waited a long time while half the officials of the *ampoe* fussed around trying to make radio contact with the military. A small radio could not get through, so they brought into play the district's principal communications system. The long and the short of it was that we got permission for the trip. But that was not the end of the story. Permission was not permissible without a permit. And now the district office had to make out a permit. This absorbed the other half of the officials for more than an hour, and necessitated visits to various rooms, kowtowing to numerous intermediate bureaucrats, and explaining our story for the umpteenth time. We were surprised that there was not some pre-printed form for making out such a permit. But either such permission-giving was rare or else things were never quite so simple. A special paper had to be invented and typed up on the spot. Finally, the document was ready, and we emerged triumphantly with it into the mid-morning light. The little letter came to have a value far in excess of what it was intended to have. Subsequently on our journey, we used it many times to sway checkpoints or obstructive *dorchodor* to gain access to restricted or closed zones.

❊ ❊

Postscript 2002

On revisiting Wiang Haeng in 2001, we found it transformed, quite unlike Kae Noi, which had changed little since the early 1990s. The dusty main drag past the school, *Sayan* and the hospital was now an asphalted all-weather road, as was the whole of the H1322 from the H1178 via Wiang Haeng all the way to Piang Luang. The days of the mudbath that people used to encounter when going down from Wiang Haeng to Chiang Dao in the rainy season had been consigned to history. Another thing of the past was a permit to visit Piang Luang from Wiang Haeng. Ruefully we remembered all the trouble we had had acquiring one for a trip to the closed border village. Now, as said in the Postscript to Chapter 1, you could access Piang Luang unchallenged – all the checkpoints had gone, or, if they still existed, they were uninterested in *farang* travellers. Wiang Haeng, Piang Luang and Kae Noi were open. Not only that, but they could be reached by public transport. These days, a stream of yellow *silor* come up every day from Chiang Dao to Wiang Haeng and Piang Luang, and there is even a daily small bus from Chiang Mai to Piang Luang via Chiang Dao and Wiang Haeng, something inconceivable in the early 1990s (it probably leaves from Chiang Mai's Chang Puak bus station)!

THE WIANG HAENG HILTON

Wiang Haeng was comprehensively modernized, or at least that part of it was that lay along the main through road, which was almost unrecognizable. The old heart of the village, by contrast, which lay W of the main road either side of the old village street running down to the *wat*, had changed little. But the section by the tarred main road was much more developed and built up, with numerous new stores. Here, the haunt of hoary old Shan chieftains even had a beauty parlour and ice-cream stall. On the east side of the main road, where once we had bought petrol siphoned out of a drum at the side of a little store, a regular little fuel station had sprung up, complete with forecourt, beside which the old store had turned into a proper shop. The old post office had been hauled out of its side street to a location on the main road, roughly opposite the fuel station. *Sayan* restaurant was defunct, but near where it used to be there was now a good daytime outdoor eating place, diagonally opposite the fuel station and next to the post office. It served up a good *raat na* for 20 baht.

On the accommodation front, the joke 'Wiang Haeng Hilton' was now also defunct, if it had ever really functioned. Curiously, at the time of writing there was, despite developments in Wiang Haeng, still no regular place to stay in 'town'. But there are lodgings possibilities nearby. Readers wishing to stay overnight locally are directed to a new guest house in Piang Luang (17 kms away – details see Chapter 3/Map 8) or to two places in Kong Lom village, some 3 kms N of Wiang Haeng on the way to Chong and Piang Luang. One of these, the far nicer and more reputable of the two, is *Khum Wiang Haeng* (*Khoom WH*), which means something like 'Wiang Haeng Residence'. It lies about 5 or 6 kms from Wiang Haeng, on the far side of Kong Lom, after the turning L for Mae Haat, shortly before Pang Po village, on the left/W side of the road (Map 7). This fine-looking place consists of six A-frame bungalows and is set in an attractive garden with trees and plants. The chalets have big rooms, hot water and their own toilets. A bungalow with air-conditioning is 700 baht/day, and one without a/c is 500 baht. The other lodging is hardly recommendable and is probably a 'bonking' place, although I did once stay in it on account of its cheapness (100 baht/room/night). It has no name, is situated in the centre of Kong Lom village, but is hard to find. You can locate it in the NE quadrant of the central 'crossroads', almost opposite both the way to Pai and a shop as well as phone box. On its side of the main road, it lies near another shop and adjacent to a small market area. The rooms are situated behind the owner's house, which is set back from the main road, is painted blue and white, and is marked by pot plants out front as well as a big satellite dish. Here, if you have succeeded so far, you will discover a row of small shabby rooms, any one of which you can take, which have a basic bed and bathroom with cold water.

Travellers wishing to access Wiang Haeng from Chiang Dao not on the longer, more problematic, roundabout route via Muang Na and Kae Noi, but directly, easily and quickly, can do so on the H1322, now paved, as said, throughout. The distance from the H1178 near Muang Ngai to Wiang Haeng centre/petrol station is 54.8 kms (see Map 9). You make a great ride on a fine road, through magnificent scenery and forest, enjoying splendid views, over a big ridge, taking in a protracted ascent and descent, negotiating hairpin bends, and passing half a dozen Lisu villages, some of which have noodle soup places. The H1322, but proceeding the other way round, from Wiang Haeng to the H1178 and Chiang Dao, also represents an escape route for any readers who, in retracing this first leg of the journey in this book, have accessed Wiang Haeng and Piang Luang via Kae Noi, but who do not wish to proceed on the very tricky route from Wiang Haeng and Kong Lom to Muang Noi and Pai, but prefer to return to Chiang Dao, completing a satisfying loop. These latter readers will have to read the following route detail and also Map 9 'backwards'.

THREE PAGODAS

Route detail: H1178 – Lao Wu – Wiang Haeng (via H1322) (Map 9)

km 0.0   At junction H1178/H1322, turn off 1178 left/W into 1322 for Wiang Haeng

km 13.2   Lisu double village of **Mae Ja Tai** and **Mae Ja Nuea** (*tai* = south, *nuea* = north). The southern part lies to the L of the road, the northern half to the R

km 20.1   Some kind of wildlife place (L)
          After it, a steep corkscrew ascent for 2 or 3 kms

km 23.8   Way left

km 26.2   Watershed conservation office (?) left side of road
          Another office (R), possibly some kind of wildlife conservation training school

km 27.6   Lisu village of **Khun Khong**, with petrol and noodles

km 28.5   Lisu village of **Pang Klang**, with noodles

km 32.5   Up on top, at viewpoint (R): great views of forested mountains all round, especially 140° or SE to Doi Chiang Dao massif, which resembles an upturned molar tooth

km 32.8   The signs and mini pagodas indicate the boundary/start of Wiang Haeng district
          A kind of pass

km 35.3   Upland Lisu village of **Lao Wu** mostly on L side of road, but with some roadside stalls also on R side, selling vegetables
          Down and along ridgetop

km 39.5   Telecommunications mast (R)
          After the aerial, big descent begins

km 40.3   Spirit house (L)

km 41.0   Green-roofed *sala* and viewpoint (L). Site of vehicle that has crashed over side of road and cliff, lodging in trees: near *sala*, down L
          Views down into Wiang Haeng basin
          Corkscrew bends

km 43.3   Old army camp and checkpoint (L)

km 47.6   Lisu village of **Mae Tae** nearby (R)

km 51.8   On valley floor: way L to offroad Huai Chang village and forestry office (+ 11 kms)

km 53.2   Way R by *sala* to nearby **Pang Kwai** village and project

km 53.6   Police box/checkpoint (R) by lake
          School (L)

km 54.3   Main village street of Wiang Haeng (L) with *wat* and pagoda at far end

km 54.8   **Wiang Haeng** centre, with petrol station and store (both R), and with shops, post office and eating place (all L)

3

POPPY MEN

WARLORDS MO HENG & KHUN SA

Piang Luang

We started immediately for Piang Luang (Map 8). As far as Chong, the way retraced the route we had come in on from Kae Noi. We passed the checkpoint just outside Wiang Haeng, the log godown, and – three kms out from Wiang Haeng – **Kong Lom** village. Then, three kms further along the dirt road, we drew up at the implacable **Pang Po** checkpoint, where the Frenchmen had been turned back a couple of days previously. It seemed to us that the two soldiers remembered us from our trick the day before. But there was nothing they could do. They scrutinized our permit and waved us through. How sweet were the licit illicit kilometres after the barrier!

Between the villages of **Mahatat** and **Muang Pok**, we noticed something we had not seen when coming from Kae Noi. A steep flight of steps with serpentine dragon-headed *naga* on each side led abruptly up from the roadside to an ornate hilltop pagoda with a commanding view over the paddy fields and the distant border mountains. It was Pratat Saen Hai (km 8). A *pratat* is a particularly important pagoda, said to house an authentic relic of the Lord Buddha. As such, this pagoda would attract pilgrims all the year round. After Muang Pok came **Chong** (km 11), and there again was the dun-coloured monastery with the seven-tiered roof, as well as the turn-off east for Kae Noi. From now on up to the border, the front tyre of the Honda carved a new furrow on the flat stony road. Passing next through **Ban Mai**, we entered an amphitheatre of cultivated hillsides, dotted with Chinese tombs. The mountains closing around us were the border. After a couple more kms, we suddenly drew up at the gates to **Piang Luang** (km 16).

The entrance to the village was an obstacle course of barriers and other obstructions. Bridging the road was one of those wooden portals which mark the approach to many rural Thai and hill-tribe villages. The soldiers at the box checked our permit and made us surrender our passports. The reason for this, they explained, was that policemen in or beyond the village might confiscate them, compelling us to carry heroin in order to get the documents back. This was a sign of the contempt with which the Thai police were viewed not just by the military. After the army checkpoint at the outskirts of Piang Luang, there were no further controls right up to the border.

Piang Luang was a thriving, relatively large, mixed KMT and Shan place. In spite of the Shan *wat* in the village, the visitor might have been forgiven for thinking he had stumbled into a small market town in Yunnan, southern China. Things were more developed than we had expected. Numerous stores lined the long main street, there was moderate traffic, and everyone enjoyed electricity. But while the village was more advanced than the KMT outposts of, say, Pa Taang on the Laos border or Mae Or north of Mae Hong Son town, it was nowhere near as developed as Doi Mae Salong. Many of the dwellings were still single-storey and made of mud or wood with leaf or tin roofs. Their door frames were decorated with the same paper banners and mottoes we had seen in Kae Noi – red strips bearing gold-leaf characters. In the main drag, there were tea houses with KMT veterans in faded military fatigues and peaked caps, drinking amber China tea from glass tumblers, smoking water pipes, reading Chinese newspapers from Taiwan, or simply passing the time of day. We found several noodle soup shops and stopped for lunch in one of them. A tasty bowlful of Chinese egg noodles was accompanied by a side dish of pickled cabbage and toasted sesame seeds. Especially west of the main street, we found big Chinese homesteads built around square courtyards, and in many spots Piang Luang was enhanced – like Mae Salong – by the red-leafed Christmas plants or poinsettias so favoured by the Chinese (red signifies good luck).

Outside one store, a very old Chinese lady with a bent back and miniscule bound feet was sitting in the sun. When we asked if we could photograph her (see photo section), she spent a long time arranging her cap, collar, cuffs, rings and bracelets until everything was just right. Pleased as punch at the unfamiliar attention, she gave us two coconut patties from her granddaughter's shop. On a more disquieting note, we noticed several fairly new MTXs, emblazoned with signs like 'P6', which suggested that they might have originated from motorcycle hire places in Pai and have been stolen from biker-trekkers. It would be very difficult for a foreigner or even the Pai owner to locate a bike in Piang Luang, let alone recover one from the nearby Shan State.

Most of the villages along the border of the Shan State and Thailand are associated in some way with the warlords and private armies operating on the Burmese side. Piang Luang is no exception. Its history is intertwined with the fortunes not only of the KMT, but also of the two veteran Shan opium barons Mo Heng and Khun Sa. The village is identified especially with Mo Heng. For the purposes of further illuminating both Piang Luang and this 'Golden Triangle' stretch of the border, I include next a thumbnail sketch of him and his activities. Again, hurried readers will be forgiven if they skip over the following section as well as the pages after it devoted to Khun Sa.

✳

Warlord Mo Heng
The wobbly Shan leader Mo Heng, also widely known as Gon Jerng or Korn Jerng, was born in Burma in 1926. During his early years, he belonged to or founded a succession of small political parties and rebel armies – a switching which came to characterize his whole career. An early move of his, surprising considering his subsequent fervent anti-communism, was to become a member and then a commander of the Communist Party of Burma (CPB). But at the age of 30 he transferred into Shan nationalist politics, joining in 1958 the Noom Soek Haan or Young Warrior movement. This small underground

resistance group, in the vanguard of the wider Shan nationalist uprising, was based on Piang Luang, and Mo Heng's long association with the border outpost dates from this time. It was while with the Young Warriors, fighting against the Burma army, that he lost his left arm. A period in mainstream Shan nationalist politics followed, with Mo Heng rising through the ranks of the Shan State Army (SSA), the principal army of Shan nationalism at that time, and ranging far and wide in the Shan State. But in 1968 he broke with the SSA and returned with a following of 1000 men to Piang Luang.

Here, in the same year, Mo Heng reunited with the original 'Young Warrior', one Chao Noi, and together they formed in 1969 the Shan United Revolutionary Army, which had as its HQ the Pang Mai Soong camp just behind Piang Luang. Soon, however, SURA vice-president Chao Noi, dismayed by the course his partner was steering, dropped out of the organization, leaving the army almost exclusively in Mo Heng's charge. For the next 15 years the SURA, Mo Heng's single greatest achievement, became virtually synonymous with him and also with Piang Luang.

In the late 1960s and early 1970s, Piang Luang was a different place from what it had been in the late 50s. Meanwhile the Kuomintang refugees had arrived, and now the frontier village housed a sizeable detachment of soldiers of Gen. Li's KMT Third Army, whose GHQ was stationed at nearby Tam Ngop (ENE of Wiang Haeng and Kae Noi). Already disaffected with the brand of Shan nationalism that mainstream bodies like the SSA were purveying, and seeing which side his political bread was buttered on, Mo Heng underwent in 1969 a radical change of heart, falling in with the KMT. After all, were they not, as he had also become, virulently anti-communist? Mo Heng's expedient but unholy alliance with the alien Chinese army, which lasted as long as his SURA, led him to be sharply criticised by other insurgent leaders. He had sold out, betrayed the Shan cause. The former plucky underground rebel commander had turned into a mere adventurer, no longer the revolutionary idealist of yore, but just another warlord.

The criticism was not wide of the mark. For while it was true that the SURA frequently clashed during the 1970s with the communist CPT along the north-western Shan-Thai border, Mo Heng and his pocket army operated out of Piang Luang in easy concert with the KMT, the two forces financing themselves through trafficking opium and jade or through taxing contraband crossing the border at Piang Luang and Mae Or (another village under their joint control further west), and doing each other's dirty work across in the Shan State. Actually, the cosy coexistence of the SURA and the KMT in Piang Luang was something of a three-way affair, for quietly colluding with the two militias was the Thai army. Just as the Siamese authorities had welcomed the KMT as a buffer against Burmese communism and also as a check on their own CPT, so they sanctioned the presence of Mo Heng's anti-red SURA, turning a blind eye to its more or less open drug-trafficking activities. Martin Smith (1993) reports that when he visited Piang Luang in 1984 he found a booming town with a thriving black market, frequented by hundreds of traders and colourful hill-tribe people. Opium and heroin were both freely available, and he saw a Thai army colonel giving training to SURA troops.

THREE PAGODAS

The long SURA-KMT marriage of convenience lasted until 1984, when Mo Heng embarked on a new piece of adventurism. Opium king Khun Sa and his powerful private Shan United Army (SUA), which like the KMT and SURA had been tolerated by the Thais in their border territory as part of their counter-communist strategy, had recently been expelled by the Thai army from the kingdom. In 1982, they pushed the overweening warlord out of his stronghold in Ban Hin Taek (near Mae Salong) back into Burma. The repercussions were dramatic, felt the length of the Shan-Thai border by all the many peoples living there. As the SUA swept south-west in a deadly scramble for new land and to control new cross-border trafficking routes, minority groups as far down as Mae Or were battled and displaced, including the KMT, the Wa, the Lahu and various Shan factions. Mo Heng and his SURA at Piang Luang were no exception. By 1984, Khun Sa was knocking insistently on their back door. He had overrun the territory behind Piang Luang, interdicted the (for the SURA) vital caravan and trafficking route leading back from the village into the Shan State, and begun a blockade of Mo Heng's HQ. The stranglehold was such that SURA income slumped by 80%. 1984 was also the year the Thais moved against the KMT, not shunting them over into Burma, but simply emasculating them – although in one sinister incident 30 KMT inhabitants of Piang Luang were mysteriously massacred by Thai army rangers. Seeing the star of the KMT on the wane, and with Khun Sa menacing triumphantly at his rear, Mo Heng could not help but read the signs. In an opportunistic about-turn characteristic of him (and typical of the tortuousness of Shan rebel politics), he made a series of abrupt changes. As easily as he had once sided with the KMT, now he suddenly terminated his 15-year alliance with the Chinese Nationalist remnants, dissolved his SURA, made a call for Shan unity, and formed a new faction, called the Tailand Revolutionary Council (TRC). Based like its predecessor at Piang Luang, the new body would, the Shan leader declared, have no part in narcotics trafficking. But that was not all. Only a short time later, in early 1985, Mo Heng merged his fledgling TRC with Khun Sa's SUA. The new organization, now some 4000 soldiers strong, retained the name (temporarily) of Tailand Revolutionary Council, and Mo Heng even became its president. But the real power lay with Sa, who took charge of finance and the military. Within two years, the new outfit of the two Shan warlords was renamed the Mong Tai Army or Army of the Tai (Shan) Land.

With the amalgamation of Mo Heng's and Khun Sa's armies, Piang Luang effectively fell under the dominion of South-East Asia's pre-eminent warlord, Khun Sa. From 1985 on, the new force engaged in unchecked drug trafficking, acquiring through the resulting wealth an awesome arsenal of modern weaponry bought on the Thai markets. Soon, virtually the entire Shan-Thai border from Takilek/Mae Sai in the north-east to Mae Or/Mae Hong Son in the south-west was under the control of the two warlords. Numerous photographs in MTA propaganda show the short, pug-faced; one-armed, chain-smoking Mo Heng in the shadow of the taller, open-faced, affable, imperious, chain-smoking Khun Sa, the two of them taking a salute, reviewing an MTA passing-out parade, or sitting around the conference table. Finally, in 1991, at the age of 65, the inveterate turncoat (although lifelong devout

Buddhist) Mo Heng died, leaving Khun Sa in sole control of the MTA, the Piang Luang border crossing, and the Shan hinterland behind the village.

❋

The forbidden temple of Fah Wiang In

Piang Luang was not only a village with a history, but a place of architectural interest. Just beyond it lay the remarkable Wat Pratat Fah Wiang In (Map 8). This Shan monastery-temple was singular in that it exactly straddled the border. No one tried to stop us going beyond Piang Luang, so we ventured on to see what happened. It was certainly exciting travelling down a dirt track not knowing whether we had crossed over into Khun Sa territory. The road dropped down from the KMT townlet, proceeded for a couple of kms to a settlement, and then forked. We asked where we were. It was **Lak Taeng**. Ahead went straight to the border, and left went up a steep track to the temple.

Wat Pratat Fah Wiang In consisted of many buildings, but its large celebrated pagoda was on a hill in Thailand while the *wihaan*, the building containing the Buddha images, lay on a second adjacent hill in Burma or the Shan State. The frontier ran precisely through the middle of the *wat*, between the two hills. While we were looking around, we were taken in hand by a small serious man in his late twenties, who wanted to show us the complex. We asked him if he was a guide. He said that it was his duty to show visitors round, and he declined any payment. His name was Toeng-Leng, he was Shan, and it transpired that he was a guerrilla from warlord Khun Sa's Mong Tai Army!

We looked first at the pagoda. This impressive ornate affair was surrounded by a curious circular building (see photo section). Inside, the building was divided up into 12 segments, each forming a little 'chapel' containing a mural. The 12 chapels referred to the lives of the Buddha, and each painting depicted a scene from one of his reincarnations. The murals were garishly painted in a naive surreal style. In one, a man was disappearing into the earth, the ground cracking dramatically around him. It was hard to know exactly what was happening in each picture because the captions were only in Shan. The pagoda was not old. It was built in 1969 to commemorate some eminent Shan monk. A glass case in the circular building housed his bones together with a wax effigy of him wearing his old glasses. More recently, Mo Heng used to come here and to the *wihaan (viharn)* to pray, ever accompanied by an armed bodyguard, and since 1991 the pagoda had contained his remains too.

Most of the other buildings at Fah Wiang In also looked fairly new, although at the back of the compound there were some old wooden constructions that might have been part of an original *wat*. The *wihaan* contained three golden Buddha figures. One of them was a splendid piece in the Shan style, with an extravagant bronze winged crown. Toeng-Leng said that there were 101 monks in the monastery, most of them boy novices. We saw some of the lads in their saffron robes running around behind the *wihaan*, trying to fly kites. We also saw a number of white-clad shorn-headed nuns. Our companion expressed the hope that when the whole monastery was completed, his state might have achieved independence. Unfortunately, real independence would probably remain a pious hope, as Rangoon liked to remind the Shan when the Burma army passed this way. They had fired artillery at the *wat* a year or two previously. One shell which had not detonated hung near the *wihaan*. Its casing served as a gong. With a grim irony, the junta forces liked to return to Wat Fah Wiang In to make their presence felt exactly at the time of *poi sang long*, the joyous Shan festival when boys become novice monks.

There were some other, secular buildings on the side of the monastery compound that lay in the Shan State. One was a printing press. All flew the Shan nationalist (MTA) flag – a green, red and yellow tricolour with a central white moon. Immediately below the monastery hill was a school, which we were invited to visit, and the buildings of Pang Kham Ko village. Behind this village, the logging road wound off down a narrow secluded valley towards the Salween river. Immediately to our left and right, Toeng-Leng pointed out, at the head of the valley, were two MTA posts, guarding the pass. Khun Sa's Pang Mai Soong camp lay nearby.

Our soldier friend told us something of his history. When he was young, he had been sent to a Christian school in Chiang Mai along with 20 other Shan boys. He had been sponsored by missionaries, who wanted to encourage him to become Christian. After school, he had wanted to study further in college, but he had been recalled by Khun Sa along with the other boys to defend Hin Taek, Sa's GHQ at that time, which was being attacked by the Thai army. Subsequently Toeng-Leng had been sent by his leader to fight alongside the Karen National Liberation Army opposite Mae Sot district against the Burmese *tatmadaw*. So his education had been broken off. He said that of all the people he had fought against, the Wa Daeng (Red Wa), now Khun Sa's arch-enemy, frightened him the most – literally almost to death. This was because they were tenacious fearless fighters. Once Toeng-Leng had been caught by the Thai police in Mae Hong Son. He had been imprisoned there until Khun Sa's men had bought his release. We noticed that whenever this quiet MTA soldier mentioned Khun Sa, he always used the reverential Shan title *chao*, meaning something like 'His Grace' or 'His Excellency'. Thus Toeng-Leng was of the opinion that His Grace was now in the process of stepping down from being leader. His Excellency was getting tired of being vilified by the world's press as 'the opium king', 'King of the Jungle', and so on. Now Toeng-Leng was based at Pang Kham Ko, where as a reserve he was on permanent call. His duty meanwhile was, along with other soldiers, to show visitors around Wat Fah Wiang In. It seemed to us that this burgeoning temple complex, together with the school at its foot, was something of a propaganda showpiece for Khun Sa and his Shan nationalist rebel cause.

We did not want to leave Piang Luang without having a brief look at the actual border crossing to Sa's territory. So we left the *wat* and went back down to Lak Taeng. Beyond the houses was an area where the log lorries were serviced and repaired, and beyond this, in a gloomy sinister defile, the frontier itself with a checkpoint. This latter was nothing more than a squalid cement blockhouse, a couple of leaf and tin-roofed shacks selling noodle soup and other goods, and crude wood and barbed wire gates, blocking the 'road' (see photo section). From time to time the gates were opened to let through a pick-up, which was thoroughly searched. Bicycles and small motorbikes also went back and forth, as well as pedestrians. An odd assortment of people hung around the checkpoint. One bent old Chinese man with grey hair offered us jade, amber, anything... What did we want?

The checkpoint used to be manned by rebel SURA/TRC/MTA personnel, but now half a dozen Thai *tahaan praan* rangers were in charge. It was the duty of these elite black-uniformed troops, trained in jungle survival and much feared by minority hill groups, to guard Thailand's most sensitive border areas. To us, however, they were friendly enough. Three of them sat on a bench at the side of the road, peeling a mound of garlic. With their loose neckerchiefs and floppy hairstyles, they looked far from intimidating, reminding us rather of effeminate boy scouts. Like Somsak of Wiang Haeng district office, the boys were from Khorat. We asked them about the possibility of crossing to the other side. More interested in their garlic-peeling, the rangers had no objection. The temptation to flit across the border was great. But Somsak's admonition not on any account to cross into Khun Sa territory rang in our ears. Also we remembered the warning words of the guards at the entrance to Piang Luang. For once discretion really did seem to be the better part of valour.

❊

Warlord Khun Sa and the 'Golden Triangle'

No account of the Thai-Burmese border would be complete without a sketch of Khun Sa. It is this colourful warlord's fiefdom which abuts Thailand for almost the whole of the north-westerly Shan stretch of the border, from the Lao frontier in the east to Mae Hong Son town in the west, and it is his intimidating presence which is most mightily felt in the 'Golden Triangle' region.[1] No account of Piang Luang, either, would be complete without an outline of Khun Sa. The village marks one of the few vehicle crossing points into and out of his territory, meaning that now the Shan narcotics kingpin has come to be just as closely associated with Piang Luang as once his right-hand man Mo Heng was.

Khun Sa was born as Chang Chi-fu in 1933 or 1934 in the Loi Mo district of Mong Yai State, one of the 30 or so former Shan principalities of Burma. Although Sa has always liked to see himself as a champion of the Shan cause, he is actually only half-Shan. His mother was a Palaung Shan, but his father was Chinese, the paternal ancestors hailing originally from the old Chinese-Shan principality of Norng Sae (Talifu) in China. Both Sa's parents died while he was still young, although his mother survived her husband long enough to remarry a local noble. It was on the strength of the stepfather's nobility, as well as because there was a tradition of district chieftainship in his real father's family, that Sa assumed the honorific *khun*, meaning 'lord' (princeling). Playing down his Chinese background with a view to improving his Shan credentials, he then dropped the name Chang Chi-fu to become known as Khun Sa.

---

[1] Situation valid until 1996. A post-1996 update is given in a postscript at the end of this account.

THREE PAGODAS

The orphaned boy was brought up amid the tea plantations of Loi Mo by his paternal grandparents. A formative influence on him was oppression by the KMT when they virtually occupied the Shan State after 1949. The sight of Nationalist intruders one day expropriating mules from his grandfather apparently led the young Sa to vow that at some time he would drive the KMT from his homeland. It has been said that the future warlord learnt his trade from the KMT, either working under or for them, but Sa himself denies this, maintaining that, always a freedom-fighting Shan nationalist, he had mixed it with the KMT from the start. Whatever the case, the KMT came to be his arch-enemy for a full 30 years.

Khun Sa set out on his career as a drugs warlord in the early 1960s. At that time he had a small clandestine rebel outfit with Shan nationalist and liberationist leanings. Two interlinked factors transformed his band. One was the legitimization of his group as a *ka kwae yae* or 'village defence force', and the other was the entry of his band as a KKY into the opium trade. At that time Rangoon, worried by the situation in the Shan State, where the KMT were rampant, the Shan *sawbwa* (traditional feudal princelings) were becoming increasingly restless, liberation groups were mushrooming, a general full-blown Shan uprising seemed imminent, and the Communist Party of Burma (CPB) was flexing its muscles, sought to win over militias such as Sa's with the twin aim of having fewer hostile groups to deal with and of gaining allies able to help with security. The deal was that if the forces would police their local areas and check both the Shan insurgents and the CPB as well as the KMT, Rangoon would sanction the militias, turning a blind eye to whatever dubious activities they might be involved in.

The *ka kwae yae* scheme, invented by Gen. Ne Win and the Burmese authorities, backfired. Neither the Shan insurgents nor the CPB were halted. There was no lessening of lawlessness, either. Rather, the idea, which eventually produced about 20 'local defence militias', many originally little more than bandit bands, ironically launched some of the most notorious warlords and their armies in the 'Golden Triangle'. A massive proliferation of weapons and drugs in the Shan State followed. Far from policing their patches, the militias simply abused their positions to line their pockets and strengthen themselves.

With no one was this more the case than with Khun Sa and his fledgling Shan United Army (SUA). Blessed by the authorities, the warlord prospered inordinately. Masquerading for a decade as the leader of a kind of volunteer home guard, he bought opium up in the Wa sub-state and transported it, escorted by his embryonic army, down to the Thai-Burmese and Thai-Lao borders, where the refineries and export possibilities were. The mule trains grew bigger and bigger, with the result that more and more profit flowed to his force, allowing him continually to expand it. He already had in his pocket his own Loi Mo district and corners of the Wa sub-state. Soon he added Kengtung and territory down by the Burmese-Lao border.

An irritating problem for Khun Sa in the early years was that he had to pay taxes to his hated fellow traffickers the KMT when his opium mule trains passed through their territory or arrived at their outposts along the Thai border. But now his caravans became so large and his SUA so powerful that he was no longer minded to pay the Chinese. The challenge for supremacy was not lost on the trafficking Kuomintang, who, seeing their main means of survival threatened and in a bid to snuff out the upstart warlord, attacked one particularly large (16-ton) shipment of opium, sparking the infamous Opium War of 1967 (more details in Chapter 1 under 'Brief History of the KMT in Burma & Thailand'). The attack, which resulted in a bitter four-day battle with heavy losses all round, was won by neither side. The larger Opium War was similarly inconclusive. It rumbled on for years afterwards, with the SUA and the KMT vying for control of the trafficking and smuggling routes in the Shan State and across the Burmese-Thai amd Burmese-Lao borders.

A great survivor in the 'Golden Triangle', Khun Sa soon bounced back from this upset, as he did also from another setback. In 1969, he was arrested by the Burmese in the Shan State capital of Taunggyi, apparently on corruption and trafficking charges. For four years, he was held in Mandalay prison until his right-hand man, Chang Su-shoen, abducting two Russian doctors working at Taunggyi hospital and holding them hostage, extorted his release. Sa did not return home immediately, but stayed a year or two longer in Rangoon. Finally, around 1975-76, he managed to escape, resurfacing next at Hin Taek (subsequently renamed 'Toed Thai' by Thai officials), a village which lies a few miles inside Thailand (ironically, not far from the KMT stronghold of Mae Salong). For the next six years, Ban Hin Taek became the Shan opium warlord's principal HQ. Given that Hin Taek was on Thai soil, and given Khun Sa's notoriety, it might well be wondered why the Thai authorities allowed, even welcomed, him – just as in 1961 they had embraced the trafficking ragtag KMT 3rd and 5th Armies – into the kingdom. The reason was the same as for their acceptance of the KMT and should likewise, as we saw in Chapter 1, be understood in the light of contemporary political events in Thailand and her neighbouring countries. Many of the latter had fallen or threatened to fall to the communists, and it was feared that Thailand, which had its own growing communist insurgency, might also so fall as the next domino. In particular, Bangkok was afraid that a strong Communist Party of Burma (CPB) might link up with the Communist Party of Thailand (CPT), with potentially dire consequences. Anti-communist forces like those of the KMT, Khun Sa's SUA, Mo Heng's SURA and the Karen KNU/KNLA could police the Thai border and act as buffers between the CPB and CPT, a role they successfully fulfilled. And so the logic of Bangkok's strange move was that Khun Sa and his SUA were tolerated as a useful plank in Thailand's anti-communist border-security strategy.

Meanwhile the *ka kwae yae* scheme had been wound up by the Burmese in 1973, and for half a dozen years the SUA, while Khun Sa had been incarcerated, had been out of his control. Now, at Hin Taek, the warlord set about rebuilding his private army. He re-immersed himself in the narcotics business as never before, and, basking in the patronage of various high-ranking Thai army and police officers, operated with impunity out of his new stronghold. But the best news for the SUA leader was that his arch-rival, the KMT, was in decline. Around 1973, both the burgeoning CPB People's Army and the Burma army definitively dislodged remaining Chinese Nationalists from the Wa sub-

THREE PAGODAS

state and the Shan State, pushing them over the border into Thailand and ending their 20-year-long control of opium trafficking in Burma. Khun Sa, reinvigorated and poised in Hin Taek, stepped in to fill the vacuum. Where once the KMT had controlled 90% of the heroin issuing from the 'Golden Triangle', now he was in control of 70% of it. In the mid-1970s, Khun Sa emerged as South-East Asia's premier drugs warlord, a position he was not to relinquish for at least 15 years.

The warlord's notoriety began to embarrass his Thai hosts. Not only was Hin Taek a funnel for vast amounts of drugs passing into Thailand and on out to the wider world, but Khun Sa's SUA was assassinating the odd CIA and US Drugs Enforcement Administration official, angering the Thais' main ally, the Americans. There were other considerations, too. The threat from the communist parties of Burma and Thailand was receding by the early 1980s, making the SUA less indispensable. But what really stung the Thai authorities into action was the discovery that Sa was in cahoots with the Burmese communists – the very people he was supposed to be undermining (he habitually traded with everyone). Worse still, he moved freely through CPB-controlled territory and was even reportedly harbouring Chinese arms for the Thai communists. In January 1982, crack Thai army rangers and BPP troops launched a massive attack on Hin Taek, backed up by tanks, artillery and warplanes. In the ensuing fierce three-day battle, scores were killed and wounded, but the strike was successful, and a thousand SUA men retreated over the border into the Shan State (Sa, it is said, was tipped off by powerful Thai friends and escaped). The Hin Taek heroin-producing hub was smashed, and the opium king dispatched from Siamese soil.

Never a man to be worsted, Khun Sa retaliated against his former hosts by sending 200 SUA commandos to sack Mae Sai and by stopping and burning dozens of vehicles on the main Mae Sai/Chiang Rai road. On the Burmese side of the border, he initiated 1983-84 a reign of terror, fanning the smouldering border war with the KMT, attacking and displacing the militias of various small ethnic groups, such as the Wa, and creating the biggest shake-up along the Shan-Thai border since the arrival of the KMT. In one memorable action, an SUA hit squad blew up, as we recall, the Fah Ham residence in Chiang Mai of Gen. Lao Li, the commander of the KMT 3rd Army. When the dust had settled along the border, Khun Sa had established new bases notably at Doi Larng (opposite Mai Ai), at Ho Mong (also known as Mong Mai, situated near Mae Or or 30 kms north of Mae Hong Son town), and at Piang Luang. At the latter place, as we know, his SUA units bottled up warlord Mo Heng and his SURA, the upshot of which was that the pocket SURA was swallowed up in 1985 by Khun Sa's bigger SUA, the new combined army subsequently being renamed the Mong Tai Army (MTA) or 'Army of the Tai (Shan) Land'. Both at Doi Larng and Mae Or, Sa's strongholds were compromised by adjacent Wa positions, but at Piang Luang the warlord was in sole control. Mo Heng's old base, the starting point for three main trafficking routes into Thailand – one down through Kae Noi, one down through Wiang Haeng, and one down to Pai – must have been the jewel in Khun Sa's crown.

POPPY MEN

By 1985, Sa dominated nearly the whole 200-km-long Shan-Thai frontier. His trafficking flourished correspondingly. He claimed to control two thirds of the cross-border narcotics trade with Thailand, approximately 1,000 tons of opium a year. As the money rolled in, his MTA swelled. Soon it comprised some 6,000-8,000 properly trained and heavily armed men. Khun Sa was the uncontested opium king of the 'Golden Triangle'. The only force which could perhaps have moved against him was the Burma army. But, as in earlier decades, Rangoon's stance was curiously hands-off, causing him little grief. In 30 years, Khun Sa has had, compared to all the other rebel groups in Burma, a remarkably easy ride with the authorities. Possibly they remembered his early 'work' for them as a KKY commander. Perhaps they thought the game of pursuing the powerful warlord into his remote jungle kingdom not worth the candle. But probably they had reached some kind of understanding with him. It was reported in the 1980s that at secret meetings with him senior Burmese military figures had agreed that he could pursue his trafficking activities unmolested if in exchange he would allow free passage through his territory for the teak which Rangoon had begun selling to the Thais for desperately needed foreign currency. The haemorrhage of logs in the early 1990s through Piang Luang would seem to substantiate such a deal. With the Thais, too, Sa now enjoyed again a surprisingly sweet relationship. Perhaps because he was no longer on their territory, they had no special quarrel with him. Rather the reverse was the case. The hardwood was coming through, as were the regular shipments of white 'N° 4', which yielded hefty kickbacks for army and police officers at the border crossings and on the mountain roads leading down from the frontier. At the instigation of the Americans, the Thais put a price on Sa's head, but the bounty was so laughable that no one bothered to try to collect it. It would have been an easy matter to do so, as the warlord had a safe house in Mae Hong Son town and even, apparently, property off the Sukhumvit Road in Bangkok. Of the Thais, Khun Sa scoffed: "If you feed them, they are friendly" and "Why should they fight or capture their moneytree?"

Around 1987, the 'Prince of Death' or the 'Poppy Man', as the world's press liked to dub Khun Sa, sought to clean up his image. He tried to attenuate the significance of opium growing, the drugs trade, the MTA, and his cause. He invited journalists to his GHQ, now at Ho Mong, who were surprised to find not a warlord of legendary ruthlessness, but an astute, articulate and affable host, a man who took pleasure in promoting Buddhist and Shan culture. Treated to French brandy, satellite TV and Taiwanese pop songs, the visitors were shown the orchids and strawberries Sa liked to cultivate. The reason so much opium was grown in the 'Triangle', the Shan champion explained, was simply economic dependency. "If you ask the peasants to stop growing poppies, they will have nothing left to barter for rice." He himself was not an opium warlord, but a Shan nationalist and freedom fighter. With the MTA, he was fighting a war of liberation against Rangoon for an autonomous Shan State. Sa did not deny his involvement in trafficking drugs, but claimed it was a necessary evil. He had only entered the narcotics trade to fund his army and finance the struggle. Actually, he was anti-drugs and wanted nothing more than to eliminate the curse of opium from the Shan State. He reminded the journalists – and through them the world at large – that on several occasions he had proposed to the US that they buy from him the entire opium crop of the 'Golden Triangle' in exchange for economic aid. For US $100m a year for five years, the Americans could stop the flow of heroin from the 'Triangle', and the Shan State would benefit from an aid programme which would eradicate the poppy, substitute other crops, and develop the Shan economy. "If I can win the Shan State, eight million Shan will be happy, but if I solve the drug problem, the whole world will rejoice." Sa reiterated his offer, but as on previous occasions it was turned down by Washington, which did not deal with 'criminals'. This was a pity, as his offer, which stood for some years, could well have been genuine. But the problem was that the warlord had become so much tainted by the corruption of the narcotics world that few believed his offer, and his remarkable change of heart did anyway come rather late. Cynics pointed out that Sa was only changing his tune because his share of the world narcotics market was declining in the face of a flood of drugs from places like Columbia. But perhaps also an ageing Khun Sa, with his eye on the history books, wanted to acquire respectability before he quitted the stage.

Khun Sa's virtual monopoly of drugs trafficking along the Shan-Thai border ended in the winter of 1989/90, when a new opium war flared up, this time between the MTA and Khun Sa's other great rival, the Wa. The two factions had already skirmished sporadically throughout the 1980s, but the confrontations, for example at Mae Or (Mae Hong Son), had been of little consequence. Now the jostling for power and for control of the frontier was deadly serious. The difference was that late 1989 the WNC Wa of the Thai-Burmese border, who already enjoyed the backing of the KMT, were substantially reinforced by a body of Wa Daeng or 'Red Wa', Wa who up in the Wa sub-state had for years sided with the Burmese communists, but who now in the wake of the 1989 CPB mutinies and the demise of Burmese communism came south from the Wa homeland. Together, the two Wa factions formed the United Wa State Army under Ai Siao-su, leader of the WNC. The new UWSA attacked Sa's MTA, notably on the Doi Larng ridge, with a view to muscling in on Khun Sa's scene and getting a bigger slice of the drugs trafficking cake. In warfare that continued and intensified until 1991 – the bitterest fighting, the MTA conceded, that it had ever been involved in – things did not go entirely Sa's way. He was obliged largely to pull his troops out of his main Ho Mong base near Mae Hong Son/Mae Or so as to relieve his beleaguered Doi Larng stronghold, and in the end the Wa captured half of the strategic ridge.

In mid-December 1993, Khun Sa invited a large number of Shan leaders and observers to his Ho Mong HQ, where provocatively he declared the independence of the Shan State. A constitution was promulgated and a 70-seat two-house parliament instituted, with Sa, his relatives and lieutenants holding key offices. All Rangoon-issued laws were annulled, and all SLORC junta troops on Shan land were required to leave. Sa invited recognition for his newly independent country from the UN and the nations of the world, and he crowed that in the years ahead the MTA would be strengthened to as many as 100,000 guerrillas.

POPPY MEN

The Burmese responded to all this bravado with a swingeing offensive against Khun Sa. In the dying days of 1993, thousands of junta troops gathered on the west bank of the Salween, closing off a 120-km section of the river. Fighting started opposite Wiang Haeng, precipitating the flight of hundreds of refugees (especially Lisu) over the border at Piang Luang, where they were housed in camps at Chong. Rangoon claimed that it had seized two refineries belonging to Sa. Sa, holding many of his troops in reserve to protect his other refineries, rushed a sizeable number of MTA guerrillas to block the Burma army. They ambushed a column of 1,000 SLORC soldiers crossing the Salween in longtail boats, killing many. At the height of the crisis, Sa warned the Burmese that if they advanced, he would destroy Takilek (opposite Mae Sai) – no idle threat, considering his earlier sacking of Mae Sai. At the same time, he claimed that the offensive against him was merely cosmetic. The two refineries seized were not his, but had been set up by the Burmese so that for effect they could then be captured. This may well have been true. The MTA spotted *farang* (probably US DEA officials) among the Burmese on the west bank of the Salween, suggesting that the offensive and the seizures had been stage-managed to impress the DEA (and congressmen back home) with a view to justifying American aid to Rangoon. And, indeed, in early 1994 the offensive seemed to peter out. Not that, as things turned out, the Burmese had any need to pursue and crush the opium king, for just two years later he fell into their hands without a shot being fired. And with this we come to the latest development in and seeming end of Khun Sa's long career.

Khun Sa postscript 2001

In the first days of 1996, the whole 'Golden Triangle' area and the world at large was rocked by the unexpected and dramatic news that Khun Sa and the MTA had surrendered to the Burmese enemy authorities. The Thai newspapers were full of stories and pictures of the unthinkable: Burma army troops entering and taking over the veteran warlord's GHQ at Ho Mong, meeting no resistance. A week into the new year, a ceremony was held at the jungle stronghold, at which Khun Sa, accompanied by some of his senior lieutenants, officially handed over to a Burmese delegation, led by Maj.-Gen. Tin Htut (the junta's Eastern Force commander), a nominal 33% of the Mong Tai Army arsenal and a large part of the MTA's troops. The ceremony must have been some party, as 2,000 MTA men were present together with 600 *tatmadaw* soldiers. At the event, the opium king presented his Burmese counterpart with a list of 4,431 MTA members, while among the 3,400 weapons on display, waiting to be turned over, were 15 Russian-made SAM-7 surface-to-air missiles, rocket-propelled grenade launchers, a home-made 105-mm mortar, machine guns, mortars and 1,000 AK-47 and other rifles. Rangoon walked not only into Ho Mong, but also into other former MTA positions, including part of strategic Doi Larng and Doi Saeng (near Mae Hong Son).[2]

---

[2] In March 1997, so the *Bangkok Post* reported, a group of 42 former MTA soldiers gave themselves up to the SLORC in the Takilek area, bringing the total of those who had surrendered to Rangoon up till that time to 14,606.

THREE PAGODAS

Appearances, however, belied the underlying reality. It emerged slowly that the ageing, puffy-faced, baggy-eyed Khun Sa had not 'surrendered' to his 'foe' of four decades, but had actually struck a deal with them. For their part, the Burmese had not found the capture of Ho Mong a pushover; they had not even been pushing against an open door – Sa had invited them in. He had even sent pick-up trucks down to the MTA Ta Sob Taeng base on the River Salween to collect the 600 SLORC troops attending the handover. As further details emerged, it transpired that the deal was reminiscent of other deals Sa had made in the past.

Khun Sa submitted a ten-point proposal to Rangoon, the main provisions of which were that he would hand over his army, his weapons and territory in exchange for an amnesty in respect of his and his followers' criminal record as narco-terrorists, for a peaceful retirement, and for not being extradited from Burma to the US to face drug-trafficking charges.[3] Sa hoped also that those of his MTA soldiers who surrendered would be accepted as volunteers in the Burma army. For the Burmese, Tin Htut said that his and the MTA troops would now join forces to develop the Shan State, and that Rangoon had already sent a first consignment of 50,000 bags of rice to the region. From the capital came official noises that, since Khun Sa and the MTA had finally heeded the authorities' appeals to them to lay down their arms, they could be sure of a constructive response from the junta. If there was to be a trial of Sa, it would be a token affair, put on for the consumption of outsiders. The warlord would be detained for a while, before being quietly let go.

Khun Sa's critics interpreted the deal as a sell-out and a last dirty move by the wily merchant of death. It was the final chapter in a history of accommodations and pay-offs and was absolutely in keeping with his past performance. The warlord had always been less a Shan nationalist and more an opportunistic businessman at heart. He must have carefully weighed up his options and decided to take his chances with the Burmese. After all, his traditional bolt-hole, Thailand, had an extradition treaty with the US. As one detracting Sa aide said, the MTA leader had bribed his way to retirement. He had been wheeling and dealing with the Burmese for years, so the latest deal, involving a pay-off to a Burmese general to the tune of millions, came as no surprise. Since 1992, Khun Sa had been sweetening the general commanding the region 500,000 kyat a month (thousands of dollars). Or as Karen supremo Bo Mya put it, it was remarkable how in the dry seasons of 1993/94 and 1994/95, when the Burmese were launching major offensives against the MTA, their actions just came to nothing (leaving them free in the latter winter to concentrate on taking the Karen HQ of Manerplaw). But that was because Khun Sa bought them off with tens of millions of kyat. Furthermore, the warlord and the junta not only came to an understanding on the battlefield, but collaborated in the narcotics business. As a result, Rangoon would never hand

---

[3] In 1989 and again in 1992, Sa and 19 associates were indicted in New York on such charges, and in early 1996 the US backed up the indictment with the offer of a $2 million reward for information leading to the arrest of the warlord, who was accused of having supplied roughly half of Burma's annual opium crop of some 2,000 tons. The 1989 indictment related to the seizure in 1988 at a Bangkok port of 1.05 tons of heroin!

Sa over to the Americans because at any trial the opium baron would spill the beans about Burmese involvement in the drugs business. And why should they hand over Sa to collect the $2 million reward when Sa would pay them many times that amount? The latest deal at Ho Mong was not surprising at all. Khun Sa had always been a lackey of the Burmese authorities. He had started out as a 'village defence force' leader under Rangoon's *ka kwae yae* scheme, and was now returning to the fold.

The question arises as to why, beyond the considerations just mentioned, the irrepressible Khun Sa – the paramount survivor of the treacherous world of Shan narco-politics – should undergo his profound change of heart after almost four decades of defiant autonomy. The answer is that around 1995 he suffered a serious setback, which, compounded with other worries, apparently caused his heart to go out of the struggle. In June of that year, several thousand MTA fighters, led by Shan nationalists, broke away from Khun Sa, complaining that he devoted too much time to the drugs trade at the expense of Shan nationalist objectives. So little had been achieved in the nationalist struggle that they wondered if he was not in it purely for other reasons. Another grievance was that within his movement Sa seemed too often to promote only followers of Chinese extraction. The dissension within the MTA was further aggravated when in January 1996, on the announcement that Khun Sa had struck a deal with Rangoon, hundreds more Shan MTA men defected, refusing to surrender and remaining in their strongholds. They accused their leader of a sell-out and of betraying the Shan people, and began to form a new liberation movement with new leaders. In a wave of secondary defections, some soldiers from both groups of renegades then went over to the Shan State National Army, proceeding to Piang Luang and elsewhere, while others simply left army life to make their way as civilians. In newspaper reports the name of a former top aide of Sa's, Maj. Gun Yord (Gun Yod, Kan Yod, Gun Jade), cropped up repeatedly as the figure around whom the dissenters were rallying.

Other worries were of a military nature. The UWSA was currently in the ascendant, having made more inroads into Khun Sa's traditional territorial and trafficking preserve. Since 1989, the 'Red' Wa had been party to a ceasefire agreement with Rangoon, were even cooperating with the junta. In the winter of 1993/94 and 1994/95, the Burma army had launched two offensives against him. Even if he had managed to buy the Burmese off in the short term, in the long term they were determined to crush him and secure the Shan State and the Thai-Burmese border for themselves. Thus it was not just that Khun Sa's two most serious enemies were now deployed against him, but were deployed in alliance. Indeed, now that Rangoon had the Karen theatre of operations under control, having taken Manerplaw in 1995, they were free to turn their undivided attention to him. Among the rebels in Burma, Khun Sa had become the prime target, and the heat was on.

And then there had been logistical and commercial setbacks. In 1994, a dozen of the opium king's senior sidekicks involved in trafficking heroin to Chinese gangs operating out of Taiwan and Hong Kong were arrested in Thailand, seriously compromising Sa's marketing arm. Altogether the Thais had become less accommodating. They had considerably tightened their control of the border at his back, cutting the main routes across and making it more difficult to sell heroin and to resupply the MTA. Income was down, and the soldiers were becoming disgruntled.

All these worries no doubt led Khun Sa to conclude that it was finally time to throw in the towel. Even successful warlords are not proof to the ravages of time. Amid changing circumstances, they get old and have to retire. Approaching his mid-sixties, a Khun Sa dejected about the split in his organization probably felt he no longer had the energy to yoke together the sundered halves or fight new fights with an insistent enemy. The weariness of age had come upon him, and he felt the war to protect his drugs trade was a lost cause. Preferring the SLORC devil he knew to an unknown fate in Thailand or the US, he decided to retire in Burma and accordingly began making a series of overtures to the Burmese government. Delegations went down to Rangoon, one led by Khun Sa's uncle, Chao Khun Saeng; a ceasefire was mediated; Sa began to step down from (or was relieved of) key MTA positions; SLORC representations arrived at Ho Mong; Sa sounded out his Shan elders about ceding to Rangoon; and the Burmese authorities started building a house for the warlord in the capital. On 5 February 1996, Khun Sa reportedly went to Rangoon to check the progress of his new living quarters. Meanwhile he stayed with the followers who had remained loyal to him in Ho Mong, protected by his new patrons. He said that his retirement wish was to be in a place where he could not be chased, where he could raise chickens and tend his vegetable garden. And, indeed, in 1997 Khun Sa was reported to be living luxuriously in a junta-provided house in Rangoon, running several businesses, including a gems operation! At the same time, there was some deterioration in his health, and he was undergoing medical treatment for diabetes. In March 1998, the old warlord was admitted to a hospital in Rangoon, suffering from diabetes and high blood pressure.

By 2001, Khun Sa may himself have bought freedom and immunity in Rangoon, but the net was closing in on many former associates and henchmen of his, some of whom were still active in the drugs trade. On 9 January of that year, Yang Wan-hsuen, popularly known as Lao Tai, was arrested by the Thais at the request of the US authorities in Mae Sai, where he was hiding in a house on the banks of the Sai river. Aged 55, he had been a former secretary and a close aide of the warlord. He had also been head of the SSA political affairs section, still had connections with local drug dealers trafficking in heroin and 'speed', and was one of the US's most wanted narcotics traffickers. He was taken to Bangkok, where he was destined to go to stand trial in the US on drug charges. Just a few days later, Peng Hui-lan, aged 54, was arrested in Bangkok along with five others at the request of the US and in collaboration with the US DEA on heroin-smuggling charges. A minor wife of Khun Sa (who had many wives, his first wife dying from cancer about 1996), she was believed to be the head of the gang arrested. Peng and the others were seized at a Chinese restaurant in the *Windsor Hotel* in Bangkok's Sukhumvit Road. She was charged with possessing 1.4 kg of heroin and was also wanted in the US in connection with a shipment of 57 kg of heroin to New York earlier the same month (January 2001). Other associates wanted in the US besides Khun Sa and the above are Wei Siao-gang (current leader of the UWSA), Chang Hsue-chuan (the SSA's chief-of-staff), and Lamdab Namsuwakhon (a drug dealer and former Sa aide). By 2001, thirteen narcotics traffickers had been arrested and extradited to the US to stand trial at its request.

By 2001, not much was left of Khun Sa's once so powerful empire. The MTA was disbanded, with the bulk of it apparently merged into the Burma army, and some parts gone over to the SSA and other Shan factions. Virtually the whole of the section of border that the warlord once controlled on the Burmese side was now in the hands of the Burmese and the Wa, who were largely collaborating. The *tatmadaw* and the UWSA controlled Takilek (opposite Mae Sai); the UWSA occupied territory opposite Mae Fah Luang, replacing Burmese troops who previously held the area; the UWSA now had the refineries, once run by Sa, opposite Hua Mae Kham (near Hin Taek); the Burma army were on the top of Doi Larng mountain, once a key stronghold of the MTA, while the UWSA were all over the Doi Larng ridge, even building a new town at their permanent Mong Yon HQ opposite San Ton Du (above Mae Ai town); the Burmese were at Nor Lae, while there were UWSA troops on Doi Laem opposite Doi Ang Karng and also opposite Nong Ook; the Piang Luang border crossing was in the hands of the Burmese, and the territory either side controlled by the UWSA; Burma army soldiers on Doi Daeng opposite Pang Ma Pa had been replaced by UWSA troops; Ho Mong was occupied by the WNA, although the Burmese and UWSA were knocking on the door; and the border ridge by Mae Or as well as the territory opposite Mae Or was likewise controlled by the WNA (Maha San's pocket army).

The departure of Khun Sa and most of his MTA from Shan territory and the drugs scene does not mean any lessening of the flow of narcotics from the 'Golden Triangle' – far from it. The area's production of some 2,000 tons of opium a year (equivalent to 200 tons of pure heroin) and of millions of amphetamine pills, is much too lucrative a business for no one to be interested in maintaining it. The principal inheritors of Khun Sa's and the MTA's refining and trafficking capacity have been, as indicated, the 'Red' Wa and their UWSA. But the Burmese junta itself, in cahoots with the rampant Wa Daeng, has also been widely implicated in the 'Golden Triangle' drugs trade, propping itself up with the vast amounts of black money deriving from the trade.

✳

Before our trip to this section of the border, we had wondered why Piang Luang (but also Muang Na and Kae Noi – and in early 1994 Wiang Haeng, too) was so firmly closed to outsiders. In retrospect, as we made our way back to Wiang Haeng, the reason, or rather cocktail of reasons, was obvious. There was the danger of cross-border bandits and robbers, of the kind who lurked around Kae Noi. There was the intermittent danger of attacks and shelling by the Burma army. There was the risk for outsiders of being mistaken by the KMT or the MTA (if *farang* crossed the border) for hated US DEA officers. There was the matter of the massacre of KMT people at Piang Luang, which the authorities no doubt preferred to remain a secret. But the real murky secret was the trafficking in the area. Kae Noi was a drug-smuggling village like other KMT border settlements, and Piang Luang was a veritable funnel for heroin passing from Khun Sa's territory into Thailand. The drugs came over the border in pick-ups and in secret compartments cut into the Burmese teak on the log-transporters. And it was in this respect that the Thai authorities quite especially did not want outsiders snooping around Piang Luang. They did not want the lid lifted here on an easy relationship with the notorious Khun Sa, nor on the collusion with him of corrupt Thai police and army officers (on one police truck we saw drums of acetic anhydride, a chemical used in the heroin-refining process), and not either on the questionable tripartite cooperation of the Thais, the illegal Rangoon junta and Khun Sa in the shameful matter of the logging – something internationally condemned.

❖ ❖

Postscript 2002

Route detail: Wiang Haeng – Chong – Piang Luang – Lak Taeng – Wat Fah Wiang In/border (Map 8)

km 0.0   Centre of **Wiang Haeng** with petrol station (R) and with row of shops plus noodle place (L)
          Head N up main asphalt road for Piang Luang

km 3.1   In **Kong Lom**, turning L in village centre by shop & phone box for Muang Noi and Pai (Map 10/Chapter 4). Opposite the turning (R side of road): the house, set back, behind which there is a row of basic rooms for rent

km 3.4   On a bend in the road: way L for Karen village of Mae Haat and Mae Haat Waterfall

c. km 6.0 *Khum Wiang Haeng* 'guest house' or small resort (L), a short distance before Pang Po (details: see Postscript to Chapter 2)

km 6.8   **Pang Po** village, its checkpoint gone in 2001
          Mahatat village

km 8.1   **Wat Pratat Saen Hai** with its golden pagoda and monastery-temple (up steps R)

km 9.1   **Muang Pok** school (L) and health centre (R)

km 11.3   In **Chong** village with its two fuel places (L) and shops: turning R for Kae Noi (Map 6)
          Ban Mai (= New Village)

km 15.9   Portal and entrance to Piang Luang. Checkpoint (L), ineffectual these days. Just before entrance: new health centre (R). Big school and play area/sports ground (also R)
          In main street: Shan-style *wat* (L)

km 16.6   Centre of **Piang Luang** in long main street
          Restaurant top end of main street (R)
          At T-junction, go R
          At next T-junction, go R again, following main way
          Main road swings L and down

km 17.5   On a bend: *Piang Luang Guest House* (R)
          Road, giving over to dirt surface, continues 3 kms to border

POPPY MEN

Lak Taeng village
Way L up to **Wat Fah Wiang In**
km 20.4   Border, border gate, Thai army checkpoint. Across border: Shan State,
Burma ('Union of Myanmar'). By the checkpoint: another way steep up L
to Fah Wiang In monastery-temple

In 2001, as already indicated in Chapters 1 and 2, much had changed or normalized in
connection with **Piang Luang**. A good paved road (H1322) went all the way to it,
starting down near Chiang Dao and the H107, and proceeding via Wiang Haeng. The
border KMT place was open to outsiders, and all the checkpoints (at Na Wai, Muang
Na and Pang Po, as well as at the entrance to the village itself) that used to prevent
farang from reaching the dubious outpost had gone or lost their teeth. Regular public
transport even went there. Piang Luang was serviced by several *silor* a day which started
at Chiang Dao, and by one small daily bus that departed from Chiang Mai.

At the entrance to Piang Luang, we found that the checkpoint by the portal was
still in operation, just, but was ineffectual – at least during the daytime – and took no
interest in *farang* visitors, occasionally checking local people only. The whole village was
much more developed than in the early 1990s, with far more stores and increased
activity. Piang Luang had turned almost into a small town. The long main street was
prosperous, and busy during the day, although it went pretty dead after 7pm, when the
shutters came down. Numerous motorcycle taxi boys congregated in the middle of the
main street, touting for people to take hither and thither, probably even into Burma.
Exploring W of the townlet, we found a massive reservoir, near the top end of which
lay a Chinese school (busy in the evenings), a temple, and a big clan house.

At the top end of the main drag, just before the T-junction, there was a good
restaurant (R/east side of road), which served fried rice, noodle soup with *pak dong*
(pickled chillied cabbage), omelettes and other dishes until about 9pm. In 2001 the lady
owner spoilt us here, bringing a succession of free extra titbits (it was Chinese New
Year). For the last two or three years, there has been a proper guest house in Piang
Luang, called *Piang Luang Guest House*, so it is easy now to stay in town. To find it, go to
the top end of the main street, turn R at the T-junction, then R again at the next T-
junction (see Map 8), and follow the main road round and down, ignoring a couple of
side streets. You will find the GH on your right, on a corner of the road, almost at the
end of Piang Luang and at the start of the way to Lak Taeng. It is a motel-style place,
built around a yard. The yard is slummy, prices are somewhat inflated, and at first sight
the rooms are nothing special. Initially, we were put off, but don't rule the lodging out.
Quite apart from the fact that there is nowhere else to stay in town (at the time of
writing), it is not so bad after all. The uniform cement rooms (200 baht/night for a
room with cold water, 250 baht for hot) are fairly basic and austere, but they have big
beds, their own bathrooms, and furniture, look clean, and are provided with towel,
soap, flip-flops and drinking water. The place is run by an old man and some young
girls, and sometimes there is a resident young Chinese girl prostitute!

In 2001, Wat Fah Wiang In and the border crossing were visitable. To reach them,
proceed out of the top northern end of Piang Luang, passing the guest house and
negotiating a couple of S-bends (Map 8). You come to the outlying settlement of **Lak
Taeng**, which we found to be likewise much developed, no longer a collection of
bamboo huts with grass roofs but a community with regular Chinese houses. Beyond
Lak Taeng and shortly before the border, a way goes steep up L to **Wat Fah Wiang
In**. The round pagoda and the Buddha figures (which may have been moved to the
Thai side) were visitable, but the part of the monastery-temple lying in Burma was not.
During our visit, we noticed groups of Thai soldiers discreetly standing and sitting
around, keeping a watchful eye on the local proceedings. Everything seemed ultra

relaxed, so Doug and I decided to stroll across to the Burmese part of the *wat*. Immediately, the Thai soldiers called after us and made us return, which we did. They pointed out some Burmese soldiers just across the little intervening valley, whom we had not noticed and who had quickly stirred into action. Wat Fah Wiang In is a hazardous flashpoint, as it has always been, so tread carefully up here. It is volatile not just because of the Burma army, but also because of constant dubious local goings-on, as was underscored precisely at the time of our 2001 visit. A man, carrying a heavy load, came running from the Burmese part of the *wat*, across the dip, to the Thai part. He dropped his load and urgently communicated some message to the Thai *tahaan praan* soldiers we were talking to, who at once jumped up, seized their guns, and began running to where the man had come from. At the same time, one of them radioed for reinforcements, who came screeching up in military vehicles, to run after their fellow soldiers. In the hullabaloo, shooting could now be heard not far away. It seemed that there had been some incident on the border between hill-tribe people, possibly involving smuggling. We never got to the bottom of the affair because an officer advised us to leave and return to Piang Luang for our own safety.

But next day all was quiet again, and we came back to view the border itself. Here, in the intervening years, little had changed from the point of view of layout, although the political situation was now quite different across the border. The same buildings and shops still congested the defile of the crossing point, and the same wooden gate with barbed wire blocked the way. But where earlier Khun Sa and the MTA had controlled the territory on the other side of the border, now the Burma army and the UWSA did so. The Burmese held the border crossing itself, as well as Wat Fah Wiang In and pockets along the border (e.g. the post above Muang Na), while the Wa, with whom the Rangoon junta was in cahoots, controlled most of the stretches in between.

When Khun Sa surrendered to Rangoon in the first days of 1996 at his principal HQ in Ho Mong, the Burma army took over many former MTA positions, including Ho Mong. Whether junta troops directly inherited Khun Sa's position at or opposite Piang Luang is not clear to me. They may well not have done so because in early February of that year many MTA troops, refusing to follow Khun Sa and accusing him of selling out to the Burmese, broke away, on the one hand uniting with other MTA splinter groups, and on the other allying with the SSA. About 1500 of the renegades moved from Ho Mong to positions at Piang Luang as well as at/opposite Hua Mae Kham and Ah Long (Mae Fah Luang), both further north. Nevertheless, the *tatmadaw* must have taken control not too long afterwards of the Piang Luang crossing and of most of the border opposite Pang Ma Pa, Piang Luang, Wiang Haeng, Kae Noi and Nong Ook for two reasons. In the late 1990s, the Burmese were in full control of the crossing points at Piang Luang and Nong Ook, as they still are now in 2001 – witness the status quo. And by the end of the year 2000, these Burmese positions were taken over – with Rangoon's tacit approval – by the UWSA, which could only have happened if the Burma army already occupied them. At the same time, the Wa mopped up any sections of border opposite Pang Ma Pa, Piang Luang, Wiang Haeng, Kae Noi and Nong Ook not in Burmese hands, seizing them from the MTA remnants and other Shan forces such as the SSA, clashing with the latter, as they still are sporadically at the time of writing. So, broadly speaking, the UWSA is now in control of this stretch of the Thai-Burmese border, with their mentors, the Burmese, at a few key points. Thus, in November 2000, the Wa were in Pang Sua Tao village, located 2 kms from the Thai border, opposite Wiang Haeng district, and they were creating merry mayhem opposite nearby Pang Ma Pa, as we discovered when we redid the Wiang Haeng to Pai trip (Chapter 4). Where the Wa are, so are also the drugs, and it is certain that Wa heroin-refining and amphetamine-producing factories are currently operating opposite Piang Luang and other places such as Kae Noi.

4

SPIRIT WELL & SPIRIT CAVE

Wiang Haeng – Kong Lom – Muang Noi – Pai – Soppong – Luuk Kao Laam – Bo Pi – Mae Hong Son

B ack in Wiang Haeng, we were refreshing ourselves at *Sayan* when we had a piece of luck. It was a Friday, and employees from the district office, the post and telecommunications offices, and the hospital opposite were leaving work for the weekend. Everyone was in a grand mood, all the more so because next day was a Buddha day, a reason for special celebration. No one was more buoyant than a fellow in his mid-twenties who was roaming around on a large white trails bike looking for diversion. This was the excellent Witit Terkae, a Karen from the nearby village of Mae Haat. He spotted us immediately, parked his machine, and introduced himself. He was a hospital employee, although his actual place of work was the health clinic in Karen Mae Haat. He was involved in family planning and in the past had worked in UN-sponsored hill-tribe development schemes. A broad-faced, short-haired chap, who had enjoyed education in Chiang Mai, he now lived in Chong, where his wife ran a shop selling domestic appliances, also doing some tailoring on the side.

Witit was instantly likeable. He seemed overjoyed to meet a *farang* and began showing us numerous kindnesses. He paid for our tea and snacks, pointed out to us (three-up on his motorbike) hidden aspects of Wiang Haeng, and invited us for nips of pre-prandial *lao kao* at the store next to *Sayan*. As the evening wore on, he became more and more eager, his altruism, embarrassingly, seeming to know no bounds. To our eternal shame, we began to grow suspicious of this rather flash, Thaiized character. What could he want of us? Why should he take such an interest in us? He liked to meet foreigners, he explained, was teaching himself English and wanted to practise what he had learnt. But more than that, he wanted *farang* visitors to get a good impression of Wiang Haeng and Thailand. When he had met Westerners in the past, they had all too often left complaining of this or that, which had hurt him. We also got the impression that this keen-minded Karen-Thai was simply bored of everyday life up in remote Wiang Haeng district. He was looking for contact, interest. But if on that Friday evening we were made for him, much more so he was made for us. On all our travels down the border, we hardly met a more helpful generous man.

We were worried that, with the school closed for the weekend, it might be awkward to continue staying in the primary school sickroom. "Don't worry about that," Witit said, "the janitor Rak-kiet is a friend of mine. We'll go down and sort it out." ("Don't worry" and "so-and-so is a friend of mine" were favourite expressions of his.) And just as we had feared, when we got back down to the school, Rak-kiet had disappeared and all the teachers had gone down to Chiang Dao or Chiang Mai for the weekend. However, Witit knew where the janitor's private house was – in the middle of a pineapple field halfway between Wiang Haeng and Kong Lom. On the way out to the pineapple plantation, we suddenly turned off the main road, still three-up on the trails bike, into a long side track running down to an isolated building in the middle of some fields. It was Wiang Haeng Christian Church. Behind the simple box church building was a long motel-like block, where the priest lived. "What are we doing here?" we asked our new friend. "Don't worry," Witit said, "the priest is a friend of mine. You can stay here." And indeed the priest and the Karen seemed to be on good terms. Within a short time, it was all fixed up that we should stay in the guest room of the pastor's block.

While Witit went off to regulate things with the janitor and at the same time recover our backpacks from the school, we made acquaintance with the priest. Most obligingly, this chubby-faced, quiet-spoken man, called Somkiet, unlocked a simple spartan room with a large double bed and electric fan. There was nothing else in the room except nails in the walls for securing a mosquito net. But the priest, although he was really cooking his supper in the kitchen, set about rustling up blankets, sheets, pillows and even pillow cases. At the back of the block, he showed us a *hongnam* cubicle (wash and toilet facilities combined), and soon we were showering with rainwater from a tank warmed by the sun. On a table on the veranda at the front of the building, jars of tea, coffee and Ovaltine appeared, together with a clump of bananas and a pyramid of oranges. There, waiting for Witit, we chatted to our new host.

After two nights in the sickbays of primary schools, all this was luxury indeed. Here was the real 'Wiang Haeng Hilton', and we told Somkiet so. It was nothing, he demurred, just simple Christian hospitality. From time to time Westerners, mostly Americans, came up from Chiang Mai to express solidarity with his mission or help him plant church rice, and he had meanwhile learned what *farang* liked. We voiced our fear that we were putting him to a lot of trouble. Not at all, he smiled, there was not a lot to do up here, he did not get many visitors, and he was glad of the company. He elaborated about the church and his work. The church had been built by missionaries between 1985 and 1991. They had left two years previously, leaving him in charge as the first Thai priest. The church had 49 members, mostly Lisu people. He held a service for them once a week. There was another church in the village, a Baptist mission for the Karen faithful. While Somkiet was speaking, we noticed that he had outsized Buddha-like earlobes – hardly appropriate for a Christian minister. Another odd thing was that the priest had put into a cassette player a tape of Christmas carols (it was the Christmas period), which played over a loudspeaker system he had rigged up. So, as we chatted on the veranda and watched the oriental sun go down over the mountains behind Chong and distant Kae Noi, we were regaled with 'Jingle Bells' and 'God Rest Ye Merry Gentlemen' – in Thai, of course.

SPIRIT WELL & SPIRIT CAVE

Witit knew of a second restaurant in Wiang Haeng, better than *Sayan*, and insisted on taking us for supper there. It was a new place, set back from the main road and positioned by a small artificial lake. It belonged to a teacher ("a friend of mine") and as yet had no name. From Somkiet's veranda we could see its fairy lights winking in the distance. There was a direct way over to the restaurant from the church, and so, guided by Witit, we picked our way under a full moon, through the dry stubble of harvested rice paddies, towards the lights.

The little lake was being used to breed freshwater fish, and it was not long before a trout couched in coriander leaves and a fiery fish *tom yam* soup in a steamboat were on the table. Best-quality Sangthip whisky appeared, a bucket of ice, soda, more dishes of pork and fresh ginger, and of stir-fried mixed vegetables, and soon we were well into a feast that must have cost the health worker a week's wages. But Witit was in his element, kept saying how much he liked *farang*, and what a pleasure it was for him to see us happy. As the Sangthip began to course through his veins, his English improved remarkably. All sorts of stories came out. One concerned his father. Years ago, his father had been walking down to Pai when he had been bitten in the bottom by a tiger. The wound had hurt so much that doctors had given the poor man opium to alleviate the pain. Unfortunately, the father had then grown addicted to opium. With the breadwinning father incapacitated, and the family having to buy ever more opium, they had all become impoverished. Witit told of how he and his mother had had to make long treks alone in search of opium, sometimes as far as Pai (60 kms away). It was only when the father had finally died that the family's fortunes had improved. This background may have explained Witit's motivation in life and relative affluence.

We were the guests of honour at the restaurant, and the teacher-owner brought to our table a plateful of *yaku*. This was a Shan confection made specially to offer to monks on Buddha days, such as was the morrow. It was a brownish sticky cake, like flapjack but softer, and made of glutinous rice, sugar cane, coconut and peanut. The wedge-shaped slices were dusted with sesame seeds. Trying the *yaku*, we learned that some of Witit's relatives had dug up in their gardens both at Mae Haat and Chong pipes, pots and other relics from the ancient Lawa people. Our ears pricked up. The few surviving Lawa now lived in a mountainous area much further south, near Mae Sariang (see Chapter 8). If what the Karen said was true, the finds would seem to indicate that at one time, either pre-dating the arrival of the local Shan (Tai Yai) and Lan-Na Tai (Tai Yuan of northern Thailand), or contemporaneously with these two Tai groups, the Lawa had lived right up here in Wiang Haeng district, constituting the original inhabitants of the area.

Witit recounted details his mother had told him about the Japanese in Wiang Haeng during the Second World War. They had pressganged local people to act as porters in their invasion of Burma from Thailand. But they could not have had things all their own way in this isolated area. Recently, a mass grave of Japanese soldiers had been unearthed at nearby Muang Noi. We asked Witit where that was. It was a Karen village halfway between Wiang Haeng and Pai. Witit had relatives there. This casual titbit of information made us sit up. The village seemed to lie on our projected onward route. The detail was all the more interesting because we had once tried to get up by motorcycle to Wiang Haeng from the Pai end, but had failed miserably. The track had been so difficult that we had given up after about 20 kms. Our abiding fear was that we might be frustrated again on this crucial link down to Pai. Was there a way down to Pai from here, we asked, and what was it like? For the first time that evening, Witit's face clouded over. There was a way, but it was very bad, and dangerous. We could not possibly get our Wing down there. Even in a 4WD truck it was virtually impassable. No one went down there. The only sensible way to get through was on foot. But to halfway Muang Noi it was more than 30 kms – an awful long way to trek in one day. The outlook seemed bleak. "But don't worry about it," our Karen friend said, seeing our crestfallen faces, "let me see what I can do."

We wanted to leave Wiang Haeng for Pai the next day. But the following day Witit had arranged with a friend to go down to Chiang Mai in a pick-up truck he owned. He was torn between honouring his arrangement and trying to help us. The more we discussed the problem of getting through the mountains to Pai, the more the spice of an adventure with us attracted him. Finally the matter was settled – fantastically in our favour. He would take us on the Saturday, if it was possible, in his truck as far as Muang Noi. There he would leave us with his Karen relatives and return the same day to Wiang Haeng. We would have to find our own way down the second half of the route to Pai. His trip to Chiang Mai he would delay until the Sunday, and on that Sunday he would also be able to take our redundant motorbike with him in the back of his pick-up to Chiang Mai, returning it to the hire shop. The plan could not have worked out more perfectly for us. But Witit declared himself very satisfied, too. He would still get to Chiang Mai, but would also have the pleasure of a day out with us. In the euphoria of the moment, another bottle of Sangthip appeared, and we all drank too much late into the night.

❊

When Witit finally arrived the next morning, he was in high spirits. We could tell from his breath that he had already been drinking. We took our leave of Somkiet the priest, left the Honda with him, and made a small contribution to his church effort. Then, in Witit's ageing blue pick-up, we blasted down the dusty stony road, past Rak-kiet's pineapple patch, in the direction of Piang Luang. Almost immediately, the truck drew up at a shophouse in Kong Lom village. "A friend of mine," Witit said, "don't worry." We did worry, because in front of the house there was a table with a litter of glasses and half-empty Mekhong whisky bottles on it. Around the table sat half a dozen men, clearly determined to waste no time in celebrating Buddha day. We feared either that we would have to join the party or that the noisy crew might want to come with us. But only one man was to accompany us, a Thai in his twenties called Ekerin Poon Nu.

SPIRIT WELL & SPIRIT CAVE

Witit and the lean wiry-haired Ekerin disappeared into the house. Presently, they emerged wearing military combat gear and bearing provisions for the trip. Witit had asked me what I liked eating, and I had said, not giving the matter much thought, but trying hastily to settle on something as little inedible as possible, "Chiang Mai sausage". So they put into the truck sticky rice, chilli dip, a bottle of Mekhong whisky and, taking me literally, a long coiled Chiang Mai sausage. Behind the seats in the cab, they also stowed "just in case" an assault rifle, two pistols and three hand grenades, while into the open back of the truck they tossed, for good measure, a hunting gun, wrapped in a sack. We questioned the two about this mini arsenal, and Witit confessed that he was terrified about the trip – not so much about the outward journey to Muang Noi, but about the way back, which they would have to do in the night. He would never have gone with us on his own, which was why he had asked his friend to come along. Ekerin was a regular Thai army soldier, in fact a paratrooper who had been trained by the Americans.

Soon we were on our way (Map 10). At a junction in the centre of **Kong Lom**, a side road went off south-west, out past Wat Kong Lom, across a bridge, through the new satellite settlement of **Kong Lom Mai**, and towards the hills. The road, already a narrow dirt track, bumped through some outlying fields, before starting to climb. Then, twisting and turning around the hillsides, it climbed over three ridges in succession. The way, a major heroin-smuggling route from Piang Luang down to Pai, passed through completely uninhabited mountainous forest, part of Huai Nam Dang National Park. During the 28 kms from Kong Lom to Muang Noi, we passed not a single hut or vehicle or person on foot. The absence of vehicles, even 4WD machines, was hardly surprising – the route proved, as Witit had predicted, virtually impassable. The main problem was that on the central ridge section the track degenerated into a series of precipitous rutted gulleys. The two boys in the cab picked out a way for the truck as best they could. We stood in the back, clinging onto the roll bar, being tossed this way and that. The wheels inched from boulder to boulder, grinding up, teetering, and lurching forward. The vehicle underside scraped repeatedly on the rocks. On the steepest downgrades, where the surface was gravelly, the pick-up slithered, its rear end threatening on the curves, where the outer edge fell away, to tip off the mountainside. Alarmed, we made ready to jump from the vehicle should this happen. Initially, Witit and Ekerin were worried, too. Witit said later that they had wanted to go back, but had not been able to find anywhere to turn round, and so had had to continue. But as they got into the expedition, they warmed to it. The two friends were like boys out on an adventure. We saw them through the rear window of the cab chattering, joking and, maniacally it seemed to us, passing the Mekhong from one to the other, which they drank straight from the bottle.

Presently, they drew up on an elevated flat piece of track. Ekerin had seen something he wanted to take a pot-shot at. He came round to the back and aimed the hunting gun up into the tree tops. None of us could see what it was that he wanted to shoot. There was a loud report, and a bird flapped away. Then the sizzling countryside fell eerily silent again. We kept looking over our shoulders into the endless lonesome *mai teng* and *mai rang* trees, wanting to press on. But the boys decided it was an excellent spot for a picnic. They began fiddling around, as Karen do, slashing at the vegetation with their survival knives and unpacking the food on the pick-up's tailboard. While the soldier recharged his hunting gun, Witit hacked off two sections from a fat bamboo and fashioned two drinking cups. I had brought a plastic bottle of purified water with me and was not amused when he poured half of the precious liquid into the green cups and threw the rest away. Taking my plastic bottle, he then sliced it in two, making two more crude drinking vessels. Decanting half the water from the bamboo sections into the two new plastic 'cups', he then liberally topped up all four with whisky, and we each had a drink. The boys thought the makeshift forest bar a hoot. Then the Chiang Mai sausage came out. And so, with slices of sausage and balls of sticky rice in one hand, and our warm whisky in the other, we had an impromptu lunch standing around the truck on a heroin trail in the middle of nowhere (see photo section).

Waving a machete with a piece of sausage spitted on the end, Witit pointed out wild orchids growing from the treetops. They hung down like dark clumps of weeds from the uppermost boughs. Through gaps in the woods, he indicated pink sakura trees and yellow *buatong* (Mexican sunflowers) growing on the mountainsides. Ekerin narrated mad stories about his commando training with the Americans. For some reason he and the other soldiers had had to stand for days on end in water. And when during their jungle survival training he had subsisted on centipedes and rats, the softie GIs had munched throughout on secret chocolate bars. A couple of kms short of our halfway goal, we passed a turning north-west (right) to the Karen village of Kiu Nor and a small dam. After that, a descent brought us to Muang Noi, almost exactly midpoint between Wiang Haeng and Pai.

Muang Noi

A relatively large village with a mixed Shan and Karen population, Muang Noi straddled the River Pai. A new bridge was being built over the water, and it was impossible to drive across to the western side. So Witit parked his pick-up in the grounds of the new health centre. His idea was to get us billeted there, where the medic in charge was "a friend of mine". But alas, the day being a Saturday (moreover a Buddha day), the friend had gone away for the weekend, and the building was locked up. Picking our way on foot through the scaffolding of the new bridge, we searched around the houses on the other side. Finally, the boys lighted on one poor unsuspecting household, and we all crowded in. The owners were Karen, evidently distantly related to Witit. What was happening and what was being arranged was quite inscrutable to us, and so we kept our own counsel. But it seemed that some corner of the large wooden dwelling would be our bedplace for the night.

We wanted to go out and explore the village, but Witit and Ekerin had other ideas. Soon the four of us were sitting cross-legged on a platform at the rear, while the lady of the house brought plate after plate of snacks. The boys intended to continue the day as they had started it, and once more laid into the whisky. Most of the snacks were either too fiery to eat or made of things one would not want to eat anyway. But a plate of roast buffalo morsels was tempting, if only to soak up some of the afternoon alcohol. Unfortunately, a scruffy young chicken also had designs on this. Numerous domestic animals besieged the platform, but none was more persistent than the chicken – or *chor* in Karen. With a constant cheeping and fluttering, it kept returning to the platform, strutting among the plates and pecking at them. We shooed it away a few times, and when that became tiresome, Witit picked it up and threw it across the backyard. Undeterred, the brazen chicklet returned. Ekerin moved to teach it a lesson, and in its panic it placed a scaly foot exactly in the middle of the roasted buffalo morsels. We thought the paratrooper was going to wring the bird's neck, but he simply cloched it with a heavy pot, from under which it cheeped inconsolably, denied access to the snacks. The *chor* was in prison, we suggested, which set the boys chuckling again...

Finally, when it was already dark, our two friends broke off the party, saying that they had to return to Wiang Haeng. They grew steadily more serious as we neared the truck. We tried to persuade them to stay the night and start back early next morning. But they would not hear of it. They checked their cache of weapons, took leave of us, and disappeared into the night-time jungle. The thought of the two of them trying to drive up that atrocious way in the dark made us apprehensive too – and with justification. When, a year later, we saw Witit again, he said that they had not reached Wiang Haeng until two in the morning. In fact, they had almost not got back at all. He did not elaborate, and we felt sure that they had had an accident. At all events, we never saw the blue pick-up again (Witit had "sold it – it was getting rather old"), and in our minds there was no doubt that the Karen and his soldier friend had written it off on that return journey.

Our lodging in Muang Noi was not a typical Karen house raised on stilts, but a regular two-storey building made throughout with wooden planking. The disorder was great, and every room looked like a lumber room. Normally when passers-by stay at a Karen dwelling, they sleep on a communal platform at the front. But we were allocated pride of place upstairs in a lobby, where the family shrine was. There, under a shelf decked with Buddha figurines, flowers, a miniature bespectacled monk and a mysterious old tea caddy, we unpacked out rucksacks and rolled out our sleeping bags. In the backyard there was a barnlike shack – probably the original house. In this, a very old man and woman lived, the parents of either our host or hostess. They never moved from the shack and tended three blackened kettles, which were permanently on the go on a fire that burned night and day. Washing was either in the River Pai or with a pot and dipper on the platform at the rear, where we had had our little party. The dipper was half a tin can nailed to the end of a stick, and with this we tried to have a wash.

Seeing that no more food would be forthcoming that evening, we went to the aged grandparents and made Ma-maa instant noodles with their boiling water. The granny smoked a pipe throughout, and the grandpa constantly rolled his own green cheroots. The impudent chicken was on the loose again, and, darting around on the bare earth floor, it ran the gauntlet of gobs of spit from the ancient pair. Neither of them could speak a word of Thai, and we could speak no Karen, so communication was reduced to an amiable exchange of signs. Electricity had reached Muang Noi three years previously, and our house had one of the few TVs in the village. Back in the living room of the main house, we found 25 people of all ages sitting in a crescent around the box, but also crowding the doorway and hanging in through the windows. A Thai thriller was showing, and we noticed that many of the viewers took the film literally. Gasping and flinching when something dramatic happened, they had difficulty telling TV make-believe from reality.

The next morning, inspecting Muang Noi, we realized what an attractive place it was. With the tight valley of the River Pai running through the middle, the settlement was surrounded by lush vegetation and dominated by nearby Doi Pa Pueng (meaning 'Beecliff mountain', Toe Nae Lae in Karen), a wooded hump with a sheer north-facing cliff. It was also a traditional village, many of the Karen inhabitants wearing their costumes. The women had on red hand-woven tube skirts and terrycloth turbans, while the men were dressed in baggy black pants and jerkins, their attire topped off by a ubiquitous bobble hat. At the high end of the village, we found a fine small monastery, surrounded by flowering *sh'bar* bushes and *lantom* trees. In the midst of their heady perfume, a monk explained to us that Muang Noi was about 40 years old and originally Shan. A few Karen had then arrived, followed by more, until they predominated. They had intermarried with the local Tai Yai, creating a truly mixed Karen-Shan village. We learned from the bonze something of advantage to us. Most days, a lorry came up to the dam from Pai. Usually it went back down the same day – he could not say when – and we might be able to get a lift with it.

We were doubtful whether the lorry would come on a Sunday, but nevertheless thought it worth trying to intercept the vehicle. So we went back down to collect our backpacks. On our way through the simple leaf-roofed houses, we came upon a disturbing sight in somebody's front yard. Although the late-morning sun was very hot, a wood fire was blazing. A man was lying next to the fire, so close that his clothes were singeing. He was wrapped in innumerable blankets, had on three woollen balaclava helmets one over the other, and his feet were bound up in hemp sacking. The bundled figure looked like the Michelin man or a mummy, and the only part of him which was visible was a panel of face, which was waxy white and had a black moustache. The man was shaking uncontrollably and over and again asked for the fire to be made hotter. He was bitterly cold, he complained, and had a terrible headache. Of course, the man had malarial fever. The circle of onlookers explained to us that the fever came on always at the same time of day. Why don't you go down and get the doctor, we suggested, fearing that the man might die. That was the problem, they replied, the doctor had gone away for the weekend.

We took up position by the road in a corner of the health clinic compound. Opposite was Muang Noi's tiny 'Private Licensed Post Office', no more than a shed. It was just as firmly shuttered as the clinic. Behind the post office was the timeless veering precipice of the Beecliff outcrop. It seemed to mock us in our wait in the blazing midday sun. We searched incessantly up the dusty track, but no vehicle came. It was incredibly boring and frustrating waiting there. The seconds and minutes and hours ticked slowly by. The only thing to contemplate was the grisly detail that Witit had told us – that our waiting station was the place where, when the health centre had been built a year or two earlier, workers had unearthed the mass grave of Japanese soldiers who had been massacred in the Second World War. They were probably killed by Karen as the Japanese withdrew from Burma back into Thailand at the end of the war. In 1945, Karen and Karenni underground forces, organized and armed by the British, killed an estimated 12,500 troops of the Japanese 15th Army, as it retreated in disarray through Burma's eastern hills and back across the Thai-Burmese border.

In the end, our waiting was rewarded. At teatime, an orange lorry came bumping towards us from the direction of the dam. We waved it down and asked if we could ride to Pai. The driver was happy to take us, and as the back was full of oxyacetylene cutting and welding equipment, he bade us climb up into the cab. And so we began the second half of the trip down to Pai (Map 11). It seemed every bit as bad as the first half. Immediately after Muang Noi, we splashed through two fords and passed an outlying hamlet or part of Muang Noi. Then the lorry broke its way over a couple more ridges of the type we had crossed earlier. The flora was part jungle, part highland woods, the trees being a mixture of pine and teak, *mai teng* and *mai rang*. The most severe section of the entire 55 kms from Kong Lom to Pai was probably around the Lisu village of **Huai Chang Tao**. Here, a dozen wickedly steep climbs and descents were aggravated by a succession of hairpin bends. This had been our waterloo on that previous attempt at the route, coming from Pai. The driver carefully edged the lorry around the bends. After the Lisu village (38.5 kms from Kong Lom), we passed the first of two checkpoints. Both were manned intermittently, our driver explained, their sole purpose being to catch drug smugglers. On the day we passed them, both posts were deserted. After one more ridge, we finally left the mountains, coming down into valley country at the Shan village of **Tan Chet Ton** (= seven palm trees) (km 49). From there, it was a straight run on through the villages of **Si Don Chai** and **Wiang Nua**, across the River Pai, to Pai town itself and its central crossroads (km 55.3).

✻

Pai

Pai was a dreamy squat little place, set in a hot wide basin. Lying almost exactly halfway along the 200-km H1095 route from Mae Ma Lai to Mae Hong Son, this Shan town was enjoying a mini boom. For the increasing number of people proceeding anticlockwise round the Chiang Mai – Mae Hong Son – Mae Sariang – Chiang Mai loop, the town made an obvious first stopping point. There was not a lot to do in Pai, either in the town itself, or in the immediate vicinity. The central grid of streets, lined with single and two-storey houses, could be walked all round in half an hour or so. Some people used the town as a base for trekking in the mountains further afield. Pai lay on the edge of a well-trekked area to the north, north-west and also west. Others came here to raft or canoe on the River Pai. But most were drawn to Pai as a place where they could 'hang out' for a week or two. In choosing tranquil low-key riverine Pai in preference to Chiang Mai, Pattaya, Phuket or other overtly touristy resorts, they were not making a mistake.

One diverting feature close at hand was the KMT Chinese village of Ping Ang Choeng, renamed by the Thai authorities **Santichon** (= peaceful river). Situated west of Pai, four or five kms up a dirt road, the village was unusual for a KMT settlement in that it was in the lowlands and not up on the mountainous border. We were told that the 20-30 Chinese families had recently been resettled there from notorious Hin Taek, where they may have been 'friends' of Khun Sa. This might have explained the frosty welcome and veiled looks we received when we briefly visited Ping Ang Choeng and tried to ask questions on a little afternoon sortie from Pai.

We stayed a couple of days in Pai, and at first the little town captivated us. The laid-back atmosphere was relaxing, and there was minimal traffic and pollution. After Kae Noi, Wiang Haeng and Muang Noi, it was also undeniably pleasant to re-enjoy the creature comforts of relative civilization. *Own Home Restaurant* provided a remarkably varied menu with good friendly service. One could spend an inexpensive week here eating one's way through molee Indian curry, barbecue chicken, Thai stir-fries, moussaka, Burmese food and Japanese tempura. And *Charlie's Guest House*, centrally located in the main street, proved an adequate lodging, with hot showers, an attractive inner courtyard with garden, and somewhere to hang out one's washing.

But gradually Pai palled on us. Above all, it was an unreal place – indeed, all 'Pai in the Sky', as the name of one guest house had it. For such a small rural community, it had a disproportionate number of guest houses, trekking agencies and restaurants. They had mushroomed to service all the *farang* who now saturated the town. However, these were not the seasoned travellers and trailblazing bikers of yore, but (at the risk of sounding patronizing) couples pushing infants in buggies, maladroit elderly tourists, and groups of pink-skinned youngsters, fresh in from their home countries, hobbling around with blisters after a first trek and bitten all over by mosquitoes and bedbugs. Our room at *Charlie's* was actually no more than a box, utterly devoid of furniture, and for this they charged prices rivalling those in Chiang Mai. In the self-regarding *Tai Yai* restaurant, we met arrogance and contempt from the Thai-Shan owner. Woe betide anyone who went there as a *farang* with a Thai wife or girlfriend. He would be served last or not at all and made to understand that he was *persona non grata* in the company of a prostitute, which was odd, as the owner seemed to be married to a *farang* woman, and the insinuation could equally have been made the other way round. Pai also had a drugs scene. Some of the trekking guides could be seen in dim corners pushing the dope that had found its way down from the Shan State. Correspondingly, not all the people 'chilling out' in Pai were there only to enjoy the river view or the local atmosphere. Finally, after 8pm the townlet was dead – unless one joined the throng in an establishment with the authentic Shan name of *Chez Swan*. Here, a pretentious French menu and inflated prices were matched by the clientele inside. The sight of them through the glitzy windows, posing and regarding each other, made us want to scurry on the next morning.

SPIRIT WELL & SPIRIT CAVE

Pai – Soppong – Luuk Kao Laam

The next leg of our journey was to take us along the H1095 first north-west to
Soppong and Luuk Kao Laam, and then south-west to Mae Hong Son town
(Map 12). From Chiang Mai, there were two ways to far-flung Mae Hong Son.
A circuitous southerly route took in Hot, Mae Sariang and Khun Yuam, an all-
day journey by bus of nearly 400 kms. And a shorter, more difficult route went
north via Mae Ma Lai, Pai and Soppong, some 250 kms. Until recently, virtually
all traffic for Mae Hong Son had taken the southerly road, painfully negotiating
the famous 1800 bends on the way. But with the completion of the 1095 road
in the early 1990s, more traffic had started to use the northerly route. The
H1095 was originally laid out by the Japanese in the Second World War as a
way of supporting their war effort in Burma.[1] It was to take another 50 years
before this tortuous dirt track through the mountains and jungle was to
become properly serviceable. At the time of our journey, the road was
asphalted throughout except for a small section between Pai and Soppong.

With our Honda Wing back in Chiang Mai courtesy of Witit, we decided
to travel on by bus. Of course, when the stumpy orange mountain vehicle
pulled into Pai bus station mid-morning, it was already full. But, tossing our
backpacks onto the pile of luggage and other bundles near the rear door, we
managed to squeeze in next to an elderly monk. The holy man, supposed to be
a model of abstinence, was using the opportunity of the stop to surreptitiously
smoke a worldly Khrong Thip cigarette out of the window. We soon
discovered the disadvantages of bus riding in Thailand. It was dreadfully hot
and cramped. For a long-thighed *farang*, the tightly packed seats meant having
to sit either legs wide apart, suggestively, or legs parallel and to one side, female
fashion. Whatever way, as the bus jolted and shuddered along, it was physical
torture.

---

[1] Most parts of the H1095 follow the former Japanese route. Using Thai labourers, the Japanese
army built during the war some 300 kms of trail in the area, from Mae Ma Lai to Pai, to Mae
Hong Son, to Khun Yuam, and from Khun Yuam to Burma via the Ban Huai Ton Noon pass,
the trail being designed to allow Japanese troops easier access to Burma. In Thailand,
Kanchanaburi town and province, as is well known, are closely associated with the Japanese
occupation during WW2, especially on account of the Thailand-Burma 'Death Railway' and the
'Bridge over the River Kwai'. But much less known is that Mae Hong Son province, too, has a
considerable and interesting wartime history, a lot of which centres on Pai as well as on Khun
Yuam. It is reckoned that at least 500 Japanese troops died in these two districts or in Mae Hong
Son province as a whole. The Japanese army set up bases in Pai district, the main one being near
Pong Nam Rorn hot springs, with others scattered from Ban Napa Kha to Pang Ma Pa district.
Shan-style Wat Pa Kham in Pai town was used as a Japanese field hospital from 1942-45, and the
surrounding area housed livestock and markets, where soldiers bought vegetables. There was
even a small mint in Pai to produce Japanese coins and banknotes. The old metal Ta Pai bridge
across the River Pai on the approach to Pai town (as you come from Mae Ma Lai), which today
you can still see standing beside the new concrete bridge, was constructed by Japanese troops
and Thai coolies. At its western end, there used to be a large Japanese military camp, and at its
eastern end a cemetery holds the remains of many Japanese soldiers. Interestingly, some parts of
the bridge structure were brought from the old Nawarat Bridge across the Ping river in central
Chiang Mai city. See Chapter 8 under Huai Pong and Khun Yuam for more details about the
Japanese in wartime Mae Hong Son province.

THREE PAGODAS

Progress was very slow. In fact it took a good two hours to complete the 40-odd kms to Soppong. This was partly on account of the twisting and climbing, but also because every mile or so the bus stopped to pick up or let down passengers, who were mostly hill-tribe people. Soon the central aisle and the standing area near the backdoor were chock-a-block with Lahu, Lisu and Karen in their colourful costumes. In the crush, we lost sight of our luggage. These mountain people never travelled except with a great deal of encumbrance. The women had snoozing infants in slingcloths on their backs. The men had their shoulder bags, cardboard boxes with animals in them, and small boys to look after. All had bundles of vegetables, which they stowed under the seats, or sacks of maize or rice, which they sat on. They had their pipes or their betel-chewing paraphernalia with them and juggled all this with packed lunches of sticky rice and boiled eggs or dried meat. Somewhere behind us a cock crowed.

Interesting as it was to literally rub shoulders with these tribespeople, the encounter had its less appealing side. Teeth blackened from years of betel-chewing and maws reddened from the latest mouthful leered at us from close quarters. If the mountain people were near a window or door, they would lean out to eject a stream of carmine juice. Sometimes the children could not wait until the bus stopped, but peed straight onto the floor. At the end of long journeys, the mountain buses were often awash not just with plastic bags and soft drink cans! Nor were the hill people very good travellers. Perhaps because they were unused to the motion of the bus, they easily got sick. Unfortunately, when we later came to retrieve our backpacks, we found that someone, probably a hill-tribe child, had deposited the contents of their breakfast on the bags.

The tribespeople got on and off the bus in the most unlikely places. We would round a corner, and there would be a little band of Lahu or Lisu flagging us down in the middle of nowhere. Then they rode a mile or two, perhaps to go to a field or to visit friends, and would alight by a tiny path leading off into a wall of jungle. The bus was driven by a young man in sunglasses and minded by a couple of busboys, who hung the whole time right out of the doors. Every time the vehicle stopped, they leapt down and placed wooden chocks behind the wheels. Then, with a shout of "Bai" to the driver, they would snatch out the chocks, scamper alongside the bus as it moved off, and jump aboard. Occasionally, the chocks were used for a novel purpose. On particularly steep upgrades, the vehicle, engine labouring, edged forward so slowly that the boys were easily able to walk beside it. Then, just as it was about to shudder to a halt, they popped the chocks behind the wheels, the driver stirred the gears, selected first, the bus moved forward again, and they pulled the chocks away, clambering in.

On the run out from Pai, the hot air of the valley floor blew through the bus as if from a giant hair-dryer. But as the road gained height, and the baking flat fields gave way to the stepped paddies of narrow secluded valleys, the warmer air was interspersed with wedges of cool. Soon we were in the damp chill of the high jungle and mountain forest. Incredibly slowly, the bus climbed to almost 5000 ft, finally emerging on top at Pang Ma Pa police box. The pass was marked with stunning bluish vistas of wooded mountain ridges receding miles north to the Burmese frontier. And then it was 2000 ft down the far side of the ridge, past Lisu people on hillsides harvesting ginger, towards Soppong.

People around us began acting strangely at this point. Rummaging in their bags, many produced handkerchiefs or scarves, which they tied around their heads in such a way that only a slit was left for the eyes. The effect was sinister, and to anyone passing we must have looked like a busload of bandits. The reason soon became apparent. Suddenly the bus plunged into the last unmade section of the 1095. Where there was no oncoming traffic, this did not matter much. We simply left a terrible dusty wake. But when a vehicle did come by, the bus was filled with a 30-second blinding choking cloud of orange laterite particles. It was just our luck that on one of the hairpin bends, 12 inches deep in the treacherous bulldust, we came across a convoy of log transporters. The bus juddered to a halt to let the groaning beasts past. They ground up round the hairpin slower than walking pace. Indeed, the swarthy Shan or Burmese crew accompanying them were easily able to run back and forth past the vehicles, managing the convoy and warning oncoming traffic with red flags. As each transporter passed the bus, its engine blasted us with hot air and another whirl of orange powder. By the time we got to Soppong, nobody cared much anymore about trying to keep clean. In particular, the monk beside us seemed quite unfazed. But then the dirt was exactly the same colour as the saffron of his robes.

The bus left the H1095 to stop in **Soppong**, which lay slightly offroad. A busload of orange zombies disembarked to dust themselves down and seek food and refreshments. While others took a hasty fried rice or noodle soup, we settled for hawker food at the side of the main street and found a girl selling *salapao* – steamed white rice dumplings with a filling of minced meat or black bean. Soppong was a small one-street Shan place. Muslims also lived there, and they may have been the descendants of migrant *jiin haw* traders, as we saw Chinese lettering on some notices. Apart from the shops and a couple of primitive fuel stations, there was not a lot else. As usual, the police station was the biggest building in town, and in front of a mini hospital stood a large sign in Thai warning of Aids in Mae Hong Son. The bus was an important line of communication in a place like this, bringing not only mail and the latest gossip from the district towns, but also entertainment in the form of visitors. So for 15 minutes, as long as the bus stopped, the local people studied us while we studied them. The ambience of Soppong struck us as peaceful, colourful, relaxed, idyllic.

Spirit cave

A notable and – to my mind – very interesting feature of Soppong and of the wider local area is a series of caves, many of which show signs of having once been inhabited by ancient people, and some of which also – famously – contain the remains of mysterious archaic coffins. The karst limestone mountains of Mae Hong Son province favour the formation of such caves. The Australian John Spies, who has lived locally for many years, who runs *Cave Lodge* guest house near Lot Cave just north of Soppong, and who has a professional interest in these caves, claims to have visited more than 200 caves in the province, of which no fewer than 80, so he says, contain the preserved remains of prehistoric coffins, while 20 sites are adorned with ancient art, and 20 are littered with stone tools. Two celebrated caves are Lot Cave and Nam Lang Cave. **Lot Cave** (also written Lod Cave, in Thai 'Tam Lot' or 'Tham Lot', pronounced *lawt*) lies about 8 kms north of Soppong near Ban Tam or Cave village. It is a massive 400-m-long cave with a broad stream flowing through it, said to be one of the longest known caves in mainland South-East Asia. The cave is much visited, and apparently you can walk right through it. It has a chamber with coffin remains.

Nam Lang Cave (also known as Mae Lang Chan Cave, called 'Tam/Tham Nam Lang' in Thai, and also popularly known as **'Spirit Cave'**) is located some 30 kms west of Soppong, south of the H1095 road, near the village of Ban Nam Khong, which takes its name from the river that intersects the H1095 at Mae Suya village (Map 12). I have never been to this cave, but I understand that it stands near the Nam Lang, a side stream that runs into the Khong river. Reportedly, the cave is set high in a cliff, its entrance lying some 120 m above the Nam Lang or 40 minutes' steep climb up from the Khong river. It is a whacking 9 kms long and in terms of volume is said to be one of the largest caves in the world. Like Tam Lot, the cave contains the remains of ancient wooden coffins. Nam Lang Cave was discovered or, rather, made famous by the renowned archaeologist Chester Gorman, who started excavating it in the late 1960s. He christened the cave 'Spirit Cave', by which name it is widely known, and did so because the local Shan and Lahu believed that *pi* or spirits dwelled in the cave, being responsible for leaving the coffins there. In digs, Gorman sieved through layers of sediment on the cave floor to unearth evidence of human occupation of the site dating back 8,000 or 9,000 and maybe 12,000 years. He revealed remnants of a race of hunter-gatherers, uncovered stone tools, and in the upper layers found pottery. Spirit Cave could well have been inhabited up until the end of the Iron Age.

Also in Nam Lang Cave, but from a later cultural phase, Gorman found the remains of some twelve ancient teak coffins. Like the coffins discovered in Lot Cave and other caves in the region, these are between 1,200 and 2,200 years old – some say up to 4,000 years old. John Spies reports that most of the coffins were once supported by posts and cross-beams above the cave floor. Together, the coffins of Mae Hong Son province are in at least 50 different styles and often have ornately carved handles on their ends. Some have no handles, but bear a human face carved in a heart shape on the lid. The coffins range in length from 9.5 m to just 80 cm, with most being between 2 and 7 m long.

Since Gorman's day, archaeologists have found that most of the coffin cave sites have human bones and teeth mixed with burial goods and possessions of the deceased, reflecting a practice still seen in some tribal peoples today. Other things that have been found include ground polished stone adzes, iron tools, plain iron and bronze bracelets and ornaments, stone and glass beads, cowrie shells, large amounts of pottery (some shards of which have cord markings on them), and fragments of lacquered teak containers. The adzes date to 3-4,000 years ago, a time which was a turning point, when hunter-gatherers, armed with the stone tools, first began to easily clear forest for crops and houses. The locally made iron tools and jewelry date to around 2000 years ago, when they were ubiquitous. The bronze, the stone or glass beads, and the shells were imported from abroad, demonstrating well-established prehistoric trade routes – the beads may have come with traders from India.

Some of the cave sites in Mae Hong Son province have, as said, rock art, which is mostly simple paintings in red ochre of people and animals. At a few sites, handprints, stencils and abstract designs have also been found. The art may have been done by Stone Age cave dwellers, making it up to 3,000 years old. Altogether, the coffins, artefacts and art paint an interesting picture of past existence in the area. Cave sites with coffins are not unique to the region, as they have also been found at Chiang Dao and in Kanchanaburi province, and, outside Thailand, there are reports of similar sites in Burma, China, Vietnam and Borneo. Apparently, people stopped using the caves near Soppong as cemeteries about 1,200 years ago or c. 800 AD, although it is not clear why they did so. Nor is it clear who the people were who inhabited the caves, placing coffins in them

To me, it seems plausible that the people who used the caves and placed the coffins in them were the Lawa, an ancient people who are said to be indigenous to the area of present-day Thailand, who may well have been the descendants of the original hunter-gatherers, and who today still live in the mountains not so far from Soppong (to the south, below Wat Chan village). It seems unlikely that the coffins were placed in the caves by some other people since come and gone. Until recently, the Lawa used to bury their dead, along with their personal possessions. Reportedly, shards of cord-marked pottery have been found at a Lawa cemetery. The Lawa are well known for having once mined their own iron ore, smelted iron, and done iron work. They continue to weave cloth, including burial blankets. And there are isolated pockets of Lawa still living down in Kanchanaburi province. It would not surprise me at all if DNA extracted from an ancient tooth from a cave burial site near Soppong, when compared with DNA from contemporary local peoples (the Lawa, Shan, Lan-Na Tai or Tai Yuan, Siamese Tai, Lahu, Lisu etc.), should show a definite link only with the Lawa, connecting them with those prehistoric dwellers of Lot Cave and Spirit Cave. I have detailed these local caves and their ancient coffins at some length both because the subject is intrinsically interesting and because they shed interesting light on Thailand's past, but also because they seem linked to the Lawa, who figure later in our journey's story (Chapter 8). But back now to the story itself.

In Soppong's main street, while we were still snacking beside the bus, a long mule train sauntered past, heading west. Out on the main road again, we soon overtook the laden beasts, led and cajoled by their Shan minders. Beyond Soppong, at the side of the 1095, a new piece of town was beginning to spring up. Probably it would soon usurp the main town itself, with the original section declining into a quiet backwater. After that, the jungle swallowed up the road again. Seeing that we were nearing our next destination and did not know exactly where to get off, we asked one of the busboys to warn us. When he heard that we wanted to visit the mysterious Bo Pi (*bo pi* or *baw pee* = 'Spirit Well'), he grew concerned. "Aren't you afraid of the spirits?" he asked. The bus climbed up again several kms, before emerging into a marvellous terrain of blue-black lumpy mountains with extensive vistas. It was the finest scenery between Pai and Mae Hong Son. To the south of the road lay a deep valley with a tiny picturesque village in the bottom, nestling at the foot of a towering mountain. At this juncture, a dozen kms out from Soppong, the bus drew up. It was time for us to get off. Bo Pi was somewhere down there by the village. We extricated our luggage from the pile and clambered down, watched by all the passengers, who wondered why we should alight in the middle of nowhere. And then the bus departed, leaving us alone in the midst of this karstic fairy-tale landscape. We watched it disappear, a drum of diesel and much other clobber lashed to its roof-rack under a net.

✳

Luuk Kao Laam

A short distance back down the road (and, 53 kms out from Soppong or exactly halfway to Mae Hong Son), we found a track leading south to the valley floor. We followed it down for a couple of kms. The afternoon heat was blistering, and we were hungry from having eaten only *salapao* dumplings. As we approached the small village, we had the impression that we were walking into an unsuspecting nest to disturb it. The houses and their surroundings were utterly silent and peaceful. We passed a closed-up primary school and entered a deserted dusty village square. There was one tiny shop, but it was locked up. Finally a boy came, bringing a key. Then his mother arrived. The shop was disorderly, with almost nothing for us to eat or drink. The village, a Lahu settlement, was called Luuk Kao Laam. Most of the people were out in the fields. We felt slightly dissatisfied, sitting in front of the shop, but the next piece of news disappointed us even more. Somehow we had imagined that Bo Pi was this village or perhaps part of the mountain behind it, but it transpired that Spirit Well was some way off in the mountains, too far to go there and back before dark. Nor was there anywhere to stay at Spirit Well. Thus, if we wanted to visit it, we would have to stay the night at the village and walk there next morning.

It was too late to climb back up to the road and go on to Mae Hong Son, so we decided to embrace the fate of Luuk Kao Laam. A clinic near the square was closed, but we found a second school, which was functioning. Inside, one solitary teacher was surrounded by a score of Lahu elementary pupils. As soon as we poked our heads in through the door, lessons were hopelessly disrupted. The teacher, a young Thai, felt he had to attend to us, and the children grew excited. In his living quarters to one side of the classrooms, the man made a wood fire so that we could boil water to make instant noodles. Then, while we ate around the smoky hearth in his kitchen, he tried to rescue his class. The children kept coming to look at us, and soon he called an end to school for the day, preferring anyway to chat with us. Learning of our plan, he offered us the school storeroom for the night. The room, wedged between his bedroom and a classroom, had a pallet bed and a wall of teaching materials, all covered with dust, but otherwise it was not bad accommodation.

There was not a lot to see in Luuk Kao Laam, and when we had finished our inspection, we went for a wash. The washing place was outside the village. It consisted of a deep well with an old plastic oil container on the end of a length of rope. A group of adolescent Lahu girls were taking their evening shower there. In clinging wet sarongs and with streaming long black hair, they soaped and scrubbed and tipped icy water over themselves. We tried to do likewise, much to their amusement. With the day drawing to a close, we took up position in a little pavilion overlooking the central patch. People were returning from the fields, young men were playing football, kicking up the dust, and children came to toy with us. The youngsters, with slightly hooded eyes, were forward and unafraid, and we realized that they were used to seeing *farang*. Altogether, during our overnight stay, we found the Lahu of this village a boisterous, loud, confident, self-reliant people. In an incomparable setting, Luuk Kao Laam was near the main road and accessible to the one or two Suzuki hire jeeps that turned up most days with tourist visitors. But if the children were cheeky and the adults inured, there was no begging and none of the souvenir stalls and ethnic tat found in some hill-tribe villages.

Our supper was a repeat of our mid-afternoon lunch, only augmented. A woman sold us some greens from her field, and the teacher picked herbs from the school garden. Once again around his kitchen hearth, we enjoyed a much tastier Ma-maa instant noodle soup, supplemented with mountain rice and tins of tuna and sardines we had bought in Pai. A final touch of luxury was Lahu *lao kao* mixed with the electrolytic soft drink Sponsor – a vernacular gin and tonic. While we were eating, people began arranging folding chairs in the largest classroom at the other end of the school building. And soon half the village crowded in. It was a meeting called by the headman. Two things were on the agenda. A cow had been stolen outside the village and slaughtered on the spot, and the assembly was to decide what should be done. And the next day was to see a visit by the governor of Mae Hong Son province, who was coming to distribute aid to the village. The meeting had to draw up plans to receive him.

A party of Hill-tribe Development Authority men had already arrived in advance of the governor, and tiring of the deliberations at the other end of the corridor, they came to join us. They brought with them bottles of local hooch, and soon a party was in full swing. Many Lahu, hearing the conviviality and seeking respite from village politics, also came by, cramming the little wooden kitchen. Finally, the *pu yai baan* himself absented himself from his own meeting to investigate the rival moot. Squatting on the bare earth floor in pride of place, he sucked on a silver-banded pipe. The Hilltribe Development men in their high spirits had invented a game, whereby lots had to be drawn to see who could ask us a question. By chance the headman pulled out a winning lot. He said: many Lahu girls and also some boys wanted to marry *farang*, and what did I think of the idea? I pointed out to him that, tantalizing as the idea was from the point of view of both the Lahu and the *farang*, there would be some big problems. How would the couple communicate, and where would they live? A Westerner would hardly be content with life in Luuk Kao Laam, and the Lahu lass or lad would hardly want to go and live in a strange faraway country. The headman pondered the matter, poking the fire. Then he asked about English football. Hearing that we lived near Ipswich, his face lit up and several times he attempted to formulate 'Ipswich Town'. Apparently very satisfied with the exchange, he then got up and returned to his session. "If there is anything you need, just come and ask me", he said. His meeting went on very late, as did numerous follow-up gatherings around wood fires all over the village. People stood, wrapped in blankets, under the brilliant moon and stars, warming themselves on the embers, smoking and turning over the issues discussed earlier. Some may well have stood there all night, but we retired to our platform bed. As we slept, condensation dripped off the tin roof onto our heads. In the dead of the night, we stirred in our sleep to hear someone enter the school and creep around...

Preparations for the governor's visit continued from an early hour. The folding chairs were removed from the school to the dusty central arena nearby, where they were set out in rows. The Thai flag was run up a white pole. Everyone fussed around. These visits by the authorities can sometimes spell bad luck for anyone else passing by. Life is disrupted, nobody has any time for you, and the village takes on a prettified artificial gloss. It has often been our fate to arrive somewhere just before a member of the Thai royal family was due to descend. But on this occasion, the visitation had its upside. The entire village, from the tiniest toddlers to the hoariest elders, had turned out in their best festive Lahu costume, something they might otherwise have done only during their New Year celebrations or for a wedding. Some 200 people had hunkered down to wait, in lines of 15 or 20, alternating male/female, and with the youngest on the right and the oldest on the left.

These were Sheh Leh Lahu, a distinctive sub-type of Black Lahu. The females wore black baggy pants, leggings, and a three-quarter-length jacket, open at the front and with long vents at the sides, which gave the impression of having three tails. The black tunic was strikingly edged with white, and often the arms were trimmed with red and blue banding. The front opening was fastened with large ornamental silver discs. Most of the older women had their hair drawn up in topknots and wore white towel turbans. We noticed characteristic silver earrings in the shape of a pendent 'S', the lower part whorled like a coiled snake. The men were in black baggy trousers, the legs joined Hmonglike down to the knee, leggings, open loose black jackets, and red sashes. A few of the oldest men also had turbans, while babes-in-arm were fussed with the most exquisite little caps. The Lahu are handsome, angular-faced people, and these colourful Sheh Leh formed as impressive a hill-tribe gathering as any we saw.

Finally, a small convoy of vehicles swept in, half a dozen heavily armed bodyguards leapt down, sealing off the entrances to the square, and the provincial governor with a posse of minions went to the front of the crowd. He made a short speech and then personally distributed the presents – blankets and other useful things for the adults, and packages of biscuits and sweeties for the children. Afterwards, the gathering broke up and everyone intermingled. It must be said in favour of the governor that this busy man, no doubt fulfilling a tedious duty, was kind enough to come over to us and exchange pleasantries. And then suddenly the suave dignitary, quilted in an anorak against the early morning chill, was back in his minibus. The convoy swept out of the village in a cloud of dust, probably heading for another three or four such distributions, and the official visit was over.

Bo Pi – 'Spirit Well'

Seeking out the headman, we asked him if he could find someone to guide us to Bo Pi (bo = well, pi = spirit). That was not so easy because the local people were frightened of going there. But he collared a couple of boys who were among the children who had twitted us the previous evening. They were both eleven years old (see photo section). One, called A-pichai, had Mongoloid eyes and no hair on his head except a little on top, the back and sides having been shorn. Taking our revenge on him for the evening before, we said that he looked like a pineapple. The other lad, Jak-gaek, a beautiful chubby-faced boy with a sense of humour, found this endlessly amusing. He began chaffing his friend, just as we chaffed them and then they us, setting the tone for an anarchic expedition.

A footpath ran out of the back of Luuk Kao Laam and began climbing steeply. We thought the scramble could not last for long, but it was relentless, quite knocking the stuffing out of us. The heat from the mid-morning sun was sweltering. Our mouths were soon dry and our bodies bathed in sweat. The path threaded its way up a headlong jungle-lined gorge. Every so often it passed the out-of-village pig pens of the Lahu, and at each one we stopped to get our breath back and cool off. The boys meanwhile would long since have arrived at the pens, and, catching them up, we would find them idly fiddling with a twig, their faces still with a fresh cool bloom. Each time, they chirped mischievously: "What kept you so long?" After 30 or 40 minutes, the stiff climb ended, and we reached a col. There was a secluded poppy field in it, and we stood among the poppies enjoying the faint breeze wafting up from the other side.

Beyond the poppies was a resting area with bamboo benches among some trees. After that, the path descended into a remote hinterland. Through the trees, we could see mountains, isolated valleys, the odd patch of hillside under cultivation, cliffs and forest. We asked the boys where the path ultimately led. It went to a waterfall, they said, otherwise they did not know. They thought that a long way off was a Lisu village. We were certain that there were extensive poppy fields in that hinterland. Descending from the col, we came to a fork. The fork was marked by fresh banana palm leaves on the ground and the smoking remains of a fire. Lahu had caught a wild boar there yesterday, the boys explained, and they had cooked it on the spot.

There was more than one 'spirit well' in the area, and A-pichai and Jak-gaek showed us first a small one. Hidden in the trees, it was a deep dark shaft in the mountainside. Into it the boys dropped rocks, which hit the water in the bottom with a splash. But nothing prepared us for the real Bo Pi. Climbing up to a rocky rim in the forest, we suddenly peered over, not so much into a well, but into a mighty chasm. Here, one hour out from Luuk Kao Laam, was a massive 'unnatural' hole in the mountainside, the bottom appearing to have sunk 150 metres into the earth. There was no way down into Bo Pi, as the sides all around the chasm were sheer or overhanging cliffs. At the foot of the tallest cliff, the one shouldering uppermost into the mountain, was a great gloomy cave. It looked like the bowl of some giant theatre or stadium. The mouth of the cave was full of boulders, while hanging down across the mouth, like curtains before the bowl, were stalactites and creepers. Some of the air roots falling from the cliff face high above were hundreds of feet long. Trees and bushes grew far below on the floor of the 'well'. It was as if, when the mountainside had collapsed in on itself, they had simply continued to grow in their new subterranean location. The boys dropped rocks into Bo Pi, and after a free fall of several seconds the boulders splashed resoundingly, as if into a lake. But apparently there was no water down there, and the noise must have come from the rocks smashing through the tree tops.

Peering over the rim gave us vertigo, and when we realized that the rocks we were clinging to were overhanging, we retreated a bit. Stumbling upon Bo Pi was altogether bizarre, like looking into a prehistoric volcano or into some monstrous aberration from science fiction. Few Lahu came here, and none had climbed down into the bottom of Bo Pi or would ever do so. They believed spirits lived in the well and were frightened of them. Local people frequently heard cries and roars issuing from the well, echoing off its walls. They thought these were the howlings of restless spirits down there, but also of numerous wild animals supposed to lurk in the depths. We told A-pichai and Jak-gaek they should stop throwing stones into the chasm, or they would upset the spirits, which would come and get them in the night. With boyish bravado they declared all that stuff and nonsense, and yet at the same time they grew thoughtful. While they were contemplating the possibility of being snatched in their sleep, we crept round behind them and suddenly made a ghostly bellowing sound. They leapt up in alarm, nearly over the cliff, and it took them a long time to see the humour of the joke.

If no Lahu had been into Bo Pi, it seemed that almost no one else had been down there either. Evidently, there was no way in except to climb down the cliffs. But at Luuk Kao Laam, people said that recently two *farang* with ropes had passed through the village, intending to explore the well. Apparently, they had successfully descended, but one of them had then fallen ill, suffering either a mild heart attack or a heat stroke. Of course, these events simply reinforced the Lahu in their beliefs about Bo Pi. In fact, Spirit Well is what is known geologically as a collapsed doline. Over aeons, underground streams created a cavern inside the limestone mountain, the roof of which then collapsed. There are numerous such dolines in the karstic landscape of this and other areas of Thailand (e.g. Nan province), and Bo Pi is one particularly dramatic example.

On the way back to the village, we met two Lahu women resting on the benches in the col. One of them was the mother of Jak-gaek. When she heard that the two boys had been dropping rocks into Spirit Well, she grew very angry. She cuffed the pair repeatedly, saying that the spirits would get angry and misfortune would befall their families. For all their trouble, our high-spirited duo had got a bad fright from us and a maternal scolding. By the time we got back to Luuk Kao Laam, they looked thoroughly disgruntled. So to cheer them up, we gave them 20 baht each, and they scampered off triumphantly.

✢

Luuk Kao Laam – Mae Hong Son
Back up on the main road, we figured that it would be some time before a bus came from Pai, so we decided to try our hand at hitch-hiking. Within minutes, a wealthy Thai couple pulled up in a flashy speeding pick-up truck. They were going all the way to Mae Hong Son and bade us hop into the back. Thus, the second half or remaining 53 kms of this leg of our journey we enjoyed from the vantage point of an upmarket Toyota or Nissan, or whatever their vehicle was. With our backs to the cab and the wind howling past our ears (bobble hat time again), we watched the mountains and jungle slip by. The remainder of the H1095 was every bit as spectacular as the earlier stretches. On the ridgecrest soon after Luuk Kao Laam, there was a roadside *sala* with a view over the same inky green mountainscape rolling north that we had admired from the bus the day before. Beside the *sala*, Lisu people, brightly attired in blues and pinks, were selling largely unidentifiable field produce on mats laid out on the ground. Then an exhilirating elevated road with hairpin bends brought us slowly down to the Nam Khong river and the village of **Mae Suya**. Just beyond the village, in a claustrophobic landscape of towering monoliths, our hosts pointed out to us a cave hermitage set at the foot of a cliff face. A solitary monk lived in this grotto temple, long twisted lianas hanging across its entrance. After the cave *wat*, called Wua I think, the steep twisting road set about climbing over two more ridges.

Ascending one of these, we came upon a disaster. Just before a blind bend, there were pieces of bush on the road – the Thai warning of some mishap ahead. Cautiously rounding the corner, we found a log transporter upside down in the drainage channel at the side of the road. Evidently, it had come too fast down the hill and lost control on the corner. Twenty or so wheels stuck up in the air, and the load of teak logs was spilled everywhere, including on top of the lorry. The cab was crushed beyond recognition. It was clear that the driver and probably a couple of mates were dead inside, and we did not dare to look too closely. Our friends stopped their pick-up to find out if anything could be done. They were told that the police had been alerted, who had not arrived yet. It would be some time before they or an ambulance could come from faraway Mae Hong Son. The atmosphere among the people standing around the lorry was noticeably gloomy, but as there was little anyone could do, our hosts motored on. For a while, mindful of this *memento mori*, they proceeded carefully, but soon it was business as usual again, rushing headlong downhill and screeching round corners, often on the wrong side of the road. Later, in Mae Hong Son, we chanced upon some people who knew that an Austrian motorcyclist had been the first to come upon the accident. According to the Austrian, the driver and his mate had managed to scramble out of the cab with only minor injuries, having a remarkably lucky escape.

On the far side of the second ridge, a dream road swung down through jungle and woods, passed the scenic village of **Huai Pa** with its Shan-style *wat* set on the valley floor amid coconut palms, and skirted the touristy and uninteresting **Tam Pla** or Fish Cave (km 90), to emerge at **Pang Mu** and the valley of the River Pai. There remained a final small ridge to climb over, after which, 106 kms of jungle and mountain from Pai, we approached Mae Hong Son. Forking left in the outskirts, we suddenly found ourselves riding up the long main street into the town centre.

❖ ❖

Postscript 2002

In the first days of 2001, Doug and I, when re-researching this leg of the journey, decided to search out the Karen Witit and see him again. We finally tracked him down to Chong. But we did not find him in his wife's family's house at that village, but in a tumbledown hut in a field about one km away. Now aged 34, he was dressed in peasant's clothing, and at first we feared that he had fallen on hard times. But the hovel was surrounded by crop fields and sited at the edge of some large ponds, and in the fields he cultivated garlic and yellow beans, while in the ponds he grew fish. At the hut, he also raised chickens. Often he slept in the disorderly hovel, occasionally with his wife, otherwise in their house in Chong. Although he had no inkling of our sudden unannounced arrival, he remembered me instantly after all the intervening years, even formulating my name – correct in every detail regarding first name, family name and title – by way of greeting. This power of spontaneous recall struck me as truly remarkable both in its own right and because he used to see many a *farang* in the old days and had seen many since. But perhaps my name was burnt indelibly into his memory for another, wrong reason, that the journey with him to Muang Noi had been unforgettably awful.

We went from the hut to his Chong house, a spacious well-to-do affair that also housed his wife's extended family. Here we discovered that his generosity, hospitality and also capacity for alcohol were undiminished. He cooked up a meal of several dishes with his own hands and bought in some bottles of beer, most of which he drank himself, growing expansive in his talk as he did so. Although he had not properly used his English for quite a few years, this too was remarkably well preserved. He had stopped his health job at Mae Haat seven years earlier, just as he and his wife had meanwhile given up their electrical appliance shop in Chong, as well as another such shop they had had down in Chiang Dao. For three years, he said, he had run a restaurant and bar in Wiang Haeng, something he had always dreamed of doing, and here he had served and met many *farang*, another favourite activity of his. But he had given that up, too, to become a farmer. "The price of garlic is very high, and I can make more money from growing crops", said Witit, whose face had been burnt black by the sun and whose hands had coarsened from his new work outside in the fields.

I asked the Karen about his Thai paratrooper friend. Ekerin, he said, had given up being a ranger soldier and had become a forestry official at Mae Haat. This led us to reminisce about the trip to Muang Noi. At this, Witit's face clouded over, just as it had done years ago. But it was not because, as he confessed, he had destroyed his truck on the way back in the dark, but because a friend of his had been shot and killed a year previously (1999) on the Wiang Haeng to Pai route. This news, in turn, made me apprehensive all over again about (re)doing the stretch. Whilst the murder of Witit's friend was probably a local affair, with no implications for *farang* travellers, nevertheless the route remains a hazardous one, to be treated with respect, and our likeable old friend Witit Terkae implored us to be very careful negotiating it.

Wiang Haeng/Kong Lom – Pai

Any readers contemplating travelling this stretch should be aware that it is, as it has always been, one of the most problematic and potentially dangerous legs in this book, which should only be attempted (if ridden) by highly experienced motorcyclists with dirt skills. The 55-km-long route (measured from Kong Lom) passes from NE to SW through the middle of Huai Nam Dang National Park. The Karen village of Muang Noi, situated almost dead centre in the park, lies halfway along the route. In the early 1990s, the stretch used to be negotiable with four-wheeled vehicles (high-ride trucks, 4WD jeeps etc.). Witit drove to Muang Noi and back (with difficulty) in his pick-up, and at the time we saw another truck, from Piang Luang, busting its way through. Now the way is impassable to four-wheeled vehicles, even 4WD trucks, but is still bikable – just.

This is not to say that the whole of the stretch is unnavigable on four wheels, only the central section. Thus forestry and military vehicles proceed from Kong Lom to the fork and checkpoint at km 9.9, before branching NW towards the border in Pang Ma Pa district, and plenty of trucks and lorries go from the hydroelectric power plant near Muang Noi and from Muang Noi itself down to Pai and vice versa. But no 4W vehicles now drive the intervening link. In my diary, I wrote of the Kong Lom-Pai leg that it was the motorcycle trip from hell and one of the worst that I had done in 13 years of biking in Thailand. It is all second and first gear riding, and the first half, the 28 kms from Kong Lom to Muang Noi, took Doug and myself on Honda Wave bikes 3 hours, while the second half to Pai, likewise 28 kms, took us 2 hours. Allow 5 hrs for the leg, excluding any lunch stop in Muang Noi, or, better, allow all day, especially if you want to check out Muang Noi and Huai Chang Tao villages.

Nevertheless, the stretch is rideable, and the soldiers at the army post at km 9.9 told us that in the dry season *farang* bike it about two or three times a month. They almost always come up from Pai. And, indeed, that is the easier way round to do the trip because you are mostly riding uphill, which is less difficult, whereas the way from Kong Lom to Pai is mostly downhill and more difficult. Biking from Pai to Wiang Haeng also has the virtue that you have the sun behind you, whereas from Wiang Haeng to Pai you have the sun in your face, which is hotter and less good for viewing the route and scenery. The stretch from Kong Lom 10 kms to the military post is not too bad, and the second half of the trip from Muang Noi to Pai is better than the first half. The worst and most difficult section is the few kms immediately after the army encampment (c. km 10-15).

Route detail: Wiang Haeng – Kong Lom – Muang Noi – Huai Chang Tao – Tan Chet Ton – Pai (Maps 10 & 11)

From centre of **Wiang Haeng** with petrol station and store (R) and with row of shops plus noodle place (L), head N up main asphalt road in direction of Chong and Piang Luang.

After 3.1 kms, in **Kong Lom** village, look for a turning L/SW by a shop and phone box, which is the:

km 0.0   Start of the way for Pai (Map 10)
Proceed down street

THREE PAGODAS

At a fork by Wat Kong Lom, go R and over a bridge

km 1.2   At second fork, go L. The cement-section road soon gives over to dirt
A very bad way heads out through the houses of **Kong Lom Mai**, then through orchards, banana groves and mixed woodland
A sandy 4WD track gradually ascends

km 4.2   At a junction, a way comes in from the R, apparently from the Karen village of Mae Haat
Up through conifers

km 9.9   Junction on hairpin bend. At the junction: an army encampment and checkpoint. In January 2001, the military had a machine gun, mounted on a stand and loaded up with a belt of bullets, pointing at the junction. From the junction, the way R, past the barrier, goes 10 kms to Mae Haat watershed conservation office, 17 kms to a reforestation office, 24 kms to the Lahu village of Pai Song Ngae, and 28 kms to Doi Pak Kut and Pang Ma Pa watershed conservation office. Undoubtedly, there is an army base up this long side trail. On a previous occasion (December 1993), I went along it to the end, enjoying great views. The route tracks up a spur of Huai Nam Dang National Park almost to the border. Doug and I asked if we could repeat the adventure, but the soldiers manning the checkpoint and in the camp laughed. It was absolutely impossible, they said, because the UWSA were all over the border up there, and it was very dangerous. This made us fearful about the rest of the way to Muang Noi. That was OK, they asserted, if we could manage the route with our bikes – it was in a poor state. The way L at the junction and checkpoint (round the hairpin) was/is the way to Muang Noi and Pai.
After the junction/checkpoint, the way seriously deteriorates, just as the soldiers said. Scarcely used any more, except by the odd motorcycle, it is steep in places and deeply rutted, the worst section being the few kms immediately after the checkpoint.
Way – no more than 6 ft wide – continues endlessly through forest and jungle, with zero traffic, although one motorcycle did pass us coming from Pai
Descend a long way off mountain
Then track flattens out

km 26.5   Junction with sign pointing back "Wiang Haeng 30 kms". At junction, way R goes 4 kms down to Mae Pai hydroelectric power station, while L/straight continues 1 km to Muang Noi

km 27.8   Muang Noi health centre (R) and junction. At the junction, go R across bridge over River Pai for centre of **Muang Noi** village (Karen & Shan), main street and a big school (up L). Street continues on out of village to Huai Hia (2 kms); Karen Huai Hok (6 kms); Lisu Pi Ru (= spirit hole), from where you can walk SW down past Lisu Sa Ngam to the main 1095 highway; and Lahu Nai Khong, from where you can walk to Soppong. Organized trekking from Pai passes through Muang Noi and these villages. Undoubtedly, on a normal weekday, you can get a noodle soup in Muang Noi. Just before the health centre and junction (as you reach Muang Noi from Kong Lom), there is a little shop (R) with soft drinks. Petrol is also available in the village.

km 27.8   From health centre/junction, go S out of village, past a *sala* (L) (now see Map 11)
Cross a first ford over the Huai Hia stream (I think)

More houses (L)
Fields (R and L)
km 29.3   Cross second ford
km 29.6   At a fork with a *sala*, go L
km 30.0   "Huai Hia Protection Unit, Huai Nam Dang National Park" (L)
Third fording of Huai Hia
After Muang Noi, the way is better, not so steep, wider, although with some poor stony up- and downgrades
km 37.8   *Sala* and way down L to Lisu village of **Huai Chang Tao**. Between Muang Noi and Huai Chang Tao, my travelling companion Douglas gave a lift to a Lisu man, who offered him opium, cannabis and other narcotics, and invited him to come and take the same in his village – you can tell that you are nearing the big drugs place of Pai!
km 38.3   Another way in L to Huai Chang Tao
Wooden bridge
km 38.5   "Huai Chang Tao Protection Unit, Huai Nam Dang National Park" (L) with defunct checkpoint and barrier
Long winding ascent with some severe upgrades, climbing from river up over a final ridge
Protracted rocky winding descent slowly into Pai basin
km 49.1   Valley floor and Shan village of **Tan Chet Ton** (= seven palm trees) with cement-section road
km 49.2   At T-junction, go L (R brings you to the main H1095 road)
On a proper tarred road, proceed roughly S straight through a couple of strung-out rural villages, ignoring many turnings R and L
km 54.6   At a second T-junction, go R or approximately SW
Cross bridge over River Pai and pass school (L), then *Own Home* restaurant (L)
km 55.3   Reach a crossroads in the centre of **Pai** town, with main street running from L to R or roughly E to W.[2]

These days, **Pai** has mushroomed even further, being a rare spot in Thailand to have defied the economic collapse of post-1997. There are now scores of places to stay both in and around the town. This does not necessarily mean that it is easy to find a room, especially during the high season, when large numbers of *farang* travellers descend on the Shan townlet. In the first days of 2001, we had trouble finding any suitable overnight accommodation, in the end settling on a mediocre place a few kms away from the town centre. In my diary, I read that my venom for the phenomenon of Pai is unabated. I write that it is a monstrous excrescence, a sprawling phony hateful grotesquerie, awash with guest houses, restaurants, bars, bakeries, Internet cafés, blues and jazz joints, 'Thai massage' places, acupuncture shops, and so on. The town is swarming with affectedly laid-back, dope-smoking, spaced-out, counter-culture, hippie types and weirdos in Pink Floyd T-shirts and Rastafarian hats, being served by a lot of

---

[2] Readers contemplating doing the trip the other way round, from Pai to Kong Lom/Wiang Haeng should start as follows. In Pai main street, at a central crossroads, go NE down a side street, past *Own Home* restaurant (R) and a school (R), over a bridge across the River Pai, 0.7 km to a junction, where a proper road branches left/NW, while the original road veers off right. Take this first proper road L, pass through a couple of strung-out rural villages, and continue c. 5.4 kms to Tan Chet Ton village, where you turn R (NE) into a side street, initially paved. Now it is 21.4 kms to Muang Noi and 49.2 kms to Kong Lom (52.3 kms to Wiang Haeng) – see Maps 11 & 10, reading them 'backwards' or from top to bottom.

spaced-out, po-faced Shan in baggy hill-tribe trousers, running all the way to the bank. You might as well be in the Khaosan Road in Bangkok, or on Ko Samui or Ko Pha-Ngan at the time of a full-moon beach party, or in Bali, or even Ibiza. I think there is no place I dislike more in Thailand and certainly in northern Thailand. This is not because I have anything at all against counter-culture types, but because of the concentration of such types in Pai, the phoniness of the place, the pervasive drug culture, and the incongruity of the Pai counter-culture relative to the region. With so many things of beauty and interest to enjoy in the area, so much local culture and history to discover, and so much adventure to be had, why hang out in utterly Westernized Pai?

We revisited the Chinese village **Santichon**, near Pai. To reach it, go to the crossroads in the NW part of town (the crossroads on one corner of which lies the excellent *Nong Bia* restaurant), take the side road which runs W up past the hospital (L), and continue a few kms, branching L at a fork shortly before the village. I think, after all, the place may not be named 'Santichon' after the Thai *santi chon*, which means 'peaceful river', but because this is an approximation of the Chinese 'Shanti Shoon' (shaan di tsoon). The KMT village was much more developed than a decade earlier, some new buildings and the paved main street having been paid for with money from Taiwan. People were hardly more forthcoming than on the previous occasion, despite Doug's valiant attempts to soften them up with his command of Chinese. They said that they were Gen. Lao Li Third Army descendants and that the village was now over 20 years old. Someone related that the inhabitants had spent 30 years in Burma before coming straight over the border to here, which I do not entirely believe. They may have crossed near Nong Ook, before being relocated from there to Santichon. For some reason, the people of this KMT village are particularly cagey, and I have yet to get to the bottom of the place. It is hardly worth visiting if you have already seen Piang Luang or Kae Noi.

Highway 1095 has long since been sealed right through from Mae Ma Lai to Mae Hong Son. Indeed, it has meanwhile been upgraded in many places and now represents the main route from Chiang Mai to Mae Hong Son, with a fair amount of traffic using the road and, by contrast, relatively little using the old southerly route on the H108. By 2002, the new part of Soppong beside the main road had, as expected, mushroomed considerably, usurping the original section offroad and relegating it to a backwater that even the buses did not bother to visit any more. West of the old part, **New Soppong** extended for a good kilometre along the H1095, mainly on the left/S side. It had numerous shops, eating places, guest houses, and an extensive market, which was a magnet for hill-tribe people from far and wide – a good point for observing tribals. You could shop here for all kinds of fruit and vegetables, and buy nice things like passion fruit juice and wild honey. The busy colourful place had even become a stopoff for tourists.

5

TUK-TUKS IN SHANGRI-LA

Mae Hong Son

In spite of a recent boom, Mae Hong Son (the last syllable is pronounced 'sorn') remains essentially a backwater idyll. Cut off in the far north-western corner of Thailand and almost 1000 kms from Bangkok, this small town lies on a broad valley floor, surrounded by hills and mountains. Immediately to the north is the Burmese border and the Shan State, and to the west, also across the 'Myanmar' frontier, is the Kayah State, controlled by the Karenni army. To the east and south stretch vast tracts of mountainous jungle and forest.

The town sometimes goes by the name of 'Muang Saam Mork', meaning 'town of the three mists'. This arises from the fact that in each of the three seasons of the year it can be affected by a different kind of mist. In the winter, ground fog grips the valley, which only burns off when the sun gains its mid-morning strength. In the hot season, the air is heavy with the spicy-smelling smoke of slash-and-burn agriculture. And in the wet season, fine misty rain blankets the town. It is a continental climate up here with relative extremes of weather. At night in the cool season, temperatures can drop to zero, with frost in the hills. In the hot season, especially in March and April, they can soar to a baking 40° + Celsius. In the monsoon season, the heavens open, and it can rain heavily for days on end.

The origins of 'Muang Saam Mork' are said to lie in elephant corralling. Records show that in 1831 the then ruler of Chiang Mai sent an expedition to this region to survey the western border. The expedition set up camp on the banks of the River Pai at Pang Mu, a few kms north of present-day Mae Hong Son town. The explorers found the locality populated with Shan or Tai Yai people (= big Tai, as opposed to the Tai Noi or Siamese Tai of central Thailand). Mixing with them, the new arrivals came to appoint the Shan Pa Ga Mong as leader at Pang Mu (*mu* = wild boar, pig). But then they discovered that an area not far south was rich in elephants, and set up a second camp there. Here, too, the camp intermixed with the indigenous Shan to grow into a regular settlement, and Pa Ga Mong's son-in-law, San Khon, was appointed leader. The two Shan headmen became involved in logging, floating teak wood down the Rivers Pai and Salween to sell in Burma. Father and son-in-law grew rich, and their respective villages developed, especially San Khon's. Known as Muai Tor (after the celebrated temple with six pagodas on the hillside to the west – the ruins can still be seen today), the elephant village expanded so

111

THREE PAGODAS

rapidly that in 1874 the Chiang Mai authorities declared it a town. In 1893, the region achieved provincial status, being incorporated in 1900 into the northern Siamese *mon ton* or 'circle' of Payap.[1] Muai Tor, renamed Mae Hong Son after a local river, became the provincial capital. Then, as now, both town and province were predominantly Shan. In the course of this century, migrant hill-tribe and other minority people have moved into the province, resulting in a mix of an estimated 50% Shan and 50% Karen, Lisu, Lahu, Hmong, and KMT. Thais of modern-day Thailand hardly show up in these statistics at all, and where they do exist, they are confined largely to the towns (Mae Hong Son, Mae Sariang and Pai). Today in Mae Hong Son town, with its population of about 7000, the Siamese account for only some 2% of the townsfolk, whereas 98% are Shan. This is another factor which gives the town its different 'exotic' feel.

If sheer remoteness and exotic ethnic feel are one appeal of Mae Hong Son, Jong Kham lake just south-east of the centre is another. Held by some to be the prettiest lake in Thailand, its banks have been landscaped and planted with colourful tropical flowers and bushes. At the rear of the lake, tall palm trees overhang the water, and behind them, in the background, loom the first of the scrubbily wooded mountains which recede hundreds of kms south and east from this oasis.

On the southern bank of the lake, two magical monasteries lie side by side. Viewed from across the water, **Wat Jong Kham** sits on the left, while its twin, **Wat Jong Klang**, sits on the right. The original building of Jong Kham was apparently constructed in 1827 by a local Shan chieftain and his wife, *pra ya* Singhanat Racha and *chao* Mae Nang Mia. Said to be the first temple to be built in the province, it takes its name from the fact that its pillars used to be decorated with gold (*jong* = pillar, *kham* = gold). Jong Klang, on the right, started out as a pavilion where people could rest, before being turned into a *wat* in the 1860s. A room in this temple houses a celebrated collection of 30-40 antique wooden figures. Between three and four feet high, the dolls represent people from the Buddha story. They have come from Burma and the Shan State – the Shan ones are tattooed. Together, the two temples form a chaotic complex of wooden tin-roofed buildings and golden pagodas. They are built in that ramshackle Shan-Burmese style which tops off the *wihaan* with tiers (more than eight high in this case) of rusty corrugated sheeting, adorned with intricate iron filigree. If one sits beside Lake Jong Kham in the early evening, looking out over the crimson sprays of flowers to the deepening green of the palms and the gathering purple of the mountains, watching the fish come up to nibble at an insect supper, contemplating the dark gold reflections of the pagodas rippling lazily in the surface of the water, one might be forgiven for thinking that one had stumbled upon Shangri-La.

In the late 1980s and early 90s, Mae Hong Son used to be an inside tip passed on by the few who were prepared to access it from Chiang Mai either

---

[1] A *mon ton* or 'circle' was an entity higher than a *changwat* or province. In the late 19th and early 20th centuries, Lan-Na (northern Thailand) was divided administratively into the two *mon ton* of Maharat and Payap. Maharat comprised Nan, Prae and Lampang, while Payap included Chiang Mai, Chiang Rai, Lampoon and Mae Hong Son. The 'circles' were disbanded in 1932.

TUK-TUKS IN SHANGRI-LA

on the rough northerly H1095 route via Pai on trails bikes, or on the gruelling southerly H108 route via Hot in a 12-hour bus ride. But word of the town's mystique got out, and now a steady trickle of visitors passes through. The handful of guest houses and small hotels of just four or five years ago has mushroomed into more than 30 places to stay of all types. Similarly, where in the past so few people arrived that in the evening over a beer on the main street it was possible to spot the newcomers individually, now Airbuses disgorge parties of package tourists, who are ferried down to the brand-new *Tara Imperial Hotel* or *Holiday Inn* at the bottom end of town, and buses plying both the northerly and southerly approach routes let down clutches of travellers. What have they all come for, and what will be their effect on the town? Mae Hong Son is only a small rural place – rather boring unless one is a connoisseur of atmosphere – and there is not a lot to see outside town.

In many ways Mae Hong Son typifies developments in Thai tourism in the 1990s. A relatively small destination is being allowed to boom, but with little regard for planning or the longer term consequences. Get-rich-quick seems to be the order of the day. Whether sleepy backward places like this can cope with the boom, and even whether the boom will last, is open to doubt. In some places, the tourism might perpetuate itself, not grounded in anything much the locality has to offer – mini Las Vegases in the middle of nowhere (like the 'Golden Triangle' at Sob Ruak) – but in others the bubble will probably burst. How on earth can a landlocked town of 7,000 Shan justify some 30 resorts, hotels and guest houses? And even if the tourists do come for a while, might they not suddenly switch to somewhere else – not Mae Hong Son but Luang Prabang or Phnom Penh or Hanoi?

Interestingly, Thai Air has recently suspended its Airbus flights to Mae Hong Son on the grounds that they were not cost-effective. The suspension met a storm of protest from the local hoteliers and restauranteurs who had just invested so much money. But the volume of visitors was not quite as expected, and some of these pretentious places will no doubt go to the wall. Indeed, as we walked round some of the new guest houses, it was noticeable how empty many were and how the owners came running out onto the street to try to entice us in. On the other hand, there is a long-term development strategy for Mae Hong Son, which might have these investors laughing all the way to the Thai Farmers' Bank. As with Mae Sai in the northernmost part of Thailand, there are plans to connect the provincial capital with selected locations in Burma. Airlinks could be forged with Loi Kaw in the Kayah State, with Taunggyi in the Shan State, and with famous Mandalay.

❖

The friendly Thais who had given us a lift to Mae Hong Son dropped us outside the bus station in the main street. Our first task was to fix up somewhere to stay. Eschewing the numerous new overpriced guest houses, and not wanting to make the rounds of the popular traditional haunts, we decided to try the discreet *Sanguan Sin Hotel* (*sanguan sin* = preserve art). Old rooming houses like this usually have plenty of beds available at modest prices.

113

THREE PAGODAS

Sidestepping the touts who were hanging around the bus station to intercept new arrivals and bring them to the guest houses, we set off south down the main street (the Khunlum Prapat Road) towards the central intersection. A turn east into the Singhanat Bamrung Road brought us quickly to our goal. In a dusty, rather squalid yard, we found a large wooden building, but no reception. A knock on the door brought out a woman, but she appeared to speak no Thai, let alone English. However, she knew well enough what we wanted and led us across the yard to another wooden building opposite. We passed through a scruffy storage room and went upstairs. In a dark corridor with rooms leading off on both sides, the woman opened a door. This was to be our lodging. It was 60 baht for the room, and any number could stay in it. The bed alone would have comfortably slept three.

Just as there was no reception, so also there was no communal room, and no food either. We closed the door and sat down on the bed. The room was a large gloomy box with dark teak beams and slatted wooden walls. A small neon tube clung to the ceiling, but its garish light hardly penetrated the dusty corners. A small mirror hung on a nail on the wall. The windows and gaps between wall and ceiling were covered over with ancient fine wire mesh, but this was full of holes. On wires over the bed, somebody had strung up a mosquito net, but it too was full of holes and, judging by the dust accumulated on it, had not been used for many moons. We had the impression we were sitting in a lumber-room. The walls of our box were so thin that it was possible to hear straight into all the other lodgings along the corridor. Over the passage someone coughed, and in the room next to ours a fan whirred. Periodically people shifted on the bed.

The teak building had heated up all day in the sun, and our lumber-room was like an oven. There was a fan, a ridiculous little thing placed on a chair, but it made no difference. Perspiration formed on our foreheads. It seemed a good idea to cool off with a shower. But that meant grappling with the mysteries of the traditional Thai ablution. A corner of the room had been partitioned off, and inside this dank cubicle were the famous earthenware pot and dipper and next to them a French-style toilet with a hole and two footpads. Beside the toilet was a slime-encrusted cement tank with more water in it and a second plastic dipper. As a concession, perhaps to *farang*, there was a crude shower nailed to the wall with a spray head like that of a watering can. The cold-water-only shower nevertheless dribbled warm water that had heated up in the pipework. As a luxury, there was even a small wash basin. It might be supposed that there was not much scope for sabotaging a wash basin. But, no, the cock-eyed tap, when it was turned on, rotated freely in its socket. Getting it to work was a matter of holding the barrel with one hand and turning the tap with the other. Then it was possible to wash hands and face – except that the waste water shot straight down through the plughole and onto one's feet. From there it drifted lazily across the floor and disappeared who knows where.

Sleeping was hardly easier than washing. Owing to a lack of ventilation, the heat in the room was still appreciable towards midnight. Getting our own mosquito net up seemed to involve stringing it first in every conceivable wrong way. Perspiration again began to bathe our bodies, and it was nearly time to brave the shower again. But finally the net was up, and we lay down stark naked on top of the bed with the fan on. The heat made sleep difficult, although later in the night the temperature dropped noticeably. We tossed and turned, falling in and out of a light sleep. All night long some creature seemed to call from the neon strip light. Mic-mac, it went, mic-mac, mic-mac, five times in all, and always on the fifth call making a slight downward attenuation. It was a gekko, of course, but in our fitful hallucinating sleep it could have been a bird or some local monster emerging out of the three mists... Suddenly I awoke with an intense sharp pain on my thigh, as if someone was sticking pins in my skin. I reached for the torch and in the beam saw a column of small orange ants crossing the sheet and climbing over my body. Finally, the refreshing coolness of dawn was conducive to deep sleep. But almost immediately a dreadful racket started up. Loudspeakers blared out Thai and Western pop music, and there was a repeated hammering as if someone was making furniture in the middle of the night. The ballyhoo seemed to be going on right outside our room. Later, when we went to investigate, we found that the hotel backed directly onto Mae Hong Son's main daytime market.

It was the racket of the market kicking off between 5 and 6 am that soon drove us to exchange the *Sanguan Sin* for the *Siam Hotel*. Situated at the northern end of the main street, this friendly hotel had nice big cool rooms for 120 baht, which were ideal for sleeping in. The *Siam* was a typical Chinese place. Inside a characterless cement block, the rooms, on two storeys, surrounded a central hallway, in which guests parked their cars, trucks and motorbikes at night. The decor was all cream and brown and pale green, and if the hotel was a little spartan and functional with its institutional tiling, it was at least clean. There were good ceiling fans in the rooms, the bathrooms and showers were adequate, and, amazingly, soap and toilet paper were provided.

The restful nights at *Siam* put us more in the mood for enjoying the market. Mae Hong Son's market was one of the most interesting we saw anywhere on our border travels – on a par with the bazaar of Mae Saam Laep on the banks of the River Salween, or the black market of Sa Kaang Thit, south of Um Pang, in Burma. But it was not so much the variety of fruit and vegetables, meat and fish, sweetmeats and smoking requisites, household goods and clothes, that was interesting, as the unparalleled mix of people milling around. The market rapidly became for us the most exciting feature of the town, and soon no morning was complete without an hour or two spent sitting by the back entrance (facing the airport runway), watching the people and the goings-on. This was where dust-laden 4WD trucks came in to park, having come down from outlying villages up in the mountains, on the border, even from across the frontier in the Shan and Kayah States (by the same token this was the place to look for lifts to those rough places). There were turbanned Shan, baggy-trousered Hmong, moustachioed Chinese, Khun Sa agents from Ho Mong, aloof-looking 'long-neck' Padaung women, broad-faced Karen with their shoulder bags, suave educated Burmese people of uncertain origin (perhaps dissident students or military men), Lisu ladies in azure and cerise, hirsute wild-eyed Wa youths, people large and small, young and old, upright and bent, decorous in their costumes or rough-looking with squint eyes and tousled hair. The conversation was a hubbub of Shan, Thai, Chinese, Hmong, Lisu, Karen, Kayan, Burmese, Wa... Trucks were being loaded up with wholesale items for resale in hill-tribe villages or with consumer goods to be taken into Burma. Drivers had brought down truckloads of produce to be sold in the market or directly off the tailboard. Rolls of 500-baht banknotes were flashing such as one otherwise only ever saw in gangster films. And here and there in the crowd were individuals conspicuous for their masses of heavy gold jewellery and Rolex watches. These were people who could only have got so rich locally from trafficking heroin or jade or armaments.

In the pre-boom days, a walk up Mae Hong Son's long main street was like a stroll up the main drag of a wild west town. On each side there was a line of two-storey shophouses, many of them still teak, and people looked out inquisitively, coolly, as if to say: What brings you to Shanville? But in 1992 we were horrified to discover that the very first *tuk-tuks* had arrived, a sure sign that a sea change in the fortunes of the town was underway. These are those bizarre motorized tricycles, half motorbike and half car, that typically ply the streets of Bangkok or Chiang Mai. Now the dusty streets of Mae Hong Son were reverberating to the characteristic sound of their two-stroke engines, and the locals in their shopfronts were breathing in not the mists of the three seasons, but the reeking blue fumes of the three-wheelers. One would have thought that the town was small enough for people to be able to get about on foot. Can it really be that there is no development officer who cannot see that the *tuk-tuks*, far from providing a service and thus encouraging tourism, will actually only drive visitors away?

The arrival of the *tuk-tuks* had been accompanied by a proliferation of tour agencies, motorcycle rental places, bakeries, restaurants and souvenir shops up and down the main street. Mostly the eating houses were run-of-the-mill, of the sort to be found in Pai and elsewhere. But one stood out: *Fern Restaurant* at the bottom (southern) end of the main drag. This distinguished place with superb decor was serving up gourmet cooking. We tried mixed seafood in a delicious curry sauce of lemongrass, fresh green peppercorns and spring onions. Amidst all the innovations of Mae Hong Son, however, old favourite details remained. At the entrances to the side streets, thickets of crude hand-painted signs still sought to lure the newcomer to various guest houses. And the pavement boards still advertised treks or whatever with a novel syntax: DEAR TRAVELLERS! WHO DON'T HAVE MUCH TIME? WHY YOU DON'T COMMING HERE. WE ARE DON'T DISAPPINTED. FREE MAP OF MAE HONG SON. SIGHT SEEING – KAREN V., PLA CAVE, HOT SPRING. TREKKING – MEO, SHAN, K.M.T. V. NEAR BORDER. CAR, MOTORCYCLE, BICYCLE, GUIDE – FORRENT TO CHEAP ASK HERE. Who could resist such blandishments?!

We were walking up the main street one morning when a *farang* woman approached. She appeared not to be a tourist, and we fell into conversation with her. It turned out that she and her family lived in Mae Hong Son and that she would be very pleased if we came round one evening to eat with them. She seemed a pleasant enough lady, so we took up her offer and that same day, towards evening, went round to her house, armed with a family-sized bottle of Coke. The house was a local affair, raised high in the air on stilts, up a side alley.

TUK-TUKS IN SHANGRI-LA

It soon became clear to us that she and her husband were American missionaries, that they had just returned from a stint in the bush and had not had any real contact with Westerners for the best part of a year. From time to time in remote places, we had suffered as a result of these proselytizing zealots – we had been mistaken for missionaries ourselves and been made to feel very unwelcome. So we took a dim view of their cultural imperialism, and an evening with Norma and Marvyn did not bode well. But in the event things turned out pleasant enough.

The American duo had five children – three girls and two boys. The bashful youngsters were exactly stepped in age and height, so that when they were lined up against the living-room wall to be introduced to us, they fell away from top left to bottom right in a perfectly sloping line. Norma explained that she and her husband were educating their children themselves, and from a meagre cache Marvyn brought antiquated books for me to inspect which introduced the elements of physics, the countries of the world, and so on. There was an air about this hospitable couple which reminded us of self-sufficient American pioneers heading out west in waggons, taking with them all their worldly possessions, their culture and their education.

The children were very curious about me, as if they had been starved of 'white' company. In particular the oldest child, a girl of about 15 or 16, sized up the visiting *farang* the whole evening. So this was what a real young man was like, she seemed to be thinking to herself. The children were also quite embarrassed about their parents' religiosity, even the youngest. During grace, they fidgeted uncomfortably, sneaking glances to see what our reactions were. "Lord bless this good food, which in Your bounty and wisdom You have seen fit to place on our table", Marvyn intoned. "May the sweet Lord protect my good wife Norm, our five fine children and our household. We endeavor to follow You in Your ways. And we think especially today of our new friends, Chris and Daeng, who You have sent to share our table, and we ask You to include them in Your blessings, and hope that You will go with them when they leave on their further travels..."

The children were looking increasingly at the food, which was in danger of getting cold. But finally the prayer was over, and we all tucked into a weird combination of American and Thai dishes. There was jackfruit curry, fried morning glory, brown rice, but also corned beef hash and our two litres of Coke. During the meal, the oldest girl grew in confidence in her relations with me. The initial stolen glances developed into a sly unmistakable flirtation. I felt sorry for her. In her staid homespun schoolgirl frock, she was bursting into nubile womanhood. Brought up to be clean-living, and deprived of contact with boys of her age, she was fairly smouldering with sexual frustration. During supper, we made the mistake of asking Marvyn how he and his family came to be in Mae Hong Son. His rambling screwball answer had us looking at our watches, thinking of a beer in the night market, and more than ever pitying the children. "When many years ago I was a college student in the state of Ohio, the good Lord saw fit to send to me a pretty girl who was to become my dear and loving wife, and we resolved to follow together the ways of the Lord, and..." The story went on a full ten or fifteen minutes, until the sharper-minded Norm began noisily clearing away the dishes. We never did find out how he and they came to Mae Hong Son.

How god-fearing Norma and Marvyn would have viewed Mae Hong Son's famous *poi sang long* festival we could only guess at. This Buddhist celebration, held all over Thailand during the school summer holidays, marks the time when a number of boys, aged between 10 and 16, are ordained novices. The expression 'poi sang long' is actually Shan (in Thai it is called *buat naak* or *buat luuk kaew*), and at some Shan places like Mae Hong Son town and Wat Fah Wiang In behind Piang Luang the festivities take a particularly extravagant form. The young postulants are paraded round town, their heads shorn, on the shoulders of relatives, mostly older brothers. However, they do not wear the simple white robes seen elsewhere in Thailand, but are dressed up in fancy costumes. They put on white jackets adorned with sequins, rosettes and medallions, and sport turbans, lavishly decked with flowers. The boys' faces are so prettily made up with red lipstick, green eyeshadow and rouge that the uninitiated onlooker could be forgiven for mistaking them for fanciable girls! They flutter fans before their faces and make their way up the thronging streets under high festive parasols. The swaying procession is accompanied by a band, beating out a throbbing frenzied rhythm on cymbals, drums and gongs. Many people dance as if possessed. Alcohol and sweat are on the air. Slowly, the ecstatic parade makes its way through the streets, ending up at Wat Jong Kham by the lake. Later in the day, the boys exchange their finery for monks' robes, after which they take their first vows.

In the middle of the main street, on the east side, there was a small all-day food market. Three or four stalls fronted a cavernous gloomy sheet-metal building, inside which the food was prepared and relatives of the cooking ladies watched TV. A dozen folding tables and chairs stood between the food stalls and the road, and these proved an excellent place to watch the town proceedings over a drink or a Thai meal. Perhaps because of the food market's position or its modest prices, it tended to attract *farang* travellers. Here Germans and Dutch, Aussies and Poms sat, a Singha beer or a fruit shake in hand, swapping information or trading tales. But it was popular with local people too, who dropped by to pick up a snack of pork satay or charcoal-grilled corn-on-the-cob. Right beside the tables was Mae Hong Son's central police box. A conspicuous sign read: WELCOME TOURISTS, WE'RE PROUD TO SERVE YOU, but an enquiry revealed that none of the three or four policemen could speak a word of English. Dressed smartly in their uniforms, they lounged around, fiddled with their walkie-talkies, disappeared on mysterious errands on their Honda mopeds, or discreetly indulged in a bottle of Mekhong whisky at 'their' table behind the kiosk.

Mae Hong Son is dominated on the west side by Doi Kong Mu. The top of this 1500-metre-high mountain is shared by **Wat Pratat Doi Kong Mu** and some soaring telecommunications masts. A landmark of the town are the temple's two pagodas. Both house the relics of eminent monks. The larger one, built in 1860, contains the remains of Pra Maha Mok Kallana Tera, which were brought here from Burma by the builder Chong Tong Su and his wife Lek. The smaller pagoda was built in 1874 by *pra ya* Singhanat Racha, an early local Shan ruler. It is said that the hilltop used to be a hideout from which Karen bandits once made raids on the Shan townspeople. A flight of steps makes a direct ascent up the front of the mountain to the two *chedi*. It is a stiff climb, but worthwhile for the wonderful views west over jungle and forest towards the Shan State. The view east reveals the 'town of the three mists' laid out at the foot of Doi Kong Mu, with the mountainous hinterland beyond (if you look at 130° or SE, you can see on the horizon part of the ridge of celebrated Doi Pui, Mae Hong Son province's highest mountain). Down at street level, from the tables of the food market, the monastery can be seen high above the rooftops. At night, lights on the pagodas and on the masts twinkle magically in the darkness.

One evening we were sitting after supper at one of these tables. An assortment of acquaintances had gathered, of the kind one meets on the road. There was the middle-aged civil servant from Australia, who had suddenly decided that there was more to life than pen-pushing. This likeable fellow was having the time of his life and subsequently ran off with a Chiang Mai waitress. There was the lanky Dutchman who divided his year between the Netherlands, where he had a psychiatric practice, and the Far East, where he indulged his proclivity for young men. There was the Thai airforce man from Khorat, who in a way untypical of the gregarious Siamese was travelling round the north-west on his own. And there was the wheeler-dealer from Germany, drifting round the kingdom in the company of a fractious dark beauty he had met down south on the island of Ko Samui. The German had vague revolutionary ideas, but uppermost in his mind at that moment was a plan to live in a boat moored off Pattaya or Puket. He thought that in this way he could live cheaply both inside and outside Thailand, avoiding all the problems of visas and taxation. We were going through the viability of his scam when a Western monk, shorn and in saffron, shuffled past. The *farang* bonze caused a momentary stir in the languid ebb and flow of the conversation. Why did the German not turn to the cloth, we suggested half seriously, perhaps that would answer his needs? It was still distinctly warm, we were sitting in our shirt sleeves, the ice was melting in the bucket, the policemen were fiddling nearby, sweetcorn and *gai yang* were grilling over the charcoal, and the lights on Doi Kong Mu were winking up above. Suddenly the Australian, his mind roaming over past, present and future, said: "It's fantastic here. We should drink in the beauty and atmosphere of this idyll. In the years ahead, it's memories of evenings like this that we'll have to live off."

* *

Postscript 2002

A decade on, not a great deal has changed in Mae Hong Son town. It has grown somewhat and is more prosperous. It seems not to have been much affected by the post-1997 economic crash. Nor did the flow of tourists drop off, as I had surmised it might. Tourism has been sustained and even boosted in Mae Hong Son by the dubious industry centered on the 'long-neck' women, which has meanwhile consolidated. So, these days, the town is a bit of a tourist trap, has gone slightly upmarket and upprice, with more gaggles of elderly and often (sorry) gross-looking package tourists ambling up the main street to look at the souvenir shops after an evening meal in their hotel and a day out at Fish Cave as well as at one of the villages of the 'long-neck' women.

On the guest house front, *Sanguan Sin* is defunct, and its useful alternative, the *Siam Hotel*, has – alas – jumped on the tourist bandwaggon and doubled its prices. Another overpriced lodging is *Pira*, scenically located down by Lake Jong Kham and with an attractive bar-café out front, where a mediocre room goes for 250 or 300 baht. Travellers looking for cheap good-value places to stay can find several lodgings near the lake: *Jongkham GH*, *Rimnong GH*, *Johnny* and *Prince GHs*. When I last looked by, *Jongkham*, in the street north of the lake, had scruffy bungalows, but nice, if small, clean row rooms with fan for 150 baht/night. The latter contained a mattress on the floor, were separated by woven bamboo walls, shared spotlessly clean toilets and hot shower, and had a nice sitting area out front. *Rimnong* (= lake edge), across the lake and near the twin temples, was a ramshackle, noisy, jovial, slightly squalid place with rooms for 100 and 150 baht, and with a chronic water/shower problem. There are several other GHs in the side streets west of the main drag.

On the restaurant front, *Fern* is as inviting as ever, and another good eating house is the centrally located *Kai Muk* (Mook). The partly covered all-day food market in the very centre of town, by the police box, now goes by the name of 'Jong Kham Bazaar', has been upgraded and completely covered over, and operates mostly in the evening. There are some useful cheaper food stalls here, and *Don Enterprises* has an extensive interesting menu, if you can handle the owner's special brand of oily obsequiousness. *Buatong* restaurant, which for many years lay opposite *Siam Hotel*, has been renamed *Ji Ji* after lady owner Lek's daughter, and has moved to a location near the post office and opposite *Seven-Eleven*. It has the same interesting menu, fair prices and slow service, perhaps because everything is freshly prepared in succession by Lek herself. Her molee curry is especially toothsome and recommendable.

There have been other developments in this community of cool Shan people. The 'town of the three mists' is now wired. Several Internet places have sprung up, and two cheap ones (15-20 baht per hour) can be found near the central crossroads at the start of the side road (on the left side) running west from the crossroads. Mae Hong Son also has an abundance of motorcycle rental shops, most of which lie near the centre. Prices are slightly higher than in Chiang Mai. A well-organized place operates in the main street, opposite the Thai Farmers' Bank. Reckon on paying 150-180 baht/day. The town has also sprouted more souvenir shops, and a relatively new feature is the infestation of mainly Lisu hill-tribe women, who lay out their brightly coloured needlework and other tat on the sidewalks of the main street and down by the lake. Aficionados of *nakrong ying* (what I like to call 'singing girls') can find two raucous seedy 'singing restaurants' in the upper west part of town, on the street above *Pen Porn GH*. Thailand's Aids problem is said to be nowhere more acute and dangerous than in Mae Hong Son.

The missionary friends with whom we dined many years ago subsequently moved to a larger house and started a mission with a nursery. On the subject of religion, I recently found a pleasant forest *wat* that is very little known – Wat Kiu Kamin. It lies on a wooded hilltop ESE of town, opposite Doi Kong Mu. Access to the peaceful secluded monastery-temple is difficult both in terms of finding the route and in terms of the steepness and roughness of the way. Poke around in the streets behind Lake Jong Kham or behind the Shell petrol station to locate the access. Up on top, you will be rewarded with a large imposing outdoor Buddha figure and a grand pagoda, both of which look west over the town, and with a place to relax and gather your thoughts.

6

DARK SECRETS

THE WA

Mae Or

When we were supping with the two American missionaries in Mae Hong Son, they suggested we visit the border KMT village of Mae Or, some 45 kms to the north (see Map 13). It was a good day out, they said blithely, although the way up there was no piece of cake. "Chris", Marvyn baited me, "if you're a connoisseur of raw frontier places, you'll love Mae Or. To get to it", he continued, "backtrack down the H1095 in the direction of Pai, pass Pang Mu village and the Pai river bridge, and turn left (west) after about 10 kms. If you miss that turning, there is a second chance after 17 kms. If you reach the Fish Cave, you have gone too far." We jotted down the instructions on a scrap of paper.

As we knew the route to be demanding and had not yet retrieved our Honda Wing, we decided to hire an MTX trails bike locally. Perched high on the yellow contraption and with a minimum of encumbrance, we set off, exactly following the missionaries' directions. We passed through the spread-out village of **Pang Mu** (from which Mae Hong Son originally sprang some 165 years earlier), tanking up at its Shell fuel station, and crossed the wide bridge over the shallow River Pai, which purled westwards, ultimately to flow into the River Salween in Burma. Then, sure enough, we found the turn-off Marvyn had mentioned, rather more than 9 kms out from Mae Hong Son town centre. Now a country road, filthy with rust-coloured bulldust, but traversing a pretty landscape with paddy fields, looped through the rural villages of **Kung Mai Sak** and **Mae Sa Nga**, arriving after a further 9 kms at **Mork Cham Pae**. The streets of this large Shan village confused us, seeming to go round and round the houses. But soon we joined the other (metalled) route in from Highway 1095 and found our way again. Pointing us now north out of the place, villagers told us to follow the signs for Pa Sua Waterfall.

We motored on through a weird moonlike landscape, in which the trees and bushes on each side of the road had been discoloured orange and beige from the dust of the road and looked frozen and lifeless, as if turned to stone. At the base of a looming ridge lay the village of **Huai Khan** with a roadside shop. I always assumed that this was a Shan place, but in fact it may be inhabited by – in Thailand – rare Pa-O people. Beyond it, the way began to climb up and up. We were beginning to wonder what all the fuss was about when, shortly before Pa Sua fall, the water in our MTX boiled. The engine overheated and, with a complete loss of power in the throttle, we ground to a halt. The bike would not restart, so we stood awkwardly by the side of the dirt track, letting the engine cool down. By good fortune, we had a litre of drinking water with us, which we poured into the radiator. The disadvantages of the fancy MTX, compared to the simple air-cooled Wing, were becoming clear. When the MTX was serviceable again, we completed the upgrade, before descending slightly to the fall, which lay to the right (east) of the trail (26 kms from Mae Hong Son).

Arriving here, we ran into a German couple just leaving. We suggested riding on together as a foursome, but they said that they were going down again. They had only wanted to see the fall. Judging by their dispirited faces and by the dirt on their machine, it looked as if they had crashed somewhere higher up, had argued together and decided to cut short their trip. And off they went. Before continuing, we stopped to look at Nam Tok Pa Sua or **Pa Sua Waterfall**. Steep earth steps climbed down to the fall, where half a dozen cascades poured into basins full of water. After the hot dusty ride, it was luxury to be able to bathe in these and then dry off on the burning grey slabs of rock. The dip was a trifle eerie. Apart from ourselves, there was not a single soul at the secluded chutes, and, lingering on the rocks, we had the impression that unseen eyes were watching us from the dense jungle all round or that perhaps someone was quietly cocking a rifle. The fact that our motorbike was out of sight also made us apprehensive, and sent us scurrying on.

Now the road climbed again, passing a dam and reservoir on the right side (km 27), before heading into a series of corkscrew bends with some extreme gradients. The worst part of the ride was upon us. On one of the fierce upgrades, bits of wrecked indicator light and rear-view mirror lay strewn in the dust, suggesting that this had been the Waterloo of the German couple. Our guess was that the climb was so steep that with two aboard they had run out of power, had stalled and crashed. Profiting from their mishap and remembering our own spill on the way up to Kae Noi, we decided that one of us should scramble the bike up the worst sections, while the other toiled up behind on foot. Our prudence paid off, but did not save us from a tumble anyway, for if we tricked the mountain on the way up, it claimed us on the way down. The problem was that always on the severest inclines and in the tightest corners there was six inches of bulldust covering round fist-sized stones. If going up was rather like riding up a scree, coming down was like motorcycling down a ski run. The brakes, of course, would not hold the bike, and the engine would not slow the machine sufficiently either. So, with the front wheel skittering, there was nothing to do except let go and hope for the best. We were doing just that, when the front wheel hit a stone, flipped to one side, slipped, and over we went, adding our quota of plastic and glass to the shards in the dust. But never mind, a new mirror was only 60 baht in Mae Hong Son and the footrest could be straightened out for free. Wise people simply unscrewed the mirrors from hire bikes on trips like these.

DARK SECRETS

Not much higher up, on another protracted upgrade, our MTX overheated for the second time. We had refilled our plastic bottle at the waterfall and once again topped up the radiator. We cursed the showy macho-looking machine and vowed never to take one again. While we were waiting in a shady corner for the MTX and also ourselves to cool down, strange people kept surprising us by issuing from the jungle all around and walking slowly past, staring. They were hill-tribe hunters, probably Karen, and were armed with stovepipe guns and machetes. We thought of the raiders who not so long ago used to infest Doi Kong Mu. Standing in the middle of nowhere with a broken hire bike made us feel vulnerable.

But soon we were on our way again. The road now cut deep through stunning jungle scenery. The sides of the narrow dirt trail were lined with an encroaching wall of green-gold *mai rai* and *mai sang* bamboos, cracking and singing in the heat. Thrusting up through these were young banana palms, their vanes a delicate translucent pale green. Overarching the palms were tall *mai bong* bamboos, their ends hanging down like coachmen's whips. And towering above all of them were the mighty *mai huak* bamboos (the ones used for builders' scaffolding) and the lofty trees of the forest. The vibrant colours were a feast for the eye – the brilliant green of the vegetation and the intense orange of the trail contrasted vividly with the delphinium blue of the sky.

With the worst section over, we reached next a T-junction (km 30), where a way left (west) went to **Pang Tong**, the site of one of the King's country palaces. But we proceeded right, continuing north-east and north, finally emerging into highland plateau country. The mountains and hills all around were largely denuded, and the colours seemed flatter, bleached out by strong UV irradiation. It was a more sober landscape up here and pleasantly cooler. The road continued at a high level until it reached **Napapaek**. This Blue Hmong village was memorable for the many black pigs roaming around and also for a *wat*, which, oddly, was a Shan one. A little shop was serving noodle soup, Hmong-style. A way off left (west) through Napapaek went to the Blue Hmong village of Huai Ma Kua Som, to the mixed hill-tribe model village of Pang Ung, and ultimately to the Karenni and Shan refugee settlement of Pang Yon across the border. At Napapaek, our MTX tripmeter had clocked up 36 kms from Mae Hong Son centre, which left another 8 kms to Mae Or.

Pang Tong Forestry HQ passed us to the west, and on the approach to our destination there were indications of some agricultural assistance project. Finally, a lonesome signed portal in the middle of the countryside and surrounded by plantations of low tea bushes welcomed us to Mae Or itself (also often spelt 'Mae Aw'). We rode on, passed a couple of unmanned barriers, and finally entered the Chinese village by a black burnt hillside on the left. Opposite this was a strange lake, with a lot of dead trees sticking up out of it. They had been drowned during the creation of a reservoir right next to the village. People later told us that the lake was essentially natural. Water had already been there, and all that had happened was that it had been 'improved' by the construction of an embankment through the middle. And in fact, to the east of Mae Or we later found the other half of the original lake. A mysterious sign on the embankment announced that it was called 'Richpool'. This was an attempt, which had gone wrong coming through Thai, at 'Misty Lake'! In the cold early mornings, the reservoir was covered with mist. At a T-junction, we went right to reach the centre of Mae Or (44 kms from Mae Hong Son).

❖

Mae Or

Mae Or lay in a basin, ringed around by high deforested hills. Windswept and eerie, the mountains stood there in silence, as if hiding some dark secret. This remote settlement seemed like the end of the world, and it was certainly the end of Thailand in the far north-west of the kingdom. The village was a bleak backward collection of long low huts with split bamboo walls. Here and there were mud hovels with grass roofs. All had bare earth floors. Some dwellings had small gardens around them, with roses blooming. Others had tall treelike constructions next to them. We studied these, as we had never seen them before. They were long poles with spars at the top. From the spars, pieces of meat were hanging on string. They were drying in the sun and wind. It seemed as if each pole bore an entire dismembered pig or cow. Nothing was missing. The hooves and tails were there along with lumps of drying brown flesh. Silhouetted like gallows against the mountains, these 'meat trees' reinforced the sinister atmosphere. As at Napapaek, we found numerous animals running around – the same black pigs, black and white ducks, turkeys, chickens and dogs. But there were not many humans to be seen. A few old men were smoking in dark corners, but they ignored us.

All this was a far cry from Piang Luang, even from Kae Noi. And Mae Salong, the leading KMT outpost (in fact, the largest Nationalist Chinese enclave outside Taiwan), was a veritable metropolis in comparison. The reason for the backwardness of Mae Or was no doubt its sheer inaccessibility. The dirt road up had been engineered by the Thai army for security reasons and, while suitable for military vehicles or shanks's pony, was not much good for anything else. But another factor was that Mae Or was still relatively young compared to the major Kuomintang villages of 1961 vintage. Founded in the early 1970s by people breaking away from Nong Ook (Aroonothai), near Kae Noi, it had not had as long to develop. Then there was the fact that Mae Or, piously renamed 'Raakthai' (= love Thailand) by the Thai authorities, was a dangerous flashpoint, where warlord Khun Sa's Mong Tai Army, the Wa National Army, the KMT and the Thai army were all entrenched in a four-way stand-off. Because of sporadic fighting in the border hills immediately behind the Mae Or, the village had been closed off from external influences until recently. If the outside world could not get in, few people could get out. Hardly any of these Gen. Lao Li Third Army veterans or their descendants had Thai ID cards, which meant that they could not travel down to trade or attract business in. The benefit for the visitor, of course, was that Mae Or, still undeveloped, remained an authentic Kuomintang settlement.

We were absolutely filthy with orange dust from the ride up, and so went over to the far side of the reservoir to clean up. Here we found a little jetty, where we could wash and try to freshen our clothes. We shook out the laterite powder, dipped shirts and headscarves in the reservoir, and laid them out to dry in the sun. On the hillside behind us (south side of lake) were some official-looking buildings. Presently, we climbed up to have a look. One complex was a new health centre. The other was a paramilitary BPP base. Both were quiet. Behind them, a little path led up to the top of the hill. We climbed up and on the summit found some of the *dorchodor* soldiers engaged in building a new temple. That in itself was not interesting (the *wat* contained a Buddha figure in the Shan style), but the view north over Mae Or to the border was.

A BPP officer joined us to explain. Like a commander surveying a model of some theatre of war, his finger pointed out over the basin. The village at our feet consisted of about 120-130 houses or families. The border mountain behind the village to the right, Doi Lan, was warlord Khun Sa territory. The mountain opposite to the left was Wa territory. Here two arch-enemies sat facing each other eyeball to eyeball, just as they did on Doi Larng, near Mae Ai. Mae Or itself, of course, was occupied by Khun Sa's former arch-enemy, the KMT, who were now allied with the Wa. Periodically, fighting flared up for control of both the hinterland, with its trafficking routes, and the border, with its access to Thailand. The last time this happened, Khun Sa's MTA bombarded Mae Or, many shells landing unexploded in the reservoir, where they lay to this day. It was impossible to go up into the hills around Mae Or or to walk along the border because each of the three parties (MTA, WNA and KMT) had laid mines, and none knew where each other's minefields were. Ironically, the situation was actually worse than that. Each rainy season, earth got washed over the mines, meaning that the parties no longer knew where their own mines were. It was literally a minefield up there. A day or two before our visit, a truck had been blown up by a landmine when driving along one of the mountain tracks. One person had been killed and the other passengers injured. But we did not need reminding of the dangerousness of Mae Or, for in February 1990 two *dorchodor* friends of ours from the Pang Mu BPP camp similarly ran over a landmine up here. When we met them shortly afterwards, one had a leg and an arm in plaster, and the other had had a leg amputated. The reason why the village was so hotly disputed was, of course, that it was strategically important in the heroin-trafficking business. It was a funnel by which drugs, emanating from Kokang and the Wa sub-state and passing down through the Shan State, entered Thailand, reaching Mae Hong Son and the wider world by the very road we had come up. This, then, was the dark secret of those sinister bald 6000-foot hills just behind Mae Or – they were the scene of landmines, night-time heroin shipments, and deadly skirmishing.

After the rough and tumble of the ride up, we were hungry and thirsty. But a strange thing about Mae Or was that there was nowhere to eat or drink. We searched around, but could not find a shop anywhere. A gaggle of children had slowly formed and began following us. We asked them where we could get a Coke, and they took us to the house of an old Chinese lady. This ample Kuomintang matriarch was making chopsticks at a table outside. Wearing a straw hat and wielding a machete, she was not to be hurried and went on to cut another three or four sticks, before finally condescending to fetch two warm Pepsis, for which she overcharged us. But we were in no mood to argue.

THREE PAGODAS

Most of the children drifted away, but one or two remained, seemingly fascinated by us. One was a girl with a Tibetan-looking face, and the other was a bewitching lass of 14 with a remarkably dark complexion and flashing white teeth. She immediately caught our eye. We bought them each a drink, and the four of us talked for a while. Where adults from the migrant minority peoples frequently spoke no Thai, their children often could because they were taught the language of their adopted country at school. The dark-faced girl was so arresting that we asked her if we could take some pictures. Although hopelessly bashful, she did not mind, and so under the watchful eye of the matriarch we composed some portraits of the photogenic nymphet. Probably unbeknown to her or the villagers, she was strikingly beautiful. Her black-yellow skin was framed by jet-black hair, her almond-shaped eyes slanted slightly upwards, the nose was petite like that of a Siamese cat, and her teeth fractionally glinted out of sensuous everted lips.

We commented to our 'model' on the duskiness of her skin. She was not at all surprised and confessed that her nickname was 'Darkie' (as in English). This was an allusion to a well-known brand of Thai toothpaste. On both the tube and the box, there was a picture of a negro with a soot black face and gleaming white teeth, together with the brand name 'Darkie'. Every time the villagers had seen the girl, they had been reminded of the toothpaste and begun to call her by its name. The nickname 'Darkie' had stuck. (Recently there was some legal wrangle over the right to use this brand name, resulting in the toothpaste suddenly being rechristened an enigmatic 'Darlie'.)

The fuss we were making of Darkie, tilting her head and arranging her hair, made her the centre of attention among the people who had gathered around. For a moment or two she was a film star. That was nice because we found out that her family was very poor, almost the poorest in the village. Darkie had to work for another household, doing the washing and the washing up, in order to pay for her clothes and schoolbooks. Her real name was Tiamjit Sae Li. She had two brothers and two sisters. One of the sisters worked for some people down in Pang Mu. In exchange for the work, they sent her to school. The sister only came back up to Mae Or once a year. We asked Darkie if she or her family ever went down to Mae Hong Son. They never did, she replied, because they were too poor to pay the fare.

After the soft drinks and the photographs, Darkie took us to her home to meet her mother. The 'house' was a broken-down bamboo hovel with a grass roof, even more abject than those around it. In front were two or three black pigs in a makeshift pen. It was gloomy inside (no electricity, of course), but after a second or two we could make out the main features. A blackened kettle was sitting over a fire in a hearth. On the hard earth floor, a pail of water was standing with several white discs of bread in it. These, we were told, would be grilled for supper. The beds were simple platform beds with a mat of split bamboo over a wooden frame. Darkie's was at the front of the hut in a room which was open to the sky. The grass roof had fallen in, leaving gaping holes. It must have been freezing sleeping there at night. The mother was sitting on a stool chopping away the outer layers from the stem of a young banana tree. These would be eaten by the pigs, while the tender core would be eaten by the

126

family. She apologized for the state of the house, adding that she had built it herself. Then we learned the main reason why the family was so impoverished. Her husband had died six years earlier. With the principal breadwinner gone, she had been left to bring up five children on her own.

Looking at Darkie and seeing how much she differed both from her mother and her brothers and sisters, we wondered if she was not just fatherless, but perhaps the orphan of another family, or a wildcard – maybe the product of a liaison between her mother and a dark stranger up in the Wa hills to the north. Given the chequered history of the migratory minority peoples from Yunnan and north-east Burma, this could well have been the case. Confirmation of our suspicion came when we once showed our Darkie photos to a perceptive KMT man in Mae Salong. "Why, she looks just like a Wa girl!" he exclaimed. Of course, we could not question Darkie, any more than we could quiz the mother, and so for the moment the dusky beauty's dark past remained a secret.

✻

The Mae Or part of our story would not be complete without an account of developments a few years later (February 1994), when we revisited the village. Taking a lift from Mae Hong Son market with a young Hmong man called Pan-na, who for 50 baht each drove us all the way to the border in his pick-up, we arrived on the last day of the Chinese New Year. On the way we noticed changes. After Huai Khan, a new metalled road was being blasted up into the mountains, scarring the hillsides and destroying quantities of jungle and forest. Napapaek had expanded, with a new first section, and electricity pylons now ran all the way to Mae Or, providing it with power. At the entrance to the KMT village itself, we found a new store, and on the north-east side there was a brand-new wooden school. But the most welcome innovation was that in the centre some simple shops and eating places had sprung up. We took lunch in one of the latter, and a lady fried up for us a delicious plateful of ribbon egg noodles, dried Chinese mushrooms, greens and deep-fried dried beef. An accompaniment of *pakkad dong* or pickled cabbage was served, and the meal was washed down with endless tumblerfuls of golden China tea. The beef seemed familiar somehow, and then we remembered it was the product of those 'meat trees' we had once seen.

While we were lunching, a Thai police truck screeched to a halt in the dusty central compound. Two policemen got out and began searching around, making enquiries. A lot of villagers came over to see what the fuss was all about. We gathered that the policemen had stopped two Hmong youths on a motorcycle down on the 1095 road and had discovered that they were carrying heroin. The Hmong had fled, trying to escape up the Mae Or road. But the police had followed them, chasing them through Napapaek all the way to Mae Or, where their escape route ran out. The punishment in Thailand for heroin-smuggling is death by Heckler & Koch machine gun, so the youths were in fear of their lives. At first the policemen did not find them. But they were clever. They waited around all afternoon in quiet corners, drinking tea and whisky

127

with the locals. Finally, one of the boys crept back into the village and was caught. It was common knowledge by then that the two lawmen intended to extort a large sum of money from the Hmong in exchange for not turning them in.

When the commotion had died down, a grey-haired Chinese man walked past, whom we had once met in Nong Ook. It turned out that he worked in Mae Or health clinic as an acupuncturist. When we had last seen him, he had been visiting relatives in that other KMT outpost (it was from Nong Ook that in the 1970s people broke away to form Mae Or). He was pleased to see us, and we fell in with him. He gave us a tour of the village, showing us things we had not previously seen. Near the secondary piece of lake, there was a mushroom farm. The fungi did not grow from compost beds, but from notches that had been cut into a ramshackle army of upright wooden logs. Around the village, there were orchards, where temperate fruits were cultivated. Tea was also grown and processed at Mae Or.

In every household, people had pasted fresh red and gold paper banners around their door and window frames. And in each front yard, a pine sapling had been planted in the dirt. Our greying friend explained that these were practices associated with the New Year celebrations. The Chinese believed the saplings brough them 'greenness' – health and prosperity. The young pines did not remain in the yards forever, but were removed after a week or so. During our walk, we ran into the commander of the BPP base above the lake. The afternoon was progressing, and he asked us how we were going to get back down to Mae Hong Son. A Hmong man was coming to collect us in his pick-up, we lied through the teeth. That was good, the *dorchodor* chief replied, because *farang* were not supposed to stay up at Mae Or overnight. Actually, we intended to try and sleep a night or two at the village, and when the commander was gone, we asked the KMT veteran if there was anywhere to stay. Not really, he said, but just for tonight, while the celebrations were ending, we could stay in the health centre. There were a couple of medics temporarily camping up there while they organized a hygiene course for the village housewives, so the place was opened up.

The acupuncture man showed us our lodging. It was in a spacious lecture hall, where every morning the hygiene course took place. There were no beds, but we could use some of the tables. While he fetched a pile of blankets, we put four tables together in the centre of the hall. The problem would be not to fall off in the night, and so we formed a barricade by placing chairs all round the tables, their backs facing inwards. The medics had made tea and coffee outside on the balcony. While we were chatting out there, we spotted something we had not seen before. It was a very tall bamboo pole on a forward hillock to the west of the village. On top was a white flag. We supposed that it indicated a BPP lookout post or defensive position. Oh no, our Chinese friend corrected us, it was to orient Wa soldiers and let them know that they were near a safe haven. Questioning him about this, we discovered something which we had not remotely imagined of Mae Or, and which was not mentioned in the guidebooks, was not, indeed, generally known at all: that the village, besides containing KMT people, was a rare Wa place. Now that we knew it, the fact seemed blindingly obvious, and we kicked ourselves for having overlooked such an important feature during our first visit. And so by chance we wrested from Mae Or its deepest secret, one of the best-kept secrets of the whole Thai-Burmese border.

Seeing our interest, the KMT man pointed out to us a wooden building near the entrance to the village. That was the Wa National Army HQ, and we could go and make ourselves known there. He gave us the name of a man to ask for. The building was actually not so much a military headquarters, but a Wa hospitality house and a kind of pension, where Wa guerrillas injured in fighting could recuperate. Inside we found a man sleeping on a mattress who had been traumatized in a battle, and also an intelligent young Wa man who had been working down at the Three Pagodas Pass with a French aid organization. He spoke good English and said that he was staying in the building while he passed through Mae Or. When we had explained ourselves, he called out of a side room two WNA officers. Both were wearing jungle-green camouflage jackets, and both had the black brown faces characteristic of Wa people. One, simply known as Jerng, had a rugged face and the wild, piercing, evil, slightly hooded eyes that we have also come to associate with Wa people. The other was Major Ta Kong Mong (alias Ying Kuang Sae Jao), the area commander of the WNA troops stationed over the border, opposite Mae Or. If Jerng looked fearsome, impressive, diabolical, Kong Mong was altogether softer and more sympathetic (photos of both in photo section). A taciturn round-faced fellow with boyish hair falling forward over his forehead and a hesitant sloping moustache, he had a roguish way which immediately attracted us. It seemed that he also warmed to us because, although we had no business with the WNA, he took us under his wing.

More tea appeared – one could spend all day drinking tea in these villages – and we sat in a circle around the teapot and glasses in a big room, the walls of which were decorated with Kachin Independence Organization posters, Karen National Union calendars, and suchlike. We asked Kong Mong about the Wa and Mae Or. Wa people first came south to the Thai border around 1973 in the wake of the Communist Party of Burma takeover of their homeland, but they did not move into Mae Or until the early 80s. At one time, there had been a joint KMT/WNA force of 300-400 soldiers garrisoned at the village, but now the WNA was back on the Burmese side of the border. We learned that the meagre body of troops was currently stationed opposite three places: Mae Or, Pang Yon and Nai Soi – all local to Mae Hong Son. At present, 36 Wa families lived in Mae Or, accounting for a third of its inhabitants.

In some albums of old photos, we saw a lot of pictures of the same tall slim man. That was Maha San, Kong Mong explained. Described by some as the last 'king' of the Wa, and by others as just another Shan warlord with another private army (the Wa are also involved in opium-growing and trafficking), the legendary Maha San was the most famous and important Wa person alive. The son of the last feudal lord (*sawbwa, chao fah*) of the Wa mini state or principality of Ming Noen (also referred to as Ving Ngun), the princeling Maha San was leader of the Wa National Army and chairman of the Wa National Organization – the WNA's political wing, which was affiliated in

THREE PAGODAS

Burma to the ethnic rebel NDF grouping. Here were photos of a younger Maha San in combat gear, directing a battle or reviewing troops, or with an open shirt and smoking a cigarette with Shan leaders at the conference table. Kong Mong surprised us by saying that Maha San was his brother. At first we did not take him seriously, thinking that he was using 'brother' in the same loose way that Thais used 'cousin'. But it turned out that the two were indeed real brothers, not even half brothers.

❊

The Wa

The homeland of the Wa is the Wa State or, more accurately, sub-state, an utterly remote mountainous area in north-east Burma composed of hundreds of former microstates or principalities or fiefdoms, ruled by erstwhile *sawbwa* or feudal lords. If, geographically, it is wedged between the River Salween to the west and the Chinese border to the east, and between Kokang to the north and the Shan plateau to the south, culturally it is overshadowed by the Chinese and the Shan. No reliable statistics exist for the number of Wa living today. Propaganda we acquired from the WNO optimistically put the figure at 2-3 million. A more accurate estimate might be 1-2 million (including Palaung-Wa), which would take into account half a million Wa thought to be living over the Chinese border in Yunnan. Several thousand Wa live along the Thai-Burmese border, about 17,500 (in the form of Lawa) exist in Thailand itself, near Mae Sariang, and the remainder, perhaps half a million, either live in the Wa sub-state or have intermarried with and been assimilated into various other ethnic groupings.[1] In Burma, through intermarrying, through internal political dissension, through being divided and ruled by other occupying forces, and through serving away in other peoples' armies, the Wa have become widely dispersed and fragmented. They are one of the most obscure, neglected and marginalized of all the minority peoples in South-East Asia.

It is thought that the name 'Wa' has Shan origins and was adopted from the Shan by the Wa themselves. But the Wa are not related to the Shan (Tai Yai), or to the Thais of northern and central Thailand (Tai Yuan, Tai Noi/Siam), or to the Burmese or Chinese. Like Thailand's ancient Lawa, they are classified as belonging to the Palaungic branch of the Mon-Khmer group in the Austro-Asiatic family of peoples or linguistic superstock,[2] and as such are related especially to the Lawa and also to the many other fragmentary groups of Mon-Khmer ancestry. Again like the Lawa, they claim with considerable justification to be the oldest people of the region, the indigenous

---

[1] Diran (1997) gives the figure of over 100,000 Wa living in Burma, while acknowledging that other estimates, e.g. Howard (1999), put the number at 300,000+ Wa living in Burma, with up to two million altogether in the whole region. Yet other sources put the Wa population at 800,000.
[2] Howard (1999) subdivides the Palaungic linguistic stable into the Angkuic languages, which comprise Samtao and Thai Loi, and the Waic languages, which include the two Wa tongues of Parauk and Vo and also Blang. People who speak Parauk and Vo, he says, are often known as Wa, which is perhaps another way of saying that Wa people speak the Waic languages of Parauk and Vo.

130

inhabitants of a territory that probably included northern and central (present-day) Thailand, the Shan State, and maybe habitat further afield (Laos, China, Vietnam etc.). It seems likely to me that the Wa and the Lawa were originally one and the same aboriginal *Urvolk*, usually called the L'wa, which was subsequently sundered for historical reasons into the Lawa to the south in 'Thailand' and the Wa to the north in the Wa homeland in 'Burma'. With the Lawa and other Mon-Khmer peoples, the Wa share distinctive outward features not evinced by Tai, Chinese and other Sinitic peoples. They do not have Mongoloid 'slit' eyes and smooth paler skins, but very dark pigmentation, hairiness of the face, and 'craggy' angular features.

During British colonial times, which lasted from the start of annexation of Burma in the 1820s until Burmese independence in 1948, the Wa principalities, as Howard (1999) writes, were largely outside British administrative control until well into the 20th century, and the Wa were never brought under effective British control. In 1885, the British captured Mandalay and then began asserting control over neighbouring Shan territories. By 1887, the southern Shan states or principalities were securely under British influence, and many of the other Shan microstates were visited in 1887-88 by a military expedition, which established British control over them. But this was no direct, heavy-handed or oppressive control. Rather, allowing the local *sawbwa* or princelings to continue ruling, the British established a structure of indirect rule over the Shan states, which 1887-95 they demarcated into five categories, including the southern Shan states and the northern, which themselves included various Wa principalities and the ethnic Palaung sub-state of Tawngpeng. In 1893, the Sino-British Boundary Commission surveyed some Wa territory, but the British made no immediate effort to establish a colonial presence among the Wa. It was only as late as 1937-42 that they established colonial administration in a few Wa areas, although this was minimal. After the Second World War, during which the Wa were only marginally involved in the fighting, the picture was hardly different – the British still only established very limited administrative control. And thus the Wa were still largely autonomous when Burma gained independence in 1948.

Why did the intrepid and assiduous British explorers, military and administrators scarcely venture into core Wa territory in some 60 years? One reason undoubtedly was that the Wa principalities were so remote, mountainous, rugged, inhospitable and economically unpromising. Probably it seemed that they contained nothing much worth bothering about, or that the effort that would be involved in developing or exploiting the Wa homeland would be too great. But another reason may have been that the Wa were were formidable and feared headhunters. Perhaps significantly, the British only really began to make inroads into the Wa heartland during the late 1930s, when Wa headhunting was reported to be in decline. In Burma, the colonial British generally considered the Wa to be the most primitive of all the many peoples of the country. To be fair, however, they drew a distinction between what they called the 'Tame Wa' and the 'Wild Wa'. The 'Tame Wa' had settled outside the Wa heartland, in communities especially in southerly Kengtung and Manglun, but also elsewhere. They had abandoned headhunting, and some of them had converted to Buddhism.[3] The 'Wild Wa', by contrast, inhabited the northerly isolated mountainous territory of today's Wa sub-state, were 'uncivilized' and pagan, practised headhunting, and evidently resisted colonial rule. The fact that the Wa traditionally inhabited remote intractable terrain, indulged in headhunting, had a reputation for being wild and 'primitive', and were left largely untouched by the colonial British in Burma probably accounts for the dearth today of ethnographic description of the Wa and for the absence so far of any systematic anthropological research on them.

The Wa custom of headhunting, which continued to be practised until quite recently, is the only thing that is at all widely known about these people. Diran (1997) reports that as late as the mid-1970s headless corpses could be found on the road to Kengtung, while 300 human skulls lined the road approaching a village called Laklai. The grisly practice may relate to Wa mythology, which apparently associates the custom with the legendary founders of the Wa race. But the hunting and displaying of both human and animal skulls was connected especially with the belief that they guaranteed successful crops and hunting (were some kind of fertility symbol), and totemically ensured both that evil spirits would be warded off from villages and that a community or house would be protected. Freshly hunted heads were left until the flesh had rotted away, after which the skulls were ceremoniously placed in rows in a sacred grove outside the village, where they would be positioned in niches in posts. The heads of strangers, e.g. of an Indian merchant, were particularly prized because the Wa believed that the spirits of such deceased would be unable to find their way out of the hills, enhancing the protection afforded.

The Wa sub-state is probably the most backward region in Burma, and that is saying something, as Burma itself is one of the least developed nations in the world (bracketed along with other LDN-status places such as Ethiopia and Chad). The Wa homeland is characterized, as indicated, by high mountain ridges, which plunge into valleys 2000-5000 feet deep. Traditionally, the Wa are slash-and-burn agriculturists, and this swiddening combined with extensive cultivation (of maize, buckwheat, beans, rice, cotton and vegetables) has left many of the hillsides deforested, denuded and severely impoverished. But the soil is in any case poor and best suited to the cultivation of the opium poppy, which is the main cash crop of the Wa. So Wa territory is impoverished, its inhabitants rely a lot on hunting and fishing, also on animal husbandry and poppy growing, and opium caravans pass through the Wa sub-state (still), proceeding from Kokang, down to the Shan State, where many refineries are, to the Thai border. The Wa exchange opium for missing foodstuffs and also metal, which like the Lawa they know how to work. In common with many tribals, they chew betel nut, which stains their teeth black – unsightly to us, but traditionally a sign of beauty and dental vigour for the Wa. Wa culture is conspicuous for its lack of art.

---

[3] Nowadays many Wa are Christians. In 1935, the American evangelist Harold Young, branching out from a base in Kengtung, the Shan State, opened the first Baptist mission in the Wa sub-state.

DARK SECRETS

Also like the Lawa, the Wa favour siting their villages on the higher mountain slopes, at altitudes above 1000 m, away from streams, which they apparently consider to be a source of fever. The settlements can be quite large, up to 300 houses. Traditionally, they were protected by a 6-ft-high earth rampart covered with thickets of thorn bushes, and a deep hidden ditch was often dug around the village perimeter for added protection (a defensive system reminiscent of the moated ramparts at Wiang Haeng!).

Photos of Wa women in Diran's *The Vanishing Tribes of Burma* show them wearing a traditional costume that is basically all-black in colour with some red. They have a short, black, long-sleeved jacket with a front opening. The left flap is crossed over the right, and the jacket is sparsely decorated except for the elongated left lapel, which is adorned with little pompoms, hairclips, buttons, safety pins, small silver hemispheres etc. The women also have a long black wrap-around skirt, the bottom half of which is unadorned, while the top half is heavily decorated with horizontal, mainly red and black banding, giving the impression of an apron. The women are also wearing black turbans lavishly decorated with flowers and horizontal swathes of beads, and some sport long dangly earrings. However, in the back of Diran's book, in the section 'Ethnographical History' (1997, p. 217), an old black-and-white photograph taken around 1905 shows a group of 'Wild Wa' dressed in a quite different costume. The women are wearing a short, very simple, short-sleeved smock, with a V-neck but no front opening. They also have a three-quarter-length wrap-around skirt, simply adorned with a hem and two or three horizontal bands (the colour of the decoration is unclear because the photo is in B + W). Around their stomachs, there is a white-looking multiple-strand sash, reminiscent of the waistbands and hoops of the women of the Palaung tribe, to whom the Wa are related. They also sport simple turbans, bracelets on their wrists, and silver bands around their upper arms. But the most extraordinary thing about the attire of these Wa women is their earrings: all of them have unwieldy 6 to 12-inch-long silver tubes, some slightly cone-shaped, passing through holes in their ear lobes. Some of their menfolk are wearing similarly bizarre outsize earrings, which rather resemble bent coat-hangers! The men's costume is altogether similar to the women's, consisting of the same shift and skirt, although almost completely undecorated.[4] I continue the account of the Wa in a more narrative anecdotal form.

---

[4] Three grainy old black-and-white photographs in Howard (1999, p. 94), themselves reproduced from Scott and Hardiman (1900/01) and Scott (1911), show groups of Wa men and women, whose attire is in part similar to that of the Wa people shown in Diran's 1905 photo. The three pictures probably predate the historic Diran shot and may stem from the late 19th century. Discrepancies between the two attires might derive from the fact the costumes shown in Diran's photo are best dress, while those seen in Howard's pictures are everyday. In Howard's photos, we can see (middle illustration) a group of women, among whom there seems to be a naked boy in a loincloth, who are wearing long-sleeved jackets and three-quarter-length skirts, the latter decorated with three or four horizontal bands. Below them (bottom photo), we see a group of five women (maybe the same women as in the middle picture) wearing similar dress. In the top photo, a group of 20 headmen can be seen, all wearing loose long-sleeved jackets and apparently longyis. Most of the men have turbans.

THREE PAGODAS

Kong Mong invited us to take supper with him down in the centre of the village. When we walked down at 7pm, it was already quite cold, and we could see our breaths. On the last evening of the Chinese New Year, the celebrations were petering out, but there was still some fun and games. A lot of people were roaming around, including WNA soldiers who had crossed over from their camp on the other side. Jumping-jack fire crackers were being let off, men were gambling in smoky dens, there was traditional dancing, special food was being eaten, and the youngsters danced until the small hours in a disco rigged up in the large *sala* or meeting-pavilion of the central compound. The Thai hit pop song of the moment was played over and over again until everybody was thoroughly sick of it.

Outside a Wa house near the noisy central compound, several tables had been set out. People kept dropping by to eat, drink tea, and chat. We sat down at one of them and were joined by Kong Mong's wife, Chang Soe, and their two children, a boy and an older girl. Chang Soe, a fearsome-looking lady with a bullish face, was actually much kindlier than she appeared. The best thing about her from our perspective was that she was a mine of information. Kong Mong was very helpful, even spoke some English, but he was not by nature forthcoming, and on that particular evening his mind was half on the gambling, to which he sloped off at intervals. So it was from the Thai-speaking Chang Soe that much of our insight into the Wa came. Under our very noses, a wild Wa boy with a stubbly moustache and hair gathered up in a topknot prepared a chicken. He killed the bird in the kitchen, the unprotesting animal dying without so much as a cluck. Soon its feathers were off, it was in pieces, and the parts were being washed in water. The boy seemed especially interested in the bird's organs and innards. Nothing was wasted. In particular I remember him carefully holding lengths of intestine up to the light, whether to check that they were clean or to read the omens it was not clear. We were drinking some pleasant Chinese peach *lao*, and after an hour the chicken was served up chopped and fried, and folded into spaghetti-type egg noodles. There was also tofu and mushroom soup, tofu strips stir-fried with vegetables, omelette, and the fiery pickled vegetable accompaniment *pak dong*. It was a feast fit for a king.

Quizzing Kong Mong, we tried to piece together the complicated family background of this noble Wa scion. His grandfather was called Ta Hlang and his father Maha Pong. Maha Pong, the last *sawbwa* of Ming Noen, had married three times. By the first wife he had had his oldest son, Maha Kwang, now deceased. By the second wife, Ye Lu, who was still alive in Taiwan, he had had

---

Howard quotes Scott as saying that in warm weather the northern 'Wild Wa' wear few clothes, going about almost naked except for ornaments, of which there are a few in everyday life and many on ceremonial occasions. The men, Scott says, wear a narrow loincloth with tassels at the end. In cold weather, 'Wild Wa' men cover their shoulders with a blanket, while their womenfolk dress in a skirt that tends to be short or worn short. The southerly 'Tame Wa', Scott continues, wear clothes instead of ornaments! The women dress in jackets and skirts, while the men wear either Shan attire or loincloths and sometimes a blanket. Lowis (1919) would seem to corroborate this by saying that northern Wa dress is very scanty, whereas the more southerly 'Tame Wa' cover themselves fully. Scott mentions five different groups of 'Tame Wa' (Hsin-lam, Hsin-leng, Hsin-lai, Hta-mo and Mot-no) and that each has a distinctive type of loincloth, striped or chequered in various patterns.

the three brothers Maha San, Kong Mong and Kong Ko. Maha San, as the most senior surviving son, had inherited the title of Maha (*maha* is an honorific similar to *khun* or *chao*) and for a while had also taken over the father's name of Pong. By the third wife, father Maha Pong had had one son Maha Ja. Maha Ja was widely referred to as 'the younger brother', and the interesting thing about him was that in 1986 he joined Mo Heng's and Khun Sa's TRC (later MTA). This was strange as the Wa and Khun Sa were bitter enemies. But even more bizarre was the fact that Maha Ja was commander of Khun Sa's Doi Lan MTA base just a stone's throw from Mae Or. Brothers from the same family commanded mutually hostile forces living next door to each other! There were also two daughters (sisters) somewhere along the line, but one was dead, and the other, Nam Cha, lived in Taiwan with her mother. Chang Soe disappeared to return enthusiastically with three ancient black-and-white photos. One showed Ye Lu ('Ama'), Kong Mong's mother, an ample round-featured lady. The others were pictures of Ta Hlang, the grandfather, and Maha Pong, the last *sawbwa* himself. Here were old feudal chiefs with Fu Manchu moustaches and straggly chintuft beards, with white turbans, and with angular faces which seemed slightly European. Looking at these faded photographs was like looking back into some incredibly exotic and mysterious past, like having a direct link with the times of Kublai Khan or Marco Polo.

While we were poring over the photos and trying to disentangle the family relationships, another couple came to join our table. We did not take much notice of them at first – a lot of people were coming and going. The woman, fresh and attractive, looked Chinese, while the man, with his dark pitted face, had to be another Wa. "More Wa people for you", Kong Mong said lightly, mischievously, "and part of the family too." They were all watching me trying to sort out a family tree in my notebook. "And where do you fit in?" I quipped, addressing the man and pointing to the mess of lines, "Who are you?" "I am Maha San", said the dark face in a deep soft resonant voice, "and this is Janoo, my wife." We looked up, stunned. Here we were suddenly, all unprepared, face to face with the leader of the Wa, the illustrious 'king' in exile (see photo section), whose house in Chiang Mai, we subsequently discovered, was sought out by a succession of Shan leaders, NDF chairmen, dignitaries, politicians and journalists.

As we got over our surprise and came to terms with our good fortune, we learned that Maha San and his wife had come up to Mae Or to take part in the Chinese New Year festivities. Many Wa were celebrating there along with the KMT, but in addition, Janoo, it transpired, was of mixed Wa and Chinese extraction. Maha San and his wife were every bit as affable and helpful as Kong Mong and Chang Soe, and from them, on this and other occasions, we learned much else about Maha San himself, his family, his life, the Wa, their history and culture. Maha San was 49 years old (in 1996), was born in Ming Noen, and had three daughters. It surprised us to hear he was so young because he looked older. When we later put this to Kong Mong, the brother confessed that Maha San had once been addicted to opium, which had aged him. We noticed also a vain touch. The princeling dyed his grey hair jet black. Nevertheless, this tall, slim, in some ways boyish man, with hooded cracklike eyes and a wedge-shaped face reminiscent of that of his father and grandfather, was every bit the distinguished personage we had expected. The nobility did not end with him, for his wife Janoo was the sister of the formidable Mrs Li Ching (Li Yi Sing). That Chinese-Wa lady was married to Ai Siao-su, son of the last Wa *sawbwa* of Yawngbre, and together the couple commanded the other major (larger) Wa faction down on the Thai border, the Wa National Council – recently incorporated into the United Wa State Army. The two Wa princeling leaders, therefore, with their separate pocket armies (the 'Red' Wa UWSA was not affiliated to the NDF), were related through the sister-wives.

We commented to Maha San and Kong Mong that they looked so unalike that we could not believe that they were really brothers. They were, they countered, it was just that Kong Mong took after their mother, while Maha San looked like their father. On the subject of semblances, we produced our photos of Darkie. Both brothers recognized the girl immediately. They confirmed what we had come to suspect, that our poor 'princess' was (at least in part) Wa. Her mother was KMT, while her dead father had been Wa. She was the spitting image of her father, they said. We asked our hosts what they thought of the road construction, which in the end would reach Mae Or, bringing with it tourism, which would change the village. We had learned at the district office in Mae Hong Son that Mae Or was due for development. The cultivation of temperate fruits and tea-growing would be further promoted, and the village was to be officially designated a place of touristic interest. It was possible that ultimately Mae Or might become another Mae Salong. Kong Mong and Maha San were aware of the potential disadvantages, but in general they thought that the village was so backward that things could only go up. There were lighter moments too. Suddenly, the BPP commander came by, stopping at our table. Of course, he remembered that he had forbidden us to stay overnight and that we had promised to skedaddle. But he said nothing, either because he saw who we were with or because he did not care. He helped himself to our peach whisky and talked a lot about how he liked young girls. Then he continued on to the disco. What with all the fruit *lao* and tea, as well as the teeth-chattering coldness of the night, we all had to keep slipping out. Once, when I returned, I said that in English we called this 'going to see a man about a dog'. "In Wa", Maha San replied, "we say that we are going to shoot a rabbit." "There won't be many rabbits left around here in the morning", Kong Mong finished, and everybody laughed.

One thing that puzzled us was the connection between the Wa and the Lawa. They were the same race of people, Maha San explained, only separated by history. There had been a time centuries earlier when Wa people lived all over northern Thailand. But they had been squeezed first by the Mon and then by the conquering Tai (Tai Siam, Lan-Na Tai or Tai Yuan, Tai Yai or Shan, and the numerous other sub-groups of the Tai). Many Wa had migrated north, inhabiting the mountains which were now the Wa homeland, but some had stayed on as Lawa, being progressively confined to the mountains north-east of Mae Sariang. Latterly a few Wa were moving back down south again. The languages of the Wa and Lawa were closely related, and our friends claimed that old people of the two groups could still communicate. The obliging Chang

Soe jumped up again, running to fetch a beginners' book in Wa. What surprised us about it was that written Wa was set down using the Roman alphabet – a practice shared, apparently, by Kachin. Kong Mong gave us the little book, and it led to an interesting discovery later in our journey.

The Wa had been living alongside the Shan so long that Wa culture was now in many respects Shan. They were Buddhists, although there was still a degree of animism (no ancestor worship), and the Wa New Year and other celebrations tended to follow Shan customs. Wa National Day was on 21 January. We asked about the traditional costume of the Wa. Without our noticing, Kong Mong instructed the lady (named Nang Ching – see photo section) whose house we were sitting outside to go and change, and presently she emerged in full costume to answer our question tangibly. There was a handwoven maroon wrap-around skirt, with wide black and thin gold banding. She wore also a close-fitting black velvet jacket, which had two long central flaps – like ties – hanging to the knees. The jacket was abundantly decorated with silver pearls, buttons, dangles and a butterfly. Down one side hung a cherry red sash. On reflection, I am inclined to view this costume as partly inauthentic, or as an embellished beautified upmarket modern version of traditional Wa female attire.

*

Maha San and recent Wa history

Maha San's life and the recent history of the Wa, of how they came down to the Thai border and to Mae Or in particular, are very much of a piece. Traditionally, the Wa sub-state had been an inaccessible mountain region peopled by wild headhunters and ruled by hundreds of feuding clannish *sawbwa* princelings or chieftains. Ming Noen (= silver mine), the fiefdom of one of the most important Wa *sawbwa*, was where Maha San was born in 1947. Burmese Independence, a year after his birth, would have been little felt up in the Wa hills, but another contemporary event, the arrival of the KMT from 1949 onwards, certainly was. Thousands of heavily armed Chinese Nationalists, fleeing Mao's communist revolutionaries, poured across the Sino-Burmese border into the Wa homeland. The marauding invaders were so much more powerful and cohesive than the fragmented locals that they quickly established themselves as an army of occupation, ironically providing for a decade the only effective overall 'government'. The present close relationship between the Wa and the KMT along Thailand's north-western frontier dates back to the forced cohabitation of the two groups in Wa territory during the 1950s. Around 1960-61, the Chinese People's Liberation Army together with the Burma army jointly swept the KMT (those who had not been evacuated to Taiwan or who had not already migrated south) from the Wa sub-state, driving them down to the Thai border.

The beginning of the Shan nationalist uprising (1959-61) brought the unwanted attention next of the Burmese. The Wa have traditionally identified with the Shan, and their land is normally considered a sub-state within the Shan State. Where earlier many chieftains had fallen in with the KMT, now they sided with the Shan nationalists. The Burmese intervened, disarming some *sawbwa* militias, but encountering resistance in others. The Wa of Ming Noen, led by a youthful Maha San and his older brother Maha Kwang, successfully fought off the Burma army. The early 1960s also saw the start of infiltration of the Wa hills by communists from China. Many Wa, disillusioned with the outgoing KMT, and not wishing to side with either the Shans or even their own Wa nationalists, were attracted by the promises of the communist newcomers. A people traditionally disunited in themselves were now split in their allegiance to at least four political forces: the Shan, the Burmese, the Wa nationalists, the Chinese communists – even a few KMT stragglers.

The communists flourished. Mutating in the mid-1960s into Communist Party of Burma units, they set up their North-Eastern Command in the Wa sub-state, based on the 'capital' Pang Sang. As the period of the KMT invasion ended, the era of CPB occupancy began. The central authorities in Rangoon, seeing the confusion on their north-eastern border and alarmed at the growth of the communists, intervened anew. In the ensuing war between the CPB People's Army and the Burma army, Wa territory was split. One tactic the Burmese used to regain overall control was the *ka kwae yae* scheme. This was that strategy, employed in the Shan State (netting Khun Sa), whereby hostile ethnic groups, in exchange for not supporting active insurgents, could gain legitimacy for themselves as government-backed local defence militias. Once on Rangoon's side, they could continue to police and tax their patches, as well as pursue whatever other interests they had (trafficking), confident that they would not be molested by the authorities. One Wa leader to take up the offer was the 22-year-old Maha San. In 1969, he marched his Ming Noen force of nearly 1000 rebels over to the government side, pledging loyalty to the Union of Burma. At the time, as he explained, it seemed the most expedient thing to do. He was under threat from all sides – from the Shan State Army, from the Burmese, from Khun Sa's trading militia operating nearby, and now from the CPB. The switch also seemed the best way of halting the advance of the communists in the Wa sub-state. But as things turned out, the move was unfortunate in more ways than one. The Wa cause was further split, the CPB proceeded to triumph completely, and the *ka kwae yae* militias were anyway disbanded in 1973. The Ming Noen princeling had backed the wrong horse.

1973 was altogether a watershed in the history of the Wa people. It was the year when the Burmese communist takeover of their homeland became complete. Rangoon was checked, the SSA was marginalized, and the last KMT stragglers were definitively ousted. The seizure also spelled the effective end of traditional Wa *sawbwa* power and rule. The Wa people themselves were divided vis-à-vis the CPB, hopelessly so. The majority decided to go along with the communists. They believed the party line that, in supporting the People's Army, they would be fighting for a free and independent Wa state and would be in the vanguard of a movement to liberate the whole of Burma. This section of the Wa, under the leadership of the Wa chieftains Kyauk Ni Lai and Pauk Yo Chang, formed the origins of the Wa Daeng or 'Red' Wa. But a sizeable portion rejected the CPB. An estimated 10,000 families fled south and west, a veritable Wa diaspora. Maha San led about 2,000 refugees down through the

Shan State to the Thai border, while Ai Siao-su (Ai Hsiao-hsu), another Wa *sawbwa* son, brought a further party. Kong Mong, Maha San's younger brother, followed later. The Wa settlements along the Shan-Thai border date back to this flight.

For Maha San, the years after 1973 were time in the political wilderness. He settled first in an important Shan rebel base opposite Mae Hong Son and near Mae Or (Mong Mai or Ho Mong, I think). There, in 1976, he formed his Wa National Army, which he sought to build up with a view to retaking the Wa homeland. Meanwhile Ai Siao-su had settled along the Thai border further north-east. He founded his own faction, the Wa National Council. Both militias enlisted a steady stream of recruits from the Shan State, notably from among the thousands of refugee Wa families. But it was the WNC, soon to become a rival of Maha San's WNA, which grew faster. Even in exile the Wa remained divided.

In 1978, following a split with his Shan hosts, Maha San moved to Piang Luang, where he found Mo Heng's Shan United Revolutionary Army in cahoots with Gen. Lao Li's KMT Third Army remnants. Assisted by the two armies, the Wa princeling continued in his attempt to build up his WNA, but some of his commanders were unhappy about the collaboration and broke away. The refugee Wa, already divided into WNA and WNC, fragmented even further. Around 1981-82, in a tripartite agreement with Mo Heng and Gen. Lao Li, Maha San decamped with his pocket army to Mae Or. The WNA was given the task, relieving the SURA, of controlling both the Mae Or border crossing and the vital caravan route from the crossing back to the River Salween. In those days, whoever held the crossing point could levy a tax of 100 baht per head of cattle passing through Mae Or and 400 baht per horse carrying jade – not inconsiderable sums.

A year later, in 1983, Maha San allied the political wing of his WNA, the Wa National Organization, with the important National Democratic Front. Neither the SURA, nor the KMT, nor even Ai Siao-su's WNC, were members of this anti-Rangoon alliance of some dozen ethnic insurgent organizations, based at Karen rebel GHQ in Manerplaw, and so Maha San contrived to alienate himself yet further. It was while he was away fighting with the Karen (who through the NDF were now allies of his) that Khun Sa, dislodged from Hin Taek in Thailand and having swept down the Shan-Thai border, seized the Mae Or border crossing point and wrested control of the Salween caravan route from the Wa. In 1984, Maha San returned to try to recapture the Mae Or gateway.

War raged around Mae Or in the early months of 1985. The WNA, aided by the Mae Or KMT and by mortar units sent up by the Karen, battled with Khun Sa troops. Hundreds of soldiers on each side were killed or wounded in pitched battles, shelling and hand-to-hand fighting that went on sporadically for some years. The result was a compromise. The Wa did not recover the Salween route, but they did regain the westerly half of the Mae Or border crossing, while Khun Sa held on to the easterly Doi Lan half. The result is reflected in the disposition of Wa/Sa forces at Mae Or at the time of writing [1995].

THREE PAGODAS

Up in their corner, the other main Wa faction on the Thai border, the WNC, was similarly embroiled in the 1980s in bitter conflict with Khun Sa. Retreating from Hin Taek, Sa's army pushed the WNC off the Doi Larng ridge. However, during the decade Ai Siao-su's Wa flourished in a way that Maha San's did not. Besides recruiting widely, they received military help from a variety of sources – the KMT Third Army, Kachin and Shan groups, and the Red Wa of the Wa homeland. The latter in particular were a source of powerful reinforcement. Following the CPB mutinies in 1989 and the demise of Burmese communism in the Wa sub-state (indeed throughout Burma), the Red Wa sent down some 1500 ex-CPB regulars to bolster the WNC. They were seeking an outlet for their opium and also to compromise Khun Sa. And there, conveniently, was Ai Siao-su's faction already sitting on the Thai border. Now the Wa army of the homeland and the WNC joined up to form the United Wa State Army, currently the strongest of the Wa forces. It was due to this merger with the ex-communist Wa that Ai Siao-su's men themselves became 'tainted' with 'redness' and known in the Thai press as Wa Daeng (unlike Maha San's WNA). They muscled in on Sa, aiming to recapture the strategic Doi Larng heights. In the winter of 1989-90, the long-smouldering Opium War flared up anew, with bitter fighting continuing into the early 1990s. But the Red Wa were only partly successful, seizing back the south-westerly Doi Laem half of the heights. At the time of writing [1995], the Wa Daeng face Khun Sa in a tense stand-off on the ridge, a disposition very similar to the WNA/MTA confrontation down at Mae Or.

In 1989, up in the Wa sub-state, Wa troops, who formed the bulk of the CPB's fighting force, were in the forefront of the Burmese communist mutinies. They stormed the CPB GHQ in Pang Sang, smashed Maoist and Soviet communist icons, and drove the old CPB leaders and cadres into China. The present era of an inscrutable incumbency in the Wa sub-state by Wa (Daeng) themselves began. Surprisingly, their leader, Kyauk Ni Lai, negotiated a ceasefire in the same year with the SLORC junta in Rangoon, the deal being that if the central authorities allowed the Wa to develop their territory and conduct 'business' as they saw fit, the UWSA would not attack Burma army troops and would refrain from allying with other ethnic insurgent groups. The situation in the 1990s was almost *ka kwae yae* territory revisited.

Six months after the 1989 mutinies, Maha San and a delegation of WNO and Karen officials travelled up to the homeland with an escort of 100 to test the political waters and see if all the various Wa factions could not be consolidated and perhaps brought into the fold of the National Democratic Front. Their reception was not what they had expected. First, Maha San found that his old manorial family home in Ming Noen had gone – not destroyed, but dismantled to provide materials for other buildings. Then, in Pang Sang, he was arrested by Kyauk Ni Lai's men and put in jail. The reasons for this were several. The Red Wa, although no longer communist, were still left-inclined and suspicious of an old feudal lord like Maha San. Further, Kyauk Ni Lai was apparently piqued by the popular support the son of the last Ming Noen *sawbwa* still enjoyed. When the local peasants heard of Maha San's presence, they came crowding to touch their forelocks to the former princeling. But in addition a rumour had spread that Maha San and Khun Sa had allied and that the two of them were coming north to take over Wa territory. The fear was not entirely unfounded, for Maha San had indeed made overtures to Sa, going to him in 1987 for talks and to arrange some kind of a truce between their two armies. The rapprochement had been such that Khun Sa had facilitated the passage of Maha San's delegation up through MTA territory to the Wa sub-state. In the end, Maha San escaped from prison. One account says that he bribed his jailors, another that he was released by the Wa Daeng for fear of the prince's popular support. Whatever the case, Maha San fled to China, where he made his way south through Laos, to return to Mae Or in 1990. There he has remained until the present day, periodically visiting NDF HQ at Karen Manerplaw, and with lieutenants like Kong Mong nurturing his few hundred 'democratic' WNA troops.

With his NDF credentials, Maha San may well be more politically correct than his main Wa rival on the border, Ai Siao-su. Yet the tide is running with the other leader and the UWSA. Whatever his distinction and draw, Maha San with his WNA remains reduced and isolated, a fragment among fragments. His fate is typical of the fate of the Wa as a whole. As Chang Soe put it pointedly, the Wa are incorrigible side-changers. First they are with the KMT, then the Chinese communists; now it is the NDF, now the Burmese; one moment it is the CPB, the next Khun Sa; for a while it is the Shan, and then the Karen. But the Wa have switched allegiance once too often – even by the convoluted standards of local Shan politics. They are their own worst enemy. For in the process they become factionalized, fragmented and marginalized. However, looking at their plight in another way, nothing has changed. The Wa are now what they were in the old days, a disintegrated collection of rival groups, the only difference being that some are now down on the Thai border.

✣

We did not want to leave Mae Or on the second subsequent visit without finding out what had become of Darkie. Since our original visit, the bashful maiden must have grown up into a marriageable young woman. What had happened to her in the meanwhile? Was she perhaps a humble washerwoman in Pang Mu or Mae Hong Son, or might she now be married with a 'darkie' of her own? We went round to the family hovel and asked her mother. Darkie was no longer in Mae Or, but had gone down to Chiang Mai to work. The mother did not know exactly where or at what. Her unconcern about her daughter struck us as odd. Our disappointment at not seeing Darkie again turned to alarm and then despair when the mother narrated vaguely what had happened. Some 'people' had come up from Chiang Mai to Mae Or to take the girl down to 'work'. It was a depressingly familiar story. Then the mother produced a letter from Darkie. We noticed straightaway that the postmark was Bangkok, not Chiang Mai. The mother had not seen this, but only complained that she never heard from her daughter and that Darkie never sent her any money. Inside was a sad little letter with a Bangkok address, which we noted down. It said: "I am alright. I miss you all. Don't worry about me..." and so on. But there was no mention of her work or the people she was working for.

Hill-tribe settlements, rural Thai communities and the villages of the Burmese hinterland are full of examples of poor gullible parents being tricked of their daughters by scouts making an attractive downpayment and promising that the girls would be given a nice job and would be able to send back money at regular intervals. And Bertil Lintner in his *Land of Jade* has reported that impoverished Wa peasants used to settle a debt to (mostly Chinese) moneylenders by forefeiting their daughters as slaves. We had visions of Darkie sold into slavery, a poor mountain girl working in the brothels or sweatshops of Bangkok. Of course, the true explanation could have been more innocent, but somehow the details did not add up. The next time we were in Bangkok, we tried to follow up the address. The trail led to teeming impenetrable Tonburi. There we spent an entire afternoon with local *tuk-tuk* drivers, getting ever deeper into a maze of appalling slums and sweatshops. Sometimes, when we scented we were getting close, the quarter was manifestly Chinese, encouraging us to hope that perhaps after all Darkie was 'merely' working as a maid or a nanny with a family connected with the KMT of Mae Or. But we could not find her, and in the end we had to give up. The address simply did not figure, leading us to conclude that it was false. So we never found out what happened to our dusky Wa friend, and we were left fearing the worst. Darkie's was a true Wa fate and the darkest secret of all.

❊ ❊

Postscript 2002

These days, Mae Or is much more accessible than it used to be in the late 1980s and early 90s. A good road, paved throughout, goes all the way to the border village, although it is still winding and very steep in places. Inexperienced riders, casually hiring a motorcycle in Mae Hong Son, should take great care on this road, especially coming back down, where they should remember to change down through the gears at the appropriate places (don't rely solely on the brakes). Several yellow public-transport *silor* or pick-up trucks go daily to Mae Or from the back of Mae Hong Son's main daytime market (the side facing the airport runway), returning of course from Mae Or to town the same day. It is 44 kms from the central crossroads in MHS town to Mae Or centre, and you proceed basically due north. It seems now that en route you enter or pass through 'Fish Cave and Pa Sua Waterfall National Park' – almost a case of Thai national park mania having gone over the top! On account especially of the King's palace at Pang Tong and of some associated highland royal projects, everything is pretty manicured up there these days, particularly after Huai Khan village and Pa Sua Waterfall. There are rudimentary places to stay overnight in Mae Or and also at other nearby villages. The trip to atmospheric Mae Or remains a great day trip out from Mae Hong Son, especially by hire bike. You can get Yunnanese chow there and buy local products.

Route detail: Mae Hong Son – Mae Or (Map 13)

km 0.0   Main crossroads (with traffic lights) in centre of Mae Hong Son town
         Proceed N up main street past *Siam Hotel* (R)

km 1.1   At edge of town, where bypass joins from left at traffic lights, fork
         rightish/straight (see Map 13), journeying up H1095
         Pass a turning (L) by a police box, which is one of the three ways to Sob
         Soi, Nai Soi and the principal 'long-neck' village of Mai Nai Soi
         Cross a small ridge in forest and come down to village of **Pang Mu** with its
         Shell petrol station (L), a place to tank up for the trip

km 7.7   Cross bridge over River Pai, flowing from R to L

km 9.2   Turning L for Mae Or just after km-marker 199. Go L, leaving main H1095
         road

km 9.9   After 700 m, at another junction, go R (way L is a second route – used to be
         the main way – to Nai Soi and the 'Long Necks'), and follow a cement-
         section road round the scenic valley floor, through the two rural villages of
         Kung Mai Sak and **Mae Sa Nga**, to the bigger Shan village of **Mork
         Cham Pae**

km 18.3 You pass Mork Cham Pae school (R), looping around the houses
         In village centre, go L at junction (way R goes back to H1095 and Tam Pla
         or Fish Cave)
         Proceed N past health centre (R) on long straight section of road, through
         attractive woodland

km 22.3 Reach village of **Huai Khan** with *wat* (L), school (L) and shop (R). Huai
         Khan may well be a rare Pa-O place. Great views N of massive ridge to be
         climbed en route for Mae Or and border

km 24.5 The great climb begins
         A first upgrade, then down to:

km 26.1 **Pa Sua Waterfall** (down offroad R), worth a visit with its half dozen
         chutes, scenically set

km 26.5 Sign indicating (entrance to?) 'Fish Cave and Pa Sua Waterfall National
         Park'
         Buildings (L) probably belonging to park
         Second upgrade, steep and winding

km 26.9 Dam and reservoir (R)
         Steep up again

km 30.1 T-junction. Way L goes a short distance to **Pang Tong King's Palace**,
         Pang Tong Centre, Pang Tong Royal Development Project and a Wildlife
         Sanctuary office. If you turn L, you go very steeply up to a barrier and
         checkpoint. There is an overpriced entrance charge to proceed past the
         barrier to the places just mentioned. At T-junction, go R for Napapaek and
         Mae Or
         Continue to climb third or fourth upgrade

km 33.8 View ahead of border ridge

km 35.2 'Agro-Tourism Visitor Centre' (L), a kind of showcase place connected with
         an agricultural project
         Descend to:

km 36.3 **Napapaek** village (Blue Hmong) and junction. Shops and noodle soup
         places. At junction, the way L goes to Ban Dong (Pang Ung village, I think)
         and Ruamthai village (probably the Blue Hmong place of Huai Ma Kua
         Som). A sign indicates *Ruamthai Guest House* in the latter place. Go
         R/straight for Mae Or

THREE PAGODAS

km 38.0   Track L goes to more Pang Tong Royal Reforestation and Agricultural Project offices (forestry office and agricultural cooperative office)

km 42.1   Portal and entrance to Mae Or outside village. Tea bushes L and R of road. Border mountain immediately above Mae Or visible ahead/rightish Lake (R)

T-junction. Go R, weaving your way along little streets, paved and unpaved, and through houses

km 43.9   **Mae Or** centre, big *sala*, shops and eating places

Mae Or

In ten years, Mae Or has really changed very little, remaining relatively undeveloped. Because the access road has greatly improved, because there is a regular *silor* service from Mae Hong Son town to the border village, and because the KMT Chinese outpost figures in the offerings of the tourist agencies down in MHS town, more visitors get to Mae Or these days. But they number only a steady trickle, or a few each day, and stay only for an hour, limiting themselves to the central part around the big meeting-pavilion, where they look around and perhaps eat some Chinese food. The rest of the village you can have to yourself, and before about 11am and after 4pm you can have the whole place to yourself. Some of Mae Or's houses have been upgraded, but the main change has been the advent and development meanwhile of a clutch of little restaurants and of a couple of places to stay. The 'restaurants', which variously serve noodle soup, fried rice and *chow mien* (noodles with meat and vegetables), always accompanied by China tea, are dotted around the central 'square'. As you approach the big *sala*, there are a couple on your right. The first is run by a young Wa lady, called Nang Ching, who sells noodle soup in front of her house and runs a well-stocked store beside it. Diagonally opposite her and across from a phone box is a little eating place and tea shop run by a friendly man called Huang Yun (Huang Yoon/Yuin, meaning 'Yellow Cloud'), who speaks a fair amount of English and whose menu board is written in English. At the far (eastern) end of the little square, behind the *sala*, is 'Niang Restaurant', run by Kong Mong's wife, Chang Soe.

The shops mostly sell things for the villagers, but also items and locally cultivated/manufactured produce of interest to the passing traveller. Mae Or tea is very good, most of it being oolong, and Kong Mong told me that the leaves are sun-dried, not cured in an oven as is apparently the case at Mae Salong. You can buy dried Chinese mushrooms, Muslim egg noodles (in a packet like spaghetti), and the *pakkad dong* or spicy pickled cabbage (in Chinese *yeng chi* or *yen tsai*) that I like so much, and which is served as an accompaniment to food.

Nowadays you can stay in Mae Or without having to get permission from the military and without having to resort to ruses such as camping inside the health centre, but this could be more tricky than might first appear. An alternative would be to stay at *Ruamthai Guest House*, somewhere near Napapaek (for many years there used to be a Hmong 'guest house' in Napapaek itself). In 2001, there seemed to be two places to stay in Mae Or, if you can locate the owners. Both are by the lake. To find the first, turn right (east) into a side track as you enter the village, just as you come to the lake. There are some huts on the hillside, on the south side of the lake, opposite a teacher's house, signed 'room and foods'. The second, currently signed 'Mr Sawat GH' (used to be called 'Suwan Aram'), lies across the lake, on its north side, by the water's edge. You pass the group of three or four fenced-in mud huts (right side of track) on your way to the central *sala* and 'square'. I have stayed in neither of these places. Visiting Mae Or on a couple of occasions in recent years, I once pitched my tent in front of the health centre (with the permission of the official in charge), washing inside the building, at the back. On the elevated platform before the health centre, you enjoy a marvellous

DARK SECRETS

view across the lake and village to the border mountains. No one in the military camp adjacent to the health centre took any notice of me whatsoever. And in February 2000, during Chinese New Year, I camped in the grounds of the school (NE corner of village, school closed during the festivities), and again no one objected. It is worth stopping overnight in places like Mae Or because you get a much better insight into the people and life there than on a flying one-hour visit.

There is no better time to visit a KMT outpost than at Chinese New Year. Many people, especially youngsters, who for the rest of the year are living and working away, come home. Friends and relatives even come from Taiwan. There is a lot of excitement, fun, eating and drinking, hospitality and generosity. Various kinds of sweetmeat are made and offered. In Mae Or, no chicken is safe – at every house chickens (the black ones) are sacrificed, offered to the spirits, and eaten. New red and gold mottoes are put up, and the old ones torn down. Conifer saplings are planted before the houses, and candles as well as incense lit in front of the greenery. Presents, especially of money in red envelopes, are exchanged, and pretend banknotes burnt. There is a lot of drinking, gambling, dancing and exploding firecrackers.

Here I interpose a touching new anecdote, which provides a telling insight into realities at Mae Or and all along the border between Thailand and the Shan State, Burma, even at the turn of the millennium. In mid-1999, a penniless Shan couple living in Mae Or Luang (6 kms from Mae Or, in the Shan State) came to Chinese Mae Or with a little girl of theirs, just one month old at the time. They were too poor to bring up the child, which they knew would die from poverty and malnourishment, and so wanted to sell her. Darkie's mother was interested in buying the baby, but in the end someone else – a Wa woman whose husband had died ten years previously – got the child. This woman, not least because she was caught by surprise, did not have much money to pay for the baby. But the parents, being desperate to unburden themselves, were content to accept a low price. They all agreed on a cost of 446 baht (£7.50), which, apart from the fact that 446 was a lucky number, was a nominal arbitrary amount. When I saw and photographed the baby girl in January 2000 (see photo section), she was seven months old. Her name was Supsanah (Li Guai-joen in Chinese), and she was going to be nicknamed Joen-Joen.

Behind Mae Or, there is a track that runs north, out of the village, a short distance to the border, where it passes through a col between Doi Lan (R) and another mountain (L), crosses a pass, and descends steeply five or six kms all the way to Mae Or Luang. This village, whose name means 'greater Mae Or', is the original place after which Chinese Mae Or was named. Undoubtedly, it was at first larger than the KMT outpost, but whether it still is now I do not know. Shan and hill-tribe people live there. The path to the border and Mae Or Luang is unguarded, as it has always been, and there is nothing to stop you hiking to the village. I once walked a fair way down the trail, but got no clear view into the valley or of Mae Or Luang, and gave up because I was afraid of being intercepted by Khun Sa MTA militiamen, who at the time were on Doi Lan. Also, I got some funny looks from men with laden donkeys coming the other way. Do not attempt on any account to reach Mae Or Luang. Apparently, there are always a few Burmese soldiers in the village. You might also be captured on the way by the Red Wa UWSA. And there are old minefields across the border. As indicated, the Mae Or Luang/Mae Or crossing is an important traditional gateway from the Shan State to Thailand, through which goods, drugs and people are channelled, just as they have been for some time. These days quite a few people come across to Mae Or, sometimes from deep within Burma. They look for work, friends and opportunities. If they find nothing in KMT Mae Or, they move on to Mae Hong Son town, and if they find nothing there, they continue to Chiang Mai, travelling and settling illegally. A few stop in Mae Or.

145

THREE PAGODAS

Darkie

More people have asked me about Wa girl Darkie and her fate than have asked about any other person in this book or in any of my other books. She seems to have captured the hearts and imaginations of readers like no other figure encountered. We thought that we would never see her again, but after many years we tracked her down and met her again. So here is an update of the story of Darkie, whose fate fortunately turned out to be not as grim as we had feared. In 1999, Kong Mong said that she was working in a brush factory in Chiang Mai. We located the enterprise, called Shining Star Co., in the heart of the city's night bazaar area, in the Loi Kroa Road. A huge irony or coincidence was that Shining Star, Darkie's place of work, was in a building, moreover in exactly the same rooms, that we had once stayed in for many weeks a decade earlier, at the time we had first discovered Darkie. How the strands of destinies can be strangely intertwined! It transpired that these rooms were actually the offices of the company, while the factory proper was in Fang. Shining Star made sweeping brushes, exporting them especially to Japan, and Darkie worked in the offices along with two or three other girls, generally helping out. The enterprise was owned by a daughter of Gen. Lao Li, and so this daughter of the famous KMT Third Army general was Darkie's employer and boss.

When we walked through the door, the Wa lass was surprised and very pleased to see us, and she remembered exactly who we were, even though so many years had passed meanwhile and she had been only 14 years old at the time of the first encounter. She said that she had, indeed, gone down to Bangkok in about 1993, when she had been 18, where she had worked for a year as a nanny with a Chinese family. Then she had returned to Mae Or. But she had only stayed in her home village briefly. Because she had had nothing to do there, Kong Mong had taken her to Lao Li's daughter, who had given her employment. Now she worked at Shining Star and also went to a school to learn some English, a few words of which she spoke. We asked Darkie where she lived, and she said at the compound of Lao Li, in Fah Ham district! Remarkable: 'our' Wa friend ends up in Gen. Li's residence! Here she worked as a housekeeper, and Lao Li's daughter was again her boss. She had two jobs, helping out both at the brush factory and at Lao Li's place, where she cooked, cleaned and looked after the ancient senile general himself, one of the very few people who were allowed into his sickroom. For all this, she earned a bit more than 2000 baht per month (less than £50), although her board and accommodation were free.

We saw Darkie again in 2000 and 2001, in the former year taking her back to Mae Or, which she visited only rarely, and even staying with her in her mother's house. We gleaned some further information about the dusky beauty. Her Wa father died when she was eight years old, and she had a treasured photo of him. This father was her mother's first husband, by whom the mother (a very small, round, jovial, Chinese lady) had three children, including Darkie. The mother then remarried, her second husband being a Chinaman, by whom she had two more children. This man, Darkie's step-father, now lives not in Mae Or, but in another KMT village, Mai Nong Bua (Xing Shoon), which is near Nong Ook, and where he looks after lychee orchards. Because the mother had five children to bring up alone, Darkie was partly raised by Kong Mong's wife, Chang Soe. When we were in Mae Or with Darkie, we noticed how even now she quasi referred to Chang Soe as 'Mother', helping herself without asking to food out of that lady's larder as if it belonged to her real mother. Darkie is the oldest of her mother's five children. A younger sister of hers, who works in Mae Hong Son town, is married with a baby boy, who is looked after not by his young mother, who almost never sees her child, but by Darkie's mother up in Mae Or. Darkie has a brother in Chonburi and a second wild-looking brother, aged 20 in 2000, who resembles her, and who works with her in Lao Li's compound.

A decade on, the house that we had originally found Darkie and her mother living in – a ramshackle hut of wood, bamboo and grass – had just been rebuilt with breeze-blocks and tin roofing. The new dwelling, still simple and spartan, cost 55,000 baht (less than £1,000 at the time of writing), but the kitchen remained to be renovated, for which the mother needed a further 10,000 baht, and the house still had no toilet or washroom of its own, meaning that the mother, the sister's baby, Darkie, we and anybody else had to go to a neighbouring house for ablutions.

Meanwhile, of course, the Wa girl had grown up. In 1999 and in the years following, we found not the shy urchin-like 14-year-old schoolgirl of yore, but a self-possessed, confident, forthcoming and very nubile young woman in her mid-twenties (see photo section). Here was a friendly, winning, spontaneous, proactive, fun-loving, alert, vital and tactile girl, nicely turned out, with a stylish short haircut, in a fetching blouse and tight white jeans, and with curves in all the right places – quite the author's muse! All the more surprising, therefore, that in 2001, at the age of 26, Darkie was still not married, had no children, and seemed even to have no boyfriend. "She's a dark horse, unpredictable, not like the others", her mother said; "she won't be married before 30, for sure." All the more surprising, too, that, as a grown-up, independent woman-of-the-world, she was – the more we looked into her situation – to all intents and purposes a slave and prisoner of the KMT 'mafia' in Lao Li's compound. Along with four or five other girls, she worked long hours every day for very little money. On the one evening, she could not come out to eat with us because as part of her duties she had to go and sit through the night at someone's bedside in hospital, and on another she had to stay in and serve some KMT friends of Lao Li. When she could go out, she had to be back by 9pm, i.e. was effectively gated like a little girl every day, "because at that time the guard dogs are let loose in the compound, and no one can come or go anymore". But this was a girl who at her age should be out going places, doing things, clubbing, being with boyfriends and having fun. This, then, was the new dark fate of our Wa friend. We asked her how she saw her future unfolding, and she said resignedly that she expected she would work a few more years down in Chiang Mai or wherever, and then return to Mae Or – there was nowhere else to go. Alternatively, she might go or be sent to Taiwan, which could easily happen, as many 'Thai' KMT and Wa do go there. And this, then, was the dark fate that probably lay in store for dusky Wa girl Darkie.

Maha San & Kong Mong

Around 1998, Maha San moved from his house in the centre of Chiang Mai, near the Ta Pae Road, to a new place on the outskirts of the city. Rather incongruously for the leader of a rebel pocket army or even for a Wa princeling from Ming Noen, he took up residence in a very suburban house on an estate near the start of the highway for Chiang Rai. But he still visits Mae Or, usually about twice a month. In 2001, he was spending more time up there. Because the political situation opposite the KMT village, in Burma, had radically changed and was still changing, and because the Wa star was in the ascendant, there was more for him to do. The Wa National Army, he said, was about a day's walk from Mae Or. But I think Maha San did not so much go to see his troops in the field as direct things from Mae Or. When not eating in Kong Mong's house, he was to be found in the WNO house near the entrance to the village and close to the lake, surrounded by his entourage of WNO/WNA officials and secretaries.

Meanwhile Kong Mong's position had completely changed. I saw him in January 1999, and he looked older and thinner (see photo section), and had taken to resting during the day. Over many glasses of tea, he told me that he was not much active with the WNA now, but grew tea and had eight pigs. He had tried to grow lychees and peaches, but had failed because cattle wandering around the village ate the trees and fruit. "I don't sit around all day drinking tea and talking, you know", the smiling rogue said unconvincingly. At Chinese New Year 2000, I found Kong Mong very frail. He was suffering from a liver complaint, which recurrently made him ill, after which he got better again, although each time he had a relapse the illness grew worse, latterly necessitating stays in Mae Hong Son hospital. To try to put matters right once and for all, he had gone to Mae Sot for a useless course of treatment with traditional herbal remedies. This had caused him to start wasting away and become seriously ill. He had gone into a coma, after which he had been transferred to a hospital in Chiang Mai, where conventional medicine had saved him. Kong Mong's problem derives from too much whisky drinking and smoking earlier in his life.

I know that for some reason or other Kong Mong has always liked me, seeming almost to adopt me as a son. At Chinese New Year 2000, he invited me into his house to eat with him, just the two of us alone. Special dishes, cooked by Chang Soe, were served, and he encouraged me to eat, gently putting choice morsels on my plate, while hardly eating himself. I did not know it at the time, but in retrospect I can see that this was something of a last supper together, for a year later things had taken a significant turn for the worse. In early January 2001, Doug and I returned to Mae Or, where we found that Kong Mong and Chang Soe had moved to a new and much more substantial house behind *Niang Restaurant*, south of the school. At the house, we found Kong Mong's aged mother, Ye Lu ('Ama'), from Taiwan (she looked just like Kong Mong), but there was no sign either of Kong Mong or his wife. Upon asking, we learned, alarmingly, that Kong Mong was in Mae Hong Son hospital's intensive care unit, suffering from liver failure. Aborting our visit to Mae Or, we went straight there.

In a corridor outside Kong Mong's ICU room, which he shared with three other critically ill men, we found Chang Soe, her and Kong Mong's children, and some other relatives. They were camping there with blankets and food in the way that relatives do in Thai hospitals. We asked if we could visit Kong Mong, which was possible if we waited. While we were all waiting, Chang Soe said that the present relapse was by far the worst of all the crises Kong Mong had had, and she was very pessimistic. Finally, we were allowed to his bedside, where we found a shocking spectacle. All over his body – a dark-skinned body that looked surprisingly young and fit – wires and tubes were going in and coming out. There was a big ventilator tube in his mouth, a small tube in his nose, drips going into his arms and legs, wires connected from his chest to a heartbeat monitor showing 120/minute, a urine tube, and so on. Kong Mong was breathing violently, as if gasping for breath, and beads of perspiration stood out on his forehead. In that hot quiet room, he was completely oblivious to us, preoccupied with unsuccessfully fighting the last battle for his life. I subsequently discovered that he died a few days after our visit, at Mae Or, in that same January 2001. It was a strange sad end far from his birthplace for a WNA major, a *sawbwa*'s son, and a man from the Wa sub-state.

✻

The Wa and recent politico-military developments at Mae Or, along the Shan-Thai border, in the Shan State, and in the 'Golden Triangle'
We already know from our account in Chapter 3 of warlord Khun Sa and his Mong Tai Army how events stood with the Wa, especially the 'Red' Wa and their United Wa State Army, until the mid-1990s. In 1985, Sa was the uncontested opium king of the

'Golden Triangle' and controlled virtually all of the Shan-Thai frontier, from Takilek opposite Mae Sai in the north-east to Mae Or in the south-west. He had drugs refineries opposite Hua Mae Kham (near his old GHQ of Hin Taek), he had a base on the Doi Larng ridge (opposite Mae Ai), where other refineries operated, he was in control opposite Nong Ook, Kae Noi and Piang Luang, his new GHQ was at Ho Mong (also known as Mong Mai, located 30 kms north of Mae Hong Son town and a good day's walk north-east from Mae Or Luang and Mae Or), and he had a post on Doi Lan, right next to Mae Or. The Wa, by contrast, controlled small pockets opposite Santisuk (also known as Li Ching, north-east of Taton, Santisuk being the HQ of Ai Siao-su's WNC), on the Doi Larng ridge, near Doi Ang Karng, and opposite Mae Or, where Maha San's WNA was stationed.

But five years later, as we recall, the balance shifted considerably. Ai Siao-su's WNC pocket army was substantially reinforced with a contingent of 1,500 Wa ex-CPB regulars who had come down from the liberated Wa sub-state, the two forces combining to form in late 1989 the new UWSA. Wanting more of the drugs and trafficking action, the UWSA muscled in on Khun Sa's scene, in 1989, 1990 and 1991 causing the old Opium War of 1967 to flare up again, this time not between Sa and the KMT, but between Sa and the Wa. Khun Sa had managed to dislodge the Wa from Doi Larng, but now the UWSA managed to recapture the south-westerly Doi Laem half of Khun Sa's strategic Doi Larng ridge. They made other inroads into his empire, too, for example forcing Sa largely to abandon his Mae Or base, and altogether compromised his power and control along the border.

Between 1991 and 1995, Khun Sa's power and control was further checked, and by default that of the Wa grew. His MTA was rocked by dissension and schism. In early 1995, Gun Yord, a former close aide to Sa, broke away from the MTA with some 1,000 militiamen to form the Shan State National Army.[5] And Sa was under pressure on two fronts, from the Burmese as well as the Wa. In the winters of 1993-94 and 1994-95, the junta launched two offensives against the Shan warlord. The Red Wa had been in a pact with Rangoon since 1989, and the two unlikely bedfellows were increasingly cooperating. Not only were Sa's two principal enemies struggling against him, but they were in alliance with one another, with the result that the Wa did not have to waste effort fighting against the Burmese, and that their strength was all the more enhanced vis-à-vis the MTA. In early 1993, the UWSA was particularly strong on Doi Laem (near Doi Ang Karng), and claimed to have 35,000 toops at its disposal, of which 6,000 operated along the Shan-Thai border.

But it was in early 1996 that the balance tipped decisively and dramatically in favour of the Wa, when Khun Sa capitulated to Rangoon, signed over what was left of his MTA to the Burma army, and allowed the *tatmadaw* to take over his Ho Mong GHQ as well as many other positions. With the demise of Sa and the MTA, obviously their power and control of the Shan-Thai border ended. Suddenly the 'Golden Triangle' looked very different, and a new era was ushered in. Now the main players were the Burmese, especially their associates the Wa (mainly the UWSA), and some minor Shan factions such as the SSNA and SSA. Post-Khun Sa, a politico-military vacuum was left in the Shan State and the 'Golden Triangle', which in the next five or six years, up to 2002 and the time of writing, the Wa increasingly filled.

---

[5] In January 1996, at the time of Khun Sa's subsequent accommodation with Rangoon, another 500 MTA troops, dissatisfied with his 'sell-out', defected to Gun Yord's SSNA. And in February 1996, a further 1,500 MTA soldiers refused to go with Sa into the arms of the Burmese, moved from Ho Mong to positions at Piang Luang, Hua Mae Kham and Ah Long (Mae Fah Luang district), and likewise apparently teamed up with Major Gun Yord, whose breakaway faction now numbered reportedly 4,000-5,000.

THREE PAGODAS

At first, the Wa were not able to profit greatly from the realignment. This was because the Burmese themselves mostly stepped into Khun Sa's former positions. They took over Ho Mong and installed themselves on Doi Larng, as we know; they inherited Doi Saeng (near Mae Hong Son) and the border crossing at Piang Luang; they had positions at Nor Lae (near Doi Ang Karng) and behind Doi Pahom Pok; and they camped on mountaintops, e.g. opposite Muang Na. Some of these positions the Burma army still holds today. An upshot of this replacement of Khun Sa by the *tatmadaw* was the start of an exodus of Shan people from the Shan State to Thailand (more below). In February 1996, for instance, following the junta's takeover of Ho Mong, some 200 Shan civilians (mostly women, children and the elderly) fled across the border to escape harsh treatment by Burmese troops. They brought stories utterly in keeping with the *tatmadaw*'s brutal record that their men had been forced to work as porters and their women raped. At the same time, the Shan inhabitants of the nearby villages of Mai Huo Ha and Mae Or Luang sought refuge in Mae Or, settling about 300 metres from the KMT outpost.

The Burmese takeover of Sa's former positions caused rancour among the Wa. The UWSA had been fighting against the MTA for these facilities, and rightly or wrongly had hoped or expected to get them. The 'Red' Wa had been the first of all Burma's ethnic rebel groups to sign a ceasefire with the SLORC, back in 1989, had generally cooperated since that time with Rangoon, had helped the Burma army in its two-year offensive (1993-95) against Khun Sa, providing food and ammunition and taking heavy casualties in the campaign, had themselves made steady progress against the MTA since mid-1995, had told the SLORC of the UWSA's planned offensive against Sa at the end of 1995, and had apparently been promised by Rangoon mortar rounds and access to government-held roads with which to attack the MTA. But now they felt cheated by Rangoon, outmanoeuvred in its deal with Khun Sa, and denied the fruits of victory that they held to be theirs.

There was talk of the UWSA abandoning its ceasefire agreement with the Burmese, something the Wa could do almost with impunity, because they had grown strong meanwhile, and were to grow immensely stronger in the following years (1996-2002). Altogether, the Wa were becoming and now constitute a time bomb for Rangoon. Although many Wa drugs went into Thailand, much trafficking was also done through China. The 'Red' Wa had close ties with corrupt Chinese officials and could easily source weapons from China through these contacts and with their drug wealth. Further, many Wa still harboured a long-standing hatred of the Burma army, based on a traditional animosity between the Wa and the lowland Burmese. All these things remain true today. The Wa had and have sufficient weapons and manpower for a renewed war with Rangoon for control of the 'Golden Triangle' area.

Probably for these reasons, the junta allowed the Wa to occupy more and more territory along the border and to take over the former Khun Sa positions that it had inherited, at the same time increasingly climbing into bed with the Wa. The Burma army delegated much military responsibility to the UWSA, almost allowing the latter to conduct proxy operations against the SSA and SSNA, MTA remnants, the Thais and others. The UWSA took over Sa's positions and drug refineries opposite Hua Mae Kham, where in early 2000 it was reported to be building a new town. By the end of 2000, it seems largely to have taken over positions opposite Nong Ook, Kae Noi, Wiang Haeng and Piang Luang, relieving the Burma army. At the same time, UWSA soldiers took up positions opposite Mae Fah Luang and Pang Ma Pa districts, likewise replacing Burmese troops. Opposite Wiang Haeng, they were garrisoned at Pang Sua Tao village, 2 kms from the border, and opposite Pang Ma Pa on Doi Daeng. The UWSA occupied the whole of the Doi Larng ridge and the narcotics-producing facilities there. Next to Doi Larng, at Mong Yon (opposite San Ton Du village, above

DARK SECRETS

Mae Ai town), Wei-Siao-gang[6], the new leader of the UWSA, began building another new town, which was to be the 'Red' Wa's permanent base, and in October 2000 Khin Nyunt, Burma's intelligence chief, met Wei in Takilek to view the new military HQ. In early 2000, there were newspaper reports that the UWSA was constructing a further whole new town roughly opposite Ai Siao-su's village of Santisuk, although this could be the same as Mong Yon or perhaps the new town opposite Hua Mae Kham. And at the same time news came that the 'Red' Wa had been given control by the Burmese of half of Takilek (opposite Mae Sai). Here, behind Takilek, they were building yet another whole new Wa town, even employing Thai architects, doctors, teachers and other skilled people, who, it could be read, were having problems with their work conditions, finding themselves unable to return to Thailand!

Opposite Mae Or, Maha Ja (the 'younger brother' of Maha San and Kong Mong), who had for some time sided with Khun Sa, commanding the MTA camp just across from Mae Or, switched post-1996 to the WNA, whose control of territory opposite Mae Or increased. Under some agreement, Khun Sa's former GHQ at Ho Mong went from Burmese control to being run by theWNA, with Col. Maha Ja as the town's ruler. But by late 2000 tension was rising in Ho Mong because a detachment of 800 UWSA troops had arrived, sent by Rangoon to 'secure' the town and other nearby border places. As far as I can understand, the UWSA may now be in control of Ho Mong, and Maha Ja may have switched again from the WNA to the 'Red' Wa. Nevertheless, the WNA still controls areas opposite Mae Or, and perhaps Maha Ja remains with Maha San's force. All this makes little difference anyway because, after all, the WNA and the UWSA are just different arms of the same group of people.

By 2002, therefore, the UWSA and to a very limited extent the WNA were all along the Shan-Thai border, exactly as their arch-rival Khun Sa and his MTA had once been. The Wa controlled the Wa sub-state and, except for pockets controlled by Shan factions, controlled much of the Shan State both with the Burmese and under their patronage. They have now become very powerful and may have up to 100,000 troops. Where the UWSA is, so also are drugs production and trafficking. With the tacit approval and probable involvement of the Burmese junta, these activities, too, have now become very big with the Wa. The UWSA is one of the world's great drug cartels, and its leader Wei Siao-gang along with his brother(s) is the new uncontested opium king of the 'Golden Triangle' and the area's most powerful warlord. Just opposite Wiang Haeng, in the highly productive districts of Mong Pan, Mong Ta and Mong Ton, opium is grown everywhere, and the resulting drugs pass in quantity through Piang Luang and also across the border into nearby Pang Ma Pa. A few years ago, UWSA factories at Doi Larng and Hua Mae Kham were said to be producing at least 140 kgs of heroin a month. The border area opposite Mae Fah Luang district is also currently regarded as a major exit point for Wa drugs destined for Thailand. Lately, the production of heroin has been either partly replaced by or supplemented with the manufacture of metamphetamines ('speed' pills, Ecstasy etc.), and these are swamping Thailand by the million. A report in 2000 estimated that the production of 200 million

---

[6] The UWSA's long-time commander Ai Siao-su retired some time in the early 1990s (for an account of him, of his 'warlordess' wife Li Ching, and of recent Wa history seen from their perspective, the reader is referred to Chapter 6 of my cultural guidebook *Around Lan-Na*) and was replaced by Tei Kung-ming, who was murdered in China in 1996. He, in turn, was replaced by Wei Siao-gang (Wei Hsueh-kang) and his brother Wei Siao-long (there is said to be a third brother, Wei Siao-yin), who are the current powerful and notorious leaders of the UWSA. Both were bitter long-time rivals of Khun Sa in the 'Golden Triangle' drugs trade, and Wei Siao-gang is wanted by the Americans to face drug-trafficking charges in the US. The brothers live at Mong Yon.

amphetamine pills in 1999, of which only 40 million were seized, would rise to 250 million in 2000, and that there were about 50 UWSA narcotics factories on the border opposite Chiang Mai and Chiang Rai provinces alone. A year later, in 2001, this estimate had been upwardly revised from a production of 400 million amphetamine pills in 2000, of which only 25 million were seized, to 600 million in 2001, with some 100 small drugs factories in the same area. The flood of drugs into Thailand, with its impact on the country's users, is becoming so great that the authorities are talking of a grave threat to national security. Believing that the problem has reached a critical level, they are considering setting up a special military force to pursue traffickers in the border areas and to launch surgical strikes on the factories to root out the problem. A Thai-Burmese border situation that is already tense in many places and in many respects would then become even more fraught, with the prospect of a new Opium War, this time between Thailand and the Wa and/or the Burmese.

The pre-eminence in the Shan State of the Wa and of their Burmese mentors has serious implications for the Shan, first in terms of dealings with the Shan nationalist factions, and second in terms of displacement of the Shan population. For now that the UWSA and the Burmese no longer have to contend with Khun Sa, and given that the Burmese have largely routed the Karen rebel KNLA further down the border, they are free to pay more attention to the Shan outfits. As far as I can make out, in recent years there have been four or five such factions in various places and at various times, all broadly under the umbrella of the Shan State Army. There has been the SSA itself, led by Col. Yod Suek (Suk/Sook), who in 1998 was chairman of the Revolution Council of Shan State, and whose base is primarily opposite Pang Ma Pa district (Mae Hong Son province), close to Piang Luang. The nationalist SSA seems to have had a strict anti-drugs policy, combating narcotics and destroying UWSA drug-prodiction facilities. There has been Maj. Gun Yord's SSNA, mainly based opposite Mae Fah Luang district, i.e. in places across the border between Taton and Mae Sai. Troops under another commander, Chao Gong Juen, have also been opposite Mae Fah Luang. And there have been Shan factions led by Jai Nong and Loen Hoeng. These other outfits seem to have been less anti-drugs.

Over the years, these Shan nationalist anti-Rangoon militias have harassed the Burma army, and especially during 1999 and 2000 they strongly disrupted drug trafficking. In March 1998, they moved against the junta opposite Chiang Mai and Mae Hong Son provinces, and sought to seize Ho Mong back from the Burmese, precipitating fighting. In an action that heralded ominous future developments, the Burmese had been trying to push minorities in ten local villages to other areas. This and the fighting caused 400 ethnic refugees to flee over the border to Thailand's Pang Ma Pa district. In November 2000, Shan rebels destroyed an amphetamine warehouse, arrested six Lahu volunteers and Burmese soldiers, and seized weapons as well as 200,000 speed pills. The Burmese, believing that the Thai army was responsible, retaliated in a clash that left two Thai soldiers wounded and one Burmese soldier dead. And in December of the same year, Chao Gong Juen, who had regularly skirmished with Burmese and UWSA forces, raided the Lahu border village of Ah-bi, with all his actions embarrassing the Burma army's area commander Maj. Myo Chit.

The Burma army and the UWSA teamed up to counter the SSA, SSNA and the other Shan rebel groups, and take over their territory. Late November 2000, Wei Siao-gang, backed by Rangoon, sent five of his UWSA battalions or 1,500 troops from his Mong Yon HQ to the area opposite Pang Ma Pa under SSA control, to wrest it from Yod Suek, silence his force, and control the opium fields and trafficking. Earlier in the same year, several hundred Burma army troops were deployed in anti-SS(N)A actions opposite Mae Fah Luang. And in February 2001, Rangoon sent an additional 1,000 soldiers to the same area in preparation for more attacks, while a further 1,000 junta

DARK SECRETS

troops as well as 500 UWSA men settled opposite Fang (Doi Ang Karng area) and Mae Ai (Doi Larng area) for more actions against the Shan rebels.

One of these operations against Shan forces blew up into a serious frontier incident between Burma and Thailand. It happened on the border, opposite Mae Fah Luang district (Chiang Rai province), near the village of Pang Noon. The Burma army had wanted to capture a Chao Gong Juen Shan rebel base close to Pang Noon, which had been impeding drugs trafficking. But to do so, it needed to intrude onto Thai soil and make use of a Thai army forward position at Pang Noon and located about 500 m inside Thailand, where some 20 BPP soldiers were stationed. The Burmese asked permission to use the position as a rear base for their assault, but this was refused. Believing that the Thais were providing assistance to the Shan soldiers, the Burmese, whose force in the operation overall numbered several hundreds, captured the Thai Pang Noon base around 8-9 February 2001. The Thai BPP soldiers managed to escape unharmed. On 10 February, the Thai army heavily shelled the outpost, killing some 50-80 Burmese troops. In a secondary action, which escalated the incident and which was widely seen as retaliation for the Pang Noon shelling, Burmese soldiers posted on high ground in Mae Sai district, at Wat Pratat Jong Kham (a temple area claimed both by the Burmese and Thais), launched a surprise attack on Thai troops deployed nearby. During the action, mortar rounds landed and exploded in busy touristic Mae Sai, and rifle fire also hit the town. Two Thai civilians were killed, 7 others wounded, and 9 Thai soldiers also injured. Reportedly, a million bahts' worth of damage was caused to a temple, a school, government installations, a shophouse and a tourist's car. Local people were evacuated temporarily, armoured cars were deployed in Mae Sai and its main street, and the border crossing between Mae Sai and Takilek was closed, as were many other border checkpoints in Chiang Mai and Chiang Rai provinces, to prevent supplies reaching Burmese troops. At the customs checkpoint in Chiang Saen, for example, no petrol, rice, medicines, cars or motorcycles were allowed across, and in Takilek the prices of daily necessities soared.

Such offensives, actions and incidents characterize the current picture of Burma army/UWSA dealings with the SSA/SSNA, and vice versa. They also illustrate the current wider situation down the Shan-Thai border, which after some years of relative lull is becoming 'hot' again, and getting hotter. And what of the future for the Shan rebel factions? Against the pre-eminent might of the Burmese and the Wa, they would seem to be boxed into a corner in the Shan State. They may hold talks with the Wa, or they may be ousted by the Wa altogether. In the light of a typical recent rift among the factions, the latter possibility seems more likely. In late January 2000, Yod Suek pulled his SSA out of the alliance with the other groups, saying that his faction was the only one serious about combating drugs and pursuing Shan nationalist aspirations, whereas Gun Yord's and Jai Nong's militias were not, a stance that would hardly further their joint political cause. And so the incredibly tortuous story of Shan narco-politics goes on.

The other implication in the Shan State of the pre-eminence of the Wa and their Burmese accomplices for the Shan concerns the displacement of the Shan population. As more and more Wa people move down into the Shan State and to the Thai border, increasing numbers of Shan are voluntarily migrating into Thailand, to the land of their Tai cousins, or are being forced out of their traditional territory to elsewhere, including Thailand. With the complicity of Rangoon, the Wa are relocating or being resettled to the Shan State and the border region so as to consolidate the Wa presence, power, activity and success there. Thus, in early 2000, reports spoke of 500-600 Wa families making their way down from the Wa sub-state to inhabit one or more of the new Wa 'towns' being built at Mong Yon, opposite Hua Mae Kham, near Santisuk, and behind Takilek. In December of the same year, Thai newspapers reported the

153

southbound migration from Pang Sang and the Wa homeland of some 200,000 Wa people – a figure that is probably exaggerated. And in early 2001, it was said that 10,000 Wa people were being relocated to the Thai-Burmese border areas to boost opium and amphetamine production, a migration that was apparently intensified by the forced resettlement by the Burmese government of Wa people to Mong Hsat (opposite Fang and Mae Ai districts) – sinister developments indeed. Shan migration into Thailand (Chiang Mai and Mae Hong Son provinces) has, actually, already been going on for several years, and has mainly been of an economic nature. But the new movement is of another order and more for political reasons. An estimate in February 2001 put the number of Shan who had already crossed at 300,000, with a further 120,000 expected to arrive during 2001, making this unchecked influx as a result of the power transition in the Shan State one of the greatest mass movements of people in South-East Asian history. Talks on the issue had already started with the United Nations High Commissioner for Refugees.

The prospect along the Shan-Thai border is hardly promising. Attempts by Thailand to defend itself against the Wa flood of drugs by neutralizing traffickers and production sources could draw the country into hostilities with the UWSA and/or Burma. As the kingdom gets swamped by Shan and other refugees from the Shan State as a result of Wa and Burmese machinations or, worse, ethnic cleansing (another dark secret) – an inundation that comes on top of the huge recent influx of Karen refugees – it could again get drawn into some kind of showdown with the Burmese. The Wa's massive upgrading of drugs involvement plus the substantial movement of their people would seem to indicate some grand design either on the part of the UWSA or on the part of the 'Red' Wa with the Burmese, as if the Burmese wanted to transform the Shan State and the Wa intended to enlarge their homeland. Meanwhile, the Wa are becoming so powerful that it is doubtful that the Burmese, should their understanding with the UWSA fall to pieces, could control the dubious 'Red' Wa. The Wa probably know this and feel that they have got one over on the Burmese, their traditional enemy. With the Wa, Rangoon is certainly playing with fire, and the result of its cosying up to them could be that the time bomb of the Wa ultimately explodes in the junta's face. The Wa sub-state and the Shan State might be the scene of a regional conflagration as the Burmese go to war with the Wa.

7

THE DRAGON & THE WIND

THE 'LONG-NECK' PADAUNG & 'LONG-EAR' KAYAW

Mai Nai Soi

Returning to Mae Hong Son from Mae Or, we stopped off at the Border Patrol Police base in Pang Mu, where two soldier friends of ours were stationed. These were the pair who had been injured in the landmine explosion up near the border. It was in their camp that we first heard about the presence of 'Long-Neck' or 'Giraffe' people in the Mae Hong Son area. The incapacitated *dorchodor* and their chums thought that three 'Long-Neck' women were living clandestinely somewhere in Pang Mu. But it must have been just a rumour, because an intensive search for them turned up nothing.

The 'Long Necks' are Padaung people from the Karenni ('Kayah') State in Burma. They are a minority sub-group of the Karenni or 'Kayah' peoples, who in turn are sometimes subsumed as Red Karen under the overall Karen or Karennic race. The Padaung are celebrated because some of their women wear polished bronze rings to elongate their necks. Normally, these Karenni could not be seen anywhere except deep in Burma, but on account of the Burma army campaigns against the many ethnic insurgencies in the country during the late 1980s and early 90s, a few had fled to the Thai border to live in the outermost reaches of Mae Hong Son province. Because these Padaung were refugees, they would return sooner or later to their homeland in the hills north-west of Loi Kaw, or so it was thought.

The obvious intrinsic interest of the 'Long Necks', combined with the fact that they might be only temporarily accessible, made us all the more anxious to try to track them down. We continued our enquiries in Mae Hong Son town, and here all roads seemed to lead to a company called 'Singha Tour'. Evidently this outfit had the 'Long-Neck' junket all sewn up, to the extent even of being in cahoots with the Karenni Army (KNPP) guerrillas who controlled the far side of the border and 'minded' the Padaung refugees. We learned from *Singha* that 'Long Necks' could actually be seen in two places. One group, the one more regularly visited, was located south-west of *ampoe muang* at a place called Nam Pieng Din. Reaching them involved a river trip and apparently crossing over into the Karenni State. The other group lay north-west of Mae Hong Son at the village of Mai Nai Soi (= new Nai Soi), also known as Nupa-ah. This second village could be reached with difficulty by 4WD vehicle or motorbike, and lay a couple of kms just inside the Thai border.

THREE PAGODAS

Singha Tour could take us to "see the 'Long Necks'" at Mai Nai Soi for 600 baht each. This seemed a whopping amount for a couple of hours with some colourful people, located, by all accounts, not so far from Mae Hong Son. So we politely declined and determined to try to reach the refugees on our own. In fairness to *Singha*, half the fee went to buying off the Karenni Army, a toll that the freelancer could not avoid either. Also, the way to Mai Nai Soi proved so poor that the tour agency really earned their money.

Knowing now the name of the 'Long-Neck' village, there remained only the problem of finding out how to get to it. In the office of the tour company, we noticed a rough map drawn on the wall. Making a mental note of it, we later checked it against a military map at Pang Mu BPP base. The 24-km run began by heading out north from Mae Hong Son on Highway 1095 (Map 13), just as we had started for Mae Or (a new shorter route is described in the Postscript below). Three or fours kms out of town, after passing a roadside reclining Buddha, the route then turned left at a police box. Now a gravelly dirt road wound through woods and banana groves, passing the Shan village of **Tungkong Mu** with its school, until it surprisingly reached a 200-metre-long suspension bridge. This slender footbridge over the valley of the River Pai was just wide enough for a motorcycle. Beneath the bridge, there seemed to be a ford, but in late December it looked to us too deep for conventional vehicles. We saw men standing knee-deep in swirling water sorting boulders and sand, probably for building purposes. Four-wheel vehicles avoided the ford by taking an alternative, longer, more northerly route, initially linked with the way to Mae Or (Map 13).

After the scenic suspension bridge, the track narrowed to a woodland path, but soon it rejoined a metalled way (Map 14). The Shan village of **Sob Soi** came next, with its new-looking Burmese-style temple, after which we turned left or roughly south-west, joining the way that four-wheel vehicles used to access Mai Nai Soi. Most of the rest of the route (Map 15), which headed west and then north-west, followed a horribly dusty road, with some steep gradients. The trail curved round the mountainside in the company of the Pai river (left side of road). In the morning sun, the pale yellow powdery road surface ran out blindingly bright before our front wheel. The vegetation on either side had become coated with this lemon dust, giving it the same weird frozen lunar quality we had seen on the way to Mae Or. We soon discovered why – empty logging lorries thundered along here heading for the border to reload. When they came, they raised an indescribable dust cloud, so thick that we were reduced to a fumbling crawl. But never mind, the particles soon settled, and then the morning sun shone with renewed splendour on the lush welcoming countryside. It was fine biking along here. The MTX was behaving itself, and we, without a care in the world, felt glad to be alive.

Nai Soi, the Shan village before Mai Nai Soi, was a fair-sized place. Some of its inhabitants had distinctly Burmese, dark-skinned faces. They wore *longyis* and had cheeks daubed with *tanaka*. The houses were typical of those in a 'model village'. Their entrances had wooden portals, each bearing a sign, inscribed white on blue, citing the names of the relevant family members together with a line or two of sententious sugary poetry. A Shan-style *wat* in the village passed us on the left, and on the way out of Nai Soi we were surprised to find an inviting-looking eating place. More remarkable still, its menu board, hung out in front, was in English. Our greed got the better of us, and we dismounted for a 20-baht mid-morning lunch of chicken with ginger and green peppers, accompanied by rice and a bowl of bouillon, all freshly cooked. But it was fortunate we stopped because the food situation in the 'Long-Neck' village turned out to be poor.

After Nai Soi our troubles began. A river had to be forded four times. The water was not so deep, between six and twelve inches, but the stones on the bed were round and slippery. The shallowest places skirted weirs, making it a delicate manoeuvre to thread a way through the shallows, but without wobbling over the weirs. Of course, at the fords there were lots of people, especially children, watching riders get their shoes wet and occasionally tumble with their bikes into the river. The trials of the fords were followed by the tribulations of the forest path. A narrow steep-sided track cut through cool damp jungle. By turns muddy and gravelly, the path included for good measure some testing upgrades. Along here, just in front of us, two adult elephants suddenly lumbered out of the trees, together with a mahout – a sure sign that we were in Karen or Karenni territory. At intervals, suspicious-looking individuals dotted the trail, seemingly up to no good. And altogether this bumpy ride became increasingly scary. The final test was a treacherous boghole. It could not be avoided, as the sides of the path were too steep. So the choice was either to pick a way along the rim of the slimy hole, pushing the bike as we went, or to boldly ride straight through it. With relief, we emerged into a clearing and spotted the entrance to the 'Long-Neck' village.

❖

Mai Nai Soi (Nupa-ah)

There were, in fact, two sets of houses at Mai Nai Soi. The first was the Padaung settlement, but behind it, well hidden one km along a jungle trail, lay an extensive new Karenni refugee camp, complete with school and field hospital. While the 'exotic' 'Long Necks' were in danger of being overexposed, with photos of the same two or three women appearing ever more frequently in the press and travel brochures, the 'ordinary' Karenni of the refugee camp behind were conveniently kept out of sight. The entrance to the village was a short 'street', with a row of bamboo huts on each side. Two of these were rudimentary shops, selling water, drinks, Mekhong whisky, instant noodles, biscuits and so on. Another was the home of so-called 'Miss Silver', and a fourth was a guardbox/reception point belonging to the Karenni Army (KA/KNPP).

As we drew up, Miss Silver appeared from her hut to intercept us. This Shan lady acted as an interface between the Padaung and visitors, and she straightaway escorted us to the army box. There a couple of Karenni soldiers, vaguely dressed in fatigue uniform, demanded the 300-baht entrance fee *Singha Tour* had told us about. We argued with the guards about this. The charge was a lot even by Western standards, and extortionate for Thai or Karenni circumstances. But apparently there were no exceptions to the toll, although by mentioning *Singha Tour* we did exact a 50-baht discount. The fee was all the more galling when we discovered that Thais were able to enter the village free. It was small consolation for such blatant racial discrimination that part of the money apparently went to supporting the Padaung village, while another part went to the school and hospital behind. No doubt the major portion flowed to the war chest of the anti-SLORC Karenni insurgents.

Miss Silver came from Burma and at the time of our visit had been living in Mai Nai Soi for a year. She was 45, divorced and had four children. A son was at school in Chiang Mai, one daughter was with her, and two other children were in Burma. We never found out what her real profession was, but she may have been a teacher. A sharp businesswoman, Miss Silver was cheerful, obliging, informative and likeable. With her squint eye, she mixed a certain coyness into her forthrightness. In the village, she was a lifeline for visitors because she was the only person to speak some English (although very little Thai), whereas the Padaung spoke neither English nor Thai. The Shan lady took us in hand and showed us round the village.

The Padaung settlement consisted of 15 families and some 20 houses, and had been in existence for three years. The village was located in a narrow valley, out of which three or four hills rose steeply on all sides. Most of the houses were sited on one favourable hillside, but others stood on the valley floor. Nupa-ah, to use its Kayan name, lay deep in jungle. All around, thin silvery trees shot straight-as-a-die to an immense height. Even among the dwellings, numerous trees had been left standing, providing shade. The houses were made of bamboo with grass and leaf roofs, and nearly all were raised off the ground on stilts. Some were quite large. At first sight it was an idyllic scene here. It was peaceful and cool, green and shady. A stream trickled through the village, and smoke drifted up from fires both inside the huts and out. Fertile vegetable patches and pig pens were dotted around. Chickens scratched and fluttered, and children played marbles in the dust. Closer inspection, however, revealed that the camp was already quite polluted. Plastic bags and bottles, Coke cans and other rubbish lay everywhere, even in the stream. These did not come from visitors, but from the Padaung themselves. Accustomed to banana-leaf wrappings, they did not appreciate the non-biodegradability of plastic or aluminium packaging. Of course, there was no mains water supply – water came from the stream – and there was no electricity either. After all, this was a refugee village, a temporary camp. The people did not want to be there, but had been forced by the Burmese *tatmadaw* to flee to Mai Nai Soi from their real homes.

One of the 'Long-Neck' ladies in the village, Ma Nang (see colour portrait photo), could speak a smattering of Thai, and she confirmed this last point to us. It was pleasant enough in Nupa-ah, she said, but she was homesick and like the other Padaung villagers wanted to see her relatives again. Home was a five-day walk away. The main problem was that, as refugees, they were not allowed by the Thai authorities to own land or work. This meant that they had to rely on handouts from relief agencies and earn what they could from tourism. They did not object to visitors coming to the village; nor did they mind being 'on display' and being photographed (about 100 visitors a month came on average, and sometimes 50 a day in the high season, but during the monsoon months few or no people). The tourists even provided the bored Padaung with some welcome distraction. What they objected to was not being able to earn their own money and keep.

Some wild allegations have been made about the plight of the 'Long Necks' in Thailand. Some have said that the Padaung are compelled to stay in Thailand by the Thai tourist authorities to promote tourism in Mae Hong Son province. Others have written that the Padaung are virtual prisoners of the Karenni Army/KNPP. Certainly there have been some unsavoury incidents in the recent past involving 'Long-Neck' women, and in general their plight resembles that of another exotic minority, the *pi tong luang* or 'Spirits of the Yellow Leaves' (Mrabri people near Nan). Tim Forsyth in an article in the *Bangkok Post* (9-11-91) reported that seven 'Long-Neck' ladies were taken from Burma by a Shan man from Soppong to be sold to a resort near Chiang Mai, where they were to be exhibited in a kind of human zoo. The Shan was arrested and the women taken to Mai Nai Soi. And we witnessed a piece of exploitation of the Padaung on the day of our visit. A handful of the bizarre-looking women – actually mostly children – were going to be taken down to Mae Hong Son to be shown at a fair. When towards evening we saw them in the back of a pick-up waiting to set off, we were reminded of a group of Mrabri we had once seen being taken away from the jungles of Nan to be exhibited like freaks in Chiang Rai. But otherwise the allegations hardly square with what we learned. The 'Long Necks' had fled their homeland because Rangoon had moved against ethnic minority rebels there. Padaung men had risked being pressganged into portering munitions for the SLORC troops. Their land had been extensively mined, and as if to prove the point, the headman at Nupa-ah, one Alphonso Zawthet, had only one leg, the other having been blown off when he had recently stepped on a landmine. The truth may be that, now that the Padaung refugees are in Mai Nai Soi, it is very convenient for both the Thai tourist authorities and the KA to have them continue to live there. Maybe a deal has been struck over their heads – the Karennis can have their refugee village in exchange for tourists being able to visit the exotic ladies. The Padaung, while not being prevented from going, have probably not been encouraged to leave either. Whatever the case, one certainly hopes that they can safely return to their homeland soon.

❋

The 'Long-Neck' Padaung

The Padaung (Padorng, Padong) are classified as belonging to the Karennic branch of the Tibeto-Burman ethnic group within the larger Sino-Tibetan family of peoples or linguistic superstock. Although placed among the Karen peoples, they have little in common with the predominant Sgaw and Pwo Karen, who mostly come to mind when one thinks of Karen people. The Padaung are sometimes called Kayah and apparently refer to themselves as 'Ka-kaung' or, as Scott and Hardiman put it in their *Gazetteer of Upper Burma and the Shan States* of 1900, as 'Kekaawngdu', both of which apparently mean 'people who live on the hilltop' (H. R. Spearman in his *British Burma Gazetteer* of 1880 refers to them as 'Ta-roo'). As is well known, the practice of some Padaung women of lengthening their necks with bronze rings has given rise to the tribe being popularly named the 'Long-Neck' people and also the 'Giraffe' tribe. The custom has also led to their becoming the best-known of all Burma's many hill tribes. An intriguing observation made by Joachim Schliesinger in his *Ethnic Groups of Thailand: Non-Tai-Speaking Peoples* (2000) is that the existence of the ancestors of today's Padaung was reported as early as the late 13th century, by Marco Polo, who saw long-necked women apparently from the Padaung tribe in Pagan.

The majority of the Padaung live in their homeland in Burma, and a few have lived in recent years in Thailand at the north-westernmost extremity of Mae Hong Son province, close to the Burmese border. In Burma, they inhabit the Karenni or 'Kayah' State in the east of the country – Michael Howard in his *Textiles of the Hill Tribes of Burma* (1999) says that the Padaung also live in Mongpai (Mobye) sub-state. In the Karenni (Kayah) State, which they share with Kayah, 'Long-Ear' Kayaw (or Bre), Yinbaw, Paku and other peoples, they inhabit a hilly c. 250-sq-km area above the Salween river, north-west of Loikaw town. Here, they are centred in seven settlements around their largest village of Bangpe, which is four or five days' walk from the Thai border. In Thailand, the 'Long-Neck' people can be found in three villages in Mae Hong Son province (all close to Mae Hong Son town, in Muang district): in the villages of Mai Nai Soi, Nam Pieng Din and Huai Suea Tao. In 2001, when I re-researched this chapter, I heard that there were Padaung now living in a fourth village in Thailand, near Taton in Chiang Rai province (might be the Karen village of Muang Ngam), but I have not checked this and so do not know whether it is true.

Estimates vary as to how many Padaung live in the Karenni State, in Thailand, or altogether. In the early 1990s, I was told that only some 7,000 'Long-Neck' tribespeople existed altogether, of which only a few score lived as refugees on the Thai border, and from another source I learned that 30,000 Padaung were to be found in the Karenni State. Schliesinger (2000) gives the same figure of 30,000 for Padaung in the Karenni State, Howard (1999) states that more than 40,000 of them live there, and Richard K. Diran in his *The Vanishing Tribes of Burma* (1997) reckons that there are up to 50,000 Padaung living in the Karenni State and Shan State borderlands. By 1995, according to figures issued in that year by Chiang Mai's Tribal Research Institute, the 'Long-Neck' population in Thailand had grown appreciably to 500. In 2001, Thai friends of mine who do business with the Padaung and frequently guide tourists to the three 'Long-Neck' villages in Mae Hong Son estimated that there were about 60 houses in Mai Nai Soi, some 30 in Nam Pieng Din, and roughly 20 in Huai Suea Tao, which would indicate a total population of more than 500. In January 2000, the Karenni refugee camp near Padaung Mai Nai Soi contained 13,393 people, substantially augmented by people fleeing successful recent offensives against Karenni rebels across the border. 'Long-Neck' refugees began arriving in north-western Mae Hong Son province post-

THE DRAGON & THE WIND

1988, in the wake of the SLORC's seizure of power in Burma in that year, and as a result of subsequent turbulent events and consequences. Near their homes, fighting erupted again between repressive junta troops and rebels from the ethnic minorities. It was the continuation of a decades-old pattern in the Padaung homeland of Karenni insurgency, conflict, upheaval, displacement, the presence of the brutal *tatmadaw*, and latterly logging, from all of which the 'Long-Necks', like the 'Long-Ear' Kayaw, suffered considerably. Especially the armed nationalist movement the Kayan New Land Party locked horns around Padaung villages with the SLORC and its successor, the SPDC.

In the Padaung homeland, settlements are sited at an altitude of between 1,000 and 1,300 metres. By all accounts, 'Long-Neck' villages are relatively sophisticated, planned and clean, with well-aligned streets – somewhat in contrast to Mai Nai Soi as we first found it. The houses, which like many a hill-tribe dwelling are made of wood and split bamboo with leaf roofs, are raised off the ground on short stilts. Following Scott and Hardiman (1900), who deemed the Padaung "most zealous agriculturists", commentators describe the tribe as being assiduous and skilful in their crop-growing practices. Around their elevated village sites, they terrace every available piece of land on the hillsides for irrigated wet-rice cultivation, growing dry mountain rice too. Despite their heavy neckrings, the women hoe the fields and carry out a wide range of other chores, such as fetching water, walking long distances to market to sell their produce, and spinning and weaving cloth. The Padaung also cultivate maize, potatoes, vegetables, fruit and cotton. They raise buffaloes, oxen, horses, pigs, chickens, ducks and dogs, and also hunt boar, deer, bears and monkeys. Traditionally, as Scott and Hardiman (1900) note, the 'Long-Necks' are keen traders, exchanging their rice and cotton for salt and betel from Taungoo, and playing an active part in the local markets. You can see the legacy of this in the main daytime market of Mae Hong Son town, where from the outset the 'Long-Neck' women have gone about their business in a brisk self-assured way – not at all shy self-effacing wallflowers, even though they are highly conspicuous and many people goggle at them.

In Thailand, because of their refugee status and for reasons of forest conservation, the Padaung are allowed by the authorities neither to cultivate the land nor have regular jobs. Accordingly, they derive their income and hence food as well as daily necessities from agency handouts, from the steep entrance charge to visit their villages, from posing for photographs, from dancing at local fairs, from selling drinks and snacks from their 'shops', and from selling souvenirs made either by themselves (textiles etc.) or by someone else (little 'Long-Neck' dolls etc.). As is well-known, the 'Long-Neck' women are now one of northern Thailand's top tourist draws. They spend a lot of their day being photographed countless times by visitors. Surprisingly, they do not seem to mind this much, regarding it as part of their work. In 2001, I found the Padaung women and girls remarkably unjaded and friendly despite ten years of being snapped and gawped at (which is not to justify this human zoo activity).

Consistent with what they grow and hunt, the Padaung eat rice, vegetables, curry, pork, chicken and jungle game such as snakes. They make rice whisky, but like Karen people as a whole do not cultivate or smoke opium. Some adults

161

chew betel nuts, leaving their mouths stained red and causing them to expectorate red juice. In Mai Nai Soi, we found that men, women and children alike spat incessantly, first loudly clearing their throats – an unedifying performance from such beautiful-looking people.

Traditionally, the Padaung have been animists or Buddhist-animists. But they have had a Roman Catholic mission in their homeland for about 100 years, with the result that many have converted to Christianity. This, in turn, has had the effect of causing a decline in the wearing of neckrings and in other practices in many 'Long-Neck' communities. Ten years ago, apparently only one family out of the 15 then living at Mai Nai Soi was Christian, the rest being animist, but this situation might now have changed, especially with the arrival of more families. Up behind the 'Long-Ear' Kayaw corner of the village, the presence of St Joseph's Catholic Church, a small wooden affair, testifies to the Roman Catholicism, unless the church is used mainly by the Kayaw, many of whom are Catholic converts. Schliesinger (2000) reports that the Padaung have both male and female shamans, called *jamu*, and that the tribe buries its dead.

The Padaung have their own language, but can speak Karen and some Burmese for communicating with regular Karen, Kayah, Kayaw and others. Ten years ago, in Mai Nai Soi, it was difficult communicating with the Padaung because they could speak no Thai or English, and we could not speak any Karen, Burmese or Padaung. Conversation and enquiries had to be channelled mostly through Miss Silver. In 2001, the picture was quite different. Following extensive exposure to Thai officials, locals and tourists as well as to foreign visitors, some 'Long Necks' could speak good Thai and quite a lot of English.

Regarding the costume of the Padaung, it has to be said that the 'Long-Neck' women make one of the most extraordinarily impressive sights of all the peoples in the world. Apart from the famous neckrings, what else makes up their costume? The women wear a simple, crotch-length, short-sleeved, V-necked smock, trimmed around the neck, down the front and at the end of the sleeves with a thin line of magenta or wine-red decoration. In Mai Nai Soi, I have seen smocks in two colours: at the top, extending about six inches below the shoulders, there is a white panel, below which, all the way to the bottom, there is a much larger magenta panel – perhaps this type of shift belongs to the women's best costume (see Footnote 2). A few tassels hang from the bottom of the two-colour smock. Their skirts are knee-length, dark indigo in colour, and again simply decorated with one or two horizontal magenta lines at the bottom.[1] Going about their everyday business, Padaung women wear terrycloth turbans decorated with coloured scarves and threads, and for show purposes – as at touristic Mai Nai Soi – like to adorn their hair with brightly coloured headscarves in red and yellow or any colour. Sometimes the women wear indigo leggings, which extend from the upper part of the calf to above the ankle. The chins of the ladies rest on a small square flap of material or pad, which prevents their chins chafing on the top of their neckrings. The pads are

---

[1] To provide a historical perspective on this, J. G. Scott (1911) observes that the female Padaung smock is V-necked, short-sleeved, usually black in colour, and ornamented by a coloured border and sometimes embroidery, while the skirt is striped red and blue, and stops short above the knee.

often edged with beading, and from their corners dangle threads, more beading, tassels and pompoms. The decorative cloth rectangles have the effect of 'presenting' the wearer's head. On their forearms, above the wrist, women and girls alike wear several wide tubular silver armbands, supplemented by other bracelets. Padaung women wear gleaming bronze rings not only around their necks, but also – traditionally – above both the knees and ankles. You do not often see this these days, instead finding golden coils of varying lengths below the knee and above the calf, which are reminiscent of the legrings worn by the Kayaw. The combined effect of the neckrings, legrings and armbands is to give Padaung women a somewhat armoured look.

Mature Padaung women wear up to 28 or even 32 of the famous neckrings (normally about 22). Actually, this neckband is not, as if often thought, a set of rings at all, but is one continuous spiral or coil of polished Burmese bronze (could that be brass?). A full spiral on a mature female is some 30 cms or 1 ft high, and weighs between 4 and 5 kgs. In Mai Nai Soi, we were told that the first rings are put around a girl's neck when she is about seven years of age. Initially, 4 or 5 are put on, more being added at intervals. I do not entirely believe this because in the village you can see infants younger than that running around with 2 or 3 rings. It is said that up to the age of about 20 the girls can remove the rings permanently. Were they to do so, they would have to wear blankets around their necks for a while to support the neck, but the neck muscles would regenerate themselves. After about 20, a girl can no longer dispense with the rings. The rings are widest at the bottom, where they sit on the ribcage, thinnest in the middle, and wider again under the chin. Traditionally, they have a separate vertical loop at the back, whose function is unclear – it looks as if the loop is meant to be used for chaining the wearer to a tree or similar object! Someone told us that new spirals came only from Burma, and that there was a shortage of them for upcoming young girls. Old Padaung ladies, it seems, take their rings with them to the grave.

By no means all Padaung women lengthen their necks. During our first visit to Mai Nai Soi in the early 1990s, we found only 17 females wearing the neckrings in the village, although far more women than that were present. One of them said that back in their homeland about 500 more women still wore the rings. Evidently, the wearing of the neckrings is a matter of family tradition. If the mother and grandmother wear them, then the daughter might do so too. But there is no inevitability in this, and increasingly mothers ask their daughters if they want to continue the tradition. Increasingly, the daughters refuse. When they wear the cumbersome rings, they stand out at school, and it is not practical for them to take part in activities such as sports. Latterly, this picture is undoubtedly different in the 'Long-Neck' villages in Thailand, where the wearing of neckrings is being encouraged for touristic reasons. Nevertheless, overall the long-neck tradition might well die out before too long. Reportedly, the Burmese are discouraging the neckrings in the Karenni State, with the result that the number of women wearing them there has sharply declined recently. It seems that missionary activity over the last 100 years in the Padaung homeland has also contributed to a decline in the long-neck tradition. The ladies at Mai Nai Soi say that in Burma only two or three Padaung villages now continue the neckring custom. Ironically, if this ancient cultural tradition does survive, it might be because it is saved by tourism in Thailand and perhaps at a later date in Burma!

As said, the gleaming neckband is often mistakenly thought of as a set of separate rings, when in fact it is a continuous coil. Another misconception attaching to the rings is that they elongate the neck. In reality, they squash down the woman's ribcage, making the neck look longer, as a Belgian researcher found out and as can be seen from X-ray images in an article published in the *National Geographic* magazine. In Mai Nai Soi, you can buy duplicated accounts of all this, probably excerpted from the above source.

When you look at 'Long-Neck' women, you cannot help but be struck by a haunting melancholy beauty. They have prominent high cheekbones, modelled angular faces, flattish broad noses, and lovely coffee-coloured skins. Their eyes are intelligent and their mouths wide. Because of the neckrings, their heads are pushed up and away from their bodies, making the heads seem detached. To my mind, this gives the Padaung women a remote, serene, unintentionally haughty and supercilious look. The fact that they cannot easily turn their heads adds a slightly pained expression to their demeanour, as if they were all suffering from a crick in the neck. Further, many of the 'Long-Neck' women, their bodies seemingly depressed away from their heads, look unusually thin and elongated. J. G. Scott (1911) summed up this impression in a memorable way: with their pin heads, long brass-bound necks, and sloping shoulders, they reminded him of a champagne bottle!

There remains the simple and obvious question of why Padaung women wear the neckrings. Is it cosmetic or what? A lot of apocryphal stories have been circulated in connection with this. A well-known one runs that in the old days, when the Padaung men went hunting for four or five days in the jungle, tigers would come into the village and drag off the women in the hunters' absence. The women took to wearing rings to prevent themselves from being seized by the throat by the tigers. Another popular explanation is that in times of yore the villages of the Padaung and other minority groups were the subject of raiding parties conducted by bandits and the region's dominant peoples, who wanted to kidnap women as slaves. Padaung men put rings around their womenfolk's necks and chained the rings to a tree or house to prevent them from being so seized. When we once put these interpretations to Thai-speaking Ma Nang, one of Mai Nai Soi's leading ladies, she laughed. The real explanation, she said, was to do with Padaung mythology. According to this, man was the wind, while woman was a beautiful dragon. The original dragon-woman was impregnated by the wind to give rise to the first Padaung people. Ever since that time Padaung women had worn rings around their necks and legs in imitation of the first beautiful dragon-mother figure. Beyond all this, the rings undoubtedly do have a cosmetic function – Padaung girls and ladies believe that the adornment makes them more beautiful, and are proud to wear the rings. In Mai Nai Soi, we noticed how these days the neck coils also have a practical purpose. They are the preferred place where the Padaung women keep their banknotes. When once, before leaving the village, we went to buy a handwoven scarf from the village's oldest 'Long-Neck' lady, she promptly tucked the 100-baht note down behind her rings.

In 2001, when I revisited Mai Nai Soi, I noticed that some Padaung women seemed to have developed a new costume feature. They had added to their head attire a kind of high pointed headpiece, a bit like the spike on a *Pickelhaube* (an old German military helmet)! At first I took this to be a vulgar, kitschy, fanciful new invention, but meanwhile I have discovered that this is not the case at all (see colour portrait photo of Padaung girl Ma Ja). The spike is a piece of traditional decoration, and the refugee Padaung are rediscovering or merely continuing a past practice. Two old black-and-white photographs in Richard K. Diran (1997, pp. 218 and 219), dated 1920s and 1905, show 'Long-Neck' women with their hair done up on the tops of their heads, ornamented with beads and discs, and surmounted by the silver spike.[2]

❖

I return to the narrative account, interrupted earlier, of our first visit to Mai Nai Soi, in the early 1990s. Most of the Padaung men were away from the village, either hunting or helping to build in the Karenni refugee village nearby. Others were over in Burma serving in one of the rebel armies. As we walked from house to house, we found the 'Long-Neck' women busy with their domestic tasks. They were cooking or sewing, fetching water or returning from a wash. Some were sitting making baskets or putting together roofing panels. Others were engaged in one of the stages of weaving. These weaving ladies sat before their huts spinning yarn or operating simple looms on the entrance platforms to their houses. We found the oldest lady of Nupa-ah putting the finishing touches to a 4-ft-long scarf. We tried to speak to her, but all verbal communication was impossible. Later, as said, we bought the finished, brilliant red scarf from this lovable diminutive grandma for 100 baht. Many of the 'Long Necks' had samples of their weaving for sale outside their houses – scarves, shoulderbags and lengths of skirt material. They made attractive mementoes and also had the virtue of directly supporting the refugees.

After a tour of the village, Miss Silver took us next to look briefly at the Karenni refugee camp. It lay five minutes beyond Nupa-ah along a jungle trail. The beginning of the path was marked by an immense tree. With intergrowing sections, and as if rippling with muscles, the tree was sacred and had a small shrine in front of it. Once a year, the Padaung villagers cleaned up the base

---

[2] A similar historic photo in Michael C. Howard (1999, p. 72), which was the frontispiece of J. G. Scott's 1911 *Handbook*, shows a group of nine Padaung women with the same pointy headdress. (Actually, the more I look at this picture, the more it seems to me to show the same women as in Diran's 1905 photo, just rearranged.) Around the base of their headdress, they have a double row of beads or baubles, at the front of it they sport double discs or bosses, one above the other like a pair of lamps, and on top of the whole is the spike. Some ornamentation of the women seems to differ from that seen today, e.g. they wear a single long strand of baubles or pompoms dangling front centre from their chins, at the bottom of which is a single large boss. There are other differences, too. But I notice, further, that some of the women are wearing the two-panel two-colour smocks that we saw the Mai Nai Soi women sporting, suggesting again that an apparent innovation is just a continuation of traditional practice.

area, and two elders sacrificed a chicken or other animal to the spirit of the place. Further up the path, we came to a fork. Left went to a military checkpoint, beyond which the land was mined, and right went to the refugee camp. Some 1,000 Karenni lived in this new village. The neat construction of the houses and the orderliness of the whole camp contrasted immediately with the general scruffiness of the Padaung settlement.

High up on a hill, to the right of the entrance, we spotted a small wooden church. With its cross and prominent Virgin Mary, it testified to the fact that many Karenni are Catholics. There was also a field hospital, a large wood and bamboo hut with a leaf roof, which was staffed by a doctor and three nurses. The camp school, with 172 children divided into six classes, was a serious, well-organized affair. The 96 boys and 76 girls studied Karenni, Burmese, English, maths, geography and science. Their teachers had names like Koo Rae, Tha Wo, Boo Moe, Hser Moo and Ki Mia, but also Victoria and Monica. The headmaster's name was Aung Win, and at 30 years of age he was the oldest member of staff! Now (in 2000) that the camp housed more than 13,000 refugees, the numbers in this school must be substantially larger.

Wanting to stay longer than an hour or two in Mai Nai Soi, we asked Miss Silver if it was possible to sleep overnight. Yes, we could – the village had a guest hut, which we could take for 20 baht. We hid and locked our motorbike in the Shan lady's vegetable garden, and in the late afternoon she took us to the hut, right in among the Padaung. We immediately realized our mistake, but with night falling it was too late to set off back for Mae Hong Son. The hut was primitive indeed, and the facilities worse. That night at the 'Long-Neck' village was possibly the worst we spent anywhere during our journey – worse than Kae Noi and worse even than nights later spent deep in the jungle on the way down to the Three Pagodas Pass.

Leaving us with some *pak gaad* greens, which she thought we could fry for supper, Silver indicated with her boss eye that the washing place was in the stream. Then she departed. We could have stayed and eaten with her, she volunteered cheerily, but that evening she had to accompany some 'Long Necks' down the fair in Mae Hong Son, and she would not be back till late. When we had got over the shock of the hut, which was a broken-down bamboo shack on stilts with one entire side open to view, we examined the *pak gaad*. This was a green vegetable with yellow flowers, but the leaves were limp and faded, and the flowers had black specks all over them. Never mind, perhaps they would taste good when fried up with oil and fish sauce. But where was the oil? There was none. Perhaps we could buy some in a village shop or borrow a drop from the Padaung. But this problem was as nothing compared to what we found when we went next to inspect the 'kitchen', adjacent to the hut. It clearly had not been used for months, possibly years. Two or three rusty blackened pots, full of dust, lay on the ground. But beyond that, there was nothing – nothing to clean them with, no spoons or plates, no matches, not even firewood. Even to begin to cook a meal, we would have had to go looking for wood, borrow an axe, and begin chopping up firewood. The situation was hopeless. We gave the mouldering greens to some pigs and marched off down to the shop, prepared either to eat biscuits for the evening or to starve until next day. This was an experience which taught us henceforth always to carry with us emergency supplies.

From one of the shops down at the entrance to the village, we bought some instant noodles and other things. The shop, it transpired, was run by a Shan pharmacist and doctor. When we explained the situation, he altruistically invited us to spend the evening in Miss Silver's hut. "Just push open her door," he said, "and you will find oil, fish sauce and other things in her kitchen." Who were we to decline? The charcoal embers were still glowing in Silver's earthenware brazier, so we stoked up the fire, boiled water for soup and tea, and ended by getting a passable supper. By 7pm the village was quiet, and an hour later the jungle-bound settlement was dead. Fearing that soon everyone would be asleep, we stumbled back up the paths in the darkness, stopping at a couple of Padaung houses to beg candles, matches and an oil lamp. And then we made ready for a long night.

In the light of the oil lamp, we dimly made out that someone had kindly deposited mats and a heap of blankets in our hut. We laid these out on the creaking uneven bamboo poles of the floor, strung up our mosquito net, and at 8.30 settled down to sleep. Once or twice figures appeared in the darkness at the open side of our hut, peering in at the two strange visitors in their net with the flickering pinpoints of light. But then they disappeared. All night long chickens and other animals scuffled around under the hut. The last thing I remember was the background orchestra of jungle frogs and grasshoppers, against which a little girl in her hut nearby was singing a plaintive Padaung song.

✻

In January 2001, when I revisited Mai Nai Soi for the purposes of re-researching and revising this book, I discovered that there were not just striking Padaung 'Long-Neck' people there, but a small group of rare and hardly less impressive Kayaw 'Long-Ear' tribals. I do not think I missed them the first time around, rather I believe they arrived at the village after my initial visit, maybe in 1994. Their small enclave of just some ten houses lies towards the far end of Mai Nai Soi (relative to the entrance), on the right side, slightly up and away from the central street, and near the small school. Very little is written or known about these interesting people, and a great deal of detailed anthropological study remains to be done on them. I include here a limited and probably defective account of the Kayaw, based on what I have gleaned from the scant literature and on what I saw and learned at Mai Nai Soi.

The 'Long-Ear' Kayaw

The Kayaw are classified as belonging to the Karennic branch of the Tibeto-Burman ethnic group within the larger Sino-Tibetan family of peoples or linguistic superstock. Although placed – like the Padaung – among the Karen peoples, outwardly at least they have little in common with the predominant Sgaw and Pwo Karen, who mostly come to mind when one thinks of Karen people. Visually, the Kayaw are surprisingly similar to the Padaung, the women's costumes of the two groups resembling each other in many respects. This might lead one to suppose that the groups are closely related. But evidently they are not. The Kayaw of Mai Nai Soi say that in Burma they live "far away" from the Padaung. Also, although the languages of the two groups are related Karennic tongues, the Kayaw and the Padaung by all accounts cannot understand each other. Nevertheless, it may well transpire that the two peoples are more closely related than they think, perhaps emanating from some common ancestral ethnic group.

The Kayaw have been given many names, but they call themselves 'Kayaw', reportedly pronounced 'Kayow'. Thus they have also sometimes been termed: Kayow, Bre, Brè, Brek, the Bres, Blimaw, Laku and Bwe. Much confusion attaches to these names and to the delimitation of the Kayaw group, which remains to be sorted out. The consensus now is that they should be called 'Kayaw', with the only legitimate alternative name perhaps being 'Bre'. The Kayaw have also been lumped together with or confused with the Manoo-Manaw people (Manu-Manaw, Minoo-Minaw etc.).[3] The term the 'Long-Ear people' or 'Long Ears' has apparently been coined in analogy to the 'Long-Neck people/tribe' or 'Long Necks' for touristic purposes in Thailand's Mae Hong Son province. It is a lazy, lurid and convenient handle with which the tour agencies can identify and sell the group to visitors, and by which tourists can easily grasp and remember the tribe. Of course, the appellation 'Long Ears' refers to the practice of Kayaw women of putting big silver rings in holes in their ear lobes, which distend the lobes, and from which the women like to hang heavy earring adornment, lengthening the lobes and ears.

The homeland of the Kayaw is in Burma's Karenni State (dubiously rechristened 'Kayah State' by the Burmese authorities), where they live apparently on the western edge of that state, which they inhabit along with more than a dozen other ethnic groups, including the numerous Kayah, the Padaung, Yinbaw and Paku. The Karenni State is a rugged region in eastern Burma, situated between the Shan State to the north, the Karen State to the west and south, and Thailand to the east. According to Howard (1999), the Kayaw – or Brek, as he calls them – live in the mountainous Kantarawaddy and Kyebogyi districts of the Karenni State. Many Kayaw prefer to inhabit remote forest areas, deep in the hills, a wary behaviour that may stem from a past fear

---

[3] Diran (1997) talks about the Bre, whom he subdivides into the Kayaw and the Manoo-Manaw, two closely related sub-groups. Schliesinger (2000) says that Manoo-Manaw is a Burmese term for the Kayaw and himself wonders if the Manoo-Manaw are not a sub-group of the Kayaw. Bwe, he writes, is a problematic term, used in English sources to describe all non-Sgaw/Pwo Karen groups in the Karenni (Kayah) State. As such, its use to describe the Kayaw is mistaken. Howard (1999), the emphasis of whose book is mainly historical, calls the Kayaw 'Brek', but, as far as I can understand, he seems to confuse the Brek with the Bwe, about whom he talks as a separate tribe. The descriptions he gives of the Brek indicate the Kayaw, and yet he says of the Bwe that a few now live in Thailand, when in reality it is a few 'Brek' (Kayaw) who live there. Citing 19th-century commentators, Howard seems to divide the Brek into three sub-groups: the northern Brek, the southern Brek, and the 'Mano', who live to the east. The impoverished southern Brek wear no brass adornment and may, in fact, be a separate group, perhaps the Kayah. The more prosperous northern Brek, who wear brass Padaung-style adornment, would seem to be the real Kayaw. The 'Mano' are not further discussed, unless they are the 'Manumanaw' he mentions separately elsewhere.

of being kidnapped by slave traders or from a desire to remain untouched by external influences.

Since the mid-1990s, just a handful of Kayaw have lived in Thailand, where they dwell – as far as I know – only in Mai Nai Soi village, Mae Hong Son province, mixed up with the 'Long-Neck' Padaung there. Schliesinger (2000) says that they began to arrive in that village in 1994, apparently lured by someone to boost the appeal of the place as a tourist attraction. Kayaw women I spoke to in Mai Nai Soi said that some of their number had been there as long as the Padaung, arriving with the latter. They came "about eight years ago" or roughly 1992-93, before which they had lived as refugees on the border. These figures do not entirely add up (information given by hill-tribe people rarely does), and undoubtedly new arrivals have meanwhile joined the original contingent. In Mai Nai Soi, there are, I think, ten Kayaw houses with an estimated 30 people, perhaps a few more. Apparently, they came from a village called Geko, which lies five days' walk from the Thai border. Howard (1999) reckons that around 17,000 'Brek' or Kayaw live in their homeland in the Kantarawaddy and Kyebogyi districts of the Karenni State (with some 3,000 Manoo-Manaw living in the western part of Kyebogyi district). Somewhere else I read that there were 14,758 Bre or Kayaw in Burma (and 6,104 Manoo). Whichever set of figures one chooses, the population of the 'Long Ears' remains relatively small. Their territory, like that of the Padaung, has suffered in recent years, precipitating the flight to the Thai border and Thailand of a few Kayaw. More could well follow in the future. The Kayaw homeland has been mixed up in the decades-old insurgency of many ethnic groups (here the Karenni) against Rangoon, has seen government anti-rebel operations and warfare, has witnessed the garrisoning of brutal SLORC troops and the displacement of Kayaw people,[4] and has been subject to widespread deforestation caused by Thai logging companies operating with concessions granted by the SLORC.

The Kayaw in Burma are agriculturists, who grow both wet and dry rice, as well as cotton, fruits and vegetables. Reportedly, they are much given to tippling rice whisky. Of course, the refugee Kayaw in Thailand are prevented from owning land, growing crops and taking employment, and – like the Padaung – must make money from posing for tourist cameras and selling souvenirs to visitors. Traditionally, the Kayaw are animists, but many have converted to Christianity, becoming Christian-animists. There have been Catholic missions in the Kayaw homeland, and the converts are mostly Roman Catholic, with a few Baptist. As with the Padaung and the Karen peoples as a whole, Kayaw society is matriarchal and matrilineal, with a matrilocal marriage system, i.e. lineage is reckoned through the women. When you stand in front of Kayaw women, you are struck by just how short these stocky round-faced ladies and girls are.

---

[4] You can get a vivid insight into the fate of Kayaw, Kayah, 'Bwe Kayaw' and Manoo-Manaw villages at the hands of the SLORC by logging on to Internet pages, such as 'SLORC Activities in Ler Ba Ko Village', posted by the Karen Human Rights Group (search for Kayaw, or KHRG, or human rights in Burma). The above page gives detailed population figures as well as the religious denomination of the ethnic groups in a series of displaced villages.

THREE PAGODAS

The costume and jewellery of the 'Long-Ear' Kayaw women is among the most beautiful of all the adornments of the many hill tribes in South-East Asia (see two colour pictures in photo section). Remarkable about it, too, is just how deeply rooted in tradition and resistant to change it has been over time, and certainly over the last 100 years or so. A historic black-and-white photo, dated 1907, from the British Library/Oriental and India Office Collection (reproduced in Richard K. Diran's *The Vanishing Tribes of Burma*, 1997, p. 221), as well as photos in the *National Geographic* magazine of March 1922 and in a book of 1967 about the Karenni peoples, all show Kayaw women wearing a costume virtually identical with that seen today in Mai Nai Soi.[5]

The attire consists of a red, V-necked, short-sleeved smock with much thin vertical striping in white and yellow. At the end of the sleeves there is a fringe of loose strands. Below the smock, a short, above-the-knee, wrap-around skirt is worn, indigo in colour, with sparse vertical markings in various colours, and with triple banding in red and yellow just above the hem. The waist is encircled with sashes consisting of swathes of red and white beads. Around their legs and in a manner very reminiscent of the Padaung, Kayaw women wear two sets of shiny brass or bronze rings (coils actually) on each leg. The first, comprising about half a dozen 'rings', sits just above the ankles, while the second, numbering 12-18 'rings', which flare towards the top, sits between the upper calf and the knee. This second, larger brass spiral is fringed at the bottom by lacquered black cotton rings, by a string of white beads, and by a circle of tiny bells. The women wear four silver bracelets around their wrists, sometimes interspersed with more black lacquered rings. The ears are pierced and the hole plugged with a large silver ring, from which dangle composite strands of red, white and blue (or red, white and green) beads as well as a loop of beads. But the tour de force of the female Kayaw costume is the jewellery around the women's necks and down their fronts. The neck is encircled with a kind of composite choker, made up of more black, lacquered, cotton or rattan coils, which is decorated at the top with cowrie shells and at the bottom with a single string of white or any-colour beads. Also at the bottom of the 'choker' is a string of mainly red and green beads, from which hang old silver coins. The neck is further encircled with between 6 and 12 wide, loose-fitting, bronze-coloured, metal hoops. As if all that were not enough, several more necklaces extend down to the navel, some strung with large heavy silver beads, some with small green and blue beads, and some with more silver coins (old Burmese and Indian coins and rupees from British imperial colonial times).

---

[5] Diran (1997, pp. 132-135) also contains some excellent modern photos, taken by him in Burma in the mid-1990s, of Kayaw costume, including a shot of a man in traditional dress. The earliest account of Kayaw costume that I have found, written by a certain W. H. L. Campbell (quoted in Howard [1999, p. 77], who reproduces it from Scott & Hardiman [1900, p. 533]), likewise describes dress similar to that worn today. The women, Campbell says, have an attire like that of the Padaung, wearing a white-and-pink-striped smock with a narrow pink border, below which is a short, deep blue and red skirt. Brass tubing, he continues, is coiled round the leg from the ankle to the knee, and from above the knee to halfway up the thigh. Large brass hoops are worn round the neck, and ear plugs in the ears. Campbell further speaks of the men wearing a pair of short, red-and-white-striped trousers, while their legs are ornamented below the knee with thin, black-lacquered, cotton coils.

Finally, a distinctive pendant hangs mid-chest, comprising two or three flat, semicircular or crescent-shaped, silver objects that are reminiscent in their outline of a set of buffalo horns, and which are both engraved and repoussé with various designs. Sometimes 'Long-Ear' women wear many rings on their fingers.

The traditional costume of Kayaw men, as shown in one old and one present-day photo (Diran, 1997, pp. 221 & 133), consists of a smock similar to that of their womenfolk, except that it has a white ground with plentiful thin vertical red striping; shorts (or possibly a short wrap-around skirt) likewise in white, with all-over red and grey striping; a headband made of red, white and blue beads; either a topknot or a turban; a modest number of black lacquered coils around the neck, as well as a couple of necklaces made of cowrie shells, beads and old coins; earrings; silver bracelets; and more lacquered cotton or cane rings around the legs, just below the knee. In the old photo, dated 1907, Kayaw men can be seen wearing simple, white, very short jackets with long loose sleeves.

❊ ❊

Postscript 2002

Thailand's population of Padaung 'Long-Neck' people live, as said, in the villages of Mai Nai Soi, Nam Pieng Din and Huai Suea Tao, all near Mae Hong Son town (as well as possibly in a fourth place up near Taton, north of Fang town). I think the 'Long-Ear' Kayaw live only in Mai Nai Soi, a situation that could change in the future. I cannot vouch for what happens at Nam Pieng Din or Huai Suea Tao because I have only ever been to Mai Nai Soi, but plenty of visitors go to the other two places as well as Mai Nai Soi. Most regular tourists are taken to one of the 'Long-Neck' villages by an agency, paying a premium for the privilege, but many more enterprising travellers make it there under their own steam. If you want to see the Padaung and/or the Kayaw, it makes sense to go on your own because you can then stay as long as you like. You can ride a hire motorcycle to Mai Nai Soi and Huai Suea Tao, but accessing Nam Pieng Din also involves a boat trip. There are entrance charges for all three villages. In 2001, it cost 250 baht per person to enter Mai Nai Soi and Huai Suea Tao, and 400 baht to visit Nam Pieng Din, an all-in charge that included the boat ride. To reach Nam Pieng Din and Huai Suea Tao, proceed as follows. From Mae Hong Son town's central crossroads, go south out of town on the H108, in the direction of Khun Yuam, past some large buildings, 2.1 kms to a well-signed junction. Turn right/W at the junction and proceed another 1.4 kms, ignoring a turning right near the beginning, through Soppong village, to a fork by a shrine in Ta Pong Daeng village. At the fork, right will take you to Huai Suea Tao and left to Nam Pieng Din. In the latter case, you go 10 mins by vehicle from MHS town to an embarkation point beyond Ta Pong Daeng, and then 1 hr by boat down the River Pai to Nam Pieng Din, which lies near the border, separated from Burma by a mountain. Obviously, I cannot tell you more about reaching Nam Pieng Din and Huai Suea Tao because I have not been to the two places. To access Mai Nai Soi village by a new, slightly shorter and more direct route than the one we first took, proceed as below. Overall, the 20-km-long way is much improved and paved almost throughout, as far as the temple in Nai Soi village (km 18).

THREE PAGODAS

After the *wat*, you negotiate the last 2 kms on a dirt road, which is every bit as awful as it was 10 years previously – rutted and bumpy with bulldust. Of course, the authorities could easily have sealed the way through to the Padaung settlement, but for some reason they have not. I suspect the last stretch is left as it is to give tourists the exciting impression that they are going into the wilds! Mai Nai Soi lies NW of Mae Hong Son town.

Route detail: Mae Hong Son – Mai Nai Soi (Maps 14 & 15, also 13)

km 0.0 Main crossroads (with traffic lights) in centre of Mae Hong Son town
Proceed N up main street towards *Siam Hotel* (R)

km 0.4 After *Siam Hotel*, turn left into Phachachonuthit Road (Map 14)
Go past *Jean's House* (L)
Ignore a side road joining from L
At a crossroads, go R, down and over a bridge to a

km 0.9 T-junction, opposite which is the Shan-style temple of Wat Don Chedi
At the T-junction, go L
You pass *Yok Guest House* (R)
At the bottom of the hill, before a bridge and MHS prison, go L into a new road, identified at its start by km-marker 0 and a sign saying 'Welcome to Tambon Pang Mu'
You pass *Rim Tarn House* (R) and a cement works (L)

km 1.9 At a fork marked by a phone box and a big blue road sign, go R/straight. You go up, then down, and out into countryside, with a mountain ridge ahead. Ignore a side turning (R)

km 3.8 In the Shan village of **Tung Kong Mu**, at a crossroads, go L by a Shan-style *wat* (at this village, the old biking way from MHS to Mai Nai Soi joins from the R somewhere – see Map 13)
Follow the road round
At the next junction, go L
You come to the River Pai on your R side
Follow a cement-section road past *Mae Nam Cottage* (R) and a shrine (R), through woodland to a

km 6.3 New concrete bridge over the River Pai, to the R of which lies the old suspension bridge once used by pedestrians and motorcyclists

km 7.0 In the Shan village of **Sob Soi**, at a T-junction, you join a broader road. The way R proceeds 6.7 kms to link up with the way to Mae Or, Mork Cham Pae village and Fish Cave (Map 13). (By the same token, this is where the third way to Mai Nai Soi joins from the R, the roundabout route that four-wheeled vehicles used to take before the new concrete bridge was built over the Pai river at Tung Kong Mu.) Go L at the T-junction (now see Map 15)
Pass through more woodland

km 7.7 Where Sob Soi village ends, you pick up a new asphalt road. Follow it for some distance, passing

km 12.0 Some nice forest and jungle (L)
You skirt round the valley, with the R. Pai following you on your L side

km 16.2 Health centre

km 17.3 Shan village of **Nai Soi**

km 17.7 After the school, turn R

km 18.1 Shan-style *wat* (L)
Barrier
After the barrier, go L at a fork onto a small dirt road
Ford river a couple of times

THE DRAGON & THE WIND

At a T-junction, go R
Proceed through bulldust and down through forest to a
km 20.3   Car park (R), shops (R) and barrier
Ways going R, L and straight ahead
By the checkpoint, go past the barrier, down 200 m, to the 'Long-Neck'
village of **Mai Nai Soi**

Mai Nai Soi

In 2001, the Padaung refugee village was still situated in the same place and in the same valley as ten years previously. Its position regarding the entrance fee, Karenni minders and subventions to the KA or KNPP had been regularized. The settlement was larger with more Padaung inhabitants, and meanwhile a small group of 'Long-Ear' Kayaw had joined the 'Long Necks'. Their 10 houses are situated towards the far end of the village, up right and near the school, and below the little church. Otherwise, Mai Nai Soi was more orderly now, less scruffy and littered, more civilized. It was also more commercial, with almost every Padaung house selling skirts (these looked to me like Tai Lue-design textiles!), postcards, information packs explaining how the necks of the Padaung women are lengthened, and souvenir Padaung dolls, keyrings and pens (not made by the villagers).

Miss Silver was no longer resident in Mai Nai Soi. She had moved several years previously to work in a tour agency in Mae Hong Son town. Her services are hardly necessary anymore because many Padaung now speak quite good Thai and even some English. Ma Ja, for example, who is the celebrated daughter of the well-known 'Long-Neck' lady Ma Nang, speaks a lot of English and plenty of Thai. She is altogether something of a polyglot, claiming to speak – besides the above languages and Padaung, of course – also some Burmese, Chinese, Japanese and even "a few words of Spanish". Now aged 19 and unmarried with no boyfriend, as she told us, Ma Ja – like her mother Ma Nang and the other Padaung women and girls – proved unexpectedly friendly and unjaded, despite all the visits from tourists over the years. She took a great interest in the photos I had taken of her and her mother in the early 1990s and reproduced in the first edition of *Three Pagodas* – this even though the 'Long Necks' in Thailand have been photographed millions of times and must be among the most snapped people in the world. Ma Ja and Ma Nang very happily and good-humouredly posed for fresh shots, imploring me bring copies on my next visit. When I expressed surprise that they should want photos of themselves in spite of all the postcards of the Padaung around them, they said that "we never get copies of the pictures people take of us. Visitors come, snap and go, and we never see them again." Unlike what she had said ten years earlier, Ma Nang told us that the Padaung now wanted to stay in Thailand and not return to Burma.

8

WORSTED IN WIZARDRY

THE LAWA & THE KARENNI

Mae Hong Son – Khun Yuam – Mae La Noi – Mae La Oop – Mae Sariang

Taking leave in our minds of the poised 'Long-Neck' ladies, of Darkie and our new Wa friends, we headed off from Mae Hong Son to Mae Sariang on the next leg of our journey. We had meanwhile recovered our Honda Wing from Chiang Mai. Riding south on it down Highway 108, we were also saying goodbye to the Shan section of the Thai-Burmese border. Until midpoint Khun Yuam, Karenni or 'Red Karen' territory (the 'Kayah' State) would shadow us to the west across the border,[1] after which we would move into regular Karen country, on both sides of the border. For the rest of our journey, therefore, from Mae Hong Son all the way down to the Three Pagodas Pass, the Karen world was to be our new milieu.

What the trip down to Mae Sariang lacked in eventfulness, featuring only one town and a handful of villages en route (see Maps 16 & 17), it made up for in terms of scenery and riding pleasure. Especially the first half of the 160-km-long journey was a motorcyclist's dream (a detailed updated account of the route to Mae Sariang is given in the Postscript below). To the left/east side of the H108, from the latitude of Mae Hong Son town to that of Khun Yuam, lay the rugged and little-known Mae Surin Waterfall National Park, founded in 1981 and sparsely peopled with mainly Sgaw Karen and a few Hmong tribespeople. Not far out of Mae Hong Son town (main crossroads in centre of main street = km 0, see now Map 16), and before Pa Bong, a sign pointed right (west) down a dirt road to the village of Huai Dua and the River Pai – an area used in the shooting of Vietnam War-style films. Then, after **Pa Bong**, the H108 began to climb steeply through some hairpin bends until it reached a viewpoint (km 17.3). From here, one could look out headily over paddy fields in a small basin far below, into an impressive, steep-sided ravine, dammed at

---

[1] The Karenni or 'Kayah' do not loom large in this book, figuring only tangentially in connection with the two Karenni tribes mentioned in Chapter 7, the Padaung and the Kayaw, and so no fuller treatment of them is given. However, for the sake of completeness, a thumbnail sketch of the Karenni and their state, as well as of the Karenni rebel organizations the KNPP and the KNLP, is given at the very end of this chapter (8), after Postscript 2002.

the mouth, which sliced back into the mountainous eastern hinterland. In the trees near the viewpoint's *sala* or pavilion, a statue – some kind of Shiva or jungle rishi figure – also gazed out contemplatively into the mysterious-looking V-shaped valley. A bearded fellow in a tiger skin, he had chosen a scenic position for his woodland meditation. After the viewpoint, in a protracted descent, the narrow road twisted down to Huai Pong.

This initial section of the leg accounted for many of the celebrated 1800 curves between Chiang Mai and Mae Hong Son (coming by the 365-km-long southerly route via Hot). Stopping in some places, we were able to line up four or five bends in a row, making a nice picture with the telephoto lens. The snaking road breasted endless ravishing wooded hillscape, before plunging like a roller coaster through an alternation of mountainous jungle and valley floors. These secluded floors, stepped with bright green paddies, were a sudden tonic for the eye. But the H108 was also a poor road – at least at this end. Its surface was filled with countless potholes, and its edges had frayed away, reducing the metalled part to single track. When an oncoming vehicle appeared, someone had to swerve out into the dust. It could not be long before this first section reverted to dirt road, after which reconstruction work would begin, lasting years.

Huai Pong (km 36) was a small place with a history. During the Second World War, it had been an important staging post for troops of the Japanese Imperial Army headed for Burma. Just south of Huai Pong, about one km outside the village, a large cemetery lay under the H108, containing the bodies of Japanese soldiers who had been killed or who had died hereabouts. A memorial to them stood on the right (western) side of the road, which was inscribed with Japanese characters saying: 'Fellow Warriors, may your souls be blissfully in heaven.' To one side of the memorial, a board displayed photos of war-related finds dug up at Huai Pong (more information about the Japanese in Thailand during WW2 can be found below, under Khun Yuam, and also in Chapter 4 under Muang Noi and Footnote 1).

After Huai Pong, a rather better road continued on down to **Mae Surin** village (km 53), which lay beside the Mae Surin, a river that flowed down from famous Mae Surin Waterfall in the mountains to the east. Like other villages between Mae Hong Son town and Khun Yuam, for example Pa Bong, Mae Surin was a picturesque little community of wooden houses and a Burmese or Shan-style *wat* nestling in coconut palm trees. Now, speeding along some protracted straight flat stretches, the H108 crossed plateau land to reach the district town of Khun Yuam (km 66 or not quite halfway to Mae Sariang). At the outskirts, a gravel road (the H1263), with a plethora of signs at its mouth, struck left/east to numerous villages and faraway Mae Chaem, as well as to the local sights of Mae Surin Waterfall and the so-called 'Buatong Fields'. The latter two are well-known and much-vaunted attractions in Mae Hong Son province. Mae Surin Waterfall (see Map 16), which gives its name to the national park to the north of it and which is said to be the biggest waterfall in Thailand, lies beyond the 'Buatong Fields', which are fields of blooming *buatong* (Mexican sunflowers) that every November carpet the hillsides near the Hmong village of Mae U-kor.

175

THREE PAGODAS

Khun Yuam

We were seduced into stopping over for a night in midway Khun Yuam not by the town itself, but, unusually, by a guest house. This was not *Peekmai Guest House* and restaurant at the bottom end of town (left side), nor the shuttered block halfway down the main street (a defunct hotel, I think), but a tucked-away ranch-style complex at the northerly top end – a veritable oasis in an accommodation desert. It was run by an ageing Frenchman and was called, appropriately enough, *Ban Farang*. Amiable solicitous Monsieur Roger had an eye for detail and a feeling for ambience. His rooms were clean, comfortable and well-appointed, with thoughtful extras. This was the only lodging we ever found which had a UV mosquito electrocutor in every room. The place was a-twitter with an entourage of Shan girls, some from Burma. The pretty, round-faced Burmese-Shan lasses in the kitchen spoke not a word of Thai, let alone English, but they had learned to turn out a respectable *cordon bleu*.

Khun Yuam's busy main street lay tipped down the side of a steep hill. There was not a lot to see here. Although not immediately apparent, the town was a big logging centre, with Union Par Co. one of the key operators. Every third or fourth house down the main drag was involved in some way with the extraction and processing of hardwood from nearby Burma's virgin forests, and many of the shops were little more than fronts for dubious timber middlemen. No doubt, much of the teak stripped from the forests of the homelands of the Padaung and Kayaw, if it did not come over the border at Mai Nai Soi, crossed near Khun Yuam. Parked before the houses were dirty battered logging lorries, the trailing rear axle section of each one jumped up onto the back of the main lorry as if the two parts were copulating.

In spite of the fact that Karenni territory lay to the west, Khun Yuam was actually a Shan outpost. The charm of the town was that it had remained traditional. Many of its buildings were still wooden shophouses. In the evenings tall thin *tai yai* housewives in conical hats sold savouries or sweetmeats directly out of their front rooms. Like Pai town and Huai Pong village, Khun Yuam had been another important staging post in Mae Hong Son province for Japanese troops during the Second World War. In the town itself, Wat Muai Tor had played host to a Japanese field hospital, and a wartime airfield had been laid out nearby (still visible). Some seven kms west of Khun Yuam market, in Tor Pae village, Wat Tor Pae had been the site of a large Japanese camp by the River Yuam, which had doubled as a gathering area for logs and rafts. There was a cultural centre in Khun Yuam (signed), which had an indoor museum housing some 500 exhibits relating to the Japanese wartime occupation, including rifles and other weapons, overcoats, lamps, boxes and personal items.

After Khun Yuam (km 66), a flattish, relatively good road snaked for a long way down a valley. A succession of mountainsides and valley-floor paddies was punctuated by the villages of **Muang Pon** (km 77), **Hang Pon** (km 83), **Ta Hin Som** (km 88), Karen **Nong Haeng** (km 90) and **Mae La Luang** (km 112), the last an assimilated Lawa place. The Honda was in its element, swinging through exquisite sunlit oriental countryside. We breasted groves of red-flowering lacquer trees, but there were also depressing sights – a number of massive log depots. Stopping once for a rest, we found at the roadside a carpet of outsize, dried-out leaves, measuring 2 ft long by 18 inches wide. They cracked like poppadoms under our feet. Further on, a Karen boy waved to us with a 5-ft-long brown snake he had caught. And then a truck overtook us, with a fully grown bull elephant in the back. At the moment the vehicle hauled past us, the beast decided to do a mighty piss, with the result that on our run in to Mae La Noi we had a free shower.

Thirty kms short of Mae Sariang, **Mae La Noi** (km 131) was another assimilated Lawa village. The survivors here of the ancient Lawa race were now physically and culturally virtually indistinguishable from local Thais. Our plan, before reaching Mae Sariang, was to investigate a place called Mae La Oop, which was a mountaintop Lawa village not far offroad from Mae La Noi that was said to have remained traditional. Seeing that we were about to head off into the hills again, we took a good lunch – inasmuch as noodle soup and fried rice can ever make a good meal – at one of the roadside eating places in Mae La Noi, also stocking up with a few emergency provisions in its little market. Here, *songtaew* drivers were sitting around, waiting for people from the surrounding hill villages to finish their shopping before returning home, and we quizzed them about the way up to Mae La Oop. For once, they were gratifyingly precise. The way was a dirt road (the H1266), which started just 400 metres south of Mae La Noi and went east 25 kms up into the mountains (Map 18). The route was not a bad one.

*

Side trip to Mae La Oop

The drivers were right. Just beyond the bridge at the bottom end of Mae La Noi, a fair dirt road began wriggling its way (Map 18) into the vast highland wilderness that extended right across to Mae Chaem and the Doi Intanon massif (Thailand's highest mountain). Gently but uninterruptedly, it climbed out of the River Yuam valley all the way up to Mae La Oop. The outlying villages of **Pa Maak** and **Huai Rin** gave way to the halfway Karen settlements of **Huai Maak Noon** (right/south side) and **Mae Sa Kua** (left side). The latter village in particular enjoyed an incomparable setting. About one km north of the track, it was an island cluster of roofs on a hilltop in a sea of forest. Tiny glints of Karen cerise – from washing hung out to dry in the sun – could just be made out between the brown leaf rooftops in the endless canopy of green. Beyond it, further to the north, the isolated settlement was back-grounded by bluish mountain ridges.

Presently, the road emerged from the forest cover into denuded upland country. Bald rounded mountaintops, covered only with scrub, receded mile after mile in every direction. Here and there, in the steep folds between the hillsides, lay out-of-the-way patches of terraced paddy. The headman of Mae La Oop later confessed to us that the Lawa themselves were responsible for this deforestation, having over the centuries cut all the trees down for housebuilding and firewood (although British logging companies operating out of Burma many years ago may also have had a hand in it). The elevated trail continued for some distance through this bleak open cool terrain until, rounding the shoulder of a mountainside, we suddenly caught sight of our destination. Mae La Oop, a concentration of wooden dwellings, lay across a valley, perched on the crest of a ridge like some precarious Tibetan outpost. It was but a short ride further until, 25 kms from the H108, we came to the eyrie. Signs at its entrance said that the dirt trail continued to the Karen villages of Huai Ha, Huai Horm and Du Lo Boe, as well as to the remote Lawa hamlet of La Ang (a further 16.5 kms). Ultimately the high-altitude dirt road would be pushed through to Mae Hae Tai, linking the area up with distant Mae Chaem.

Mae La Oop

With 160 houses and the benefits of electricity, Mae La Oop was a relatively large and developed Lawa settlement. There were a couple of tiny stores, a fair-sized school at the bottom north-westerly end, a small temple, a health centre and some kind of government development building. But otherwise it was a traditional place, similar, for example, to Chang Mor – another typical Lawa village. The main street, an uneven surface of stamped earth and humps of polished rock, ran the length of the flat ridgecrest. From time to time dust squalls, caused by strange hot-air turbulances convecting up out of the valleys, scorched along it. Black pot-bellied pigs rooted around everywhere, along with dogs, chickens, buffaloes and cows. We even saw sheep in Mae La Oop. These domestic animals were kept for eating or trading, but also for sacrificing. Essentially the houses lined the main street on each side. Simple primitive affairs, high on stilts and mostly with grass roofs, they were nevertheless solidly built of wood and had spacious front platforms. From their mountaintop eyrie at nearly 4000 ft, these Lawa enjoyed spectacular views to the north and south.

Near the village centre, we found a group of people busy with ropes, levers and plumb lines, erecting the frame of a new house. We stopped to quiz them about accommodation. Everybody – man, woman and child – gathered round. They had dark coppery careworn faces, and virtually all except the infants were smoking short pipes. The women and the older men were in some sort of costume, and the children all had hacking coughs. Most of the females were diminutive, and in general these people looked downtrodden, but they were very friendly. There was nowhere to stay in Mae La Oop, they reported, and no eating places either. We suggested the headman. Ah, the *po luang*, they said (a dialect word for *pu yai* or headman), yes, we could try there. It was the tin-roofed house over there with the new extension.

The headman, a pleasant fellow in his forties called Boonyeuan Promsermsook, was happy to let us camp in his new extension if we did not mind the total lack of furnishing. With no alternative, we naturally gratefully accepted his offer. His wife and daughters moved to bring us refreshments from the gloomy smoky kitchen at the back. We expressed a desire to clean up a little first. Immediately, we ran into the two major problems of staying in a Lawa village – food and water. Living on a mountaintop might be defensively sound and agreeably cool, but it was hardly practical waterwise. Whereas most other hill-tribe and minority peoples douched themselves regularly towards

178

sundown, the Lawa seemed never to wash at all. Of course, no rivers or streams ran up here, but there were large circular cement tanks around the village, which collected rainwater. The Promsermsook family directed us to one of these near the school. But three months out from the end of the rainy season, the tank was already empty. We brought our problem to the village schoolteachers, and they invited us to wash in the 'bathroom' under their house. But the modest plastic urn in their *hongnam* held hardly enough water to rinse our hands, let alone take a bodywash. Increasingly peeved, we returned to the *po luang* to report our fruitless errand. He referred us to a cubicle near his house which contained a cement trough, half full of water. But this had clearly not been used for some time. The water was infested with small wormlike organisms jackknifing hither and thither. Preferring to remain dirty for two or three days than to risk picking up some frightful tropical disease, we gave up the idea of trying to wash in Mae La Oop. It was not pleasant later that evening having to slip into our sleeping bags caked in sweat and dirt from the ride. The situation was salvaged to some extent the next day, when we discovered a spring some way down the mountain. A 20-minute walk down a zigzag path brought us to a pipe sticking out of the hillside, which dribbled water. Here we were able to clean up a bit, but we saw no Lawa doing likewise.

The headman and his womenfolk were exceptionally hospitable, bringing food three times a day. But it was always cold rice, a kind of marrow soup, a saucerful of tinned sardines, and bananas. We were glad of our emergency provisions from Mae La Noi, although instant noodles and coconut cake for breakfast, lunch and dinner was not a big improvement on the recurring marrow gruel. The food problem in Mae La Oop was not helped by the fact that the drinking water (from heaven knows where) came from dirty old oil cans. Also the water, tea and even *lao kao* was drunk from metal goblets and glass tumblers ingrained with grime, while the food was served on enamelled tin plates which looked as if they had never been properly washed up. The situation was little different at Chang Mor, another Lawa village we once stayed in. It struck us as remarkable that a people so ancient as the Lawa and with an early history apparently so illustrious should now be so backward and unfastidious. Theirs seemed to be a civilization in steep decline.

Out on the balcony we had noticed chains and padding which looked like elephant working tackle, and we asked Boonyeuan if the Lawa used elephants and if he himself had any. They did use them, he replied, for dragging logs, and he himself had two elephants. Actually, until recently he had owned four, but had sold two in order to pay for his extension. While we were sitting on the bare wooden floor, eating our Ma-maa noodles and toying with the pee-coloured marrow soup, a succession of people called by to consult with the *po luang*, but mainly to gawp at us. They included the teachers, who were finalizing arrangements for some celebration on the morrow, village elders come to pass the time of day with their chief, women suckling babies, and half the children of Mae La Oop. After a while, Boonyeuan brought from the kitchen some home-made rice whisky, which his wife was in the process of distilling at that very moment. We had brought with us a 'flattie' (half bottle) of Mekhong and added it to the supply. The Lawa made their *lao kao* out of rice, yeast and palm

179

sugar only, and were partial to it, the headman being no exception. He liberally helped himself first to our Mekhong and then to his hooch. It was the beginning of an evening of conviviality which went on until the small hours.

During the protracted session, the *po luang* and elders related some interesting stories about the Lawa, tales that the assembled party obviously relished hearing, although they had undoubtedly heard them many times before. One, rehearsed by an old man in our 'inner' circle, was a celebrated story concerning the origins of the Lawa. The race had actually once lived in the Salween valley area, he said, but had been chased out of it into the Yuam river valley by an extraordinary huge boulder. To escape the rock, the Lawa had then run up the narrow bed of the Mae La Noi river, but it had still pursued them. Finally, the boulder had lost sight of the fugitives and paused. A bird told the Lawa people that they were safe where they now were, because the rock could not find them. This was how the Lawa had come to live in the inhospitable mountains above Mae La Noi. But the boulder was still in the stream where it had stopped, which was why, when people used the path down the bed of the Mae La Noi river, they fell silent near the big boulder, for fear that it might start chasing them again if it heard their language. The story was evidently an attempt to account in mythical terms for a major displacement or migration of the Lawa in their distant past.

A second elder narrated another mythical dispersal story, which is undoubtedly grounded in historical fact. There was a time, before Mon and Tai rulers governed 'Thailand', when the Lawa had had their own kings, who had controlled the whole region. The last of these had been a certain Khun Luang Wilanka. When the burgeoning Mon kingdom of Haripoonchai or Haripoonjaya (today's Lampoon) had grown so powerful as to threaten the Lawa and their domination, a local power struggle had ensued between the Lawa and the Mon. It was determined that the struggle should be settled by a magic contest between Wilanka and the Mon queen of Haripoonchai, a lady called Chaam Taewi. Unfortunately, Wilanka had lost this contest, and, worsted in the wizardry by the Mon queen, he and his people had beaten a hasty retreat into the mountains to the west of Haripoonchai.[2]

This story led a third man to narrate a favourite Lawa legend. He spoke of a fabulous hidden Lawa treasure hoard (a trove that had perhaps been stashed either in the wake of the victory of the Mon over the Lawa, or, later, following the conquest of the Lawa and the Mon by the Tai). There used once to be a book, complete with maps, which showed where all the treasure of the Lawa, mainly silver, was buried. Unfortunately, one of the Siamese kings had got hold of this book and hidden it. He had then died, and the inventory had been lost

---

[2] Holt Hallett heard the Lawa legend of the vanquishing of Wilanka by Chaam Taewi (or Khun Luang Viranga/Milunga/Me-lang-ta and Queen Chamadevi/Chamatawi/Cham-a-ta-we/Sam-ma-tay-we, as they are also formulated) during his journey through Siam and past Lawa villages in 1876. A more detailed version of the legend is given by him in his book *A Thousand Miles on an Elephant in the Shan States* (1890, pp. 49-50), which he wrote to describe his journey. More can be read about Queen 'Chaam Théwi' in *An Asian Arcady* (first published in 1926, see pp. 263-68) by Reginald LeMay, who travelled in Siam around 1913-15. A further version of the Wilanka/Chaam Taewi legend, which in addition refers to the ancient capital of the Lawa, Muang Lameng, is given in Hallett's book (1890) on p. 58 (or see Footnote 2 below).

for generations. But there was a rumour that the treasure book had recently been found in Chiang Dao Cave...

The talk of the treasure encouraged a few people from the party to slip away and return with family heirlooms. The Lawa have a tradition of skilled silversmithery, and soon the floor was awash with argent artefacts. One one old man in particular emptied out of a *yaam* a cascade of items. As he was old, single and childless, he offered to sell some of them to us. Here were chunky Lawa bracelets; pairs of large cup-shaped earrings; sets of antique Shan betel boxes, repoussé with animals and mythical figures, and engraved on the base with Shan or Burmese lettering; characteristic Lawa pipes in silver and wood, in the shape of a U-tube and embellished with silver wire; and a strange Lawa coronet in the form of an expandable band, decorated on one side with a kind of upstanding diamond or star.

We remembered that our acquaintance Maha San, the spiritual leader or even 'king' of the Wa, whom we had met in Mae Or, had maintained that the Lawa people were closely connected with the Wa, just as the Wa and Lawa languages were similar. Our session with *po luang* Boonyeuan and the elders of Mae La Oop seemed a good occasion to test out this idea on the Lawa. Neither the headman nor the other older men were surprised. Boonyeuan said that the Lawa were able imperfectly to understand Wa people. Many words in their languages were the same or similar, for example the words for tree, house and dog (*khao, nyie, soh*). To put the matter beyond doubt, we fished out the beginners' Wa book that Maha San's clan had given us. The book, which was written in the Latin alphabet, led to an interesting discovery. From the book, we read out a list of Wa words and phrases, which some of the older Lawa present were able to identify for us in Thai. But their recognition of the Wa words and the link between Wa and Lawa was more remarkable than this. The literature says that Lawa has no written form. That may be true traditionally, but not in terms of recent history. When we handed the Wa booklet to our hosts, one or two of the oldest men were able to read it, even though the texts were rendered in the Latin alphabet. So these Lawa elders were not just understanding Wa, but also understanding it in written (Latin) form. They must have been able to read it on the basis of written Lawa, perhaps similarly systematized in the last hundred years (by missionaries?).

It was already after midnight, late by hill-tribe standards. Many people had drifted away, but some remained, unwilling to pass up any titbit relating to their mythology, history or culture. Eventually, even these lingerers disappeared, leaving just the *po luang* and ourselves. We were weary and would gladly have retired too, but headman Promsermsook insisted on just one more nip of *lao kao* – to round off such a pleasant evening. Finally, he got up too, and, our heads reeling from an excess of tipple with insufficient substance in our stomachs, we crawled into our sleeping bags. Our dreams were a welter of rolling boulders, treasures troves, King Wilanka, and Wa words.

Only an hour or two later, at 5.30am, we were awakened by clumping across the wooden floor. We tried to hide our heads inside our sleeping bags, but to little avail. Wailing Lawa music regaled us from a cassette recorder, and outside millions of cicadas made a piercing racket in the trees. Poking our heads out after a while, we found the headman sitting exactly where he had been the evening before. He was cleaning and playing with some kind of rifle, making a loud snick every time he pressed the trigger. A bottle of *lao* already stood in front of him, together with a small glass. It was as if he had not moved the whole night long. There was a silver workshop in Mae La Oop, the headman mused. He himself would be busy with the teachers that morning, but we might like to visit it on our own. We breakfasted on more stewed marrow and cold rice, and then, eager for a wash, searched out the dribbling pipe down the mountainside. Refreshed, we set off up the main street to investigate the silversmithery.

The workshop was located in a house near the entrance to the village. It was only a small affair. With a set of primitive tools, two young men were transforming small stamped bullets of silver into bracelets, fine chains and exquisite round repoussé boxes. It was not so much these objects that interested us as a strange stone artefact which the boys showed us. This was antique and fitted pleasingly into the palm of the hand when one wrapped one's fingers around it. It was smooth to the touch and seemed to us to be vaguely shaped like a duck. Smirking, the young men explained that the stone imitated a woman's genitalia. It was only when we examined it more closely that we saw their point. The stone was articulated. A male half fitted snugly into a female half. The two could be wiggled slightly, but not parted. The stone was an erotic object which a boy fondled in his hand when he went to flirt with a girl. It was supposed to bring him good luck on his errand.

In many houses in La Oop, women were weaving on their balconies. The Lawa were not just fine silversmiths (and workers of iron), but also skilled weavers. Their looms were of that simple type (backstrap, body/back-tension looms), where one end was attached to the house wall, while the other formed a backrest. When a woman, sitting on the floor, leaned back against the rest, she tautened the warp strings and could then weave across her lap. The women were mostly weaving material for skirts and shoulder bags. With La Oop being a traditional Lawa village, one of the joys of a visit there was the spectacle of the women and older men in costume. The clothes were not at all like Wa costume. Rather they seemed to us to show some Karen influence – the Lawa are reckoned to have borrowed much over recent centuries especially in terms of their attire from the Karen, something which *po luang* Promsermsook flatly denied. A description of traditional Lawa costume is included in the account of the Lawa people and culture below.

During our time in Mae La Oop, we searched the faces of the Lawa inhabitants. Sometimes it seemed to us that the wide-eyed children (see photo section) looked like 'Yellow Leaf' Mrabri infants we had seen over in Nan province, while some of the girls had Darkie's beauty. Other times, we thought we saw in their mothers the placid round faces of Khmu and Lao women, while the men, with their dark angular faces and (for Orientals) unusual hairiness of face and limb, resembled the wild sharp-featured hirsute Wa. But these people remained enigmatic. Here was a race, like their cousins the Wa, waiting to be much better understood. And if their history was rather obscure, the investigation and archaeology of Lawa prehistory had scarcely even started.

WORSTED IN WIZARDRY

Almost the most puzzling question was how a people apparently once so prominent and even civilized could now be so reduced and entropic. Their ancient faces were unmistakably careworn, and behind the openness, friendliness and hospitality there was an undeniable squalor. The villages were impoverished and disorderly. Their agro-economy was near subsistence level, with many Lawa men working as itinerant labourers. Sanitation was poor, and clothing was mostly dirty. Kitchens were gloomy and soot-encrusted, and cups and plates were unbearably grimy. The food was unappealing, and water was lacking. The Lawa, like the Wa, Mrabri and many other fragmentary Mon-Khmer peoples, seemed to be a tribe hopelessly compromised in history by the appearance of other races, in this case by the Mon, Khmer, Tai, Burmese, and latterly even Karen.

✻

Some notes on the Lawa people, their history and culture

The Lawa are one of South-East Asia's many splintered, fragmented and in some cases entropic Mon-Khmer peoples. They are an ancient, important and very interesting tribe. Being of Mon-Khmer stock, they are not related ethnically to the Thais of Thailand or to the many other Tai peoples. They claim with justification to be – and are widely considered to be – the indigenous inhabitants of Thailand, existing in the northern part of that present-day country before the arrival of the Mon, the Khmer and the Tai themselves.

The Lawa people go by and in the past have gone by several other names, including – as Schliesinger (2000) reports – the L'wa, Luwa, Lua, Lowa, Lavu'a, Lava and Milakkha. But the tribe, to add my own halfpennyworth of information based on casual enquiries, does not call itself Lawa, or the Lua commonly and sloppily used by Thais, or the L'wa of old Tai chronicles, but La-wua (in Mae La Oop) and La-voe (in the traditional and isolated Lawa village of Ho Gao, which lies north-west of La Oop, beyond La Ang and in the direction of Mae Chaem).

Within the Mon-Khmer group, which is itself subsumed under the overall Austro-Asiatic family of peoples or linguistic superstock, the Lawa are generally classified as belonging to the Palaungic branch. Within this specific branch, they are closely related to the Wa people, the Palaung tribe, the Lamet, and other minority peoples, while as part of the larger Mon-Khmer group the Lawa are less closely related to the Mon (of south-eastern Burma and western Thailand), to the Khmu (of Laos and Thailand's Nan province), to the Lua or Htin (of Thailand's Nan province and Laos' Sayaburi province), to the Mrabri or 'Stone Age' 'Yellow Leaf' people (of Thailand's Nan province and Laos' Sayaburi province), and to other peoples. Schliesinger (2000) states that the Lawa themselves can be divided into two sub-groups, the Moi Bi and Ao Ta, although I have never heard of these.

As a Mon-Khmer tribe, the Lawa are of a racial stock quite other than that of the Thai. They are short stocky mountain peasant people with the strikingly dark skin pigmentation that is characteristic of Wa-related groups, and with the angular or 'craggy' facial features and hairiness that is uncharacteristic of smooth-skinned Mongoloid, Sinitic or Tai peoples such as the Thais, Chinese, Hmong, Yao and Akha.

South-East Asia is one of the most diverse and complex ethno-linguistic regions in the world, and there is still considerable controversy among scholars about the classification of its peoples – including the Lawa, Wa and other Mon-Khmer tribes – into the various families (or superstocks), groups (or phyla or sub-families) and branches. Just as this is the case, so the history and migration of the Mon-Khmer peoples and, more specifically, of the Lawa is also controversial and obscure. Thus, one can read in the literature that the Austro-Asiatic peoples, of which the Mon-Khmer form the majority, began moving into mainland South-East Asia some 6,000 years ago (4,000 BC) via northern Vietnam, from where they migrated south and west as far as India. Or that the Mon-Khmer peoples came from India about 4,000 years ago (2,000 BC), proceeding to occupy large parts of South-East Asia and Yunnan province in China. Doing so, they partly mixed with pre-existing Melanesians (themselves a mixture of Proto-Australians and very early Negrito types), giving rise to the visibly negroid blood of Indo-China's Mon-Khmer peoples.

And of the Lawa one can read that they derive from a common aboriginal ethnic source going back thousands of years that also included the ancestors of the Khmu, Lua (Htin) and maybe Mrabri, and which perhaps inhabited southern Yunnan, from where they migrated southwards as a result of pressure from the Tai. Or that the forerunners of the Lawa were of Polynesian-Micronesian stock, and migrated northwards from the south. Or that, similarly, the Lawa, like other Mon-Khmer peoples, scattered northwards more than 2,000 years ago from regions in southern Thailand, Malaysia, Cambodia and Vietnam. And then one can surmise that the more recent ancestors of the Lawa neither migrated from India nor Yunnan nor Vietnam nor the south, but developed out of palaeolithic and neolithic people who had resided locally for thousands of years. This might then link the ancestors of the Lawa or the Lawa themselves with the people who lived in the caves near Soppong and elsewhere thousands of years ago, and who later buried their dead in wooden coffins in the caves 1,200-2,200 years ago and maybe up to 4,000 years ago (see Chapter 4). These origins do not necessarily entirely exclude one another, as some of them might form a sequence, with the people moving around.

The position of the Lawa in more recent history is clearer. Whether or not they came from Yunnan or India or Vietnam or the south, or developed out of pre-existing local people, by probably 2,000 years ago or longer and certainly at least 1,500 years ago, the Lawa were living in what is now northern Thailand as one of the area's first residents and as the largest and first identifiable (Mon-Khmer) ethnic group. Their territory centred on the area of present-day Chiang Mai, where they seem to have had their capital. Arguably, in their heyday, they occupied the whole of northern Thailand (possibly as far south as Bangkok), the Shan State area in Burma, eastern Burma as far as the Salween river, parts of Yunnan (Sipsong Pan-Na), and northern Laos, possibly extending even as far as the China Sea. More archaeology should eventually settle the extent of their large kingdom.

WORSTED IN WIZARDRY

For hundreds of years, the Lawa had a flourishing civilization. In Thailand, they seem to have had 'cities' at or near places such as Chiang Saen, Chiang Khong, Chiang Mai, Lampang, Prao and maybe Mae Sariang, 'cities' that ultimately gave rise to these Thai towns. The Lawa claim with justification to have founded Chiang Mai, a claim that the Wa also make independently, based on their lore. Various kinds of evidence back up the dual assertion. Just west of Chiang Mai, to the south of an imaginary line drawn between the city centre and Doi Sutep, lies a ruined ancient city, called 'Muang Lameng', which is said to have been the former Lawa capital prior to the arrival of the Tai. I do not know if any of its remains are still visible today, but around 1914 Reginald LeMay visited them, as he relates in his *An Asian Arcady: The Land and Peoples of Northern Siam* (1926, p. 80) and found 'fosses and portions of ramparts'.[3] The sites of other ancient towns surround Chiang Mai, which may or may not have been Lawa. James McCarthy, who was in Chiang Mai especially about 1890, writes in his *Surveying and Exploring in Siam* that to the north of the city lay the once famous Muang Timan, on the downfall of which the present city came into existence. The Lawa claim to have built the giant pagoda Chedi Luang in Chiang Mai (and may have built its twin in Chiang Saen). In 1797, when the Lan-Na Tai king Kaawila moved his royal court from near Lampoon back to Chiang Mai after a 22-year absence, ceremoniously re-entering the city, Lawa were given pride of place at the head of the procession, suggesting that they had some special connection with Chiang Mai. And until about 1850, perhaps likewise acknowledging that the Lawa were the original owners of the land, the kings of Chiang Mai used to pay nominal tribute to the Lawa, granting certain Lawa villages special rights and taxes.

In the middle of the 8th century (possibly in AD 767 or 769), the Mon princess Chaam Taewi (she of the legend of the magic contest with the Lawa leader Wilanka) came from Lopburi to found and be the first ruler of

---

[3] Before LeMay, Hallett also wrote of this putative ancient Lawa capital, which he may likewise have visited (some 40 years earlier, about 1876). In his *A Thousand Miles on an Elephant* (1890, p. 120), he writes: '...between the city [Chiang Mai] and Loi Soo Tayp [Doi Sutep] are the ruins of Muang La Maing, the ancient capital of the Lawas, of which nothing but the ramparts and ditches remain.' Earlier in the same book (p. 58), Hallett relates a legend which both refers to Muang Lameng (or Muang La Maing, or Muang Lamung) and also links the ancient Lawa capital with the Lawa king Wilanka and the Mon princess Chaam Taewi, the feuding duo of another legend mentioned above. 'On the [Tai] first entering the [Chiang Mai] country, they found the city of La-Maing, which had recently been founded by Melang-ta [Wilanka], the king of the Lawas, deserted. At that time, the whole of the country to the south of the Burmese [Tai] states belonged to the Lawas, who resided in the hills in the dry season and cultivated the plains in the rainy season. Overrunning the plains at the time when cultivation was not going on, the [Tai] occupied La-Maing, the ruins of which adjoin the present city of [Chiang Mai], as well as Lampoon and other similarly deserted Lawa towns. The Lawa king gathered a great army in the hills to drive the [Tai] out of his country, but finding them strongly entrenched and in great force, he offered to form an alliance with them if they would cement it by giving him in marriage Nang Sam-ma-tay-we, the beautiful and accomplished daughter of the...prince of Lampoon. The [Tai] chief haughtily rejected the offer of the Lawa king, and marched with a great host into the hills, attacked Me-lang-ta, scattered his army, and slew him. The place where he was killed is known as La-wat, "the Lawa destroyed"; and the king became the Pee Hluang [*pi luang* or great spirit] or tutelary deity of the region, and resides in a cave... to the north-east of [Chiang Mai].'

185

THREE PAGODAS

Haripoonchai or Haripoonjaya, a city state just a few miles south of the Lawa capital, where the town of Lampoon (Lamphun) now stands. From Thailand's Mon period, many legends survive which indicate that the Lawa had a close relationship with Mon Haripoonchai. Expanding into northern Thailand, the Mon encountered a numerous and dominant people called the L'wa, who were ruled by a powerful chieftain, who had his capital near the site of present-day Chiang Mai. For a while, no doubt, the Lawa and the Mon lived harmoniously side by side – there was room for everybody. But as the Mon presence became more insistent, the Lawa resisted the creeping conquest. However, they must have been reduced or checked in some way, or perhaps they withdrew to areas where there was no Mon presence. If the magic contest legend is correct, the L'wa must have suffered some kind of eclipse.

The Mon civilization of Lopburi and Haripoonchai (Lampoon) flourished for several centuries, with Mon Haripoonchai enjoying a golden era from about AD 1160 to 1280. But at the beginning of the 11th century, Lopburi became a vassal of the Khmer empire, initiating campaigns between the Mon and the Khmer, with the Mon presumably trying to liberate Lopburi, and with the Khmer seeking to add the Haripoonchai kingdom or principality to their empire. So things went on until the start of the 13th century, when Khmer military power waned in central Thailand, and the situation eased for Lampoon. Altogether, Mon pre-eminence at Haripoonchai lasted some 500 years, from c. AD 769 until about the middle of the 13th century and the advent of the Tai. The arrival of the Tai in proto-Thailand spelled the essential demise not only of the Mon, but also of the Lawa.

The Tai came to Lawa and Mon-occupied 'northern Thailand' from Nan Chao, a predominantly Tai state to the north-east that flourished AD 650-1250 in south-western China, in the area of the present-day provinces of Yunnan and Sichuan. Actually, they had already been migrating south-west in dribs and drabs from that area for some 200 years, between about AD 1050 and 1250. Many reasons have been put forward to explain why so many Tai left Nan Chao, but a crucial factor was undoubtedly the conquest of the state by the Mongols under Kublai Khan in 1253. The Tai migrated first into what is now Laos, and from there westward across the Mae Khong (Mekong) river into today's Shan State, Burma, as well as south-westward into 'northern Thailand', likewise crossing the Mae Khong. The Tai spread out in 'Laos', parts of the 'Shan State', the future Lan-Na or northern Thailand, subsequently central and southern 'Thailand' or future Siam, what was later Isaan, and elsewhere.

It is thought that the Tai first entered proto-Thailand somewhere near Chiang Saen, where they established a bridgehead settlement at or near what seems to have been a pre-existing Lawa place. For a record indicates that a Lawa town bearing the name of Muang Nguan Yang or Ngoen Yaang was founded at the site of Chiang Saen by a certain Paya Anurudha and 1000 followers about AD 850. On the other hand, another record tells that Chiang Saen was the place where around AD 1050 the Lawa set up an independent state, again known as Ngoen Yang, starting there a dynasty under a king called Lao Chok or, in Pali, Lava Chakkaraja or Lawa Changkarat. Yet other ancient chronicles identify this Lawa king Chakkaraja and his dynasty with the legendary principality of Yonok, said to have been situated either at Chiang Saen or somewhere opposite the town, on the east bank of the Mae Khong. Thus, for perhaps 200 or 400 years, depending if one counts from AD 850 or AD 1050, Ngoen Yang or Yonok was ruled by a score of Lawa Chakkaraja's successors, who culminated in Khun Chuang, termed in chronicles 'the hero-king of Yonok', who is said even to have mightily extended the borders of the principality north to the Tai territory of Sipsong Pan-Na and north-east into Muang Puan (the modern province of Chiang Kwang in Laos). These details suggest the perhaps surprising might and territorial extent of the Lawa even at the time of the Mon Haripoonchai kingdom and of the southward filtering Tai.

Upon reaching 'northern Thailand' and the 'Shan State' between AD 1050 and 1250, the Tai initially doubtless lived quietly by themselves – again, there was space enough for everyone – or lived under the tutelage of residual Lawa chiefs and Mon princelings. But as their numbers grew and they became more established, they increasingly assimilated and then dominated the locals they encountered. Powerful Tai chieftains began setting up small independent principalities, such as Payao. Reportedly, one of the largest of these was the same legendary Yonok, whose capital is thought to have been situated either at present-day Chiang Saen or just across the Mae Khong from it. We might conjecture that the Tai took over Yonok or Ngoen Yang from the Lawa and their local Chakkaraja dynasty.

Between around AD 1250 and 1300, the Tai finally preponderated. The most significant of the incoming Tai chieftains was Mengrai, the famous king of Thai and especially northern Thai (Lan-Na) history. Becoming king of Yonok in 1259, he left the Chiang Saen area three or four years later to set up in 1262 or 1263 Chiang Rai, which means '(King Meng) Rai's City', which was to be the capital of a new realm of his. He then captured Chiang Khong from the Lawa, founded Fang in 1274, and advanced south to wage war on the Mon city state of Haripoonchai, taking it after a protracted siege in either 1281 or 1292, after which the principality's last Mon ruler fled south. With Yonok (Chiang Saen), Chiang Rai, Chiang Khong and Haripoonchai now all Tai, the northern Thai kingdom of Lan-Na was born in the latter decades of the 13th century. But Mengrai's greatest achievement was still to come. In 1296, just north of Haripoonchai, he founded 'New City' or Chiang Mai. Mengrai and his successors ruled variously out of Chiang Rai, Chiang Mai and Yonok (Chiang Saen), until in 1350 they moved their capital definitively to Chiang Mai. By 1400 at the latest, virtually the whole of Lan-Na or northern Thailand was ruled by the Tai (to be precise, by the Tai Yuan), dominated to a greater or lesser extent by Chiang Mai. Conversely, the 500-year-old era of the Mon was over, and the even longer incumbency of the Lawa, which had lasted perhaps 1,000 years or more, was also finished.

The Lawa were progressively squeezed from the Chiang Mai area, important parts of Lan-Na, and seemingly the territory of today's Shan State. Historical documents from the time of the Tai kingdom of Chiang Tung (Kengtung in today's Shan State, Burma) not only record the existence in the region of the Lawa, but note that at the end of the 13th century King Mengrai sent troops to expel them. They fled into the hills away from the fertile areas under Tai control, especially into the extensive mountainous hinterland to the north-west, west and south-west of Chiang Mai, where the remnant descendants of those L'wa live to this day. But they were also exiled (or merely continued to live) e.g. north-west of Chiang Mai at places like Wiang Haeng, and north-east of Chiang Mai at places like Wiang Pa Pao. Some Lawa became servants of the royal families at the court of Chiang Mai and at the befriended court of the Chiang Tung kingdom.

As said earlier, the Lawa and the Wa peoples are closely related to each other ethno-linguistically. They themselves know this and, as we 'proved' in Mae La Oop, can imperfectly understand each other, despite having been separated for hundreds of years and having developed different traditions over time. Given this, it is plausible that the Lawa and the Wa descended from one and the same people. This *Urvolk* or original people must be the L'wa of the period from roughly 2000 years ago to AD1400. But how did they become sundered? How is it that the Lawa now inhabit the mountains north-east of Mae Sariang while their cousins the Wa mostly live in the Wa sub-state in north-east Burma, close to the Chinese border (even if pockets of Wa have recently come to live along Thailand's northern border with the Shan State, Burma)? They are separated by a considerable distance, comprising the whole of the Shan State and a good chunk of northern Thailand.

If the above sketchy historical account is correct, two or three explanatory scenarios suggest themselves. Conceivably, some of the L'wa were once living in what is now the Chinese province of Yunnan, just as the rest occupied a much wider area of Indo-China, but were pushed out of 'Yunnan', across the Mae Khong river, and into the mountains of the Wa sub-state, by some other, more powerful group, perhaps the Mongols, where the ousted L'wa became the Wa. Perhaps the L'wa *Urvolk* basically inhabited 'northern Thailand', but, with the arrival of the Tai and the establishment of the Tai kingdoms of Lan-Na and Chiang Tung, was split in such a way that one half was relegated to the plateau between Chiang Mai and Mae Sariang to become the Lawa, while the other half was pushed north, across the 'Shan State' to the inhospitable 'Wa' mountains between the Salween river and the Chinese border, where they became the Wa. But the most likely scenario, so it seems to me, is that at the time of the advent of the Tai the L'wa were living not just in 'northern Thailand' but also to the north, up on what is now the Shan plateau or the Shan State (as well as elsewhere), forming an unbroken population across the whole wider area. Here, on the 'Shan' plateau, they were squeezed north by the incoming Tai Yai (or Shan) arriving with the Tai Yuan (or Lan-Na Tai) as the overall Tai peoples migrated south and west. The Tai Yai established the Tai kingdom of Chiang Tung, while the L'wa were split off from their brothers and forced up into the 'Wa' hills, where over hundreds of years they became the Wa. Here, they declined to become the relatively primitive Wa of Burma, while in the rugged hinterland east of Chiang Mai the 'Thai' L'wa declined to become the reduced Lawa ethnic minority that we know today.

These days, in Thailand, the Lawa are really only to be found on the plateau north-east of Mae Sariang. Here they live in some two dozen villages, eking out an existence. I say 'really only' because actually Lawa live almost all

188

over Thailand, but over the centuries they have been assimilated either completely or largely into mainstream Thai society. (By no means all the L'wa ancestors of the Lawa fled or were pushed into the hills at the time the Tai conquered Lan-Na. Many, perhaps the majority, stayed roughly where they were, knuckling under to the new Tai masters.) Most Lawa, therefore, have long since been thus submerged in mainstream Thai society. Examples of places that are Lawa but largely integrated, such that in them you would not know that they were Lawa, but would mistake them for regular Thai villages, are Mae La Luang, Mae La Noi, Kong Loi, Bo Luang, Bo Sali (near Mae Waen, south of the H108 Mae Sariang/Hot road), Hua Lin (west of San Pa Tong) and Wiang Pa Pao (halfway between Chiang Mai and Chiang Rai on the H118 road – the Lawa here are said to have come from Chiang Tung/Kengtung). Thus, authentic, unassimilated, identifiably Lawa villages, where some people even still wear traditional tribal costume, exist only around the Mae La Oop – Ho Gao – Chang Mor triangle, although there are reportedly relatively unassimilated Lawa villages elsewhere in Thailand, notably in parts of Kanchanaburi province. In 1989, Chiang Mai's Tribal Research Institute put the number of unassimilated Lawa in Thailand at 7,845, accounting for 1.42% of the country's hill-tribe population. By 1995, a census of Bangkok's Department of Public Welfare had raised this figure to 17,346. In 2002, this number is probably closer to 20,000. Provincewise, Lawa are to be found mainly in western Chiang Mai (Mae Chaem district) and eastern Mae Hong Son, but also in Chiang Rai, Lampoon, Lampang, Utai Tani, Supanburi and, as said, Kanchanaburi.

Lawa villages vary in size from relatively large, like Mae La Oop, with some 160 houses to quite small, with perhaps 20 houses. These villages are typically built at an altitude of 3000-4000 ft, many on ridge tops or crests. As we have seen, this gives the inhabitants a good view and traditionally an element of safety, but it leads to problems with the supply of water. Village houses are primitive dwellings, solidly constructed of wood, raised high on stilts, with grass roofs (increasingly the tendency is to use galvanized metal sheeting) and spacious front platforms or balconies. The roofs of many Lawa houses are decorated with a galae, which is a wooden V-shaped gable-end traditional to the Lawa and apparently taken over from them by the Tai. To enter a house, you climb up a wooden ladder onto the balcony. The balcony is used for preparing food, for washing up (the bits fall through to the chickens and pigs underneath), and for drying washing. Ladies weave on the balcony, or make roofing panels, and visitors can sleep there too. Inside the house there is basically one big room, which has areas partitioned off to form sleeping cubicles for family members. There is little or no furniture. The central feature is the hearth, which is a shallow wooden box on the floor containing sand and smouldering logs. The family cook here, sit around it, eat, relax, smoke their pipes, keep warm in winter, chat to friends, and frequently sleep. Hanging above the hearth is a bamboo tray, used for smoking bits of meat. A feature of Lawa houses, as you will find out if you stay in one, is that people have little privacy. In a village, everybody freely wanders in and out of everybody else's house all the time, even if the owner is not there.

THREE PAGODAS

The Lawa have a near-subsistence agricultural economy. They grow rice (practising wet-rice cultivation with irrigated/inundated fields), maize, sweet potatoes, marrows, Chinese mustard, aubergines, chillies, and other vegetables, and raise buffaloes, pigs and chickens. Like all the hill peoples, they hunt wild animals. Recently, encouraged by the authorities, they have started cultivating cash crops such as cabbages, kidney beans, carrots and coffee beans. The occasional Lawa village grows opium for its own use and as an illegal cash crop (I have seen one such village with several poppy fields), but the Lawa are not traditionally associated with opium. They have become clever at constructing terraced paddy fields in steep awkward terrain. Traditionally, many Lawa men have worked – and still do work – as itinerant labourers in other towns and villages and, for example, in mines. The headman at Lawa Chang Mor village said that he once used to work in a tin mine near Om Koi, while at the Lawa village of Ho Gao about a third of the inhabitants will be working away (mostly in Chiang Mai) at any one time (for accounts both of Chang Mor and traditional Ho Gao, see my guide book *Trek It Yourself in Northern Thailand*, Treks 20 & 23).

The Lawa diet is very simple and monotonous, as we discovered. Almost every day, three times a day, they eat rice, marrow soup, chilli dip, a dried fish and sometimes some stewed or smoked meat from a sacrificed animal or from the hunt. They do not have regular cups of tea or coffee as we do, but instead drink water drawn from a spring and kept in old plastic engine-oil containers. The Lawa are big drinkers of rice whisky, which they distil themselves from rice husks, water, yeast and palm sugar. Of an evening, sitting on the floor with friends around the hearth, they will drink this home-made hooch with a kettleful of China tea, brewed on the fire.

If you were a Lawa woman, your typical day would be as follows: you would get up at first light, get the fire going in the hearth, and cook breakfast – fresh sticky rice and squash soup. Then you would either do the washing and look after your many children, or, more probably, go to your field, in which case the grandparents would look after the children. Your field is on a mountainside often far away, involving a long trudge in the hot sun. On your way back from hoeing, weeding, harvesting or whatever, every day you gather a heavy load of firewood, which you lug back uphill on your back to the village. You fetch fresh spring water – down in the valley, of course – or cajole your children into getting it. You pound rice in the rice stamper under your house. At regular intervals, you distil rice whisky under or in your house. It takes about 3 hours to make 2½ bottles. You won't drink this yourself, but your husband, the headman and friends will polish it off in an evening. From time to time, you weave smocks and skirts for yourself and your daughters. You rarely wash, or so it seems to *farang* visitors, you smoke your pipe all day long, and to the Western outsider your pots and pans look filthy, greasy and soot-encrusted. You are quiet, uncomplaining, and accept your hard lot. If you are young, you probably dream of marrying a Western boy and fleeing to live like a princess in England or Germany or Switzerland.

Lawa men build houses, saw up timber, carry it to the village, also work in the fields, go hunting and fishing, slaughter and butcher wild and domestic animals, make gunpowder, go away to labour, otherwise gamble and have a lazy time smoking and drinking. Some men, as we saw, are engaged in silversmithery, for which the Lawa are famous. They produce objects on their own account (e.g. the decoration for Lawa pipes), but mainly to order for outsiders. Dealers from Chiang Mai come by with ingots of silver, leave their requirements, and later call to pick up the finished articles. Lawa smiths make fine silver chains, bracelets, necklaces, earrings, and repoussé boxes. If as a tourist you buy silverware in Chiang Mai in the Night Bazaar or in one of the handicraft factories, there is a good chance that it was made by a Lawa man in a Lawa village. Other men work as blacksmiths, forging machetes, chains and suchlike. Metal working has traditionally been a celebrated and distinguishing feature of the Lawa. In 1876, the English explorer Holt Hallett (as he says in his book *A Thousand Miles on an Elephant in the Shan States*, 1890, pp. 55-56, see also p. 143) observed them manufacturing elephant chains, machetes, muskets, spears, ploughs and other metal articles in Bo Luang village, and reports that they mined and smelted red iron oxide near Chang Mor, transporting the ingots by elephant to their villages. Evidently, there was a ready demand for the resulting wrought iron products all over Siam. This Lawa metal work was carried out not just north-east of Mae Sariang, but elsewhere in northern Thailand. Thus Hallett finds Lawa people mining and working iron, for example, in the Wiang Pa Pao area, around Mae Suai (north of Wiang Pa Pao), and in the Mae Lao valley (south of Chiang Rai in the direction of Pan and Payao). The availability of cheap Thai iron caused this work by the Lawa to lose its former importance.

The Lawa are not Buddhists, but animists, i.e. they believe in spirits, which reside in things. If they are Buddhist at all, they are animists who have acquired a veneer of Buddhism. In this respect an element of controversy attaches to the religion of the Lawa, for there is a school of thought which believes that, far from being basically animists who have overlaid their animism with Buddhism, they are actually fundamentally Buddhists who fell into animism after their displacement into the hills by the Mon and Tai. Whatever the case, it cannot be denied that in Lawa villages you can often see traces of Buddhism in people's houses – little shrines, Buddha figures and amulets on shelves. Some Lawa, like a number of their Wa cousins, are Christians, having been converted by missionaries. There are Christian Lawa and churches, for example, at Mae La Oop, Ho Gao and Ho Mai. In the mid-1990s, there were 46 converts in Mae La Oop, won by a missionary who had meanwhile gone, leaving a Lawa priest in charge.

Animist Lawa believe in a pantheon of spirits, including the spirits of the sky, the mountain, forest, village, village entrance, house, field, people, the human body, and of many natural phenomena, such as the virgin jungle, trees, fallen trees, streams, landslips, spiders, ants, and so on. The Lawa also venerate their ancestors. Signs of animism in a Lawa village are, besides the sacrificing of chickens and other animals, so-called Solomon's seals (star-shaped bamboo objects) above the lintels of houses, mirrors beside house doors, and cotton strings around people's wrists, ankles and necks. These are all devices for warding off evil spirits. Spirits can be bad as well as good. While the good ones need humouring or propitiating, the bad ones require appeasing. This is done by offering food to the spirits or, as indicated, by sacrificing animals to them. In Mae La Oop, two ceremonies, held annually, are especially important. One is to honour the ancestors, and every July the villagers offer one buffalo to the spirits of their forebears. The other is an offering to the spirit of the village. Made every 10 November by the two oldest inhabitants of La Oop, it involves the sacrifice of eight pigs or cows or whatever – the type of animal is rotated, while in other Lawa villages the number of animals offered differs. It is entertaining watching the Lawa put out food as offerings for the spirits. Within seconds a passing dog has bolted the food. The sacrificing of animals and proffering of food has another amusing aspect, though not for the poor animals. As the headman of Mae La Oop said: "The spirits don't have very big appetites, nor do they like chillies, so when we make an offering, we take a pig or a cow if we can and add chillies, and then we have a jolly good feast!"

Illness is also a spiritual matter: it is a sign of some disharmony between the ill person and the spirit world. When a person is ill, either some spirits are missing from the afflicted person's body, which have to be coaxed back into the body, or some evil spirit has entered the person's body, which has to be exorcized. Another Lawa belief pertaining to the body and spirits is that certain people are inhabited by the spirits of tigers. This enables them to carry out amazing feats of strength or endurance. They can, for example, cover great distances very fast, and are held actually to be tigers. The Lawa further believe that the entrails of animals can be read to see if the omens are good or bad, e.g. for ploughing or starting the harvest.

The Lawa are monogamous, and divorce is unusual. Upon marriage, a girl goes to live with her husband's family – residence is patrilocal, just as lineage is patrilineal – although sometimes a couple set up a new house of their own. She does not move in with him if he is remarrying, when understandably she will not want to live in the house of his ex-wife. In that situation, he might move into her house. People mostly marry in the winter. In the winter of 1993/94, for example, ten couples got married in Mae La Oop. Girls marry young, soon after puberty, when school is finished, i.e. when the girls are 13 or 14. The suitor's family pays the bride's family a bride price. This involves a certain amount of silver in the form of old coins and family heirlooms. The giving of the bride price is largely symbolic and ritualistic. The silver heirlooms come back again to the man's family, remaining in the family and being handed down through the generations. In Mae La Oop, headman Boonyeuan showed us a bag containing some of his family's heirlooms, which he had 'given' to his wife's family when he had married his wife. In it, were old silver Indian rupees bearing the heads of 'Queen and Empress' Victoria and Kings Edward VII and George V. The coins must have come overland from the former British colonies of India and Burma. But more interesting for us were some examples of old Thai currency. These were the celebrated 'dog's penis' pieces, so called because of their shape. One was stamped 2411 (1868), making it 134 years old in 2002. Another interesting detail concerning marriage is that some of the older Lawa villagers, for example in Mae La Oop, are married to Khmu and Khmer people. The latter sometimes come across from Thailand's Nan province, from Laos or from Cambodia to marry Lawa or at least to trade with them, subsequently intermarrying with them. This might seem surprising until one remembers that all three minority groups are from the same Mon-Khmer stable. Ancient channels of communication and trading connections still remain open between them, however tenuous.

When a member of their community dies, the Lawa do not burn the body Buddhist-style, but bury it. Evidently, in the past they interred corpses, together with items belonging to the deceased, in wooden coffins made out of hollowed-out logs. After the death there is a wake, animals are sacrificed, and people eat and drink. The corpse is kept in the house of the deceased for a day or two, and the village youngsters process around it singing. This processing is an eagerly anticipated opportunity for girls and boys to flirt together and touch each other accidentally on purpose (I think these customs may have come from the Karen, who do likewise). Lawa funerals are not very solemn affairs. The former custom of the Lawa of burying their dead in hollowed-out log coffins, which was observed by Holt Hallett in 1876, when he visited Lawa villages such as Kong Loi and Bo Luang,[4] might well link the Lawa – as was suggested above and also in Chapter 4 – with the prehistoric people who buried their dead in mysterious wooden coffins, thought to be between 1,200 and maybe 4,000 years old, in caves in many parts of northern Thailand, notably near Soppong. By the same token, the Lawa might be the descendants of these ancient people.

Some Lawa villages have special clannish hereditary chiefs (akin to the *maha* of the Wa and the *sawbwa* or *chao fah* of the Shan), with power and status being passed down through certain 'noble' families. The Thai authorities are currently trying to stamp out this feudal practice by democratizing the way such chiefs and also conventional headmen are chosen. Peter Kunstadter (1965) reports that these special families enjoy a *samang* (= *khun*, *chao*) lineage, some claiming to be able to trace their pedigree back to the last Lawa king or at least to one of his princes, although in reality they can probably trace their descent back only ten generations. Some villagers owe allegiance to these chiefs, the *samang* receiving payments of meat and money. With their ritual knowledge, the *samang* are also held to be the local guardians of Lawa culture. Another person important in Lawa society is the *lam*, a spiritual leader or shaman who is often the oldest man in a village. The *lam* and to a lesser extent the *samang* are able to summon up the spirits.

Lawa women, we said earlier, are given to weaving on their balconies and, like Karen females, are champion weavers, working at simple backstrap looms. They mostly weave material for their traditional skirts and shoulder bags. Nowadays, Lawa tribal costume is not worn every day in all Lawa villages (we speak here, of course, only of the two dozen separate-identity villages northeast of Mae Sariang, not of assimilated Lawa places elsewhere). It is still worn

---

[4] Hallett visited these and other Lawa villages 125 years ago during a fact-finding journey he was making from Moulmein via Mae Sariang and Chiang Mai to Chiang Saen. He wrote up this journey in his *A Thousand Miles on an Elephant in the Shan States*, first published in 1890. His observations on the Lawa practice of burying their dead in hollowed-out log coffins appear on p. 49.

every day in the remoter, more conservative villages, such as Pae, Ho Gao and to a lesser extent in Mae La Oop. It is worn mostly by the women, especially the housewives and older women. Lawa men mostly do not wear their traditional costume any more every day, wearing it only on special occasions. The women who still wear costume every day have a workaday version and a kind of Sunday best version for celebrations. Interestingly, Lawa women's best traditional attire does not resemble the costume of Wa women, as far as the latter is known.[5]

Lawa women typically wear a black (dark indigo), knee-length, tube skirt with horizontal wine-red or pink banding (but also sometimes of azure or white), which often shows a kind of linked chain motif or warp *ikat* (tie-dye) decoration; a shiftlike, short-sleeved, V-necked smock, coloured white or fawn; indigo leggings, held in place by some kind of band; and, above the leggings but just below the knee, black-lacquered cane rings. Sometimes they also wear indigo armlets ('leggings' for the arms), held in place by a silver band, while all Lawa women like to sport heavy silver bracelets around their wrists. The most distinctive thing about Lawa women are their multiple strings of small beads worn around the neck, which are usually coral in colour, although you can also see red, yellow and azure necklaces. The swathes of coral beads are often supplemented by big necklaces strung respectively with many silver chunks, smaller silver beads, and old silver coins (see photo section). In large holes in their ear lobes, they wear cylindrical silver earrings, cup-shaped on the outer side. The costume is completed with a white or pink shoulder bag and mandatory little pipe.

The men (on ceremonial occasions) wear simple, baggy, off-white, heavy cotton trousers and an open jacket – the ensemble resembling a judo outfit. Some Lawa men still wear another kind of 'clothing', tattoos. Traditionally, they bear two tigers on their backs to fend off evil spirits, and down their thighs – from waist to knee – they have densely tattooed emblems (such as cat figures), which make it look as if the men are wearing black lycra cyclists' shorts!

✻

Mae Sariang
After Mae La Oop, we backtracked 25 kms down off the mountain to Highway 108, picking up our original route from Mae Hong Son via Khun Yuam to Mae Sariang. This we did at the H1266/H108 junction just south of Mae La Noi, from where it was but a further 30 kms south to Mae Sariang. The last stretch of the leg proved without incident, with a good flattish road

---

[5] For an account of Wa dress, see Chapter 6. Holt Hallett (1890, pp. 52-53) provides a brief description of Lawa women's attire as worn in 1876. Possibly, it approximates slightly to traditional Wa costume. 'The Lawa women are the only natives in Indo-China whom I have seen wearing their hair parted in the middle... Their hair is gathered up and tied in a knot at the back of the head... Unlike the Siamese and Zimmé Shans [Lan-Na Tai of Chiang Mai], the Lawa women wear upper clothing for decency's sake, and not solely for the sake of warmth. Their dress consists of a short skirt reaching to their knees, and a black tunic having a dark-red stripe on the outer edge.'

passing through yet more forest and taking in the two villages of **Tung Ruang Tong** and **Mae Tia**. Had we not spotted road signs suddenly reading 'Hot: so-and-so-many kms', we would have sped clean past Mae Sariang on a bypass. A last-minute turn west just after a big petrol station slewed us into the beginning of Mae Sariang's long main street, the Wiang Mai Road.

Until the 1960s, when the H108 was first built, the town, like Mae Hong Son, was another pretty inaccessible place on the remote north-western fringes of the kingdom. Even afterwards, few penetrated here unless they were cattle dealers or Karen National Union/Karen National Liberation Army and Thai army officers come to liaise about border security. Things remained that way until the late 1980s, when the town began to figure in the itineraries of people making the Chiang Mai/Mae Hong Son loop. In the early 1990s, a handful of intrepid travellers realized that Mae Sariang lay not only on the road north to Mae Hong Son, but at the gateway to the marvellous new H105 border route south to Mae Sot. But these visitors and the ever-so-slight boom they brought with them scarcely more than stirred the spot's age-old calm.[6]

What at first seemed to us an unremarkable backwater quickly grew on us as an intriguing little nest. Like Nan, Mae Sariang was an authentic, laid-back, minding-its-own-business kind of place which could easily in its own right claim the visitor for a pleasant relaxing stay. The town's variety of religious buildings told that its 7,500 inhabitants were a good mix. As we scooted around the streets, we found Burmese/Shan-style temples for the Shan and Thai populations, a mosque in the market area for the Muslim Indo-Burmese and Chinese, and a Christian church in the main street in part for the Karen. A 10-ft-high phallic *lak muang* or town pillar, standing in front of the old police station and covered in squares of gold leaf, was a focal point for animist tendencies. This old police headquarters, situated in the Mae Sariang Road next to the new station, was a fine teak building. It was one of the many old wooden houses and shophouses still standing which made the town so pleasing to the eye.

Our hunt for accommodation in Mae Sariang was characteristic of the search that had to be embarked upon every time one arrived in a new provincial town. Proceeding down the Wiang Mai Road away from the H108, we spied first a promising-looking place called *New Mitaree* or *Mitaree Guest House N° 2*. The reception was spick and span, and a Chinese lady led us down a lot of clean corridors past pristine rooms. The odd thing was that they were all unoccupied. Finally, we came to the room she had singled out for us, and inside we found very agreeable accommodation with a hot shower. It seemed a

---

[6] Readers still interested in the historical perspective might like to know that the beginnings of Sariang were possibly Lawa. When in 1876 Hallett passed through the 'town', which he refers to as 'Maing Loongyee', using its Burmese name, he found – as he says (1980, p. 35) – the remains there of the two ancient cities of Yain Sa Lin. These remains, which he visited, lay about one mile south-east of the town. The ancient cities were surrounded and divided from each other by moats and ditches, and their area was much bigger, so he says, than 'Maing Loongyee' itself. They were situated on a knoll, and their western ramparts had been swept away by encroachments of the river (probably the River Yuam, but it could also be the Mae Sariang river). The remains might date back to the 13th century or earlier and sound as if they might be Lawa.

bargain at 120 baht per night. But back at the reception, we discovered the scam. Fortunately verifying the rate before we moved in, we learned that the room was suddenly 240 baht – 120 per person. Of course, we showed the lady a clean pair of heels. But who would have wanted to stay in this complex anyway? In the maze of concrete corridors and rooms, a guest would have felt about as comfortable as Rudolf Hess in Berlin's Spandau Prison.

We called in next at the *Mitaree Hotel* in the town centre. A large typical Chinese establishment, it must have been the original which spawned the *New Mitaree*. For an acceptable sum, the management wanted to put us in the shabby hotel annexe. Everything inside and out was painted pale green, and our room neighbour would have been a bent old Indian man, renting by the month. Checking out the beds in every room, we soon discovered the reason for his bowed posture. They all rose at the foot and head ends. Sleep would have been impossible except by lying on our backs. While we continued to scout round town, a youth on a moped drew level with us. He was touting for custom for a guest house with the singular name of *See View* and invited us to come and have a look. But when we got there, there was no sea or lake or indeed any view to see, except a sand quarry with a row of parked tipper trucks.

Mae Sariang GH had acceptable rooms but no hot water, and *Hunter GH* had appeared last year, only to disappear again this. It was all typical of the lodgings scene in Thailand. Places mushroomed overnight, to go under just as suddenly, and standards went up and down like a yo-yo. Our quest ended at the *Riverside GH*, a typical traveller hang-out. The four-storey building was built on the steep south-eastern bank of the River Yuam. A bamboo bridge from the main house crossed the sluggish flow to a spur of scrubby parkland on the far side. Here, in a bend of the river, a clutch of primitive bamboo bungalows supplemented the bedrooms in the house. Overlooking the Yuam and the parkland was a pleasant balcony restaurant with a travellerish menu, listing dishes half *farang*, half Thai. Around the walls were maps and details of local tours, together with a mini library of well-thumbed paperbacks and magazines from countries around the world. In this relaxed place, there always seemed to be someone to chat to.

After a first night in one of the cool gloomy spartan rooms underneath the restaurant, we moved across the river into a bungalow. The bungalows were much favoured by 'smokers', and in the one next to us a serious withdrawn Japanese boy had settled in for the season. To get a hot (= lukewarm) shower, we had to stagger over the swaying bridge to the bathrooms in the main building – no piece of cake at the best of times, but in the dark or after Mekhong (or a good smoke) a hazardous adventure. One of these bathrooms had a feature to titillate the exhibitionist. The window, glassless but barred, looked directly into a cage of monkeys. Precisely at the moment one was stark naked and trying to adjust the shower, they came to the window and stared in. Another titbit amused us at the *Riverside*. One morning, we were having breakfast on the balcony when two girls, aged about 14, both very ordinarily dressed in jeans and T-shirts, tried to come in. They were prostitutes, apparently Karen. The lady at reception threw them out, but they remonstrated, saying that they had been in before and they only wanted to meet some men. She shooed them away again, but just as they were going, she relented, saying that they could come in if they paid 5 baht each.

With accommodation sorted out, the next priority was food. *Renu* restaurant in the main street had inviting décor, but always seemed empty. *Ruan Prae*, an eating place in a side street just a stone's throw from *Renu*, boasted a celebrated cook, but was never open. Which left *Intira*, (near the central crossroads, with traffic lights) the restaurant almost opposite *Renu*. It was *Renu's* misfortune to be situated facing *Intira*, for without doubt *Intira* was the most satisfactory and popular eating place in Mae Sariang, and to my mind was one of the best no-nonsense restaurants in all Thailand. It had good food, prompt service and fair prices, which meant that no evening was complete without a meal and a drink in it. The diminutive fetchers and servers were assiduous and rewarded faithful customers in discreet ways – large portions or discounted bills. The décor was unprepossessing, and yet the place hummed equally with local people and *farang* visitors. The food was not connoisseur's fare, but their fried beef in tomato sauce or renowned chicken with basil and chillies was most acceptable, and their *tom yam goong* (hot and sour prawn soup) or delicious chicken in sweet green curry sauce outstanding – great bowlfuls for 50 baht.

Opening onto the busy main street, the Chinese-run *Intira* could be a noisy place. But sitting there of an evening just before New Year watching the local people and events outside, we could begin to get our finger on the pulse of Mae Sariang, appreciating its real *raison d'être*. Convoys of cattle trucks rumbled loudly up the main street, beginning a long night journey to the slaughterhouses of Chiang Mai or Bangkok. Audis, BMWs, Volvos and Mercedes, fabulously expensive by the Thai standards of the time, were parked at the roadside. Groups of traders and dealers made their way from them into the girlie 'singing place' adjoining *Intira* to drink Chivas Regal and dally with skimpily dressed floosies. It was a mini Mae Sot, and as with Mae Sot, located further south down the border, the number of gold shops and flash luxury cars in Mae Sariang, disproportionate for such a backwater place, betrayed that it was a booming trading centre, living off a prolific and dubious cross-border traffic. The town, although small in itself, was the hub for this trade, which funnelled across the frontier at the nearby village of Mae Saam Laep. Through this controversial border station down on the River Salween, which we were soon to visit (Chapter 9), and through Mae Sariang, cattle and teak as well as other valuable commodities flowed in an endless stream from Burma (specifically Kawthoolei or the Karen State) into Thailand, while quantities of consumer goods flowed the other way.

❈ ❈

THREE PAGODAS

Postscript 2002

Meanwhile the H108 has been upgraded and is now a good road, paved throughout, all the way to Mae Sariang. Once you leave Mae Hong Son town and its outskirts behind, there is still very little traffic on this road, which makes its way through endless forest. Between Khun Yuam and Mae Sariang, there are some particularly beautiful sections in January, when many trees are aflame with orange flowers. I do not know whether it is an illusion brought about by the fact that one is heading south, but the stretch to Khun Yuam seems to be mostly downhill. It is 66 kms to that little town and then a further 95 kms to Mae Sariang (161 kms in total or about 163 kms to Mae Sariang town centre).

Route detail: Mae Hong Son – Khun Yuam – Mae La Noi (Maps 16 & 17)
km 0.0   Main crossroads (with traffic lights) in centre of Mae Hong Son town
          Proceed S down main street, link up with bypass coming in from R, and pass Shell fuel station (L) (Map 16)
          After about 2 kms, you pass a well-signed turning right for Ta Pong Daeng, which is the start of the way for the Padaung 'Long-Neck' villages of Nam Pieng Din and Huai Suea Tao
          Soon out of Mae Hong Son town, you pass through nice forest
km 6.1   Turning left/east for Mae Sakoet and an entrance to Mae Surin Waterfall National Park. A very taxing motorcycle trail through the park traverses a string of Karen villages, including Huai Hi, ultimately to reach after 85 kms Wat Chan village, from where you can continue another 55 kms down to Pai or a further 140 kms via Samoeng to Chiang Mai. I have described this exciting route, which duplicates much of the 'Old Elephant Trail' from Mae Hong Son town to Chiang Mai, in my *Trek It Yourself in Northern Thailand* (Treks 24 & 25)
km 11.1   Entrance (R) to **Pa Bong**, down R. The village with its Burmese-style *wat* is attractively set amid coconut palms, and near it lie some hot springs, which can be visited. The H108 bypasses Pa Bong
km 13.3   Way in L 3.5 kms to dam and Pa Bong Reservoir. From the dam, you can trek E through the jungle and up the valley of the Samart river about 3½ hrs to the isolated Karen settlement of Huai Goong Mai (no vehicle access) and then further to other villages (see my trekking guide *Hinterlands*, Trek 16)
          In the basin, near the paddy fields, and just before the H108 starts to climb up: an electricity station (L) connected with the dam and hydroelectric power generation
          Winding ascent to
km 17.3   Viewpoint and *sala* just offroad (L), with great view E of dam and up the ravine of the River Samart
km 30.7   Way R to Mai Sang Nam and Ban Glua (+16.9 kms), and to other villages
km 30.9   Way L 11 kms to the Hmong village of Kao Huai Nang Po, popularly known as Miao Microwave on account of its mountaintop siting near a telecoms mast
km 35.8   **Huai Pong** village
km 36.9   Memorial (R) to Japanese soldiers killed in WW2, and board with photos of wartime objects dug up at Huai Pong

km 53.3   **Mae Surin** village, another attractive community of wooden houses in coconut palms with Shan-style *wat*, sited beside River Surin. From Mae Surin: way R to villages offroad. In January 2001, there was a refugee camp somewhere near Mae Surin, housing 2,817 Karenni from Burma

km 57.5   Way R goes at least 38 kms to Pratu Muang village and other places en route. Also up this side road: Doi Wiang Gla Wildlife Sanctuary HQ (4 kms from H108) and a forestry station (28 kms)

       A few kms before Khun Yuam: **Nong Pa Koa** village

km 64.0   On the edge of Khun Yuam: way L (H1263) to Mae Surin Waterfall, 'Buatong Fields', faraway Mae Chaem, and many villages en route. From the H108/H1263 junction, marked by a forest of signs and a police box, it is 20 kms to the Hmong village of Mae U-kor with its *buatong* or Mexican sunflower fields, and 37 kms to the spectacular waterfall with a drop of 250 m

km 65.9   **Khun Yuam** main street

In **Khun Yuam**, *Ban Farang Guest House* lies in the upper part of town, near the top end of the main street. As you hit Khun Yuam, coming from Mae Hong Son, you reach a kind of roundabout. The GH is near this roundabout, in a side street going R off it, where it lies on the L side of the road. *Ban Farang* ('Foreigner House' or 'Frenchman's House') remains a nice spacious place, still functioning. The main house is styled like a chalet, and near it are a couple of pretty, attractively furnished *sala*, in which meals are taken. Unfortunately, upon enquiring in January 2001, I learned that kindly Frenchman-owner Monsieur Roger had died about four years previously. Conflicting accounts were given about his demise – a typical Thai scene! One woman working there said that M. Roger had had a motorcycle accident and had had a leg amputated in Chiang Mai, where he had died, but his Thai wife reported that he had had a heart problem and that she had put him on a plane to France, where he had died. Meanwhile the young wife and her Eurasian daughter by the Frenchman still lived in and ran the GH/restaurant, but I found the rooms and food there even more overpriced than before, and the service as well as food not as good as earlier. Enterprising *Peekmai Guest House*, at the bottom end of town (L side of main street) towards the end of Khun Yuam, has a restaurant with a fair range of moderately priced dishes, but I have not stayed in its rooms, so cannot comment on the accommodation.

km 65.9   Khun Yuam main street (km-readings continue from above; see Map 17) After *Peekmai GH* (L), fuel station (also L) – a place to tank up for the 100-km ride to Mae Sariang. After Khun Yuam, a considerable winding descent to Ta Hin Som

km 77.4   Proceed through woodland country to village of **Muang Pon**

km 80.2   Way R/west to some 9 villages, the furthest 28 kms away

km 82.9   **Hang Pon** village

km 88.0   **Ta Hin Som** village

km 90.5   **Nong Haeng** village. Just 200 m beyond Nong Haeng:

km 90.7   Way L/east to a hot spring (several little bubbling stinking pools in some scrubby grass) and to Pa Pueng cave. After Nong Haeng (from roughly km-markers 173 to 185), you enjoy for a dozen kms a great ride down a forested valley with some picturesque stepped paddies nestling on the valley floor

km 97.9   Road left to Huai Yuak, Mae To Glang and other villages, maybe a dozen in all

THREE PAGODAS

At about roadside km-marker 185: the scenic valley ends, you climb over a low ridge, and then descend a fair distance to

km 112.0 **Mae La Luang**, an assimilated Lawa place. Somewhere W of Mae La Luang (NW of Mae Sariang), at Sa La, lies (in 2000) another refugee camp, apparently containing Karenni and regular Karen people plus rebel Burmese ABSDF students. I am not sure if Sa La camp is the same as Mae Khong Kha camp in Salween National Park, accessed from Mae Sariang, or not. If it is, it housed (in January 2000) 10,531 refugees from Burma

km 118.5 Way R to various villages – road goes in only 5 kms, apparently

km 131.1 **Mae La Noi** with its roadside market and shops both L and R of the H108

km 131.6 Just 400 m beyond market, across a bridge: junction marked by a petrol station (L). Straight on continues on 108 road 29 kms to Mae Sariang, while L/east is the H1266 dirt side road to Mae La Oop (continuation of route on H108 below, after side trip to Mae La Oop)

Route detail: Mae La Noi – Mae La Oop (Map 18)
In 2001, the H1266 side trail to Mae La Oop was paved to begin with, after which it was dirt, as before. However, although still stony and bumpy in places, it was more of a regular dirt road, these days fairly well used by traffic, including public-transport pick-ups (*silor/songtaew*), which go up to Mae La Oop at intervals from Mae La Noi market, returning to Mae La Noi.

km 0.0 Junction H108/H1266 just 400 m south of Mae La Noi market, by fuel station
At junction turn L/east into H1266 side road
Paved road runs out past regular rural lowland villages of **Pa Maak** and **Huai Rin**, before giving over to fair dirt surface

km 11.3 Temporary forestry office (R)

km 11.6 Way R/south to Karen village of **Huai Maak Noon**, which lies close to the road, and also to more distant Mae Kwang and Huai Poeng, not visible

km 13.8 Scenic Karen settlement of **Mae Sa Kua** about 1 km offroad L/north. Two ways lead to it, a footpath and then a track

km 16.6 Way R to a waterfall

km 21.9 Way L to Mae Sa Ping Tai (possibly Mae Sa Poen Tai), c. 9.5 kms distant
Regular stony dirt road
Great view R of ridgetop Mae La Oop across valley
Way L to Mae Nga village (I think) and some kind of herb-growing farm

km 25.9 Junction and *sala* (R). Way R leads into Mae La Oop's long main street, while L is the continuation of the H1266 on a poor surface (in 2001) to the Karen villages of Huai Ha, Huai Horm (offroad) and Du Lo Boe, as well as to the ridgetop Lawa village of La Ang (16.5 kms beyond Mae La Oop). Just beyond the junction, there is a pagoda and a curious pink Chinese-looking house

Mae La Oop
Revisiting Mae La Oop in 1999, I found that there were some changes, although in most respects it remained a traditional Lawa settlement. Just outside the village, near the *sala* by the entrance, a motorbike repair shop had sprung up. The surface of the protracted main street, formerly of dirt and worn rock, had meanwhile been paved over. Along the main drag, there were a few more shops, including two useful ones situated more than halfway down, on a bend by a telephone box (R side of road). In the main street, you could now buy petrol from a little fuel booth. The number of

houses must have increased from the 160 of yore, and they, like the stores, were now noticeably more developed. People said that the Lawa of La Oop had prospered from a couple of years of good cabbage crops, and had invested their earnings in their buldings.

As you go W down the village's long main drag, you come (after the two shops and phone box) to a fork. Branching L here brings you to a compound and a small *wat* at the end of the street. If you look roughly ESE from the elevated compound, you can see the village of Dong Gao down in the valley. Branching R at the fork brings you via a twisting road down to fair-sized Mae La Oop school and ultimately a big new health centre. The village headman's house is also to be found in this north-westerly corner.

If you fancy staying overnight in Mae La Oop, consider doing so at one of three places. You could try lodging in the house or annexe of headman Boonyeuan Promsermsook, as we once did. Or you could try the new health centre, where Nittaya, Doug and I put up in 1999. We were invited to sleep inside the building on the floor, but in the end, preferring to have some privacy early the next morning, erected our tents in the grounds of the secluded and quiet centre. But the best accommodation possibility might be to stay in one of the two shophouses (the left-hand one) that lie in the main street right next to the phone box. Here, a young man sometimes puts up *farang* passers-by on the floor of his house, providing blankets. He is Yoon Sen, nickname Yanae, a clued-up *farang*-friendly chap, who has even been to Sweden on a student exchange, one of only two people from Mae Hong Son province to have done so.

Route detail: Mae La Noi – Mae Sariang (Map 17)

km 131.6 Back down at junction H108/H1266 just 400 m south of Mae La Noi market, by fuel station, resume journey south, as earlier, picking up km-readings where left off. Road makes a considerable ascent, before descending all the way to Mae Sariang

km 137.5 **Tung Ruang Tong** village

km 143.2 **Mae Tia** village
Longish, rather uneventful stretch until run-in to Mae Sariang
Big fuel station and forecourt (L). Roughly opposite this, there are quick ways in R to the centre of Mae Sariang
Otherwise continue on H108 a short distance until a

km 160.6 Complicated junction, where straight on continues on H108 to Hot and Chiang Mai. Leave H108 by turning R. Now go R again into Mae Sariang's W/E-running main street, avoiding a way L, which is the start of the H105 route for Mae Sot
Head W a good km up the main street (the Wiang Mai Road), past a market area (L), *Lotus Guest House* (L), the main post office (L), and *Intira Restaurant* (L) to a crossroads and then a T-junction, the last three lying in the centre of town

km 162.0 **Mae Sariang** town centre

Mae Sariang

Into the new millennium, the town remains an appealing, unspoilt, comfortable, laid-back, little nest. It has almost everything the traveller needs – a plethora of places to stay, good restaurants, a big covered day market, shops and a couple of small supermarkets. Near the bus station, there is a striking monastery-temple (Wat Si Boonruang), and close to the market and bridge over the River Yuam lies an impressive Burmese/Shan-style *wat* (Wat Kitti Wong). You can use the town as a base for organized or independent trekking, either on foot or by motorcycle, making excursions to the Lawa to the north-east and the Pwo Karen to the ESE (see my *Trek It Yourself in Northern Thailand*). You can visit the border village of Mae Saam Laep, from where you can make exciting longtail boat trips up the River Salween. And you can go north to Mae Hong Son or south to Mae Sot. Yet, strangely, Mae Sariang has not caught on as a tourist destination. Thus you will find no droves of older package tourists à la Mae Hong Son, and no crowds of younger trekkies, druggies and alternative types à la Pai. These days, the town is visited by no more than a steady trickle of traveller types, who pass through Mae Sariang on hire motorcycles or in rented jeeps when they are doing the Chiang Mai/Mae Hong Son loop either clockwise or anticlockwise, usually staying just one night in town, breaking their journeys. Now that the Burmese and their DKBA henchmen have secured most of the border to the west of Mae Sariang, and that the KNU/KNLA is out of most of Kawthoolei (the Karen State) and its 'capital' Manerplaw, cross-border trade at Mae Saam Laep and the town has dropped considerably in recent years, with the result that Mae Sariang's economy has taken a visible nosedive, although Burmese cattle still pass through and the town remains full of gold shops.

For such a modest place, Mae Sariang has a disproportionate number of guest houses and hotels. There are simply too many of them for the small number of visitors passing through, and more are being built – a kind of commercial suicide. Most of these places are, in my opinion, of mediocre quality. Traditional *farang* traveller haunts are *Riverside GH*, *Mae Sariang GH* and *See View GH*, but none of them are anything to write home about. The tucked-away *Riverside*, overlooking the Yuam river, has, as said earlier, a nice elevated reception-cum-eating area, but the rooms below stairs are dismal, and the lodging has gone downhill in recent years, changing owners at least once. Nearby *Mae Sariang* is pretty basic, with cold-water rooms around a compound, and is partly used these days by Thai truckers. *See View*, across the River Yuam and just out of town, has rather seedy hot-shower rooms in a motel block, and a ranch-style restaurant. It is not as good as it might at first appear, is a bit of a hard sell, and the staff/owners tend to overorganize guests. Accommodation at these three places goes for the usual prices.

Lotus GH, which is located towards the eastern end of the town's long main street (the E/W-running Wiang Mai Road), not far short of the big four-way junction by the H108, is hardly worth considering. Set in the run-down surroundings of a former entertainment and brothel complex, it is not really a proper GH, and the staff at reception habitually try to overcharge visitors. Nor would I stay at nearby *New Mitaree GH* or at the old original *Mitaree Hotel*, which are not my style, especially when there are now nicer places in town. If you want a hotel, *Kamolsorn Hotel* (the building covered with lights) somewhat on the south side of town, in the Mae Sariang Road, beyond the police station, looks promising, and when I last asked, fan rooms went for 350 baht/night and air-con rooms for 450. Otherwise, stay at the new *Northwest GH*, which is currently easily my favourite and the best lodging in Mae Sariang, and which lies diagonally opposite the *Riverside*. Brand-new in 2001, it is an all-wood building with nice clean tidy fan rooms, sharing well-appointed hot-water bathrooms and a pleasant sitting area below, and all for 120 baht only. Almost opposite *Northwest*, the same owner (I think) is finishing what promises to be an even more impressive, all-wood house, which by the time you read this will probably be the best lodging in town, unless it is intended to be a riverside restaurant.

❖

WORSTED IN WIZARDRY

A thumbnail sketch of the Karenni (Kayah) people & state, the KNPP & KNLP
The Karenni State is a thinly populated, mountainous region in eastern Burma, located between the Shan State to the north, Karen territory to the west, the Karen State (Kawthoolei) to the south, and western Thailand to the east. Historically, the area always enjoyed relative political independence, which partly derived from the fact that it was ruled by strong hereditory chieftains or princelings, akin to the Shan *sawbwa*. The Burman king Mindon acknowledged this independence, which was also formally recognized in 1875 by a treaty of the British during their annexation of Burma (the Karenni State area came under British administration in that year). As a result, the Karenni State was never fully incorporated into British colonial Burma, and its principalities and ruling feudal *sawbwa* essentially retained their sovereignty right up until Burma's Independence, with minimal British administrative interference. The Karenni State was created as a single state out of the former Karenni principalities in 1948, following Independence. It was already named as such in the 1947 constitution, which guaranteed both it and the Shan State, in recognition of the traditional independence of the Karenni and Shan territories, an extraordinary right to secede after a period of ten years within the Union of Burma. *Sawbwa* rule would continue with this ongoing independence. The Karenni might have been satisfied with all this, except that in August 1948 the Karenni leader U Bi Htu Re, whose Karenni faction unilaterally declared the independence of the Karenni States mid-1947, was assassinated by Rangoon militiamen, triggering an armed nationalist uprising in the state, which has continued from August 1948 up to the present. In 1951, under the Constitution Amendment Act, the Burmese authorities, in an attempt to downplay the Karen pedigree of the Karenni peoples and negate the force of Karenni independence sentiment, renamed the Karenni State as the Kayah State (a piece of nonsense with no ethnic foundation and widely ignored by the Karenni, the KNPP, serious anthropologists and others), and in 1974 demarcation of the Kayah (Karenni) State was constitutionally confirmed, although the right of secession was finally written out of the constitution. Outrage at this, coupled with the failure of successive governments in Rangoon to meet Karenni grievances, stoked the rebellion.

The Karenni State is home to a group of more than a dozen ethnic minority tribes, who are collectively generally known as the Karenni or Kayah peoples. Calling them Kayah is rather confusing because the Kayah are one of these tribes in their own right (the largest, with a population estimated at more than 150,000), making it clearer to call the group Karenni peoples, among whom the Kayah constitute the most numerous tribe. 'Kayah', used to describe both the peoples and their state, is a fiction invented by Rangoon for its own nefarious purposes. These peoples are generally known collectively as Karenni or also as 'Red Karen' on account of the predilection of the dominant Kayah tribe for wearing red in its costume, notably in its women's shawl. The Karenni group of peoples include, as said, the Kayah, but also the 'Long-Neck' Padaung (see Chapter 7), the 'Long-Ear' Kayaw or Bre (likewise see Chapter 7), the Manoo-Manaw, the Yinbaw, the Lahta or Zayein Karen, and the Paku. The Karenni tribes form a substantial sub-section of the overall Karen or Karennic peoples, but are not the same linguistically or culturally as the 'regular' Karen (comprising the Sgaw and Pwo sub-groups of Thailand and Burma, as well as the 'normal' plains-dwelling Karen of southern Burma), who form the majority of the overall Karen ethnic family.

In the half century since the start of the insurgency, the Karenni State has suffered – like other parts of Burma – from considerable conflict between Rangoon and the rebels. The turmoil has embroiled the many local ethnic groups, as we saw with the Padaung and Kayaw in Chapter 7. Whole communities have been compelled to relocate, many hill tribals have fled *tatmadaw* campaigns against ethnic rebel forces, and government troops have increasingly swamped and militarized the Karenni State with a view to both controlling it and also opening up its vast forest resources to exploitation by Thai logging companies. During the 1990s, large tracts of the State were shamefully clear-felled by these companies, making use of concessions granted by the SLORC in a deal engineered by the unprincipled Thai deputy prime minister 'Logger' Chaovalit. A haemorrhage of Karenni teak and other hardwoods came over the border at Mai Nai Soi, Mae Sakoep (west of Mae Sariang), at points north-west of Khun Yuam, and at other places. During 1994-95, ceasefires were agreed between the SLORC and the three principal Karenni rebel armies, but any real peace has yet to materialize. Karenni people have continued to flee eastward towards the Thai border and into Thailand, where in the mid-1990s about 12,000 of them lived in refugee camps. A few details gleaned from the *Bangkok Post* give an insight into recent events.

The ceasefire agreement which the KNPP signed with the SLORC mid-1995, which gave the rebel force de-facto control of most of the Karenni State, was already declared null and void by the Karenni just a few months later. Normally, when insurgent groups agree ceasefires with the Burmese, the latter grant the compliant rebels economic autonomy within their territory, as has been the case with the 'Red' Wa.[7] And this was how the Karenni understood things. But in their case the SLORC thought otherwise and demanded control of the valuable timber trade with Thailand. In June 1995, Rangoon sent troops to the relevant areas "to halt illegal logging and exports", whereupon the Central Committee of the KNPP accused the SLORC of violating the terms of the peace and reconciliation agreement, abrogating it. Just before Christmas 1995, clashes erupted between the Burma army and Karenni forces opposite Khun Yuam and Mae Hong Son districts, which over New Year and into the first days of 1996 escalated into heavy fighting. The *tatmadaw* took over the KNPP's stronghold at Doi Ti Sakoe, opposite Mae Hong Son town. KNPP troops sought to dislodge Rangoon soldiers from the mountainous U-lae tract. There was fighting between the two sides at Tanakwai village and at the Tanakwai Pass (north-west of Mae Hong Son town, close to Mai Nai Soi village). Here, Hills 900, 904, 908 and 921 were the scene of the combat. A 1600-strong SLORC force was attempting to move onto highland held by up to 500 Karenni. On Hill 900, 50 KNPP troops mortared SLORC positions on Hills 921 and 908. The *tatmadaw* responded with artillery fire from Hill 904, using Chinese-made weapons, including 189-mm cannons. The exchanges could be heard 30 kms away in Mae Hong Son town. A force of 400 Karenni rebels managed to recapture one of the stronghold hills taken by the Burmese, dubbed 'Rambo Hill', which they were able to hold on to. But the much larger SLORC force continued to rain down shells on the border hilltop, and analysts feared that the Karenni would not be able to hold out for long against it, especially because a further 1,000 Rangoon soldiers had meanwhile arrived from the Shan State as reinforcements. During the fighting in the area, another 1,500 Karenni villagers sought refuge in Thailand. And so things continued in the years thereafter.

The Burma army was largely successful in its offensives against the Karenni, just as it was further south in the Karen State against the KNU/KNLA. A sign of this is

[7] The United Wa State Army (UWSA) was the first ethnic rebel group to sign a ceasefire agreement with the SLORC, in 1989. The accord between the Wa and Rangoon has proved the longest-lasting, still in place – surprisingly – at the time of writing, in 2001. The Shan State Progress Party (SSPP) also entered into a ceasefire agreement with the SLORC in 1989, and was followed by the Pa-O National Organization (PNO) and the Palaung State Liberation Party (PSLP) in 1991, the Kachin Independence Organization (KIO) and Kayan New Land Party (KNLP) in 1994, the New Mon State Party (NMSP) in 1995, and, as said, the KNPP (temporarily) also in 1995.

that by the end of January 2000 there were reportedly four 'Karenni' refugee camps in Mae Hong Son province, holding a total of 34,456 people who had fled the fighting between the KNPP and Rangoon. The camp near Mai Nai Soi in Muang district contained 13,393; that at Mae Surin village, Khun Yuam district, housed 2,817; that at Mae Khong Kha in Mae Sariang district held 10,531, of which some may have been Burmese ABSDF students and regular Karen; and the camp at Mae Lamaluang in Sob Moei district contained 7,715, many or all of whom may actually have been KNU Karen. Nevertheless, the Karenni continue their struggle. During a search in January 2000 of a Karenni village called in the *Bangkok Post* 'Pang Traktor', which must be Mai Nai Soi refugee camp, a cache of 302 sticks of TNT were discovered, weighing about 67 kg, and thought to belong to the KNPP, as well as 1,600 litres of illegally distilled whisky – at least the 'Red Karen' have something to sustain their spirits!

The Karenni National Progressive Party (KNPP) & the Kayan New Land Party (KNLP)

Founded in July 1957, the **Karenni National Progressive Party**, which has been headed by notable veteran Karenni such as Baptist KNPP Chairman Saw Maw Reh and one-time KNPP Chief of Staff and Karenni Foreign Minister Abel Tweed, is the largest and most successful of the Karenni rebel armies, which have also included the KNLP and the Karenni State Nationalities Liberation Front (KSNLF). With its GHQ sited for many years at Huai Plong on the River Pai, its main aim has been to re-establish the historic right of independence once legally enjoyed by the Karenni State. In the late 1960s and early 70s, the KNPP became involved in the burgeoning cattle and black-market trade with Thailand, a good slice of which funnelled through its checkpoints along the east bank of the River Salween. With income from this source, it built up its military wing, the Karenni Army (KA), reaching a peak strength of 1,000 armed troops. However, around 1974/74 there was a debilitating split within KNPP ranks concerning what the movement's stance should be to communism and the CPB, then making advances in the region. Some thought the organization's aspirations should be nationalist, others communist. In the end, the KNPP did not side with the CPB, but instead joined with other movements to form in 1976 the important NDF, of which it was a founder member. The KNPP suffered another blow in 1977, when the KNLP, a close cousin organization of the KNPP, resigned from the NDF to adopt a pro-CPB line. This led to renewed uncertainty about what the movement's relations should be to the CPB.

The controversy resulted in a second, more serious split in 1978, when fighting between two KNPP factions broke out in the Karenni State, one pro-CPB and the other anti. The KNPP long enjoyed widespread support throughout the Karenni State, but the violent dissension cost it dearly, and afterwards it never regained its former strength. Late 1978, the pro-communism faction of the KNPP broke away to form the Karenni State Nationalities Liberation Front (KSNLF), which trained with the CPB and began operating as a communist outfit to the north, west and south of the Karenni State. However, we are talking small numbers here – in 1988 the strength of the KNPP was 500 men, while the KSNLF had 150 troops. Meanwhile, the KNPP remained true to its purely nationalist aspirations, standing only for Karenni people and for an independent Karenni State. Following Gen. Saw Maung's bloody military coup in 1988 and the institution of his repressive brutal SLORC, both the KNPP and the KSNLF were reinvigorated, gaining many new Karenni recruits. The KNPP was also reinforced with a battalion (number 303) of ABSDF Burmese rebel students. In the winter of 1989/90, the SLORC mounted its most swingeing offensive hitherto against KNPP as well as KNU and NMSP bases down the Thai-Burmese border. This was both in response to the perceived threat of the DAB and in order to clear the way for cross-border logging. During the campaign (in 1989), the KNPP's GHQ on the Pai river fell to Burma army troops. Since 1990, the KNPP has mounted guerrilla actions far and wide in the Karenni State against the SLORC and its successor, the SPDC.

The **Kayan New Land Party** (KNLP) was formed on 8 August 1964. As far as I can understand, it has always been based in the relatively narrow confines of the Mongpai (Mobye) sub-state on the border between the Karenni and Shan States and peoples, whereas the KNPP has been more widely based throughout the whole of the Karenni State, up to the Thai border. Here, enlisting both Buddhist-animist and Christian tribesmen, the KNLP has been closely associated with, has enjoyed the particular support of, and has recruited from the 'exotic' Kayan or Karenni tribes such as the Padaung and Yinbaw. It has always been a pocket outfit, initially having a hard-core force of 200-250 armed volunteers. Nevertheless, it has survived several major SLORC offensives, perhaps because it is highly mobile, flitting especially among the more traditionalist villages of the Padaung. Early on, the KNLP was won over by the arguments of the CPB and – unlike the KNPP – for many years had a communist orientation, although it was never as ideologically dogmatic as the CPB. Always hard-pressed to source arms, it sometimes acquired them from the CPB. In textbook Maoist fashion, it concentrated its efforts on working with rural farmers and peasants. It has been allied with – besides the CPB – the communist-oriented KSNLF and the Shan State Nationalities Liberation Organization. In 1976, the KNLP became a founder member, along with the KNPP, of the landmark NDF, but it left this a year later to pursue its communist line, which was essentially incompatible with NDF membership. In general, the KNLP has resisted fusion with its fellow Karenni and Karen organizations. In the aftermath of the 1988 SLORC coup, the KNLP and its CPB allies were joined in the Shan State by 250 rebel Burmese students, who formed there under the wing of the KNLP the small Democratic Patriotic Army. In 1994, the KNLP signed a ceasefire agreement with the SLORC, as did some other ethnic rebel groups in the first half of the 1990s, but how long this lasted or whether it still holds I do not know. In view of the continuing flow of refugees from KNLP base area, it must seem that the agreement was soon broken.

In February 1994, I stayed in Pang Yon, a Karenni refugee village straddling the border just south-west of Mae Or and Napapaek, putting up in the house of Karenni Army (KNPP) commander Jo Lae. Exploring away from the settlement, with its 100 huts and 500 people, I stumbled upon a wooden prison, holding two men, and guarded by one soldier. It was so well built amidst the trees and jungle that at first I took it to be some senior functionary's house. But the way into it was by a hole with an 18 x 18-inch 'catflap' at ground level, through which the inmates had to crawl on their stomachs to get in and out. One of the prisoners was a KNLP commander, seized and imprisoned by the KA/KNPP for reasons I did not understand – perhaps it was because the KNLP had cosied up to the SLORC, signing a ceasefire agreement with the junta. An older man with a pitted face, he spoke fluent English. Inside the cage, his notebooks, pipe and other belongings lay on the floor. "Like you, I'm just visiting here, but on a long visit", he quipped, and in fact he had already been in the little prison in Pang Yon nine months.

9

REBEL HQ

THE KAREN PEOPLE & REBELLION

Mae Sariang – Mae Saam Laep – Manerplaw

Prince Maha San had recommended to us in Mae Or that we should visit Manerplaw. Said to mean 'Victory Field' or 'Land of Victory' in Karen, Manerplaw (I shall adopt the established spelling rather than 'Ma Noe Plo' or similar) was the GHQ inside Burma of the insurgent Karen National Union and its military wing, the Karen National Liberation Army. It was also the HQ of the National Democratic Front, the principal anti-government alliance in Burma of a dozen ethnic rebel organizations, of which the Wa National Organization was one. Maha San, leader of the Wa and chairman of the WNO, thought that on the strength of our connection with him we stood a fair chance of reaching this supreme rebel HQ. He had given us the names of contacts en route who might help us and the name of somebody to ask for when we arrived. All this set in train a little side trip from Mae Sariang south-west to the border which we would certainly have abandoned, so terrible was the way, had not the ultimate goal been so alluring.

Negotiating the notorious H1194 'road', we had first to get down to Mae Saam Laep, the cross-border trading village that lay beside the River Salween, which formed the frontier between Thailand and Burma west of Mae Sariang. The 46-km ride down the H1194 (Map 19) began innocuously enough. The route started in the south-western corner of Mae Sariang, by Wat Kitti Wong. crossing the Yuam river bridge, and swinging west (past *See View GH*), south and then – after some distance – west again. Near the start of the route, the trails to the Salween hamlets of Mae Khong Kha and Mae Sa Koep branched off north. Our way wound out through the fringes of town, past outlying villages, and through lurid green paddy fields. A modest paved affair, it afforded a glimpse of rural Thailand in the wide fertile valley of the River Yuam. The lakeside *Baitong* restaurant yielded to an isolated petrol station, and after the village of **Huai Sing** the paved section of road gave over to orange dirt.

Huai Po was followed by Tatafang police station, where for some inexplicable reason an amiable policeman politely saluted us. The H1194 now plunged into forested hill country, climbing up some distance to a low pass, before descending at length into marvellous jungle scenery. In a ravine, tall trees, covered with moss-like epiphytic plants, dripped with lianas and air roots.

THREE PAGODAS

Several herds of emaciated cows, 20-50 strong, came against us. Driven by solitary Karen boys with knapsacks, they had wandered from deep inside Burma, crossed the Dawna Range, ferried or swum the Salween, and were now nearing the end of their epic journey. Sadly, beyond Mae Sariang only a truck ride separated them from the slaughterhouses of Chiang Mai and Bangkok.

To better cater for the trade in Burmese livestock (and also timber), the 1194 was slowly being improved. In this middle section, we came across a number of bridges under construction. The roadbuilders' encampments lay at intervals beside the route. It was not long before we reached the cutting edge of the improvements. Bulldozers and graders were hacking a way along the side of the valley through virgin jungle. Now we were routed onto an old track along the ravine floor. Ominously, it was strewn with large boulders which had rolled down from the workings above. This was the first hint of the trouble ahead. Weaving our way through the rocks, we suddenly drew up at a river. On the other side, in some trees, lay a ramshackle Karen settlement, named **Huai Kong Kaat**. We could see that the track picked up on the far bank, passing through the dozen huts. Clearly the river had to be forded. Children at play gleefully spotted a *farang* coming, and in an instant the whole village had turned out. Luckily, we rode without mishap through the water and on up through the hovels. As we passed, not one person moved or said anything, which was strange. Later we learned that *farang* hiking to Mae Saam Laep had several times been robbed in this ravine, some near the hamlet.

After Huai Kong Kaat, the real nightmare began. The track ran for seven or eight kms down the bed of the river (the River Saam Laep), dishing up a mess of mud, water, sand, gravel, stones and small boulders. Where the bed widened, the river broke up into a network of rivulets and islands. Here the track kept losing itself, and we cast around trying to find a way through. In a short space, the water had to be forded between 50 and 60 times. It was filthy exhausting work, and these last few kms alone took us on our Wing the best part of two hours. What was particularly galling was the knowledge that before long people would be swanning down this valley in minibuses on a fine new road. Towards the end, we even nearly missed the way into Mae Saam Laep, which veered off to the right up the river bank. Continuing on down the riverbed, we all but ran into the Salween. But that would not have mattered – it was the way the cattle and the trading trucks came.

Mae Saam Laep

Ascending the right-hand bank, we passed through one of those wooden archlike portals that typically mark the entrance to obscure villages, and then hit the first houses of Mae Saam Laep. A sign by a police box required visitors to report with their passports and enter their names in a register inside the box. However, the policeman on duty seemed unconcerned, and we rode on into the narrow main street. This was a long winding rutted mud road, clinging, like the outpost itself, to the precipitous eastern bank of the Salween. It was immediately noticeable that both the number of stores and the profusion of their merchandise was quite out of proportion to the size of the isolated village, which was strange, until we remembered that Mae Saam Laep was one of the principal gateways by which goods entered and left the Karen State, or Kawthoolei, in Burma. Indeed, with Rangoon itself seeking increasingly to cash in on these gateways (Kawmoorah, Wa Lay and the Three Pagodas Pass, for example, all fell – temporarily – to the Burma army at the start of the 1990s), Mae Saam Laep was rapidly becoming the most important of all. It was all the more important because it serviced Kawthoolei's 'capital', Manerplaw.

A steep flight of steps led down from the narrow main street into the Salween river bed. Outside the rainy season, the famous river withdrew here into a narrow central channel, lined on each side by black craggy rocks.[1] With the waters receded, extensive banks of white sand lay exposed. They were so dazzling in the intense light that we had to screw up our eyes. The strong dosage of UV radiation had blackened the skins of the local people and burnt out the colours all around. Down on these scorching sandbanks, we found to our surprise numerous small blue lorries. They were no ordinary vehicles, but were covered in searchlights and had their exhaust pipes and air filters sticking up above the cabs. For a moment, we wondered if they actually crossed the Salween, but, considering the depth of the river and the power of its current, that was clearly impossible. Also, the trucks were all waiting for something, although far and wide there seemed to be nothing that they could possibly be waiting for. It was enigmatic and suspicious. In the shade of some of the lorries, the owners and their families were sitting having lunch. We quizzed them about the mystery, but got only evasive answers. Finally, one man volunteered that he was expecting some cattle "and other things". The lights and exhaust systems were designed for the way back down to Mae Sariang. Often the trucks ploughed back up the riverbed in the night. When I photographed one of them, a man came over and harangued me, saying that I should confine myself to taking pictures of nature, not of his truck. We began to feel uneasy in this out-of-the-way place, which was clearly not just a trading post but also a smuggling point, and which had been repeatedly fought over by the Karen and the Burmese.

It was a motley collection of people hanging around at Mae Saam Laep. The fact that there was no sign of any authority, other than the solitary policeman at the entrance to the village, hardly lessened our feeling of disquiet either. Nowhere was this more the case than in the market area, laid out on the sand at the foot of the village. Two lines of makeshift stalls with leaf roofs curved down towards the river. Of course, there were many Karen in the village, but they were mostly not the traditional hill type one met all down the Thailand's western border, with their red and white costumes and shoulder

---

[1] My *Encyclopaedia Britannica* says that the River Salween (called Nu Chiang or Nu Jiang in Chinese) is Burma's longest river. It rises in eastern Tibet in the T'ang-ku-la mountain range, and flows generally south for about 2,400 kms (1,500 miles) through China and eastern Burma. In China, it passes through Yunnan province, and in Burma it cuts through the Shan State and Shan Plateau. For a short distance, opposite Mae Sariang, it forms the border between Thailand and Burma. The river empties at Moulmein into the Gulf of Martaban and the Andaman Sea. The Salween is a wild and picturesque river which, because it often flows through narrow deep gorges and is obstructed by dangerous rapids, is mostly unnavigable for boats and has never been a major waterway, although it has been used for floating teak logs either down to the sea or latterly from Burma to Thailand.

bags. They were wearing no costume at all. There were Thai wheeler-dealers taking advantage of the cross-border trade and smuggling. There were unaccountable black-faced Burmese in *longyis*. There were Indo-Burmese Muslims with little beards, their dark faces and white eyes peering out of the gloom of their shops, scrutinizing us. Some of the women and girls in the market were heavily made up and in fancy clothes quite incongruous for such a rough place. They were prostitutes, waiting to accompany a flush trader or grimy backwoodsman to some shabby hut. At the bottom of the market alley, by the water's edge, we found a shack even with a snooker table in it. It was flanked by two gambling dens, in which groups of men squatted on the sand floor around mats, which were divided up into sections marked with symbols of chickens and other things. The dice, with corresponding symbols on their sides, were watched intensely, and, depending on how they fell, caused substantial banknotes to change hands. Gambling was supposed to be illegal in Thailand, but we got the impression that in this respect, as in many others, the authorities here turned a blind eye. Anything went in Mae Saam Laep. It was extraterritorial, controlled by neither the Thais, nor the KNU, but a law unto itself. The village was altogether one of the rawest, most riveting and exhilirating corners we found anywhere on our journey.

The market was a cornucopia of merchandise which even Mae Sariang could hardly match. For such an isolated spot, the colourful assortment of fresh produce, groceries and other household items was all the more remarkable. But, on the other hand, the village was where Karen potatoes met Thai condensed milk, and dried Burmese prawns from the Andaman Sea intersected with yellow noodles come down from Yunnan, China. Overestimating the facilities of Manerplaw, we made a mistake in not stocking up with some of these provisions. A vegetable and fruit stall was piled high with immaculate cauliflowers, the choicest *mangetout* peas, tomatoes, potatoes, cabbages, shallots, garlic, green aubergines, ginger, green and red chilli peppers, pineapples, coconuts, oranges, water melons and jujubes. Next to it was an Aladdin's cave of cooking oil, bottles of pork fat, shrimp and fish paste, fresh fish, dried fish, eggs, peanuts, Singha beer, *lao kao*, bottled water, black tea, rice, noodles, bread rolls, blocks of cane sugar, tubes of ground pork meat, dried bananas and mushrooms, prawn crackers, and sachets of sunflower seeds for snacking on. Packs of dark brown discs caught our eye, and we enquired what they were. *Tua nao kap* or "rotten bean squash", a lady laughed, using northern Thai dialect. They were compressed roundels of dried-out yellow bean mash, used for making curry sauces and chilli dips. And then there was a smoking counter. Bundles of Burmese Best Thukita cheroots, 50 for 10 baht (a terrific bargain), were stacked up alongside mounds of loose tobacco and cartons of Thai Khrong Thip cigarettes, contraband Marlboro and various Burmese and Chinese brands (for example, Fortune, Hunter, Horse and Xinxing). A round-faced Burmese-looking girl minding the stall was also doing a brisk business in arcane betel chews. From a variety of pots, she took different kinds of brightly coloured paste, which was spread on green leaves. There were *plu* leaves to be smeared with lime, and *siri* leaves. They were then folded up, bought by the customer, and chewed either on their own or with betel. The litter of messy tins and caked spatulas on the spattered counter was a bit like an art class in an infants' school. And all this was not to take into account the ironmongery stalls, clothes shops and refreshment stands.

At the end of the market alley, by the Salween, there was a small bay, where some 25 longtail boats of all sizes were moored (see colour photo). Some were very large, and it was these which were used for bringing the livestock across the river, either transporting the animals on board or swimming them over with their heads roped to the sides. Teak logs were manhandled across in a similar fashion, and of course the *hang yao* provided a regular service for people, ferrying them and their goods back and forth, as well as up and down the river. On the far side of the swirling fast-flowing Salween, directly opposite Mae Saam Laep, there was little except mountains and jungle. A clearing on the other bank was littered with hardwood trunks waiting to be floated across. Behind them, on a knoll, stood two buildings – perhaps a Karen 'customs' point, where taxes would be levied on everything passing through. A track went off past the knoll into the interior. Looking back towards Thailand, we could take in the whole of bustling sinister Mae Saam Laep in one sweep. The longtails with their Thai or Karen flags and massive engines lay moored to the 'beach'. The empty trucks waited sizzling in the sun. The gambling sheds and market straggled across the sand to the steep hillside. The tiers of wooden houses of the village proper perched precariously on the hillside on long stilts. And above the village, a small Burmese-style *wat* crouched in the background.

At the upper end of the market, in a small eating place, we ordered *raat na* or noodles with pork and greens in gravy. While we were waiting for the food to arrive, we noticed a pair of booted feet sticking out through a curtain across a doorway. Behind it a walkie-talkie could also be seen hanging from a chair back. Presently, a KNLA officer emerged, rubbed his eyes, and continued with whatever he had been doing before his nap – perhaps travelling upriver. As we ate, a continuous stream of men went past the chow shop, humping sacks of rice and other necessities down to the longtail boats. We asked our cooking lady about accommodation in Mae Saam Laep (it was this lady who told us about the robberies on the road in from Mae Sariang). She said that there had once been a guest house in the village, but that it had burnt down in mysterious circumstances. The headman sometimes let out rooms, but if we wanted, we could stay in her house. We thanked her, saying that we were hoping to travel on. This led us to ask her if she knew how we could find our contacts. Maha San had told us of some dissident Burmese students operating clandestinely in Mae Saam Laep, who should be able to help us on our way. The village was a large confusing place, we explained, and it would be difficult for us to hunt out the contacts on our own. The cooking lady knew exactly who we wanted and, lowering her voice, indicated where we could find them – at the back of a certain shop.

Sure enough, when we asked at this shop, two Burmese men in sarongs appeared. Communication was difficult because they spoke no Thai, although one of them had a smattering of English. But they soon understood what we wanted. They themselves had no direct link with Manerplaw, they explained, but were agents for the ABSDF HQ of Daungguin (Dagwyn), 30 minutes by boat upstream (north). Why did we not go there instead? Lying, we said that we wanted first to go to Manerplaw for New Year, but would come on to them afterwards. It was a stroke of luck that we never visited their camp, for a few days later it was attacked by SLORC forces, a number of student rebels perishing. The two men bade us sit down while they went to make enquiries. The contacts seemed to us to be not quite all they had been cracked up to be, and we began to fear that we would never get to Manerplaw. But we were wrong. Soon they returned and reported that everything was arranged. Suddenly, we were overtaken by events. A *hang yao*, which we could travel on, was now waiting for us. It would leave for Manerplaw in five minutes, and we should get down to the water immediately. There was a big problem with our motorbike, we remonstrated. "Should we leave it here, or take it with us, or have it transported back to Mae Sariang?" "Give us the keys," one of the duo pressed, "we will sort it out." We surrendered our £1000 hire bike to unfathomable people we had never seen before, hurried to get our backpacks from the noodle restaurant, and strode down to the longtails. We arrived to see the Honda being lifted aboard one of them, where it was lashed down. We climbed in too, along with a dozen other passengers, and within minutes the boat set off with a great roar of its outsize engine. We had not even had time to ponder the wisdom of our move, let alone make a few hasty purchases for the trip. As we headed off to an unknown fate in a murky region very far from anywhere and embroiled in a civil war, we reflected that, well, at least there was no turning back now. On the backrest of one of the boats' seats was painted in English: BE HAPPY AND SMILE. In the circumstances, it was the best and only thing to do!

*

Fifty baht each bought us a thrilling two-hour boat trip south down the Salween (Map 20). It was a ride precisely along the border – the west bank was Burma or 'Myanmar', while the east Thailand. The river itself was claimed by the Burmese. These *hang yao* plied the Salween at a fair lick. When an oncoming boat zipped past, there was scarcely time to see who was aboard. Our longtail bore mostly Karen people who had been shopping or trading, but there were also two Burmese monks, as well as a girl who was returning home from college for the New Year break. The boat was manned aft by an expressionless driver and fore by a youth with a paddle, who was drunk. Between the passengers and the driver was a mountain of prawn crackers in cellophane bags. Someone in rebel Kawthoolei obviously had a soft spot for the crunchy titbit. The bows of our craft sliced through the water, sending up each side an arced curtain of glistening iridescent droplets, while in our wake a long plume of spray was churned up by the single thrashing propeller. The riverbanks to left and right alternated clumps of black jagged rocks and sandy coves. Tiny settlements flashed by, white pagodas punctuated the hillsides, people were fishing with nets in the shallows, and here and there a sawmill stood at the waterfront. Passing the sawmills, all on the Burmese side, we could see how the cut timber was floated across to Thailand on bamboo rafts. Tributaries came down to meet the river on both banks, and sometimes a track ran up from the water's edge. Ahead, the monolithic peaks of the Dawna Range loomed. Not far after the Thai village of **Mae Haat**, set in an area of reforestation, we came to a major confluence. It was where the Moei river flowed into the Salween. The princely Salween, which had been running north to south, now turned north-west into the Burmese heartland, while the knavish fast-flowing Moei, which unusually ran north, headed off upstream (south) along the border towards distant Mae Sot. We struck off into the mouth of the Moei.

Amost immediately we came upon a serious KNLA checkpoint, mounted on the Burmese bank. Armed rebel soldiers in sunglasses ordered the longtail to pull over. They checked the papers and business of everybody aboard, and of course we fell into their hands. A tense five minutes followed. Diagonally opposite on the other bank stood a Thai military post. We could see its soldiers watching us and the proceedings through binoculars. The situation was difficult not least because the Karen guards could speak no Thai, while we could speak no Karen. Altogether Thai was of little use down here – English, if anything, was the fall-back language. But these boys could speak no English, either. Judging by the way they were shaking their heads, things did not look promising, and we were convinced that they would send us back. After all, what business had we up here, especially at GHQ Manerplaw? The guards seemed particularly unhappy about the motorcycle and our backpacks. It was clear to them that we were no ordinary trippers from Mae Sariang taking a spin out on the river. Shouting across the water that separated the boat from them, we tried to explain in Thai and English that Prince Maha San had sent us and that we were going to visit the Wa representative at Manerplaw. But nobody had heard of Maha San or knew of any Wa representative. There were a lot of ordinary Karen civilians hanging around the checkpoint, waiting with their bags for a boat north. Now the words 'Maha San' and 'Wa' were on everyone's lips. The people, like the guards, chewed over the concepts, tentatively, unsure whether the taste would prove bitter or sweet. Suddenly, it bore in on us just how obscure Maha San and the Wa actually were, at least down here in Karen territory.

Finally, the KNLA soldier in charge delivered his verdict in Karen. One of the two monks leant over and relayed the message to us in broken English: "Cannot go further, must to go back now." We grew very dispirited. It seemed such a shame to have got all the way to Mae Saam Laep and then, with the aid of the ABSDF student contacts, so far downstream, just to be repulsed by a handful of youths on the riverbank. At this point the college girl intervened. She elicited from us what our purpose really was. As she could speak Thai and Karen, she was able to clearly convey to the guards what we wanted. They appeared to relent. Did we have any documentation with us? We handed over our passports, which they scrutinized. As they appeared now to be in two minds, we further passed over for good measure Maha San's personal card and a wallet of photos we always carried with us. The card spelled out Maha San's membership of the NDF, while among the photos was a shot of myself with a KNLA commander we had met on another occasion. Somebody recognized the commander, and that did the trick. To everybody's relief, the boat moved forward again.

THREE PAGODAS

We breasted some rapids, rounded a large island midstream, and passed some kind of staging post, situated by a confluence on the Thai side, where possibly the River Yuam ran into the Moei. It was not long before the longtail slowed down to stop apparently in the middle of nowhere. There was a beach, an escarpment behind it and, growing on top, a lot of trees. The driver motioned us to get out. We queried if this was Manerplaw. It was, confirmed the other passengers. Nobody else got out, although one or two people who had been waiting on some rocks got in. All the men present helped us lift the Honda onto the beach. Then the boat sped off, leaving us stranded with a motorbike in Burma. It was all quite different from what we had imagined. Where was the famous GHQ, where were all the houses and soldiers, and where was the checkpoint processing new arrivals? In the shade of a large boulder we spotted two youths with rifles. We also noticed a rickety sign on two poles in Karen lettering. We asked the boys what it read. "Manerplaw", they said. "Where is the village?" we enquired. "Up the escarpment", they replied, uninterested. Our surprise, upon arriving at Manerplaw, at not finding what we had expected was just the first of a series of re-evaluations we were obliged to make at rebel HQ.

Manerplaw

Pushing the Honda across the sand and stones to the foot of the escarpment, where we left it for the moment, we climbed up a steep flight of earth steps to emerge at a control post, hidden in the trees. Opposite it was a 6-ft-diameter satellite dish aimed heavenwards, but full of fallen leaves. The checkpoint, a wooden hut with a tin roof, was manned by a youngster. Like his predecessors on the river, he spoke only Karen. Unlike them, he was not at all concerned about us, or, rather, he did not really know what to do with us. Finding that he put no obstacle in our way, we wandered on through some large wooden houses and stumbled all at once on the heart of Manerplaw. Around a parade ground-cum-playing field were a number of substantial office buildings, while on the far side was the Karen National Liberation Army General Headquarters itself. We were amazed at how easy it was to breeze into Manerplaw, the resistance nerve centre that the Burma army had spent years trying to capture.

Looking for some reception or information bureau, we strolled around. No one challenged us, which was remarkable as we could have come with a bomb for GHQ. But then there were not many people around anyway. The overriding impression we got of Manerplaw was not of a bustling fortified garrison, but of a cool relaxed spot, shady under trees – the pervasive tranquillity broken only by the distant growl of longtails on the Moei. We had timed our visit to coincide with New Year. This was not because of any special celebrations here (nothing special did happen – the Karen New Year was two weeks later), but because we wanted to avoid the (Western) New Year in Thailand. The celebrations for this had degenerated in recent years into a national bunfight, with mayhem in places like Chiang Mai, widespread drunkenness, and carnage on the roads. In Manerplaw, we had picked the right place to come. Battered old trucks with no number plates languished in sleepy sunlit corners, the clack of a typewriter drifted lazily out of an office window, giant butterflies wafted by, and on the hour a muffled bugle sounded somewhere.

Poking our heads into a few windows, we asked where reception was. Over in the corner of the parade ground, people said. Everyone was friendly, orderly, civil. Sure enough, there was a reception point across the ground, but it was unattended. It was while we were looking there that we began to notice sentries discreetly dotted around, at intersections or on corners, especially in the vicinity of the GHQ building. In a house marked Karen Women's Organization, we asked if there was an information office anywhere. We were pointed back in the direction we had come from, towards the Moei. Behind an empty barrack house, we found the office. It too was deserted, although after a while a man appeared. When we had introduced ourselves, he sat us down to fill up a long form, one for each of us. It was not easy to do this. The questions asked: 'Purpose of visit?', 'Intended length of stay?', 'Representing which organization?', 'Rank?', and so on. We could hardly write: 'Just popping by to have a look'! The forms were borne away by the man to another building. After a quarter of an hour, another man appeared, apparently some secretary. He asked us all the same questions, but ended by flabbergasting us with the enquiry: "And which minister is it that you have come to see? You understand that the ministers are busy people, but I will try to secure an appointment for you." Actually, we had no desire to interview any minister. We wanted only to form a writer's impression of Manerplaw. But to say so would have undermined our credibility, and so, not quite daring to go for C-in-C and KNU president Bo Mya himself, we blurted out almost at random "the Minister for Education and Culture". A meeting with this gentleman was duly arranged for the afternoon of the following day. The encounter with the information office and the secretary revealed another unexpected aspect of Manerplaw – it was a grave bureaucratic place. It was as if, through sheer bulk and weight of paperwork, the Karen authorities were trying to substantiate a world which did not quite properly exist.

The secretary escorted us next to Manerplaw's hospitality house. A simple wooden affair with a nice veranda, this was soon to be replaced by regular accommodation being noisily hammered together next door. Washing was done outside from a cement water tank with the aid of a dipper, while sleeping was attempted in a series of cubicles, separated by 6-ft-high wooden partitions. These cubicles – a kind of dormitory for officers – had no roofs (except for the overall roof of the building high above), and were screened off from the corridor by flimsy curtains drawn across the doorway. Journalists and TV crews from all over the world came to Manerplaw to get the latest news at source of the long-running insurgency. During our stay in the hospitality house, we overlapped with two radio reporters from Germany. They were a pair of humourless spinsterly ladies, one older and one younger, and when they were not going from one appointment to another, thet sat fiddling on the veranda with their notebooks, cassette recorders, water filters and other paraphernalia. They were snobbishly contemptuous of us, not deigning once in three days to recognize our presence, let alone mouth a friendly 'Hello'. It was as if they thought that we were somehow poaching on a patch they wanted all to themselves, as if our presence somehow detracted from their feeling of exclusivity. A seasoned female aid worker we met elsewhere in Kawthoolei said that the behaviour of the two Germans was typical. Probably Manerplaw was the only part of the border they had seen. The more trivial the journalist, she said, the more self-important and snooty they were. She had met at HQ some of the world's most famous reporters, and they were invariably the friendliest.

To stay at the hospitality house we were charged a hefty (by local standards of the time) 200 baht per person per day, although that did include three daily meals. Clearly the sum was a nominal one, with the fat constituting an involuntary contribution to the war effort. We rather got the impression that the new 'guest house' being built next door was to put up not just delegates to the occasional NDF or DAB conference, but possible future tourists. The Karen authorities had perhaps spotted some potential in that.

The secretary indicated to us a way round the escarpment by which we might bring our motorbike up to our lodging. After we had settled in and washed, we went to retrieve the Honda. We also took a first scout round Manerplaw. Again we were struck by the calm of this well-established place. Lofty mature trees surrounded the central parade ground, shading the various organizational and command buildings. Perhaps the trees were planted in 1975, the date KNU/KNLA GHQ was first established in Manerplaw. It was difficult to imagine that the area had repeatedly been the scene of bitter fighting. Yet the air-raid shelters everywhere (mostly bunkers dug sideways into earth banks), as well as the series of checkpoints on the tracks out north and south, bore witness to the fact. The last such attack had been in 1991. Unlike many other gateways to Kawthoolei,[2] which had fallen in the late 1980s and early 90s to the SLORC *tatmadaw* (mostly quickly being retaken by the Karen), Manerplaw had never been captured. But this was hardly surprising. Owing to its position, the place looked virtually impregnable. Situated furthest to the rear (east) of the Karen State, it lay sandwiched between the protective waters of the Moei border river to the east and the shield of the Dawna mountains to the west, beyond which, further west, lay the Salween river. The jungle-clad slopes of the towering Dawna range rose straight up immediately behind the KNLA GHQ building itself.

Manerplaw's quietness was also in part due to the fact that not many ordinary people lived there. We had expected an extensive village, bustling with children and animals. But we found a community of about 100 houses with only two or three tiny shops – a far cry from Mae Saam Laep. In fact, Manerplaw was not a regular village at all and much less the capital of the Karen State, as is sometimes assumed. It was primarily a military camp, with all the earnestness and spartan regimen that that implied. Certainly, there were people in Manerplaw, about another 1000, but they were all troops stationed in barracks mostly north of the centre. However, things did liven up a bit towards evening, when people returned from working in the fields and some soldiers came back from day exercises.

---

[2] Kawthoolei (Kawthulay, Ko Thu Lae) might mean 'bare burnt-black country', i.e. a land that must be fought for, or 'green/flowery land'.

REBEL HQ

There were two primary schools in Manerplaw and a secondary school not far away. On the north side was a Baptist church, and power came from a hydroelectric plant, generating locally. Besides the KNLA GHQ building itself (see photo section), as well as the hospitality house and the information bureau, our tour of inspection turned up a communications centre, an administrative office, a clinic and a couple of central barracks. Away from the village centre were a series of buildings, all of wood and bamboo, housing the representations or headquarters of numerous organizations, including the Karen Youth Organization, the Karen National Defence Organization, the Palaung State Liberation Front, the important Democratic Alliance of Burma (DAB), the National Democratic Front (NDF), and many more. The NDF HQ was itself home to an alliance comprising the Arakan Liberation Party, the Chin National Front, the Kachin Independence Organization, the Karenni National Progressive Party, the Karen National Union (KNU), the Lahu National Organization, the New Mon State Party, the Pa-O National Organization, the Palaung State Liberation Party, the Shan State Progress Party, and Maha San's Wa National Organization, together with all their corresponding armies. Inside the NDF HQ was a colourful array of the flags and emblems of all these political parties and military wings (see photo). The DAB HQ (see photo) was home to an even bigger alliance, which included the NDF and a number of other movements. Manerplaw was the meeting place of a veritable pot-pourri of ethnic groups and military factions, and, walking around, one could on any one day bump into a sample of representatives from them. The danger at rebel HQ, a danger that not a few visitors succumbed to, was of getting sucked into an endless investigation of these fascinating minority groups and their insurgent efforts. Many were the people in the village who spent days on end consulting, asking questions and taking notes.

On returning to our lodging, we found our supper already laid out on a table in a gloomy back room. The pattern was always the same. The food, prepared by some cooking boys, was put out irrespective of whether the guests were there to eat it or not, so that if the guests were late or the meal was early (which happened most of the time), the food was left to go cold. We sat down to the cold supper with an unaccountable American, who was "just passing through". The joyless German women preferred to eat on their own out front on the balcony. The offering was threefold. There was a meat and potato curry, cabbage fried with tomato, and omelette. Rice, of course, was also served, and coffee afterwards. Unfortunately, the meat was almost exclusively fat and gristle, and the curry was swimming in oil.

Later on our journey, we were to enjoy some fine Karen cooking, and *Yang* hospitality in general was to prove unsurpassed among that of the minority peoples, but this first meal at Manerplaw was an introduction to typical run-of-the-mill Karen fare. Unlike Thai or Chinese cooking, it was more in the style of Burmese food – heavy, bland and greasy. In three days of breakfasts, lunches and suppers, there were some variations. Chicken replaced beef in the curry, cauliflower was fried with tomato instead of cabbage, noodle was served as a change from rice, and once for breakfast we had an intriguing deep-fried rice pillow, filled with chick peas. But always the dishes were cold and greasy, the chicken (for example) consisted of pieces of chopped up neck, and no meal was complete without egg in some form, mostly fried or boiled. We took to putting the boiled eggs in doggy bags for redistribution during our walks. The fare proved no problem for the punk-style American. He ate it like a horse, and we began to wonder if he was not a soldier of fortune who had just returned from the front and weeks of jungle diet. In the matter of food and drink, we made another discovery about Manerplaw – it was a dry village. The reason for this was that the leaders of the KNU and KNLA were predominantly Baptist and Seventh-Day Adventist, and had imposed a prohibition on alcohol at GHQ. Nowhere was beer or whisky to be had, not even *lao kao*. So our New Year's Eve in Kawthoolei passed off completely teetotal!

The next morning we explored on foot the tracks running south and north of Manerplaw. To the south, the impressive new HQ of the Karen Youth Organization was fronted by a series of signs bearing the slogans: TO HAVE MORE UNITY AMONG THE ETHNIC GROUPS, TO BUILD UNDERSTANDING AMONG THE FUTURE LEADERS OF THE ETHNIC GROUPS, TO EXCHANGE CULTURE OF DIFFERENT ETHNIC GROUPS and TO DEFINE PLAN FOR FUTURE ACTIVITIES AMONG THE GROUPS. Some serious youths inside tried to embroil us in a heavy political discussion in broken English right after breakfast. We found a little shop and also a couple of 'cafés'. Outside the KNU Finance Department – Supreme Headquarters, a wooden building with plaited bamboo walls and a leaf roof, a battered Toyota pick-up was parked in the shade of a banana palm (see photo). The vehicle's front bumper, headlight mounting and front offside bodywork was lashed on with a rope running up to the roll bar, while on a side panel some wag had sprayed 'OK'.

The dusty jungle track south was punctuated by a series of checkpoints and barriers. Being near to GHQ, they were not trivial affairs, but on the other hand no one tried to stop us in our exploration. After the NDF and DAB offices, we found Manerplaw's church, called the Redeemer Church. A side track, signposted 'Daw Aung San Suu Kyi Road' in honour of the Nobel Peace laureate and heroine of Burma's 1988 democracy uprising, led down to the Moei. Also on this road, a tranquil side ravine housed the representation of the All Burma Young Monks' Union (see photo). A flamboyant sign on the portal overarching the entrance to the *pongyis*' compound read: LONG LIVE HOLINESS – REVOLUTIONARY AREA. Burma had a tradition of militant monks, and the ochre robes we could see hanging in the ravine would have been no strangers to bloody front-line action. A tiny sawmill also lay to one side of the route. Here two men, their bodies glistening with sweat in the morning sun, were laboriously sawing a tree trunk lengthways with a 6-ft-long, double-handled saw. The resulting beams were remarkably true, and from time to time they paused in their slow rhythmic efforts to oil the blade.

An hour's walk out from Manerplaw, we came to a third checkpoint. Situated high up on a Dawna mountainside, it had a commanding view over the Moei. The guardhouse and barrier were manned by a lady soldier and a boy, both of the KNLA. The Karen military had servicewomen, and some of them could be seen at HQ. She was holding an automatic weapon, while he in true *Yang* fashion was puffing at a cheroot. Both could not have been more than teenagers. She looked about 17 or 18, while he, with his boyish round face and quavery deep voice which sounded as if it had just broken, must have been only 14 or so (see photo). The girl was also singular in that she was barely 4 ft tall and had a squint eye, which could not have helped her shooting – or perhaps it did. He, a spindly playful creature with hair down to his shoulders, was hardly taller. The lady sentry was dressed in camouflage jacket and trousers, a wide-brimmed hat and flip-flops, while the boy had regular army trousers and boots, a military cap with KNLA badge, but also an ordinary civilian shirt and a kind of tea towel tied around his waist. We could not help wondering how effective they would really have beeen if the enemy had suddenly appeared round the corner. Conversation with the two was impossible, but they were happy enough to sit with us for a while on a table next to the sentry box. We passed on to them our boiled eggs from breakfast. These they peeled and ate on the spot, dropping eggshell into the dust. The soldier girl's flip-flops fell from her feet. Incised into the top of each was the enigmatic message I KISS. Whether 'I' was 'I' (me) or '1' (one) we never discovered.

Investigating the track north was a different kettle of fish. If the southern end of Manerplaw was the political quarter, the northern was the military. Over the road up here was a series of arches which all bore the message in stark white letters on black: GIVE ME LIBERTY OR DEATH – KNLA (see pictures in photo section). We walked under them humbly. They were a grim reminder of the seriousness with which the Karen took their struggle for self-determination, of the whole *raison d'être* of Manerplaw, and of the deadliness of the 40-year-old insurgency against Rangoon. But passing under one arch, we could not resist a smile. A large pot-bellied pig trotted beside us. Did the looming slogan apply equally to the *Yang* porker?

Beyond the arches, we came across Kawthoolei Military Training School with its adjacent barracks. The KNLA emblem (two horns and a drum superimposed on a sunburst) blazed from a coat of arms above the entrance to the school (see photo). The barracks were simple affairs. Each was a wooden longhouse, raised on stilts, with a roof, but open at the sides except for a low wall. Inside, the length of the two long walls, each soldier had a metre or two of space for his bed and belongings. Opposite the school was another parade ground-cum-football pitch (the Saw Ba U Gyi sports ground). A match was in progress between Karen soldiers and some guesting Shan troops. The clothes of the spectators were an interesting mix of green camouflage fatigues and checked *longyis* or sarongs. Between the pitch and the river stood an open-air lecture hall. The Four Principles of the Karen struggle, almost exactly as first formulated in 1950 by Saw Ba U Gyi (the first prime minister of the provisional Kawthoolei government of the day) were pinned up in here: 1. FOR US SURRENDER IS OUT OF QUESTION, 2. THE RECOGNITION OF THE KAREN STATE MUST BE COMPLETED, 3. WE SHALL RETAIN OUR ARMS, and 4. WE SHALL DECIDE OUR OWN POLITICAL DESTINY. A military cemetery adjoining the hall was a poignant reminder of those who had embraced death in the pursuit of liberty. About 200 overgrown graves were marked by simple wooden Christian crosses, almost every one with RIP etched on it. The details on the crosses showed that most of the deceased were Karen and Mon, as well as ABSDF student guerrillas. The dates of their deaths were variously 1990, 1992 and 1993.

At sundown, we returned to the guesting Shan soldiers, now off-duty. There were hundreds of them. On the breast pockets of their jungle-green uniforms, bright yellow flashes announced: SNPLA (Shan Nationalities People's Liberation Army), while their shirt sleeves bore red sunburst badges, and their caps had red stars. Evidently part of a new or renamed army, it was, we were later told, a Pa-O outfit which had joined the Shan. To us, many of the troops looked like Wa. They were wild-looking men of all ages and sizes (see photo in photo section). Their skins were black-brown, and many had wispy chintuft beards or moustaches. Some were already quite old and greying, while others were mere boys of twelve or less, their voices not yet broken. There were men with bits of ear missing and decayed brown teeth, others with scarred lips and squint eyes. These pitiful people almost made a more profound impression on us than anything else in Manerplaw. Scattered in the scrub around their barracks, they had divided up into groups of three or five or ten. Many had improvised windbreaks to shield themselves and their camp fires from the chill evening breeze. Those who had not already gone to rest in the long huts were cooking, or brewing tea, or strumming guitars, or cleaning their weapons, or smoking, or lying in hammocks made of old rice sacks. Hanging from the trees or lying on the ground was every kind of gun and grenade launcher. It was as if troops had decided to set up camp for the night in the middle of a battlefield. Passing from fire to fire, we tried to see what the groups were cooking. It was always the same. Youths squatting in broken-down shoes or in cracked rubber ankle boots were stirring two pots, one containing a stew of green leaves and salt, the other rice. It was a meagre diet to sustain them in a hard boring life.

Earlier that afternoon, we had made our visit to the Minister of Education and Culture. By mistake, we arrived for our appointment half an hour early. This was because we had not noticed a 30-minute discrepancy between Thai time and Burmese standard time. The minister turned out to be Saw Shwi Ya Hae, the Karen Central Committee member who in 1989 led the first NDF delegation up to the Wa State in the wake of the CPB mutinies to see if the Wa defectors could be brought into the democratic fold. Shwi Ya Hae welcomed us into his wooden house near the Moei escarpment. An assistant accompanied him, and at a table in an ante-room a male secretary picked out keys on an ancient typewriter. There was evidence of duplicating equipment, and dusty piles of roneod pamphlets lay stacked up on the floor. The minister, in regular civilian trousers and a fashion camouflage jacket, bade us sit round a large table. He had short hair and a military moustache, and spoke good English. An urbane, educated, soft-spoken man, Saw Shwi patiently answered our many questions about the Karen, their history and culture, and the insurgency. Some of what he said has gone into the two following accounts of the Karen people and their culture, and of the Karen rebellion. Readers impatient to continue with the travelogue may care to omit the lengthy digests.

❖

Karen people and culture

The Karen (in the widest sense of the word – the stress is on the second syllable: Ka-*ren*) are usually classified as belonging to the Karennic branch of the Tibeto-Burman group in the overall Sino-Tibetan family of peoples, although their inclusion in the Sino-Tibetan ethnolinguistic superstock is controversial for some scholars. Taken as a whole, the Karen or the Karennic group comprises a range of tribes that are more or less closely related, and which include the Sgaw Karen ('White Karen'), Pwo Karen, Pa-O ('Black Karen', Taungthu Karen), Kayah Karen (Karenni, 'Red Karen'), 'Long-Neck' Padaung and 'Long-Ear' Kayaw (Bre), as well as other minority tribes. Of these, only the Sgaw, Pwo and Pa-O are really numerous. The Karennic branch is sometimes divided into two sub-groups of Karen: the Sgaw-Bghai and Pwo. Using this distinction, Howard (1999), for example, lists under the Sgaw-Bghai sub-group: the Sgaw Karen themselves, the Kayah, the Padaung, Kayaw, Lahta, Yinbaw, Paku and others; and under the Pwo sub-group: the Pwo Karen themselves and the Pa-O. Some of these taxonomic attributions are themselves controversial, and there are fragmentary tribes (such as the Manoo-Manaw) that have yet to be definitively ascribed. When the word 'Karen' is used in this book and chapter (the same goes for the Thailand guide books and much other literature), it mostly does not refer to the Karen peoples as a whole (the Karennic branch), but specifically to the dominant Sgaw Karen, with the Pwo Karen, Padaung etc. being named as such. Thus the Karen of Chapters 9 to 16, the Karen of Manerplaw, of the rebellion, of Wiang Haeng district, Muang Noi village and the settlements south of Um Pang are really the Sgaw Karen, with the word 'Karen' being used in a limited sense. Accordingly, the observations made below about Karen culture refer essentially to the Sgaw (for a brief account of the Pwo Karen, see my guide *Trek It Yourself in Northern Thailand*, pp. 254-258).

It is said that the Karen as a whole do not have a name, such as 'Karen', for their race, although Schliesinger (2000) says that they call themselves the "Pga K'Nyaw", which may be of Chinese origin. The Sgaw Karen, he continues, call themselves the 'Kanyaw', which would seem to be the same as the term just mentioned, although elsewhere I have read that they call themselves 'the Sgaw people', referring to their Pwo cousins as 'the Pwo people'. The Pwo Karen are said to know themselves as the 'Plong' or 'Plong Su' people. The word 'Karen' was coined in the past by American missionaries and British colonial administrators in Burma, who first made the Karen known to the outside works through their work and records, starting in the early 19th century. In Thailand, the Karen (Sgaw and Pwo alike) are referred to by the Thais as 'Kariang' or 'Kaliang' or just 'Yang'.[3]

The origins of the Karen as a whole are obscure. For such a large family of peoples, they are singular in their lack of a recorded early history – they are a race almost with no history. It is not known where they originated or through which territories they passed as they migrated to their present area of habitation. As they moved, they seem neither to have left any mark on the indigenous groups they passed through, nor to have gained any traces from those races. Karen culture shows, for example, little or no Sinitic influence or evidence of association with the Chinese, unlike the culture of many peoples, say, the Yao or Hmong or Wa. It bears, if anything, traces of contact with the Burmese, Mon, Lawa and British. This might mean, of course, that the Karen did not dally with other races during any migration.

One school of thought associates the origins of the Karen with the Gobi Desert area, which they may have left a very long time ago. Karen legends speak of their race coming from 'Tibi Kobi', which could be Tibet and the Gobi Desert. Another believes that the Karen originated in the upper reaches of the Yellow River in China, from where they migrated down to what is today's Yunnan province, where they possibly settled for a longer period, before being pushed further south by other peoples advancing behind them from the north. A third theory is that the Karen might have passed through Cambodia. This idea is based on the fact that a celebrated part of Karen culture is its bronze drums, which are associated with Cambodia and which may have been taken over from that cultural territory. Most scholars believe that the Karen originated either in south-east Tibet/China near Tibet or in south-west China, although none of their race live in these places today.

In the former case, they then migrated to south-western China, from where in both cases they moved to the Mae Khong (Mekong) river valley area (the stretch now forming the Lao-Burmese border), with which the Karen are traditionally associated. From here, they migrated west and south into Burma, perhaps 2,000 years ago or maybe in the 6th or 7th centuries AD, but in any case well before the arrival of the Burman, whom they predate.[4] The Burman migrated into Upper Burma in the 9th and 10th centuries AD (they began to build Pagan in AD 849), and as they did so, they displaced the Karen first into central 'Burma' and then to the south-east. It is generally assumed that the Karen first moved from 'Burma' into 'Thailand' in the 18th century, but they may well have done so far earlier. According to some sources, Karen settled in the vicinity of present-day Chiang Mai as long ago as the 8th century AD, quite some time before the Tai, which would make them the earliest settlers of Sino-Tibetan stock in 'Thailand'. In any case, they began migrating (again) in

---

[3] 'Kayin' is a generic term used by the Burmese which equates with the English word 'Karen' and refers to the Sgaw and Pwo. 'Kayin-ni' is a Burmese term for 'Karenni' or Red Karen.
[4] The Karen date their present era back to 739 BC, making it longer even than the Buddhist era, let alone the Christian one (in 2000 AD the Karen year was 2739, the Thai year 2543 BE), but what this date refers to and whether it refers to the origins of the Karen people or to their most recent migration into Burma is not clear.

appreciable numbers into Siam/the Lan-Na kingdom in the middle of the 18th century, a fact documented in written annals.

Migrating eastwards, across the Salween river and into territory that is now Thailand, the Karen apparently first reached areas of present-day Mae Hong Son province. Here they found themselves settling in land that was occupied in places both by the ancient indigenous declining Lawa people (see Chapter 8) and by Shan (Tai Yai) people. They managed to settle among and live peacefully with especially the Lawa, and today, in Mae Hong Son province, both Sgaw and Pwo Karen live cheek by jowl with the Lawa (as well as, of course, with the Thais, Shan and other minority groups), continuing to get along with the Lawa and even intermarrying with them. You can see this both south and especially north of the H108 road (the section between Mae Sariang and Hot towns). In these areas, there is considerable evidence of Lawa influence in the costume, ornamentation and implements of the Karen, as well as of Karen impact on the Lawa. Subsequently, the Karen migrated east across the border in other places up and down the Thai-Burmese frontier, and they are still doing so today (e.g. at Mae Salid and into Om Koi district) on account of continuing oppression of them by the Burmese military junta and as economic migrants.

Today, the picture regarding Karen areas of inhabitation and population figures is very complicated and confusing. They live only in Burma and Thailand, but are not spread additionally over, say, Laos, China and Vietnam, as are some Indo-Chinese tribes. In Burma, Karen (in the wider sense of the overall Karennic family of peoples) inhabit large areas of Lower Burma, from the Arakan Yoma and Delta region right up to the Pegu Yoma highlands, the Shan State and the Thai borderlands. After the Burman, they must constitute the second-largest ethnic group in the country. There may be 4 or 5 million Karen in Burma, possibly 6 or 7 if the 'Red' Karen of the Karenni ('Kayah') State and the Pa-O of south-western Shan State and elsewhere are reckoned in. But if the vast majority of Karen live in Burma, a substantial minority – perhaps 350,000 of them (disregarding hordes of refugees) – inhabit Thailand, living in a swathe of territory down its western border with Burma. These 'Thai' Karen account for fully 50% of the country's 'hill-tribe' population, making them easily the kingdom's most populous highland ethnic minority group.

More specifically, in Burma, an estimated 1 or 2 million Pa-O[5] (who actually do not have much in common with the other Karen peoples) live, as said, in the south-western part of the Shan State around Taunggyi, but also in other parts of the country. The relatively small group of Karenni (Kayan, 'Red Karen') tribes live in the Karenni State and also to a limited extent in southern Shan State, of which the Kayah themselves constitute the biggest tribe, numbering some 150,000 - 200,000 or more. 'Regular' mainstream Karen (i.e. non-Karenni/Kayan, non-Pa-O) live west of the Karenni State and also to the south of it, in the Pegu hills between the Irrawaddy and Sittang rivers; in the Karen State (Kawthoolei), which lies south of the Karenni State, and runs

---

[5] Howard (1999) puts the figure at c. 560,000.

down Burma's eastern border with Thailand from roughly the latitude of Mae Sariang to the Tenasserim Division; in the coastal Tenasserim region all the way down to Victoria Point; and in southern lowland Burma, in the plains of the Irrawaddy, Sittang and Salween deltas.

Most 'Burmese' Karen are Sgaw and Pwo. An estimated 2 million or more Sgaw live in Burma, and an estimated 1.2 million Pwo live in the country, mainly in the Irrawaddy Delta, making them largely lowland Karen in Burma at least. Among these 'regular' Karen, we can make an important distinction between 'ordinary' plains-dwelling Karen, who form a majority, and more traditional hill Karen, who form a sizeable minority. The former live all over Lower Burma, and some are relatively assimilated into mainstream Burmese culture, wear no costume, and may not even speak Karen any more or speak it as a second language. It has been said (Howard, 1999) that in Burma 3.5 million people speak a Karen language (in the widest sense), of whom about 1.3 million speak Sgaw and over 1.2 million speak Pwo. Burma's hill Karen live mainly in the remote mountainous terrain in the east of the country, up and down the border with Thailand, especially in the Karen State, but also in the Pegu hills, between the Irrawaddy and Sittang rivers. They speak mainly Sgaw, and wear traditional costumes in the characteristic red (e.g. the men's smocks, married women's blouses) and white (girls' shifts) that one associates with Thailand's Karen. About a million Karen, or roughly a quarter of Burma's Karennic peoples, live in the Karen State.

The c. 350,000 Karen to be found in Thailand are nearly all 'regular' Karen, i.e. non-Karenni/Kayah and non-Pa-O. There are a few of the latter in the kingdom, as we saw in Chapter 7, but they make up only a tiny minority. Schliesinger gives the following figures for the 'exotic' Karen tribes residing in the country, whose numbers should be added to the 350,000 just mentioned: Kayah 2,500, Pa-O 900, Padaung 500 and Kayaw 30. These 'regular' Karen are all traditional hill or 'tribal' Karen and often or always wear the distinctive red-based costume, or parts of it. Essentially, they are the same as their brothers just across the border in Burma's eastern reaches. Thailand's Karen live all down the country's western border with Burma, spread across some 15 provinces, from broadly the latitude of Chiang Rai town in the north to Prachuab Khiri Khan in the south. They are all Sgaw and Pwo Karen. Depending on what figures from which source you follow, the Sgaw make up the great majority, accounting for 80% or 70% (c. 245,000 people in the latter case) of the total, while the Pwo constitute a fair-sized minority, accounting for 20% or 30% (c. 105,000 people) of the total. The Sgaw Karen live throughout the area of western Thailand designated above, but the Pwo live only, I think, south of a line drawn between the towns of Mae Sariang and Hot. Many Pwo live in Mae Hong Son and Chiang Mai provinces, in a cluster of some 20-30 hill villages just below the H108 road, although there are other Pwo communities, according to Schliesinger (2000), down in Tak, Kanchanaburi, Ratchaburi, Petchaburi and Prachuab Khiri Khan provinces, as well as over in Lampang province. Because this book is written mainly from the perspective of Thailand and focusses on the western border area, I shall henceforth largely disregard the Karen of Burma except in that they figure in the border journey,

Above: Shan pagoda at Wat Fah Wiang In, on border, near Piang Luang
Below: Shan Buddha figures at Wat Wiang Haeng

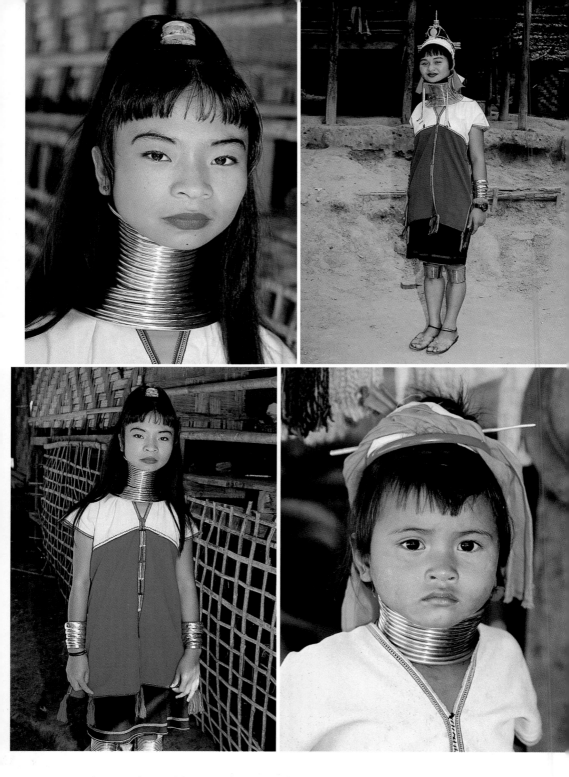

Above right: Padaung "Long-Neck" girl Ma Ja in costume at Mai Nai Soi
Above left & below left: Young Padaung woman at Mai Nai Soi
Below right: Padaung infant girl with first neck rings

Padaung "Long-Neck" girl Ma Ja, aged 19, at Mai Nai Soi

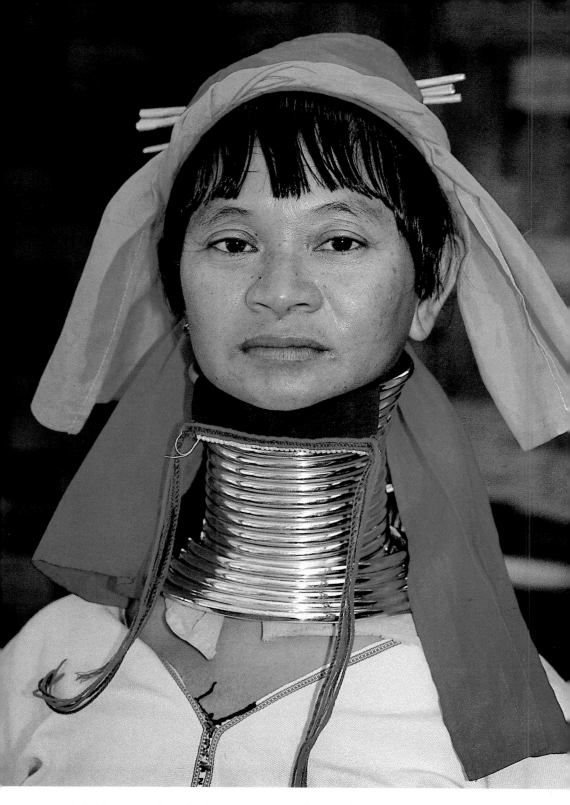

Ma Nang, aged 48, Padaung "Long-Neck" mother of Ma Ja, at Mai Nai Soi

Rare Kayaw "Long-Ear" lady at Mai Nai Soi –
Kayaw women's costume and jewellery is among the most beautiful
of all the adornments of the many hill tribes in South-East Asia

Above left: Kayaw "Long-Ear" woman at Mai Nai Soi -- note the leg rings
Above right: Lawa woman in best costume -- note the pipe & cup-shaped earrings
Below: Lawa man & women in traditional attire -- note his sword

Above: Longtail boats on River Salween at Mae Saam Laep –
view north, with Burma (L) & Thailand (R)
Below: Lawa girl tending field of opium poppies

Above: Three Karen women in jungle between Lae Tong Ku & Kui Le Toeng
Below: Trekking through jungle towards the Three Pagodas Pass:
Nittaya crossing part of Suriya border river near Kui Le Toeng

Telakhon cultist hunter in jungle near Lae Tong Ku

Above: KNLA commander Mor Thaing Chor flanked by two Telakhon
rishi cultists in betel grove near Lae Tong Ku
Below: The Three Pagodas Pass in 1993 (now more developed)

Top: Wiang Haeng main road in 1992, in morning mist. View N towards
Piang Luang with "Sayan" restaurant (L) & old fuel booth (R)
Centre & below: Armed forest protection boys at Wiang Haeng in front of
"Sayan" and shop make ready for a first patrol

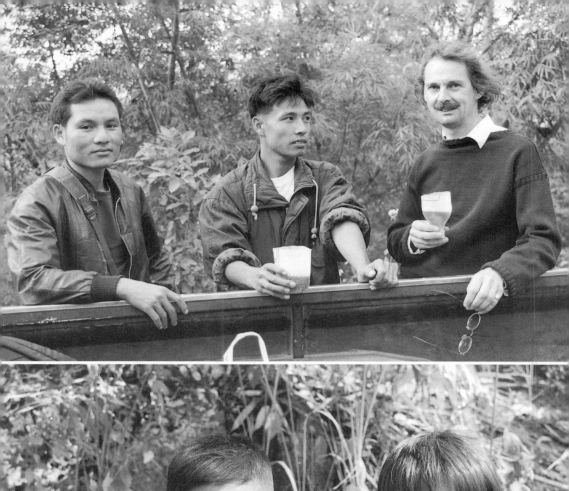

Above: Karen Witit Terkae, Thai paratrooper Ekerin Poon Nu & author
between Kong Lom and Muang Noi in the truck that got destroyed
Below: A-pichai & Jak-gaek (R), the Lahu boys who guided us to Bo Pi (Spirit Well)

Above: Wa National Army officers Jerng & Kong Mong (R) in 1993 at Mae Or
Below: Baptist Karen Joi-ih (R) with KNU Karen driver at Ti Po Mo

Prince Maha San, spiritual leader or figurehead "king"of the Wa
& chairman of the Wa National Organization (photo taken 1993)

Darkie as a nubile 25-year-old (in 2000) – quite the author's muse!

Above: Troupe of female Karen folk singers at Jo Ta, Burma,
attending Karen New Year celebrations (January 1994)
Below: Karen boys posing with KNLA truck at Jo Ta (near Sa Kaang Thit), Burma

Above: KNLA Kawthoolei Military Training School, Manerplaw
Below: KNU finance office, Manerplaw

Above: Northern entrance to rebel HQ, Manerplaw
Below: Manerplaw: view south across Saw Ba U Gyi sports ground – note the
high defensive Dawna peaks immediately behind rebel HQ

Above left: KNLA girl and boy soldiers guarding southern entrance to Manerplaw
Above right: Shan Nationalities People's Liberation Army soldier at Manerplaw
Below left: KNLA commander Saw Tae Tu at Sa Kaang Thit (Ban Mai)
Below right: Author's last photo (1999) of Kong Mong two years before his death

Above & below: ABSDF rebel Burmese students' office & library
at Po Pa Ta, Burma

Above: View (2001) from Wa Lay into DKBA-controlled Palu, with portal,
border crossing checkpoint, & dangerous DKBA soldiers
Below: Border crossing & checkpoint at Lak Taeng, near Piang Luang

Above left: KNLA commander Mor Thaing Chor at Kui Le Toeng, Burma
Above right: Sooksi from Boeng Kloeng, one of our KNLA guides
Below: KNLA commander Saw Kyi Shwi with author at Mae Ta Ro Ta, Burma

Above left: Telakhon rishi disciple at half-moon ceremony, Lae Tong Ku
Above right: Toom Yai, our Telakhon cultist interpreter at Lae Tong Ku
Below: Telakhon rishi sect *wat* at Lae Tong Ku

The Telakhon rishi man-god (*pu chaik*) of Lae Tong Ku

concentrating on the Karen of Thailand and of the area each side of the border, i.e. mainly on the traditional hill Sgaw Karen.

The Sgaw and Pwo Karen sub-groups[6] have their own languages, which are considered to be mutually unintelligible, although they, along with the other Karen tribes, can apparently communicate with each other through a common standard Karen language (or, in Burma, through Burmese, or, in Thailand, through the northern Thai dialect). Based on Sgaw, the standard Karen language has both a spoken and a written form. Written Karen is very similar to written Burmese. This is because the American Baptist who put Sgaw Karen into writing in the early 19th century used the Burmese alphabet.[7] The Karen like to borrow words from Burmese, Thai, Mon and Shan.

The hill Karen both of western Thailand and of the eastern border regions of Burma are often referred to as 'hill-tribe' people. But, strictly speaking, this is a misnomer since they do not really fulfil the basic criteria for classification as a hill tribe (such as the Akha or Hmong). Thus the Karen are not true mountain dwellers, living high up, nor are they migratory, nor do they mostly rely on slash-and-burn agriculture and on dry rice cultivation. Both the Sgaw and Pwo Karen of Thailand live in villages sited in the low highlands and lowlands, typically at a medium elevation of around 500 metres above sea level. Their villages tend not to move, and a sign of their essential permanence is that there are Karen villages in Thailand that are over 200 years old. As non-migratory people living in settled villages, the Karen are sedentary farmers who practise wet rice cultivation in established terraced paddies even with irrigation, and grow orchards.

A Karen village can comprise as few as 3 or 4 houses (I have seen such hamlets) or as many as 100, with the average settlement having perhaps 20-30 households. Villages typically have no central shrine or meeting place or ceremony ground. Karen houses are raised off the earth on stilts, are made of wood and split bamboo with grass roofs (or these days often with roofs of

---

[6] The ethnographers Paul and Elaine Lewis (1984) report that the Pwo, according to the testimony of their own folk tales, regard themselves as the guardians of the entire ('regular') Karen culture. Further, they consider their more numerous Sgaw cousins to be, as it were, the male lineage of the Karen race, whereas they are the female lineage. Perhaps this accounts for the noticeable tendency of the Pwo, among both females and males, to greatly beautify themselves in terms of costume, accoutrements and cosmetics!

[7] Western missionaries created written forms of a number of Karen languages, the first being developed in 1832. The American Baptist Mission to Burma started work in that country in 1813, while the first European Christian mission began work among the Karen of the Tenasserim Division in 1825. An especially important early Baptist mission among the Karen was set up at Bassein in 1835 in the south-western part of Pegu Division. By 1925, the number of Baptist missionaries in Burma had grown to 220, most of whom left during the Second World War. Some returned after the war, but most were subsequently forced to leave again. These missionaries left behind some 250,000 Burmese Baptists (data from Howard, 1999). Besides doing their proselytizing work, they opened mission schools and trained Karen and other tribals as clergy, teachers, medics and administrators. To communicate with the ethnic minorities and ultimately to provide them with versions of the Bible in the ethnic languages, they had of course to learn their languages, an upshot of which was written versions and basic dictionaries of the languages. Another result of the influx of Christianity was the emergence among the Karen of several millenarian movements (more below).

galvanized corrugated tin sheeting), and have spacious, partly covered verandas that are used for preparing food, sometimes for eating, chatting and weaving, and for accommodating guests overnight. Most households are nuclear, consisting of a husband and wife plus their unmarried children, but not three-generational, as with other ethnic minorities. Diran (1997) and Schliesinger (2000) report that in the old days Karen used to live in longhouses, accommodating 20-30 nuclear families, each occupying its own room, which faced a central corridor running the length of the house, and that in some remote areas of Burma a few of these longhouses can still be found.

As indicated, the Karen eschew slash-and-burn agriculture, preferring to develop stepped wet rice fields where feasible, and practising an ecologically enlightened crop rotation. They also have maize fields, vegetable gardens, tobacco fields, and chilli as well as sesame plots, and are celebrated for cultivating sugar cane. In many a Karen village, you can see harvested sugar cane being passed through a mangle and the resulting juice being boiled up and evaporated to produce slabs of brown unrefined sugar. On the hillsides, they further grow some dry mountain rice, but not poppies – the Karen are not involved in opium, either in producing, refining, trafficking or selling it. But their (mostly subsistence) economy is not only agricultural. They raise livestock, for sacrificing, eating and selling, and, famously, keep elephants. The Karen are the only people in Thailand still to keep elephants in the ordinary way – authentically, for working, and not for show or tourist purposes. Wherever one goes in Karen country, especially in the border or remoter areas, it is not long before one encounters the lumbering beasts. Only relatively rich Karen have elephants, as the animals are expensive to keep, and in *Yang* society elephant owners enjoy high status. The tuskers are used for transporting goods through the jungle and over the mountains, as well as for hauling logs. Sometimes they are hired out, complete with their mahouts. The Karen are famed for their mahouts all over Thailand and South-East Asia. Some Karen men work for Thais as wage-labourers, while *Yang* women, who are consummate weavers, sell their handicraft. They create their cloth, from which they make clothes, shoulder bags and blankets, on simple backstrap looms (like the Lawa).

Karen people can be very hospitable. This is especially true of the Sgaw Karen and in particular of the Sgaw of the border areas. In my experience, based on extensive travelling among the Sgaw all down the frontier, both on the Thai and Burmese sides, these Karen are the most hospitable of all Thailand's minority peoples. Many border Sgaw, I have found, will give you food and possessions down to their last penny, perhaps a sign of the fact that they have been caught up for years in a war situation, express solidarity with each other and with any visitors who happen to come by, and follow a more happy-go-lucky existence. However, based on my limited experience of the Pwo Karen, among whose villages I have trekked, I cannot say that this generosity applies to them. The Pwo, it seemed to me in many cases, would not give except in exchange for money. This impression was backed up by a missionary I once met near Mae Sariang, who had worked several years locally with the Pwo. He said of them that they would not do anything for nothing, and told me the story of a Pwo man who travelled with a gravely ill friend to

226

Mae Sariang hospital, but who would only give the friend a life-saving transfusion of his blood if the friend paid him handsomely for it! Karen hospitality is at its peak during their New Year celebrations, which are usually in January.

Karen kinship is matrilineal, while residence is matrilocal. Initially, after marriage, a man goes to live with his wife's parents, after which the new family will become nuclear. The Karen are mostly monogamous people, and are altogether rather chaste. Divorce is uncommon, and after divorce remarriage is unusual. The Karen marry for life. A child born out of wedlock is a serious matter. Pre-marital sex, even overt contact between unmarried boys and girls, is frowned upon. Karen maidens, pretty with their round faces, have a studied coyness about them. This is not to say that young people have no opportunity to dally. Festivals, the harvest, work in the fields and sessions around the evening fire making *jaak*-leaf roofing panels provide a chance to get to know members of the opposite sex. Notably funerals are an occasion for such contact. At these, the body of the deceased, wrapped in a bamboo mat, is placed on a bier in a house, and unmarried Karen boys and girls process round and round it in groups of four, three, two and one, chanting songs to help the deceased on his or her journey to the land of the dead, but at the same time making good use of the protracted opportunity to tease, flirt and touch one another. Many a Karen youth has been heard to wish that someone would die soon, so that he would have a chance to go a-courting again.

Most 'Burmese' Karen are Buddhist or Buddhist-animist, while the Karen of Thailand are predominantly animist. The animist hill Karen believe in 'the old way' – bodies of belief and spiritual practice established by their ancestors and differing (at least superficially) from village to village. They believe in a variety of spirits, which must be propitiated with offerings and animal sacrifices. Above all, harmony must be preserved between the spirit world and life down here on Earth. Chief among the spirits is the 'Lord of Land and Water', who has a special shrine somewhere outside the village – the only such shrine, as otherwise there are no altars either in the houses or villages of animist Karen. Also important are: the household spirits (i.e. the ancestral or matrilineal spirits, who guard over the members of the household and the house itself), the spirits of the village and locality, the jungle spirits, the 'Crop Grandmother' spirit, and the spirits which indwell certain singular features around the village. Offerings are made to the spirits by the village priest or, as appropiate, by the female lineage heads.

The priest or shaman, whose position is essentially hereditary, is a key figure in a hill Karen village, much more so than the headman, who in Thailand often has little more to do than fulfil the thankless task of interfacing with the authorities. The priest is the ritual and spiritual leader of the village, fixes dates for and officiates at important annual village ceremonies, watches over the moral conduct of the villagers, requires sacrifices when the moral code has been broken, arbitrates in disputes, has a say in the allocation of fields, and generally arranges for and guarantees the harmony of the community. A striving for and the preservation of harmony both within the village and between the village and the spirit world is, as indicated, a basic theme of both

Sgaw and Pwo life and a paramount desire among the Karen, which is why the shaman-priest, being the guarantor of it, is so important.

An important part of Karen mythology is the figure of the orphan. It is an objective correlative for the downtrodden state which Karen believe they languish in, a state most keenly felt especially by those living down the border with their long experience of conflict and oppression. They understand that – through their own negligence and oversight – they have become dispossessed. A corollary of this feeling is the idea that one day their time will come and Karen will regain their rightful inheritance. The redemption theme finds expression in a number of other myths. There is the myth that one day the time of the 'Karen king' will come and all Karen will live in a magnificent palace in a great city. There is the myth of the 'white brother', who will come from across the sea, bringing back the 'writing' or the 'Golden Book' lost by the Ur-Karen. There is the Karen legend of a single god, Y'wa, and of a 'Garden of Creation'. Such comforting prophecies have given rise to a number of millenarian movements among the Karen during their history, and a Karen sect inspired by such millenarian thinking exists in Thailand south of Um Pang (the Telakhon rishi sect, visited in Chapter 14).

The notions of the foreigner saviour, the lost scripture, the single god and the garden of creation have had another far-reaching outcome for the Karen. Missionaries arriving among them for the first time (in the early 19th century, as we saw in Footnote 7 above) could not believe their luck. Some even thought that in the Karen they had found one of the lost tribes of Israel. The Karen for their part were relatively predisposed to the teachings of the newcomers. Some saw the appearance of the 'white men' from across the seas, clutching their Bibles, as the fulfilment of their old millenarian myths. But in addition, the message of the missionaries' Christianity seemed largely to confirm the substance of their own prophecies. The result was significant conversion of the Karen. Today an estimated 15-20% of Karen on both sides of the Thai-Burmese border are Christian. Most of the missionaries have been American Baptists. In the conversion of the Karen, the Baptists have scored their greatest success to date in the history of their proselytizing.

One effect of the conversion of Karen has been some improvement in their lot. Having to sacrifice fewer domestic animals to the spirits, some families have enjoyed a better standard of living. In Burma, there have been other effects. Many Karen across the border have picked up a good education from the Baptists – Baptist (later Judson) College in Rangoon used to be popularly known as 'Karen College'. And altogether the Christian Karen are more educated, 'developed', urbane and better informed about world affairs than their animist counterparts, in addition having in many cases some knowledge of English. Nowhere is this more apparent than in the leadership of the Karen National Union and of the Karen National Liberation Army, the political and military wings of the Karen movement in Burma struggling for independence and its own state of Kawthoolei. Virtually all its most senior personnel are Christian. Those few who are not Baptists are Seventh-Day Adventists.

REBEL HQ

From the traveller's point of view, perhaps the most intriguing – and certainly the most visible – aspect of the Karen is their costume. The Sgaw and Pwo Karen wear similar but nevertheless rather different costumes. Because the Pwo do not figure in the journey in this book, with only Sgaw Karen villages being visited, I concentrate here on Sgaw attire and reduce a description of Pwo costume to a footnote.[8] Traditionally the Karen, both the Sgaw and the Pwo, make their own clothes with cloth hand-woven at home. Unmarried Sgaw girls of all ages wear long white cotton shifts usually with a band of red or pink or cerise or similar colour woven into it just above the waist, and with other red trimming down the sides or around the neck and arm holes. Married Sgaw women wear smocklike overblouses and saronglike tube skirts. The smocks are simply cut, sleeveless or short-sleeved, and made of cotton. They are usually indigo or black in colour and have a lower portion of varying width which is embroidered in red. This embroidery on the lower panel can be more or less heavy, either filling the space completely or just putting simple patterns on it. There is other red trimming around the V-shaped neck hole and arm holes. The blouses are further embellished with white Job's-tear

---

[8] Like Sgaw maidens, unmarried Pwo girls also wear a long white cotton shift, but embellish it more heavily than their counterparts. The adornment is in red or shades of pink and often takes the form of an all-over lozenge pattern on the lower portion of the dress, or panels across the collar bones and breast, or yokelike strips down the shoulders. Pwo girls used to wear their hair long and tied in a knot on top of the head, like their mothers, but now they mostly wear it short in the style of the ubiquitous bobcut of all schoolgirls in Thailand. Women, as said, wear their hair long and twisted up in a topknot, concealing the bun under a turban often of white or green or red material, or of terrycloth in any colour. When Pwo females are not wearing a turban, their hair is often generously decorated with silver hair clips.

Married Pwo women wear sarongs and sleeveless or short-sleeved overblouses or smocks. The sarongs are tube skirts of a plain red or cerise or pink colour with more or less horizontal banding. The smocks are typically in wine red and often with bold patterning. All the Pwo women that I have seen in Thailand had smocks that were a fairly plain red except for the yokes, which were ornately patterned. They also wore detached black sleeves to protect their arms, and Lawa-style leggings on their lowers legs from knee to ankle. Their arms are laden with dozens of twisted bronze or silver bracelets, worn in two places: on the forearm, especially above the wrist, and on the upper arm, above the elbow. In this respect, the Pwo are reminiscent of the Padaung 'Long-Neck' women, and perhaps the two groups have borrowed from each other or ultimately derive from some common ancestor tribe.

These days, most Pwo men simply wear casual Western-style clothing, such as has been largely adopted by both tribal and Thai men all over the kingdom. Traditionally and on special occasions, they wear sleeveless V-necked smocks in red or red-and-white, and a sarong or Thai peasant-style trousers. An old Pwo man I once stayed with wore such a shirt in dark brick red with short sleeves. Traditionally, young Pwo bachelors have worn their hair long and pulled across the head to be tied at one side, rather in the fetching manner of the male cultists of the Karen Telakhon rishi sect at Lae Tong Ku, south of Um Pang (see Chapter 14). Altogether, Pwo youths, when dolled up, remind one of the pretty acolytes of the jungle sect, suggesting connections between the cultists and the Pwo. Many Pwo men are densely tattooed from waist to knee, and some women are tattooed too.

All the Pwo women I have seen wore around their necks multiple Lawa-style strands of silver beads reaching down to about mid-chest or elbow level. They also sported chokers of black or white beads, from the front of which a furry tassel sometimes dangled. Some women wore earrings with long dangles of multicoloured fluff and pompoms. Altogether, Pwo women cut quite a dash, especially when got up in their best costume and liberally made up with lipstick, which they even apply to their cheeks to make marks like duelling scars.

seedwork. The narrow, knee- to ankle-length tube skirts are basically red and have all different kinds of horizontal banding, sometimes with *ikat* or tie-dye patterning. These blouses and skirts are subject to variation in colour and decorative design in different parts of Karen territory. Sgaw women wear their hair long, gathering it into a bun at the nape of the neck. They also wear turbans, typically white and of terrycloth, giving the impression of having arranged a small bath towel or baby's nappy on their heads. Women and girls like wearing multiple strands of small beads, which typically hang down to mid-chest. Women further favour decorating themselves with cylindrical silver earrings, which have a cup-shaped outer part (like Lawa earrings).

The traditional costume of Sgaw men is nowadays less often seen in an everyday context than the women's garb, but is still visible on special occasions. The men wear simple hip-length cotton sleeveless shirts, typically in brick red and often with vertical stripes or banding. Sometimes the striking red *Yang* male smocks, which are often for sale in markets and tourist shops (e.g. in Mae Hong Son town), have a fringe at the bottom. Sgaw men wear either knee-length sarongs or Thai peasant-style black trousers. Sometimes they, too, sport a turban. It has to be said that the tendency among men, especially the younger ones, and also to a lesser extent among young Karen women, is to drop the traditional costume in favour of the ubiquitous Western-style jeans and T-shirt, or, in the case of the women, in favour of cheap and cheerful printed garments picked up in local markets. No self-respecting Karen, either Sgaw or Pwo, and no matter whether man or woman, would be seen, when going walkabout, without their shoulder bag and often without their little silver-embellished tobacco pipe. Pipe-smoking, combined with betel-chewing, leads to a favourite habit of the Karen, rather off-putting to Westerners, of spitting through the cracks in the slatted floors of their houses!

❊

The Karen rebellion

The 45-year-old Karen rebellion[9] is one of the longest-running and least known-about insurgencies in the world. That would be remarkable enough, except that the Karen insurgency is just one of some dozen other continuing ethnic uprisings in Burma, which altogether form probably the world's longest civil war. Virtually since the country's independence from Britain in 1948, rebel armies have been at war with the central Rangoon-based military dictatorship of Gen. Ne Win (since 1988 Gen. Saw Maung's SLORC, and since late 1997 the SPDC) in the frontier regions all round the Burman heartland. The totalitarian, 'Unionist', 'Socialist', essentially Burman junta cannot tolerate the secessionist, federalist, democratic aspirations of the minority peoples, with the result that for three generations a combined insurgent force of 25,000 - 30,000

---

[9] This account was written in 1995, and so the details in it are valid up until that time or, more exactly, until 1994, when it was researched. Some things have meanwhile changed, especially in the light of the subsequent fall of Manerplaw and other Karen border bases, and of political changes. Thus, for a more accurate and up-to-date picture, the account should be read in conjunction with the update details in the Postscript below.

guerrillas have been pitted against some 200,000 troops of the Burma army in a vicious war of attrition, which has claimed the lives of an estimated 10,000 people a year on average, including civilians. The war would probably have been concluded years ago in the junta's favour except that Rangoon is fighting on numerous fronts in remote jungle or mountain areas against motivated guerrillas who are battling on their own patch for their very existence. Also, although the Burma army or *tatmadaw* is numerically far superior, it has never had enough soldiers to win this kind of war – military analysts calculate that to win a guerrilla war an army must outnumber the rebels by at least 10 to 1. For their part, the insurgents might easily have won earlier had they not been so disunited both among themselves and even within their own individual ethnic groupings. The Karen, along with the Kachin, constitute at the time of writing the biggest faction among these groupings, and many of the most important developments in the civil war have happened on Karen territory.

The Karen uprising dates back to the late 1940s – to the time of the end of the Second World War, the second Panglong conference (1947), and Burma's Independence from Britain (1948). The Karen people's dream of the right to self-determination and of an independent state actually goes back further than this, but it was in the immediate post-war period that their aspirations became more sharply focussed, even seeming realizable. During the Second World War, Karen troops in the British Burma Army had remained loyal, fighting alongside the Allies or operating underground against the Japanese occupiers and collaborating Burmese. Afterwards, they naturally looked to the British for reward, only to be disappointed. But in any case, within three years the colonial masters were gone. The Panglong conference, which was supposed to regulate the federation of the ethnic minority territories in a Union of Burma, similarly failed the Karen. It did not create a Karen State, but instead made convoluted provision for a special Karen region to be established at some future time. Worse still, the projected territory would not enjoy the crucial right to secede after ten years such as had been granted to the Shan and Karenni States. It was remarkable and cruel that at a conference so momentous provision for the most significant and pressing of Burma's minority peoples should have been so fudged. The Karen quickly understood that they would get nothing except through armed struggle. Hostilities were not long in coming. In January 1949, the Rangoon HQ of the KNU (a union of all the Karen organizations of that time) as well as Karen quarters both in the capital and elsewhere were attacked by Burmese government troops. The decades-long insurgency had begun.

Fighting flared up in many places. In the early days, the Karen had a string of outstanding successes, capturing towns and even coming within an ace of taking Rangoon itself. In territory under their control, they proclaimed the establishment of a Karen State. At Toungoo, they instituted a provisional Kawthoolei government, with Saw Ba U Gyi, the originator of the 'Four Principles' of the Karen revolution, as the first prime minister. Later, in 1953, at the KNU's First National Congress, held in Papun, they announced the formation of a new Kawthoolei Governing Body, informing the Thais that along the Siamese western border a Kawthoolei Free State was to be created, for which recognition would be sought from the United Nations. The initial triumphs were the result especially of a strong military. Just before the outbreak of hostilities, Karen National Defence Organizations, local defence militias still operative today, were set up throughout *Yang* territory. And when fighting did start, units of the Karen Rifles in the Burma army mutinied, defecting en masse to their own side. As they joined their rebel brothers, they took with them not only their weapons, but valuable military experience gained from fighting alongside the British in the Second World War. This was to stand the Karen people in good stead in the long years of warfare ahead, as it still does today. The modern KNLA remains modelled on the British Army of the Second World War, and many KNU and KNLA leaders, including Karen supremo Bo Mya, even now are veterans who saw service with the British.

The early successes, however, were followed by reversals. As the Burma army recovered itself, towns captured by the KNU were retaken by Rangoon, often later to be seized again by the Karen. The 1950s marked the beginning of the deadly cat-and-mouse game the Karen military and government forces have played with each other ever since. On the political front, too, there were problems. During the 1950s and 1960s, the KNU, until it regained pre-eminence in the 1970s, was eclipsed as the vanguard party of the Karen by the left-oriented Karen National United Party. Maoist ideology and an out-of-character alliance with the CPB were the order of the day. A left-right split between the pro-communist KNUP and the strongly nationalist, pro-Western, anti-communist KNU weakened the Karen movement, from which it did not recover until the rise of the present-day Karen leader, Bo Mya. But with that we arrive at the modern era of the insurgency.

Five factors in particular have determined the evolution of the Karen struggle from the mid-1960s until today: the emergence of the modern KNU and its armed wing, the KNLA; the rise of Bo Mya; economic considerations, especially the boom in trade across the Karen-Thai border; the notorious 'Four Cuts' campaign of the Burma army; and the formation of two major alliances – the NDF and the DAB. The rise of the phenomenal Bo Mya and the emergence of the modern KNU are essentially the same story. Unlike many other KNU luminaries, Bo Mya never enjoyed a university education. His was a case of local lad made good. Born in 1926 as an animist Sgaw Karen in the Papun hills, he attended a village elementary school, breaking off his education early. Growing up in the dying days of British colonial rule in Burma, he was just a teenager of 15 or 16 when the Japanese invaded the country in 1941-42 and only 23 when the Karen rebellion erupted. For a short time during the Second World War, Bo Mya worked with the Japanese. Having personally witnessed some of the atrocities committed by the Burma Independence Army against his local kinsfolk, he considered this to be his best course of action. But it was not long before he transferred to the side of the Allies. His service with the British until they left at Independence made a profound impact on the future Karen leader. The outbreak of the rebellion in 1949 saw Bo Mya go underground to join the struggle. The 1950s and early 60s were the time of his meteoric rise through the ranks of the insurgent army. His military prowess and daring exploits in the eastern hills of Kawthoolei were to become the stuff of legend. While another prominent Karen commander, the wily Shwi Soe, came to control Duplaya district (the 6th Brigade area of Kawthoolei's Eastern Division), Bo Mya was rewarded with Papun-Pa'an (7th Brigade area), adjoining to the north. The two areas, accounting for the whole of the Kawthoolei-Thailand border, from approximately Mae Saam Laep in the north to the Three Pagodas Pass and beyond in the south, were to assume a critical importance in the struggle. Then, in 1963, with his main base at Kawmoorah, Bo Mya was promoted almost overnight to commander of the entire Eastern Division.

An event in 1964 profoundly altered the commander's cast of mind, in-deed had far-reaching consequences for the political direction of the whole Karen cause. The animist Sgaw married a Seventh-Day Adventist Karen and converted to Christianity. One immediate upshot was the first of two 'coups' which Bo Mya staged in the 1960s and 70s. The coups stamped the KNU with the definite rightist pro-Western stance it has since had. In the first days of 1966, Bo Mya ordered all KNUP troops out of his Eastern Division. At a stroke, the whole Dawna region of the Karen State fell into his hands. He re-placed the administration of the KNUP with a new Karen National Liberation Council, filling its posts with anti-communist hill Karen like himself. Little is remembered today of the short-lived Council, except that its military wing, the Karen National Liberation Army, gave its name to the modern Karen army.

Within a year of the coup, some KNUP officials, including party chairman Maan Ba Zan, returned to join Bo Mya. The KNUP and Bo Mya's Council fused to become the Karen National United Front, the immediate precursor of the modern KNU. Initially, the new body retained elements of the old KNUP ideology, but over the next ten years and in a protracted tussle between the two leaders the communist baggage was progressively dropped until everything was to Bo Mya's liking. Among other things, the name Karen National United Front was changed to Karen National Union, and the goal of a left-sounding 'people's democracy' was replaced by that of a more rightist 'national democracy'. Finally, in 1976, at Manerplaw, it was decided that the KNU should accept aid not just from any country (meaning communist ones too), but only from Western 'capitalist' nations. It was at this stormy Manerplaw meeting that Bo Mya staged his second 'coup'. He definitively ousted Maan Ba Zan, who had been KNU president. Bo Mya already had under his khaki belt the positions of KNLA Chief of Staff, Minister of Defence and Minister of Foreign Affairs. Now he added the KNU presidency. By the mid-1970s, his grip on the Karen movement was complete.

Bo Mya's inexorable rise to the position of uncontested Karen leader was not without its foundations. Always a military hardman, since his early days he has enjoyed a reputation as a formidable, ruthless, even wild guerrilla commander. With a house at Manerplaw overlooking the Moei, latterly the supremo has not been afraid to exploit his reputation and power. His, it has been said, is an authoritarian, rather undemocratic style of leadership, not given to tolerating open disagreement or real debate. Announcements and policy changes, some senior figures have complained, are apt to be made without prior consultation. Since his marriage and conversion, Bo Mya's pronounce-ments have been increasingly interlaced with Christian sentiment and Biblical allusion. He has come to seem like a patriarch of the Karen movement, moreover guarding over the mores of his people (at least around Manerplaw) with a prudish, conservative, Old Testament eye. The Karen chief has something in common with the few other military strongmen who have ridden out Burma's civil war – one thinks of Khun Sa, Brang Seng, even Ne Win himself – and he has not escaped the criticism from friend and foe alike that he approximates to a warlord who in Kawthoolei has built up a private fiefdom. But it would be wrong to dwell on these criticisms. To the mass of hill Karen, this charismatic, anti-communist, anti-narcotics leader is a legendary father figure. Unlike other KNU leaders, university-educated and from the plains, he is 'one of us'. His great achievement has been to unify and galvanize the downtrodden neglected people of the eastern hills, at the same time revolutionizing the Karen movement.

Under Bo Mya's leadership, the KNU burgeoned dramatically. The Karen, along with the Kachin, came to pose the biggest threat militarily to Rangoon. The KNLA swelled to a force of thousands of well-equipped soldiers, an army only ever eclipsed in strength among Burma's insurgents by the CPB People's Army. In particular the 6th and 7th Brigade areas bordering Thailand, which had been the weakest of the KNU, were transformed, and not just transformed, but now turned into the strongest of all the Brigade districts. These had been backwaters of the Karen State scarcely touched by British or Japanese rule, let alone Burmese. But suddenly Papun-Pa'an and Duplaya were catapulted into the vanguard of the Karen revolution.

The rise of a powerful modern KNU, together with its forceful leader, was facilitated by a dramatic change in the economic fortunes of Kawthoolei. This key factor in the Karen struggle must be seen against the background of the collapse under Ne Win and the SLORC of the Burmese economy. Ne Win's oddball programme 'The Burmese Way to Socialism', introduced in 1963-64, led to a quarter century of ruinous economic and political mismanagement. Companies were nationalized across the board, half a million Chinese and Indian businessmen (middlemen vital to the well-being of the economy) fled the country, whole trade sectors folded, there were shortages of everything everywhere, and in a series of bizarre demonetizations of the Burmese currency thousands of people lost their precious savings overnight. Burma rapidly became the 'Albania of Asia' and in 1987, as one of the world's ten most impoverished nations, was admitted to UN Least Developed Country status, alongside Ethiopia and Chad.

The economic ruin gave rise to a massive black market, which in turn engendered a vigorous cross-border trade. What was lacking at home was obtained from neighbouring countries, notably Thailand. And what could not be properly traded domestically was diverted over the frontier. But the frontier areas were almost exclusively controlled by the various ethnic rebel armies. So all the new trade, having to pass through their territory, fell into the hands of the insurgents, who taxed it. It is ironic that Ne Win's misguided strategy ended up so handsomely benefiting people he sought to crush. Nowhere was this more true than in Kawthoolei. In peak years in the 1980s, the value of Burma's black economy nationwide was estimated at a staggering $3,000 million p.a. or

40% of the country's GNP, while taxes arising from two-way traffic passing through KNU Eastern Division were estimated at an annual £50m – a fairytale sum for such an impecunious backwater.

Local Karen commanders cashed in on the unexpected bonanza. From the 1960s on, customs gates were opened at Mae Saam Laep, Kawmoorah, Palu/Wa Lay, the Three Pagodas Pass... everywhere along the lengthy Karen State-Thai border. A 5% levy was imposed on the flood of livestock, hardwood, jade, antimony, dried prawns and so on flowing out of Kawthoolei, and on the medicines, foodstuffs and consumer items (such as fabrics, transistor radios and watches – anything unobtainable in Burma), flowing in. Some of these border trading posts, for example Kawmoorah or the Three Pagodas Pass, grew into bizarre jungle emporia, and the odd commander amassed a personal fortune, again raising the suspicion of Karen warlordism. It was not just the Eastern Division which was transformed. Sleepy backwoods towns on the Thai side of the border, such as Mae Sariang, Mae Sot and Sangklaburi, boomed on the back of the Burmese black economy. Mae Sot, in particular, became a pivot of the bustling new cross-border trade.

Obscure Papun-Pa'an and Duplaya, then, were awakened from their age-old slumber, suddenly to become of leading geographic an economic significance in the Karen struggle. But the Eastern Division's change in fortune had a further consequence. Bo Mya's old stamping ground was transformed militarily. The ever-increasing revenue from the taxes on trade flowed largely to the KNLA war coffers. The border strongholds of 6th and 7th Brigade areas became not just jungle emporia, but flourishing arms-trading centres. First, American Vietnam 'surplus' and then Chinese-made Khmer Rouge 'surplus' found its way to these centres, where it was either bought with the new wealth or passed on to other rebel armies in Burma. The outcome has been that the KNLA has sometimes been better equipped, especially in the field of communications, than the Burma army itself.

The response of the junta to a robust KNU (and other rebel movements) was to initiate its infamous 'Four Cuts' campaign. Originally, this was a renewed effort on Rangoon's part to silence the Karen (and other insurgents) through a series of decisive offensives. Subsequently it was an attempt to wrest control of the border from them, so that the Burmese military itself – and not its enemies – could profit from the lucrative cross-border trade. Latterly, the new SLORC has wanted to reap the benefits of the various concessions it has made to Thai logging and other companies. It should not be forgotten that until recently the only access Rangoon had to Thailand the length of the Karen and Shan State borders was puny Myawaddy (Mae Sot) and Takilek (Mae Sai). The Four Cuts campaign as a whole dates back to the late 1960s. The idea was to neutralize the rebels by systematically clearing territory controlled by them. The insurgents' supply lines were to be interdicted, their access to funds and food from their rear areas interrupted, their lines of communication severed, and their means of recruitment disrupted. Ne Win set up special new task forces to effect these 'four cuts' – the feared Light Infantry Divisions. In a series of brutal offensives, the LID's singled out large squares of land and then went through them, burning and destroying, confiscating, terrorizing and killing, resettling and pressganging. Today, some dozen of these anti-rebel strike forces exist – they have bizarre designations such as 77th, 88th and 99th Division (probably so numbered for auspicious/superstitious reasons).

Nowhere was the campaign more vicious than in South-East Burma. In the early 1980s, Rangoon moved with full vigour against the Karen, and also against the Karenni and Mon. For a decade, the Burma army operated like some foreign marauding army, attacking its own people in their own country. For the onlooker, it was hard not to conclude that the motivation for the Four Cuts was racial, even genocidal. All the KNU strongholds along the Dawna Range came under attack. Mae Ta Wo (Ban Ta Song Yang), just south of Manerplaw and in the heart of Karen country, fell, cutting north-south links between KNLA 7th and 6th Brigade districts. Later the Three Pagodas Pass fell, along with Palu/Wa Lay, Kloe Dae and Mo Po Kae. Other bases, such as Kawmoorah, were overrun by Rangoon, but quickly recaptured by the Karen. Manerplaw was attacked and bombarded, but never taken. The success of the campaign spelt a serious setback for the Karen, if not disaster. Up and down Kawthoolei, the scene was one of devastation, with villages torched and fields ravaged. Tens of thousands of Karen refugees poured across the border into Thailand, while scores of thousands more sat poised (as they still are) to follow. The fighting badly affected cross-border trade, causing KNU revenue from taxes, vital for financing the struggle, to dip by some 60%. In the grim *tatmadaw* offensive of 1992, an estimated 10% of the KNLA was wiped out. By the early 1990s, the Karen were reeling from a series of blows from which, many commentators feared, they might never fully recover.

The insurgents' response to such systematic destruction was to close ranks and form first the National Democratic Front and then the Democratic Alliance of Burma. The NDF was formed in the KNU's new Manerplaw GHQ in May 1976, at the time when Bo Mya's grip on the Karen movement was becoming complete. An alliance of a dozen ethnic insurgent organizations, the Front for the first time united minority armies from all around Burma. NDF members demanded a Union of Burma with states federated on the basis of Western models, although separatist calls were later toned down. Cohesion and effectiveness grew during the 1980s, especially when the formidable KIO with its 8,000-strong army returned to the NDF fold. A high-water mark was the link-up in 1986 of the NDF and CPB, meaning that for a while an unprecedented 30,000 guerrillas were allied against Rangoon. However, the alliance with the CPB rankled with anti-communist Bo Mya, and so the pact was short-lived. This was not the supremo's only irritation. Despite being its president, he grew impatient with the NDF itself. Perhaps the Karen strongman had grown too used to having his own way, or perhaps he had genuine reason for disillusion with the Front, but disagreements arose between his KNU and the other members, and Bo Mya threatened to take the Karen out of the NDF. But it never came to that, for these bickerings were suddenly overtaken by the great Burmese democracy uprising of 1988 and by the foundation of the DAB.

The popular uprising of 1988 was the result of a number of long-standing economic and political resentments. In particular, it was triggered by two recent demonetizations, which made large banknotes worthless and overnight cancelled people's savings. Pro-democracy demonstrations began in towns and cities all over the country. Fuelled by long pent-up frustration, they escalated in an explosion of anger beyond the wildest expectations. The darling of the rallies was the charismatic and beautiful Aung San Suu Kyi. She soon became, almost by default, the focus of the people's aspirations and the leader of the whole democracy movement. The junta's response was characteristic – a brutal crackdown. Attacks and massacres followed, and there were waves of round-ups and disappearances. Suu Kyi was put under house arrest and held incommunicado. In the midst of the turmoil, Ne Win announced his 'retirement' after 25 years of misrule. In September 1988, in a bloody coup, Gen. Saw Maung seized power and replaced the veteran strongman. Claiming to have saved Burma from chaos and a communist takeover, Saw Maung announced that the country, now to be called Myanmar, would be ruled by a State Law and Order Restoration Council. The new SLORC continued with more of the old military repression and intensified its Four Cuts against the ethnic rebels.

In spite of all this, democratic elections had been promised, and in 1990 Saw Maung surprised everybody by allowing them to go ahead. The SLORC was perhaps convinced that by fair means or foul it would win. It vowed it would honour the election outcome and permitted numerous political parties to be formed. They came to be dominated by Suu Kyi's National League for Democracy (NLD). The result of the election was a victory for Suu Kyi and the forces of democracy as overwhelming as the uprising of two years previously. But the SLORC notoriously reneged on its promise and failed to hand over power. Suu Kyi, who by rights was Burma's new leader, remained in custody. New waves of arrests were made, all opposition was silenced, and a climate of fear as chilling as any since Independence overtook the country again.

The events of 1988 and 1990 played into the hands of the insurgents. Activists from the cities, having experienced at first hand the brutal clampdown of their own military, and exasperated by SLORC political treachery, went over to the rebels. These were not disgruntled minority people, but Burmese citizens. Many were educated professionals, but the bulk were students. It is estimated that about 10,000 went underground in the jungles and mountains controlled by the ethnic armies, about half making their way to Kawthoolei. Here, they immediately started guerrilla training with their hosts, impressing with their alacrity. Aided by the KNU and the NDF, the students founded late 1988 in Kawmoorah the All Burma Students Democratic Front. This renowned organization resolved to work with the NDF. A score of special ABSDF battalions were formed (half of them in Kawthoolei), and they went into battle alongside their insurgent colleagues. Some students were killed in action – witness the ABSDF crosses in Manerplaw cemetery. Others did not go out on patrol, but became medical orderlies or village teachers.

It was in the wake of the 1988 democracy uprising that the important Democratic Alliance of Burma was formed. Established in November of that year in Manerplaw, its chairman was, once again, Bo Mya. The DAB was founded to accommodate along with its military core of NDF members another dozen new dissident Burmese organizations, like the ABSDF. At the inaugural session, the biggest meeting of insurgent leaders ever held in Burma, groups such as the General Strike Committee, the All Burma Young Monks' Union, the Committee for the Restoration of Democracy in Burma (a group of prominent Burmese exiles) and many more, were admitted to the umbrella alliance. The DAB repudiated Saw Maung's SLORC, called on all democratic opposition to come over to the Alliance's side, and in effect set itself up as a provisional alternative government. Indeed, in 1990, anticipating that the democracy elections would be rigged, it instituted a provisional Government of Burma, led by Bo Mya, and began drafting a federal constitution. Burma-watcher Martin Smith reports that at the end of 1990 a group of prominent Burmese MPs arrived at the DAB HQ to announce their own 'national coalition government'. Declaring a ceasefire with the Alliance, they then allied themselves with the DAB. They claimed to have the backing of scores of other MPs in the land and argued that it was they, as MPs, who along with the DAB truly spoke for the country's populace. The final turn of events, then, in the civil war was that the insurgent forces of the DAB, the NDF and the KNU had come together not just with Burman people, but also with Burmese 'elected' popular representatives.

With this, the story of the Karen insurgency comes up to date. At the time of our journey down the border, the Four Cuts offensives were still in full swing. But shortly afterwards, there was a lull in the fighting, a kind of precarious informal truce between Rangoon and the KNU. A breathing space suits both sides. With the new problems nearer to home on the streets of the cities, Rangoon welcomes an opportunity to withdraw some troops, particularly as many are in dangerously exposed forward positions with tenuous supply lines. The KNU, on the other hand, like other ethnic insurgent groupings, is growing increasingly war-weary after more than four decades of fighting. Does the struggle have to last another whole generation, Karen leaders ask? In a letter to Saw Maung which broke a silence of a quarter of a century, Bo Mya spoke of the fundamental goodwill of the KNU. The war could not be solved by military means, he correctly indicated, but had to be resolved politically. Whatever their intentions (time to regroup, divide and rule?), at the moment the SLORC seems keen to enter some kind of dialogue with the rebel groups. But it will only negotiate separately, group by group. Some insurgents are unilaterally coming to an understanding with the Burmese authorities. Others, like the Karen, are only really willing to negotiate with Rangoon multilaterally, within the framework of the DAB or NDF.

❖ ❖

Postscript 2002

Route detail: Mae Sariang – Mae Saam Laep

Meanwhile the 45-km-long H1194 route from Mae Sariang town centre to Mae Saam Laep centre (Map 19) has been upgraded and paved throughout, except for a short 200-m stretch just before the village itself, where the small Saam Laep river must be forded three times. Gone are the scores of confusing mucky river crossings down on the ravine floor, and now you can scoot there in an hour on a mostly good, scenic road that takes you somewhat up and away from the Saam Laep river valley, across a ridge and through forest. There is some room for confusion on the southbound initial stretch, as far as Tatafang police station, because two ways – the original route, meanwhile upgraded, and a brand-new semi-finished highway – intertwine, although both head in the same direction. *Silor* now go at intervals from Mae Sariang to Mae Saam Laep, returning to Mae Sariang, and the fare is 50 baht each way.

	In the SW corner of town, near the big covered day market and the Muslim shops, locate Burmese-style Wat Kitti Wong, go past it, keeping it on your left side, and cross the big bridge over the River Yuam
km 0.0	Just beyond the bridge, turn L into a side road, at the start of which a sign announces that it is 46 kms to Mae Saam Laep. The side road takes you past *See View GH* (L)
km 1.2	At a T-junction, go L for Mae Saam Laep
	At a second junction, swing R, following the main way
km 5.3	At a fork, go L (someone said that the way R went to Mae Khong Kha, but it might just be the second way to Mae Saam Laep)
	At another fork (the original road and the new one come back to back here), keep L and continue on out S through villages and rice fields
	Cross and recross the new highway
km 17.4	On the old road, now heading W, you pass Tatafang police station (R)
km 19.9	Police house (L), opposite which is the start of a dirt side road (R) for Khun Mae Khong Kha (not the same, I think, as Mae Khong Kha village down on the River Salween), 8 kms distant, and Mor La (10 kms)
	Continue past police house on bumpy but paved H1194 through fine forest
	Climb up a long way on the improved 1194, then descend
km 27.6	Signs indicating boundary of Sob Moei district
	You come down to a river (the Saam Laep) and bridges
km 35.1	Forestry conservation/development station (R)
km 36.8	Karen village of **Huai Kong Kaat** (R) with school and *sala* (both R)
km 39.8	Small dam and reservoir (R)
km 40.6	Some kind of agricultural or forestry station (R)
km 43.1	Leave the elevated tarred road to drop down a dirt side way (R) onto the valley floor, which you cross obliquely, fording the river three times, to pick up on the other side of the little valley a cement-section road, which soon leads into Mae Saam Laep village. If you continue on the main tarred 1194 road, you pass what look like some Karen refugee huts and 'shops', after which the road curves round, ascending, before coming to its end at km-marker 0. It is worth continuing the short distance to the end of the H1194 because you come out on top of a headland, from where there are excellent views N of the River Salween, up the valley of the wild Salween, across the confluence of the Saam Laep and Salween rivers, and over Mae Saam Laep,

THREE PAGODAS

which nestles below, on the far side of the confluence, with its new strange-looking 'promenade'. Beyond km-marker 0, the H1194 turns into a dirt road, which leads S to Pratat Mae Saam Laep pagoda and probably Karen villages (unverified)

On the cement-section road into **Mae Saam Laep** village, pass through the entrance portal and proceed down the narrow winding main street, lined each side with shops, until you drop down to a

km 44.8 Big wooden *sala* or open-sided sitting pavilion and the beginning of the promenade, running a few hundred metres N

Mae Saam Laep

In January 2001, the transformation of this outpost was total, making it virtually unrecognizable. Almost all of the bustle as well as many of the features of the old Mae Saam Laep of the early to mid-1990s had gone, while a few new ones had been added. In this remote border station, traditionally so important for the rebel Karen military of Kawthoolei and for the Karen of eastern Burma in general, which had been fought over in the past by the KNU/KNLA and the SLORC as well as latterly by the KNLA and the DKBA, everything was altogether smaller, lower-key, more organized and less exciting. All the sprawling makeshift market extending from the main street, across the sand, to the river had gone, and beyond it most of the longtails had vanished, too. There was little call for them any more. Now that the DKBA controlled Manerplaw and the Rivers Salween and Moei south of Mae Saam Laep to Manerplaw and beyond, no one went to the former GHQ any more, or came shopping from there to Mae Saam Laep. Just a few boats went north up the Salween on occasional tourist trips. Across the river, opposite the village, there was now nothing except a Burma army post. Some cattle still came across the river from Burma from time to time, and there were still a few cattle traders and fetchers with their trucks, but not the convoys of yore. Otherwise, the row of mostly Indo-Burmese Muslim shops in the snaking main street were still there. And half a dozen boatmen waited in a little open-sided hut near the water to take people for longtail rides upriver (and also downriver as far only as the confluence of the Salween and Moei rivers). Every day, they said, some tourists came to Mae Saam Laep for boat trips, but it was a very quiet place now.

New was the rather incongruous 'promenade' beside and overlooking the Salween, slightly reminiscent of that beside the Mae Khong (Mekong) at Chiang Saen. At its southern or 'town' end stood the splendid new *sala* mentioned earlier, which bore an inscription speaking of all the wood that had been taken out Salween National Park. Near the pavilion was *Baan Mae Saam Laep*, some kind of guest house or information centre with food and drinks, although it was closed on the day we visited. Halfway up the promenade, looking down on it, was a new health centre, while at the far end stood a *grom pamai* (forestry protection) office, part of Salween National Park. Apparently, it was possible to stay at the office at a rip-off cost of 800 baht per night with blankets and 400 without. If you want to stay overnight in Mae Saam Laep, which would undoubtedly be interesting with great views of the Salween late afternoon and early morning, try the 'guest house' place or any house, or put up a tent somewhere. Beyond the National Park office, a long path ran through a concatenation of shanty Karen dwellings. Lining one side of the promenade was a row of poor shops and noodle places, many run by dejected KNU people from either Thailand or Burma. When I showed these Karen some of the photos that I had once taken of Manerplaw, of KNLA commanders and KNU officials, and of Mae Saam Laep in the old days, they grew less despondent and enthusiastically called their friends, who gathered round, feted me, and for a few moments glimpsed how things used to be. Then the excitement subsided, and reality supervened again. Basically, Mae Saam Laep had become a straggling refugee village, with many downcast KNU people. One thing that had not changed there was that the place was as swelteringly flatteningly hot as ever.

The boatmen confirmed that it was possible to take a longtail boat downstream, as said, as far as the confluence of the Salween and Moei rivers, but that further, to Manerplaw, was out of the question because the journey was too dangerous. When I asked about going beyond Manerplaw, all the way to Ban Ta Song Yang (as done in the journey of *Three Pagodas*, Chapter 10), they laughed out loud at the sheer lunacy of the idea. "But you can go a long way north, upstream," they said, "that's no problem. There are no DKBA up there. The Burma army controls the Burmese side of the river, and it is safer. You can go to Mae Khong Kha and Mae Sakoep, and to other places beyond that, as far as Jo Ta village, after which the Salween goes off into Burma. All the villages up that way are Karen." The boatment reeled off to me a list of places and times to reach them, which on reflection do not add up. But the last, Jo Ta, may be about five hours by boat from Mae Saam Laep, or so the men said. On the way, you would pass Mae Khong Kha, Mae Sakoep, U-da, Bo Ga Doe, Mae Yae, Wae Ji and No Pa Na, before reaching Jo Ta. They quoted 5,000 baht per boat for a return trip to Jo Ta, where you could stay overnight. A fine expedition would be to get together a few people, charter a boat, share costs, and make a 2-day return trip up the Salween to Jo Ta.

In 1998, in one of their notorious, terrorist, sabotage, mayhem, cross-border raids, the DKBA destroyed half of Mae Saam Laep. On 31 March, a number of their guerrillas crossed the Salween from Burma at 1pm and torched a restaurant in the village's market, possibly in retaliation for a previous incident in which Thai army rangers arrested DKBA men on border intrusion charges. Fanned by strong winds, the blaze quickly spread to destroy more than 100 houses, the living quarters of rangers and border officials, and buildings belonging to a border health centre. It took villagers, soldiers, local police and officials more than five hours to put out the fire, which caused damage worth an estimated ten million baht.

In the light of what has been said above and, in particular, of what will be said below, it is clearly impossible now (since early 1995) to boat by longtail from Mae Saam Laep to Manerplaw, visit rebel GHQ there, and then continue by *hang yao* from Manerplaw south up the Moei river to Ban Ta Song Yang. The murderous and treacherous DKBA is in control of the western Burmese bank of the Moei between the Salween/Moei confluence and Ban Ta Song Yang, and of Manerplaw itself. Nobody goes to Manerplaw these days, and even if you managed to get there, you would be unlikely to find much, with most buildings apparently razed to the ground. In addition, the Burma army has established artillery positions on some of the Dawna mountaintops down this stretch. From the latitude of Manerplaw, the DKBA has conducted banditry, raiding, pillaging, kidnapping and intimidation across the Moei on the eastern Thai bank. The upshot of this is twofold. First, I have not been able to retravel and re-research this key leg of the journey down the Thai-Burmese border, with the result that I am unable to revise and update the material relating to it – travelwise at least (some updated politico-military details are given below). Second, readers wishing to retrace part or all of the journey will be unable to travel this leg. Nor, until the situation changes dramatically in the future (currently unforeseeable) should they attempt to do so, which could prove very dangerous or even fatal. Instead, in the Postscript to Chapter 10, I give details of the stretch from Mae Sariang to Ban Ta Song Yang proceeding via the H105 road, which traveller-readers should take instead of the double boat trip via Manerplaw.

❋

241

THREE PAGODAS

Karen rebellion update
The fall of Manerplaw & Kawmoorah, and the loss of KNU 6th Brigade area

The changes and upsets in the Karen rebellion in the years up to 1994 were as nothing compared to the calamity that overtook the cause and major sections of the Thai-Burmese border during the winter of 1994/95. Most affected were the long-suffering Karen and especially borderlands of their Eastern Division. At the end of November 1994, the SLORC junta broke its two-year unilaterally declared ceasefire with Burma's rebel groups and began attacking the Karen, Mon and ABSDF dissidents. That in itself would not have mattered so much – after all, it was nothing new. Much more worrying was that simultaneously conflict broke out in early December within the Karen movement itself. Some Buddhist soldiers of the Karen National Union grew increasingly discontented with regard to their Christian counterparts. They felt that they were being passed over for promotion and that the Christian-dominated leadership of the KNU was practising religious favouritism. Rumours circulated that the Christians were persecuting Buddhist Karen civilians and soldiers, and there were reports of each side attacking the other. The Buddhists began focussing themselves on the so-called River Junction Pagoda, a pagoda and *wat* on a strategic hill at the confluence of the Salween and Moei rivers. Run by a prominent abbot, Myiang Gyi Ngu Sayadaw, the confluence monastery in turn became a source of irritation for the Christian KNU leadership. Not only was the abbot gathering hundreds of disgruntled Buddhist Karen around him at a sensitive point, but he was also building temples and pagodas in other parts of Kawthoolei, some in militarily restricted zones. The leadership, which suspected the hand of SLORC in all this, objected that the temples compromised KNU security, allowing the enemy to infiltrate Karen territory. For a few days the crack was papered over, with an agreement between the two factions.

But then, in the dying days of 1994, a sizeable number of Buddhists definitively split off from the KNU. Five hundred armed guerrillas and hundreds of followers took over River Junction Pagoda as their base and proclaimed an organization of their own, the Democratic Kayin (Karen) Buddhist Organization/Association or DKBO/DKBA ('Kayin' is a Burmese term for 'Karen'). The mutiny was a serious, possibly fatal, blow to the Karen movement. Not only was it now riven and weakened by internal dissension, but the defectors seemed to have gone over to the side of their 'Buddhist brothers', the Burmese enemy. As if that were not enough, an organization apparently in the pocket of the SLORC also controlled the KNU's vital Salween-Moei supply line from Mae Saam Laep to Manerplaw. Confirmation of the treacherous alliance was not long in coming.

In the last week of January 1995, the Burma army launched a three-pronged attack on KNU positions up and down the border. The aim was no less than finally to capture rebel HQ. After a week of fighting, the unthinkable happened. Manerplaw fell, an event that not only stunned the Karen and their NDF/DAB allies, but triggered a chorus of protest and condemnation around the world. Six other bases north and south of the insurgent nerve centre were also captured, precipitating the flight of thousands of refugees and many KNU leaders into Thailand. Few documents could be saved, and there were reports of the 'capital' being torched as the defenders withdrew.[10] During this latest SLORC campaign, about 10,000 - 15,000 new Karen refugees crossed the border (an estimated 5,000 from the Manerplaw area alone), pushing the total of displaced Karen in Thailand in the mid-1990s to some 70,000. There was no mistaking the hand of the *tatmadaw's* LIDs in the seizure. Possible

---

[10] For a detailed account of the fall of both Manerplaw and Kawmoorah (see below), especially from a signals intelligence (SIGINT) perspective, see Desmond Ball (1998), chapter 8.

smarting from outraged world reaction, the SLORC sought to play down its involvement, claiming it had merely provided logistical support for the Buddhist Karen renegades, who had actually made the attack. Judging by the suddenness of the fall, suggesting that there had been an unexpected assault through a side door from Karen kinsfolk to the north, the DKBO would indeed seem to have been implicated.

Following the fall of Manerplaw, KNLA troops withdrew to Kawmoorah (Kawmura, Ko Mu Ra), reinforcing the defenders there. The Burma army had already laid siege to the base in December 1994. Now, on 30 January 1995, they began attacking this last Karen outpost in the northern sector. Although of little strategic value, Kawmoorah had great symbolic importance not just for the defending Karen, but also for the SLORC, which desired to take it at all costs. Over the years, the junta had lost hundreds of troops trying to rush this virtually impregnable old stamping ground of Bo Mya. Situated some 20 kms north of Mae Sot (opposite the Thai village of Wang Kha), it lay on a piece of land backed on three sides by a horseshoe of river (the Moei) and connected to Burma by a thin neck of land. This strip, mined and booby-trapped, with three rows of trenches and a dozen layers of barbed wire entanglements, and overlooked by ten two-storey reinforced concrete bunkers, was called by the Karen 'the killing zone'. With some 1,000 KNLA and ABSDF soldiers on one side of the zone and 1,500 SLORC troops on the other, the scene was set for a vicious and protracted battle.

After a week of preparations, the Burmese began round-the-clock shelling of the camp with up to 100 artillery pieces in an attempt to grind the resisters down. Thai army observers reported hearing 120-mm mortars, 130- and 155-mm howitzers, rockets and heavy Chinese-made siege guns. Possibly as many as 50,000 shells were fired during the two-month siege, more than 1,000 of which landed in Thailand. Then, on 9 February, the *tatmadaw* launched an unsuccessful frontal 'suicide' assault on the defences. The Karen believed that many of the 200 attackers had been drugged, so impervious did they seem to the danger, and reported that civilian porters had been used as 'minesweepers'. After the attack, some 40 dead and 60 wounded littered the 600 x 500-m area of 'no man's land' between the two forces, among them apparently Buddhist KNU renegades. It was at this time that further up the border Daungguin (Dagwin), the ABSDF headquarters so hated by the junta and situated 30 kms north of Manerplaw (near Mae Saam Laep), fell to the SLORC. Before evacuating their HQ, the student fighters torched their buildings. For the KNLA defenders at Kawmoorah, the last straw was when, as they alleged, chemical shells (possibly tear gas) landed around their bunkers. On 21 February, the thousand rebels withdrew, leaving the Burmese to cut through the fortifications and take the last major Karen stronghold on the Thai-Burmese frontier. The KNU survivors regrouped further down the border, vowing now to resort to guerrilla warfare in the southern sector. They would conduct operations in Tavoy and Mergui, and threatened to target key installations, such as the proposed Burma-Thailand Unocal/Total gas pipeline.

Following the fiasco and with the wisdom of hindsight, analysts pointed out that the KNU should have seen trouble coming. The leadership had, indeed, been too Christian-dominated, whereas the bulk of the KNU rank and file was animist or Buddhist. Bo Mya was out of touch with his people, he had grown too autocratic, and his KNU seriously lacked democracy. Suddenly, many realized that no real party conference had been held since as far back as 1974. Bo Mya countered by saying that the disaster had happened not because of any weakness in the KNU, but because of the treacherous machinations of Rangoon. The trouble at River Junction Pagoda had been fomented by SLORC agents, who had financed the DKBA's operations, setting Karen against Karen. Manerplaw and the other bases in eastern Kawthoolei had fallen not because of a lack of democracy, but because the junta, aided by the Buddhist

THREE PAGODAS

Karen, wanted to clear the border area of opposition prior to developing it. The Burmese wished finally to reap the full benefits of their logging concessions to the Thais and above all intended to cash in on the lucrative business of selling power to their energy-hungry Siamese neighbours. But they could not build dams across the Salween or lay the Unocal/Total gas pipeline from the Gulf of Martaban to the border pass at Pilok village (near Sangklaburi in Kanchanaburi province) if the KNU controlled the area. Critics of Bangkok noted that it was this – the routing of ethnic minorities and not any political reform of the junta – that was the real fruit of Thailand's hollow policy of 'constructive engagement' with the SLORC. Even as Manerplaw fell, the Thai government was signing a 30-year agreement to buy annually $400m of natural gas from an illegal dictatorship. And while Kawmoorah succumbed to its pounding, senior Thai army officials, no doubt mindful of their private business interests, were inviting SLORC top brass to visit the kingdom "to strengthen ties between the two countries".

The calamities of the SLORC's dry-season offensive of the winter of 1994/95 were followed in early 1997 by disasters scarcely less grave, when the Burma army attacked and overran KNU 6th Brigade district (Duplaya). At the same time, from early 1997 to the time of writing (2001), it set about 4th Brigade area, further south. With 'Mae Saam Laep', Manerplaw, 'Ban Ta Song Yang', Kawmoorah and other northern sector places in the bag or under DKBA control, it wanted to control Karen-held southern-sector borderland opposite Mae Sot and Um Pang district in Tak province, as well as opposite Kanchanaburi, Ratchaburi, Prachuab Khiri Khan and Chumpon provinces.

In the wake of the Manerplaw and Kawmoorah fiascos, 6th Brigade area became the new KNU stronghold. As far as I can understand, Bo Mya moved his GHQ to a place called Ti Ka Ploe (Htee Ka Pler), a jungle clearing near – I think – Klo To and Sa Kaang Thit (see Map 26 & Chapter 12). Abandoning the idea of a permanent stationary GHQ, such as Manerplaw, he had a set of mobile HQs and camps at Ti Ka Ploe, Ti So Ki, Mae Ta Ro Ta (near Boeng Kloeng/see Map 28 – Mae Ta Ro Ta is visited in Chapter 13), and other places. But in a series of lightning strikes as part of a concerted all-out offensive, SLORC troops took these camps and HQs in just a few days mid-February 1997, seizing the whole of 6th Brigade area from Um Pang (or Kawkareik in Burma) down to Ti Lai Pa (close to the Three Pagodas Pass – see Map 29 & Chapter 16).

The attack was preceded by a lull and, possibly, by a piece of Rangoon trickery and espionage. Ti Ka Ploe, which had been the venue on 31 January of a celebration to mark the 48th anniversary of the Karen revolt against Burma's central government, was visited by a 12-man delegation from Rangoon, despatched for a new round of truce talks with the KNU. But less than two weeks later, GHQ Ti Ka Ploe and the other places came under unexpected attack. The Thai newspapers reported that 700-800 porters were pressganged into carrying weapons and supplies for the assaults, while at Ti Ka Ploe some 500 Karen rebels faced about 1,500 Burmese troops. In 6th Brigade district as a whole, reportedly 11,000 KNU guerrillas were fighting against 15-20,000 tatmadaw soldiers, while overall the KNLA was said to have 15,000 troops still at its disposal. About 13 February 1997, the Burmese, who were besieging Ti Ka Ploe, heavily bombarded the camp with artillery and mortar shells, to which the Karen replied with mortar fire. But in the face of overwhelming SLORC forces, the KNLA burnt down its new GHQ and retreated, deciding that it was better to fall back than lose men in a vain defence.

As they attacked Ti Ka Ploe, the Burmese also assaulted and took Ti So Ki, which was a KNU 6th Division forward operational base, and Sa Kaang Thit (Ban Mai) with its large black market. Reportedly, the Indo-Burmese Muslim traders of Sa Kaang Thit

244

market (just across the border from Klo To) were forcibly moved by SLORC troops to a new settlement at Patein in Burma's Kya-in Seikkyi district, although they might also have fled across the border into Thailand, to Nupo Towa hamlet (next to Klo To village), where many Muslim refugees were said to be sheltering. A few days before the attacks on Ti Ka ploe, Ti So Ki and Sa Kaang Thit, about 3,000 Karen civilians fled to Nupo Towa. During the two assaults on Ti Ko Si and Sa Kaang Thit, Burmese gunners shelled the Nupo Towa refugee camp, with several 82-mm mortar rounds falling in and around it. This caused the evacuation of both the Muslims and the many Karen, as well as of 200 local Thai villagers, to a safer place. Overall, the influx of refugees from Burma/Kawthoolei into Thailand resulting from the February 1997 SLORC offensive on that part of KNU 6th Brigade area opposite Um Pang district numbered some 2,000 Muslims and 8,000 Karen. Initially sheltering at the villages of Nupo Towa/Klo To, Nong Nok Ped, Nu Po and Ti Jo Si along the Um Pang/Boeng Kloeng road, they were all soon moved to a new large refugee camp at Nu Po village (Map 27), which dates from this time. The number of refugees coming from Burma into Thailand as a result of the 1997 SLORC offensive on the whole of 6th Brigade area (not just that section opposite Um Pang) numbered some 20,000.

A few days later, on 17 February, another blow befell the KNU, when some 300 KNU rebel fighters (the Burma army said 400, the KNU 70) surrendered to the *tatmadaw*, taking with them 280 rifles and 15 mortars. They were the first group of the KNU's 6th Brigade to 'defect' and gave themselves up at Myawaddy, opposite Mae Sot town. Evidently, the guerrillas did not so much surrender as lay down their arms, dispersing without being detained – something of a propaganda coup for the SLORC. The KNU sought to explain away the painful event by saying that the '70' had committed crimes, knew that they could not remain in the KNU, quit it and defected to the Burmese. But the incident might have been a symptom of policy differences at that time between hardline KNU leader Bo Mya and powerful moderate vice-president, Shwi Seing (= U Ba Tein/Ba Tein/Padoe Saw Ba Thin?) over how to deal with Rangoon (more below).

The loss of their GHQ at Ti Ka Ploe, as well as of Sa Kaang Thit, Mae Ta Ro Ta and other camps, was a further serious military setback for the KNU and the Karen cause, following which they announced that henceforward they would be resorting to (were, in fact, obliged to adopt) hit-and-run tactics and guerrilla warfare, at which they had always excelled. But the future hardly looked promising. Having taken KNU 6th Brigade district, the Burma army now switched it attention to 4th Brigade area, opposite the Thai provinces of Kanchanaburi, Ratchaburi, Prachuab Khiri Khan and Chumpon. After February 1997, this southern part of the Karen State came under attack and continued to be assaulted. In 1997, eight *tatmadaw* battalions of 350-400 troops each were already being deployed against the 4th Brigade area, while another six Burma army battalions were attacking KNU strongholds at Chong Kamiu, opposite southerly Chumpon province, where the KNLA's 11th and 12th Battalions were located. This was bad news indeed, for these territories were at the time the KNU's primary source of income, which was derived from fisheries, logging and mining. In early 2000, the battle for this southernmost sector was still going on. The *Bangkok Post* reported that it was being subjected to numerous all-out Burmese offensives, causing around 2,000 villagers to flee into Ratchaburi and other nearby provinces – business as usual. And I think that at the time of writing, in 2001, the struggle still continues down there.

The consequences of the convincing Burma army victories and fatal KNU-internal splits of the last six years, from 1995 till 2001, are heady and sobering. If, after relinquishing its 6th Brigade area, the KNU loses its 4th Brigade area, which is its last remaining sizeable piece of territory, it will have lost almost all of its territory and stationary bases in Burma, which once stretched all the way from Mae Hong Son

THREE PAGODAS

province down to Chumpon and Ranong provinces. The loss of these lands will make it very difficult for the Karen rebel movement to operate or survive militarily, politically and financially. That means, in other words, the total defeat of the KNU and the collapse of the Karen insurgency after 50 years of struggle. From Rangoon's point of view, it will mean that for the first time ever it will exercise full central control – with the help of the highly dubious DKBA and UWSA outfits – of the whole of Burma's 2500-km-long common frontier with Thailand. For the Thais, it will mean that the entire ethnic buffer zone between them and their traditional enemy, the Burmese, which used to be provided by the likes of Khun Sa, the Karenni and the Karen, will be gone.

Political developments

Other developments in the story of the Karen rebellion between 1994/95 and the time of writing include the following. Between 9 and 12 January 1996, the third Central Committee meeting of the DAB was held at the HQ of KNU 6th Brigade area. At the meeting, which was attended by 15 of the 19 groups belonging to the alliance, the Pa-O People's Liberation Organization was voted in as a twentieth member, and ABSDF students were elected to senior DAB positions. Around the same time, the KNU and Rangoon met in the Mon State capital of Moulmein, the first such meeting between the Karen rebels and the Burmese government since the failed negotiations of 1963. In an interview given at the time, Karen supremo Bo Mya said that he would give up the armed struggle and support the SLORC if Rangoon restored full democracy to Burma. A year after the DAB meeting, the NDF congregated. At the week-long session (8 - 17 February 1997), there was heated discussion as policy differences surfaced over how to deal with Rangoon. KNU leader Gen. Bo Mya wanted to continue a hard line against the junta, while KNU vice-president Shwi Seing advocated a more moderate stance, arguing for a start to negotiations for peace with the SLORC. By about that time, many ethnic rebel groups had entered into ceasefire agreements with Rangoon, leaving the Karen increasingly isolated as the only major insurgent group to reject the junta's peace overtures. Perhaps in keeping with this altered climate, at the NDF meeting Bo Mya was replaced as NDF leader by Shwi Seing. Nevertheless, the conference pledged to reject the SLORC's ceasefire agreements, which, it said, amounted to no more than divide-and-conquer tactics, and which only provided Rangoon with greater freedom to operate in the ethnic areas and to ethnically cleanse the border. At the end of the year, in November 1997, the SLORC (State Law and Order Restoration Council) was abolished and replaced with the sweeter-sounding State Peace and Development Council (SPDC). The junta may have wanted to put a more pleasing peaceable complexion on itself, in keeping with the ceasefire agreements, but of course underneath it was just the same old brutal repressive military dictatorship.

On 27 January 2000, Karen personnel changes went a step further when, at the end of a 10-day congress held opposite Tak province (6th Brigade area), the KNU elected the civilian Padoe Saw Ba Thin (U Ba Tein, = Shwi Seing?) as its new leader, replacing Bo Mya, who became vice-president, but who simultaneously remained defence minister and vice-chairman of the Central Executive Committee. Lt-General Tamalabaw was retained as supreme commander, while Padoe Mahn Sha was appointed secretary-general. The replacement of the rotund Bo Mya, who was aged 73 at the time and who had led the KNU for 24 years, almost marked the end of an era. But Ba Tein, also aged 73 in 2000, was seen as more conciliatory, more of a compromiser, than the hardline autocratic Bo Mya, and it was hoped that his appointment would inject more democracy into the Karen movement, win back some disaffected Karen leaders, strengthen the KNU, and perhaps have more success with

Rangoon. Graduate of a mission school and a fluent speaker of English, Ba Tein vowed that he would work for a political solution with Rangoon, but would never surrender to the junta.

In December 2000, the Washington-based National Coalition Government of the Union of Burma (NCGUB), a Burmese government in exile, marked the tenth anniversary of its foundation by vowing to push for the end of the SPDC junta. The NCGUB was formed in December 1990 by opposition MPs who were forced to flee Rangoon and Burma in that year during the SLORC's bloody anti-democracy crackdown. Initially, the MPs were given refuge on the Thai border by the Karen before they were granted asylum in the US. They accused the junta of wickedly campaigning to abolish Suu Kyi's National League for Democracy, which handsomely won the elections of 1990, of wrecking the future of the country by stifling student education, of hijacking and trampling underfoot the election results for more than ten years, and of allowing Burma to deteriorate in the political, economic, social, educational and health fields. They resolved to continue the struggle for a genuinely democratic system in the country.

In keeping with this sentiment, at the turn of the millennium things turned somewhat against Rangoon and in favour of the NLD and the ethnic rebel groups. For late 2000, the International Labour Organization (ILO) imposed sanctions on Burma, undoubtedly shaking the SPDC regime and apparently forcing it to rethink. The ILO required Rangoon to stop forced labour and bring legislation in line with the related Convention No. 29, and it allowed member states to take steps to compel Burma's compliance. The sanctions worried the junta because they could isolate 'Myanmar', cut inward investment, and hasten the SPDC's demise. The junta had reason to be worried because recently the US, the EU and Japan have indeed implemented the threat of sanctions, and have also latterly adopted a wait-and-see policy before giving backward Burma any more aid. In addition, since the great SLORC anti-rebel offensives of 1997, foreign investment in Burma has plummeted. The Western economic boycott may have been instrumental in easing the SPDC's pressure on the opposition, even if it has hardly helped the Karen in KNU 4th Brigade area. The screws on the junta were tightened a further twist in January 2001 first by a 5-day visit to Rangoon of UN envoy Razali, a veteran Malaysian diplomat respected by the Burmese, and then by the arrival there of a European delegation, which came to assess political progress and press for more liberalization.

Signs of a change of heart on the junta's part have been secret meetings, confirmed by Razali to have taken part, between Rangoon and Suu Kyi/the NLD. The meetings, which are the first talks between the SPDC and the opposition since 1994, are aimed at building a framework for a landmark dialogue between the two sides with a view to breaking the decade-long (since the 1990 crackdown) political impasse. Also, the Burmese authorities released in January 2001 from Rangoon's Insein prison 84 members of the NLD. Further, the junta has stopped its virulent attacks in the press on Suu Kyi, the NLD and Bo Mya. Where Suu Kyi used to be called 'a democracy witch', 'a Western Mae Daw Gyi', 'a Western puppet', 'Mrs Airs' or just 'Suu Kyi', in December 2000 the newspapers started using her full name 'Daw Aung San Suu Kyi'. And where Bo Mya was once dubbed 'Nga Mya' (nga was used in the past with slaves), he was now referred to as 'Gen. Mya'.

Nevertheless, in August 2000, Suu Kyi was blocked by the authorities in a nine-day stand-off when she tried to travel outside Rangoon, she was confined to her house when on 22 September 2000 she tried to travel to Mandalay by train, and has remained under virtual house arrest for years, right up to the time of writing. Also, despite the NLD releases, an estimated 1,700 political prisoners remain held in Burmese prisons. In addition, the campaign against Karen 4th Brigade continues. Further, analysts believe

THREE PAGODAS

that the current thaw in relations between and dialogue between Rangoon and the opposition is just a show for the new Bush administration, the EU, and Japanese investors. After nearly 40 years, Burma-watchers maintain, the junta will hardly meaningfully loosen its grip on power. And, indeed, it is difficult to see how the uncompromising nothing-but-democracy Suu Kyi/NLD and the equally uncompromising military, both of whom believe unshakably in their cause, could compromise. The bottom line is that the military just want to stay in power, while 'The Lady' will accept nothing short of full democracy.

Refugee camps

Two repercussions of the fall of Manerplaw and of KNU 7th Brigade district, the February 1997 offensive against and fall of KNU 6th Brigade area, and the campaign since that year against southerly KNU 4th Brigade territory have been the flood of mainly Karen refugees across the border from the Karen State into western Thailand, where a series of camps have been set up to house them, and the advent and activities of the DKBA, which have impacted on the camps. Karen refugees in camps in Thailand near the border are nothing new. For as long as I have been visiting the country and the western border area, I have come across camps holding Karen civilians and guerrillas fleeing SLORC troops engaged in their annual dry-season offensives against the KNU. But these camps were mostly relatively small and temporary, and their inmates mostly soon returned to Burma when the *tatmadaw* withdrew or the rains came or the KNLA seized back the overrun territory. Thus, for example, in February 1990 I found a brand-new camp at Mae Klong Ki (north of Um Pang – see Chapter 11), which was gone the next year, and in January 1992 I saw a camp, likewise just being built, at Boeng Kloeng (see Chapter 12), which in February 1993 had vanished completely. And until the winter of 1994/95 the numbers in the camps were probably relatively small and volatile. These were not so much proper settled camps where the authorities were in charge and aid agencies ministered, but makeshift places hastily erected by the refugees themselves, who soon returned home. But with the fall of Manerplaw in early 1995 and the loss of the territory opposite Um Pang district in February 1997, all that changed. Now large numbers were involved and seriously organized camps began to be built.

Following the January 1995 campaign, as already said, 10-15,000 new Karen refugees fled into Thailand, 5,000 from the Manerplaw area alone, pushing the total in the mid-1990s to some 70,000. And after the February 1997 offensives against 6th Brigade territory opposite Um Pang district, another 20,000 sought refuge on Thai soil, increasing the total at the time to over 90,000 and maybe more than 100,000. It was feared at the time that if SLORC operations in KNU 4th Brigade area were successful, a further 50,000 could stream into the kingdom, and at the time of writing this could still happen. These refugee figures are the highest since the Cambodian conflicts in the 1980s. Diran (1997) says that if the illegal migrants into Thailand (mostly Karen, Shan, Karenni and Mon) are reckoned in, the figure of 100,000 rises to half a million or more. The genuine refugees are housed in a dozen or so camps down the Thai-Burmese border. From 1997 on, the authorities amalgamated and moved deeper 'inland' (away from the border) many camps in the provinces of Mae Hong Son, Tak and Kanchanaburi, to protect them from cross-border DKBA attacks. My own view is that if you look at some of these camps, as I have done, the figure of 100,000 refugees down the western border, such as is constantly given in the press, must surely in 2001 be higher that. For reasons best known to themselves, the Thai authorities seem to prefer to give figures lower than the real ones, just as they keep the existence of the camps quiet. This may be because they do not want a lot of international bodies nosing around, or because – less charitably – it is their intention to repatriate the refugees as quickly as possible without anyone really noticing. In 2001, I counted about a dozen Karen/Karenni refugee camps, and there may well be others that I have not seen or heard/read about.

Going from north to south, they are: (1) the Karenni camp at Mai Nai Soi (mentioned in Chapters 7 and 8), near Mae Hong Son town, Muang district, where in January 2000 some 13,400 people were held. (2) The small Karenni camp at Mae Surin village, Khun Yuam district, housing in January 2000 nearly 3,000 people. (3) Possibly a camp at Sa La, west of Mae La Luang, containing Karenni and ABSDF students – or it might be that locals were confusing this with the Mae Khong Kha camp. (4) A camp near Mae Khong Kha, WSW of Mae Sariang town, Muang district, with more than 10,500 people in January 2000, who may be a mixture of Karenni, regular Karen and some Burmese ABSDF students – there was a proposal in early 2000 to move this camp, which was in Salween National Park, out of the park, because some of the refugees had allegedly been lured by illegal loggers to cut and process trees. (5) A camp near the village of Mae Lamaluang (Mae Wa Luang on H105?), south of Mae Sariang, in Sob Moei district, which in January 2000 comprised nearly 8,000 refugees, all of whom must have been KNU Karen, mainly from the Manerplaw area, which lies nearby to the west. These camps in Mae Hong Son province alone hold at least 35,000 Karenni and Karen. (6) The massive Mae La camp (Map 21 and see Chapter 10), situated 60 kms north of Mae Sot, Tak province, on the west side of the H105 road, which in January 2001 housed at least 30,000 and maybe up to 50,000 KNU Karen and Muslim Indo-Burmese refugees, making it the biggest refugee camp in Thailand since the wars and upheavals in Indo-China in the 1970s – it stretches for 3.7 kms from one end to the other! (7) Mawkier (Mawker, Mo Kia/Mo Ker/Mor Goe) camp, south of Mae Sot, in Tak province, Pop Pra district, which has in the past housed 7,000 refugees from places such as Palu (opposite Wa Lay), but which was destroyed on 23 March 1998 by the DKBA – I suspect that its inmates were moved to Um Biem camp. (8) Um Biem camp (Map 23, see Chapter 11), 85 kms south-east of Mae Sot, in Tak province, beside the H1090 road, just after the village of Rom Glao N° 4, which when I visited it in 2001 housed some 8,000 and maybe over 10,000 people, mostly KNU Karen. (9) Nu Po camp (Map 27, see Chapter 12), 63 kms south of Um Pang, in Tak province, near Nu Po village, beside the dirt road to Boeng Kloeng, which when I visited it in February 2001 had 7,000 - 8,000 or maybe more refugees, who were mostly KNU Karen and some Muslim Indo-Burmese from KNU 6th Brigade area. (10) Tong Yang camp, near Tong Yang village, in Sangklaburi district, Kanchanaburi province, west of Sangklaburi town, which houses mostly KNU Karen, maybe Mon people, and in 2001 the parents of the famous God's Army child-soldier twins, Johnny and Luther Htoo (I have not seen this camp and have no population figures for it). (11) The camp near Tam Hin village, in Suan Pueng district, Ratchaburi province, which in 2001 housed over 8,000 mostly Karen refugees, and which has been mixed up with the recent trouble and killings in that area (more below). And (12) the nearby Maneeloy camp or 'holding centre' – same as (11)? – at Suan Pueng, Ratchaburi province, which contained perhaps 500 ethnic Burmese pro-democracy dissident students, and which was earmarked for closure by the end of 2000. Beda (Preeda), the member of the Vigorous Burmese Student Warriors (VBSW) who took part in the siege of the Burmese embassy in Bangkok in October 1999 and also in the seizure of a hospital in Ratchaburi in January 2000, used to live at Maneeloy. Maneeloy was/is a holding centre in the sense that the students were being held there, under the care of the UNHCR, prior to resettlement in third countries. About 2,000 of them would eventually be resettled, with the US agreeing to take some 1,500, and Australia and other countries promising to take the rest. However, first they had to be sent to Maneeloy. Most of the 2,000 students were in Bangkok, where several hundred had given themselves up for

THREE PAGODAS

'holding' and then resettlement, but an estimated 1,200 were still in hiding. These camp population figures add up to some 110,000 refugees and maybe many more.

DKBA activities

As we saw earlier, the Karen renegade DKBA came into being in the winter of 1995/95, climbed into bed with the SLORC, and was instrumental in the fall of KNU GHQ Manerplaw to the junta. Since that time, this small, disreputable, highly dangerous outfit, which can only survive because of its *tatmadaw* patronage, has conducted a series of murderous terroristic cross-border raids. Its sphere of influence runs from the Manerplaw area, down to Boeng Kloeng, and maybe as far south as the Three Pagodas Pass or beyond, but the DKBA must be very thinly spread and probably concentrated in a few pockets. Thus they must be in Manerplaw itself and on the western bank of the Moei between 'Ban Ta Song Yang' and Kawmoorah or Myawaddy, e.g. opposite Mae Salid, they have a presence at Pa Toei (opposite Nong Luang) and at Sa Kaang Thit (opposite Klo To), and they control the border crossings at Palu (opposite Wa Lay) and Boeng Kloeng, at both of which places I saw armed uniformed DKBA men in 2001 with my own eyes.

In the early days, the DKBA was responsible for a number of attacks across the Moei border river south of Manerplaw, especially in the Ban Ta Song Yang area. They raided villages, e.g. Mae U-su and Ti No Ko, and struck terror in Karen refugee camps. Travelling between Mae Sariang and Mae Sot between 1996 and 2001 was sometimes a hazardous business, and when I rode down the H105 at that time, I often found the route bristling with Thai army camps and checkpoints, which occasionally were unwilling to let me continue. An infamous DKBA action happened in early January 1996 at the Mae La refugee camp, when DKBA renegades apparently attempted to kidnap Major General Ta Lu (Hta Lue), aged 71 at the time, who was a former KNLA quartermaster general. This Karen elder, who was paralysed, was dragged from his bedroom by five DKBA men who came knocking on the door of his house just after midnight. They tried to force him to walk from the house and camp, but when they found he could not walk or when he resisted, one of them shot him in the chest, killing him instantly. Evidently, the DKBA wanted to take Ta Lu back to Burma as a hostage to compel Col. Bena, a KNU staff officer and also Ta Lu's son, to join the DKBA and press for the return of Karen refugees to Burma. The five kidnappers were seen to be part of a group of 20, armed among other things with five RPG rocket launchers. The party had forced a Karen to guide them to the general's house, and on their way back to Burma they robbed another Karen's grocery, taking rice and food.

At the end of January 1996, the DKBA threatened more such attacks. Lt Col. Sa Thwe, leader of the DKBA, said that his force would step up its actions against Thailand if the country continued to offer refuge to KNU troops and civilians. The renegades were trying to pressurize the kingdom into ejecting the KNU and punish it for harbouring them. They were true to their word, and other incidents followed, which provide further insight into the DKBA. On 30 January 1996, during the night, they crossed the border from Burma to attack and rob villages in Ta Song Yang district, killing three people, including a Thai policeman. And they were busy again in March 1998. In that month, over 20 suspected DKBA bandits torched a police checkpoint at km-marker 152 on the H105, at Klo Ma Nae village, near Ban Ta Song Yang, at the same time killing a Thai policeman. Also in March, some 30 armed men, apparently DKBA and thought to be led by Capt. Maung Tin Aye, surrounded and robbed Mae Salid market, making off with cash and goods worth more than 500,000 baht (more in Chapter 10, Postscript). Mid-month, the DKBA again attacked Mae La refugee camp, firing ten mortar rounds into it from a jungle post inside Burma, and wounding one Karen inmate. The Thai army responded to this violation of its sovereignty by firing 33 artillery shells into the DKBA camp, killing seven troops. On 17 March 1998, when I was travelling down the H105, I came upon a DKBA incident that had just happened. Near Ban Ta Song Yang, a dead person lay at the roadside, who turned out to be a policeman, shot and killed by the renegades, who stole his weapons and money. On 23 March, in an early morning raid, some 40 DKBA troops destroyed Mawkier refugee camp, south of Mae Sot, burning it to the ground, killing one inmate and wounding nine others, and also injuring four Thai soldiers. And on 31 March 1998, suspected DKBA guerrillas crossed the River Salween, as we saw earlier, and torched Mae Saam Laep, burning down more than 100 houses and causing some 10 million bahts' worth of damage.

God's Army, 'the twins' & the Ratchaburi hospital incident

No update of events surrounding the Karen rebellion would be complete without a mention of the above, all of which recently grabbed the headlines in the Thai press as well as the imaginations of people in Thailand and around the world. The stories surrounding them, which tell of reckless actions, are a sign of the desperation of Karen and other rebels in their plight. But they were preceded in October 1999 by the drama of the seizure of the Burmese embassy in Bangkok by a group of ethnic Burmese student dissidents who wanted to both protest against the SPDC and highlight their cause. They were led by Kyaw Ni, also known as Johnny, and seemed to be members of the Vigorous Burmese Student Warriors (VBSW), a group of rebel students who a decade earlier had fled from Rangoon into the jungle and to the side of the ethnic insurgents to take up arms after the Burmese military gunned down pro-democracy demonstrators during the 1988 crackdown. In the embassy, the students took hostages, and after a tense day of negotiations with the Thai government they were allowed to leave the embassy and flee to safety in exchange for the release of the hostages, an escape that infuriated the SPDC junta, which demanded their handover. Johnny later joined the quaintly named God's Army.

The God's Army is a somewhat mystical, basically Karen rebel outfit that was formed in Burma in 1998 by members of various ethnic militias, including Karen Christians, Buddhists and animists. The group was headed by two twin Karen boys, Johnny and Luther Htoo, who were just nine years old at the time (no connection between Johnny Htoo and Johnny Kyaw Ni just mentioned). The God's Army took its name from rumours that the boys, who preached in a church, believed that God was calling them to lead an armed group to fight the Burma army. Members of the force credited the twins with magical powers, which made them bullet-proof and allowed them to become invisible. This had helped them defeat *tatmadaw* soldiers trying to capture them. Word spread, and the twins were more widely lionized by the Karen, who saw them as sons of God sent to protect the overall Karen army. There are Karen millenarian overtones in this respect for and focussing on the twins by a routed Karen army and people. As word of the twins spread, the strength of the God's Army swelled to 200 by 1998. Soon Johnny and Luther Htoo became the world's most famous child soldiers. The prominence of the twins and the legendary prowess of their little army was partly based on fact, for after the KNLA was driven out of KNU 4th Brigade territory opposite Ratchaburi province by the Burma army, the God's Army somehow managed both to put up a stubborn and successful resistance against the massive *tatmadaw* offensive, and to mount inspiring hit-and-run attacks on the Burmese military.

Two years later, in January 2000, God's Army positions opposite Ratchaburi province's Suan Pueng district were heavily shelled for several days or weeks by

251

Burmese troops. Initially, the Thai newspapers reported that the God's Army jungle base of Kamaplaw, which housed 200 fighters and 100 civilians, was overrun by the Burmese, with many people being killed, including women and children. But a few days later it reported that Kamaplaw had not been taken after all and that the God's Army had managed to hold out against the *tatmadaw*. During the sustained attack, both the twins and Johnny Kyaw Ni fled the camp and disappeared. However, it was not just the Burmese who were shelling the God's Army positions. The Thai army was, too. Boxed in from both sides and sustaining heavy casualties, guerrillas from the positions opposite Suan Pueng resorted to a drastic measure, which resulted in the Ratchaburi hospital incident.

Towards the end of January 2000, a group of ten of them crossed the border into Ratchaburi province, hijacked a bus, and went to the centre of Ratchaburi town, where they seized a hospital and held 800 patients, doctors and nurses hostage for 22 hours. The group may not in the end have included any God's Army Karen, but seemed to be mainly composed of VBSW members, who perhaps emanated from Kamaplaw. Neither the twins were involved in the action, nor Johnny Kyaw Ni, who was scheduled to lead it, but who was replaced by Beda (Preeda). As things turned out, this replacement saved Johnny his life. At least one of the gunmen had taken part in the Burmese embassy seizure the year before. The group, all of whom were apparently armed, demanded that the Thai army stop attacking them, claiming that Thai shelling had slaughtered hundreds of innocent villagers, and also called for medical treatment for fellow militia members wounded in the Thai and Burma army attacks.

The Thai authorities, smarting from an admitted serious lack of intelligence, which allowed ten gunmen to so easily cross the border and travel to Ratchaburi, and piqued that this was now a second guerrilla action after the embassy seizure, decided not to negotiate with the rebels, but instead ended the crisis by making a dawn raid on the hospital, when 48 commandos freed the hostages unharmed and shot dead all ten rebels. Overreacting, they evidently intended to eliminate the guerrillas so that they would not repeat such actions and so that other rebels contemplating such operations would know what to expect. Initial elation in the press at the successful conclusion of the hospital incident soon gave way to nagging doubts. It seemed that all ten rebels had been shot in the head, and there were reports that prior to their deaths they had all been stripped naked and had their hands tied up with electric cable. From the authorities came some rather lame and also indignant explanations of what could only otherwise be interpreted as murder. And the situation began to stink all the more when the accounts of some of the hostages themselves began to be heard, who said that they had never felt intimidated or threatened by the rebels, that the rebels had all been polite and had showed respect for the elderly, that leader Beda had been soft-spoken and considerate, that the rebels had not harmed anyone, and that at the time of the dawn rescue raid they had surrendered or at least had not seemed prepared to fight back. Insightful commentators noted that in killing the rebels the Thai authorities had dealt with the immediate problem, with the symptom, but had overlooked what drove the group to desperation, the underlying cause. And critics said that the response to the hospital incident was another indictment of the authorities consistent with their shameful cosying up to the illegal SPDC junta in Rangoon, their refusal to support or tolerate the KNU any more, and their failure to provide effective security for the refugee camps down the western border against the DKBA.

On the other hand, the rebels' cause was not helped when at the end of December 2000 members of the God's Army, in what looked like a raid that went wrong, crossed the border 3 kms into Ratchaburi's Suan Pueng district and killed six Thai villagers in Ban Wai Noi Nai. All this became too much for the Thai authorities, who now moved against the God's Army, capturing mid-January 2001 a dozen or more of their number, including the celebrated boy twins. The Thai army encircled their base, which straddled the border in Suan Pueng district, and laid siege to it for two weeks, denying the guerrillas foodstuffs and other essentials. At the same time, it issued the group with an ultimatum that they should turn themselves in within seven days or face attack. If they surrendered, they would not be harmed. Only those involved in the village killings would face justice, while the rest would be sent to Tong Yang and Tam Hin refugee camps. A first group surrendered and then a second. Johnny and Luther Htoo, now aged 12, were taken into custody, with pictures of the sweet-faced, girlie-looking, cheroot-smoking duo splashed across the front pages of the Thai newspapers, but the other Johnny was not among those taken, although three rebels suspected of having been involved in the killings were. The twins, who after their surrender debunked the myths of their magical powers and invincibility in battle, were later sent to join their parents at Tong Yang in Sangklaburi district. The capture of the group may have dealt a mortal blow to the God's Army.

Outlook

As has become clear in the foregoing, the predicament of the Karen has become acute, and their rebel cause might finally have been totally defeated. Since 1994, the KNU has lost almost all of its border territory, although it still clings on to pockets, as I discovered in 2001, when re-researching this book. Huge numbers of KNU Karen from 7th, 6th and 4th Brigade areas now languish in refugee camps in Thailand. From them, the KNU can do little in Burma. Even though it might hold pockets in Kawthoolei, it cannot move from one to the other, nor can now move from one to the other via Thailand, at the rear, as it used to be able to do. So the Karen must wait. They must wait for circumstances to change, perhaps for the SPDC junta to fall or for democracy to be restored, perhaps for sanctions to truly bite and bring about change, or for international pressure to cause the same. Meanwhile, the military cling on to power in Rangoon and the Burma army has increased hand over fist in recent years, from some 186,000 troops in 1988, to an estimated 450,000 - 600,000 in 2001, making the *tatmadaw* the second-largest army in South-East Asia. Nevertheless, Burma-watchers note that it has weakened or become less solid of late. The chain of command has been decentralized to a regional collective leadership. Regional commanders have become very powerful, operating like warlords, especially in the Shan State. The junta is beset by problems other than just financial ones. Health is on the verge of collapse in Burma, which is being overwhelmed by so many HIV/Aids cases, up to 700,000 sufferers, that a full-scale epidemic looms. And the resistance groups, despite the ceasefire agreements, and although some may be down but not completely out, remain well-armed. Of no group is this more true than the 'Red' Wa with its UWSA, which the SPDC regime cannot control. The UWSA has burgeoned to become probably the largest force outside the Burma army and the greatest threat to Rangoon. If it turns on the junta and upsets its apple cart, salvation for the Karen might come from the Wa.

10

SINGING GIRLS

Manerplaw – Ban Ta Song Yang – Mae Salid – Mae Ramat – Mae Sot

I t took us a long time to catch a longtail boat going south from Manerplaw. There were few settlements immediately upstream along the Moei, and the distances between them were relatively great. Also, the river was not easily navigable in places. But the main reason why few Karen boatmen would go beyond rebel HQ was that there was a danger of attack by the Burma army, which held some of the commanding heights down that way. We stood folornly in the morning sun, waiting with our Honda on the sand and rocks of the river bed. Finally a *hang yao*, its engine making a searing whine, came into view. We waved to it. At first, it looked as if the boat was going to pass us by, but at the last moment, after some conferring between the passengers and the boatman, it veered round to pick us up. The passengers were two solitary men, and we began to wonder if they had chartered the longtail. This impression was reinforced when we noticed that the boat simply ignored groups of Karen (much to their consternation) waving frantically for a ride with their bundles on the river bank. The two men and their expressionless boatman helped us stow and lash our motorbike aboard, and we set off.

The Moei was by turns wide and languid, and narrow and fast-flowing (Map 20). We passed a Karen village on the Thai side and then came to a ferry. This was at a point immediately below the third checkpoint that we had walked out to earlier. We wondered if the squint-eyed girl soldier and the cheroot-smoking KNLA boy were still at their posts. The boat moved into a patch of choppy water, small waves smacking under the bow. Suddenly, the driver, his face all grim concentration and his arms braced against the steering arm of the engine, headed his slender craft into some rapids. A true aim was critical. A slight error to either side, and the boat would swing round across the current and be washed backwards. The boatman misjudged. The prow veered to the Burmese side, hit the bank and got covered with earth and plants. We drifted back down the rapids until the driver recovered the boat to have another go, this time successfully, just. On these flights up rapids, the engine at full throttle, we seriously feared for our hire bike. Everything seemed so precarious.

Over the din of the engine, we shouted as much to our two fellow passengers. We should not worry, one of them replied, because these boatmen made such trips everyday, and in the dry season, when the water was lower, navigation was even trickier. The man who was doing the talking seemed to be a Karen. He wore a brilliant red *Yang* smock over normal civilian clothing and spoke by turns broken English and imperfect Thai. A large corpulent man, he had a bull neck and pug face with heavy jowls and short silvery hair. His skin was unusually dark, like that of southern Thais. Evidently, he was a man of some consequence, for he had with him a leather attaché case crammed with documents, and his companion always deferred to him. We could not help noticing the heavy Rolex watch set off on his swarthy right arm. He had a house down in Chumpon province, the man explained, and was here on business. First he was going to a refugee village upstream, after which he would return "in my boat" to Manerplaw for a meeting. But what were we doing? We explained that we had just spent a few days in Manerplaw and were now trying to get to Ban Ta Song Yang.

The longtail moved into open glassy water. To our right, the Dawna peaks reared up, covered in green vegetation, giving the Moei an emerald colour. It was a tranquil scene, stunningly beautiful, very remote, and with a slight but insistent note of danger. An isolated sawmill on the Karen bank glided by, and dirt tracks on either side came down to the water in the middle of nowhere. For long stretches, there was no one and nothing, just a solitary man in this jungle wilderness making a dugout canoe, and another fishing from a tiny raft. Ahead lay a pointed triangular mountain, and for a long time we motored towards it. Two villages appeared, the first on the Burmese bank apparently a refugee camp, the second on the Thai side a regular *Yang* settlement. It was here that our two fellow passengers got out. We made to do likewise. But the swarthy Karen businessman motioned to us to stay in the boat. The driver would take us to Ban Ta Song Yang and come back to pick him up later. We did not even have time to express our thanks because immediately the *hang yao* set off again. Presently, the driver said to us that we were very lucky. He had been instructed to take us to Mae Ta Wo (as the Karens called our destination). Normally, we would have been charged 100 baht each for the trip, even if any boat had been going there. Did we know who "the big man" was? It was Bo Mya, and we were travelling in the leader's boat. We were thunderstruck. Later, only one thing rankled with us more than the fact that we had not recognized or thanked the Karen supremo, and this was that our slide film of him and of this ravishing section of the journey was later stolen by a clerk in Chiang Dao post office.

The twin villages were followed by a long lonely stretch. Now the Moei was hemmed in by mountains on both sides. Trees and greenery grew from the steep banks right down to the water. The river roiled again, with whirlpools. Swallows, fishing up insects, winged and dipped all round the boat like dive-bombers. A tributary flowed in left between two headlands, while on the right a waterfall cascaded down dark slimy cliffs. In the shade of the Dawna peaks, it was distinctly cool even at midday. Rounding a bend, we saw in the distance the double village of Mae Ta Wo/Ban Ta Song Yang. Our longtail cruised past the first Karen section and finally, after a 1½-hour trip at speed from Manerplaw, drew up at the second Thai half. There we had to disembark. Karen boats would go no further – ahead lay pockets of SLORC-controlled territory.

THREE PAGODAS

Ban Ta Song Yang

We would have lingered at the disembarkation point, a little bay with a sandy beach, where colourful *hang yao* were moored. But the drivers, who were tinkering with the engines, shouted to us to get off the beach, immediately. The Burmese claimed the river and even the beach, and they would shoot at us if they saw us. That seemed ridiculous to us. Only a week ago a *farang* had been shot just where we were standing, the men hollered sharply, gesticulating with greasy hands. And indeed, as we rode up the escarpment that separated the village from the Moei, we spotted a sign at the top which read in Thai and Burmese 'Thai Border'. Thus it was that we re-entered Thailand.

Ban Ta Song Yang, not to be confused with the district 'town' of Ampoe Ta Song Yang 55 kms further south, was altogether a strange place. We scooted around the network of dreamy dusty alleyways, but found the village drained of life. No one was around, and no shops were open. There was not even any stand where a noodle soup could be had – a rare thing in Thailand. We approached some children to ask why the village was so quiet, but they all ran away. Old people peered at us suspiciously from the dark interiors of houses. Finally, a woman explained to us that today was the day of some special religious celebration. Everybody was at the temple. In the north-east corner of the village, we found the temple – Wat Mong Khon Khiri Kaet, a brand-new Thai affair with high sloping roofs and sited near the base of an old pagoda – and, sure enough, most of the villagers were inside.

Continuing our search for food and also for someone to quiz, we figured that the police station must be manned, so we rode in there. But the large central BPP compound overlooking the river was as deserted as everywhere else. Unchallenged, we roamed through its buildings, perused the duty book, and studied the official local maps. Our only witness was King Bhumipol, whose serious bespectacled face stared out of a large wall calendar. The station was heavily fortified, confirming that the area was a hot spot. The yard was full of sandbagged bunkers, observation points and, as all along the riverfront 'promenade' and indeed all around the village, machine-gun posts. Looking out over the pale green Moei, it was difficult to believe that these defences were necessary. Over the river, completely uninhabited, thickly forested mountains rose straight out of the water. But the threat was real enough. Hanging up in the compound, just as at Wat Fah Wiang In on the Shan border, was a large piece of shell casing, a grim souvenir of recent SLORC bombardments.

If the shell had not landed in 1984, it must have fallen in 1988. In 1984, at the beginning of the Four Cuts offensives against the Karen, the Burma army overran this area. In a carefully planned strike, 2,000 44th LID assault troops captured the nearby KNLA Mae Ta Wo base. So successful were they, setting up a garrison there, that they held on to it for nearly five years. But then, in the autumn of 1988, the Karen managed to regain the position. In the major month-long battle, which towards the end involved ABSDF student soldiers, there were heavy casualties. The silence of the mountains opposite and the peacefulness of Ban Ta Song Yang were illusory. It was but a short time since all had reverberated with the sounds of exploding shells and gunfire.

SINGING GIRLS

Back near the 'Thailand Border' sign, we found a small makeshift restaurant. Located on a knoll and called *Rim Moei*, it overlooked the border river, as well at the steep track down to the longtails. The owner cooked up a mediocre fried rice for us. At the restaurant, we found the policemen. Although it was only two in the afternoon, here they were on Mekhong whisky duty. They were drunk. They obviously thought that we could not understand Thai, for in the midst of their discussions one of them bragged loudly that he got 10,000-baht kickbacks for turning a blind eye when the teak logs came over. We had little desire to fraternize with these BPP men, and so soon left the village. The way out was a one-km-long access road, at the end of which, where it joined the 'main' road, stood a particularly splendid wooden portal, surrounded by a welter of signs. In Thai, Burmese and Karen these indicated the way to Ban Ta Song Yang school, a BPP camp, the health centre, the police station and the jetty. We particularly liked two notices which provided an ironic comment on this sinister smuggling nest. 'Welcome, visitor, to the golden honest village', one read, 'where the inhabitants' votes are not to be bought.' Another announced: 'Welcome to Ban Ta Song Yang with its famous handcuff-making workshop.'

✳

Putting the 'golden honest village' and also our two river trips behind us, we made ready to continue south by road (Map 21). We had joined Highway 1085 (since renumbered the H105). To the north, 93 kms away, lay Mae Sariang, while south, 137 kms over the horizon, was Mae Sot. Route 105, on the map a tenuous wiggly 230-km-long line running clean down the border, was a road built primarily for military 'border security' purposes. Few people used it – because of its great length and also because of robberies in the night – and in the early 1990s there was no through public transport. In fact, the road had only recently (mid-1991) been completely sealed. Without doubt, it was one of the most spectacular rides in Thailand, perhaps second only to the extraordinary Mae Sot/Um Pang 'Death Highway' (described in Chapter 11).

Much of the excitement came in the initial Mae Sariang/Ban Ta Song Yang stretch, which now lay behind us. For 60 miles, the little road climbed through a marvellous alternation of airy open bushland, cool oppressive jungle, banana palm country, forests of pink-, orange- and white-flowering trees, sun-scorched scrubby upland and eerie bald mountaintops, finally making a long descent to Ban Ta Song Yang (see Postscript 2002 below for a detailed account of this stretch). But the second central section was hardly less impressive. For some 40 kms, to just short of Mae U-su village, the road ran precisely along the border, shadowing the River Moei and the Dawna Range. Even on the final section, from Mae U-su down to Mae Sot, the H105 was never far from the border river and mountains. The motorbike dipped and swung through thrilling scenery. To the east, sunny singing mountainsides, reforested with teak saplings, rose out of the narrow Moei valley, and to the west, in the shade with the afternoon sun behind them, a succession of dark tree-clad outcrops soared almost perpendicularly straight out of the river. Karen villages crouched on each bank where space permitted. Those on the Thai side had intriguing names like **Nam Ork Ru** (= water coming out of a hole), **Huai Ma-nok, Huai Mae Nin, Ko La Haeng** and – beyond Mae Salid – Wa Kae Ra Ko, Hua Nok Kok (= great hornbill stream) and Ka Nae Chu. At intervals, in the middle of nowhere, tell-tale unmarked tracks left the side of the road to go down to the river. We could see hardwood logs piled up on the Burmese bank, waiting to come across at night – when Ban Ta Song Yang's police chief was looking the other way.

Mae Salid

It was not long before we passed through **Mae Salid Noi** (parva) to arrive at **Mae Salid Luang** (magna). At a distance of 115 kms (by road) from Mae Sariang town centre, this Karen refugee village – also spelt 'Mae Sarit Luang' – was the first place of any consequence going south down the H105 and lay exactly halfway to Mae Sot. We were surprised to find a thriving roadside market. In front of it, a number of Mae Sot *songtaew* were parked, gleaming in the teatime sun. After the poor fare at Ta Song Yang, we stopped for a snack. A Karen lady was serving up one of the most unconventional but delicious noodle soups we ate anywhere – a fiery spicy brown liquid containing noodles, vegetables, a boiled egg and dried shrimps. She told us of a new guest house in Mae Salid. It was just across the road, slightly up the hill. As it was too late to get on to Mae Sot that day, we walked across to see if we could spend the night there. They had a room, a gloomy *Yang* boy said laconically.

Mae Salid GH was not one of the greatest places we stayed in. The Karen had always impressed us with their hospitality, helpfulness and integrity, and so we were all the more disappointed with our stopover in this lodging. The guest house seemed to be in the charge of half a dozen smoking boys, friendly enough, but lackadaisical. Of course, in a remote refugee village one does not expect overmuch. Nevertheless, a place which pretended to be a guest house, charging tourists 100 baht for a room for two, could have provided better amenities. The position and outward appearance of the house was fine enough. Set in a commanding position on the side of a hill, the wooden building had a spacious balcony, from which the visitor could look out over the village and the River Moei to the Burmese mountains beyond. There was also a roomy vestibule, in which guests could eat supper sitting cross-legged on the polished teak floor. But we found nowhere safe to leave the Honda. The best we could do was, with the aid of a couple of the boys, to manhandle it up into the garden and park it overnight below the guest house balcony. But no one was really happy with this. One of boys confessed next morning that he had not slept a wink for fear of the bike being stolen in the night. Every time a dog had sniffed around in the garden, he had crept out into the moonlight to check that the machine was still there.

It was a pity that the boys' solicitude in respect of the motorbike did not extend to the accommodation and food. Our room was a stifling windowless box. With no electricity, there was no hot water, no lighting and no fan. The sole object in the wooden room was a mattress on the bare floorboards. Presumably, the cracks between all the boards were for spitting through, hilltribe-fashion. In the adjacent 'bathroom', a shower had been rigged up, but it did not work. With no water running either evening or morning, it was not even possible to fill up the lavatory bucket and wash out of that. Not that the idea was appealing – the plastic dipper was lined with green slime. The bathroom facilities were little improvement on the river, and actually it would have been better to take our soap and towel and wash in the Moei along with the refugees. All night long, a sickly sweet smell of urine emanated from the bathroom.

For 35 baht per person, the boys cooked up an all-in evening meal. From the comments in the guest book we learnt that this was always the same – stewed chicken with rice, stir-fried vegetables, and fresh fruit. That would not have been so bad, except that the stew was horribly greasy and the chicken all inedible bone with at most one nugget of tough old hen flesh adhering to it. All in all, it was food reminiscent of what we had been glad to leave behind in Manerplaw. But no matter, we were able to supplement the fare with some after-dinner titbits bought from the stores down by the road, and nibble them with glasses of *lao kao* on the balcony as darkness fell. And that was the redeeming feature of this guest house. Communication with the Karen boys was restricted (although a couple of them had a smattering of Thai and even of English), and they retired early to their own small boxes to smoke. But with the other odd traveller passing through, it was a pleasure to sit there trading stories while the sun lowered behind the Dawna peaks.

During breakfast on the balcony, one of the Karen lads pointed out to us a hill in the middle distance on the Burmese side of the border. There were orange gashes near the summit, better seen through binoculars. It was a SLORC outpost of some 70-80 soldiers. From time to time, in their boredom or lust for meat and drink, they apparently came down in this direction to ambush the Karen and steal livestock and whisky. Not so long ago, they had shelled the Karen settlement on the far bank of the Moei. Tired of the harassment, the Karen had moved all their families over to Mae Salid, although there were still about 200 KNLA troops left on the far side. Seeing the move, the Burma army had then bombed Mae Salid itself, since which time the Thais had maintained a military presence in the village. The refugees were housed in an area between the market and the river. When we visited them, we found particularly wretched and impoverished people.

A few hundred metres south of Mae Salid, we came across the first and only real turning off the H105 for 200 kms (counting from Mae Sariang). A BPP checkpoint and military encampment stood near the junction. It was an unusually serious affair, with sandbagging around it and obstacles across the road. The soldiers were friendly enough, if watchful. The side road (H1267) was a small metalled way which zigzagged 16 kms up to *Chao Doi House*. Exploring up there one year, we found a homely ranch-style lodging, nestling in a tiny secluded valley and smothered in pink *fuang fah* blooms, run by one Mr Narong, a Thai ex-policeman and former tin miner. Beyond his house, the side road rounded Mon Krating (= gaur mountain), climbed over Mon Kiu Lom (= windy col mountain) and a pass, skirted Mr Narong's disused tin mine, and descended to Mae Ramoeng, an especially old Karen village (200 years). Some maps and guidebooks show a road continuing from the village to Om Koi, a mistake supported by a misleading sign on the H1267 itself, announcing 'Om Koi 84 kms'. But at the time of our visit, there was no way through here – except on foot – and the sign actually indicated Om Koi district, not town. The isolated mountainous hinterland beyond Mae Ramoeng is the source of most of Thailand's annual 25 tons of raw opium – not an area to stray into.

*

Po Pa Ta bazaar & black market

From the boys at *Mae Salid GH*, we learnt of Po Pa Ta bazaar and black market. They lay five kms south of the H1267 junction, beyond the next village of **Mae Song** (Map 21). We would have gone clean past both had we not been alerted by a couple of pick-ups parked for no apparent reason at the roadside. From the H105, nothing could be seen of either. Behind the trucks, a path dropped down into a motley conglomeration of leaf-roofed buildings. Crammed between the highway and the Moei, this was the bazaar. A dark corridor ran through the shacks, lined on each side by general stores. At first sight, it was an Aladdin's cave down here. Everything was on sale – from dried fish to catapults, from Karen costumes to 'Best Thukhita Cheroots', from milk bread to Burmese cloth. But after a while, we noticed a uniformity in the merchandise and also that much of it had come not from Burma, as we had initially supposed, but from Mae Sot. The goods were more to provision people in Kawthoolei than to supply locals or passers-by in Thailand.

More interesting than the goods were the marketeers and general atmosphere. Outside in the sun, naked children played in the dirt, while inside men and women peered furtively out of gloomy rooms behind their stores. Did they live here, we wondered, or did they cross every day from Burma and Po Pa Ta? Were they legitimately in Thailand, or were they, like the bazaar itself, seemingly tolerated by the authorities in this one spot? Nearly all the men had black beards and skullcaps, suggesting that they were Muslim Indo-Burmese or Arakanese Rohingyas. But they could also have been recent Bangladeshi refugees, such as we later found in Mae Ramat. A tall gaunt old man told us that his grandfather had lived in India, and that the bazaar was a refugee market. While prices were cheap by Western standards, none of the stallholders was prepared to do any real bargaining.

At the back of the bazaar, a log bridge led to a steeply climbing path. Scrambling up it, we came to a track, which led down to the Moei. Here a marvellous arena greeted us, but with a strange atmosphere. There was the limpid river itself, a backdrop of sheer mountains, a long rickety bamboo bridge crossing the water (wide at this point), and on the far bank in Burma, perched atop an escarpment, the settlement of Po Pa Ta. At the foot of the escarpment, in a bucolic idyll, children were playing at the water's edge, cattle were wandering along the sandy beach, and men and women were making ready to set off in a longtail. And yet the mood of this arena seemed to us even more unfathomable, shiftier, than in the bazaar. Numerous characters were waiting around, but for what? As soon as we arrived, a crackle of small-arms fire reverberated for several seconds around the walls of the lush bowl. The shooting continued sporadically throughout our stay. What was it? As no one seemed concerned, we ignored it too (actually it was hunters on the mountainsides). The bamboo bridge and the bazaar indicated that Po Pa Ta was a regular frontier crossing-point. But no one seemed to be in charge, unless it was the KNLA. No Thai police or military were in evidence, suggesting that things were left to look after themselves – another extraterritorial corner like Mae Saam Laep. Closer inspection, however, revealed individuals discreetly positioned, watching through binoculars. But were they plain-clothes *dorchodor*, or the KNLA watching out for Burmese soldiers, or smugglers checking that the coast was clear?

The gaunt old trader in the bazaar had said that we could cross to Po Pa Ta. So we went down to the bamboo bridge. This was in two sections, which met in the middle of the river on a sandbank. There seemed to be some kind of control post on the central islet. Stepping onto the first section of bridge, which creaked and swayed above the water, we arrived at the checkpoint. In a hut, half a dozen KNLA men were sitting around, armed with M16s. An older man, apparently in charge, was chewing betel, spitting out red saliva onto the blinding sand. We asked him if we could look at Po Pa Ta. That would be alright, he said, but we would have to pay a toll. We asked how much, expecting this to be a nominal 10 or 20 baht. One baht each, he replied. But we had to leave our cameras with them, another man ordered. We had already hidden our cameras in our bags and said we had none with us. Then, paying our princely one baht each, we made to continue. But it seemed a good idea, before reaching the point of no return, to find out how much it would cost to cross back and whether there would be any trouble with the Thai police. We had heard horror stories of travellers being forced by rebel armies to pay extortionate sums to return or having trouble with the Thai authorities for having illegally left and then re-entered the kingdom. The older man with the red-stained mouth shrugged his shoulders, saying that there would be no problem with the police. And to cross back over, he would ask us to pay another one baht each. It was for using the bridge.

Not entirely convinced, we clambered over the second span of bamboo bridge and stepped off, back already after only one day in Burma – or rather the Karen State. Looking back across the water to Thailand, we were struck by the strange thought that while we were in one country, our motorbike and luggage was in another. We also enjoyed the irony that, while people up at Mae Sai were being milked hundreds of baht by the SLORC for the dubious pleasure of looking round Takilek and saying that they had been in Burma, down here you could cross for precisely two baht or even for free. Although only a year or two old, Po Pa Ta was already relatively large. Of course, it was a refugee village, full of Karen and other victims of the Four Cuts. It was depressingly squalid, unexpectedly so for a *Yang* place. We tried to take photographs in the main street, but were immediately prevented by a number of people. They said it was for security reasons, but it may also have been because conditions made a poor advertisement for the insurgent cause. In Po Pa Ta, we found the black market. Along the central 'thoroughfare' of the settlement, some half-hearted shops sold, besides Thai products, Chinese goods and cartons of American cigarettes at 90 baht (£1.50) for 200, brands unobtainable in Thailand because of the government tobacco monopoly.

Two teachers took us in hand and showed us round. They spoke reasonable English and were not Karen, but dissident ABSDF students. The nicest thing to do at Po Pa Ta, they said, was to walk in the early morning or late afternoon along the Moei, where it flowed round in a great sweep before one particularly massive monolith. They showed us their school, inside which little groups of sweetie-pie infants where distractedly wrestling with the Burmese, Karen and English alphabets. But they wanted us in particular to see what was called 'the Library'. Of the school and the library we could take as many photographs as we liked. The library was really more a propaganda centre for the KNU and especially the Students' Front (see photo section). Here were stacks of back copies of the magazine *Dawn*, stamped on the front cover 'Ye Kyam Camp, ABSDF 207 Regiment'. The magazine was the official news bulletin of the students. It followed developments in the popular uprising, sought to boost morale, and kept tabs on the SLORC, detailing Burma army atrocities and defections. On the walls of the library were portraits of democracy heroine Daw Aung San Suu Kyi, as well as photo displays of KNU and ABSDF activities. Posters proclaimed OUR HEADS ARE BLOODY BUT UNBOWED and KACHIN STATE – OPIUM FREE STATE 1991. There was also artwork depicting a fighting peacock. This emblem, taken from the old student journal 'Khut Daung' (= fighting peacock) and much touted during the 1988 uprising, had become the logo of the ABSDF.

The guerrilla student teachers were likeable fresh-faced individuals, but there was also a certain hectoring cockiness about them, which endeared them to us less. One surveyed us the whole time from behind designer sunglasses. Whether it was to protect his identity or for preening purposes was not clear, but it was not something the Karen normally did. On our border journey, we came into contact with several ABSDF groups. A similarly ambiguous message came to us from them, too. Some students, in a depressed state, had taken to 'smoking', while others tried to sponge off us, one individual once stealing from us a bottle of Mandalay Rum. But it was difficult to be harsh with these boys. In the last analysis, theirs was a hard pitiful lot. Many were educated and from professional Rangoon or Moulmein families. They had witnessed such terrible things that they had been compelled to flee to people and places they had never seen before. After the first flush of anger and the elation at having linked up with sympathetic ethnic rebels, they had come to find themselves in impoverished jungle backwaters with no future prospect except the hopeless one of endlessly more of the same. For if they returned to their home towns, they faced years in prison or worse. When they had arrived, they had expected to find plenty of arms and Western support to further the struggle, but hardly any had been forthcoming. It was estimated that the majority of Front students in Kawthoolei had contracted the malaria endemic there, some dying of it. Caught between a rock and a hard place, and accepting that they were not cut out for the rigours of jungle guerrilla life, hundreds if not thousands had fled into Thailand, going underground, mostly in Bangkok (as we saw in Chapter

9). But there they had found no solution, either. Many had been rounded up by the Thai authorities, who found them an embarrassment, put into camps and repatriated to Burma, where they had gone to their deaths or an unknown fate. Recently, those who had remained with the NDF insurgents had become a source of friction. The students, with no funds or local livelihood, were an extra burden on already overstretched insurgent resources. Some rebel leaders had found them arrogant, mere guerrilla upstarts. One ABSDF deputation which had gone to Manerplaw to complain had been unceremoniously incarcerated. The dissidents had been rocking the boat. A few students had been suspected of spying for the SLORC and, "just to be sure", had been executed. Guerrilla leaders were coming to appreciate that the reinforcements which had at first been so welcome were increasingly a liability. They drew down on the ethnic armies especial Burma army venom. When we once made an excusion from Mae Or to Pang Yon (Chapter 8, end of Postscript, under KNLP), we found that the ABSDF 601 battalion camp there had just been 'vacated'. And when we asked the local Karenni Army commander why the students had gone, he told us simply that "they were no good."

❖

Between Po Pa Ta and Mae Sot there was still the little matter of some 110 kms, 70 of them through the mountains – an exhilirating if towards the end rather relentless ride. For some distance, the H105 pursued its course beside the Moei, while the Dawna outcrops on its western bank continued to rear up one after the other like an endless serpent's back. The villages of **Wa Kae Ra Ko**, **Mae U-Su** (with its cave nearby, to the west), **Tung Tam**, **Mai** and **Mae Tan** flew past. More sandbagged paramilitary BPP posts fished us up, some checking us, others not. One group of *dorchodor* were able to solve a little mystery for us. The strange succession of stagnant ponds we had seen on the east side of the road were places where experiments were being conducted with different strains of malarial mosquitoes. We encountered elephants. In groups of three or four and supervised by their mahouts, they were on their way to or from work, probably hauling Burmese teak. The lumbering beasts, chains jangling and a youth aloft each with red-stained mouth, were a reminder that we were still in the heart of Karen country. One oncoming tusker caravan provided a comic touch. As we rode slowly past, all seven, as if consumed with curiosity, pirouetted on the spot, ending up facing the wrong way, much to the annoyance of their scolding cajoling minders.

    Ampoe Ta Song Yang (almost 150 kms south of Mae Sariang) was a relatively large place (the district seat, not to be confused with Ban Ta Song Yang village further north). In this administrative centre lying just west of the road, we found a market, foodstalls and, at long last, the first petrol since Mae Sariang. More villages with magical names followed – **Mae Khamu Noi**, **Huai Nok Kok** and **Ka Nae Chu**. Near the latter, we finally emerged from the mountains, descending into a hot plain. The air was redolent with what seemed like the fragrance of oregano and oranges. Slowly the traffic began to increase. It was an uninteresting plain, stripped of trees as far as the eye could see. A left turn, the first side road going anywhere since Mae Sariang, was the H1175 northern mountain road east to Tak, the provincial 'capital', while two turnings on the right went into the small town of **Mae Ramat** (about 200 kms south of Mae Sariang town centre). After that, a wide speed road thundered through numerous outlying villages, in one of which a way went right (west) to Wang Kha and Kawmoorah, until (km 227, or c. 229 kms from Mae Sariang town centre) at a T-junction we hit the Pan-Asian Highway. At some time in the future, this massive road was supposed to link Singapore with Istanbul, if the many intervening countries could get their act together. At the T-junction, east went to the provincial 'capital' of Tak, and west proceeded a few kms to the settlement of Rim Moei, the Moei river and the border. Beyond the T-junction lay Mae Sot (centre: km 230), which, if you discount the small places of Pai, Mae Hong Son and Mae Sariang, was the only major town on the whole of our journey between Chiang Mai and the Three Pagodas.

✻

Mae Sot

We had always imagined Mae Sot (sometimes written 'Mae Sod') to be a small cool spot by a river, at the foot of some hills. Instead, we found a hot noisy dusty place in a featureless plain. Joe Cummings (of Lonely Planet guidebook fame) once described Mae Sot to us as the wildest, most lawless town in Thailand, the place in the kingdom least under central Bangkok control. It had the highest degree of corruption among its authorities and was in the grip of powerful local mafias. Many people still carried guns. And indeed, as we soon discovered, the town had an unmistakable wild-west atmosphere, a certain raw stimulating 'anything goes' edge. The reason was its function as the isolated pivot of the region's arms, gems and drugs business. No other town down the western frontier had profited more from the prolific cross-border trade of the 1960s, 70s and 80s. Channelled through Mae Sot on its way to Kawthoolei's Eastern Division and deeper into Burma, went M16s and AK47s, consumer goods, medicines and fabrics, while in the other direction came jade, rubies, heroin, opium, hardwood, cattle, antiques and foodstuffs, as well as cheap labour and girls. In town, the KNLA bought up dextrose-saline drips by the gross, while the numerous precious stones shops around the central *Siam Hotel* formed a gems centre in Thailand second only to Chantaburi. Mae Sot's two big cattle markets, one at the H105/Asia Highway junction and the other near Mae Ramat, dealt expressly in livestock that had made the long trek over the Dawna.

On our Honda, we scouted round our new port of call – no easy matter in the chaotic traffic-choked grid of one-way streets. The town seemed like a beefier glitzed-up version of Mae Sariang or the rich twin of swanky Loei over in eastern Thailand. The streets clotted around two main roads, running parallel through the centre on an east-west axis. The more northerly of these, the Intra Kiri Road (the one with the post office and police station), took vehicles from west to east, while the more southerly one, the Prasart Witi Road, drew traffic from east to west – at least that was the theory. The latter road was perhaps the real main drag of Mae Sot, identifiable by its midpoint *Siam Hotel* and bombastic *Thai Farmers Bank*. As we went round and round trying to get some orientation, interconnecting streets fleetingly revealed miraculous gold-covered pagodas, glowing in the late afternoon sun.

Mae Sot centre was brash, modern, Westernized and tangibly artificial. Here was the vulgarity, ambiguity and sleaze of a boom town. The streets were lined with spanking rows of shophouses, all gleaming white, as if cast in icing sugar. They were the epitome of that Thai speciality 'wedding-cake' architecture – pastiches of modernist, vernacular and neoclassical design. Every shophouse flashed chunky gold trading signs in four languages – Thai, Chinese, Burmese and English. And, indeed, Mae Sot was a cosmopolitan place. *Farang* aroused little interest here. Amid Thais from near and far, Chinese merchants, Muslim Indo-Burmese traders, Bangladeshi refugees, Karen jobbers, illegal Burmese workers, Hmong migrants and many others, Caucasians were just another group. Closer inspection revealed that the wealth-creating core was Chinese-dominated. Mae Sot oozed money. Parked in front of the gem dealers, wholesalers', bakeries, supermarkets and department stores were flashy top-of-the-range Volvos and Mercedes. The liquor stores were piled high with Scotch whisky and French brandy, and in one shop we could find English toffees, but no mosquito coils.

Curiously for such a metropolis, it was not easy to find anywhere suitable to stay. There was plenty of luxury accommodation for the wealthy trader, and a number of unspeakable doss-houses, but not much in between that was pleasant, modest and clean. We thought we would give the renowned *N° 4 Guest House* a try, situated out at the western end of town (why are so many guest houses in Thailand called 'N° 4' – an allusion to the white pure N° 4 heroin?). Here, in a wooden building set in mediocre surroundings, the personnel were friendly and helpful, but the atmosphere did not appeal to us. It seemed too self-consciously laid-back, threatening to turn into a slummy semi-hippie commune. Leaving *N° 4*, we almost went to the other extreme. We decided to try the *Siam Hotel*. They had some fair-priced rooms, but unfortunately, owing to some conference or fair, these were all taken. We were deliberating in the lobby about splashing out for once on an expensive room when our minds were made up for us. Suddenly, a boy ran past and out of the front door with his hands, shirt and trousers covered in blood. He rampaged around the car park half demented – screaming, trying to staunch the flow of blood with his shirt, and vowing to kill someone inside the hotel. We learned that in the kitchen the cooks had been fighting with meat cleavers.

Back in the Intra Kiri Road, we pulled up to have another look at the guidebooks. Stopping near the post office, we noticed by chance a place called *Old House*. It looked like a guest house, but we could not be sure. At that moment, a *farang* walked out of the entrance. He confirmed that it was indeed possible to stay there. And so it was that we stumbled on the nicest accommodation we ever found in Mae Sot. Set well back, *Old House* was separated from the traffic-congested road by a deep front garden, full of flowers, bushes and creepers. Immediately in front of the house was an idyllic little beer area, covered over with a pergola. True to its name, the guest house was a sizeable old wooden building, and like all these old teak places, had that characteristic hot dusty smell that comes from dried-out teak planking, but also from the town dust that has seeped in through the cracks. The rooms and bathroom inside were basic, but the restaurant was quiet and dignified, and its atmosphere magical.

The date of that first visit to *Old House* was the evening of 8 February 1990 – in the event a fateful night both for the region as a whole and for the local Karen insurgents in particular. Having cleaned up after the ride down from Mae Salid, we sat in the restaurant. After the fare of Mae Salid and Manerplaw, the food and drink was most welcome. The tables were low, and guests sat at them cross-legged on cushions, on a polished teak floor. A demure round-faced Burmese girl brought the dishes, kneeling at the side of each table to serve them. Somewhere someone was gently strumming an acoustic guitar. At the next table, a single *farang*, in his late thirties, sat alone. We thought no more about him, and in fact, with our spirits restored from the supper, went out to stretch our legs after the ride on the Wing.

A short way beyond the guest house, there was a Chinese brothel. The entrance to this small ramshackle wooden building was lit by two dull red Chinese lanterns. Outside, from a trestle table, an old woman was serving an assortment of fortifying spirits and elixirs. In the glass jars were murky concoctions such as snake whisky and centipede wine. These were to give punters courage to cross the threshold and, once across, to get up their virility. A tremendous noise was coming from somewhere nearby, and it turned out that a fund-raising festival was in full swing in the grounds of a temple-monastery. The temple, Wat Manee Prai Son, housed one of the glowing pagodas we had glimpsed earlier. It was a large bell-shaped *chedi*, set on a square gold-tiled base and covered in mini pagodas. Near it squatted an ample smiling 'Happy Buddha', complete with belly button. In the monastery compound, an open-air cinema was projecting some gruesome film, while on the sidelines, incongruously, a troupe of Burmese dancers was performing to traditional music. From all around came the sound of competing rock bands. In the middle of the hurly-burly, monks, installed high up on the golden pagoda, were hauling a gilt rooster up a wire by means of pulleys. People put offerings in the rooster, which the saffron-robed bonzes then received at the top. A large number of surly drunken people were hanging around, people were brawling, and dogs were snapping and snarling. It was a sinister aggressive atmosphere, which seemed to prefigure the events of later that night.

Back at *Old House*, we found the lone *farang* still sitting at his low table. He was Thorben, a Danish guy. He had a military background, had once been a captain in the Danish army, and had worked as a military advisor to the Iraquis in their war with Iran. He seemed to us a sort of educated Rambo character, who preferred semi-military clothing, talked a lot, and had a thirst for adventure. He was interested in crossing illegally into Burma "for the hell of it", and had a plan to boat on his own down the Mae Khong (Mekong river). Thorben had a headful of ideas, but lacked specific direction. We, on the other hand, had a specific plan (to continue on south down 'Death Highway' to Um Pang), but, not having met anyone who had done this or who could tell us anything sensible about it, were lacking in courage. So it was as if we were all made for each other. He would get his concrete goal, and we would find the moral support we were looking for, in the form of a man with substantial military experience.

While we were talking deep into the night, laying plans and questioning the owner of *Old House* about hiring a second motorbike for our new Danish friend, we suddenly became aware of the heavy crump of mortarfire and the crackle of machine guns a few kms away. We looked at each other in alarm, but the owner said that this just happened from time to time. It was the Burmese fighting again with the Karen on the border. However, this was no ordinary skirmish. The fighting continued for hours. Thorben, assaying the timbre and magnitude of the explosions like a connoisseur, kept muttering things like "82-mm mortar" and "heavy artillery". All night long, the ground shook under *Old House*. What with a full-scale battle raging not far away, too much whisky coursing through our veins, the headiness of the plan to go down 'Death Highway', the fatigue from a long day, and the oppressive heat of the teak bedrooms, sleep was impossible.

During that night, Burmese government forces, as part of their most massive Four Cuts offensive against the Karen to date, attacked and overran both Palu, not far south of Mae Sot, and Kawmoorah, the Karen stronghold just north. Set just inside Burma, Kawmoorah lay (as indicated in Chapter 9) opposite the Thai village of Wang Kha, with the River Moei flowing in between. Rangoon had good reason to want to seize the stronghold. For years, Kawmoorah had been Karen supremo Gen. Bo Mya's 7th Brigade base, and for years, since as far back as 1965, it had been one of Kawthoolei's most significant trading and customs posts. In its heyday, up to 1,000 head of cattle and 1,000 porters a day had passed through on their way over the border, generating by local standards a stupendous income in taxes. Bo Mya had even set up a special KNLA 101 battalion to guard the customs gate. It was in Kawmoorah also, two years before this assault, that the ABSDF, so hated by Rangoon, had been founded. The outpost had been attacked before (just as it would be assaulted again, in February 1995 – see Chapter 9, Postscript, Karen rebellion update), but on each occasion the Karen had been able to repulse the Burma army. Now the situation looked much less favourable.

While some *tatmadaw* troops pounded Kawmoorah with mortars and heavy artillery, others, in an attempt to encircle the KNU stronghold, used Thailand (with the tacit support of the Thai army, led by the since discredited Gen. 'logger' Chaovalit) to attack the camp by the back door. In what was euphemistically described as a 'fighting spillover', hundreds of SLORC soldiers twice crossed the Moei into Thai territory, precipitating the flight not just of thousands of Karen refugees, but of hundreds of local Thais. The Karen, temporarily driven out, mounted a counter-attack, fighting the Burmese on both sides of the border. They managed to cut off the retreat of numerous SLORC troops, inflicting heavy casualties and leaving many dead. In Wang Kha alone, the BPP found next day 19 Burmese and six Karen dead. The newspapers reported that altogether more than 60 people had lost their lives that night. Three captured Burma army officers and five 'porters' were later taken down to Rim Moei (opposite Myawaddy), to be returned to the Burmese side, while the inhabitants of Wang Kha began filing demands for 20 million baht as compensation for their destroyed village.

The following day, Karen rebels returned to Kawmoorah with captured weapons and munitions. Unfortunately, the Burmese, in their retreat, had left a booby-trap bomb. It exploded, killing 33 KNLA guerrillas – one of the worst single death tolls of the whole Karen insurgency. Ultimately, Rangoon did not take Kawmoorah in that offensive, nor did it capture it in the following fighting (dry) seasons. But it did capture Palu, as were soon to discover (Chapter 11). On a less momentous but hardly less sinister note, there was another sequel to the events of that night in Mae Sot, which concerned *Old House*. Returning another time to town, we were disconcerted to discover that we could not find the guest house any more. Were we dreaming, or had we imagined it to be somewhere along the road where it was not? Enquiries revealed that the fine old teak building had burnt down in mysterious circumstances. Someone thought that the owner and his wife had gone to Laos. With a new 'wedding-cake' block (possibly today's *DK Hotel*) going up on the garden where the magical old lodging had once stood, we could not banish the depressing thought that the teak building had been deliberately torched to move the owners on – an arrangement of affairs Mae Sot-style.

✼

Rim Moei

For the traveller, Mae Sot was essentially a place either to be enjoyed for its atmosphere or to be used as a springboard for explorations north and south. But we spent a pleasant afternoon down at Rim Moei (= Moei river bank), the settlement a few kms west of town where the Asia Highway stopped short at the Moei and the frontier. On the far bank lay Myawaddy, one of the very few places along the whole of the Thai-Burmese border firmly – at that time – in Burmese hands (like Takilek opposite Mae Sai). That might not always be the case if the Karen ever manage to retake it, as they once tried in 1974. Then, in a pincer movement which turned into the biggest battle in the Dawna region since the Second World War, the KNU and its allies attacked the outpost from Kawmoorah to the north and Palu to the south. But after five days of savage fighting, the 1500-strong insurgent force was unsuccessful and withdrew. Sometimes, there was a footbridge across the river at Rim Moei, but we found none. We heard reports that occasionally it was possible for *farang* to cross to inspect Myawaddy, depending on the whim of the Burmese authorities. Another rumour was that Rangoon was contemplating opening up Myawaddy to tourist trade, in the manner of northerly Takilek. But from the Thai bank, there did not seem to be a lot to see across the water, and in the early 1990s Myawaddy's significance was in serious decline. Between 1991 and 1992, the value of Thai products entering Burma along the Mae Sot/Myawaddy corridor slumped from 712 million baht to 463 million. From newspaper reports, we learned of Thai-Burmese plans to construct a bridge at Rim Moei (a counterpart of the Thai-Lao Friendship Bridge at Nong Khai, over in eastern Thailand), and at the time of writing work has probably started on it (more below under Postscript).

At Rim Moei, we found a scaled-down calmer version of the frenetic Mae Sai/Takilek crossing. No frontier control posts were apparent, and yet official-looking people were hanging around on both sides, keeping an eye on things. Despite the absence of a bridge, a steady trickle of locals was passing to and fro. Nearly all were humping great packages of goods. A dozen longtail boats were moored at the river bank, and people were either using these to have themselves ferried to Myawaddy, or were simply wading across the 20 metres of thigh-deep water. On the far bank, we could see, besides the jetty, a *wat*, a school, a market, some grass-roofed houses and a lot of bamboo fencing. Much of the fencing was covered with blankets and clothing, drying in the sun. On the Thai side, a permanent market, consisting of a street of stalls, sold Burmese goods, but also Thai products required by the Karen and Burmese across the river. Imports from Burma included bags of dried prawns (not cheap), dried fish, cashews, quails eggs, bone chopsticks, jade and other gemstones, cottons, carved wood, lacquerware and kitschy souvenirs. From Rim Moei, people were taking over to Burma wholesale parcels of T-shirts, plastic bags, fabrics, Coffeemate, sugar, condensed milk and other household items.

Enjoyable down at this sleepy crossing point was just to sit and watch the leisurely goings-on. A makeshift money-changing stall was dealing in outsize 'Myanmar' notes of all colours. Women and children, in *longyis* and with gold discs of *tanaka* on their cheeks, were portering bales, sacks and boxes on their heads this way and that. An old Burmese monk (eyebrows not shaved off, unlike Thai monks), carrying a broad fanlike object to shade himself from the scorching sun, was being ferried in style across the Moei like some Chinese emperor. A wizened old lady, with a complete mini restaurant on a tray on her head, went to join him in the boat. Naked boys were cavorting in the river. Dogs stood barking at the little waves. White cows were strolling around. A black-faced man, with a pagoda tattooed on his chest and some Buddhist emblem emblazoned on his back, took to the waters, swimming past the longtails. And the youths of the gaudy *hang yao* idly tweaked the throttles of the boats' outsize engines, making a gratuitous roar of noise.

✳

A hearty meal before 'Death Highway' seemed a good idea. But if Mae Sot was not bursting with good places to stay, surprisingly it was not overloaded with great restaurants, either. The night market along the main Prasart Witi Road had numerous eating stalls, but the food was inevitably snacky, and none of them sold alcohol, so people did not linger after eating. An exceptional stall was the noodle place outside the *Thai Farmers Bank*. This mini triumph of pavement food was a feast both for the eyes and palate. An outstanding display of prepared vegetables in a glass cabinet spoke of the tasty noodle dishes to come. And behind the mobile stand, at a wobbly folding table, we once enjoyed the best *pat thai* we found anywhere in Thailand. A mixture of fried ribbon noodles, dried shrimps, chopped scallions, egg, crumbled peanuts, soy sauce and pepper was served with a side salad of fresh beansprouts, spring onions, cabbage, sprouting banana pods, and a sprig of basil.

But the best meal – and also finest evening's entertainment – we ever found in Mae Sot was at a place called *Nueng Nut* (= N° 1 Girl). Located near Wat Manee Prai Son, this ranch-style restaurant, complete with waggon-wheel decoration, was a typical Thai 'singing place'. People came here to eat and celebrate, but they also came to be entertained by the *nakrong ying* and *nakrong chai* – 'singing girls' and 'crooning men'. Here we found the good if rather pricey food we had been looking forward to ever since *Intira* in Mae Sariang. Relays of teenage Mae Sot waitresses, earning pocket money after school, brought plates and dishes while a three-piece band warmed up on stage. Savoury beef (from the Burmese heartland), stir fried in oyster sauce, was accompanied by a wonderfully fragrant *tom ka gai* – a soupy chicken curry served up in a 'steamboat'. In the steamboat, glowing charcoal, placed in a central 'funnel', continued to simmer the curry at table in a 'boat' surrounding the steaming funnel. The lemony coconut sauce yielded up nuggets of chicken breast, shallots, mushrooms, lemongrass, sliced red chillies, galangal, kaffir lime leaves and other intriguing titbits. And our glasses were continually topped up with Mekhong whisky, soda and ice by the assiduous schoolgirls.

The songs in these singing restaurants were mostly lugubrious Thai ditties, not at all appealing to the Western ear. But not at *Nueng Nut*. As the evening wore on, the singing and dancing grew ever more spirited. Neither were the singing girls (and boys) the usual wilting Siamese flowers. They were the raunchiest, most vivacious *nakrong* we saw anywhere in the kingdom. It was all another sign of Mae Sot's grittiness. Considering the fact that within earshot Rangoon's war of attrition against the Karen was entering a crucial phase, it also seemed like part of some gay apocalypse. At *Nueng Nut*, there were nine singing girls and two crooning men. They were accompanied on stage by the little band, consisting of drums, synthesizer and guitar. Each singer came on in turn to sing a couple of his or her own chosen songs or old favourites suggested by the guests. Halfway through the evening, the girls came on to sing together (see photo section), and the culmination of the night's entertainment was a suggestive song and dance routine with all nine *nakrong ying* in a line, like chorus girls. There was the languid sulky miss (much beloved of Thai men), her glossy black hair all dolled up like a film star. There was the impish little goer, perfect in all her parts, with a round face, huge mischievous mouth, tiny pussycat nose and charcoaled eyebrows. There was the leggy Karen teenager, slightly aloof, with her slender immaculate body ridiculously revealed in a red tutu. And there was the 30-year-old mum, busty, fetching, squeezed into a white dress with a flared skirt, good-natured and entering into the spirit of things.

The mum's dress had red hearts sewn all over it, another girl's blouse was see-through, and the teenager's panties were clear to see. Obviously, the function of the singing girls (and men) was more than just to sing. They paraded themselves on stage in their frilly, slinky or downright erotic outfits partly to create a floor show, but also with a view to catching the eye of the diners. And, indeed, most *nakrong* were also call-girls. However, the prostitution at a singing restaurant was not the blatant seedy kind found in massage parlours or girlie bars. Things were discreetly arranged, and outwardly everything was innocuous enough. This was why such places were frequented also by female customers, indeed whole families. The men at this table were perhaps having a night on the town, but the lady teachers at that one were celebrating a promotion. The couple over here were eating out, while the family over there was making merry because it was someone's birthday. Singing places were an integral and authentic part of Thai life.

The relationship between *nakrong* and diner was such that if a singer sang well or tickled the fancy of someone at table, the diner bought a jasmine garland and placed it over the singer's head. A popular *nakrong* often had a number of such perfumed garlands around his or her neck. The singer noticed where the admirer was sitting and, prompted by an invitation passed up from the floor, came down to join the diner at table. Often matters went no further than this, but if *nakrong* and music-lover wanted to take the singing a step further, they went off together at the end of the evening, perhaps to a motel on the outskirts of town.

Revisiting Mae Sot a year or two after that first visit, we looked in again at 'N° 1 Girl'. The place was still flourishing, although prices had risen uncomfortably. Alas, every one of the nine singing girls who had pleased us so much was gone. We produced some photographs, which caused a stir among the staff. It transpired that this girl had gone to Bangkok, while that one was now singing in Khorat, and a third was in Kampaeng Pet. The only *nakrong* who was still in Mae Sot was the impish little goer, who was pregnant! The new singing girls at *Nueng Nut* were somehow not as inspiring as their predecessors, and temporarily the star of 'Girl N° 1' was on the wane. However, another singing restaurant had opened in a side street nearby. With equally fine food, better prices and good girls, it was the new hot spot. For the time being, the real singing continued there...

✻ ✻

Postscript 2002

As indicated in Chapter 9, it has been impossible since January 1995 to travel by longtail boat from Mae Saam Laep to Manerplaw and then on to Ban Ta Song Yang (Map 20) because the DKBA and the Burma army have seized Manerplaw and because especially the DKBA controls the west bank of the Moei from the Salween confluence down to Ban Ta Song Yang, making any such double trip highly dangerous and probably impossible. Thus readers wishing to retrace the Mae Sariang/Mae Sot leg of the journey in this book, even if they can visit Mae Saam Laep and perhaps get as far as the Moei/Salween confluence, cannot currently and for the foreseeable future travel the Mae Saam Laep/Ban Ta Song Yang stretch. Nor should they attempt to do so, which could cost them their lives. Instead, they must reach Ban Ta Song Yang by travelling on Highway 105 from Mae Sariang via Sob Moei and Nam Ngao villages. I know that that is no substitute for the superlative adventure of boating a long way down the frontier River Moei. Nevertheless, be consoled that the route from Mae Sariang to Ban Ta Song Yang and beyond is highly scenic and interesting. Altogether, the 230-km-long stretch from Mae Sariang to Mae Sot is one of the greatest rides that you can make in Thailand. The way is paved throughout, except for patches where the road is being remade (a frequent occurrence), is lonely and exposed in places (very few villages between Sob Moei and Ban Ta Song Yang, and little traffic throughout), is nevertheless safe at the time of writing (although unsafe at night), and is now regularly travelled by *silor*, so that you can now ride it with public transport. The orange pick-ups leave Mae Sariang bus station every hour and charge about 100 baht to halfway Mae Salid (journey time 3 hours) and 150 baht to Mae Sot (allow all day) – some *silor* go as far as Mae Salid, others the whole way. Depending on the local military situation, which can change from month to month, reckon on encountering Thai army/BPP checkpoints down the H105, which are not interested in frustrating you for the sake of it, but only in your safety. Here are some updated and completer route details for the H105, starting with the Mae Sariang/Ban Ta Song Yang leg, which I noted down when I last made the journey in January 2001.

Route detail: Mae Sariang – Sob Moei – Nam Ngao – Ban Ta Song Yang

From the centre of Mae Sariang, proceed a couple of kms E up the town's long main street (the Wiang Mai Road), past *Intira Restaurant*, the post office and *Lotus GH* (all R), almost until you hit the H108 Mae Hong Son/Chiang Mai highway. At a complicated junction, go R into the start of the H105 road, marked by a waiting hut on the left side

km 0.0 Start of H105 Mae Sariang/Mae Sot road (now see Map 20)
Immediately cross big bridge over the River Sariang, I think
You ride out on a flat road through villages

km 12.4 Big village
Flattish road continues a long way
The river down R is the River Yuam, which flows into the Moei near Manerplaw

km 25.0 **Sob Moei** village and *ampoe* (district). Sob Moei, which means 'Moei confluence', is nowhere near the real Moei/Salween confluence, which as we know lies quite close to Mae Saam Laep

km 27.4 Start of a climb up over a shoulder
Corkscrew down to bridge and river (the Mae Rit river)
Sob Moei Highway office (R)

km 32.9 Begin to climb up again, through fine forest, then down again to

km 39.5 **Nam Ngao** village and bridge over the Ngao river. Near the village (beyond it, offroad L, I think) is *Nam Ngao GH*, which is connected with *Northwest GH* in Mae Sariang. It would make a nice tranquil place to stay (120 baht/night). At Nam Ngao bridge, you leave Mae Hong Son province and enter Tak province, which stretches all the way S to Tung Yai Naresuan Wildlife Sanctuary, S of Um Pang
Climb up into mountains on twisting narrow road, with impressive mountain views L

km 49.9 Karen village of **Mae Wa Luang** (R), with its school and health centre (both R). If you have never explored a Karen hill village, take a look at it or at Mae Om Ki further down the road. It is possible that Mae Lamaluang refugee camp lies near Mae Wa Luang. In 2000, it housed some 8,000 Karen refugees mainly from the Manerplaw area. Manerplaw is located WSW not so far from the village

SINGING GIRLS

	Hamlet offroad R
km 53.1	Way L for village of Mae La Ki (2 kms)
km 57.3	Karen village of **Mae Om Ki** (R) – take a look
	Pass through great flora
km 61.3	Way R to villages of Pang Tong (3 kms), Ka Noe Ko (3 kms) and Mae Sa Pao (8 kms)
km 64.6	Hamlet up L
km 68.3	Way R, near km-marker 161, to Mae Woei village (12 kms offroad)
km 69.3	Army checkpoint and houses
km 76.3	By km-marker 153: reforestation place (R) and maybe a *wat*
km 77.4	Along this stretch: magnificent jungle and forest (R) with orange-flowering trees (in January/February)
	You ride over the brow of a hill to encounter stunning views ahead of mountain ridges, including the Dawna range, receding into Burma/Karen State
	Down a long way
km 86.3	A rather weird inconguous place (R), called 'Pa Pa Valley Recreation, Coffee Break and Resthouse'
	You come down off the mountains to the valley floor of the River Moei
km 91.4	Side road R leads through an imposing portal 1 km to **Ban Ta Song Yang** or Ta Song Yang village (as distinct from Ampoe Ta Song Yang or Ta Song Yang district, which lies a further 55 kms further S, at km 146.2). Looking in here in January 2001, we found a situation that was defused and relaxed compared to the tense atmosphere encountered nearly a decade previously (New Year 1993/94). All was quiet and very picturesque down on the beach by the Moei, but there were no longtail boats there because it was too dangerous for the KNU Karen boatmen to go either up- or downriver, on account of DKBA attacks from across the water. At both the police station and the health centre, people said that the Burma army had a position on the top of the towering mountain directly opposite Ban Ta Song Yang, while the DKBA held sway to the N of the mountain (downstream), and the KNU controlled terrain S of it (upstream). Here, therefore, was a pocket of Kawthoolei still in the hands of the KNU.

Route detail: Ban Ta Song Yang – Mae Salid

km 91.4 Route detail and km-readings continue from junction of H105 and side road/entrance to Ban Ta Song Yang (now see Map 21). From Ta Song Yang village onwards, the snakelike wavy-backed humps and peaks of the Dawna range shadow the southbound road and also the River Moei, which for almost the next 40 kms, until about Mae U-su village, runs close to the H105 on its R side. It is breathtaking magical scenery. Since early 1995, the H105, from N of Ban Ta Song Yang to S of Mae U-su, has been subject to repeated cross-border raids by the DKBA, who have attacked and robbed villages, police boxes, refugee camps, shops and travelling vehicles, killing many Karen people, policemen, drivers and Thai tourists. I have specified some of these raids in Chapter 9 (Postscript 2002, under Karen rebellion update, DKBA activities). The attacks account for the high level of security down the stretch. At the time of writing (2001), the situation had eased and the security been scaled down. Nevertheless, as you travel, you may come across Thai army or police roadblocks, which might check you. Be guided by common sense and circumspection on this questionable stretch, as you should in all sensitive border areas in Thailand.

km 97.4   **Nam Ork Ru** (Nam Aug Roo) village, offroad
km 101.4 **Huai Ma-nok** village, offroad
km 102.9 **Huai Mae Nin** village, offroad
km 104.4 **Ko La Haeng** village, offroad
km 108.6 By km-marker 120: **Mae Salid Noi** (Mae Sarit Noi) or 'Little/Lesser Mae Salid'
km 113.5 Centre of **Mae Salid Luang** (Mae Sarit Luang) or 'Big/Greater Mae Salid'. In the centre, a way L goes steep uphill, past some little shops, 100 m to *Mae Salid GH*, while to the R of the H105, both here and a bit further down, there are a couple of eating places, some shops, and a fuel booth.

Mae Salid

When we revisited the village in January 2001, we found that hardly anything had really changed there. It was still just a small trading place, truck stop and *silor* interchange, with many downtrodden refugee Karen eking out an existence. Things seemed quieter, lower-key, than before, but that might have been because the bustling central market (W side of road) was missing. Whether it had stopped altogether, or whether it had been market day at the time of our original visit, while on our revisit it was not market day, I do not know. Remarkably, in 2001, there was still no electricity in Mae Salid, which meant that there was no street lighting at night, no refrigeration in the shops (meat, vegetables and beer were kept cool in giant plastic iceboxes), and no power in the guest house, where after dark everything had to be done by candlelight or with torches – romantic for some.

At the back of the central market area, diagonally opposite the way up to the GH, there is an eating place selling the usual stuff (noodle soup, fried rice etc.), which also has cold beers in an icebox if you fancy some of an evening at the GH. Beside the restaurant are a couple of stores. Further down the road, opposite the H1267 side road for Mae Ramoeng, there are more such places. One is another little restaurant, there are more shops, and you can tank up at a petrol booth. At the far bottom end of the set-back row of places, you can find what is left of the local market run by Indo-Burmese Muslims. As described in the main text above, this used to be an impressive bazaar, located a few kms S of Mae Salid, beside the highway and opposite Po Pa Ta village and black market in Burma. In February 1998, I found that it had been moved from there N to Mae Salid, where it still thrived. But in 2001 it was much reduced to just a pale shadow of its former self, to merely three or four stalls.

This may have had to do with a raid on the Muslim bazaar and other shops in the row, which occurred in March 1998. One night, at 1.45am, a group of about 30 suspected DKBA men, thought to be led by Capt. Maung Tin Aye and brandishing M16 and AK47 rifles, M79 grenade launchers and RPG rocket launchers, crossed over the Moei from Burma, surrounded this lower market area and robbed it, even though a BPP and ranger position lay only one or two hundred metres away. From four stores, they stole cash, 200 watches and other merchandise worth more than 500,000 baht, also injuring the market's security guard, a man called Tapi, before they fled back to Burma. It was reported that Maung Tin Aye had earlier sent threatening letters to the market merchants demanding protection money.

In 1998, the Thai military position lay halfway down the road that leads from the centre of Mae Salid to the river. It was a fairly substantial affair, with a sandbagged guardhouse, a barrier and soldiers checking everyone who went up or down the road. In 2001, this was gone, and the street was given over again to numerous cattle pens and the poor straggling Karen huts each side of the road. Instead of the checkpoint and encampment, there was a small-scale observation post, manned by a couple of soldiers, down by the Moei, overlooking the river and beach. Here, a dozen longtail boats lay moored, women and children were washing in the water, and some men were fishing from dugout canoes in the river. If you can make it down to the Moei at Mae Salid, you will be pleasantly rewarded. The river, wide here, flows round a great bend, backgrounded by impressive peaks of the Dawna Range. You can swim, wash or take a walk along the river bank. It is a picturesque atmospheric spot, reminiscent of the beach and river at Ban Ta Song Yang, where the emerald-green Mae Moei is equally resplendent.

Little had changed either at *Mae Salid GH*. Here, numerous Karen boys were still hanging around, one of whom said that the place was owned by some military guy in Mae Sot. There was a dormitory and half a dozen other simple wooden windowless rooms. The bedrooms had meanwhile acquired some enormous crude pallet beds with mattresses, big enough to sleep six side by side, but the washing facilities remained parlous. The food was unchanged – chicken in coconut curry sauce with potato, stir-fried vegetable, and rice – but it was now served from a fine big teak table in the lobby. In 2001, I paid 70 baht for my room, and the evening meal was 40 baht (actually a bargain). At the front of the GH, by the entrance stairs, you can wash through your clothes, as the Karen boys do. On the attractive balcony, they explained that the KNU held land opposite Mae Salid, and that the Burma army as well as the DKBA were positioned nearby. Here again, therefore, the KNU Karen seemed still to control a pocket of territory in Kawthoolei.

Regarding the H1267 side road to Mae Ramoeng, the position had changed completely in 2001. What used to be a mostly poor road, very difficult in places, is now paved a fair way in, to Kiu Lom and beyond, perhaps all the way to Mae Ramoeng. If you have time, ride in, especially late afternoon (tank up in Mae Salid first if you plan to do the whole 70-km+ round trip). The corkscrew up at the beginning is tremendous, the roadside flora is marvellous, and from a couple of viewpoints there are some great vistas of Burma and its receding mountain ridges, stunning at sunset. But a section of Mae Moei National Park has now been established in here, complete with office buildings and a checkpoint. If you want to venture further along the road or even to the viewpoints, which now lie in the park, you must pay an entrance charge of 40 baht. Mr Narong's *Chao Doi House* is defunct, closed down because it lay within the national park. From Mae Ramoeng, I once trekked on my own (with two Karen guides) four days to Om Koi town, one of the most adventurous things I have ever done in Thailand. I did not see any poppy fields in the wild mountainous hinterland, but I was struck by the huge number of illegal Karen immigrants from Burma who were settling there. Because Mae Moei National Park has been set up in this area, it is unlikely that any road will ever be built through from Mae Salid to Om Koi.

Route detail: Mae Salid – Mae U-su – Ampoe Ta Song Yang – Mae La refugee camp – Mae Ramat – Mae Sot

km 113.5 Route detail and km-readings continue from centre of Mae Salid Luang (Map 21).

km 114.3 Junction and police box. The H1267 side road L goes into Mae Moei National Park, to the Karen village of Mae Ramoeng, and to other villages, while straight on continues S towards Mae Sot. A brief account of the status quo up this side road has just been given

km 119.8 Village of **Mae Song** (L) with bridge over River Song, which flows into the Moei. After Mae Song, on the R/west side of the road: the site of the former unofficial bazaar and, beyond it, across the Moei river in Burma, the location of former Po Pa Ta village and black market. The bazaar was moved N to Mae Salid, as we have seen, where it dwindled. I have not checked, but Po Pa Ta has almost certainly been razed to the ground, and the bamboo bridge will be long since gone. No more little flits into Burma here. Most of the Muslims from the bazaar will now be in Mae La refugee camp (see below), as will the KNU Karen of Po Pa Ta. The Po Pa Ta ABSDF students may be at Mae La, but they could also be in the refugee camp near Mae Khong Kha, where some Burmese students are said to be housed, or in Maneeloy holding centre, or perhaps in hiding in Bangkok. Fabulous motorcycling road swings down valley, passing

km 129.7 **Wa Kae Ra Ko** village (R)
km 134.0 Near km-marker 94: way R to Mae U-su Cave and another part of Mae Moei National Park
km 135.1 **Mae U-su** (Ou-su) bridge and village
km 139.4 Village of **Tung Tam**
km 142.9 **Ban Mai** (New Village)
        Mae Tan village
km 146.2 At a junction, a side road goes R/west to **Ampoe Ta Song Yang** (Ta Song Yang District, not to be confused with Ban Ta Song Yang village further N), while straight on continues S on the H105 towards Mae Sot. If you go about 2 kms away from the main road into Ampoe TSY, you can find some eating places, especially near the market
        Mae Khamu Noi village
        Huai Nok Kok village
km 167.7 Start of giant **Mae La refugee camp** on R/west side of road
        Around roadside km-marker 58: centre of camp and entrances to it

Mae La refugee camp

As you approach this camp on the H105, both from the N and the S, you pass a series of military checkpoints, barriers and security posts, an indication of the number of people in it and of the importance of the camp. And as you pass it, you cannot fail to be impressed by its sheer size. From one end to the other, it stretches for 3.7 kms (nearly 2½ miles) and contains thousands upon thousands of leaf-roofed bamboo huts. This is not so much a camp as a village or, rather, a town, stuck out in the middle of nowhere. The camp, which is so called because it lies in *tambon* Mae La (Mae La precinct), but which is also known as Bae Ko camp and possibly as Huai Kalok camp, is surrounded by a fence that is broken by numerous entrances, each marked by a guardhouse, manned by Thai soldiers. You cannot get past these guards unless you are an official or aid worker, or unless you have acquired a pass from the district office in Mae Ramat.

The camp has at least 30,000 refugees in it and maybe up to 50,000, making it one of the largest, or even the biggest, in Thailand since the wars and upheavals in Indo-China, when huge numbers of people fled Vietnam, Laos and Cambodia to seek refuge in the country, to be housed in vast camps. Behind (west of) the camp are cliffs (part of the Dawna Range), to the rear of which lies the Moei river and border. Burma is apparently only 3 kms away as the crow flies. Across the frontier, the Burma army and DKBA are now in control, no longer the KNU. As we saw earlier, it was the DKBA which at least twice attacked Mae La camp, first (in January 1996) killing an elderly senior KNU official in a failed abduction attempt, and then (in March 1998) shelling the camp with ten mortar rounds (details: Chapter 9, Postscript, Karen rebellion update, DKBA activities).

Despite the security measures, Doug and Andrew and I wanted to go into Mae La camp and look around when we passed by in January 2001. However, we did not feel like going some 30 kms to Mae Ramat district office, trucking with *ampoe* bureaucrats, getting a pass, wasting a lot of time, and then returning 30 kms to Mae La. So we scouted round some of the entrances until we noticed one where the guards were absent. Its barbed wire-festooned gate was slightly ajar, and we slipped in, expecting to be challenged at any moment and thrown back out. But nobody came or said anything, although our presence caused astonishment and quite a stir among the inmates. So we looked around, went in deeper and deeper, still encountering no opposition, and observed the huts as well as the people, who were washing, or cooking, or doing their laundry. Finally, we got into the market area, which was a labyrinth of alleyways full of shops, tea houses and eating places, run almost exclusively by Muslim Indo-Burmese, a few of whom perhaps came from Po Pa Ta bazaar. We tried to ask people questions about the camp and taxed some Muslim men in a tea shop, who, we felt, must surely speak a few words of English. But they spoke no English and no Thai either. The camp inmates were, indeed, people from inside Burma and not so much from the polylingual border area.

Finally, someone went off to get an inmate who could speak English and help us. A young teacher called Zo Dteng turned up, who taught in the camp and spoke reasonable English. He showed us round part of the camp and the market area (see photo section). He explained that the camp was full of people from Burma, who had fled first the *tatmadaw* and its offensives against the KNU and the Karen, and then the DKBA. The camp housed mostly KNU Karen, Muslim Indo-Burmese traders, and a few ABSDF rebel students. A Thai guard at the perimeter said that the camp was seven years old, while the men at the tea house indicated 19 years or longer, which at first we did not believe, but which may well be true. Zo Dteng said that most inmates came post-1988, the year of the crushed democracy uprising in Burma. Even if Mae La was functioning all those years ago, it must be that most of its refugees arrived in the wake of the fall of the Manerplaw area in January 1995 and of the fall of Kawmoorah the following month, as well as after the SLORC offensives against KNU 6th Brigade area in February 1997. It is difficult to imagine what it must be like to live so long among so many people, in such a confined space, unable to go out much or to do work. But at least the refugees must be fairly safe. The children go to school, and the adults pick up handouts from aid agencies or trade with each other, using partly Burmese money, but mostly Thai. Most of the inmates are Christian, and there are over ten churches in Mae La camp, although there are also Muslims, who use four mosques, and Buddhists, who make their devotions at two Buddhist temples.

km 171.4 End of Mae La camp
km 179.9 Police box/checkpoint in nice cool spot, backed by cliffs
          Ride through hot flat plain
km 192.0 At junction: road L/east is H1175 for Tak. Continue straight/S for Mae Sot
km 193.4 First of two side roads L/west for **Mae Ramat** town
km 226.9 T-junction (with Shell fuel station L) and end of H105 Mae Sariang/Mae
          Sot highway. Go R and then L to bring you towards Mae Sot centre

Mae Sot
In early 2001, the town seemed bigger, more developed, and even more prosperous than some ten years previously. I had forgotten, too, just how many Muslim Indo-Burmese and Bangladeshis lived there, or perhaps more had arrived meanwhile. A whole town quarter, lying south of the Prasart Witi Road, was teeming with them. Here, throngs of men in white gowns, with skullcaps and black beards, went on errands, clinched deals, ran shops, sat in numerous tea houses and congregated around their mosque. Actually, Mae Sot is roughly divided into three layers. To the north, lies a Thai-Buddhist quarter, the centre is dominated by the Chinese, and the Muslims reside

to the south. In this southern quarter, behind *Siam Hotel*, there is a big, bustling and interesting day market, well worth visiting. Near this hotel, in the Prasart Witi Road, there are several gem shops and bazaars, which mill with multi-ethnic gem dealers from all over, who spill out onto the pavements, where ruby inspections, haggling and dealing continue. These days, a fair trickle of *farang* travellers get to Mae Sot. Although hectic and confusing at first, it is a place that grows on you as you invest more time in it. You can fly into/out of town four days a week from/to Bangkok, and there are air links with Chiang Mai. Thai Air has an office at the western end of the Prasart Witi Road, beyond *Siam Hotel*. Every day, three or four VIP and aircon overnight buses leave Mae Sot for Bangkok between 9 and 10pm (fare about 420 baht), and there is even an a/c bus plying the long route between the western border town and northerly Mae Sai, which goes via Chiang Mai and Chiang Rai.

In the middle of the Prasart Witi Road, on one corner of a crossroads, there is a motorcycle hire shop (160 baht/day or 120 baht per day if you rent for 7 days). However, I can hardly recommend it, as its bikes are mostly in poor condition, and because we had trouble with the Chinese owners, who unjustly accused us of – and tried to charge us for – bike damage that we had not caused, but which was already on the machines. Better to hire a good motorcycle in Mae Hong Son or even Chiang Mai and ride it to Mae Sot. In the evening, food stalls still line parts of the Prasart Witi Road, and a whole new section of the night food market lies in an alleyway running south from this road. If you fancy *farang* nosh, better than the long-established *Pim Hut* is a more recent Canadian-run restaurant also in a cross street between the Prasart Witi and Intra Kiri Roads, which serves very good Western and Thai food.

On the accommodation front, Mae Sot is still poorly provided for in terms of guest house-type places to stay. I have long since given up staying in the chaotic *N° 4 GH*. *Mae Sot GH*, way out east along the Intra Kiri Road has gone downhill. Apparently run by a couple of couldn't-care-less girls, its rooms are overpriced. For 100 baht, you get a horrible chicken-hutch box at the rear with a fan and outside washing, while 280 baht gets you a very poor, run-down aircon room with no hot water, indeed almost no water at all, and no wastepaper basket – you get the picture. *Bai Fern House*, a guest house with a restaurant towards the western end of the Intra Kiri Road, looks promising, but we could never get a room there, and the proprietress came over as too hard-sell for our liking. The characterful Chinese-style wooden *Suwannvit Hotel*, round the corner from the post office, and in a side street between the Intra Kiri and Prasart Witi Roads, has many rooms (150-200 baht/night with fan and cold water), but is relatively sordid and partly run by a lofty freakish woman. Unless you want to go upmarket, perhaps to *DK Hotel* (opposite the post office), probably the best deal in the end is *Siam Hotel* itself. Here, you can get a big fan room with cold water for 200 baht. It has the virtue of being central, in the heart of the action, and you can spend happy hours in the lobby or coffee shop/restaurant watching the many wheeler-dealers who congregate there.

Rim Moei

To reach it, go W up the Prasart Witi Road and continue out of town, past *N° 4 GH* (right), until you hit the big Pan-Asian Highway, where you bear L and proceed a few kms to Rim Moei and the border. *Silor* go there for a few baht from the town centre. Visiting the place in early 2001, I found it completely transformed and unrecognizable, relative to the position a decade earlier. The little market on the Thai side had turned into a whole new small town, and the compound on the Burmese side with the grass-roofed huts had likewise burgeoned into a small town. The two communities were connected by a massive new concrete bridge, arching high over the river, overshadowing the shallow water that people used to wade across as well as several sandy islets. The bridge, which is similar to the Thai-Lao Friendship Bridge across the Mae Khong (Mekong) at Nong Khai, was started around 1993, but work soon broke off because of disagreements about the boundary in the Moei river. In 1996, construction was restarted and the bridge eventually finished. It has a vast approach boulevard, reminiscent of Mae Sai's main street running up to the Mae Sai/Takilek border bridge. Huge lorries, laden with logs, come across the bridge from Burma into Thailand, and the pavements each side deliver up into Rim Moei a stream of Burmese peasants in *longyis* and with *tanaka*-smeared faces. On the Thai bank, to the N and S of the bridge, there is now a market area even more extensive than before, with dozens of stalls and eating places. You can browse among fake jewels, wooden furniture and other artefacts, before taking a Coke at a table overlooking the river. Right down by the water, among the dunes and reeds, there is a little slum area and black market, where people come rushing to sell you cartons of cigarettes and bottles of whisky. On the Burmese bank, new waterfront houses and warehouses drop straight into the river, swarthy kids swim from a promenade and beach, and on rocks women beat washing, which they then dry out on the bank, while longtail *hang yao* motor up and down the Moei. A pagoda is visible, and everywhere a hotchpotch of peoples come and go. Looking at this tranquil quotidian scene, it is difficult to imagine that just a few years ago Thai and Burmese troops confronted each other at Rim Moei in a tense stand-off, which closed the bridge and border for some time, all because of some absurd dispute about one of the sandy islets. Latterly, it has been possible for *farang* both to visit Myawaddy, across from Rim Moei, for the day and to extend/renew their visas there, rather as is usually possible in Takilek (opposite Mae Sai), assuming the bridge and border at Rim Moei are not closed because of friction between the Thais and Burmese, which occurs on a rather regular basis.

11

DEATH HIGHWAY

Mae Sot – Saw Oh – Pop Pra – Wa Lay
&
Saw Oh – Rom Glao N° 4 – Mae Klong Ki – Um Pang

The next leg of our journey was to take us further south down the Thai-Burmese border on Highway 1090 to Um Pang. Of all the trips we made on the Honda Wing, this 165-km run was the most varied and exciting – without doubt the finest ride in Thailand. A real roller coaster of a road plunged through stunning mountain and jungle scenery. Completed only as recently as 1987, the road surface was already badly deteriorated in places, adding to the excitement. Route 1090 had the alarming popular designation of 'Death Highway'. This was because during its construction a number of workers had been killed in two infamous massacres. Communist Party of Thailand guerrillas hiding out in the jungle had wanted to prevent the intrusion of the road. By the early 1990s, the area was quieter, and these days, as Joe Cummings says in his Lonely Planet guide, the route earns its nickname more from its treacherous steep twists and turns, which give rise to numerous accidents. A notorious recent example was when in early 1995 a bus from Bangkok's Santa Cruz school crashed, killing 30 teachers. However, there were other reasons why the route deserved its name. In the border areas west of the road, Rangoon continued to wage its ruthless long-standing war of the Four Cuts against the Karen people, depressing signs of which we encountered as we passed. The lonely road was preyed upon by robbers, leaving the few who ventured down the 100 miles of obscurity with a nagging feeling of unease. Specifically for us, 'Death Highway' also earned its reputation because of a fatal accident we witnessed near the beginning, and because of a certain incident offroad at Wa Lay...

Our Danish friend Thorben rustled up a Kawasaki 100, which looked so puny and beaten-up that we feared it would never make the journey to Um Pang, let alone back. We stocked up with provisions and also money. The shops in Um Pang, people told us, were very limited, and the next bank after Mae Sot was apparently (incredibly) in Tong Pa Poom, beyond the Three Pagodas and on the way to Kanchanaburi town. At the Shell petrol station sited at the far eastern end of Mae Sot's Intra Kiri Road, we tanked up, simultaneously setting our Wing's tripmeter to nought (see Postscript below for more precise and up-to-date route details). Within sight of the station forecourt, a right turn at the T-junction brought us onto the H1090 (Map 22). For some distance we sped southbound on a flat road through the plain of Mae Sot, until after 32 kms we arrived at a fork in the village of **Saw Oh**. Left continued on the H1090 another 130 kms to Um Pang, while right (H1206) branched off to the small district town of Pop Pra and the border village of Wa Lay. We decided to interrupt our journey to take in Wa Lay.

Fourteen kms down the H1206 side road, **Pop Pra**, really just an extended village, was suspiciously rich-looking, with many splendid new teak houses. It was easy to see why. Just outside was the biggest log depot we saw anywhere down the border. Precious teak trunks from Burma were piled up as far as the eye could see. There were possibly millions of them. Immediately, we understood the truth of what Martin Smith has said about the indescribable destruction of Burma's virgin forests hereabouts. He reported that in one forest reserve alone (near Palu/Wa Lay), which he visited in 1989, over 100,000 trees had been cut down – all as a result of the million-dollar concessions SLORC had sold to Thai logging companies under a greedy, shameful, ecologically disastrous scheme architected by Gen. Chaovalit. It was a depressing sight. But that was not all. The land all around Pop Pra itself was devastated, no doubt first logged and then subjected to extensive slash-and-burn. In a scene reminiscent of a First World War battlefield, charred tree stumps smouldered in acres of ash. This kind of burning often meant that Hmong people were nearby. And, indeed, the whole of Pop Pra district was full of them. Many had been resettled from villages around Um Pang – a relocation policy still in operation at the time of writing (1995). It seemed a pity that, in order to preserve the national parks and wildlife sanctuaries further south, whole landscapes had to be spoiled in the north.

For a few kms the H1206, by now a poor metalled road, proceeded through this forlorn countryside, before giving over to a dust track. On each side of the track were strange compounds. The buildings inside them were barricaded behind wire fencing and wooden palings, or screened from view by bushes. Nameplates at the entrances, discreetly indicating 'Muang Pon Co.' or 'Zilar International Trading Co. (Zitco)', gave away the occupants' business – logging. West of the road, in the distance, our old friends the Dawna mountains began to loom up. Over there, in Kawthoolei, KNU 7th Brigade area (Papun-Pa'an) was yielding to that of 6th Brigade (Duplaya). We passed a turning left to the border villages of Ya Po and Mae Ork Hu. Finally, some 57 kms out from Mae Sot, we came up against a barrier. Beside it was a checkpoint, and behind that lay a fortified BPP camp. We had reached the entrance to **Wa Lay**.

Wa Lay

The BPP soldiers wanted to know our business. We said we wished quickly to visit Wa Lay. Unaccountably, they laughed out loud, adding that a visit was out of the question. Often, these soldiers tried more to discourage *farang* from going to sensitive border villages, rather than actually prevent them, so we persisted in our attempt to get past them. However, this time they were adamant. That was a pity, not just because we had wasted time and effort coming along the dusty bumpy track, but because we had heard that Wa Lay was an interesting and important smuggling village. In fact, it faced across the border the Karen village of Palu, another major gateway (like Mae Saam Laep, Kawmoorah and the Three Pagodas Pass) to the Karen State. Traditionally, the way through Wa Lay/Palu had been the main route for Karen and Thais alike to Um Pang. Passing through a corner of Burma, it had been a short cut which had obviated the long roundabout way through Thailand on the (at that time unmade) 1090 road. Once, I think, it had been the only way from Mae Sot to Um Pang and vice versa.

Such a short cut was now impossible, the *dorchodor* explained, because the Burma army in its latest and most massive sweep up the Thai-Burmese border had just captured Palu, in fact only the night before. We reflected: first Kawmoorah overrun; now Palu gone; and, as we subsequently discovered, the Three Pagodas Pass also lost, all of them at the same time – the writing really was on the wall for the Karen. Just as Rangoon had been greedy for Kawmoorah, so it had also wanted Palu. This stronghold had been the very first of all the new Karen customs gates that had been opened to profit from the burgeoning cross-border trade of the 1960s, 70s and 80s. Established in 1964 by KNU 6th Brigade commander Shwi Soe, it had grown, like the other gates, into a thriving centre with an extensive 'black' market. There had been shops, streets, houses and timber mills, all overlooked by a wooden temple and a large white pagoda on the hill just behind the KNU base. In 1985, the Burmese had executed 40 'smugglers' near here, hoping that the example would stifle Palu's trade and also stop revenue flowing to the KNLA. In 1986, they had surrounded the outpost, burning down the timber mills a year later. In 1989, dissident ethnic Burmese student soldiers had been deployed at Palu, and now in a swingeing night-time assault the village had fallen (early February 1990). The problem was, the BPP continued, that the Burmese had not just captured Palu, but were claiming Wa Lay itself, even though the village clearly lay on the Thai side of the border river. These disputes over villages or pieces of land along the frontier occurred regularly. They arose because, with the exception of some 58 kms, the 2400-km-long Thai-Burmese border had never been clearly defined. Four treaties applied to the long frontier, including a British-Thai one of 1868. Of course, when the Burmese seized a piece of Thai territory, they backed up their claim with some old colonial map showing things in their favour. This was the basis of their pretence not just to Wa Lay, but also to the famous Three Pagodas.

Owing to the events of a few hours earlier, therefore, the situation in Wa Lay was extremely tense. All the Karen of both Palu and Wa Lay had fled, in fact everybody had fled except a few local Thai people in Wa Lay (the Palu Karen were later housed in Mawkier/Mor Goe refugee village). Presumably the Thai inhabitants wanted to look after their property and felt that the SLORC troops had no quarrel with them. Even the police and military had evacuated, withdrawing to this safer position two kms behind the village. Their instructions were not to tangle with the *tatmadaw*, to keep a low profile, and to fire only if fired upon.

The gravity of the situation was borne in on us by the presence at the checkpoint of three utterly dejected Burmese men. They were pressganged porters, who had somehow managed to desert during the night-time battle from the Burma army and had been captured by the BPP on Thai territory. They were in fear of their lives, for if the *dorchodor* returned them, they would be shot on sight and dumped in the river. None of the ten young BPP boys seemed to know what to do with the black-faced, unshaven, *longyi*-clad men. Obviously, the porters could not be returned to Burma, and yet they could not stay in Thailand, either. They had no money and could speak no Thai. The soldiers for their part could not speak any Burmese, and so communication was all but impossible. It seemed that the three porters wanted to go to Mae Sot, and the BPP were prepared to let them go, except that the men would never get past the other checkpoints on the way. For the moment at least, the *dorchodor* chain of command seemed to have broken down. But in the end, the porters would be taken to Mae Sot and returned to the other side at some safer point further up the border.

The thrill of a genuinely extraterritorial Wa Lay made us (foolishly) all the more keen to go down there. We fraternized with the BPP boys for half an hour and then badgered them again to let us go down to the village. It was too dangerous, they said. Much as the SLORC army hated the Karen, it hated *farang* even more, whom it took for spies or agents helping the insurgents. Two *farang*, a girl and a boy, who knew the locality well, on both sides of the border, had gone down to the village a couple of days earlier, but had not returned and were now presumed dead. And recently a Western TV unit, which had come to film the Karens' plight, had been shot at, with ten people injured. We asked the soldiers if they would come down to the village with us, forming an armed guard. They would not, they answered, and when we asked why not, they confessed that they were simply too scared to go.

Finally, the checkpoint guards relented. They said that we two men, Thorben and I, could go down on our own and at our own risk, but that, if anything happened to us, they would know nothing about it. We should not stay any longer than five minutes, we had to leave all our valuables at the checkpoint, and we must sign the duty book. So we divested ourselves of passports, money, cameras, backpacks and jackets, and entered into the logbook our names, nationalities and the exact time of our departure. Then, saying goodbye to everyone at the checkpoint, we set off on the two bikes. It was exhilirating riding unemcumbered down the dirt track to Wa Lay, but, while for the Danish army captain it might have been just another routine sortie, for me it was also terrifying, and I trembled like a leaf.

We rode into a street lined with low wooden houses. They were deserted, and the place seemed like a ghost village. At the bottom end, a narrow river was visible immediately behind the houses. All along its rim and in the gaps between the houses were rolls of gleaming new butterfly barbed wire. The rolls had been put there after the *farang* couple had disappeared. An old man came out of a house and said that we could get a better view round at the market place. We rode warily through the empty alleyways until we found it. It was a dusty square that sloped down to the river. A number of local Thais were standing around there, chatting but watchful. Their faces showed great surprise when they saw us. There was something eerie and chilling about this small market place, so we turned the bikes around, parked them facing uphill, towards the village exit, and left the engines running. In the middle of the square was a military post, surrounded by sandbags, but there were no faces at the observation slits. All round the square, where it bordered the river, ran the same coils of barbed wire. Behind the wire, a small footbridge, consisting of a wooden gangplank, crossed the meagre river, which was the Moei, I think. It was blocked in the middle by a boarded-up gate. Some wag had attached to this obstacle a nude pin-up of a Thai beauty queen. It was a strange conjunction of mortal danger and beauty – death and the maiden.

On the other side, just a few feet away, SLORC soldiers were roaming around. Three were loitering on the bridge itself, relaxing after the fury of the night assault. They were tall thin men, wearing ragged uniforms, belts laden with pouches, grenades, water bottles, knives and the other paraphernalia of war. One had a beaten-up straw sun-hat, and another a red bandanna, which was pulled tight behind his head in a knot. They looked a duplicitous semi-hippie outfit. Of course, they all spotted us immediately, and on seeing the *farang* stirred into activity. Inexplicably, many seemed to walk away, perhaps to go and get guns. Thorben chose this moment, of all moments, to go down to the water's edge. It seemed to me that we had already stayed too long and that we should get back to the idling motorbikes. Concerned, I asked him what he was doing – did he want to look into the faces of the *tatmadaw* fighters eyeball to eyeball? Back came the unconcerned reply that he only wanted to see what the fishing was like. Just then, there was a terrific explosion, and Thorben, myself and all the villagers were showered with water and mud. Someone on the other side had lobbed a grenade, but it had hit the barbed wire, falling back into the river. The villagers shouted "Get down, get down", and themselves lay flat in the dust. But it was not my idea to wait for a second attack, so I ran to the bike, jumped on it and retreated to a safe distance, there to wait for the Dane. I saw him go to his bike, get on it – and then stall the engine! In that burning sun-bleached square, he kicked at the baby Kawasaki for a good half minute. Finally he came up the hill, and we rode straight out of the village. "What was the hurry?" he said above the din of the engines. "They were trying to kill us", I shouted. "They were fishing with grenades", he replied. "A strange way of fishing", I retorted. "More like they were fishing for you!"

The BPP boys and the others back at the camp had heard the explosion. They all thought we were done for. In spite of what they had said, they sent out a rescue party. Two soldiers immediately came down to the village on motorbikes. But because we rode a different way out of Wa Lay from the way we had come in, they did not meet us. Soon we reached the camp again, much to everybody's relief. The two soldiers quickly got the story that we had not been captured or killed and also returned to base. We thanked them for their efforts and sheepishly gathered up our possessions. Then we rode back to Pop Pra and the fork in the road at Saw Oh village. It was the end of the little ill-advised side-trip to Wa Lay and our encounter with the Burma army.

❈

'Death Highway'
'Death Highway' proper began back at the junction of the H1090 and H1206 roads (km 32). The road headed east over a plateau, past villages, houses,

experimental farms and agricultural research projects (Map 23). Through the heat haze, mountains began to appear in front of us. Not far down the road, we found a sign pointing left down a track to Pa Charoen Waterfall. As the fall was near the road, we decided to have a quick look. We were not disappointed. It was a multi-cascaded fall with dozens of tiers and basins. But the best thing about Pa Charoen was a little mobile foodstall at its foot. The owner prepared for us an excellent *somtam*, a refreshing salad of grated green papaya, tomato, raw green beans, lemon juice, dried shrimps, shrimp paste, peanuts, garlic, fish sauce, fresh palm sugar and a prise of deadly 'mouse shit' chilli peppers.

Following Nam Tok Pa Charoen, the H1090 continued straight and long through a blisteringly hot plain of burnt fields and tree stumps. It was another environmental catastrophe up here. In every direction, the denuded shimmering beige landscape receded as far as the eye could see. The occasional charred tree trunk made the plateau look as if it had been the scene of a nuclear attack. It was the worst ecological devastation we had seen anywhere in Thailand. This depressing setting was the home of most of the Rom Glao villages hereabouts.[1] These were three settlements (two Hmong and one Chinese, I think – there was a fourth further down the H1090), all with the same name, but distinguished by a different number. Hmong **Rom Glao N° 1** greeted us first (km 45), soon followed by Chinese **Rom Glao N° 2** (km 48), but Rom Glao N° 3 we never found – perhaps it lay offroad or in the mountains. As at Pop Pra, the land had been devastated partly through logging, and partly through slash-and-burn clearance to make room for crop growing. We hoped only that the numerous agricultural projects and research farms strung along the road would somehow manage to reverse the despoliation.

It was in the midst of this desolate landscape that we came upon a tragic accident. From a distance, we saw a couple of pick-ups parked oddly at the side of the road. Some figures stood huddled near one of them, and as we approached, the story of what had happened began to emerge. There were the tell-tale long black skidmarks veering off the road, a mangled bicycle on the asphalt just beyond them, and a woman lying across the centre of the road, with a pool of blood coming from her head. She was dead. She lay face down, her hair flopping onto the tarmac, an arm up around her head as if to shield herself from a blow. What made the situation all the more unbearable was the fact that it was obvious she had died only a minute or two earlier. Her body was no doubt still warm. The bystanders seemed instinctively to know this, because they kept their distance, as if recoiling from some ambiguous object. No one had the courage to go and cover the woman up. Even passing vehicles gave her a wide berth, creeping round by her feet on the scrub verge. Her loneliness out there on the road in the sun was absolute and terrible.

Our horror began to turn to anger – anger that one of these pick-up drivers, either through speeding or drunken driving, had so casually obliterated a life. But then it occurred to us that the woman herself might have caused the accident, perhaps wobbling out of a side track into the road, not so much as

---

[1] There are numerous villages in Thailand with the name of 'Rom Glao'. They would all seem to be refugee or resettlement places because *rom glao* in Thai means something like 'umbrella shade' or 'umbrella over head', i.e. 'shelter' or 'refuge'.

giving a glance to see if the way was clear – as people so often did in Thailand. And then our anger gave way to a sense of waste, of futile loss. This woman, no doubt a wife and mother, had got up this morning as usual, but by lunchtime was dead, while her husband and children, still unknowing, were probably working in the fields.

Thailand was famously a country full of *sanuk* or fun, but there was also no shortage of death. Like two sides of the same coin, they often seemed locked together in a kind of gay Siamese apocalypse. In the kingdom, the visitor saw a delight in eating, drinking Mekhong, conviviality, going places, doing business, developing tourism and patronizing singing girls. But the pleasures had a darker side: hedonism, alcoholism, exploitation, pollution, logging, environmental destruction, graft and corruption, and AIDS. Sometimes it was difficult to escape the impression that a charming, affable, almost childlike people was cheerfully bent on self-destruction, careering down a larger 'death highway', lacking in common sense and self-control, self-indulgent and avaricious. It was a situation reflected in miniature on the roads. Carefree self-centred drivers, like children with a new toy, hurtled down an asphalt death highway, grinning behind the wheel. In 1991, some 25,000 people died in the country in traffic accidents (the majority motorcyclists), making death on the roads the number two killer in the land of smiles (second only to death from heart disease). One person died in a car or motorcycle accident every 21 minutes, like this young woman near Rom Glao N° 2. Life was cheap (8,000 baht one person told us), so why worry too much? And, anyway, did not Buddhism teach of reincarnation and many more lives to come?

The Rom Glao area was also the site of the two massacres that had taken place during the long construction of the H1090. According to contemporary newspaper reports, some 30 roadworkers were attacked and killed at km-marker 43, apparently by Thai, Hmong and Karen CPT insurgents wanting to stop the road from penetrating Um Pang district (one of the main communist strongholds in Thailand in the 1960s and 70s). The attacks were one of the factors which had delayed completion of the road for so long. Following them, the Thai authorities deployed anti-communist KMT forces from places like Kae Noi to guard the project and its construction workers. The security situation was alleviated in 1982-83 with the mass surrenders in Tak province of hundreds of heavily-armed communist rebels and thousands of sympathizers. Nevertheless, until the late 1980s, when 'Death Highway' was finally finished (a decade late), the CPT remained active in the region south of Mae Sot.

Our minds full of all these unsettling thoughts, we headed into the mountains. The road swung left and then right, ascending rapidly. Most of the traffic stopped on the denuded plateau. Anything still continuing was probably going right through to Um Pang. It was a creepy little road in poor condition. It skirted steep mountainsides, which dropped away to streams in valley clefts, hundreds of feet below. Mysterious footpaths branched off to each side, disappearing in the vegetation, only to reappear much higher up or much lower down. Soon we emerged into grassy upland country. Magnificent views opened up on all sides, with wooded hills and valleys receding like the waves of the sea towards bluish ridges on the horizon. The road snaked along mountain saddlebacks, dipping up and down between scrubby bald hilltops. In the end, it was not the plateau of the three Rom Glao villages which we found the most sinister section of 'Death Highway', but this first mountain stretch. Back at Pa Charoen Waterfall, the *somtam* lady had spoken of a robbery that had occurred the previous evening at a viewing pavilion on a hilltop up here. Now we came to the *sala*, involuntarily shivering as we rode past. Far and wide, there were no signs of human habitation. The only people for long distances were parties of careworn Hmong, beating brushgrasses at the roadside and laying them out to dry on the hot asphalt. They did not even look up as we passed.

Around km-marker 80, on a steep ugrade, we rounded a corner to find a brand-new pick-up upside down in the water drainage channel on the inside of the road. The driver, coming too fast down the other way, had evidently lost control on the corner and crashed. He was lucky that he had not gone over the edge. Strangely, his shiny pride-and-joy was being guarded by a wandering monk, who was perhaps unhappy about seeing the truck abandoned. The highway at this point had been gouged out of the rocks of the high mountainside. Soon it rounded a spur and presented us with a completely new vista over a broad secluded valley. Down a series of hairpin bends, we rapidly lost height, to roll into **Rom Glao N° 4** (km-marker 84). This shabby Hmong settlement (the fourth and last of the Rom Glao villages), which was sited exactly halfway between Mae Sot and Um Pang, was where everybody, *silor* included, stopped for a rest or a snack. Most of the village lay to the east of the road. An enterprising Hmong family had set up a makeshift canteen there, and passers-by could get a noodle soup or a drink. When Thorben and we arrived, it was well past lunchtime, and the noodle soup was all gone. However, the friendly stallholders soon cooked up three packets of Ma-maa instant noodles, adding any scraps of leftover vegetable and meat they could find. There was always a camaraderie among the people stopping at this canteen, as if to say "we are all adventurers down 'Death Highway' together".

A road sign just beyond Rom Glao N° 4 said 'Ampoe Um Pang 80 Kms' – not so far, apparently, and yet there was another cool 50 miles of steep mountain and jungle road to go, virtually uninhabited until the run in to Um Pang. Two or three hours of hard riding still lay ahead. Fortunately, the road surface was better after the halfway village, and for a while we swung speedily down the valley. Somewhere along here, a 6-ft-long brown snake slithered across our path, just before the front wheel. It was not the first time that this had happened. The snakes always seemed to wait until we were upon them, before darting across. It was an unnerving experience, which again sent cold shivers up our backs. Obviously, at speed no sudden evasive action was possible. The vision flickered through our minds of what would happen if we ran the serpent over. In its agony, it might writhe up and bite us in the ankles.

Snakes were not the only problem. On one isolated stretch of jungle, we rode into a swarm of bees. Stopping precipitately to flick them off our clothes and hair, we had the uncanny feeling that we were being watched from out of the green-gold wall either side. Were not those two spots of dappled sunlight the eyes of a tiger staring out unblinking, and was not that trembling leaf the faintest switch of a tail at the end of its motionless body? The air of the impenetrable undergrowth seemed to bring us an acrid smell, redolent of the fell of wild boar or big cats – the sour smell that assails you in certain corners of zoos or circuses. We hurried on our way. The road wound on through more jungle and new mountains. Progress was slow, the bikes began to heat up and we to tire. The strategy of the highway seemed an odd one. It did not follow the valleys, but preferred to skim from mountaintop to mountaintop. There must have been a logic in it. A rare track east (km-marker 94) was signed **Mae Klong Noi**, at km 100 we came to a checkpoint, and shortly after it another way went east to **Mae Klong Yai** (*noi* = small, *yai* = big).

Somewhere along this central section, we passed a pick-up with a dozen Hmong men aboard. The vehicle struck us as odd because it was just sitting at the roadside. The men were neither relieving themselves, nor gathering anything, but just waiting. The ones in the open back of the truck were wearing those black balaclavas which leave nothing of the face showing except the eyes, which watch out through a slit. Their sinister appearance did nothing to alleviate our fears. After we had passed, we noticed in the rear-view mirror how they pulled out and began to follow us. They shadowed us for a long way. Mostly they kept a short distance behind, but sometimes, on the steep climbs, we could pull away and get clear of them. However, on the next level piece of road they caught us up, or even overtook us. When that happened, we dawdled to let them get well ahead. But then, just when we thought we had shaken them off, we would round a corner to find them parked, as if waiting for us. Thoughts of an ambush began to nag us, and we could not rid our minds either of the massacres of years gone by or of the robbery of the previous night. Once we stopped for a longer time to definitively lose them. But when we started off again, there they were the same short distance ahead.

After a bridge over the River Mae Klong (km-marker 106), the big climb began. Up and up the road went like a corkscrew, necessitating frequent changes down into first gear. Wafts of heat rose up from our engine. We were crossing the biggest and last ridge before the descent to Um Pang. Another checkpoint greeted us (km 116), after which the road entered elevated rainforest. If the first section of 'Death Highway', up to Rom Glao N° 4, was the most sinister, this stretch was the most beautiful. As we passed from open sunny patches to dark corners, the roadside vegetation alternated between rank brilliant green foliage and cool damp recesses of dark evergreen. Massive trees rose up, standing silent, dripping, covered in lianas, moss and other epiphytic plants. Peering anew into this dense jungle, we could once again almost see the glint of amber eyes and smell the fetid exhalations of forest beasts. Our increasing tiredness from the ride, our fear of the Hmong, and the coldness both from the altitude and the rainforest made us tremble on the bikes, almost uncontrollably.

The breaks between the trees revealed marvellous views west of forested mountains, rolling uninterrupted and uninhabited, like a green carpet, right across into Burma. Suddenly, coming round from the cold shady side of the ridge (now see Map 24), we emerged into the sun and onto a short stretch of high-level road (c. km-marker 126). It was a pass, the highest part of the journey, and the most impressive piece of Thai roadbuilding we had yet encountered. A ledge had been carved out of the rock just below the ridge crest. Cautiously, it bore the narrow road around the curves of the mountainside above a precipice falling away several hundred metres on the east side. In places the roadside was unprotected, and a wrong manoeuvre here would have spelt certain death. With a queasy feeling, not looking left over the abyss, we edged forwards, hugging the inside (wrong side) of the road, hoping that no vehicle was coming the other way. In a little lay-by right under the rock face, we parked the bikes and walked on unsteady legs to enjoy the view. To the south-east also, mountains rolled away into the far distance, blanketed with virgin forest. Looking south, we could see the last 40 kms of 'Death Highway' heading off into flatter land. The route glittered silver in the sun like a river, before vanishing in the heat haze.

After the big climb: the great descent. With a series of sharp twists and turns, the highway ran down and down a spur of the ridge. The heat of the afternoon came up to meet us. Finally, the road bottomed out in the valley of the River Mae Klong. Crossing the river, we arrived at **Mae Klong Ki**, a Karen village on the eastern side of the road (km 132). While we were coming down the last hill, our Danish companion suddenly called out to us. He was out of petrol. He pulled in the clutch, coasted over the river bridge and came to a stop right outside the entrance to the village. The little Kawasaki 100 was out of fuel, and in the middle of nowhere! Certainly there was no fuel station at Mae Klong Ki. We looked at each other with consternation. Time was getting on – it was already late afternoon – and there was still 30 kms to go. On the other west side of the road, we saw a lot of building going on. Then we noticed that, facing this, on the far side of the river, there was an army camp. We recrossed the bridge, went to the guardhouse, and explained the position. The guard said that they had no petrol for us at the camp, but we could probably beg or buy some in the village. We asked about the housebuilding opposite. It was a brand-new Karen refugee camp, still in the process of being set up. The guard offered to show us round.

Everywhere men, women and children were busy fetching and cutting up bamboo poles, plaiting wall panels, thatching roofs, and hammering and sawing. In the centre of the compound stood a communal shelter. Besides being a kind of meeting place, this housed all the community's sacks of rice. Several battered pick-ups were parked around it. With the help of the Thai soldier and the leader of the group, we pieced together the refugees' story. A month earlier, when the Karen feared another Four Cuts offensive, they had sent a 'spy' to Mae Klong Ki to sound out the possibility of using the village as a fall-back position. When things had become dangerous, the women and children, together with the food supplies, had come on ahead. The men had arrived just a day or two before our visit, fighting a rearguard action as they came. This accounted for the fact that every one of these handsome friendly men looked utterly exhausted and dejected. The SLORC troops had chased them across the border to here, even though it was several kms inside Thailand. To prove the point, the men showed us bullets in the coconut trees. It was the same sad story as at Kawmoorah and Palu/Wa Lay. When things were quiet again on the other side, the Karen leader said, the refugees would return home.

THREE PAGODAS

We thanked the Thai soldier for his trouble and went across to the real village, on the left side of the road. In Mae Klong Ki, we found people willing to sell us petrol. Thorben bought a couple of litres, measured out in old Mekhong whisky bottles. With the aid of a plastic funnel, we poured the red liquid into his completely dry tank. Coming down off the mountain into the Mae Klong valley was like dropping into a different world. And, in fact, we were entering Um Pang Wildlife Sanctuary. At the village of **Wa Kru Ko** (km-marker 140), there was another checkpoint, which constituted the formal entrance to the sanctuary. Here we made as if to pass, head ducked, under the half-raised barrier, but the soldiers manning the box insisted that we sign our names and nationalities into a duty book. A sensational karstic landscape unfolded before us. To the left and the right of the road, the hilly wooded countryside was punctuated with needle monoliths, hundreds of feet high. These jagged grey Ratchaburi (also called Kanchanaburi) limestone outcrops were partially covered with trees, bushes and creepers, giving them a hirsute appearance. Many were bizarrely eroded. The effects of water and weather during their 350 million-year history had left them with clefts and pockmarks, fissures and caves. One monolith with a cave stood directly at the roadside.

Near the Karen village of **Wa Koei Ta** (km-stone 145), we found a *silor* parked by an isolated roadside dwelling. Stopping to check the distance to our destination, we noticed cartons of dextrose-saline drips being unloaded from the vehicle. Opposite, an unmarked track disappeared into the scrub, heading west towards the border. The boxes would find their way up there to KNLA troops, wounded in the latest fighting. A string of small villages ran south down the valley – **Pro Pa Do**, **Mai Pa Ka**, **Mae Klong Gao** and **Mae Klong Mai** (*gao* = old, *mai* = new). A turn-off west by the checkpoint at this last place was the beginning of the old way up from Um Pang to Mae Sot passing through Nong Luang, a spur of Burma and Wa Lay. There remained just one more village, **Mae Klong**, after which the H1090 passed a well-known local shrine on the right. It was the resting place of the spirit of a dead man, called Pra Wo. The custom here was for vehicles to toot their horns when passing, to say 'hello' to the man's spirit. We did so too, but out of relief that we had safely reached the end of 'Death Highway'. For almost immediately the road reached the brow of a steep hill and after 165 kms from Mae Sot town centre plunged down into Um Pang.

❃

Um Pang

Discounting Karen settlements deeper in the jungle, to the south, Um Pang had to be Thailand's ultimate remote village, or at least ultimate remote *regular* village. To go shopping in Mae Sot meant a two-day round trip, and anything not produced locally had to be hauled over the mountains and around Death Highway's 100 bends by truck or *silor*. For vehicles, there was no exit from Um Pang, so the way out was the way back. Tak town, the provincial administrative centre responsible for the village and local Um Pang area, was a cool 250 kms away, while Bangkok, although not so distant as the crow flies, could only be reached by a circuitous route indeed.

DEATH HIGHWAY

Until recently, Um Pang had been even more cut off. Tong Lor Toed Yotin, the old man who ran the telephone booth at the 'Five Ways' (that nodal point in the village centre where five streets met), told us why. Until 1987, when the H1090 was completed, it had been difficult to get there at all. He had moved down to Um Pang from Mae Sot in 1968. In those days there had been no road, not even a track. The journey had taken the 'short' cut via Wa Lay through Burma – a four-day walk on foot or by elephant, camping three nights in the forest on the way. In 1971, people had begun building a cart track south from Mae Sot, so that rice could be transported from Um Pang up to town in four or five days. In 1975, the first motorized vehicles had started using the new cart track. Work on turning the cart track into a proper road had been unusually slow because of local CPT guerrilla activity and because of the two massacres near Rom Glao village N° 2. As late as 1984, the 30-km route through Burma had still been in regular use, some people continuing to use it until, of course, it had been interdicted by the Burma army. In the rainy season, the new dirt road had often become impassable, leaving Um Pang cut off from the outside world for months on end. Finally, in 1987, 'Death Highway' had been metalled right through.

With the completion of the new road, Um Pang's first tourist visitors arrived. They were mostly just a few Thais wanting to view nearby Ti Lo Su (Tee Lor Soo) Waterfall. Local people also vividly remembered the first *farang* visitor, who came the same year. The number of visitors, both Thai and *farang*, had remained to this day a trickle. We estimated that during the clement season an average of one *farang* a day made it to Um Pang. Almost none came off their own bat. Nearly all arrived in small organized (and costly) parties, passing straight through the village to go trekking in the surrounding jungle or rafting down the Mae Klong river.

Um Pang village itself, with a population of 2000, was a sleepy little nest. It was one of those places, like Mae Sariang, which could grow on the visitor. A first stay perhaps disappointed. The thrill of the adventure down 'Death Highway' raised false expectations as to the excitement of the goal. But, of course, Um Pang was just another rural settlement at the end of the road. Even on a second visit, the village hardly overwhelmed. But to the patient visitor it eventually began to yield up its charms. As the romantic illusions fell away, its real self could start to speak. This magical corner, that droll character, or this unexpected detail delighted, and one wondered how one could have missed so much in the first place. The end of all our exploring would, indeed, be to arrive where we first started and to know the place for the first time, or, to put it another way, the secret of travelling was never to be in too much of a hurry. Given the chance, Um Pang could easily seduce for a week or two. Far from the madding crowd, it offered a tranquil little world all of its own. This isolated but intact Thai-Karen outpost, with its own feel and rhythm, offered nothing, but also everything.

A nexus of quiet dusty alleyways formed around the village's two main parallel streets. The houses, often with shops at the front, were mostly single-storey wooden buildings. It was a community laid out in a coconut grove, and over the homesteads towered immense palms, stirring lazily. Of a morning, the

291

odd truckload of Chinese-looking Hmong breezed in from outlying Ka Ngae Ki. Traditional Karen folk, colourful with their costumes, shoulder bags and pipes, wandered around, making purchases. A group of serious enigmatic rishi cultists from Lae Tong Ku or another sect village, clothed in green and pink, proceeded in single file past the market. Later, in the sizzling afternoon heat, while Um Pang's inhabitants napped, extravagant butterflies with four-inch wingspans fluttered in the silence, which was broken only by the whooping noises of monkeys in the trees beyond the village.

The hill down into Um Pang was lined on the left by a BPP base, a meteorological station and an agricultural office. On the right, set back, stood a fair-sized school. In front of it, the road forked, dividing into the village's two main streets. In our usual fashion, we rode round and round, getting our bearings. The right-hand (westerly) way dropped down past the post office, a fuel station, the police station, *Gift Shop*, and a daytime restaurant *Khun No* with green tablecloths. A side road running left by *Gift Shop* headed up to the central Five Ways, while the next turning right ran off past the abode of the *kamnaan* (village 'mayor') towards the bridge over the River Um Pang. Continuing straight on, we arrived at the bottom end of town. Here the road swung left, skirted the *ampoe* or district office (right), and then bore left again, bringing us to the bottom end of the other (easterly) main street. Riding up this, we passed several shops, a motorcycle repair place, a *wat*, Five Ways, a small market, more shops, and the generating station which supplied Um Pang's power (right). With that, we were back at the fork at the top end of town. In the side streets east of Five Ways, up on the hill, stood a small hospital and a second monastery. Many of the shops in the two main drags were general-purpose, selling the same ubiquitous fish sauce, tinned sardines, soap, washing powder, doughnuts... Some also supplied petrol out of drums. The price, as at the new fuel station, was a baht or two higher per litre than normal. And there was no bank to be seen.

Accommodation was in short supply, too. Somebody told us that the *kamnaan* had rooms, but in our tiredness we could not find them. Asking again for directions at *Gift Shop*, we were told by a lady that she had a house we could rent for 60 baht per person. It was just outside Um Pang, and we followed her on our bikes as she rode on a moped up the steep hill and back towards Mae Sot. After three kms, and saluting Pra Wo again with our horns, we turned left down a track among the houses of Mae Klong. Here we were given the keys to *Gift House*, a brand-new well-appointed villa in a banana grove. We could not believe our luck. We foresaw a problem with food, but the lady said we could have whatever we liked. She would bring it out to us later. After we had cleaned up, a moustachioed young man arrived with supper in a plastic bag, slung from the handlebars of the same moped. We tucked greedily into a feast of stir-fried chicken and vegetables, fresh fruit and iced beer. The young man began to serenade us with music on a synthesizer. What with the food and drink, the gentle music, the peace of the banana grove, the relaxed review of the day's events, and the balmy air of the veranda under a starry sky, it seemed as if on the fringes of Um Pang we had found heaven on earth.

DEATH HIGHWAY

The young man went by the nickname of 'So'. With his dashing good looks, So fancied himself as the local pop star (in fact he was a teacher). He subsequently presented us with a signed cassette of some of his music, entitled *So – So Easy*, and it was accomplished stuff. Through the 'pop star' and also the *Gift Shop* lady, we became friendly with So's brother Sombat, who worked in the district office. This modest sincere man was to become our most valuable contact in Um Pang, but just how he fitted into the picture only emerged later.

Because *Gift House* was rather cut-off, we decided to move the next day back into Um Pang itself. A diligent search turned up more lodging possibilities. In fact, in the end it began to seem to us that almost anybody in town would offer us floorspace if asked. We tracked down the mayor's accommodation, *Um Pang House*. It lay a short way down the road leading to the bridge. A vaguely fanciable ladyboy, working as a maid for the *kamnaan*, greeted us. She (he?) showed us first some bleak noisy rooms in a block beside the road and then, in a grassy area behind, a set of bungalows. All were over-priced, even after haggling, so we showed a clean pair of heels. As we left, we heard the *kateuy* wailing that we could have one of the block rooms for 100 baht – still rather dear for Um Pang. In the same road, we found other places to stay, but again the owners were charging inflated prices, considering the state of the rooms and the humble status of the village. The people of Um Pang did not seem much amenable to sensible bargaining, or perhaps they reasoned that visitors, trapped down here, had nowhere else to turn to. In the end, a man stopped us in the street and offered to lend us a kind of secondary garden-home he owned. He was the 2-i-c at the *ampoe*, and his house lay in an obscure back alley. Only one storey high and made of wood, it was built on piles in the middle of a small lake, on which floated a carpet of pink-flowering lilies. The lake was set in a marvellous garden, full of tropical plants. The house was reached by a gangplank from the garden. All this we could have to ourselves for just 30 baht each per day. And so for a number of idyllic days and nights we lazed in the quarters which we came to know as 'The Lilypond'.

One thing that Um Pang lacked, even the locals agreed, was a decent restaurant. From an early hour, tea and coffee were served in a shed at Five Ways, and our preferred breakfast came to be hot coffee or Milo there with coconut cake bought from a store. *Khun No* and a couple of other modest eating places in the two main streets offered during the day fried rice, *pat thai*, and noodles with meat and greens in gravy (*raat na*). In the early evening, many housewives, in traditional Siamese style, sold snacks and takeaway food in front of their houses, but what was on offer was not to everybody's taste. Down by the *ampoe*, a few stalls offered typical Thai sweetmeats. With these possibilities exhausted, the one remaining eating place was the questionable *Ti Lo Su* restaurant in the *kamnaan's* backyard, also known in northern Thai dialect – more appropriately – as *Karngtong* (= in the middle of the field).

This desultory ranch-style place, with its long wooden tables and benches on a bare earth floor, had no menu, either in Thai or English. On enquiring, we learned that we could only have whatever was available. That should have simplified things, but when we asked the lackadaisical cooks and waitresses what they had got, back came the answer: What did we want? Meanwhile they

293

fiddled up at the front with a cassette player, which crackled out lugubrious Thai songs. Of course, whatever we wanted they had not got. *Mai mii, mai mii*, they replied breezily. Finally, a stir-fry of vegetables and sliced Chiang Mai sausage was borne to our table by the same passable ladyboy we had snubbed earlier. 'She' gave us a cool look through half-closed eyes. In fairness to *Ti Lo Su*, the food improved the more we ate there. Also, the better the staff got to know us (including the willowy *kateuy*), the better the service became and the more reasonable the bill at the end of the evening.

The real problem with this eating place was drunkenness. BPP soldiers from their border posts, forestry boys from the jungle, and off-duty policemen all homed in on *Ti Lo Su* to drink away their boredom or frustration. The drunkenness in itself would not have been so bad, but all these characters passed through that intermediate stage, having supped on watery *tom yam* from a clay pot and emptied two or three bottles of Mekhong whisky, when they spotted us minding our own business, latched onto us and thought it enormously funny to ask endless forward and fatuous questions. One evening, this unwanted attention became so tiresome that we rebelled. The manageress, noticing that things had gone too far and failing to shift a pair of drunks from our table, called the police. The police arrived, but they were also drunk and started fraternizing with our importunate tablemates. Finally, the bosses of the two drunks, accompanied by a senior official from the *ampoe*, arrived, but, far from restoring order, these local eminences merely suggested that it was we who should leave "because it was not good for us to see such a thing". We were preparing to depart from *Ti Lo Su* in utter disgust when the *kamnaan* himself arrived, saving the day, or rather evening. He had brought a length of elephant chain with him and proceeded to chain up the two men, tying them to a post out in the darkness, where they cooled off at length with intermittent grumblings.

Um Pang had originally been a Karen settlement until Thais from the northern provinces of Chiang Mai, Lampoon, Lampang and Prae began to settle there. The village was at least 100 years old because records showed that in 1889, when Um Pang district belonged to Utai Tani province, it had been an immigration point for people from Burma. This might account for its name, which is said to derive from the Karen *um pa/oom pa*, meaning variously 'issue pass' or the bamboo cylinder used by Burmese travellers for keeping their immigration documents in. In 1898, Tak provincial administration made nearby Mae Klong an *ampoe* (present day Mae Klong Gao). With two district seats so close, it was inevitable that they should merge. In 1926, *ampoe* Mae Klong was subsumed under Um Pang district, but at the same time the newly enlarged *ampoe* Um Pang was reallocated from Utai Tani to Tak province.

Ampoe Um Pang now had the distinction of being the largest district in Thailand, with a surface area of 4,325 sq. kms. Its population, however, was a mere 13,000, distributed throughout some 37 villages. It was bordered to the north by Pop Pra district, to the south by Sangklaburi and Si Sawat, and to the east by the districts of Klong Lan, Laad Yao and Ban Rai. To the west, lay the Tanon Tongchai mountains, which divided off Um Pang district from Burma, with which it shared a 180-km-long border. The River Um Pang ran past town on the south side, skirting *Garden Huts GH* and flowing into the River Mae Klong somewhat to the west. This larger river ran south to join the River Mae Chan, and both ultimately flowed into the River Kwae Yai, down in Kanchanaburi province. For a while, the Mae Klong had been used for floating logs south from Um Pang district to Kanchanaburi. Almost the whole of the district was mountainous. Its agricultural economy had to make do with only some 3-5% of flatland. Local produce was sold mostly to Mae Sot. The area had reserves of tin, wolfram, lignite and antinomy, but as yet these had not been exploited. For eco-political reasons they might never be so.

About 70% of Um Pang district was jungle. With such a large area of mountainous jungle so sparsely populated, it was a largely undisturbed zoological and botanical treasure trove. Fortunately, this had not been lost on the Thai authorities. With so many other parts of the kingdom depredated from logging, slash-and-burn agriculture and erosion, they had been commendably quick to add Um Pang to other contiguous fastnesses to form one giant nature reserve. Thus, combined with Um Pang Wildlife Sanctuary to the north of Um Pang (and also south), Klong Lan and Mae Wong National Parks to the east, Huai Kha Khaeng Wildlife Sanctuary to the south-east, Tan Lot and Erawan National Parks to the south, and the vast Tung Yai Naresuan Wildlife Sanctuary and Forest Protection Zone to the south-west, Um Pang district formed the greatest and the last real wilderness in Thailand (said to be one of the most significant in Asia). A look at the map confirmed this. It was one huge inaccessible area, with not a single proper road running into it. The reserve was home to tigers, gaurs, wild elephants, bears, deer, barking deer, gibbons, leaf monkeys, wild boar, civet-like linsangs, serows (goat-antelopes), peacocks, Chinese pheasants, forest chickens, snakes and a multitude of birds. There were forests of teak, ironwood, rubber trees, betel, *mai daeng, teng, rang, pradu, tabaek,* and *takien.*

One result of the formation of this giant nature reserve was that increasing numbers of people were being moved out. There were next to no Thais living in it, so the villages which were being resettled were hill-tribe, mostly Hmong, but also some Lisu. As we saw, they were being moved north to the Rom Glao and Pop Pra areas. They were being relocated not just for the sake of creating uninhabited national parks. As Prasert Leksakhun Deelok, head of the district office explained to us, especially the Hmong were involved not just in slash-and-burn, but in illegal logging, poaching and opium-cultivation. He showed us press cuttings detailing a scandal in which local Hmong had hunted and killed a wild female elephant with a calf. On the subject of poppy-growing, as the authorities became increasingly successful in suppressing cultivation, the Hmong apparently moved deeper and deeper into the jungle to evade detection, cutting down more trees to make room for new fields. Thus, villages had been moved out of Mae Wong National Park between Um Pang Ki and Klong Lan, and we heard rumours that the Lisu villages beside the River Mae La Moong (La Mung/Ra Mong), near the hot spring, had gone. It seemed that even strategic Mae Chan Ta might not be immune from resettlement.

Karen villages did not seem to figure much in the relocation program. In a sense this was right, for if anyone could claim to be the region's indigenous people, it was the Karen. By contrast, the Hmong were migratory people who had entered the area relatively recently. In addition, however, the subsistence economy of the Karen, who were mostly lowland farmers, was much less environmentally destructive than the highland slash-and-burn economy of the entrepreneurial Hmong. Also, the *Yang* did not grow opium and certainly never poached elephants. At most, some outlying Karen hamlets would be amalgamated with more established 'central' villages, such as Pa La Ta.

Finally, a second result of the creation of this huge natural conservation area was that public access to it was under threat. Visitors, we were told, would increasingly be prevented from trekking either in it or through it. Some tracts had already been closed. The path through Mae Wong National Park from Klong Lan to Um Pang via Um Pang Ki (even marked on some maps as the H1117 road) was absolutely forbidden, the way having been closed eight or nine years previously, with all villages en route shut down. The truth of this we found out to our own great cost when we once went to a lot of trouble trying to take a short cut from Kampaeng Pet to Um Pang. Other parts would no doubt follow. Perhaps in the future it would not be possible to go beyond Ti Lo Su Waterfall, or one would only be allowed to make specific walks care of the wildlife and forestry departments and in possession of a permit issued by them. But, in addition, with villages in the jungle disappearing, any trekking, whether independent or organized, would become increasingly difficult. If a logistically important village such as Mae Chan Ta went, it would be all but impossible to get down to the Three Pagodas unless one mounted a regular expedition, with porters carrying food and tents. The upshot of all this was not lost on us. Adventure south of Um Pang seemed about to be nipped in the bud, and so if we were serious about our dream of trekking through the 200 kms of jungle from Um Pang to the Three Pagodas, there would never be a better time to try to realize it than now.

❖ ❖

Postscript 2002

In 2001, the 161-km-long H1090 route from Mae Sot to Um Pang (nearer 165 kms if you count from Mae Sot Town centre) was paved throughout, as was the 58-km-long route on the H1090 and H1206 roads to Wa Lay (about 60 kms from Mae Sot town centre). 'Death Highway' had been significantly upgraded, and when Doug, Andrew and I biked down to Um Pang in early February of that year, we encountered heavy re-engineering roadwork especially between the villages of Rom Glao N° 2 and Rom Glao N° 4, as well as between Mae Klong Yai and Mae Klong Ki, which impeded our progress, but which means that by the time you read this, you should be able to scoot all the more easily to Um Pang. Nevertheless, 'Death Highway' (but not the route to Wa Lay) remains dangerous travelwise. Serious and fatal accidents continue to happen on it all the time, and every time I go down it, I see at least one grave mishap. Many

DEATH HIGHWAY

Thai drivers simply cannot handle mountain roads and drive too fast.[2] In 2001, several trucks were speeding insanely down the twists between Rom Glao Nos 2 and 4, almost killing me. Many *silor* go every day from Mae Sot to both Um Pang and Pop Pra/Wa Lay. On the way to Um Pang, you can get fuel and also lunch at the midpoint village of Rom Glao N° 4. Wa Lay is best visited as a 120-km one-day round-trip excursion from Mae Sot and not while you are proceeding from Mae Sot to Um Pang, for which you should allow all day.

Route detail: Mae Sot – Saw Oh – Pop Pra – Wa Lay (Map 22)

From Mae Sot town centre, proceed E up the Intra Kiri Road and continue a fair way (2 or 3 kms) through the outskirts to the Shell petrol station (L)

km 0.0   Shell fuel station forecourt

Go round the roundabout, turning roughly R off it into the start of the H1090 for Pop Pra and Um Pang

A good flat road heads out through villages

km 18.0   At a confusing junction, go L/straight and up a long steep hill. The way R, which is signed for Um Pang, is merely a new alternative circuitous piece of road designed to avoid the long steep upgrade, and rejoins the original route 4 kms further down the H1090

km 21.6   At a second junction, again go L/straight. The way R is where the alternative route, bypassing the upgrade, rejoins the H1090

km 31.5   In **Saw Oh** village, turn R at the big junction for Pop Pra, negotiating the central reservation (go past it and make a U-turn, then go L). At the big junction, which is marked by a police box, the way L, continuing on the H1090, goes to Um Pang

Now on the H1206 side road, head S out of the market village of Saw Oh towards Pop Pra

Just before Pop Pra, you pass through a big portal, which lies near a waterfall (R)

km 45.4   **Pop Pra** centre and post office (R)

After Pop Pra, we passed a couple of army checkpoints in a relatively militarized area. They are more on account of the DKBA in Palu and to catch illegal Burmese migrants than to frustrate you. The old dirt road from Pop Pra to Wa Lay is now paved

Roadside health centre and also new road L 5 kms to the border villages of Ya Po and Mae Ork Hu (if you visit these places, take great care, as the DKBA are down there and the border is more porous than at Wa Lay – you would in any case have to get past a serious Thai army checkpoint)

km 57.1   Portal and entrance to Wa Lay

km 58.2   Market area of **Wa Lay** down by river

Wa Lay

Riding towards and into Wa Lay, we encountered the same desolate, end-of-the-road feel experienced a decade earlier. In the village, we followed the cement-surfaced street, bending left and then down right, to come to the market area, river, border and

---

[2] A lot of them have trouble handling any kind of road safely, due to lack of training, indiscipline, speeding, drink-driving, and a me-first lack of consideration for other road users, although overall things have improved over the past decade. Nevertheless, Thailand is still regarded as one of the most hazardous places in Asia to drive or ride on the roads. Each year, some 20,000 motorcyclists die in traffic accidents, and at least 400,000 are hospitalized. At New Year 2000/01 alone, 351 people died in the country on the roads, while 20,000 were injured.

frontier crossing to Palu, which lay immediately on the other side of the modest river. The riverside market area was a compact spot, with shops, two or three eating places, a dozen trucks, and *silor* from Mae Sot or Pop Pra. Some people said that the river, small here, was the upper reaches of the Moei, while others maintained that it was the Huai Wa Lay or Wa Lay stream. To me, the water looked too wide and voluminous to be a stream. Whichever, it was spanned by a wooden footbridge, just to the right of which, on the Thai bank, was a Thai army observation post and border control, manned by a handful of soldiers. Karen were going to and fro across the bridge and border (see colour photo), local children were swimming in and jumping into the scenic little river, while their mothers washed clothes at the water's edge. There was a great atmosphere, accentuated by Palu and the brooding menace of its occupants on the other bank, just a few metres away.

For across the river, the DKBA was in control, while its patron, the Burma army, was stationed 6 kms away. Beyond the bridge, the entrance to DKBA territory was marked by a portal, painted blue and yellow, and surmounted by three DKBA flags. The flags were white, with the letters 'DKBA' inscribed on them, while the portal bore various Buddhist symbols and lettering in Burmese and Karen, which we were unable to read (see black-and-white photo). Beside the portal stood a guardhouse, outside of which half a dozen uniformed and armed DKBA soldiers lounged on chairs, some of them boys of 10 or 11 years. Sections of Palu were visible, which was a village with simple leaf-roofed huts, a big new *wat*, and dozens of sawmills plus woodworking shops, which lined the river bank and were surrounded by mounds of red-brown sawdust. We wondered aloud to the Thai soldiers that they were not afraid, given the presence of the infamous DKBA so close by. "They depend on us for food", a ranger said, "and so cooperate with the Thai army." That did not stop them heavying it up with other people. Wa Lay has always been an eventful place, both in general and for me in particular. Now the grenade incident with the Burma army years ago was complemented by another sinister encounter. A DKBA officer, who grew irritated with my photography of the bridge, Palu portal, the guards and himself, drew his pistol, waved it around, pointed it at me, motioned and shouted at me to clear off, and threatened to shoot me if I did not, which had the Thai soldiers all a-flutter, and walkie-talkies crackling on both sides of the river. Poking around in another corner of Wa Lay, slightly downriver, we found a second bridge over the water, which was unguarded. A Karen man going over it invited me to cross to view Palu. It was quite safe, he said! Another *farang*, unaware of the threat posed by the DKBA, might have done so, to be relieved of his camera, money or worse (the KNU report that the DKBA would like nothing better than to capture a *farang* so as to extort a large ransom). But on this occasion, I could resist the temptation to cross to Burma.

The date of my original visit to Wa Lay, with the Dane Thorben, was 9 February 1990, immediately after SLORC troops first overran Kawmoorah, failing to hold on to it, and then took Palu. Just how volatile and eventful things are at Wa Lay/Palu can be seen from the following little chronicle. Traditionally, Wa Lay/Palu has been Karen and a double village on the old way from Mae Sot via Nong Luang to Um Pang. In the 1960s, 70s and 80s, Palu was a KNU 6th Brigade stronghold, an important gateway to the Karen State, and a major trading and KNU customs post. In 1987, the Burma army attacked and burned down Palu's timber mills. In 1989, ABSDF rebel students were stationed there. In February 1990, as detailed in the main text above, just before my first visit to Wa Lay, Palu was captured by the *tatmadaw*. But in 1994, when on 18 January I visited Wa Lay/Palu for a second time, the SLORC troops were gone. They had just withdrawn, a Wa Lay villager said, shortly after New Year.

The bridge beyong Wa Lay market place was open, although nothing was using it. The market area itself was empty, and many of the buildings around it looked disused.

DEATH HIGHWAY

There was still some barbed wire around, but mostly it had gone. Curiously, a checkpoint by the bridge was unmanned, and anybody was free to wander across. A makeshift wooden frontier sign announced 'Thailand', under which another amateurish board exhorted 'No Arm, No Uniform'. An old couple in a nearby shop told us we could go across. We could go to Chi Sa Lae, the Karen village 6 kms distant or, indeed, all the way to Nong Luang and Um Pang – the old way was open again... A rapid reconnoitre was irresistible, even though I had my daughter with me, aged just three at the time. On the far bank, Palu was deserted. In fact, there was nothing left of Palu, it was completely destroyed. Every building had been smashed or burnt at some time during the four years of SLORC occupation. Jungle had already reclaimed some of the old streets and households. Among the ruins were a couple of small timber workshops, and further up the road a checkpoint. It seemed to be a BPP guardbox (inside Burma!), controlling logging traffic. The guards were fast asleep. Picking our way through the overgrown ruins of Palu, and with the thought of left-over landmines or booby traps nagging, we tried to get up to the big white pagoda on the hill. But it was impossible. Over in that direction the countryside was ablaze everywhere. But we did get to the wooden *wat*. Just as we arrived, however, the burning bushes around it set fire to the temple, and before our eyes, remarkably, the monastery conflagrated. Through a door, we could see a wardrobe with mirrors in flames, and some votive banners hanging from the ceiling dripped fire. Hurrying away, we saw that the bush fire was just beginning to engulf the pagoda. It was not clear who had set fire to the area, whether the retiring Burmese or the Karen, probably the former. With the Burmese gone, Wa Lae/Palu was no less disquieting than on the first visit.

Sometime between January 1994 and the time of my third visit to Wa Lay, in early 2001, Palu must have been recaptured by the Burma army. This may have happened in the wake of the fall of Manerplaw in January 1995, but most likely it happened during the *tatmadaw* offensives of February 1997, when KNU 6th Brigade area fell to SLORC troops, who took e.g. nearby Pa Toei (opposite Nong Luang) and Sa Kaang Thit (opposite Klo To). For in early 2001, the *tatmadaw's* protégé, the DKBA, was in the saddle at Palu, with the old Palu/Nong Luang route interdicted yet again. How long the DKBA will remain at Palu, and whether the KNU can retake it, is an open question. Meanwhile the unusually chequered history of the place and area goes on. On 12 February 2001, seven mortar shells fired across the border apparently from Palu landed at 1am in a village given in the newspapers as 'Mae Kon Kane' (*tambon* Mahawan, Mae Sot district), exploding near the BPP's 346th base. The KNLA, positioned opposite Pop Pra district, launched counter-attacks on Palu, and the DKBA and KNLA slugged it out for a while. One of the reasons why Palu/Wa Lay remains so eventful is that it remains a major smuggling point on the Thai-Burmese border. Where cigarettes, gems, logs or whatever used to come across, now drugs are said to come, in which the DKBA is involved. In 2000, reportedly, hundreds of thousands of amphetamine pills were seized in 'Mae Kon Kane' village. All this will guarantee that Palu/Wa Lay remains in the headlines.

Route detail: Saw Oh – Rom Glao N° 4 – Mae Klong Ki – Um Pang (Maps 23 & 24)

km 31.5 Odometer readings continue from big junction H1206/H1090 back at Saw Oh village (see Map 23). From junction, go ESE on H1090 for Um Pang In 2001, everything much more developed along side of road

km 36.5 Way L 700 m to Pa Charoen Waterfall

c. km 38 Near km-marker 39: you enter low hills, followed by a desolate stretch with bleak tracts either side of road

At km-marker 43: site of former massacre by CPT insurgents of workers constructing H1090

THREE PAGODAS

Also near here: village of **Rom Glao N° 1**, with Hmong people

c. km 46   Chinese tombs (L) alert you to the presence locally of Chinese people
Near km-marker 48: village of **Rom Glao N° 2** with Chinese people
(left/N side of road). The entrance to this place is marked by a big school
(L) and a Burmese-style pagoda as well as a strange white pagoda (both R).
Also opposite the village, on the R side of the H1090, is a mushroom
factory. If you turn off and motor round the grid of dirt streets forming
Rom Glao N° 2, you will find the village full of spread-out, mostly single-
storey Chinese houses, many built around courtyards. In one street, there
are several stores and tea shops, generating a fair amount of bustle. Actually,
there are not just Chinese here, but also Yao, Lahu, Lisu and Akha people,
as well as Burmese labourers and Hmong shoppers, making it an ethnic
hotchpotch and also a local microcosm. Although some inhabitants we
asked denied the fact, the Chinese in Rom Glao N° 2 must in part be
descendants of the KMT soldiers sent to the area in the 1970s and early 80s
to guard construction of the H1090 from attacks and sabotage by local
Thai and Hmong CPT rebels. Perhaps after their duty, these nationalist anti-
communist KMT guards were rewarded for their efforts by the village, or
just stopped and settled there anyway. Chinese Rom Glao N° 2 is an
intriguing place that would certainly repay exploration.

km 48.3   Checkpoint (R) and start of real 'Death Highway' as you climb up into
mountains
Great views
Down into valley and up
In 2001: road often in poor state, with lots of dangerous speeding traffic.
Highway widened and improved in places

km 81.8   Midpoint Hmong village of **Rom Glao N° 4**, a place where most people
going to/coming back from Um Pang stop for lunch. Restaurant (down R)
and noodle soup place (up L). In 2001, village more built up than a decade
earlier, now with school and health centre. It is possible that the Hmong of
Rom Glao N°s 1 and 4 (possibly 3, too) were settled in these villages after
surrendering as former CPT rebels in the early 1980s
After Rom Glao N° 4, traffic lessens appreciably and road improves

km 83.2   New Hmong settlement of **Um Biem Mai** (L), followed by checkpoint

km 84.7   Near roadside km-marker 87: **Um Biem refugee camp** (L), a fairly new
place run under UN auspices (see colour photo). In January 2001, people
here told us that it was more than one year old and housed over 10,000
KNU Karen from Burma. Just before and after the camp, a series of
military posts control the H1090, but we got the impression that it would
not have been difficult to walk in and have a look round. I fancy that the
camp either dates from February 1997, when KNU 6th Brigade area in
Burma to the west was overrun by SLORC troops, precipitating a massive
influx of refugees into Thailand locally, or from March 1998, when the
DKBA attacked and destroyed Mawkier refugee camp in Mae Sot's Pop Pra
district, causing thousands of inmates to have to be rehoused, probably
partly at Um Biem

km 91.0   Hmong village of **Mae Klong Noi** (L), a strange scruffy place partly
surrounded by destroyed countryside

km 97.0   Checkpoint and barrier

km 99.7   Way L 2 or 3 kms to **Mae Klong Yai**, another Hmong village

km 103.0   Jungle

km 112.7   Police box and lots more jungle

DEATH HIGHWAY

km 117.3 *Grom pamai* (forest protection) and wildlife sanctuary office

km 122.9 The high precipitous section of road, with long views down into valley of the Mae Klong river, as well as of distant mountains W and SW (now see Map 24). The exposed stretch over the pass has meanwhile been made safer, with barriers at the side of the road
Come down off mountains through hairpin bends into valley

km 128.6 Bridge over River Mae Klong and Karen village of **Mae Klong Ki** (mostly L). You can usually buy fuel here. Start of a series of karst formations beside road. The brand-new KNU Karen refugee camp we found near the bridge in early 1990 has long since gone, and was probably vacated before 1991, with its inmates returning to Burma

km 136.5 **Wa Kru Ko** village (aka Mai Krapong) with school L, which is where Thailand's well-known folk/pop singer 'So' is a teacher (latterly headmaster)

km 139.2 Cave (L). You continue through a fairy-tale karstic landscape on valley floor

km 141.4 **Wa Koei Ta** (Wa Boei Ta) village

km 144.7 **Pro Pa Do** village

km 150.2 Start of **Mai Pa Ka** village

km 154.0 **Mae Klong Gao** village (= Old Mae Klong)

km 157.1 At junction, go L/straight for Um Pang. Side road R/west passes immediately through **Mae Klong Mai** (= New Mae Klong) and then proceeds variously to Nong Luang (Map 26) and Ti Lo Su Waterfall as well as Boeng Kloeng (Maps 26 & 27)
Mae Klong village with roadside places to stay, including *Uncle Tin's Cabin*
Descend steep hill to reach school (R) and fork at edge of Um Pang. Go either way

km 160.9 **Um Pang** centre

Um Pang

I first visited Um Pang in February 1990, returning there a couple more times in the early 1990s, and the picture painted of it above derives from those early visits. A decade later, in February 2001, the village was essentially similar, although more developed especially round the edges. Now we noticed that many houses had been rebuilt meanwhile, often using teak; that there was a big new white hospital up on the hill on the east side of 'town'; that there were many more shops; that new restaurants, tour outfits and places to stay had sprung up; that the post office had moved to the entrance to Um Pang, near the meteorology station; and that there was even a small airstrip behind or west of the post office and weather station (perhaps it had always been there, but we had never noticed it before). Quite in contrast to the food situation in the early 1990s, when the only evening 'restaurant' had been the *kamnaan's* lousy *Karngtong*, you can now eat well in Um Pang in a variety of places.

In general, the large village is set up for and used by Thai tourists, almost all of whom come to visit famed nearby Ti Lo Su Waterfall and/or go rafting. A number of *farang* tourists go to Um Pang for the same purposes. It is all Ti Lo Su and rafting, and a pushy local 'mafia' revolving round the tour agencies and guest houses, which are all in competition with one another, try to sell you the waterfall and rafting. Um Pang is a bit of a hard-sell place. I have never been to Ti Lo Su or gone rafting, but in fairness to both I am bound to say that the waterfall is most impressive and beautiful (as people have reported and as is evident from pictures), while the rafting is very scenic and thrilling. By contrast, almost no Thais bother to go to, say, Boeng Kloeng village, far south of Um Pang, on the border and in the jungle, and perhaps no more than one or two *farang* (bikers) a year go there either. Yet the village and its setting is no less interesting and beautiful, and the journey there no less exciting. I suppose it all depends

301

on what your cup of tea is. Incidentally, during the years between the early 1990s and 2001, tourism in end-of-the-road Um Pang was badly affected by events across the border in Burma, just as it was in many places down Thailand's western frontier. Following the Burma army offensives against the Karen especially in the winters of 1994/95 (fall of Manerplaw and Kawmoorah) and of 1996/97 (capture of KNU 6th Brigade area, right opposite Um Pang district), tourism down much of the Thai-Burmese border dropped by 80%, with visits to Um Pang decimated.

Excluding daytime noodle soup and fried-rice places, there must be half a dozen restaurants now in Um Pang. A fancy indoor eatery is *Phu Doi Restaurant*, located by Five Ways (centre of easterly main street). It has a good selection of well-cooked dishes in the mid-price category of about 60 baht per dish. Slightly cheaper and with a marginally smaller menu is *Food and Beverage*, a place up a side alley off the westerly of Um Pang's two parallel main streets. The cooking is good here, too, a typical dish costing 50-60 baht and a large Chang or Leo beer 45 baht. I think the *kamnaan's* place is still functioning, but there is no reason to go there any more. During the day, you can eat at *Nong Koong* restaurant, near the *wat* and *Umpang GH*, on the crossroads where the Pa La Ta road starts at km-marker 0 (opposite *Gift Shop*). It does good clean lunches for 20 or 25 baht. You can also take both lunch and breakfast at *Tom Restaurant*, at Five Ways, almost opposite the entrance to the *wat* and nearly adjacent to *Phu Doi Restaurant*. Down one side of *Tom*, you can drink ordinary Thai coffee (*gaffae tammada*) with free China tea at breakfast time, which you can take with excellent dirt-cheap hot coconut patties purchased from a vendor in front of *Tom*.

You can stay at *Umpang GH*, at the start of the Pa La Ta road, by the crossroads and km-marker 0 (diagonally opposite *Gift Shop*); at *Umpang House*, a bit further down the same road on the same left side, which belongs to the *kamnaan*, and which has a variety of lodgings, including big cold-water rooms for 100 baht; and at *Garden Huts*, further down the same road, just before the bridge, on the right and fronting the River Um Pang, where you can stay in a bungalow on stilts for 150 baht with cold water and a shared bathroom or for 300 baht with hot water and private bathroom. It is pretty down here, although the proprietress remains pushy, as she has always been. Beyond this place, across the bridge, are two resorts, which cater more for groups of Thai tourists than for *farang* travellers. We stayed at *Garden Huts* a couple of nights before moving to accommodation representing better value, i.e. offering more amenities for less money. This was *Trekker Hill*, an apparently ramshackle compound in an elevated position, up a steep hill east off Um Pang's easterly main street. Used by people taking rafting and trekking trips, it has a variety of huts and rooms. We took a room each for 100 baht that had a private bathroom, hot shower, double bed, mosquito net, Western-style toilet, soap and other nice features – great value indeed. *Trekker Hill* looks west over Um Pang and is an altogether cool place. Another similar lodging, nearby and in a comparable location, is *Khundoi Campsite and GH*, which is a misnomer because it is not a campsite, has no camping, and is in fact a guest house basically for Thais. Nice rooms here with hot water are 200+ baht or 150 shared – if we understood the staff correctly, who seemed pretty clueless and were unable to deal with our enquiries, probably because they are used to putting parties of eight into a big bungalow.

Following his serenading of us at *Gift House* on that balmy evening in February 1990, 'pop star' So – real name Sompong Muenjit, artist's name 'Khru San' (Teacher San) – went on to have considerable success with his music in Thailand. Actually more of a folk singer-songwriter than a pop musician, who played primarily guitar rather than a synthesizer, he produced a little series of recordings of his socially committed songs after the initial cassette *So – So Easy*, which he presented to us. He likewise progressed from being a teacher to being a headmaster. Born in 1959, he went to school and college in Tak province, after which he followed a distance-learning course.

DEATH HIGHWAY

His first teaching job was at Mae Klong Gao school in 1979, after which he was appointed headmaster first of the school in the Hmong village of Ka Ngae Ki (45 kms S of Um Pang – see Map 25) and then of another village school in Um Pang district. Finally, in 1992, he became headmaster of Wa Kru Ko (Mai Krapong) school, the village which we passed as we approached Um Pang (24 kms to the N on the H1090 – Map 24), where he is still in charge today.

So started singing as a response to the poverty of his school pupils. These children, mostly Karen, often came to school with inadequate clothing and no food or money for lunch because their parents were very poor. Taking pity on his wards, he decided to try to do something to help them, thinking that people should not always wait for the authorities to act, and that a teacher himself could do something to alleviate a perceived educational or social problem. After wondering what to do, he thought that maybe he could raise money to buy food and clothes for his charges through his music.

Writing songs about poor rural schoolchildren and their teachers, as well as about the changes and his experiences in Um Pang district, So recorded a first cassette, going down to Bangkok and investing all his savings of 50,000 baht (about £1,000) in the project. He made 2,000 copies of this cassette, which was called *Khru Peua Cheewit* (= teacher for life, i.e. teacher in aid of life). The album was a professionally produced version of the original home-made *So - So Easy* cassette that he had given to us back in 1990, containing all the same songs. The 2,000 copies he then tried to sell, at the same time performing in Tak's *Wiang Tak Hotel* and elsewhere both to raise more money and promote the tape. Finally, by 1993, he had sold all the copies of the cassette, recouping his investment and realizing a profit of 40,000 baht, with which he funded a school lunch project.

Meanwhile, word got around about the singing teacher, who was increasingly in demand. After 1993, So produced a second album, titled *Um Pang*, and also a third, *Pahom Jai* (= heart blanket, i.e. heart warmer). This led to an offer from a recording company to sign up with them and produce a fourth album, which could have resulted in a successful singing career, but modest So declined the offer. He did not want to do any more albums, preferring to concentrate on his teaching and pupils' welfare.

❊

Excursion (1) to Pa La Ta and Tung Yai Naresuan Wildlife Sanctuary (Map 25)

From Um Pang, readers (especially motorcyclists) might like to make a great day trip to the northern edge of Tung Yai Naresuan Wildlife Sanctuary, the first of two recommendable excursions from Um Pang. The trip proceeds 46 kms S to a sanctuary HQ, passing Doi Hua Mot (= bald head mountain) ridge and the two Karen villages of Pa La Ta and Sae Pa La, traversing a spur of Um Pang Wildlife Sanctuary, and modestly entering Tung Yai. The way is mountainous and scenic, particularly as far as Pa La Ta, after which you negotiate terrain which is hot and dry with low hills. A great new asphalt road goes as far as Pa La Ta (km 26), after which (in 2001) a new gravel highway proceeds as far as km 31.2, beyond which a badly deteriorated dirt 'road' or track continues to the sanctuary HQ. Public-transport *silor* no doubt ride as far as Pa La Ta, but not to the HQ. In fact, almost no traffic at all goes to the HQ, which is pretty inaccessible. You can only reach it with a motorcycle or jeep of your own.

In February 2001, Doug and Andrew and I biked down to the HQ on a one-day exploratory ride from Um Pang. The HQ hardly sees any visitors and is not really geared up to dealing with them, especially *farang*, but we were well received and even given some lunch, and I am sure you could stay overnight there, either in a room or in

THREE PAGODAS

a brought-along tent. When I first visited the site of the HQ, back in the early 1990s with Nittaya, there was no sanctuary office there, but a thriving Hmong village, called Ka Ngae Ki (the place where musician So had been school headteacher). In 2001, this had completely gone, having been moved out by the authorities and replaced by the HQ around 1994-94. There are a number of buildings spread over the HQ compound, one with maps, and another containing a little shop, selling instant noodles, snacks, soft drinks, coffee etc.

From the HQ, you could proceed further along trails into the heart of Tung Yai with a motorbike or 4WD vehicle, or you could trek extensively on foot. If we understood sanctuary officials correctly, the 4WD track beyond the HQ continues to a series of forestry outposts, including U-nai (7 kms), Mae Chan Ta (8 kms), U-ta Ki (14 kms), Tung Na Noi (46 kms), Huai Nam Kiao (47 kms), Ka Ngae So (56 kms) and Chong Pae (75 kms) – considerable distances. By all accounts, it is possible to motorcycle to the first three outposts (whose names do not indicate that they are near the villages of the same name), while the remainder can only be reached by 4WD vehicle. Apparently, you can walk 19 kms from Ka Ngae So to a cluster of five Karen villages, which include Mae Chan Ta as well as Chua Krao Song Bae forestry office. My guess is that this would be a roundabout and difficult way of accessing strategic Mae Chan Ta village, which is more easily and normally accessed from Mong Gua, Kui Le Tor and the Um Pang/Boeng Kloeng road (Map 27). All these details are unverified, and S of the HQ you could do some pioneering exploration.

Route detail: Um Pang – Doi Hua Mot – Pa La Ta – Sae Pa La – Tung Yai Naresuan Wildlife Sanctuary HQ (Map 25)

km 0.0   Um Pang centre and start of Pa La Ta road at crossroads near *Gift Shop* and *Umpang GH*. A km-marker at the crossroads indicates 0 km
Go W, past *Garden Huts GH* and over bridge spanning River Um Pang, and follow road round behind a hill and out of sight of Um Pang
Road climbs up

km 3.3   Way R to Sai Fon Waterfall
Between about km-markers 7 and 10: karstic outcrops and **Doi Hua Mot** (bald head mountain) ridge (L)

km 10.1   Just after km-marker 10: way L by sign 600 m to a viewpoint on a hillock. From the viewpoint, if you look at 30° or just E of N, you can see the H1090 road to Mae Sot climbing up a ridge. To the N, Um Pang with its white hospital building is visible in the valley, while to the E lies Huai Kha Khaeng Wildlife Sanctuary
A fine new asphalt road skips along the ridgetop, skirting a succession of peaklets and outcrops (L)

km 16.0   Rugged mountains dead ahead
Descend from ridge in light deciduous woodland
Pointy mountain visible

km 22.0   Checkpoint, office (L) and entrance to southern part of Um Pang Wildlife Sanctuary. Bridge over pretty river, which is the Mae La Moong (Mung)

km 22.6   Near km-marker 23: way R 12 kms to Ko Ta village. You can drive in as far as the Mae La Moong river, after which you have to walk

km 25.8   Km-marker 26: police box and centre of **Pa La Ta**, a Karen village. At start of village: a school. The river W/just behind Pa La Ta is the Mae Klong. Opposite the police box, a way goes R into the village. Pa La Ta is said to be the biggest Karen village in Um Pang district, to be about 250 years old, and to have about 30 elephants (value of each up to 150,000 baht) – more than any other local village

DEATH HIGHWAY

After Pa La Ta, the road's asphalt surface gives over to gravel (in 2001) Just before a copse: a way L goes to Mae La Moong Ki, possibly a Lisu village, near which is a hot spring. You can trek 4 hrs on foot to the village, on the way crossing the Sae Pa La river, passing through woods and forest, going over the Doi Hua Mot ridge, passing the deserted village of Ko Ki, and crossing the Mae La Moong river

km 29.8   In copse: a waterfall (L)

km 30.3   Karen village of **Sa Pa La** (R)

km 31.2   Portal and end of new gravel road (in 2001). After the portal, you pick up the old dirt road, now much deteriorated and overgrown. At the portal, Um Pang Wildlife Sanctuary ends. L of portal: a Tung Yai Sanctuary office

km 43.3   Karstic mound, near which a sign reads: 'You are entering Tung Yai'. All over this area: many white-flowering *dok siao* trees, a symbol of Um Pang

km 45.3   Guardhouse, checkpoint, barrier and formal northern entrance to **Tung Yai Naresuan Wildlife Sanctuary and Forest Protection Zone**. Here, our details were checked into a logbook. Beyond checkpoint: main **HQ** buildings set back L, and little shop set back R. The whole HQ compound used to be the site of the Hmong village of Ka Ngae Ki, which is now completely gone, amazingly

✣

Excursion (2) to Nong Luang and border near Pa Toei (Map 26)

Another – shorter and much easier – excursion that readers with their own transport might like to make from Um Pang is to Nong Luang village and, beyond it, to the Thai-Burmese border near Pa Toei, all of which lie WNW of Um Pang. It is 15 kms to Nong Luang and 21 to the frontier, making a round trip of 42 kms, enough to fill a morning or afternoon. The way is a good paved road throughout, which for the first 12 kms duplicates the start of the book's main onward route to Klo To, Nu Po and Boeng Kloeng (Chapters 12 & 13). The reasons for making the excursion are to enjoy a pleasant spin, visit en route Ta Ko Pi Cave and rural Nong Luang, and savour the atmosphere of the border and backwoods Pa Toei crossing point – if you like drinking in that frontier feeling. Beyond Nong Luang, the border is open, but open in a way quite different from the porousness that I found when I went up there once before, in February 1993. On that occasion, we were able to flit unchecked straight over the border into Burma, landing up in the Karen settlement of Pa Toei. On this occasion, because there was again no army post or barrier at the border, the frontier was still open and we could have gone across again, but some Thai soldiers at a roadside camp before the border explicitly forbade us from continuing to Pa Toei because the DKBA was present there.

In 1993, after passing the checkpoint at km 12, we rode into Nong Luang, a relatively large sleepy village that had that last-place-before-the-border atmosphere, and which – now that the old short way from Um Pang to Mae Sot through a spur of Burma (via Nong Luang and Wa Lay) was closed or no longer used, while the H1090 was open – gave the impression of having seen better times. Beyond Nong Luang, we continued riding for some distance on a road that increasingly diminished and seemed to be going nowhere. The vegetation each side was encroaching on the trail, and the few houses that we passed were either burnt down or abandoned, giving rise to an uneasy feeling in us. In what seemed like a piece of no man's land or extraterritory, we wondered if we were we still in Thailand or already in Burma. Suddenly, 21 kms out from Um Pang, we bumped over the brow of a low hill and entered Pa Toei, inside

THREE PAGODAS

Burma. We did not know this until a couple of concerned men, shabbily dressed, pointed out the fact to us. When we had parked our bike, they led us by the arm back to two home-made wooden signs that we had passed but not seen. These read, in shaky hand-painted red lettering: THE BORDER OF BURMA AND THAILAND and KAREN: THE BONDRY OF BURMA AND THAILAND. Arrows pointing in each direction were supposed to indicate that this was Karen territory, which extended either side of the 'bondry'.

The two men talked urgently, but we could not understand a word of what they were saying. However, their gesticulations seemed to indicate that there was a Burma army camp just up the road and we should on no account go any further. A few people gathered round, their eyes wide, and faces began to peer furtively out of windows and doors. All this caused us to grow worried. We thought that we may have ventured into a Burmese village, and we half expected bullets to strafe us. But then we noticed traces of reassuring Karen costume and concluded that we were after all in KNU-held territory. Besides, no one was actually trying to shoo us out of the village. Gradually, people got over their consternation, we relaxed, and things simmered down. Our two new hosts even volunteered to show us round the settlement. Fortunately, they were joined by another man, who could speak some broken Thai.

Pa Toei (or Ba Tui, as we also heard) was a ramshackle Karen place, consisting of about 20 families. It transpired that there was another larger community with the same name further up the road, probably where the SLORC camp was. Beyond that village, the trail continued up to Palu and Wa Lay. Pa Toei by the border was only two years old, suggesting that it was a new refugee settlement. People must have moved here so that they could flee at a moment's notice across the frontier into Thailand. The condition of the houses seemed to confirm this refugee status. With the exception of the headman's house, which lay closest to the red border signs, all Pa Toei's dwellings were wretched hovels. Some had graffiti carved on them, such as 'KNLA', meant to bolster up the spirits of these displaced people. But one, which took my fancy, was more lighthearted and also unaccountable. It pronounced, likewise in English, DON'T KISS ME and formed a kind of counterpart across the intervening miles and days of the enigmatic 'I KISS', which we had found incised on the lady guard's flip-flops at Manerplaw. Little stalls lining the track through the settlement were as impoverished as the houses, but they were well stocked with 'Best Thukhita Cheroots'. In an act of solidarity with the refugees, we bought a bundle of 50 to replenish our stock for the absurdly low price of 17 baht. On a more sombre note, we were introduced at one of the stalls to a beautiful young Karen woman with an infant boy, whose husband had been killed defending KNU GHQ Manerplaw in 1992.

In keeping with other border KNU Karen, the people of Pa Toei grew ever more friendly. Further into the settlement, we came across a group building a large shelter for some celebration the next day. They invited us to return if we wanted. It seemed they were already in party mood because the *lao kao* was out and there was a lot of amusement. Of course, we were unable to escape without ourselves downing a tumblerful of the white spirit in the scorching midday heat. When we did finally leave, an embarrassing and rather alarming mishap befell us, watched by half the village. While I was kicking the Honda, the kick-starter broke off and fell to the dust. The lever was sheared and could not be repaired. We had visions of being stranded with a broken motorbike inside Burma, dangerously close to SLORC troops. And that was how things would have remained, had not the good Karen of Pa Toei pushed us back up to the top of the hill and the border, from where we were able to jump-start the machine and ride all the way back to Um Pang without a stop.

DEATH HIGHWAY

In 2001, as said, the way across the border to Pa Toei was not at all blocked (it looked as if a few local vehicles or people went to and fro), but soldiers forbade us to cross. With no guards or obstacles or barrier at the frontier, it was still in this sense quite open, and technically we could have continued across. After Nong Luang, which had changed little in eight years, you continue 4.7 kms up an increasingly remote and lonely paved road, with the thickly forested border ridge shadowing your progress close at hand on your left side, to a checkpoint, above which, on your right side, a Thai army camp is positioned high up in trees. When we reached the unmanned checkpoint, no one came down from the camp to prevent us going further or took any interest in us at all. Actually, it was we who got one of the camp soldiers to come down and advise us. He said we could continue to the border – there was no one there, but we could not mistake it – but should on no account cross it. The Karen village of Pa Toei now lay unambiguously in Burma, and we should not visit it because DKBA and Burma army troops were roaming around 3 kms away or less (from the Thai camp), and owing to them the situation was dangerous. We rode on 800 m and came to the deserted frontier, which had an atmospheric feeling of nothingness about it.

The Thai asphalt road simply ended, after which a very poor dirt track went off slightly downhill, through scrub and trees, towards Pa Toei, which was not visible. To the left of the road lay an old wooden guard hut, derelict and overgrown with weeds and vines. Next to this stood a tall bamboo pole, from the top of which a Thai flag fluttered. On the right side of the road, a pointed wooden sign said simply 'Thailand', given in English on the side facing Burma and in Thai on the other. It was shadeless and very hot at the crossing. There was no one around, and the silence, except for the cracking of bamboos in the sizzling sun, was thunderous, eerie. As before, we could so easily have gone on to Pa Toei, or just a little way to look down on it... But, of course, we did not. We had the feeling that we were being watched from out of the trees. The place was spooky, and the thought alarmed us that nothing stood between us and the DKBA, who could so easily interfere with us, rob us, apprehend us, or worse.

Route detail: Um Pang – Mae Klong Mai – Nong Luang – border (Map 26)

km 0.0	Um Pang centre at crossroads near *Gift Shop* and *Umpang GH*
	Go N out of Um Pang as if returning to Mae Sot on H1090. Climb up hill, leaving village behind, and proceed past Pra Wo shrine (L) and **Mae Klong** village 3.8 kms to junction
km 3.8	Junction marked by tourist box (L). Turn L/west here off H1090 into H1167 side road
	Pass through pleasant market village of **Mae Klong Mai** and cross bridge over Mae Klong river
	Road dips up and down through hilly country, wooded with teak
	Along here, on L side, sign for Ta Ko Pi Cave. A track leads S away from the road to a fork, where you go L to reach the cave, situated 300 m from the road. Rumour has it that the cave is 3 kms long and that there is a way right through it to Mae Klong Tai
km 8.3	Checkpoint
km 12.3	Big junction, where L goes to De Lo Ki (5 kms), Ti Lo Su w/f, Mae Chan/ Klo To (30 kms) and Boeng Kloeng (74 kms), which is the route taken in the next two chapters of this book, while R continues to Nong Luang
km 13.3	Village of **Soe Ta** (or Soei Ta)
km 14.9	'Nong Long' health centre (R)
km 15.6	**Nong Luang** school (R) and centre. Petrol available here
km 20.3	Checkpoint and Thai army camp (up R)
km 21.1	End of road and border

12

THE DRIVERLESS KOMATSU

Um Pang – Klo To/Sa Kaang Thit – Nu Po – Kui Le Tor

O ne evening, when we were talking to Sombat, the *ampoe* man who was the brother of 'pop star' So, he began speaking about the village of Lae Tong Ku and of the enigmatic rishi cultist people who lived there. The village lay far south of Um Pang on the Burmese border and could only be reached on foot. The people were a small colourful Karen sect, who worshipped a divine rishi[1] or hermit-sage. This demigod lived in the village in a *wat*, and somehow elephant tusks figured in the group's religion. The people ate only the meat of jungle animals and wore their hair long, twisted up in topknots. The rishi sect was unique in Thailand and little was known about it. Needless to say, the subject fired our imaginations, and we immediately determined to reach the mysterious village.

We asked Sombat if he thought we could visit Lae Tong Ku. It might be possible, he said thoughtfully. Had he ever been there? He occasionally went there on district business, and once he had stayed a longer time because he had had to organize a census and prepare the ground for a helicopter visit by a member of the Thai royal family. We plagued the sober Sombat with many questions, and he patiently tried to answer them. How could we get there, and were there other villages on the way? What language did the rishi people speak, and would we be able to communicate with them? What about the problem of food? And did other people ever visit the village? The *ampoe* official thought that it would take us about two to three days to get from Um Pang to Lae Tong Ku and the same amount of time to get back. So a round trip would take one week. We had first to go down to the Karen village of Nu Po and then start trekking. There were villages on the way, but we would need guides. After Nu Po, there were two ways on to Lae Tong Ku – a long roundabout path remaining in Thailand, and a short cut through Burma. All the local people, of course, took the short cut, but he was not at all sure about the wisdom of a *farang* trekking through Burma, all the more so with the war currently raging across the border.

---

[1] The rishi is widely known in the Um Pang area at the *loe-si* or *lü-si* (difficult to render the Thai pronunciation exactly in 'English'), which – because Thai-speakers have difficulty with the letter 'r' and prefer to replace it with the letter 'l' – equates with *rü-si* or *roe-si* or *reu-si*, which in turn is derived from the Sanskrit word 'rishi'. The rishi of Lae Tong Ku village and of the rishi/*loe-si* cult plus associated villages also goes by the title of *pu chaik* or 'Grandfather Buddha'.

THE DRIVERLESS KOMATSU

Lae Tong Ku, we imagined, lay roughly on our route to the Three Pagodas Pass, and so it seemed a good idea to try to use the village as a first stepping stone. We plied our informant with more questions. Did the rishi community lie far from the route to the Three Pagodas, and what did he know of the territory beyond it? But here our friend's knowledge was exhausted. Lae Tong Ku was on the southernmost edge of Um Pang district. Beyond it was another district (Sangklaburi) and another province (Kanchanaburi). Sombat knew nothing about that outer darkness. It seemed, anyway, that we should at least be able to reach Lae Tong Ku. The problem now was to research the lie of the land beyond it. As this was the more obscure part of the journey and also, we estimated, the lion's share, we spent several more days in Um Pang trying to gather further information. The results were hardly encouraging. But one thing sustained us in our enquiries. We had once met someone who had trekked from Um Pang to the Three Pagodas, so the journey had to be possible. This was Wachara Liu Pong Sawat, the young owner of *Ta Mi Laa Guest House* in Chiang Khong. He had taken part in an expedition jointly organized by the paramilitary BPP and a Thai adventure club. The group had taken ten days to trek through the jungle, starting at Ti Lo Su Waterfall. He had told us that the trip had been hair-raising, so much so that in one place on the mountains he had cried with fear. Remembering Wachara's words, we were filled with apprehension, but at the same time spurred on. What we did not know until later was that the way taken by Wachara had been a different, more easterly route than the one which we finally took.

The obvious person to quiz next was one Boonlum, an ex-Thai army ranger of Um Pang who sometimes organized trekking and rafting trips. At first, he warmed to our idea, but then the complications began to pile up. Yes, he could come with us, but there would have to be a minimum of two guides. The trip would last about a week, and at his charge of so-and-so-much per guide per day that would work out at thousands of baht for the trip. On top of that, we would have to pay for the bus tickets to get the guides from Sangklaburi back to Um Pang. Or, rather, we would have to pay for them (and ourselves) to get to the bottom end, because now the one-time *tahaan praan* ranger planned to start down there and trek up. The mounting expense of the trip, not to mention the enormity of our plan, began to dawn on us. We told Boonlum that we would think the matter through, but soon anyway his interest went off the boil, and he drifted away, saying that we knew where we could find him. We then studied the guide's maps. They seemed not to accord with the accurate administrative map we had wheedled out of the district office. Also, it became clear to us that the ranger's real stamping ground was restricted to Um Pang district. Details on his map further south were sketchy. Seeing his heart go so quickly out of the project, we even wondered if he had ever trekked right through.

We turned next to the *kamnaan*. He knew nothing about what happened beyond Lae Tong Ku, but thought that from a place called Boeng Kloeng to the rishi village it was a 20-km or hard day's hike (this stretch turned out, in fact, to be a 4-hour walk). He imposed the stricture on us that we should on no account do anything unless it was sanctioned and organized by the BPP.

309

Beyond that, the village head seemed more interested in coaxing us away from the 'Lilypond' into his guest rooms. Seeing that we were not amenable, he finally suggested we try for information at the police station. At the station, just off Um Pang's westerly main street, deputy commander Rong Moet could add little to what we already knew, except to say that he thought it would be alright to proceed to Boeng Kloeng, the village the *kamnaan* had mentioned, where we should report to the BPP camp and ask about the local situation.

It was becoming increasingly clear that all roads led to the Border Patrol Police and that nothing could be achieved without enlisting their help. Accordingly, we summoned up our courage, rode to the edge of Um Pang, past the sentries at the entrance to BPP 347 base, and up to the camp offices. Here, working our way up the chain of command, we finally spoke to the base commander. This was a mistake, for, quite apart from getting nothing out of the *dorchodor*, we merely apprised them of what we were up to, with the result they they would probably radio through to the first checkpoint to turn us back. While sympathetic to our cause, the commander explained that he himself could do nothing for us, neither give us permission, nor arrange back-up. We would have to go through headquarters in Mae Sot. Not only that, but we would have to get permission from the Forestry Protection HQ in Tak. Moreover, he could not radio through for us to get permission. We would have to appear in person at the two places, make an application and wait for a written permit.

This news came like a bombshell. Had we come so far just to be sent all the way back, frustrated by bureaucracy? A round trip to Mae Sot and Tak would take at least three days, not allowing for any hitches. Worse still, the whole thing squared with what Wachara of Chiang Khong had told us, for he and his friends had had to go through exactly these official channels. There really seemed now no other option. Seeing our despondent faces, the commander then began to slightly attenuate what he had said. He himself did not mind what we did, but he had strict orders from above and was obliged to stick to them. He did not want to be held responsible for us if anything happened. It seemed to us that he was trying to communicate to us an interstice through which we might slip. It was as if he was intimating: Go if you want, but I have now put myself in the clear. We thanked him politely and left.

As a last resort, we went to Um Pang district office. We remembered how helpful Somsak, the chief of *ampoe* Wiang Haeng, had been to us earlier. Through Sombat and also through our 'Lilypond' landlord (deputy *ampoe* head), we secured an interview with the chief. But in his room, the door to our little jaunt seemed to slam shut forever. *Mai dai*, came his repeated response as we unfolded each new element of our plan, *mai dai*. The situation with the Karen was far too fluid at the moment. In short, he flatly forbade us to set off for Lae Tong Ku, let alone for the Three Pagodas. In a last-ditch attempt, we produced Somsak's letter and tried to shame him into assisting us. Could he not produce a similarly helpful letter? But the chief would not even consider the idea.

The volatility of the Karen situation that the *ampoe* chief had mentioned referred not only to the latest offensive of the Burma army against the KNLA.

THE DRIVERLESS KOMATSU

In the days before we reached Um Pang and also during our stay there, we began to receive disturbing reports of some serious incident near Mae Chan Ta, in the southmost part of the district. The newspapers were full of lurid horror stories that rishi cultists had attacked and killed a number of BPP soldiers and *grom pamai* (forest protection) officials deep in the jungle. This rather contradicted the impression we had gained from Sombat of the rishi people of Lae Tong Ku, whom he had described as quiet peace-loving folk, but there was no denying the press cuttings or what was on everybody's lips in Um Pang. On top of the discouragement which we had garnered at the hands of the authorities, all this was bad news indeed. It seemed that not only were the very people we wanted to visit embroiled in some kind of bloody conflict, but that we would absolutely be prevented by the military from going anywhere near the area for our own safety.

One newspaper report spoke of the brutal murder of five BPP soldiers and one Thai villager by members of a little-known religious group, the 'Talarku' (Telakhon). These cultists were followers of a godlike leader who lived in a monastery in the remote Karen village of 'Letako' (Lae Tong Ku). The 'Talarku' wore their hair long, tied up in a knot on the tops of their heads. For religious reasons, they ate the meat only of wild animals. The cultists were extreme in the devoutness of their beliefs, and if anyone criticized their faith or tried to put obstacles in its way, they could resort to violence. It was thought that while the *pu chaik* or *pu kyaik* (the man-god rishi) was not himself directly responsible for the incident, his most fervent followers were. Two possible motivations for the attack were given. On the one hand, the Forestry Department had been trying to prevent the cultists from entering and hunting in the wildlife preserves (i.e. frustrate their precept to eat only jungle game), and on the other, the cultists had believed that the *dorchodor* were trying to suppress their faith in favour of Buddhism. So they had moved to protect their deeply venerated way of life, and this had resulted in the killings. In nearly every detail, the newspaper report tallied with the picture we were building up of the rishi people of Lae Tong Ku.

Another account ran along the same lines, if marked by the occasional difference. 'Talarku' cultists had ransacked and burnt a forestry office in the jungle south of Um Pang, before going on to attack a nearby BPP base. The 'Karen splinter group' of 'voodoo fanatics' had hacked five BPP officers and one Thai civilian to death with machetes, and had abducted three forestry officials, who were later released. However, the incident had not taken place at Lae Tong Ku, but in and around Mae Chan Ta, a village many hours' walk away. Further, the perpetrators were not the 'whitethread' 'Talarku' of Lae Tong Ku, but members of a breakaway 'yellowthread' group, who lived in villages within the ambit of Mae Chan Ta. Numbering some hundreds, they had set up a 'hermit centre' of their own with their own rishi in the outlying settlement of Chong Pae. The rival man-god and his followers, so the second newspaper report continued, were ex-CPT communists. As to the motive for the attack, the upstart 'yellow' cultists had wanted to expand their sphere of influence to villages such as Lae Tong Ku and Mong Gua, where the 'whitethread' rishi cult was already firmly established. Ultimately, their goal was

311

to drive out the traditional 'Talarku' from such places. The killing of the BPP soldiers had been an attempt by the 'yellowthreads' to impress the orthodox 'Talarku' with their prowess and so gain influence. In the wake of the attack, large numbers of BPP soldiers had been helicoptered in to track down the culprits, resulting in the encirclement of about 300 cultists around Mae Chan Ta and the arrest of 21 of them. The 'yellowthread' *pu chaik*, however, followed by dozens of his most ardent disciples, had fled deeper into the jungle, towards Kanchanaburi province, where they were still at large.

The news of this serious incident put an even bigger question mark over our already doubtful project. It was still not clear whether it was the cultists of Lae Tong Ku or of Mae Chan Ta who had been responsible for the murders. And even if we knew, we had no idea which of the two villages we might have to pass through on our way to the Three Pagodas – perhaps through both. But, further, assuming that Lae Tong Ku was safe and that we could also give Mae Chan Ta a wide berth, we would still have to pass through the jungles of Kanchanaburi province, where dozens of murderous fugitive 'yellowthreads' were on the run. Added to this, there were all the regular problems and dangers associated with jungle trekking. The more we contemplated actually embarking on our adventure, the more they weighed down on us. Would we not get lost? Would we find people to guide us? Would we be able to communicate with them? Were there any tracks going where we wanted to go? The jungle was full of poisonous snakes, bears, big cats and other large wild animals. What was the risk with these? Especially the border areas of Tak and Kanchanaburi provinces were notorious for malaria. What was the risk of catching the disease? The same areas were a hideout for fugitive criminals and cross-border bandits. How real was that danger? And, then, it was not clear to what extent we might have to go through Burma. Sombat had hinted that to get to Lae Tong Ku we would probably have to trek some hours on the wrong side of the border, but what about beyond the rishi village? Passing illegally through Burma brought a new set of problems. The Karen in Kawthoolei were every bit as hospitable as those in Thailand, and no doubt the KNLA of 6th Brigade district could be very helpful, but in Burma we were beyond the help of the Thai authorities and at the mercy of people we could not fully know. A major Four Cuts offensive was in progress. Apparently, it had now mostly swept further north, but the situation was extremely volatile. What was the latest? Even more unfortunate that running into 'yellowthreads' would be to fall into the hands of a *tatmadaw* foot patrol, or be seen by an informer or a government spotter plane, or step on a landmine left in a deserted village.

Our round of the authorities in Um Pang had left us despondent enough. Now all these new concerns threatened to overwhelm us. In the Um Pang offices, we began to realize that the more we enquired, the more we only generated discouragement, conflicting information, disinformation, confusion, *mai ru's* and *mai dai's*. Instead of building towards setting off, we were being pushed ever further back in the direction of Mae Sot or even Tak town. However, there was one avenue, so simple and obvious that we had overlooked it, that we had not explored: just to set off and see what happened. Policeman Rong Moet had even almost suggested this. Go to Boeng Kloeng, he had said, and ask again there. Warming to this possibility one evening in *Ti Lo Su* restaurant, we figured that the worst that could happen would be that we would be sent back from Boeng Kloeng with a flea in our ear. So after relaxing for a week in Um Pang, we decided to start next morning.

The area south of Um Pang was the last great unspoilt area in Thailand, and a trek through it to the Three Pagodas Pass the last great adventure left in the kingdom. After an assessment of the possibilities and risks, our concern now was with practicalities and preparation. Real jungle trekking, Sombat told us, was more than twice as exhausting as ordinary trekking. The heat and humidity made it difficult to go very far or carry much weight. Accordingly, on the eve of our departure, we divided our possessions into two piles – the things we would leave behind and those we would take with us. The unnecessary things we bundled up and gave to our *ampoe* friend. Traveller's cheques, airline tickets, excess money and other valuables went into the district office safe. Onto the pile of indispensable things we threw: jeans, trainers, long-sleeved shirts (against mosquitoes), pullovers (cool evenings), underwear, one change of lightweight clothes (pyjamas or a sarong seemed a good idea), lightweight sleeping bags, a mosquito net, washing things, plasters, Autan insect repellent, sun cream, water purifying pills, antiseptic cream, diarrhoea pills, a wide-spectrum antibiotic, vitamin tablets, toilet paper, matches, a torch, notebooks, cameras and film.

The biggest problem, we foresaw, would be food. Of course, wherever there were people, there was cold rice to eat. Villagers may or may not offer other food. But if they did, it was another matter as to whether one could stomach it. In Mae Sot, we had taken the precaution of stocking up with tins of tuna and sardines in various sauces, and now in Um Pang we loaded up with packets of Ma-maa instant noodles. The famous packs of Ma-maa were a godsend. They weighed very little and provided a tasty snack wherever someone had a fire going to boil water.

We had long since taken leave of our Danish friend. Seeing us getting ever more deeply entangled in Um Pang, he had left to chance his arm bobbing down the Mae Khong (River Mekong) in a boat. Now all that remained was to seek out Sombat, tell him of our exact plans, and hand over our dispensable possessions. He wished us good luck and gave us a slip of paper, on which he had scribbled the name of the BPP commander in Boeng Kloeng and a couple of other words. This scrap of paper was to prove the most important of all our items of preparation, crucial to the success of the whole venture.

❧

To go forward we had first to go back. On our faithful old Honda Wing, we rode out of Um Pang a couple of kms in the direction of Mae Sot (Map 26). Tooting the bike's horn at the Pra Wo shrine for the last time, we passed the turn-off at **Mae Klong** for *Gift House* in the banana grove, where we had started out all those days ago. At the police box, we bore left/west onto the H1167 road, immediately passing through **Mae Klong Mai**. In this pleasant market village, we crossed a bridge over the Mae Klong, the river which gave

313

both this village and others in the vicinity their names. Beyond the bridge, the asphalt gave out, and a gravelly dirt road dipped up and down through hilly country, wooded with teak, in which Ta Ko Pi Cave lay to the left side. Two checkpoints followed, the second (12.5 kms from Um Pang centre) marking a junction. Straight on (west) led to the Thai village of Nong Luang and to the Karen refugee settlement of Pa Toei (Ba Tui), situated on the border (details in Postscript to Chapter 11), while left (south) – our way – headed towards Klo To and Nu Po. At the junction, therefore, we branched left to proceed down a dirt highway. Not far along this, we came across a sprawling low wooden building with a grass roof. In front of it were some of those large brown earthenware waterjars found everywhere in Thailand, as well as sacks of rice and baskets of vegetables. Bunches of bananas were hanging up, trays of soft drinks were stacked up, and many other provisions were for sale. In among them, we spotted an urn with hot water on the go. We stopped and drank a cup of *gaffae tammada* or strong Thai coffee. It turned out that this ramshackle building, resplendent in the early morning sun, was the last real roadside store for some 200 kms, until Sangklaburi.

De Lo Ki (De Lor Kee, 16 kms from Um Pang) was the first village down the southbound dirt road, a Karen place. Two more checkpoints followed and a couple of bridges. After the bridges, the way divided, left proceeding a further 27 kms to the famous Ti Lo Su jungle waterfall, and right/straight continuing to Klo To. The stretch between the fork and Klo To was as lonely and scary as any we had ridden on our journey. For 20 kms, it snaked up and down through uninhabited jungle and forest. Bizarre sinister limestone monoliths stuck up through the canopy like teeth. Behind them, to the west, lay the Tanon Tongchai border mountain ridge. The road was totally devoid of traffic. With relief, we found ourselves descending into a broad valley, past another checkpoint, to the Karen village of **Klo To**, already 40 kms south of Um Pang.

Klo To (Klor Tor), also known by the Thai name of Mae Chan (the Mae Chan river flowed past the village), lay west of the dirt road. Dominated by a white pagoda atop a karstic needle, it marked a significant unofficial border crossing point to the Karen State and Burma. Some kind of market was taking place on the playground of Klo To school, and here people told us about a big black market over the border at a place called Ban Mai (= new village). Ban Mai was seven or eight kms away, and we could visit it if we wanted. As the morning was not far advanced, we decided to have a quick look. A very bad 4WD track led past a checkpoint, over the Mae Chan river, past a military camp, to the Karen settlement of **Nupa Towa**. Spread out along the route in three sections, the village had its own white *chedi* and was enhanced by many red-flowering trees. As we continued through woods and jungle, outcroppings in the form of a razor blade reared up above the vegetation to the south. A post at the trackside with no sign on it led us to believe that we had reached the border. Picking our way through a maze of criss-crossing tracks and paths, we went down a hill to arrive suddenly at a KNLA checkpoint and customs gate. We were at Ban Mai or, in Burmese, **Sa Kaang Thit** (Sakaangthit/ Sakaanthi).

THE DRIVERLESS KOMATSU

Sa Kaang Thit (Ban Mai)

Although only three or four years old, the village was surprisingly large. Some 180 houses, 20 well-provisioned stores and a school bore witness to the fact that this was indeed a major border crossing for both people and vehicles. Sa Kaang Thit seemed to us like a mixture of Po Pa Ta and Mae Saam Laep. Set in a bowl, and backgrounded by a bald ridge, it was surrounded close at hand by three small jagged tooth mountains. Parking the bike, we wandered up and down the streets of leaf-roofed houses. In front of every store were bundles of Thukita cheroots, 50 for 10 baht, and also all the paraphernalia of betel chewing – lime leaves, pastes and so on. Conspicuous too were pyramids of cartons of cigarettes, mainly imported into Burma from Singapore. The brand names pretended to luxurious internationality, or affected the swank of American limousines. The smoker could indulge himself with Long Beach, Monterey, Fortune, Lucky Strike, Eagle, Classics, Perilly's, Monte Carlo, Hunter or Modern. Those of a Chinese smoking persuasion could light up a Duya, a Xinxing or, strangely, a Horse.

What struck us most about Sa Kaang Thit was the large number of Muslim Indo-Burmese traders and their families in this Karen village. As at the bazaar near Po Pa Ta, we were surrounded by tall dark wiry men with beautiful piercing eyes, chintuft beards and white skullcaps. Some were Arakanese *rohingyas*, others Burmese Indians, a few perhaps Bangladeshis. Mostly they were not refugees, but people who had been living in Burma a long time, who had recently been displaced. Muslims had traditionally traded along the old Moulmein/Um Pang/Mae Sot route. It was just that in the recent fighting many had been pushed up here to the border from the interior. Very possibly the Muslim Liberation Organization provided at Sa Kaang Thit one of the Muslim units that still operated within the KNLA.

We were taken in hand by a soft-spoken refined young man, who was a dissident ethnic Burmese student from Moulmein. In convincing English, he told us that there were no fewer than three revolutionary student camps in the village. Two, only a year or so old, were ABSDF camps, Battalions 206 and 216, while the third, his own, was called Sa Kaang Thit Students' Camp, consisting of 50 rebel men. Perhaps on account of his English, our Moulmein friend (name suppressed) was charged with "looking after foreign matters and supplies". We expressed to him our desire to take an early lunch in Sa Kaang Thit. We had spotted numerous Muslim tea shops, but found no regular eating place. He brought us to a Karen-run 'restaurant', called *Family*. Operated by a Mr Jo Thu, it turned out to be the local KNLA nerve centre with an adjoining KNU propaganda room. The walls were covered with information and slogans. Meant less for outside consumption and more to boost insurgent morale, the slogans announced: THE RACE IS NOT TO THE SWIFT, NOR THE BATTLE TO THE STRONG, A HOUSE DIVIDED AGAINST ITSELF CANNOT STAND (highly ironic in the light of the disastrous split that was later to befall the Karen), and THE DARKEST HOUR IS BEFORE THE DAWN.

In the black-market village, we had seen goats wandering everywhere. Now, inevitably, goat was served up for our early lunch – curried and eaten with the fingers. There was a great deal of coming and going in and around *Family*. Women and children with discs of *tanaka* on their cheeks played in dark corners. An invalid guerrilla with a wooden leg came in to read the paper over a mid-morning Hong Tong whisky. Outside, three elephants plodded past. Battered trucks arrived and departed. One delivered up a squad of heavily armed security men. Nearly all had long hair, done in pigtails or ponytails, or just loose, adding to the racy atmosphere. A minah bird in a bamboo cage chattered in Karen, while at the main table in *Family* a group of people sat huddled around a transistor radio, listening to the news in Burmese from the BBC World Service.

We were eating the goat curry when a Suzuki jeep drew up outside. The local KNLA commander, accompanied by a driver and two armed bodyguards, got out. Word had reached him of our presence and he wanted to check us out. He was Saw Tae Tu, a pleasant chap of about 40 with a square face, moustache, and red teeth. Sitting down at our table, he asked us our business. During the interview, he made no move to make himself more comfortable. He sat there with his green beret on, complete with KNLA badge (British Army style), and a much-bepocketed safari jacket, heavy with bits and pieces (see photo section). From a waist belt hung, on one side, a pistol in a holster and, on the other, a hand grenade, shiny from rubbing against his camouflage trousers. As he enquired, we noticed on one of his fingers a gold ring inset with green jade. Satisfied with our account of ourselves, he relaxed and turned the conversation to other things. Why did we not go and visit the Karen New Year celebrations at Jo Ta across the Dawna range, he asked? We explained our intention of going to Lae Tong Ku. In the restaurant, we had noticed a mysterious set of jars up on a shelf. What were they, we asked? That was *lapat tho* or tea-leaf mixture, Saw Tae Tu said. He motioned to Mr Jo Thu to bring the jars down and prepare some. It was a kind of nutty snack made of sesame seeds, peanuts, *bae yi* (split beans), *tua noi* (little peas), fried grated coconut, fried garlic, and green tea-leaf paste mixed with oil and fish sauce. The idea was to dip into each jar, taking according to one's taste, and stir the ingredients together. Doubtfully, we tried some of the *lapat tho*. It was surprisingly good. As the commander made to go, we asked him about the wisdom of leaving our motorcycle with the headman at Nu Po village, as we planned. That would be alright, he said, "and come back and see me again sometime."

✵

Back in Thailand again at Klo To, we rejoined the dirt road south to reach after a couple of kms a Karen village signed **Nu Sae Po** (now see Map 27). Here, we found the way blocked and a bridge under construction. It seemed like the end of the road. Back at Um Pang, Sombat had said that the road terminated at a place called Nu Po and that we should leave our motorbike there. We asked several people if it was Nu Po, but either they could not understand Thai, or they indicated that it both was and was not Nu Po – very confusing. Tiring of riding round the dusty alleyways of the village, we went back to the entrance by the road. We had seen a school on the top of a hillock there, and wandered up.

THE DRIVERLESS KOMATSU

Ragamuffin children gawped in silent astonishment from every window of the school building, and finally a single all-purpose teacher with some deformity came out onto the veranda. The village was Nu Sae Po, he stated. Nu Po lay another 20 kms down the road, and to get past the bridgeworks we had to make a detour through the village.

We continued on our way, passing a forest conservation office and the deserted village of Ko Ga, which had been amalgamated with Nu Po (or was it Nu Sae Po?). Otherwise, there was little else on this stretch of road, which penetrated ever deeper into forest country. The compacted gravel and dirt surface began visibly to deteriorate. The way was littered with fist-sized stones, some of which catapulted up from the front wheel. More than one struck me painfully on the shin bone. After that, the surface degenerated into soft, churned-up earth. It seemed that we must be nearing the roadhead, and as if to confirm the fact, we passed a wayside navvies' camp, two half-built bridges, and a small quarry with a rock-crushing machine. Just when we were on the verge of giving up because the way was virtually impassable, we spied houses in the trees to the right. A long 64 kms south of Um Pang, it was the Karen village of **Nu Po** – the end of the road.

We biked into this unprepossessing collection of 20 wooden dwellings, situated around a dry grassy compound, and asked for the headman. At his house, we found that he was away, but relatives said that it would be alright for us to leave our bike under the house in among the stilts, pigs and chickens. Everyone seemed very vague, which made us uneasy about abandoning a hire machine so lightly. But, remembering the assurances of both Sombat and Saw Tae Tu, we did just that. (When, finally, we came to retrieve the Wing, it was exactly where we had left it, untouched and covered with a layer of dust.)

At Nu Po, we enquired about a guide to lead us to Kui Le Tor, our next station. As luck would have it, a party had just left. A boy went round the village asking if anyone else was going to Kui, but at two in the afternoon we had arrived too late. The last people had now gone, and no one else was prepared to guide us there. This left us in a quandary. Nu Po did not look like a good place to stay, it was too far to get back to Um Pang by nightfall, and we did not know the way forward. That did not matter, everybody said in the typically blithe manner of Karen folk, we would easily find the route. All we had to do was follow the course of the new road and then turn off it onto a well-marked path, which would bring us in an hour to Kui. People went this way all the time. A group with a laden elephant had set off earlier, and we would undoubtedly catch them up. Against our better judgement, but with no satisfactory alternative, we shouldered our backpacks and set off. Right at the beginning of our adventure, we broke one of the cardinal rules of jungle trekking, never to go without a guide. The imprudence nearly led to our undoing.

We trudged a few kms through the deep orange powder of the rudimentary road. Reassuringly, small groups of red-clad Karen came against us. Especially to the east, there were breathtaking views through vivid green banana palms of spiky monoliths piercing the jungle canopy. We passed two giant yellow Caterpillar bulldozers slicing into the shoulder of a hill, shoving piles of rock and earth, and tipping them unceremoniously over the edge, where the debris rolled down the hillside into a tangled mass of bamboos and trees. From under their parasols, the drivers, faces masked by triangles of cloth, waved to us. Clambering through their worksite, we came onto a pilot track. The track was no more than a tunnel which had been smashed through the tall dense bamboos. We walked along this for another km or two, following the profile of the mountainside. Presently, we came upon a surreal sight. A third giant bulldozer, this time a Komatsu, stood unattended in the depths of the jungle, its massive diesel engine gently idling. Beyond its shovel was virgin jungle. This was the absolute cutting edge of the new road to Kui Le Tor and ultimately to Boeng Kloeng. We looked around, expecting to see someone in the trees having a snack or a nap, but there was nobody. We even waited for 15 minutes, hoping that the driver would return because we wanted to ask what had become of the path to Kui. But nobody came. It was a weird situation.

The position was further disquieting in that it was clear that our path could not lead beyond the bulldozer. That way the vegetation was impenetrable. So somehow we had missed the turn-off. We backtracked for a while until we saw what looked like a little path dropping down from the pilot road. The beginning was marked with a stick. We scrambled down the steep mountainside until the ground levelled out among trees and bamboo. For some reason we had the illusion that we were near a habitation. But there was nothing. The path fragmented increasingly until it became clear that the ways were just animal tracks through the bamboos. We stopped to look and listen. Nothing. The sweat was pouring off our bodies, our shirts were sticking to our backs, and winged insects kept bothering us by settling on our forearms and faces. We looked at our watches – nearly 4pm. In a couple of hours it would be dark. Alarmingly and humiliatingly, only 40 minutes out from the motorbike, we were already lost in the jungle. It was hopeless to go on, so laboriously we climbed back up to the pilot road. There we noticed that the stick we had seen was just one of many marker sticks, telling the bulldozer driver where to push the road. How stupid we had been! At the same time our ears picked up the low tones of the Komatsu ticking over. In fact, it was just around the corner. So, for a second time, we visited the bizarre spectacle of the machine left running in the middle of nowhere. But where before the sight of this juggernaut had vaguely sickened us because it seemed to be an instrument of the rape of the virgin jungle, now we greeted it with relief as a sign of civilization.

We trudged back along the pilot track. A night in Nu Po looked inevitable. Suddenly a battered Land Rover approached us. We waved it down. Inside were five boys with long-barrelled guns poking out of the windows. We thought we were done for, but it was just the Komatsu team returning to work. They offered us water from a dirty bottle, which we drank greedily, disregarding everything we knew about doubtful water. The boys said that the Kui path went off from the east side of the 'road', not the west, and started about one km back, near the two other machines. We cursed the imprecision of the Nu Po Karen and set off again. Sure enough, there was the beginning of the path, although it was easy to see why we had overlooked it.

THE DRIVERLESS KOMATSU

Far too late, we began the two-hour mountain trek to Kui. Essentially, the path crossed a mountain. Relentlessly, it climbed up through the trees, before dropping steeply down an even greater distance on the far side. During this long hour of clambering we met not a single person, but the way was clear enough. At the bottom, there was a river. The river at that point fragmented into a network of tree-covered islands and rivulets, and we could not see where the path went or where it emerged on the other side, even if it did. Nor was it clear whether we had to go upstream or down. So, blindly we thrashed about among the islets, watching the sun make its steady tropical descent. We picked up scraps of path, only to lose them again. In our hearts, we knew what we did not dare to admit to ourselves, that with the light beginning to fade we were lost for a second time. Categorically, we promised to ourselves that we would never again make the idiotic mistake of trekking either without the most precise instructions or without a guide.

We figured that if we proceeded downstream, we must eventually come to some village. Suddenly, 100 metres away, we saw half a dozen buffaloes being led by an old man, who had a mighty bundle of straw on his head. We hullooed to him, shouted more urgently, and chased after him. But he ignored us totally. We skipped across the islands, splashed through the rivulets and felt sure we would soon catch him up, all the more so because we saw that he had to cross a deep pool. But when we got to the pool and waded through the waist-deep water, he and his animals had vanished. It was uncanny. Were the buffaloes and the man real, or were they just some chimera? We found no further trace of them. But we did find a path. The path led through some tall trees until suddenly we came across a wooden sign nailed to an outsize tree. In hand-painted white letters, it said (in Thai): Ban **Kui Le Tor**.

❧

Kui Le Tor

Around a parched clearing, we found about 20 wooden thatch-roofed Karen houses. On the platforms of some of them, families were sitting cross-legged in a circle eating supper. It was clear to us that we would have to spend the night in this unpromising-looking place. Perfunctorily, we asked at one dwelling how far it was to Boeng Kloeng. It was far too late to set off now, the people said. The last group had left two hours earlier. Kui Le Tor, although unimportant in itself, was significant in that the way divided here, one path leading to Kui Ta and Mong Gua (the first leg of the long roundabout way to Lae Tong Ku), and the other path going to Boeng Kloeng (the first leg of the short way to Lae Tong Ku).

As was the custom in these situations, we reported to the *pu yai baan* or village headman. We clambered over the bamboo stockade marking off his front garden and addressed him as he sat with his family over rice, stewed vegetable, a dried fish and chilli dip. Fortunately, he spoke some Thai. He motioned to the covered part of the balcony behind him, where we could stay the night. Beyond that, neither he nor his family took much interest in us. They were not unfriendly, but not friendly either. We unpacked our bags and, as there

319

were obviously no toilets or washing places, went down to the river to wash both ourselves and our filthy trousers. On the far bank, we saw more houses, and in full view of these we began to wash. We balanced our clothes, comb and soap tray on a tree stump and, half in the water and half on the sandy river bank, attempted to juggle soap, shampoo and towel. While we were thus engaged, Kui Karen women came down to the river to fill up fat sections of bamboo with water for the evening. This was for drinking and cooking, and we noticed that where they drew their supplies, the river was fouled not only by our soap and shampoo, but also by big buffalo droppings.

On the way back to the headman's, we made a brief tour round the dusk-bound village. In fact, there was not much to see. Like Nu Po, Kui Le Tor was a less interesting Karen village. It did not even seem to have a shop. Of course, there was no electricity in the village and no vehicles. The only way to arrive here was on foot. All necessities had to be transported either in baskets on people's backs or by elephant. In among the houses and all over the central compound, domestic animals wandered around – buffaloes, pigs, goats, cows, chickens and cocks. As night fell, their owners herded them behind the bamboo fences of their respective plots. Otherwise, not much was happening. After a day out in the fields, the villagers were sitting around, smoking, chewing betel nut and spitting. They watched us with a kind of distant curiosity. It was a backward, impoverished, rural scene, as if the clock had been turned back 200 years. However, the clock was all set to leap forward. Soon the dirt road down from Um Pang would reach Kui Le Tor. We were told that it would cut right through this central patch. When that happened, the lives of these people would be transformed forever. They would have improved access to the outside world, but equally the outside world would have easier access to them (in the event, the new road did not pass through the village, but bypassed it a km away). In one corner of the compound, behind a house, we found the elephant that the people of Nu Po had talked about. Chatting to its youthful mahouts, we learned that the beast was going to Boeng Kloeng next morning. If we wanted to join the party, the lads said, we should turn up at 8.30am.

In a forlorn attempt to dry our jeans, we laid them over the headman's fence. Then we turned our attention to food and drink. We were famished and parched. We had eaten and drunk nothing all day except a doughnut for breakfast, a Thai coffee at De Lo Ki, morsels of goat curry at Sa Kaang Thit, and some dirty water from the bulldozer boys. Meanwhile, we had scrambled down to Nu Po, walked all round a black market, climbed over a mountain, got lost twice, and sweated profusely. But we had nothing to eat or drink except our emergency provisions of tinned fish and instant noodles. Were we to start on them so soon? We scrounged some cold rice from the wife of the *pu yai* and topped it off with sardines in tomato sauce. Bed that night was embraced with gnawing hunger pains.

The situation with drink was even more problematic. But it had a humorous side. The good lady of our hut thought she was doing us a kindness when she brought us some water poured out of a bamboo section into a bronze bowl. We thought of the river water contaminated by soap, buffalo shit and, who knows, perhaps a dead goat upstream. When she saw that we did not drink the water, she removed the bowl. Presently, we had to ask her to bring us some more water. When no one was looking, we slipped a couple of water-purifying tablets into the bowl. It took an hour for these tablets to work, and for a long time they sat stubbornly and visibly on the bottom of the bowl. Our problem was that for an hour we had to stop anyone from taking the drinking bowl away from us. For a long dry-mouthed 60 minutes we defended the bowl, pretending to drink from it from time to time and hiding it behind our backs, but when the time was up, we greedily gulped down long draughts of the purified river water. (In retrospect, with much more experience both of jungle trekking and of tribal people such as the Karen, I feel sure that the water offered to us was not from the river – that would have been for the animals or for washing – but was from a clean spring. If the water had come from the river, it would have been boiled.)

While we were minding our own business on the *pu yai's* platform, virtually the whole of Kui, on the pretext of visiting the headman's family, came round to have a look at us. People were actually much more interested than we had first thought, and yet they maintained a kind of studied indifference, stealing sly glances at us from behind pillars. The majority of our onlookers were females, and old and young alike, even quite young girls, smoked. They puffed on pipes, home-made cigarettes and green cheroots, and spat incessantly through the cracks of the raised floor. Darkness had meanwhile fallen, and we were surprised by the chill of the night-time jungle air. People began lighting fires in front of their houses. The evening's social activity seemed to consist of standing or squatting next to one of these fires, warming first one's front and then one's rear. The villagers wandered from fire to fire, exchanging the latest tittle-tattle. We decided to join the group around 'our' headman's fire. But when I stood up, I made an unpleasant discovery. I could not get my left foot into my shoe. The ankle had swollen up, throbbed painfully and was difficult to stand on. We thought immediately of the large stones which had struck my shin bone on the ride down to Nu Po. The headman and a lot of other concerned faces peered at the reddish purple ankle in the light of an oil lamp. Of course, there was nothing to be done in Kui, and it was some 75 kms back to Um Pang. But the *pu yai* muttered something about a field hospital in Boeng Kloeng and suggested we talk to the elephant boys. So, hobbling, we went over again to the house where the elephant was and began protracted negotiations with the mahouts. In the end, they agreed to take me on the tusker to Boeng Kloeng (an all-day ride) for the very modest charge of 150 baht (£2.50). In fact, they said, seeing that the beast was a female, we could both ride, although it might be difficult for the second person to find much space because the elephant would also be loaded up with goods. Apparently men may ride on both male and female elephants, but women may not ride on males.

Back at the headman's fire, the socializing went on for a long time. One thing that struck us was that nobody ate or drank anything, not even tea or water. This seemed strange, for in most societies conviviality is marked by nibbling or nipping. Again we thought: perhaps these people really were as economically depressed as they looked. Two Thai boys wandered in with torches. They were from the roadmakers' forward camp beyond the village and were looking to buy a chicken from the locals. They were involved in the surveying and marking of the new dirt road. We were pleased to see them because we were uneasy about the cool inhabitants of Kui, even wondering about the wisdom of sleeping there. But the roadmarking boys put our minds at rest. Except for the flicker of the fire and the occasional pinpricks of light from torches, the night was as black as pitch. Overhead, the stars twinkled brilliantly. It was freezing cold, and the people who were not grilling their backsides at the fire squatted huddled in blankets. In the gloom, some were nimbly assembling roofing panels out of *jaak* leaves. It was past midnight before everyone had drifted away.

Sleep was virtually impossible. My ankle throbbed painfully, and we were afraid that we might have to abort our whole expedition. We were hungry and cold, and the floor was uncomfortable. Bit by bit, we realized that we were not alone on the platform of the headman's house. In dark corners, shadowy shapes in crumpled blankets tossed and turned. What with these, the night owls by the fire, and people creeping backwards and forwards across the balcony, it was like trying to nap in a market place. There must have been up to a dozen *Yang* staying that night with the *pu yai*. The noise and commotion went on into the small hours. Between the last person coming to bed and the first getting up, there was a quiet interval of a couple of hours, but even this was punctuated by the cries of a baby, old folk coughing and muttering, people heaving themselves up on one elbow to expectorate through the floorboards, and others clambering across the platform and down the ladder to go and warm themselves on the embers of the fire. As we hovered between sleep and wakefulness, we had nightmare visions that these stealthy figures were coming to slit our throats. At four in the morning, a cock began to crow under our heads, and soon afterwards some women started operating a rice pounder directly beneath the house.

✳ ✳

Postscript 2002

The first person that I know of who trekked from Um Pang to the Three Pagodas was Wachara of *Ta Mi Laa GH* in Chiang Khong. Over the years, I have learned of a few other people who have managed the expedition. There are two ways down: an easterly route that remains in Thailand and goes via Mae Chan Ta and Sa Kae, and a westerly route which partly goes down the Burmese side of the border. Wachara would seem to have taken the easterly Thai route, while in the end we went the westerly Burmese way. A character called Dtoo, who used to own *Mae Sot GH* about ten years ago, also made it through to the Three Pagodas. Like Wachara, he was accompanied by paramilitary BPP men. I do not know which route he took or whether he went before us or after, probably before. We made a first exploratory trip from Um Pang to Boeng Kloeng and the rishi cultist village of Lae Tong Ku in January 1992, and came back in February 1993 to redo that trip and then continue from Lae Tong Ku to the Three Pagodas Pass, proceeding via Burma. In 1993, we were accompanied by an English traveller friend we met on the road, called Mike Batley. A few days after we completed the expedition, traveller friends of ours, the German Peter Scheurenberg from Düsseldorf and his Venezuelan wife Lidya, also went right through to the Three Pagodas, following the route we took. But they eclipsed our efforts because they came back to Um Pang via Sa Kae and Mae Chan Ta on the easterly route, in effect doing the expedition twice and exploring both routes, while we returned to Um Pang (to retrieve our motorbike and belongings) by bus and road via Kanchanaburi, Supanburi, Nakhon Sawan, Kampaeng Pet, Tak and Mae Sot.

A couple of years after our expedition, at the latest before February 1997, when the Burma army captured the whole of KNU 6th Brigade border area and more, from Palu to the Three Pagodas Pass, making it impossible any more to trek the westerly route through Burma, the Austrian guy Armin Hermann, who runs the *Burmese Inn* guest house in Sangklaburi, further completed the journey, taking the same westerly route that we took, and travelling from north to south. In February 2001, Kaet Tai Wongsuwan, who is the commandant of Nu Po refugee camp and army officer in charge of the whole area down that way, told me that some months earlier, maybe in July 2000 (rainy season?), a *farang* couple walked the expedition on their own, orienteering they way with the aid of an old map! They took, of course, the easterly route through Thailand, and did the trip the other way round, from south to north, starting at Sangklaburi and ending at Boeng Kloeng, from where they took a *silor* to Um Pang and on out. I do not know of any other people, especially *farang*, who have made this expedition. It is possible that in the old days the odd *farang* aid worker or medic, helping the Karen and especially KNU refugees, went from Um Pang to Sangklaburi or the other way round, but I do not count these types because they would have ridden one of the trucks buzzing up and down a 4WD track on the Burmese side of the border, which went as far north as Klo To, would not themselves have organized the expedition or conducted it under their own steam, would not have walked, and would not have visited places such as Kui Le Tor and Lae Tong Ku. So until I am challenged to the contrary, I still maintain that I was the first *farang* traveller to trek through from Um Pang to the Three Pagodas. Anyone out there want to dispute my claim or otherwise get onto the roll of honour?

Route detail: Um Pang – De Lo Ki – Klo To/Sa Kaang Thit – Nu Sae Po – Nu Po – Kui Le Tor (Maps 26 & 27)

km 0.0   Um Pang centre at crossroads near *Gift Shop* and *Umpang GH*
Go N out of Um Pang as if returning to Mae Sot on H1090. Climb up hill, leaving village behind, and proceed past Pra Wo shrine (L) and **Mae Klong** village 3.8 kms to junction

km 3.8   Junction marked by tourist box (L). Turn L/west here off H1090 into H1167 side road
Pass through **Mae Klong Mai**, cross bridge over Mae Klong river
Continue west along road – now asphalted – past Ta Ko Pi Cave (300 m L of road)

km 8.3   Checkpoint

km 12.3   Big junction, at which R/straight goes to Nong Luang (km 16) and border near Pa Toei (km 21 – details in Postscript to Chapter 11), while L goes S to De Lo Ki (signed 5 kms), Ti Lo Su Waterfall, Klo To/Mae Chan (signed 30 kms) and Boeng Kloeng (signed 74 kms – these km indications are essentially correct). Go L/south. The long-time checkpoint on the junction is defunct
A wide gravel and dirt highway, paved in places (especially at the beginning) strikes S. We were told that ultimately the road would be asphalted as far as Klo To, after which it would remain dirt

Pass limestone outcrops

km 16.7 **De Lo Ki** and roadside shop (R), phone box (L)

km 18.4 Checkpoint and entrance to southern part of Um Pang Wildlife Sanctuary

km 18.8 Junction, at which L goes past another sanctuary entrance 25 kms to Ti Lo Su Waterfall, while R/straight continues to Klo To (our route)

After the junction, you wind over a low ridge through great forest and jungle. In 2001, we encountered a lot of road work along here, which should soon be finished

Just before Klo To centre, you cross a bridge over the Mae Chan river

km 39.8 Junction and centre of Karen **Klo To** (Mae Chan). Noodle soup/fried rice place on the junction (R). At the junction, straight continues south to Nu Po, while R/west goes into Klo To village, further to Karen Nupa Towa, and eventually to **Sa Kaang Thit** (Ban Mai) across the border. It is no longer possible to visit Sa Kaang Thit. Nor is there any reason to do so. On or around 13 February 1997, the Burma army (helped by the DKBA), during its sweep up the border, overran the village, just as it seized all the other KNU villages and territory in 6th Brigade area opposite Um Pang district. It burned down all the houses and shops in Sa Kaang Thit, and precipitated the flight into Thailand of all the local Karen and Indo-Burmese Muslims. Initially, they fled to Nupo Towa, where they took refuge, but were later moved along with Karen and Muslims sheltering at Ti Jo Si, Nu Po and Nong Nok Ped (8,000 people in all, of whom up to 2,000 may have been Muslims) to a big new refugee camp at Nu Po village. Nothing much remains of Sa Kaang Thit. People at Klo To and Thai army soldiers in Nupo Towa said that it now consists of just half a dozen houses, is dangerous because some land has been mined, and that Klo To people are afraid to go there, both because of the mines and because of the DKBA. Some locals said that there was a DKBA presence in Sa Kaang Thit, others that no military force controlled it. KNLA commander Saw Tae Tu, formerly of Sa Kaang Thit, now lives both in Klo To and also Mae Sot town, where he is said to have a house. Relatives and friends of his live in Klo To, some running a KNU house and office there.

Back on the main road, at the junction (now see Map 27), you continue S from Klo To centre to reach after a further 3.4 kms:

km 43.2 Centre of **Nu Sae Po**, another Karen village

km 45.3 Wildlife Sanctuary checkpoint

km 52.3 Way R to Ti Jo Si (Tee Chor See), another Karen village, where in early 1997 many 'Burmese' Karen and Muslims sheltered as SLORC troops seized KNU territory across the border

km 60.6 Way L to Ti Po Ji (12.5 kms offroad)

km 62.2 Checkpoint and barrier, followed by **Nu Po**, a Karen village on the R side of the road. Fuel for sale in bottles at a shop. In 1992 and 1993, when we came down here en route for Boeng Kloeng and Lae Tong Ku, Nu Po was as far as you could go by motorcycle. The road ended here, and we had to leave our machine with the village headman, and then walk on footpaths. Meanwhile, the dirt road has been pushed a further 24 kms past Kui Le Tor to Boeng Kloeng, where it now stops

km 63.1 Way L to **Nu Po refugee camp**, about 100 m offroad. This large camp, run under UN auspices, contains 7,000 - 8,000 refugees and possibly as many as 10,000. The inmates are Karen and Indo-Burmese Muslims from Burma. Up to 2,000 of them are Muslim traders, many from the former black-market village of Sa Kaang Thit (Ban Mai), opposite Klo To. The

THE DRIVERLESS KOMATSU

refugees fled Burma in February 1997, when the Burma army and its fledgling protégé the DKBA seized KNU 6th Brigade area opposite Um Pang district. Coming from Sa Kaang Thit, Mae Ta Ro Ta and many other villages, they sheltered initially at Nupo Towa (between Sa Kaang Thit and Klo To), Nong Nok Ped, Ti Jo Si (between Sa Kaang Thit and Nu Po) and Nu Po itself, before being gathered together and relocated to Nu Po refugee camp in about 1998, perhaps because the initial camps came under attack from SLORC troops or were threatened with attack by the DKBA. In February 2001, Doug and Andrew and myself were invited to lunch in the camp by the commandant, Kaet Tai Wongsuwan, the big shot in these parts and a friendly helpful man, who sat us down in his canteen among some senior KNU figures. After we had all tucked into their lunch and nipped at rice whisky, Kaet deputed some lackeys to take on a tour of the camp. It was an orderly place, more spacious and less chaotic than Mae La camp (N of Mae Sot, see Chapter 10), and had a grid of streets between hundreds and hundreds of huts made of split bamboo with leaf roofs. As at Mae La, there was a market quarter with many shops run by Muslim traders. A small field hospital was in operation, and a few *farang* were resident in the camp, working for the UNHCR and other organizations. We discovered that Saw Kyi Shwi, a KNLA commander from Mae Ta Ro Ta in Burma (whom Nittaya and I met in February 1993 – see main text, Chapter 13), was housed at Nu Po camp, and commandant Kaet bade someone fetch him, but it transpired that he was temporarily "away at a meeting across the border in Burma", which shows that even though the Burmese may have seized Duplaya, the KNU still holds pockets of it or infiltrates it.

After Nu Po camp, road deteriorates for some distance, then improves again

Two more checkpoints

km 64.9   A wicked view L of precipitous outcrops in the middle distance

The road, now no more than a very poor narrow dirt trail, winds down through fabulous virgin forest and jungle

km 68.6   Massive mountain and ridge (R), called Doi Mo Ga Tu, which forms part of the border. Between Nu Po and Boeng Kloeng, you essentially go the whole length of it

km 69.1   Um Pang Wildlife Sanctuary and *grom pamai* (forest protection) office (R)

km 70.9   Way L for **Kui Le Tor** (1 km), Kui Kloe (signed 11 kms), Mong Gua (possibly 13 kms), Po Ka Ta (signed 15 kms), U-nai (signed 32 kms), Gru Bo (signed 40 kms) and Mae Chan Ta (possibly 52 kms). In 2001, the way 1 km to Kui Le Tor was a very bad trail indeed. We biked in from the 'main road' to find that the Karen village had hardly changed at all since Nittaya and I twice trekked through it nearly a decade earlier, in 1992 and 1993. It was still a small, traditional, relatively backward place, with uncertain staring people, many sitting around. An incongruous phone box had meanwhile arrived, powered by solar batteries and communicating via satellite. The headman with whom we had stayed in 1992 was still present, in the same house. For any reader contemplating trekking to Lae Tong Ku not from Boeng Kloeng and through Burma, but via Kui Le Tor and Mong Gua (the roundabout route through Thailand), he said that it was 12 kms from Kui Le Tor to Mong Gua (and then probably about the same distance from Mong Gua to Lae Tong Ku)

Details of final stretch of road from Um Pang to Boeng Kloeng (Kui Le Tor to Boeng Kloeng) are given in the Postscript to Chapter 13.

13

EXTRATERRITORIAL

Kui Le Tor – Boeng Kloeng – Mae Ta Ro Ta – Lae Tong Ku

The next morning, after putting on our cold wet jeans and breakfasting on water and peanut crunch by the fire, we made it to the elephant house at the appointed hour. There, to our annoyance, we found that the elephant and its retinue had left soon after dawn. We returned to the headman and explained the situation. "Never mind", he said, "you will soon catch them up." We thought that in two or three hours they would have got a long way and asked him to find us a guide. This he did, and soon we were on our way with a boy and two youngish men. One of the men was going to branch off into Burma, and the other two were going to fetch something from Boeng Kloeng. Karen people, no matter whether young or old, flew along the mountain paths in their flip-flops and with their *yaam* and machetes as if there were no tomorrow. It had often puzzled us why they raced along like this, but probably it was just that they were fit, were used to the heat and the climbing, and travelled light. The trek from Kui Le Tor to Boeng Kloeng was to take us a brisk three hours. Our guides told us that, after reaching Boeng Kloeng and picking up their goods, they would run-walk home in an hour. This fleetness of foot made Karen underestimate times and distances by Western standards (even more so by Thai), so that when they said that a village was "15 minutes away" or "just around the corner", actually a haul of 50 minutes still lay ahead. "Just over this hill" meant an exhausting climb over that distant ridge.

The guides set off at a cracking pace through the trees and over some dried-up paddy fields outside the village (Map 27). We trudged after them. Then, for some distance, we all splashed in single file through water and mud along a river bed. It seemed hopeless to try and keep our trousers and shoes clean or dry, and from that moment on we never again attempted to do so. Quite soon, we came across the road surveyors' camp beside a stream. This was an orderly affair, with three or four roomy bamboo huts, a field kitchen, a washing-up place, and a long bamboo table with fixed benches on each side – big enough to seat a dozen workers. Washing was drying in the sun, theodolites and other surveying paraphernalia were lying around, and we could see communications equipment. The marking boys were all out with their red sticks in the jungle. We learned that they had got so far with their surveying and marking that it now took them two hours to walk to the forward edge and two hours back. Soon the camp would have to be moved.

EXTRATERRITORIAL

Round at the back of the camp, we surprised three older men. They were tall, thin and Chinese-looking, with droopy Fu Manchu moustaches. Clearly the brains behind the operation, they were lolling in shirts and tracksuit bottoms on the balcony of their office, reading girlie magazines. Amid the tits and bums of Thai cuties were military maps and piles of paperwork, which they toyed with from time to time. In spite of their agreeable existence down here by the stream, they welcomed us as a pleasant distraction. They offered us Milo and Nescafé, pointed to a large thermos of hot water, and told us to help ourselves. A man got up and fetched mugs and a barrel of chocolate biscuits. The boss wanted to show us round. After our austere night in Kui Le Tor, we could not believe our luck. The three Karen guides fidgeted in the background.

We helped ourselves to two mugfuls of Milo and a cup of coffee, and ate about a pound of chocolate biscuits each. Then we took advantage of the roadmakers' incomparable maps. These stretched well into Burma and a good way beyond Lae Tong Ku. We jotted down the names of villages which seemed to be on our route. The men were very interested in our plan to try to strike through to the Three Pagodas Pass. They thought that from Lae Tong Ku to the Three Pagodas it should take us two days on foot (drastically inaccurate, as things turned out). Also, they said, there was a 4WD track down that way, but mostly on the Burmese side of the border. If the Burma army had not interdicted it, we might be able to make use of the trail.

As the boss showed us round the small camp, we noticed that it was a veritable arsenal of weapons. We commented on all these guns, and the boss explained that some were for hunting, but others were for self-defence. Roadmakers were popular with tigers, bears and snakes, and unpopular with some of the local people. He may well have had in mind the 'Death Highway' massacres or the recent 'yellowthread' incident. Interestingly, his team, now constructing this road, had previously engineered Highway 105 (in those days the H1085), the new Mae Sariang/Mae Sot road. The present project was slow stepwise work. It was going to take at least another two years just to reach Boeng Kloeng – a matter of a couple of hours on foot. There, the new road would stop for the moment. A plan had once existed to push the road at some time down to the Three Pagodas, but this would probably never happen, partly because it would take decades to build, but mainly because nobody now wanted a road through the famous Tung Yai Naresuan Wildlife Sanctuary and Forest Protection Zone.

Finally, we consulted the surveyors about my swollen ankle. They thought that nothing was broken, but that the bone was bruised, and that if I was care-ful, I could walk to the field hospital in Boeng Kloeng. They produced some deep-heat cream, which we rubbed in. Besides, they said airily, if we continued, we should soon catch up with the elephant, which had passed their way earlier. Fortified with the coffee and biscuits, we set off again with almost a spring in our stride. Somehow, the troublesome ankle was already feeling better.

The guides continued as we found they often liked to go, with one in front, one bringing up the rear, and us sandwiched in the middle. This was a good arrangement, because then they could not speed off, leaving us behind. Also, the leading Karen could warn of dangers, such as snakes or bees' nests, but also point out items of interest, which strangers to the jungle often did not see. The peril from snakes was very real, as on this very stretch of our trek we ran into one, just as we did on later legs. Our three guides said that they often encountered snakes and also bears on the Kui Le Tor/Boeng Kloeng path.

The path climbed up a long way through a bamboo forest. At the top was a deep narrow cutting through orange clay. It looked as if it had been worn down by generations of *Yang* walkers and elephants. In the defile we stopped for ten minutes to get our breaths back. Ahead, we heard cracking noises and low insistent cajolings. Slowly a massive bull elephant, piled high with goods, and a Karen mahout perched on top of its head, came into view. The dark sinister shape crashed through the jungle gloom under the forest canopy, its chains jangling. Everybody got well out of its way, especially the little boy, who out of fear hid behind a tree. Our guides and the mahout exchanged information, and we learnt that 'our' elephant was not far ahead. This was good news as my foot was throbbing more than I cared to acknowledge. After the bull elephant, we encountered next an officious off-duty BPP soldier, hiking alone back to Um Pang. He told us to turn back because the area ahead was troubled. He asked to see our BPP permits and even our passports and visas. While not exactly telling him to mind his own business, we largely ignored him and said that the *dorchodor* commander in Boeng Kloeng was expecting us, which may or may not have been true.

An hour out from Kui Le Tor, we emerged into open sunny upland, covered with sizzling 5-ft-high elephant grass. To the west, lay the high Burmese border mountain of Doi Mo Ga Tu (actually a ridge), which we were now to follow for some way. Appropriately enough, in the elephant grass we caught up with our elephant. The party, including the mahout, three or four Karen boys and a dog, had stopped to adjust the load. The young men were not at all embarrassed about having left without us. They merely said that the elephant had been too heavily laden to take the two of us. But it would be possible for the *farang* with the hurt foot to ride. So, in the end, one of us at least came to get on the elephant, and for free too.

The ride was not at all as I had expected, and afterwards I was never again in a hurry to get up on an elephant. I had envisaged swaying comfortably along in a wooden howdah, but the howdah was so full of sacks and cartons that there was nowhere else to ride except on the tusker's neck. Also there was no stepping aboard from some mounting block, but an unseemly scramble up the side of the animal past its ear. Even with a leg-up from the elephant and a good pull from the mahout kneeling on its head, this was a strenuous climb up the beast's neck chains. The mahout lashed our backpacks to the netted bundle of goods, shinned down his animal and led the way. All the others followed behind. It seemed awfully high and exposed on the elephant's neck. The neck was some eight feet from the ground, and, adding another three feet of human torso length, my head looked down from a height of eleven or twelve feet. Worse than that, there was nothing to hold onto. The broad smooth top of the animal's head lay immediately in front at lap level, offering no handhold; and the tops of its ear flaps were unsteady. So I gripped my legs around the animal's neck and in behind its ears, and where necessary leaned back to grab hold of the corners of the wooden basket.

Then we began to roll. As the beast lumbered slowly forward, its shoulders pummelled up and down in my bottom, making things uncomfortable after a while. Walking on the level was harmless enough, and even going up the steep narrow paths was not too bad. Each time the elephant set a front foot in one of the well-established plod marks, there was a sudden and exhilirating heave up into the air. But the slow step-by-step negotiation of the precipitous, rocky, sometimes muddy descents of the trail was alarming. As the beast set a front foot down, we seemed for a sheer second to be in free fall forwards through empty space. Going down, the animal's head did not rise to meet me, but dropped clean away. I lay back and held on tight to the lurching howdah. Another problem was that the elephant seemed to have no sense of obstacles lying across the path, which it could go past or under, but which I had to evade or duck. In fact, it seemed to take a perverse delight in making a beeline for these. Thus, I was lashed by overhanging bamboos and, had I not paid constant attention, would have been struck in the face by a thorn tree or simply dismounted by a low bough. It was while passing close to the branch of a tree that the first brush with a snake occurred. Suddenly, one of the boys behind shouted out in Karen "Snake!". But by the time this was translated into Thai and then English, I had no time to take precautions, and the ends of a branch swished past my head. When I turned to look, I saw a bright green snake with scarlet diamonds, a metre long, lurking on the foliage of the branch. The snake was a poisonous one, and it had passed within inches of my face.

Our whole progress was accompanied by a litany of calls and clicking noises, wheedlings and cajolings, entreaties and curses on the part of the Karen boys. Sometimes, to gee the old lady up, the mahout leapt up in front of me and slapped her on the head or prompted her with leg-kicks under the ears. Once, to our horror, he beat her on the skull with his machete, adding fresh cut marks to numerous old ones. But the old lady was not to be hurried and just took it all uncomplaining. In fact, she had a mind of her own, and her wilfulness led to the amusing side of the ride. She would go off down the wrong track and refuse to turn around. Or she would crash off into the pathside undergrowth and snack on something she fancied. Sometimes, not bothering to do this, she just took a titbit in passing, casually twirling her trunk around a young succulent 4-ft-high banana plant, uprooting it and chomping it on the move. Once the sly tusker farted loudly into the faces of everybody traipsing behind, and she never tired of frightening the dog. She would lash out at it with her trunk or crash her trunk down on some dry bamboos behind where the dog was sniffing, sending him scampering for dear life.

Almost my most vivid impression was of the dome of the elephant's head – perhaps because there was plenty of time to observe it. The skull seemed to have two distinct mounds or lobes, which moved independently of each other as the animal lurched along. The skin was leathery and dusty, and it sprouted hairs as bristly as those on a wire brush. The ride had a legacy which plagued me for days afterwards. Hundreds of itchy red spots appeared all over my upper body. This dermatitis may have come from sleeping in sweaty clothes or on dirty blankets. Or it might have been an attack of prickly heat. It could even have come from some jungle plant brushing against my skin. But I felt sure that it had come from the dirty head of that elephant.

Progress with the elephant was so slow and uncomfortable that after an hour I climbed down. It was going to take all day to get to Boeng Kloeng, and our guides were getting restless. In spite of my ankle, we decided to walk on. We thanked the elephant boys and presented them with a couple of tins of sardines in tomato sauce. While we were retrieving our backpacks and shouldering up, they lost no time in opening the tins. They took some fresh banana leaves from the jungle, spread out sticky rice on them, levered open the tins with machetes, mixed the fish and tomato with the rice, and ate balls of the mixture with their grimy fingers.

We journeyed on through a forest of immense trees rising up as straight as a die. Their two-metre-thick trunks were buttressed at the base with giant moss-covered vanes. Also along here were fig trees and the dense dark salacca woods that were a favourite haunt of bears. Two hours out from Kui and with still an hour before Boeng Kloeng, we came to an unmarked fork in the path. Left was our way, and right went 15 minutes downhill to the village of Bo Na Ta, in Burma. One of our guides was going there, and he took his leave. We began next a long descent through mixed country until we hit a cart track. The cart track intertwined with a watery muddy river bed, and for a some distance we splashed our way through. Down in the valley, the heat was oppressive, and we envied some children and their mothers bathing naked in a pool. At the sight of a grubby *farang* limping by, the children ran away and the mothers shrieked. Finally, we passed through a grove of betel palms and came to the first houses of **Boeng Kloeng**. Our other guide and the boy left us here. We thanked them for their patience and paid them 100 baht to be shared among the three of them (100 baht per day was approximately the going rate for guiding at that time), and they looked well pleased with their morning's work.

❖

Boeng Kloeng

Boeng Kloeng (also Beung Keung) was much bigger than Kui Le Tor. With around 300 inhabitants, it was a mixed Karen, Burmese, Indo-Burmese and Lao place. This 'Lao' puzzled us because we could not understand how people from Laos could have got so far from home. We had a theory that they were the descendants of Khmu teak workers who had perhaps been brought here from Laos in the early years of the 20th century by British logging companies operating in Thailand and Burma. But, in fact, they were just Thai people – 'Lao' was an old way of saying 'northern Thai'. The village was one of the most picturesque we saw anywhere on our journey. Set against a backdrop of rocky cliffs and pitted denticular mountains, it lay astride a long dusty, but shady and tranquil 'street' (see photo). Considering how rural and remote Boeng Kloeng was, many of the wooden houses lining this thoroughfare were surprisingly large and ornate. Some had lovingly tended front gardens with a profusion of colourful blooming plants and bushes.

EXTRATERRITORIAL

We were surprised to find the main street humming with activity. In both directions, there was a steady flow of people, old Chinese bicycles and bullock carts, piled high with rice and other goods. Even more astonishing, we found one or two beaten-up motorbikes and pick-ups. Where did they go? Did they no more than ply the main street? And where had they come from? Had they been helicoptered in? The mystery was solved when we learned that there was a track behind Boeng Kloeng, across the border (it was the track that the road surveyors had spoken of) and that most of these people were Karen refugees from Burma. In fact, in the days before our arrival there had been a massive influx of people, vehicles, food and animals into Boeng Kloeng, all fleeing in the face of a swingeing SLORC offensive. They were mostly being housed in a refugee camp at the bottom of the village near the river, and, when we went down to have a look, we found everybody in the process of settling in.

The flood of refugees and the nearby fighting made everyone jumpy. We had hardly gone a few paces up the street when a BPP boy tumbled out of a house and challenged us. Where were we going? What were we doing? We could see from his red eyes that he had been drinking. He was joined by four colleagues from the same house. They were all drunk, yet it was only noon. We told them we were going to Lae Tong Ku. *Mai dai*, they said, impossible, the whole area was active and it was from the Lae Tong Ku direction that the refugees were coming. We would just have to go back to Um Pang. We told these aggressive *dorchodor* that we would think about it over lunch, and wandered off. This first encounter with the Boeng Kloeng authorities was not encouraging, and the news of fighting towards our goal made us even more despondent. Now it really seemed that we would get no further.

While we were looking around the main street, a tall thin moustachioed character called Sampan from Ko Samui island came up to us. He was also BPP, but his attitude was much more conciliatory. He said he recognized us from *Ti Lo Su* restaurant in Um Pang, where he had seen us a couple of nights earlier. We mentioned that district officer Sombat had encouraged us to come to Boeng Kloeng and produced his magic slip of paper with the local commander's name on it. We called Sampan 'Mr Fixit' because from then on his sole concern seemed to be to want to fix things for us. He radioed through to the BPP camp base and escorted us there to meet the commander. We climbed up a long steep flight of steps and found on the top of a hill a regular fortified encampment. In a kind of open mess-building, the commander interviewed us. He wanted to know in particular if we were journalists. We flatly denied this, adding that we were a travel writer accompanied by his Thai guide. To demonstrate the fact, I produced my diaries and also the photographs we carried with us precisely to 'oil' such occasions. The commander was much taken with the pictures, and so the shots of Darkie and the 'long-neck' women came to be passed from him to Sampan and then to the assembled orderlies. We explained that we had come to visit the rishi cultist people of Lae Tong Ku and, if possible, the divine guru himself.

Our cards were on the table, and the moment of truth had arrived. Either we would now be sent back to Um Pang with a flea in our ear, or we would be officially allowed to go to Lae Tong Ku. A lot of radioing went on next.

331

Contact was made with the Karen headman of Boeng Kloeng, the BPP commander at Lae Tong Ku and the local KNLA commander across in 6th Brigade district. News from the latter was especially important not just because the next part of our trek went through Burma, but because it was feared that an attack by the Burma army exactly in that part of Duplaya opposite Lae Tong Ku and Boeng Kloeng was imminent. The rebel commander better than anyone would know the latest position. While the transceivers hissed, our BPP commander motioned to the cooks to provide us with some lunch. They dished up catfish with green chillies, rice, two cans of sardines in tomato sauce, purified water and nips of *lao kao*. While we were tucking into this little feast, Mr Fixit drew up a protocol detailing: Mr Christian, nationality, age, passport number, profession travel writer, our goal and intentions. Finally, to our great surprise, the commander said that if we went tomorrow morning everything should be alright. Further, he offered to organize a guide for us, or, if we preferred to wait a day or two, we could accompany the next detail of BPP going to Lae Tong Ku. We said we would be happy to take the guide the next morning. He shook our hands, wished us good luck, and suggested that we fill up with good water at his camp before setting off.

We could not believe our good fortune. Not only had the commander not been interested in any permit from Um Pang or Mae Sot, but he had not queried our plan. We regretted having wasted so much time enquiring in Um Pang. From the encounter we learned two things. Firstly, that the attitude of the authorities (notably the BPP) in the field could be quite different from what it was back at headquarters. And secondly, that the *dorchodor*, far from not cooperating with the insurgents (as one read in the newspapers or as was put out diplomatically for SLORC consumption), were still working hand in glove with them. Intelligence was shared, communications were good, both the KNLA and refugees freely came and went across the border, and the Thai army crossed with impunity through rebel-held Burma. But above all, from our point of view, the BPP, far from stopping us from going on, were trying in conjunction with the KNLA to help us, even apparently encouraging us (illegally) to leave Thailand and then step back in. The same helpfulness and tolerance we found all down this frayed section of border. It was a different world down here. From Boeng Kloeng on, the way was extraterritorial in both senses of the word.

As yet, we had found nowhere either to stay or take supper. We walked up and down the long main street in the hope that somehow a solution to the problem would present itself. There were four little shops, two of them well stocked, but no eating place or noodle stall. On our reconnaissance, we found the village school, the field hospital, plenty of elephants (Boeng Kloeng was a big elephant place), a *wat* and numerous houses with betel nuts drying in their front gardens. In the street, a Karen woman buttonholed us and asked us to examine the eyes of her son, whom she was dragging along behind her. The poor boy was blinded in one eye, apparently by cataracts, and had half lost the sight of his other eye. He squinted at us hopefully and folornly, and his mother implored us for some medicine to cure him. We tried to reason with her that we were tourists, not doctors, but the naive woman thought that as Westerners

332

we surely had all the answers. We told her that she should seek help at a hospital in Mae Sot or Kanchanaburi. She had already been to Mae Sot, she said, but they could not help her. The hospital had told her to go to Chiang Mai, but that had been too far away and she could not afford the journey. Our visits to remote areas often led to such painful situations.

Down by the refugee camp, where there was a constant hammering and sawing, coming and going, unloading and stowing, we met two Karen boys. They were from Jaddhur in Burma and had walked to Lae Tong Ku and on to Boeng Kloeng. Their village had been overrun by SLORC soldiers and they were not so much fleeing, as migrating. They intended to push on to Klo To, where they thought they could get some kind of legitimation papers. After that, they proposed to move up to Um Pang and Pop Pra, where one of them had a sister. They hoped to find some kind of work there or in Mae Sot. With scarcely a bean between them, the plight of these naive happy-go-lucky boys was typical of many people in the area.

Although they had never been to Boeng Kloeng before, the boys had that easy familiarity with everybody and everything which we had noticed before among the Karen, especially the border Karen. We explained that we were looking for a place to stay, but had not been able to find anywhere. "No problem", they exclaimed, "you can stay anywhere!" And within minutes they had fixed up lodging space for us on the platform of a large house near the refugee camp. Not only that, they rustled up blankets for us and even *longyis* (Burmese sarongs), so that we could wash and change. They themselves preferred to stay in another house nearby, where there were certain girls... At dusk, we used the *longyis* to wash in the river. We washed surrounded by some hundred doleful but inquisitive Burmese Karen refugees – a humbling experience. The night spent in that large strange house was, if anything, even more public and uncomfortable than the night at Kui Le Tor, but in the morning the boys brought round a tray of rice cakes coated with sticky toffee.

With my ankle still painfully swollen, it seemed a good idea to visit the field hospital. We were unlucky in this because when we stepped into the small wooden building, we learned that a Thai doctor and nurse, who had come to attend the refugees, had just left, going north. A couple of local paramedics were kicking a football around behind the hospital, and after a while they came in. They poked and twisted my ankle to see if it was broken or infected, causing excruciating pain, and pronounced that the bone was bruised. Then they rummaged around for medicines, but found that they had only two large sweetie jars full of paracetamol and antibiotics. They gave me a fistful of each free and said that on no account should I walk to Lae Tong Ku the next day.

That evening, outside Boeng Kloeng's best-stocked shop, we found a rough table and benches. It did not look like an eating table, but we sat down anyway. We had seen that the store sold instant noodles, so we bought two packets and asked the lady serving if she could prepare them for us. While we were waiting, we inspected her provisions. Amongst the more conventional items, such as the inevitable tinned sardines, we spotted Anchor beer from Malaysia, Burmese gin, and fruit liqueurs from China. There was also Nescafé, Milo, Pepsi and other soft drinks, as well as stacks of cheroots and home-made *lao kao* at only ten baht a large bottle. The evening looked more promising than the one before. Presently, the Karen owner called us into her house, where the Ma-maa noodles were steaming in bowls. To our pleasant surprise, we found in addition a mini banquet laid out for us on the floor – stewed aubergine, okra with dried shrimps, rice, and huge glass mugs of coffee. In the lamplight, we sat and gorged ourselves, watched by a sea of placid faces of all ages. The lady said that if we returned in the morning, she could make us coffee or hot chocolate for breakfast at five baht each.

It transpired that the shop was also the home of the elephant we had ridden earlier. It had arrived meanwhile with its retinue and was penned round the back. After supper, its *Yang* owner, the mahout, joined us at the rough table. We asked him to bring *lao kao*, cheroots and glasses. The man spoke broken Thai, and mixing the hooch with the soft drink Green Spot, we spent a convivial and informative evening with him and his family under the stars. The *lao kao*, he said, was made of rice and sugar cane, and was 20% alcohol. Everyone was cracking and chewing betel as usual, so we asked the man about this habit. They just chewed betel nut as we did chewing gum, for fun, the man said. The bitter taste made the saliva flow, hence the frequent spitting. But the mahout was much more interested in our story, and soon we noticed that not only his family, but half of Boeng Kloeng, Burmese refugees and all, were squatting in the gloom around our table listening. They would all have heard of the 'long-neck' women, but our tales of Manerplaw, Wa prince Maha San, 'Spirit Well', and legendary Chiang Mai had them all transfixed.

✣

The BPP commander had arranged that the man escorting us to Lae Tong Ku should come for us next morning at 9am, but the Karen guide was already waiting outside our hut at 7.30, while we were still in our sleeping bags inside our mosquito net. But we need not have worried, for after delaying him while we washed, ate sticky cakes, went to the shop for Milo, and got water from the BPP camp, he then kept us waiting while he stopped off to chat at a friend's house. Not many people went to Lae Tong Ku because it was out on a limb. For the locals, the paths beyond the rishi village went nowhere. So it was correspondingly hard to find anybody willing to go there, and often the best hope was to tag along with some passing rishi people. The first guide who was sent to us upped his price from 100 to 200 baht, after which he lost interest altogether. But we were well pleased with the second candidate, who was now waiting for us.

This was Sooksi, a fine fellow (see photo section). This tall, slim, gentle man, with short hair, a handsome square face and broad flared nostrils, was a father of five and came from Boeng Kloeng. He trekked in flip-flops, a calf-length wrap-around skirt, and a KNLA camouflage jacket. Of course, there was also the obligatory machete and Karen *yaam* or shoulder bag. We struck out with him along a muddy river bed, and almost immediately crossed into Burma (Map 28). The river bed was the border, Sooksi said. We considered what we had so often thought before – that it was this easy to wander out of the kingdom and into xenophobic 'Myanmar'. There was no fuss, no barriers and no controls. With typical *Yang* understatement, everybody had said that the journey passed through only a small bit of Burma – we understood perhaps half an hour. But, in fact, almost the whole of the four-hour trek to Lae Tong Ku was on the wrong side of the border. Had we known, we might have gone via Mong Gua because we were not interested in passing through a war zone 'just for the hell of it'. But there was no going back now.

After a short distance, we deviated from the Lae Tong Ku path and headed off deeper into Burma. We grew increasingly anxious about this and asked Sooksi what was going on. But our guide merely said that we had to meet his local commander. The land was flatter here, and although it was only ten in the morning, the temperature was rising uncomfortably. Presently, we picked up a 4WD track, which brought us into a village with the delightful name of **Mae Ta Ro Ta**. It was a diffuse Karen place, scattered among trees and bush. An hour out from Boeng Kloeng, Sooksi presented us to the local KNLA 6th Brigade commander.

The commander received us high up on the balcony of his spacious wooden house. We could see that he was a man of some consequence not just from the size of his house and the way everyone deferred to him, but from an entourage of beautiful women and girls, who looked on in the background. Saw Kyi Shwi was an affable urbane middle-aged man with a round face, balding head and gold teeth. He was dressed like our guide in flip-flops, sarong and a khaki army shirt, and even spoke some English. He bade us sit down, called for water, and frankly asked us what we wanted in this area. We told him that we were tourists, that I was collecting material for a book, that we were on our way to Lae Tong Ku, and that we hoped to press on to the Three Pagodas Pass. At first, for security reasons, Saw Kyi was unwilling to divulge his name, let alone pose for a photo. But when he got used to the idea that we were neither spies nor gun-runners, he loosened up. In particular, this vain man was not proof to the blandishments of his many comely females, so that in the end he had to relent and pose with the *farang* before the camera (see photo section).

We picked up some useful information from the leader about our onward journey. For the Three Pagodas, we would have to proceed after Lae Tong Ku to a place called Sa Kae. Sa Kae could be reached either by continuing on down through Burma, or by striking east across to Mong Gua and then south via Mae Chan Ta through Thailand. But this latter route involved a difficult mountain path, which everybody feared and avoided. As far as Saw Kyi knew, there was no direct way from Lae Tong Ku to Sa Kae. The commander's information, though substantially correct, turned out to be inaccurate in some respects. It went to show just how difficult it could be to obtain reliable data when on the move, even from well-informed sources. But what interested us particularly was how safe the next part of our journey would be, especially in view of the SLORC advance. The KNLA had scouts out, the commander said. Normally, the scouts went out every second day, but at the moment they were out every day. The path should be safe. We could have stayed for an early lunch, but we did not want to detain our guide, and something told us that we should press on while the situation remained favourable.

THREE PAGODAS

After Mae Ta Ro Ta, the three of us followed the 4WD track for some distance. We passed through a countryside of mixed bamboo, scrub and trees. The sun was reaching its zenith, making the trudge along the dusty trail devastatingly hot. Sooksi tore a branch off a bush and used it as a parasol. We did likewise. I remarked to him that we looked like a band of *pi tong luang* (Spirits of the Yellow Leaves) on the move, which amused him greatly. Presently, we left the track and rejoined the direct Boeng Kloeng to Lae Tong Ku path. Mercifully, it was shaded by overarching bamboos and trees, making the going cooler, if more humid. Most of the way to Lae Tong Ku was fairly flat, and for some distance the path followed the steep eastern bank of a stunningly beautiful river. The Suriya, which like the River Moei flowed unusually from south to north, was beautiful both because it meandered lazily through pure jungle, with rank green foliage pitching straight into the water on both sides, and on account of its remarkable turquoise colour. Upstream, into the sun, the water shimmered a glaucous colour, and downriver, it was a fuller aquamarine. Where the waters reached in under the gloom of the overhanging vegetation, they shaded off into a dark emerald.

Sometimes the path ran low, virtually along the river bank, and sometimes it skirted the precipitous hillsides high up. But always there were glimpses of the blue-green Suriya through the tree trunks and knotted lianas. Where the narrow path climbed or dropped steeply, we found again the deep plod marks of elephants, and it was not long before another such beast came against us. We scrambled out of the way as best we could. This elephant, although heavily laden, was moving at a fair speed. It was accompanied by only one mahout, perched high up on the animal's head, feet tucked in under its ears. He was a rishi cultist boy, with a topknot of hair just above his brow. Boy and animal had established a steady rhythm, and we saw now how we should have travelled the day before. As man and mount trundled past, Sooksi exchanged words with the mahout. The man had come with his elephant from Lae Tong Ku.

In a small clearing, we stopped for a rest. Our guide pointed out termite mounds in amongst the stands of giant *mai huak* bamboo. He also told us something of his life. One thing that surprised us was that his five children were relatively grown-up, and yet to us he looked no more than 30. He had four girls and one boy. Two of his children were still with him, but three were in Kanchanaburi province. One daughter was working as a labourer on a building site. While we were talking in low voices, we heard a sudden crack of bamboo from the way ahead. Purposeful footfalls drew closer. We filled with alarm. It was certainly an advancing Burma army column. Four youths, in single file, swung into view. They were wearing combat jackets and military backpacks. Even Sooksi looked concerned because he could not recognize them as KNLA guerrillas or *dorchodor*. In fact, they were four more Burmese Karen boys fleeing from the oncoming *tatmadaw*. Evidently, they had never seen a *farang* before because they were mightily taken with us. One produced a primitive pocket camera and insisted on being photographed by my side in front of the River Suriya.

After the refugees had got on their way to Boeng Kloeng, two rishi boys in their early teens caught us up. In their green skirts and azure and pink shirts, they looked striking. Scarves were wound around their heads in such a way that their topknots were revealed in an opening. Augmented to five, we set off again – a strange international band. One rishi boy took up the lead, an English *farang* and a Thai were sandwiched in the middle, and the Karen Sooksi and the other cultist boy brought up the rear. For some reason, the two rishi boys seemed disgruntled and switched restlessly at passing twigs and bamboos with their machetes. Suddenly, as we were labouring up a path through deep jungle, the leading cultist boy in front of me leapt high in the air, landing with his legs wide astride the path. I could not work out what had turned him so and stood rooted to the spot in amazement. Sooksi had seen everything. The rishi boy, just as he had been about to tread on a snake, had spotted it, sunning itself on the path. He had leapt into the air, startling the creature. The snake had slithered off down the path, but had encountered my ankles. Wriggling around the obstacle, it had then darted off into the undergrowth. The escape was perhaps even luckier than the earlier encounter with the tree snake.

All along the Suriya, we saw signs of refugee movement. People were ferrying family possessions and rice supplies across the river on bamboo rafts. Some were washing themselves or clothes in the water. Men were hastily constructing temporary shelters in the trees on the side of the river away from the enemy. And in an open, burning hot field we found a new refugee cultist village – Kui Kloe. Wherever we saw people, or people passed us, our guide and they would briefly chat. Seen from the air, this must have looked like a tenuous column of ants encountering each other, exchanging information, and passing on. At the deserted rishi village of Loe Ka Nae Ta (the people had mostly moved to Lae Tong Ku), we found a betel palm grove intergrown with wild star fruit, papaya and grapefruit trees. The white flowers of the grapefruit trees were heavy with sweet perfume. Sooksi got down some star fruits and cut off slivers with his machete, and we enjoyed a tart refreshing snack on the fly.

The last hour of the trek was the most gruelling. It was here that we learned the true meaning of Karen understatement about time and distance. Perhaps to encourage us when the path was most strenuous and we were most weary, Sooksi kept saying that Lae Tong Ku was just over that hill and that there was only another 15 minutes to go. There were two ways into the village from Boeng Kloeng – a longer flatter route in through the backdoor via a waterfall, and this steeper, more direct path, which aimed straight for Lae Tong Ku's BPP camp. We battled up an endless mountainside in the blazing sun towards a col. After four hours with the backpacks in the torrid heat, this was the killer. The sweat was streaming off our faces and bodies, and we had to stop every ten minutes, every five minutes, to drink water and get our breaths back. We each had a two-litre bottle of water with us. Nearly all of it was drunk on this last ascent. Sooksi and the rishi boys drank too, but they did not carry water bottles, rather drank from the Suriya and any passing spring they found.

Finally, in the distance, we saw the BPP camp – on the top of a hill. Behind its fortifications, a flag was flying. We crossed some baking open ground and with our last reserves of strength toiled up the hill. There we threw ourselves on a bench, all in. Red-faced, dry-throated and with sweat running freely, we tried to cool off in the faintest hilltop breeze. Sooksi looked cool and

THREE PAGODAS

fresh and amused, ready to do the same again, which in fact he presently did. Suddenly, it dawned on us to our great joy that we had made it. Three days out from Um Pang, we had reached the first principal objective of our jungle adventure – Lae Tong Ku.

✳ ✳

Postscript 2002

Route detail: Kui Le Tor – Boeng Kloeng (Map 27)
In early 1992, the projected Um Pang/Boeng Kloeng road ended at Nu Po, beyond which one had to walk. In early 1993, it had been pushed a bit further, almost to Kui Le Tor. I remember that in the latter year *silor* used to stop and unload their passengers and goods down by the river, where we had got lost and had tried to chase the man with his buffaloes. The boys had returned to the driverless Komatsu, and a year or two later, by the mid-1990s, they had of course pushed the road through to Boeng Kloeng, where it now terminates. So in 2002 it is not necessary to walk from Nu Po to Kui Le Tor and Boeng Kloeng, as the stretch can be ridden by either motorcycle or *silor*. At the end of the Postscript in Chapter 12, we left off the updated route detail for the Um Pang/Boeng Kloeng road at Kui Le Tor, precisely 1 km W of the village (km 70.9 on the road, measured from the centre of Um Pang). Now we pick up the account at that point for the remaining stretch from Kui Le Tor to Boeng Kloeng.

km 70.9 Way L to Kui Le Tor (1 km) and many other Karen villages
The road continues a fair distance (10 kms) without any special features, except that the impressive high Doi Mo Ga Tu border ridge still shadows your progress to the R. Road descends at length past a:
km 80.9 Thai army checkpoint (L)
km 82.9 You pick up an unexpected asphalt road and enter a karstic fairy-tale landscape with groves of vibrant green betel palms
km 84.2 Sign signifying entrance to **Boeng Kloeng** village
You pass along a lengthy main street, with many houses each side and more groves of tall slender betel nut palms. Two booths at far end (L) sell fuel
km 86.1 Thai-Burmese frontier and border gate

Boeng Kloeng
In February 2001, the village was completely transformed relative to what it had been nearly a decade earlier. As we rode into it and up the main street, I recognized almost nothing, except the local geography, and felt disoriented. With the completion of the Um Pang/Boeng Kloeng road, at the end of which the village lay 86 kms S of Um Pang, Boeng Kloeng had been prised out of its age-old bucolic languor and was now connected up with the outside world. Where once you had had to trek several hours to it, now trucks, pick-ups, *silor* and motorcycles – although only a handful – rumbled in and out. From the edge of 'town', where it metamorphosed into asphalt, the road, skinny and mediocre since Nu Po, swept broad and wide through the centre, right up to the border. In 2001, the *silor* fare from Um Pang to the remote southerly frontier community was about 100 baht, and the same back to Um Pang.
    If the advent of the new access road was one big difference between then and now, another concerned the main street. My slide photos record a magical narrow dirt track winding between shade-giving palms and wooden houses (see photo). This had

338

been replaced by a wide, cambered, hot and shadeless, tarred highway that struck through the heart of Boeng Kloeng, cutting it in two (see companion photo). The main drag seemed much longer than I remembered, stretching almost 2 kms from the village entrance sign at the eastern Christian end of 'town' to the border gate at the western Buddhist end. It was a long thin habitation, hemmed in to the N and S by low wooded ridges. The school, centrally located to the N of the main street, had been enlarged and rebuilt, and the small wooden field hospital where I had once had my ankle treated had turned into a regular health centre (to the left/W of the school). Also to the N of the main drag lay the *wat* (right/E of the school), which was more impressive than I recalled. A beautiful monastery-temple in the Burmese style, it nestled in a palm-shaded compound, quite near a small pagoda perched on a rock.

Boeng Kloeng had grown considerably from about 300 inhabitants in the early 1990s to some 1,000 in 2001, living in roughly 200 houses – extensive compared to Kui Le Tor or Nu Po. The refugee quarter we found in 1992 had already disappeared by 1993, but had probably reappeared a couple of times subsequently, until the events of 1997, after which the same refugees were undoubtedly definitively and for the long term housed in Nu Po refugee camp. The village now had many more shophouses and several simple eating places. You could even buy fuel at a couple of booths in the SW part of the main drag. But there was still no electricity in Boeng Kloeng – in the evening, illumination was by candles or battery-powered neon strip lights. Some atmospheric and picturesque elements remained. Bullock carts still trundled up and down the main street, some having crossed from Burma. Elephants continued to come in from Lae Tong Ku and elsewhere to be loaded up with provisions and goods in Boeng Kloeng before returning (see photo). Rishi followers from Lae Tong Ku and its associated cultist villages, with their topknots and colourful clothing, walked earnestly around, carrying out their errands, and there were girls with *tanaka*-adorned faces. Everywhere there were groves of lush green betel palms, quite especially to the N of the road near the village entrance, and in front of numerous houses people were drying and shelling betel nuts. It was a regular industry in Boeng Kloeng, with the nuts being sold in Mae Sot. We saw a cattle truck in the village, indicating that traders come to buy beef from Burma. Also, we met two Thai men from Lampang, who had come to buy 'Myanmar' beans. They said that they just waited until people brought sacks of beans across the border. The duo must have waited a long time, and the beans must have been very cheap to justify such a long and difficult journey. If you want to get an impression of what Boeng Kloeng and its main street used to be like before the arrival of the new road, explore up and down the second 'main' street, which lies S of the new main drag. A winding rutted dirt track passes idyllically through backwoods homesteads among coconut and betel palms, fording the Huai Boeng Kloeng a couple of times, which is the stream after which the village is named (*kloeng* = swamp or marsh in Karen).

But perhaps the most significant change locally, one which impacted greatly on Boeng Kloeng, was that the border crossing and territory across the frontier was no longer controlled by the KNU Karen, but by the DKBA and Burma army, who had seized the land opposite in February 1997, during the *tatmadaw's* offensive sweep up the Burmese side of the border at that time. The border at Boeng Kloeng used to be really open – I do not recall ever seeing any kind of formal crossing point or boundary or checkpoint there – and Karen as well as Thai civilians, Thai soldiers, aid officials, medical personnel and *farang* crossed at will into Burmese KNU-held territory, perhaps to visit Lae Tong Ku or Mae Ta Ro Ta, or to go N to Klo To or S towards Sangklaburi on the 4WD track that went up the border on the Burmese side. All that had made Boeng Kloeng a busy free-wheeling place. But now the cross-border traffic had stopped except for a few peasants going to and fro with produce. For fear of the

THREE PAGODAS

DKBA and Burma army, no one went to Lae Tong Ku through Burma any more, and Mae Ta Ro Ta had fallen. No KNU Karen crossed the border here any longer, and absolutely no Thai soldiers or *farang*. So no more little extraterritorial treks and thrills there now. Ordinary Thai civilians can and sometimes do cross for whatever reason (mostly trading), but, as our old friend and former guide Sooksi confirmed, no KNU sympathizer, including himself, went further beyond the crossing point (see colour photo) than the shops, about 20 metres away – if they went beyond that, they would be shot. Symptomatic of the current highly volatile situation in the Boeng Kloeng/Lae Tong Ku area was that late 2000 a Thai soldier was killed by the DKBA near Boeng Kloeng, and that on 3 February 2001, when we were staying a couple of nights in Boeng Kloeng, there was shooting at 4am just across the border from the village, while at 8am there was more of the same. Numerous similar incidents have occurred locally in recent years and continue to happen at the time of writing.

On arriving in Boeng Kloeng in February 2001, we found Sooksi very quickly, merely by showing my photo of him to people in the main street, who took us to his house. He was instantly recognizable, older of course, but with the same high-up 'plug' nose and same calm helpful manner. He, for his part, immediately recognized me and vividly recalled the trip of yore to Mae Ta Ro Ta and Lae Tong Ku. Now aged 49, while his wife was 48 (both are from Boeng Kloeng), he had greatly enlarged or rebuilt his house (N side of main street) and ran a noodle soup place in a hut adjacent to (L/west of) it. Much of the new information I gleaned about Boeng Kloeng, Lae Tong Ku and the local area came from Sooksi during tours of the village and over meals with him. Before our arrival, no *farang* had come to Boeng Kloeng for a while, he said, and during the previous year only three had visited. We took lunches in his noodle place and suppers in his house, and, to sleep, some of us put up in his house, on the front platform, while others camped in tents across the road in a field beside the house of the deputy headman, called Tan-oh, a friendly, fat-bellied chap. It was a pleasant campsite, dotted with coconut palms, betel trees and pineapple plants. If you go to Boeng Kloeng and want or need to stop a night, you could undoubtedly put up in the same places, or try the school or health centre or *wat*.

Boeng Kloeng – Lae Tong Ku (Map 28)

In 2001, we intended to proceed from Boeng Kloeng to revisit Lae Tong Ku with a view to updating the story there, and had even planned to do so once again with Sooksi. But we were prevented from going in the first instance by the BPP in Boeng Kloeng and ultimately by area commander Kaet Tai Wongsuwan of Nu Po, despite the fact that he was well disposed to both us and our cause. The reason, he said, was that in general the routes to Lae Tong Ku were currently hazardous, and that in particular the situation in Lae Tong Ku itself was currently too unstable and dangerous, with plenty of fighting locally. He was very sorry to have to prevent us from going, but would be happy to let us go another time or the following year, when things had quietened, and even to escort us there personally with some soldiers.

The upshot of this is that I am unable to update the travelogue on the basis of actual on-the-ground experience in that the story relates to the route to Lae Tong Ku and to Lae Tong Ku itself, and, further, I have not been able to retravel and revise the whole of the rest of the journey down the Thai-Burmese border, from Boeng Kloeng to Sangklaburi and the Three Pagodas Pass. So, from here onwards, my update comments are confined to what I have heard or know to be the case. Anyway, the situation beyong Lae Tong Ku has changed completely. Now that the Burma army has seized KNU 6th Brigade area across the border, it is impossible to travel down through Burma towards the Three Pagodas, rendering the westerly route that we originally took unviable. The onward journey from Boeng Kloeng could now only be done on the easterly route through Thailand. But this I have not done. Moreover, to research it and include it would be to rewrite the whole of the rest of this book.

In Boeng Kloeng, in 2001, I learned that there was a third way from the village to Lae Tong Ku, in addition to the two routes that we already know about (see Map 28). Thus (1), there is the quick way, which goes through Burma, via Mae Ta Ro Ta, partly following the Suriya river. This westernmost route is the one taken above in the travelogue. It is the flattest and shortest trail, taking about 3 hours on foot. (2) Then there is the slow roundabout way, which does not cross the border but remains in Thailand, keeping well away from the frontier. It proceeds via Kui Le Tor, Mong Gua (a Karen/Telakhon cultist village of 40-50 houses, where you would probably have to break the journey) and other settlements. From Boeng Kloeng, it is 15 kms back to Kui Le Tor and then some 12 kms to Mong Gua, after which it may be 3-4 hours on foot to Lae Tong Ku, crossing mountains and the escarpment just before Lae Tong Ku. It may be possible to hike directly from Boeng Kloeng to Mong Gua. (3) But a third way, the 'middle' route, which may have come into being because the first is blocked and the second too long, goes directly from Boeng Kloeng to the rishi cultist village. It does not cross the border, remaining in Thailand, although rather hugs the frontier. It crosses three ridges, takes 4-6 hours on foot, and is said to be arduous. The route is used mainly by local Karen and Lae Tong Ku cultists with elephants, who come to Boeng Kloeng to collect supplies, before returning.

Anyone wishing to visit Lae Tong Ku, no matter whether KNU Karen or Thai or *farang*, cannot any more use route (1), the old regular short way through Burma (not even local Karen, such as Sooksi). It has become fundamentally impossible – and looks set to remain so – because of the presence across the border of the murderous DKBA and of the Burma army. Trekking route (3), the 'middle' way, is currently inadvisable, and we were forbidden to use the path by the BPP. In 2001, commander Kaet Tai Wongsuwan told us that it was dangerous because the whole Lae Tong Ku area was subject to cross-border attacks and because DKBA and Burmese troops were given to raiding the path. In addition, he said, a *farang* had recently died of heatstroke on this tough trail. Thus, the only really safe and viable way at present is route (2), which keeps well away from the border until Lae Tong Ku. In early 2001, even this, as said, was closed to us owing to conditions at the rishi village. Reader-adventurers aspiring to reach Lae Tong Ku should invariably check first with the BPP, preferably back at Nu Po. The village and surrounding area has traditionally been dodgy securitywise. We recall the murders involving the 'yellowthreads'. While we were in the village in 1992, there was fighting to the west of it. Mid-January 2000, the Thai newspapers reported that near Lae Tong Ku a forest protection official was tied up and shot dead possibly by poachers, some of whom he had apparently caught previously, although DKBA men or rishi cultists may have been to blame. And around 1997, an acquaintance of ours from Lae Tong Ku was killed probably on the path between the village and Boeng Kloeng, as we shall see in the next chapter.

Finally, a word about **Mae Ta Ro Ta**, which we briefly visited with Sooksi in 1993, during our second hike to Lae Tong Ku. Between the fall of KNU GHQ Manerplaw in early 1995 and February 1997, it seems that Mae Ta Ro Ta was the new HQ of the KNU/KNLA, or that at least a mobile HQ was stationed there. But in February 1997, during the Burma army campaign against KNU 6th Brigade district (Duplaya), Mae Ta Ro Ta was attacked and overrun during the same offensive that saw the fall of Sa Kaang Thit (Ban Mai). The villagers together with commander Saw Kyi Shwi and his KNLA troops fled into Thailand, where they were eventually housed in Nu Po refugee camp (as we saw in the Postscript to Chapter 12), where they remain to this day. Saw Kyi Shwi has a son who is married and living in Boeng Kloeng.

14

A JUNGLE MAN-GOD

THE TELAKHON RISHI SECT

Lae Tong Ku

Contrary to our expectations, the paramilitary Border Patrol Police were excited to see us. The commander must have known that we were coming, but it appeared that the ordinary soldiers did not. They began rushing around to make us comfortable. The royal reception we had from these *dorchodor* at Lae Tong Ku was such as we experienced nowhere else down the border. Pineapples appeared, water, some round yellow peanut cakes and, marvel of marvels, cans of iced Coca-Cola. (Looking back on this, it is clear that the Cokes were not iced, as there was no electricity in the village. In our euphoria, they had seemed chilled, when in fact they must have been cooled in one of the rivers running through Lae Tong Ku.) The soldiers made us eat salt with the juicy pineapples to counteract dehydration. They took down our details in a duty book, invited us to supper that evening, and escorted us to a canteen at the foot of their eyrie.

Here, more fruit and water appeared, also a dish of tinned sardines, while a cook knocked up a large omelette in a wok. Unfortunately, when he served this on the mess table, we all saw that it was full of fried ants. Unperturbed, the chef cooked up another one. When we expressed our concern about the wasted omelette, he said that out here nothing was wasted. The boys up above would eat it. And, in fact, somebody straightway carried up the ant omelette to them, who shared it out. Surrounded by M16 weapons hanging from nails, we tucked into the new offering. At the back of the kitchen, we spied a barking deer (muntjac), tied up by one leg. The soldiers had trapped it in the night. The future did not look too bright for this poor little animal.

Sooksi left us at that point. He wanted to hurry back to Boeng Kloeng. We paid him his 100 baht and thanked him sincerely. We were sorry to see the Karen go. We could not have hoped for a more charming, informative guide. When he had gone, one of the BPP soldiers escorted us to the school, where we could stay. It was lucky that he did, for we would never have found the way ourselves. The first thing we noticed about Lae Tong Ku was just what a spread out village it was. Actually, it was more like a village within a village, with a strict cultist hub and *wat* located amid a wider outer band containing a mixture of dwellings belonging to both cultists and ordinary Karen. We thought that our walking was over for the day, but it was a good km to the school, and another one beyond that to the village proper.

The school consisted of a wooden tin-roofed building with about four classrooms, as well as a corrugated-iron latrine block. Further, there were a couple of teachers' huts, a guest hut, storeroom and mess area. Two teachers greeted us – a third was away. Our hut was a bamboo affair, raised on poles, with a leaf roof, split-bamboo floor, and no door. We hung a towel in the door frame to provide some privacy. The teachers brought blankets, mats, an oil lamp and a torch. Later, they rigged up a short strip light, powered via wires in the trees by an old car battery on their balcony. There was a dribbling tap in the ovenlike latrine block, otherwise washing was done in public from a standpipe and pail outside our hut, or in one of the rivers. Four young cultist boys worked for the teachers, and two of them were assigned to us. In particular, the pair had to look after our breakfast.

We would dearly have loved to unpack our rucksacks, wash and rest, but the teachers insisted on taking us straightaway across the playing field to the village's so-called Karen hospitality house. We got the impression that the teachers, now that the *dorchodor* had flirted with us, wanted to have their share of our company. And, indeed, there was a certain element of jealousy and ill feeling between the teachers and the soldiers. The Karen hospitality house was a gloomy wooden building, situated on the perimeter of the inner rishi village and run by an old woman. There, we were regaled in the afternoon heat with a spread of very hot food, laid out on the floor. There was grilled wild boar, barking deer curry, other unidentifiable curries, *somtam* with dried fish in it, and sticky rice. The wild boar had been salted first and was surprisingly lean and tasty. It was reminiscent of smoky bacon, but was chewy and salty, too. Politely, we ate as much of this as we could stomach. When we asked the teachers how much we had to pay, they said the food was free. At the time, we did not know how much we would come to rely on this house, nor did we fully appreciate the quality and generosity of the hospitality. It transpired that the *Yang* grandmama was famed far and wide for her welcome.

We finally got our wash and nap. When we were making ready to go up to the *dorchodor* camp for the supper to which we had been invited, the teachers came round and said it was time for us all to go over to the hospitality house again. We remonstrated, saying that we had been invited by the BPP. But they insisted, saying it would be bad form not to accept the Karen hospitality. So they trooped us across the playing field once more, and for the second time we picked at the grilled salted boar and barking deer curry. We were getting near to breaking into another of our precious reserve tins of tuna salad, nursed all the way from Mae Sot, but we thought first we should see what the soldiers served up. We ate several more times at the hospitality house, but, no matter whether it was breakfast, lunch or supper, the food was always exactly the same as on that first day.

Honour satisfied, we were free to go to the camp. We dared not ask the teachers to guide us, so we got one of the rishi acolyte boys to lead the way. It was already dark, and he headed off with his torch down a path we had not

343

taken earlier. We followed the lad downhill and up, through bits of jungle and across slimy single-log bridges over black rivers and muddy ravines. Lae Tong Ku by night was a perilous maze, punctuated by the feeble pinpoints of torchlight of Karen folk hurrying hither and thither. The soldiers again greeted us extravagantly. It seemed from their high spirits that they had already been at the bottle. They ushered us up the steep hill with its controlling daytime view over the whole area and sat us down at a table in a kind of open-sided command post. They were celebrating a colleague's birthday. The colleague was not actually present – he had gone to Um Pang – but, well, never mind. Also, they wanted to celebrate our arrival. In fact, in our honour, they had decided to take the rest of the day and the night off. The fact that the commander had also gone away had nothing to do with the matter, of course. So the camp and, indeed, the whole area was under the control of his deputy. This unshaven rogue, in his early twenties and sporting a red baseball cap, was drinking away like the best of them. If the Burma army had swept across the border at that moment, as it could easily have done, heaven only knows what would have happened.

In the corner of the command post, the soldiers had stood up a cardboard cut-out of their absent friend, and at intervals we toasted the symbolic figure with gulps of Mekhong whisky and Coke. Then the cooks proudly brought in the party meal – rice with a tureen of wonderful barking deer curry. In the space of six hours, we had already had enough muntjac curry to last us a lifetime. What made it even more difficult to force down another plateful was the thought of the little hobbled deer we had seen earlier, who would now bark no more. We asked the *dorchodor* about the eating habits of the rishi people. It was true, they said, that the cultists ate only the meat of game, not of domestic animals. They ate deer, boar, monkeys (four kinds), snakes, jungle fowl, fish – whatever they could hunt in the wild. Within the confines of the village, we would find no chickens, ducks or pigs. There were elephants, buffaloes and cows, but the people did not eat these, only used them for work. Neither did the rishi followers drink alcohol, although they did smoke. This was why the school and the army camp, even the hospitality house, were outside the real core village. Anybody who liked chicken or pork, or who enjoyed a drink, lived, literally, beyond the pale. We asked the boys why the cultist Karen did not eat domestic animals. Their answer was an explanation as apocryphal as any we heard. When domestic animals came into cultists' houses, the inhabitants cursed them. The rishi followers then avoided eating the animals because they did not want to eat their own curses.

It interested us to find out from the soldiers if *farang* ever came to Lae Tong Ku. None had come recently, although they thought that a few years previously two had somehow orienteered their way here. (A year later, when we revisited the village in 1993, the teachers said that no *farang* had been in the meantime.) Occasionally foreign missionaries came to Lae Tong Ku in a futile attempt to convert the devout rishi people. They mostly came up from Kanchanaburi and stayed only a short time. We had heard that a Karen Christian missionary woman, who spoke some English, was living near the mini waterfall, but we never encountered her. In the early 1990s, the principal trouble in the village was religious conflict between the sect and a Californian missionary, Mr Christopher. Cultural imperialists like him generated considerable ill feeling, which was then indiscriminately directed against any visitor, as we were later to discover.

When the cool evening air began to bite, the *dorchodor* rolled down tarpaulins over the open sides of our post. The atmosphere became cosier, more convivial, but also steadily more inebriated. The boys ran down to the storeroom to fetch more bottles of Mekhong, Coke and whatever titbits they could rustle up. Then the sound of distant fighting started, thundering in the Dawna Range. We hearkened to it for a while, but nobody paid much attention. Someone had the idea of trying to teach us a few words of Karen. Thus we learned: *omi* = rice, *oti* = water, *lor omi* = I'm hungry, *goh poh gah yor* = full, *tabloe dumah* = thank you very much, *soe koh* = hello, *jor lai le loh* = where are you going?, *or chua* = how are you?, but also, as the evening became progressively sillier and more drunken, things like *chi cha* = wee-wee. A helicopter dropped supplies to the BPP jungle camps every ten days. On that evening. the boys, with our help, drank up the whole of their ration of Mekhong whisky and ate nearly all the food. Afterwards, we were not invited to any more meals and drinkies at the camp. Worse still, only a few hours after our arrival, we were shamefully stotious in this ultimate teetotal village of stoics.

The next morning, when we appeared in the teachers' open-air canteen area, our two rishi acolyte boys brewed up coffee for us. From an early hour, the teachers had been blasting the immediate area through a tannoy with the Thai national anthem and Isaan pop music. This they did every morning. Seeing us arrive, they made to take us to the hospitality house, but we bridled and instead ate up the stale remains of some coconut cake we had brought from Um Pang. Over breakfast, we enjoyed the marvellous surrounding scenery. To the east, a long sheer cliff formation began to emerge from the morning mist. One of the teachers went off to school. The school was visible from where we sat, but we were surprised to see him together with only seven pupils, lined up before the Thai flag. We commented on the small number of children, and the other teacher explained that mostly the pupils did not come during the day. They went out collecting *jaak* and teak leaves to make roofing, and came to class in the evening. Altogether, there were 57 schoolchildren, aged between 7 and 15 years.

The second teacher took us on a guided morning tour of the village. Again, we were struck by the distances we had to walk and by how fragmented the place was. Often, houses stood quite isolated among the trees and fields. We saw also how relatively prosperous and established Lae Tong Ku was, compared to, say, Kui Le Tor. It was a study in self-sufficiency. There were rice and cereal fields (altogether some 100 and 50 *rai* respectively), and cotton, sugar cane and tobacco plantations. Fruit was a significant part of the local economy, people cultivating durian, grapefruit and betel trees. Of course, growing wild, were coconut and banana palms. Another important crop was chillies and sesame. In many places, we saw chillies and betel nuts drying in the sun, and in one spot we found a rotary mill, driven by an ox, grinding the oil out of sesame seeds. In many parts of Thailand, cereals were harvested more than once a year. Here, there was just one annual crop. Some of the rice and other products were sold to Karen in Burma or exchanged with them for salt, dried fish, shrimp paste and tobacco. Most families were engaged in weaving, both of cotton and bamboo. The finished cloth, mats and baskets were mainly for personal use. In one house, we watched black gunpowder being prepared. Considering that the cultists people did not eat domestic quadrupeds, we were surprised to see so many cows and buffaloes wandering around. A recent census in Lae Tong Ku (by our Um Pang friend Sombat) counted 81 cows, 39 buffaloes and also 7 elephants. But nowhere did we find a single chicken, duck, pig or goat.

The headman, Tra Nai, was out of the village at the time of our visit, but we did see his deputy, Mong Aemi. The deputy *pu yai* spoke good Thai, and we quizzed him at length. We were also introduced to a key character called Oh Sae Tae. This 65-year-old man had been born in the village and had seen four rishis come and go. It was under his direction that the fine new second monastery building had been constructed in 1991. Evidence of his skill as a craftsman could also be seen in the design of his own house. A sign of Oh Sae Tae's influence was that he was a confidant of the present rishi and owned two elephants. During our stay at Lae Tong Ku, we spoke at length both with Tra Nai and Oh Sae Tae, but also with the teachers, the BPP, and the rishi himself, and some of the information gleaned from them is incorporated in the following account.

※

History and culture of Lae Tong Ku & the Telakhon rishi sect

Lae Tong Ku, people said, was about 140 years old (in 1993), but whether this in fact applied to the foundation of the village or of the wider Telakhon rishi sect was unclear. Apparently, the original inhabitants had come from Burma. An account we found in Lae Tong Ku, written – I think – by a Thai teacher, reported that between 1852 and 1860 they had been chased two or three times out of the country by the Burmese, finally settling at the site of the present village during the 1850s. They had crossed the River Suriya, which forms the Thai-Burmese border hereabouts, one mile to the west of Lae Tong Ku, and established their village just inside Thailand, beside Kao Saam Rom mountain. Between the village and the Suriya lay a small waterfall, from which the settlement had taken its name – 'Lae Tong Ku' meant 'the village above the waterfall'. The villagers were mostly Telakhon cultist people, who in 1992 numbered 610 or 109 families (excluding a Karen refugee camp nearby), comprising 365 males and 245 females. The major discrepancy between the number of men and women was explained by the fact that the male contingent was swelled by the disciples of the rishi, many of whom came from outside the village. Lae Tong Ku lay at an altitude of 210 m above sea level and consisted of approximately 15 sq kms of houses and fields, with an additional 12 sq kms of jungle and mountain.

A JUNGLE MAN-GOD

In 1992, most of the houses were constructed of wood and bamboo. All were roofed with teak leaves, except five, which had tin roofs (a decade later, there are undoubtedly many more galvanized corrugated iron roofs, done with metal sheeting brought by elephant from Boeng Kloeng). Only two of these dwellings had 'proper' toilets (i.e. with pot and dipper), 65 had just a hole dug in the ground, and 42 had no toilet at all. Three small rivers ran through the village: the Ti Mo Ko, the Lae Pra Ko (= bat cliff river) and the Ba No Krae Ko (= lemon river). The rivers were used for washing, irrigating and drawing water. Drinking water was derived from two shallow man-made wells and from sand wells along the rivers. The water in the taps near the school was stream water piped down from the mountain. There was no hospital or health centre in Lae Tong Ku, although the BPP were sometimes able to provide emergency aid (by now, there may well be some kind of medical centre). At that time, villagers walked mostly to the clinic in Boeng Kloeng for treatment, or they waited for the mobile hospital that came three times a year (probably from Klo To to the north or Sangklaburi to the south via the 4WD track running along the Burmese side of the border). The most common complaints of both adults and children were thyroid problems, respiratory and intestinal ailments, and malaria. Lae Tong Ku was (and remains) one of the deadliest places in Thailand for malaria.

What made Lae Tong Ku interesting, of course, was that it was a centre for the Telakhon rishi sect. It was not the only such centre – there was reportedly another one or maybe more than one across the border in Burma – but it was the only Telakhon cult centre in Thailand, making Lae Tong Ku unique there, housing the only Telakhon *pu chaik* or man-god in the kingdom. The Telakhon (I have also read 'Talarku' and 'Lagu', which are probably just Thai attempts at 'Telakhon') rishi sect was another of the many sub-groups or splinter groups of the overall Karen (Karennic) family of peoples. A religion-based group, their beliefs were informed with the millenarianism associated especially with the Karen. A historical perspective sets the Telakhon cult and its representatives at Lae Tong Ku in context.

Martin Smith (1993, pp. 426-428), who in turn partly draws on Theodore Stern (1968), says that several millenarian sects like the Telakhon rishi cult have been recorded over the last 150 years in South-East Asia. There have been such sects among the Shan of Burma, the Khmu and Hmong of Laos, the Lahu of Burma's Shan State (where the G'uisha cult has given rise to a series of militant man-god prophets), and the Lua or Htin of the border area between Thailand's Nan province and Laos' Sayaburi province (where 1964-65 the trickster 'prophet' Pu Wong gave rise to a cargo cult). But the movements have been prevalent especially in Burma and in particular among the country's rural Karen, whose culture, beliefs, legends and above all downtrodden condition have predisposed them to such millenarian cults (as we saw in Chapter 9, under 'Karen people & culture'). These sects have mostly been started by messianic prophets who claimed either that they had in their possession the fabled Karen 'Golden Book' or that they alone had the powers to read such a book when the 'White Brother' of Karen legends returned.

347

THREE PAGODAS

These days, the two best known of these Burmese Karen sects are the Leke and Telakhon. Founded in 1860, the Leke sect is centred on the village of that name in Burma's Kyondo district, and is noted for its celebrated 'chicken-scratch' script of the cult's own 'Golden Book' (in fact, Smith says, this is just a hand-written school exercise book). The Telakhon sect was also founded in the second half of the 19th century, in Burma's Kyain district, by a prophet known as the *pu chaik* or 'Grandfather God/Buddha'. By the early 1960s, this cult had burgeoned under the seventh *pu chaik* man-god, who was an ethnic Pwo Karen, to become a movement with several thousand adherents. It flourished in Burma's eastern hills and also, after spreading across the border, in western Thailand, specifically in the Lae Tong Ku/Mae Chan Ta area. Now it is apparent why the age of Lae Tong Ku as a Telakhon sect centre is unclear. It remains to be established whether the cult existed simultaneously on both sides of the border from the outset (c. 1855), making Lae Tong Ku as old as the sect, or whether it existed initially and for many years only in Burma, subsequently spreading to Thailand (we recall that in 1993 65-year-old Oh Sae Tae claimed to have been born in the village, in which case it must date back to at least 1928, although such data is never completely reliable), in which case the village as a rishi place might not be as old as the cult. Over the years, the Telakhon sect developed an apparently complex system of village administration and ritualized worship.

In the 1960s, an incident among the Telakhon cultists of Burma brought the sect into conflict with the KNU. The behaviour of the incumbent (seventh) *pu chaik* changed, becoming increasingly erratic. As Smith reports, the rishi seemed convinced that the age of Arimetteya (the new order of the future – fifth – Buddha), prophesied to arrive in his lifetime, had come. Breaking the tradition of celibacy of the hermit *pu chaik*, he married and also began trying to recruit KNU soldiers to attack government-held towns as a demonstration that the Telakhon movement and not the KNU was the real organ of Karen nationalism, which naturally rankled with the KNU. In 1967, the man-god rishi, believing his followers to be protected by special charms and hence invincible, ordered them twice to attack Kyaikto town, which led to the deaths of two dozen cultists and six Burmese troops, following which the Telakhon warriors retreated in disarray. Shortly afterwards, the KNU moved to put down the cult, and the *pu chaik* was arrested, tried and executed, along with his chief lieutenant. Today, Smith continues, 2,000-3,000 survivors of the Telakhon sect linger on both in former KNU 6th Brigade district in Burma and in the Lae Tong Ku area. Here, under two junior *pu chaiks*, they continue to await the predicted return of the great *pu chaik*.

In addition to the above question of the exact age of Lae Tong Ku, some details relating to the foregoing do not add up or remain to be settled. Smith mentions that the Telakhon sect today numbers a couple of thousand or so, but in 1993 we learned that it comprised a total estimated at 16,000 followers (in Burma and Thailand). Perhaps the former is rather low and the latter too high. The rishi cultists continue to live on both sides of the border in the south of the Dawna Range, but mainly in Burma. They live in altogether 31 villages, seven of which are in Thailand, all of the latter in the remote south-western part of Um Pang district, near the Mae Chan river. In Thailand, Lae Tong Ku is the principal community of these seven and the only one with a rishi. The other six Thai Telakhon settlements are Mong Gua, Mo Ta Lua, Mae Chan Ta, Chong Pae, Ti Wa Kae and Kai Wo Ta. With no rishi in the six, their cultists go from time to time to worship the man-god in central Lae Tong Ku. The same goes for some nearby rishi villages in Burma, for example, Kui Le Toeng, whose faithful likewise walk to Lae Tong Ku, e.g. for full-moon ceremonies. But what is the position in Burma? Are there more central Telakhon villages there on a par with Lae Tong Ku, how many, and which are they? How many rishis are there in Burma, if any – one or perhaps two? Are they and their villages equal in status to the Lae Tong Ku hermit and his village, or are they more senior or more junior? Is Lae Tong Ku now the centre of the whole Telakhon cult, and is its rishi the real leader of the movement, or is he, as Smith suggested, one of a couple of junior *pu chaiks*, who continue the tradition until a single senior cult leader re-emerges? The way that the present Lae Tong Ku rishi is described as the tenth and latest in the line of *pu chaiks* going back to the mid-19th century encourages one to suppose that he is the overall cult leader. But what of any other rishis in Burma? Do they see themselves as the newest incumbent? Could there be two or three or more rishi lineages, one in Thailand and the other(s) in Burma, which perhaps share the original *pu chaik* or even some early *pu chaiks*, but which then split to form separate different lineages in Thailand and Burma, each with its own subsequent rishis?

The millenarian movements of the Karen can generally be described as animist sects that borrow widely from (1) Buddhist imagery and belief, (2) Christian prophecies of the Second Coming, and (3) the Karen legend of the 'Golden Book'. From Buddhist imagery and belief, they take especially the idea of the messianic figure of the *cakkavatti* or universal monarch, who will pave the way for Arimetteya, the new order of the future (fifth) Buddha. The Leke sect, which is said to be more Buddhist-influenced, anticipates that Ariya (the future Buddha), whom they await, will be the same as the Karen Y'wa or God. The Telakhon cult, by contrast, which is more Christian-influenced, believes Ariya to be the same as Christ. The Telakhon sect shares Buddhism's five central precepts, although interprets the first differently. Thus, where Thai Buddhism says thay you should not kill animals, the rishi cultists believe that you may, for eating. Just why the cultists of Lae Tong Ku do not eat domestic animals such as cows and buffaloes, and yet consume wild animals, we never established and remains another question to be answered, but it might be because of Hindu influences. In many ways, the Lae Tong Ku Telakhon, with their elephant cult, their ascetic sadhu or guru, their long hair, and their made-up faces, are reminiscent of some exotic Indian sects. They repeat the old Karen myth of the 'Golden Book' stolen from the Karen people by the 'White Brother', who will one day return with this book of all knowledge. Borrowing from all these Karen, Buddhist, Christian, animist and maybe Hindu sources, therefore, the millenarian Telakhon of Lae Tong Ku believe in and worship their Christlike *pu chaik* or divine rishi, as Thais believe in the Lord Buddha, and have further overlaid their composite religion with the elephant tusk cult.

349

THREE PAGODAS

The rishi cultists of Lae Tong Ku are devout people with austere practices. Each year, at the village, they hold four main religious ceremonies: at *songkraan*, prior to the rainy season, after the rainy season, and after the harvest. Also, every month, they hold three ceremonies at the time of the full moon, half moon and no moon. You can always recognize them by their characteristic topknots as well as by their costumes, which are basically Karen but with flamboyant modifications.

In the teacher's account, we read that when rishi cultists transgressed, they were first admonished and then, if they repeated the transgression, shorn of their hair and paraded round the village. On a third occasion, they were expelled from the village and the sect. The wrongdoer could be re-admitted by apologizing, by being purified with holy water, and by bringing five kgs of pure beeswax and also flowers, incense and a candle. A villager with shorn hair was not necessarily a wrongdoer. A cultist might cut off his hair to get rid of lice or fleas. When sect members died, they were not cremated as in Buddhist practice, but buried. The burial took place on the day of the death without a *wat* service. When cows and buffaloes died, the people did not eat them, but likewise buried them.

In 1993, the rishi of Lae Tong Ku had 82 disciples. These were different from the rank-and-file followers in the village or in other villages in that they lived at the monastery and learned from the holy sage. At the time of our visit, their ages ranged from 11-28. The young disciples had to serve a minimum of three years and three months and during that time could not, like the rishi himself, enter people's houses or marry. After three years of the ascetic life, they were free to leave or marry. However, if they did so, they could not then re-enter the discipleship. The newest and youngest acolytes had the hardest work to do and lived with the master himself in the original *wat* building. They fetched water, gathered wood, cooked rice and served the rishi. The older ones lived in a separate building and made baskets and other things for use in the monastery or to give to villagers. Local people sometimes brought food offerings to the *wat*. In order to become a disciple, a young man had to be bathed in the *pu chaik's* holy water and had to offer one coconut, three bunches of bananas, one kg of pure beeswax, and food. He brought, further, his personal requisites, including three knives, one axe, a sleeping mat and a pillow.

Lae Tong Ku's present rishi was titled Monnae and named Ujae (English: Ujay, 'U.J.' – I have also seen this written as Mu Je/Jae). In 1995, Ujae was aged 44 and was the tenth rishi since the founding of the Telakhon sect and possibly of Lae Tong Ku. He was a relatively new incumbent because the last man-god, hailing from Burma, had died in August 1989. Technically, Ujae was the eleventh *pu chaik*, as there had been another one, Jae Hor Wae, before the lineage of ten. But that very first one had been caught and killed by the Burmese (possibly in 1855?), and the cultists had begun counting anew with their second leader. For the record, the ten official Telakhon leaders have been (from the Lae Tong Ku point of view at least): Jae Bae (said to have died in 1852, but that does not accord with the death of the original rishi), Jor Yor, Jae Moe, Jae Lia, Gaeng Kor, Soe Tia Boei (died 1942), Jae Chouai (1942-1955), Toh (1955-1965), Du Yoh (1965-1989) and Ujae (1989-). I have read that Jae

350

A JUNGLE MAN-GOD

Bae, the first rishi, had wanted Karen men to have the chance to be ordained and study Dharma. He had announced himself the religious leader of all the Karen people and had taught a form of Dharma from Buddhist principles. It is apparent from the lineage above that the seventh rishi, Jae Chouai (died 1955) or even the eighth, Toh (died 1965), does not accord – unless the dates are wrong – with the incident mentioned earlier, in which the seventh *pu chaik* was executed by the KNU in 1967. This suggests that the rishi killed was one from Burma and not from Lae Tong Ku, which in turn implies that from some time onwards Lae Tong Ku has had its own rishi lineage, and, further, that there are at least two *pu chaik* lineages, one in Burma and one in Thailand.

Before a rishi died, he normally nominated his successor. Du Yoh and Ujae had inherited the mantle in this way. But if an outgoing *pu chaik* died without having chosen, a meeting was called of all the Telakhon villages in Thailand and Burma to nominate the successor. The rishi could not marry or visit villagers' houses, and stayed mostly in the *wat*. His daily life was to instruct the disciples and the cult followers in general. He ate twice a day, morning and evening, preferring fish, fruit and jungle bipeds (monkeys and wildfowl). In the rainy season, he ate once a day, after sunset. The leader was held to be endowed with certain magical and shamanistic powers. Illness in a villager was regarded as possession of that person by an evil spirit. The rishi could exorcize such spirits. It was said that he did not actually arbitrate in disputes, but could act rather as if the disputants had taken a 'truth drug'. The Karen came to the man-god and told their conflicting stories. They believed that whoever told lies would die. If the Telakhon sect's numbers were holding steady or were even on the increase, belief in the magical powers of the rishi himself was on the decline.

✳

Our morning round of the village with the teacher ended with a visit to the *wat*. The teacher thought he might be able to secure us an interview with the holy man, but he held out no great hope. We for our part knew that this Thai teacher was a particularly religious (Buddhist) man and hoped that he might have some leverage with the rishi. We came down to the monastery complex. It lay sheltered in a coconut grove at the foot of 'Bat Cliff' escarpment. The atmosphere was peaceful and friendly. Cultist boys and men sat or strolled around, and cows and buffaloes wandered at will. We found five buildings: the original *wat*, the new quarters constructed by Oh Sae Tae for the older disciples, a meeting place, a shed housing elephant tusks, and a storehouse for rice and food. Besides the compound itself, a further 30 *rai* of land belonged to the monastery.

At a certain point on the approach to the compound, there was an invisible line beyond which no one could go without taking his or her shoes off. We were just about to overstep this line when the teacher and some of the disciples firmly reminded us that now we should proceed barefoot in the dust. Beyond this line, at the level of the *wat*, there was a second invisible line, marking off territory which no woman could enter, not even Thai queen Sirikit. A third line, behind the *wat*, demarcated a sacred area running back to

351

the cliff, accessible only to the rishi and his disciples. Apparently, there were elephants in there, and rumour had it that in the cliff face there was a cave for the personal use of the jungle hermit.

We particularly enjoyed the colourful extravagance of the rishi followers. These were handsome wide-jawed men in bottle-green or blue sarongs, and wearing shirts which were typically green, azure, or pink (see colour photo section). Their long black hair, rubbed with coconut oil to make it shine, was twisted up behind the head and brought over the crown to be knotted above the forehead. Mostly the knot was worn centrally, but sometimes it was sported above the right eye. Almost every follower had a white or pink scarf, often fringed with magenta, which was wound around the head in such a way that the topknot appeared in a front opening. It was the habit of the cultists to beautify themselves with gold facial painting, red lipstick, earrings, necklaces and flowers in their hair, in a way that reminded me of heavily adorned Pwo Karen men I had seen, from whose culture the Telakhon sect has possibly borrowed. Altogether, they looked very pretty, and sometimes it was hard to remember that the young ones were not girls. The cultist women were no less striking. Married ladies wore wine-red sarongs and red or blue or black blouses, while the unmarried girls dressed in long, off-white, pink-edged shifts. All the rishi people, like all good Karen, never went anywhere without their cerise shoulder bags.

The original *wat* building, which, judging by its state, must have been decades old, was smaller and more ramshackle than we had imagined. It was made of old brown wood and rusty beaten-up corrugated sheeting, and was raised high enough on stilts for buffaloes to be able to wander underneath (see photo). The jungle hermitage was in the Burmese style and appeared in essence to be a deep rectangular box, although, of course, we could not look round the back. At the front was a porch, and low wings with sloping roofs abutted on each side. The whole building was surmounted by a curious stunted square wooden tower and was shaded by the trees. I was not permitted to enter this building and tried instead to look through the open door, which was about six feet off the ground. But it was so gloomy inside that it was impossible to make out anything except a photograph of the previous rishi and numerous baskets. I had the impression of peering into a dusty run-down junk shop.

As an offering for the jungle man-god, the teacher had brought some peas roasted in batter. He called into the *wat* and asked for the holy man to come out. After a while the rishi appeared from the interior gloom and sat cross-legged in the doorway. The teacher handed the 'sweeties' to him via one of the acolytes. Monnae Ujae was simply dressed in an off-white robe wrapped around his body and over his left shoulder, leaving bare a muscular right arm and shoulder. Of course, he had a topknot, but no headscarf, and we noticed cotton strings (spirit cords) tied around his wrists. His face was severe, angular, unsmiling, crosspatch. Wisps of hair grew out of his chin, his eyes were rather too close together, and the pronounced furrows which slanted upwards and outwards from the bridge of his nose made him look more diabolical than divine. Our teacher guide could not speak Karen, and the rishi no Thai, so communication was difficult. However, through one of the acolytes, who spoke some broken Thai, the teacher tried to convey that we had come all the way from Um Pang to visit the leader. But the hermit was a model of calculated indifference. He said almost nothing the whole time, avoided our gaze, and, when I tried to photograph him (with his permission), looked steadfastly at the floor beyond his knee. Finally, he cleared his throat and spat demonstratively onto the ground, whereupon he disappeared back into the gloom of his ramshackle jungle *wat*.

We were disappointed with this audience with the *pu chaik*. After having come so far, we were peeved that he had had so little time for us and had shown so little interest. It must have been a rare event for a *farang* to come and see him. But beyond that, he did not even show the common courtesy and welcome one might have expected of any holy man, whatever his persuasion, and so we formed a poor opinion of this man-god. On top of everything, I knew that the half dozen photographs I had sneaked were failures. Thoughts were running through our minds that the divine could not be interviewed or photographed, and, less charitably, that at the end of the quest was nothing. Later, we found out that the rishi had mistaken us for missionaries, and we roundly cursed all missionaries and even the pious teacher for not making things clearer.

While we were thinking evil thoughts outside the *wat*, one of the disciples shinned up the long trunk of a coconut tree and began hacking football-size nuts down. Although there were only three of us, he had to get four because one of them, after plummeting to the ground, burst open with a spectacular spray of milk. The boy then deftly lopped off the tops with a machete and presented each of us with a fresh coconut. After we had drunk the milk, he then split the green nuts in two, allowing us to scoop out the thin slimy flesh. Apparently, all visitors were at least accorded this courtesy.

Later that evening, after we had supped once more on wild boar and barking deer, we returned to the school area to find two wandering monks, an old one and a young one, who had trekked in from faraway Supanburi. We also found a couple of BPP boys who, far from inviting us for food and drink, were trying to heavy it up with us to leave Lae Tong Ku. Evidently, visitors were not allowed to spend more than a night or two in 'government property' except by prior arrangement with the authorities. In Lae Tong Ku, seeing that it was impossible to stay in a sect house, anyone passing through was more or less obliged to stay in the school guest hut. Insofar as Buddhist monks could express such feelings, the two whacked bonzes, shorn of their hair and eyebrows, looked reproachfully at us because we had taken the only free accommodation, and they were going to have to double up with one of the teachers in his hut.

The rishi boys had made a fire, and we all sat round it in the betel trees under the moon and stars. The fire was a criss-cross of dried bamboo sections, and at regular intervals everybody pushed the end nearest to them further into the centre of the fire. We were a strange gathering: a brace of wandering monks, the religious Thai teacher, the two Telakhon sect boys, an Anglo-Thai and an English *farang*. The other teacher was busy in the school, and from nearby came the drone of multiplication tables or the Thai alphabet being chanted by the pupils. We asked the two monks which route they had taken. They had wanted to go from Mong Gua to Boeng Kloeng, but had got lost after half an hour and had followed by mistake the dreaded path from Mong Gua to Lae Tong Ku. They had set off from Mong Gua at 9am and had arrived here at 4pm. The path had not been so difficult, especially coming this way round. But if one started from Lae Tong Ku, there would be a long steep climb over 'Bat Cliff' ridge.

Reviewing with the teacher our unsatisfactory visit to the rishi earlier that day, we came to speak of the confusion surrounding the two groups of Telakhon cultists, the 'yellowthreads' and the 'whitethreads'. At the same time, we were able to make more sense of the confusion surrounding the attack by rishi tribesmen on BPP soldiers. There were indeed two rival Telakhon sub-groups: the old 'whitethread' sect based here on Lae Tong Ku, and another breakaway 'yellowthread' cult, which was trying to establish itself near Mae Chan Ta. The murders had had nothing to do with either Lae Tong Ku or the 'whitethread' *pu chaik* followers living there, but had taken place in a different place, fomented by a different group of people – the troublesome 'yellowthreads'. It was said that the splinter 'yellow' group, numbering some hundreds, were partly ex-communists local to the area. They and their rival rishi, one Ti Liang Eng or Dhi Liew Eng, had set up an alternative hermitage in the far-flung settlement of Chong Pae. From here, they wanted to establish a fiefdom in the heart of the giant Tung Yai and Huai Kha Khaeng wildlife sanctuaries. Actually, there was a rumour that the new self-proclaimed 'yellow' leader was already dead. Reportedly, the upstart cultists believed that, if they carried a piece of their rishi's yellow robe, they were invincible, incapable of being hurt even by bullets. To prove the point, Ti Liang and three of his most devout followers had allowed themselves to be ceremonially shot at, with the unfortunate result that they had been killed.

Unlike the Lae Tong Ku cultists, who cooperated to a degree with the authorities, the rival sect sought total autonomy in its area, subject to the control of neither the 'whitethread' *pu chaik*, the paramilitary *dorchodor*, nor the forestry *anuraak* and *grom pamai*. But the BPP and the forestry authorities had outposts in the sub-sect's 'territory' and, provocatively, had forbidden the group to hunt the wildlife of Tung Yai and Huai Kha Khaeng or to cut down sanctuary trees to make space for agriculture. For a while, relations with the authorities had been distinctly strained. But what had brought matters to a head was not so much the belief of the 'yellowthreads' that the authorities were trying to suppress their Ariya cult, or the ban on hunting, as a particularly galling and all-too-human detail. In revealing this telling detail to us, our pious teacher friend provided an insight into the resentment he and his colleagues felt towards the BPP soldiers and also the *anuraak*. The *dorchodor* and forestry boys, not content with forbidding the cultists to hunt, had then themselves proceeded to hunt, openly flouting their own interdict. One might perhaps have expected that the BPP would engage in a bit of surreptitious poaching, but not the very guardians of the wildlife sanctuaries. Yet the *anuraak*, too, had openly hunted under the very noses of the 'yellowthread' rishi people.

A JUNGLE MAN-GOD

So it had been the hypocrisy of the military and the forestry authorities that had so incensed the cultists, triggering the violence. The mechanics of the raid we gleaned from BPP soldiers themselves. One night, 30-40 'yellow-threads' had come to the Mae Chan Ta forestry office, ordered two young men staying there to leave, and burnt the place down, including all the paperwork and communications equipment. Later the same night, between 4 and 5am, the same band of cultists had gone to the local BPP camp, about one km away. The soldiers had all been sleeping except for a sentry and one cook, who had got up to prepare the camp breakfast. The cook had seen the cultists coming and raised the alarm. But it had been too late, and the rishi followers had killed six soldiers with machetes. One soldier had managed to get out a machine gun and shot half a dozen of the assailants. The rest had run away, to Supanburi and Kanchanaburi. Those who had not been rounded up in the subsequent army action were still at large down that way.

The next morning, sick of grilled boar and muntjac curry, we went in search of food which we could buy and prepare ourselves with the aid of the teachers' utensils. In a house near Oh Sae Tae's residence, we found the beginnings of Lae Tong Ku's very first shop. We purchased there some yellow Burmese noodles, shallots and greens, and later cooked these up into a wonderful pottage, flavoured with fish sauce, oyster sauce, garlic and black pepper. It was the best meal since Um Pang. Village elder Oh Sae Tae was doing some detailed woodwork on the balcony of his house. Meeting him again, we had a piece of luck. He introduced us to one Toom Yai, who was sitting with him. We joined the two men on the balcony. The fetching 35-year-old Toom Yai, who sported a stylish bushy bobtail topknot (see photo section), spoke good Thai as well as his native Karen. Among other things, Toom Yai offered to guide us on the next leg of our journey, wherever that might take us.

The role of the elephant tusks in rishi religion puzzled us, and Oh Sae Tae, through Toom Yai, seemed to be the very person to ask about it. The story, as told to us by the elephant owner, was as follows. In the old days, a large wild elephant had frequented the village area. It was a smart animal because it used to come to the *wat* each time there was a full or half moon – the days when people brought food offerings for the rishi and his disciples. The people saw this as a sign of good luck, a sign from the Buddha, and began to incorporate the elephant in their cult. When the elephant died, the *pu chaik* of the day cut off its outsize tusks and had them carved by a Burmese craftsman. The tusks were the enormous pair in the ivories house near the *wat*. If we liked, Toom Yai and Oh Sae Tae could take us down to see them. We took up the offer at once. We also told them about our disappointing visit to the rishi the day before. The two were quite upset about this and resolved to put things right. And so it happened that we secured our second and successful audience with rishi Ujae, this time equipped with one of his confidants and an interpreter.

We waited on the benches facing the porch of the old hermitage while Oh Sae Tae explained behind the scenes to the hermit that we were not missionaries, but had journeyed with no other intention than to see him. Could not the holy man come out again and answer our questions? After a long time,

355

Monnae Ujae appeared for a second time. On this occasion, he did not skulk in the doorway, but came right out to sit cross-legged on a kind of dais between the doorway and the benches. Behind him was an array of 18 disciples in their colourful finery. We quickly realized that our second audience was an official reception, making it a somewhat daunting occasion. In other respects, however, it was the same seedy spectacle as before. The rishi sat patiently on his makeshift platform in his dirty cotton robe. Because he was sitting in a shaft of light burning down through the tree canopy, beads of perspiration formed on his forehead. As he emerged from his *wat*, he picked up a handful of betel nut and crammed it into his mouth. For a long time, he chomped on this, spitting out streams of saliva in a way that was not at all godlike. Behind him, his entourage of young girl-boys lolled around, likewise chewing betel and expectorating, but also smoking pipes and fat home-made joints. The spectacle would have been absurd or even suspect if it had not been so riveting.

Through Toom Yai, we asked the rishi as many questions as we could think of. We asked him if he could leave the village or if the sect could uproot and move to somewhere else. No, they had to stay here in the appointed place. We wanted to know if his sect was proselytizing. No, their cult was non-expansionist. How tolerant and forbearing these people seemed in comparison with the missionaries who intruded into their jungle retreat. The subject led on to the 'yellowthread' cultists, who had attacked the BPP. Here, Monnae Ujae, who had been a picture of composure, quietly picking at his toenails under our noses, became agitated. His face darkened and the lines fanning out from between his eyes deepened into that infernal frown. This was a splinter group, and they were false Telakhon people, the 'whitethread' leader hissed. They wore trousers and other degenerate things. They had nothing to do with the Lae Tong Ku group and were bad people.

The rival sect troubled Ujae in another way that was not easy for us to understand. He said that in his cult, if the rishi dreamed three times of yellow thread, he had to change the colour of his robes from white to yellow. He had recently had a second dream of yellow thread, and he was afraid that he might soon have the third and final dream. The photo we had seen of the previous leader, taken shortly before his death, showed the predecessor wearing a yellow robe. It was possible that the colour yellow was associated for Ujae with something bad, the need to nominate a successor, or some great change in the sect. The rise of the breakaway 'yellowthread' group may have seemed for him like the harbinger of some apocalyptic change.

Toom Yai explained to the holy man that I was sure that the photos I had taken the previous day were no good, and he asked if it was possible for the *farang* to take some fresh ones for his book. Ujae nodded approval. Where earlier the rishi had resolutely avoided looking at the camera, now he scowled into the lens with such a vengeful thunderous stare that I thought the lens, film and my eyeball would be burnt out (see black-and-white photo). After the photographs, the jungle hermit expressed an interest in the camera and began asking questions about it. It seemed he was taken with the idea of becoming a snapper himself. We suggested that he buy a pocket Kodak from Mae Sot, a notion which brought to his face the only smile we ever saw him make.

A JUNGLE MAN-GOD

Our last question concerned the religious ceremonies. It was answered in an unexpected way. By good fortune, there was to be a half-moon ceremony the next morning, and if we liked we could come and watch. The man-god rose to return to his hermitage. As he disappeared, Oh Sae Tae asked if we might look at the ivories. It was arranged that some of the disciples would show them to us.

The sacred tusks were housed to the left of the old *wat* building in a special shed, raised high off the ground on stilts. As the ivories lay behind the second invisible line, women were not permitted to see them. My eyes peered at floor level into the gloomy repository. Inside, were two pairs of tusks, one large and one small, and many Buddha figures, mostly rather small. The two large tusks from the local elephant were massive indeed. Standing at 155 cms high and weighing 35 kgs each, they were mounted on their stump ends and arched up and inwards, framing the smaller ivories and some of the figurines. Both giant tusks were elaborately carved with scores of standing and seated Buddha images, which diminished in size as they approached the tip. We were told that the carving had been done by a Burmese mastercraftsman. The two smaller tusks, two kgs in weight and one foot high each, had come from Kanchanaburi and were remarkable, although damaged, for their exquisite intaglio work. It looked as if a lacework of ivory had been wrought around the core of each, itself carved with Buddhas, and yet the tusks were all of a piece. There had once been a third pair of tusks at Lae Tong Ku, but these had gone to another monastery.

The two largest Buddha images were a 12-inch-high golden standing figure in the Ayuttaya style, and a similar black figure in the Burmese style. There were a pair of white jade Burmese Buddhas five inches wide by seven inches tall. In addition, there was a small Burmese clay figure two inches wide by three inches tall, covered in gold. Seven Burmese images with similar dimensions were covered with silver and had heads of gold. Further, some 30 or so other small figures resided in the shed. At one time, there had been a Buddhist *wat* in Lae Tong Ku, manned by one monk. When he had died, all the temple's Buddhas had been moved to the rishi cultist *wat*. Considering how valuable the big tusks and some of the Buddha figures were, in terms both of their material and spiritual value, it was remarkable to see them on display outside unguarded. After we had inspected the ivories house, we were again treated to a fresh coconut each.

On the fourth day of our stay in Lae Tong Ku, we got up very early and went down unaccompanied to the *wat* to witness the half-moon ceremony. People were arriving from far and wide. Some had got up in the small hours to trek from far-flung rishi hamlets. About 200 people had congregated in the temple compound. The disciples were brushing up dead leaves to make the bare earth spick and span. In several places, fires were burning, and the dust and smoke drifted up through the shafts of early morning light filtering through the trees. People were busy changing into special ceremonial clothes. The men were donning ankle-length white shifts, edged with pink and bearing four vertical red stripes, an attire which made them resemble unmarried girls.

THREE PAGODAS

People were bringing food offerings for the rishi, and these were transmitted to him by the *ukoh*, a special male intermediary. Presently, everybody sat down, sorted in receding bands. At the front were the disciples, behind them ordinary male followers of the *pu chaik*, and at the back women and children. The ceremony seemed to be conducted by the *ukoh*, for the rishi himself was nowhere to be seen – perhaps he was at the back of the *wat*. A short religious service followed. It was difficult for us non-initiates, relegated to the side lines, to see. The *ukoh* said prayers and chanted, and intermittently the assembled rishi followers chanted with him. At the end of each chanted section, they exclaimed a loud "Hey!" and as they did so, turned their upper bodies to face another direction. Occasionally, the man conducting the prayers went to the rear of the *wat*, where some bamboo posts were erected with candles on them. Their function was unclear to us. The end of the ceremony was marked by the beating of gongs and bells.

Back at the school, a visitation of BPP soldiers made it abundantly clear to us that we should quit Lae Tong Ku as soon as possible, and, as we did not want to completely outstay our welcome, we decided to go the next morning, our fifth day. The only problem was how to continue. Nobody did go on, not the rishi people, nor the *dorchodor*. We tried to glean any further information we could in the village and review our options. It seemed that whichever way we went we had to get to a place called Sa Kae, the village that the KNLA commander had mentioned back at Mae Ta Ro Ta. Going the shortest way, down through Burma, this was apparently two days' hard walk away. Beyond that, as we subsequently found out, it was a further 60 kms or three days of hard trekking to the Three Pagodas Pass. We had estimated that it would be two days on foot from Lae Tong Ku to the Three Pagodas, and the roadmakers near Kui Le Tor had confirmed this. How wrong everybody turned out to be! Lae Tong Ku was scarcely half way – a good 100 kms of jungle lay between the rishi village and the famous triple pagodas. Already, one week out from Um Pang, we were beginning to get tired and dirty and demoralized, and yet a second tougher week lay ahead. Our problems seemed only now to be starting, and we seriously wondered if we would ever reach our goal.

Once Um Pang had seemed like the end of the world. Then it was Nu Po or Kui Le Tor. Now it was Lae Tong Ku. Each new remoteness relativized its predecessor, and from this distance Um Pang, with its choice of modest shops and eating places, looked like home indeed. But would not Lae Tong Ku also become, relative to later stops, a new home? The Telakhon people and their guru demigod certainly did not see the village as the end of the world, but rather as the beginning of a world. And, in fact, after we had got used to the village and then travelled on, Lae Tong Ku did come to seem like a civilized friendly restful place. However, the comparison with Um Pang was not exhausted there. Like that distant idyll, this new one, which at first had seemed like the end of the trail, now proved that it, too, was just the beginning of a new set of routes.

There was, of course, the way we had come in, the path back to Boeng Kloeng. There was the mountain way east to Mong Gua, which the monks had negotiated. There was a way west, so we had discovered while reconnoitring, to

Kui Le Toeng, which then swung south down through Burma, possibly to Sa Kae. And there was a fourth potential route that went due south. We learned of this only on the very eve of our departure. We were sitting after supper as usual in the darkness, pushing the bamboos into the flames, when a small old man with a wispy beard stopped by chance to warm his bottom on our fire. He revealed that there was a direct route from Lae Tong Ku to Sa Kae which stayed in Thailand, thus avoiding the hazard of Burma. This was good news. But then came the bad news. It took this wiry old Karen a full nine hours to make the journey, and he was renowned as the fastest walker in the village. Carrying no baggage, he started at 5am and reached Sa Kae at 2pm. The journey had to be made in one day because the path ran through the jungle without passing a single village or house the whole way.

Examining the various possibilities from every angle, we ruled out this last one first. What the fastest Karen could run-walk in nine hours might take us with backpacks 18 or 24 hours. Obviously, we did not want to return to Boeng Kloeng. That left the path east to Mong Gua or the route south-west via Kui Le Toeng through Burma. The easterly route via Mong Gua and Mae Chan Ta we next excluded partly because it was a very circuitous way of getting to Sa Kae, but also because it passed straight through 'yellowthread' territory. In the wake of the killings, even Karen had given up walking the long jungle path (feared and rarely used at the best of times) from Mae Chan Ta to Sa Kae. Which left only the south-westerly route via Kui Le Toeng – possibly the best and shortest way, but also potentially the most hazardous, as it ran mostly through war-torn Burma.

❖ ❖

Postscript 2002

As explained in the Postscript to Chapter 13, we were unable to revisit Lae Tong Ku in 1991 on account of fighting locally, and so I have been unable to update the story there. But I did learn in Boeng Kloeng of a couple of – mostly negative – developments in the Telakhon cultist village. Apparently, Mong Aemi, who used to be the deputy headman, had meanwhile become headman, which suggests that former headman Tra Nai had died. The worst news was that our helpful and handsome interpreter-friend Toom Yai had died. He had been shot and killed within Thailand, possibly on the 'middle' path from Lae Tong Ku to Boeng Kloeng that runs close to the border. According to Sooksi, he was murdered "three years ago", i.e. in 1997 or 1998, apparently by the scumbag DKBA. His body was never found, and the motive for and circumstances of his killing remain somewhat unclear. And the days of the tenth rishi of Lae Tong Ku, Monnae Ujae, seemed numbered. We were told that he had malaria, was now very sick and thin, and would probably die soon because he refused to take any medicines or go for treatment in a hospital.

Concerning the onward journey from Lae Tong Ku to the Three Pagodas Pass, if as serious adventurers you were to try to repeat our expedition, you could not go the westerly route that we took down through Burma, which has now become impossible because the Burma army and DKBA control all the formerly KNU-held territory

THREE PAGODAS

down the Burmese side of the border from at least Klo To to Ti Lai Pa. The 4WD track that ran right down the frontier inside Burma is similarly out of commission. But you could still do the expedition, remaining in Thailand and taking the easterly route (Maps 28-30), although it would be an adventure substantially different from the one described in Chapters 15 and 16. You would go from Lae Tong Ku to Sa Kae, possibly taking two days to trek this long direct trail. Or, perhaps cutting out Lae Tong Ku, you would go from Boeng Kloeng to Mong Gua (probably via Kui Le Tor), and from there to Mae Chan Ta and Sa Kae, on each leg passing other Karen settlements (more details already given under Postscript to Chapter 13). From Sa Kae, you would walk to Ti Po Choe and Ti Po Mo (if the Thai army allows you). Then, again proceeding down through Thailand where we cut through Burma, you would hike the long leg to Ti Lai Pa, after which, because no vehicles apparently go any more between Ti Lai Pa and Sangklaburi, you would have to walk on out at length through Ko Ta Doe, Doe Nae Po and Sa Nae Pong to the H323 road and Sangklaburi/the Three Pagodas Pass. I have been told that, because the way through Burma is now impossible, the local Karen have established paths between Ti Po Mo and Sa Nae Pong, which they now walk up and down. Such an expedition on foot might take about eight days from Kui Le Tor to Sangklaburi/the Three Pagodas.

15

ELEVEN TIGERS

Lae Tong Ku – Kui Le Toeng – Muang Rae – Titabong – Ti Po Choe – Ti Po Mo

On the morning of our fifth day in Lae Tong Ku, the teachers made enquiries about a guide who might take us to Kui Le Toeng. Over breakfast, they radioed with a walkie-talkie to the BPP camp. The base commander had meanwhile returned, and it transpired that he had just had a meeting with the local KNLA commander of Kui Le Toeng as well as with the headman of that village. If we hurried, we might be able to catch them up as they walked back home.

We scampered off with one of the teachers to the beginning of the path. The path seemed to cross somebody's garden, which was surrounded by a stockade. Sliding aside a couple of bamboo poles which acted as a gate, we entered the patch. Here, at a house, we caught up with the headman. He had stopped for a natter with some Karen friends while the KNLA commander and an interpreter (just someone who knew Karen and Thai) had gone on ahead. The headman was a Burmese rishi follower in his twenties, and although he could speak no Thai, he soon understood what we wanted. We said goodbye to the teacher, thanking him and his friends for all their trouble. And so it was that we set off on the next stage of our journey (Map 28) not with Toom Yai, as we had imagined we would, but with this young Burmese cultist headman.

Strikingly handsome, like many Karen, he was dressed in an azure shirt and emerald wrap-around skirt, knotted at the stomach. A cerise *yaam*, slung over his right shoulder, hung at his left side. Around his head was wrapped a piece of cloth, something like a terry nappy, which revealed a glossy black topknot. The Karen was also wearing, we noticed, cotton wristbands and a gents watch. For some reason, the headman was carrying a 5-ft-long crowbar. He sauntered off with us in tow through a pineapple field and through a maze of criss-crossing paths. The stretch from Lae Tong Ku to Kui Le Toeng took only an hour, but it was one of the most varied and appealing treks that we made anywhere. Our spirits rose because finally we were on the move again.

The headman led us down a steep muddy V-shaped defile, through close steamy dripping jungle, through sunny airy bamboo groves, and into wooded country. In the bamboos, we met an extraordinary old cultist hunting man. He was naked except for a skirt girded up around his loins and some old plastic shoes. But he was heavily laden. He carried a green game bag, two long

361

dibbling implements, a home-made stovepipe rifle as long as himself, and, on a tumpline suspended from his forehead, a basket full of jungle produce (see colour photo). Although sweating from his exertions and bothered by insects, the old man was very pleased and also surprised to meet us. His lined face and Chinese-style moustache wrinkled up into a broad grin. Extending his free hand, he amazed us by saying "Good morning, Sir". One or two other old people had done this to us in Burma. Probably they were remembering English learned in colonial times 50 years earlier or during service with the British army in the Second World War.

In the wooded country, we met a party of three rishi cultist women coming the other way. In their magenta outfits against the sappy green background, they were the picture of beauty (see photo section). The ladies were glad to see us, for it gave them an excuse to have a rest. Like the old man, they were heavily laden. Jokingly, we tried to hump their baskets of rice and betel ourselves, but found the loads almost too heavy to lift, and yet these women were only a shade over four feet tall. The woods gave over to a bright spacious betel forest. Betel trees had always seemed to us to have a simple primordial appearance. Their slender silver trunks rose up unadorned and straight as a die to a considerable height, to be topped off by a few fronds and a couple of bunches of nuts. They were absurd plants. In their competition with one another for sunlight, they all shot up to a uniform height, producing nothing on the way, when they could just as easily have had the same competition six feet off the ground, wasting much less energy in growing.

In the middle of this betel forest, I had something of a mystical experience – not Buddha under the bodhi tree, but a Brit under a betel. We had stopped for a little rest. Each of us sat on the scrubby woodland floor, our backs propped against a betel trunk. While I was vacantly staring at the ground between my feet, my eyes suddenly caught sight of a strange crescent-shaped object in the dry leaves. Picking it up, I found that it was a small carved piece of antique ivory. It was six inches long, in the shape of a miniature tusk, and had a hole drilled through the stump end to accommodate a piece of string or a silver chain. Evidently, it was a pendant which somebody had lost. Later, in Kui Le Toeng, we showed it to several rishi cultists, and they all confirmed that it was old ivory. It was too heavy to be bone, they said, and finding such a thing was a great piece of luck.

What was remarkable about the find was that of all people I should happen to find it just in this spot. The chances of anybody at all finding it were remote, for why should anybody stop just by that tree? But the chances that a *farang*, me, should find it were billions to one, or so improbable that it seemed that somehow, miraculously, the ivory had been specially put there for me to find. But who could have put it there? The only possible explanation was that it was the rishi himself. It was as if the man-god had wanted to make a sign to us. It seemed as if through the token of the elephant's tusk he had wished to communicate his regret that he had received us so discourteously during our first visit to him and also perhaps wanted to bless our onward trip. A supernatural pattern was building up – the ride on the elephant between Kui Le Tor and Boeng Kloeng, the rishi cult of the elephant tusks at Lae Tong Ku, and now the antique ivory. In Kui Le Toeng, we got a length of string, and I wore the pendant as a lucky charm around my neck for the rest of the journey.

The remainder of the short trek was characterized by many stream and river crossings (see colour photo). The bridges over these were of three kinds. There was the greasy pole type of bridge, where we did not know whether it was better to risk the single slimy log or splash through the mud and water underneath. There was the bamboo suspension bridge, swaying high above the river. And across the wide Suriya, which we learnt was called Juai Ya Kru in Karen, there was the rickety bamboo pontoon bridge. Near the pontoon bridge, a cultist man was building rafts out of bamboo. Several examples of his handicraft were moored by the bank. We stopped to admire again the turquoise Suriya and also to pluck up courage to broach the pontoon. Before crossing, I turned to look at the path by which we had come down to the river. A short piece of planking was nailed to a tree with the word THAILAND crudely painted on it, together with a picture of the Thai flag and some words of Burmese or Karen (see photo). We were beginning the long Burmese section of our onward journey.

Kui Le Toeng

On the far bank, the path proceeded for some way through woods, passing deserted and burnt houses – the result of a recent Burma army attack. People were in the process of building them anew. Finally, we emerged into the dry dusty compound of **Kui Le Toeng**. This small Telakhon cultist village, consisting of about 40 houses, was a poor scruffy affair compared to Lae Tong Ku. Chickens scratched around, a bullock cart stood idle under a tree, and in a couple of huts women were weaving. We found two basic shops and, near them, a lot of people hanging around, we knew not why. They looked at us with a degree of suspicion. Nobody spoke a word of Thai. The late morning heat was building up. It was an uncomfortable situation.

Our guide, the young headman, conveyed to us that we should wait by the bigger of the two shops. A small veranda provided some shade, in which we sat. The shop was stocked primarily with pulses, but there were also sweeties, biscuits, torches, batteries and Coya Pearl make-up. In addition, as at Sa Kaang Thit, there was every kind of smoke for sale, both cheroots and cigarettes, including Monterey, Monte Carlo and Seven Diamonds. Glancing by chance up into the roof of the little store, we noticed laid out across the rafters a sizeable cache of automatic weapons. We were back in the war zone. While we were waiting, a number of children came to watch us. The girls, in their white full-length shifts, were wearing cosmetics, perhaps the Coya Pearl from the store. Once again we were struck by the heart-rending beauty of Karen lasses. It was a beauty all the more poignant for blooming in the midst of so much death and destruction – the death-and-the-maiden scenario again that we had encountered back in Wa Lay.

The headman returned with the local KNLA commander as well as the man who had mediated between him and the Thai commander of Lae Tong Ku (see colour photo of the three in photo section). The 'interpreter', with his bare top, terrycloth turban, hairy underlip, wispy beard and moustache, not to mention a fearsome stomach scar, looked rugged enough, but the Karen commander, one Mor Thaing Chor, was one of the wildest characters we met anywhere on our journey. Very different from the urbane Saw Kyi Shwi of Mae Ta Ro Ta, the ageing commander of Kui Le Toeng district, perhaps 60 years old, had permanently half-closed eyes, making him look as if he was sleepy or drugged out. A set of six deep lines stretched across his brow, he had dark straggly flyaway hair with wispy white sideboards, and long isolated hairs sprouted out of his chin (see black-and-white photo). In a dark blue and red sarong and with a black sweatshirt, Mor Thaing Chor did not appear to be cultist. We could scarcely believe this man capable of a spirited defence or a counterattack against a SLORC assault force, but perhaps he was the wiliest guerrilla leader of them all. A commander he certainly was because he had a transceiver with him. We spotted this by his side in a kind of green military-style *yaam*. He had wrapped it up in a plastic bag, but the tell-tale stump of a telescoped aerial stuck out of the top.

A 4WD track could be seen passing through the central compound of Kui Le Toeng, and from the bizarre trio of the commander, the headman and the 'interpreter' we learned that a solitary truck plied it some days. Coming from Mae Ta Ro Ta, the vehicle mostly terminated here, in Kui, but occasionally it went further to Sa Kae. Hearing the magical words 'Sa Kae', our ears pricked up. A whole new perspective began to unfold – the possibility of riding to Sa Kae. Apparently, it was a three-hour drive to the staging post or a full two days' walk. Naturally, hearing these times from Karen, we took them with a pinch of salt (in fact, they proved substantially correct). On the way, there were other villages. Through the 'interpreter', we asked the commander if the truck might come that day or if perhaps it had already come, but he did not know. Finally, the villagers said that no vehicle had passed by that day yet. We asked him if he could radio to Mae Ta Ro Ta to establish whether any vehicle would set off or indeed had set off, adding that Saw Kyi Shwi had suggested we approach Mor Thaing Chor for help. Patiently, the old man radioed through, not only querying the truck, but verifying our story. Hearing from his opposite number that we had indeed passed through Mae Ta Ro Ta and were 'OK', the commander relaxed a bit. However, the message he received did nothing to dissipate the general vagueness. No one knew if the truck had departed or would depart. And, with that, the little band of the wild guerrilla leader, the crowbar-bearing headman and the scarred interpreter left us.

We considered our position. We had planned to trek from Kui Le Toeng. However, seeing that a jeep track ran through the village and that, moreover, from time to time transport ran down it, walking began to seem increasingly senseless. Also, because of the vehicle, no one was prepared to guide us. It was easy to walk, the villagers of Kui said, we should just follow the track. But we already knew that tracks had a horrible way of dividing or petering out. Further, we were unhappy about spending more time in Burma than we had to, particularly on foot, and it seemed a fair distance down to Sa Kae. But, above all, we really wanted to get on. The length of the journey still to go – an estimated 100 kms – was weighing ever more heavily on us. We feared we might never get to the end of it. So the truck looked like a good option for speeding on our way. The trouble was: where was it? Even if it came, would it by chance be going beyond Kui Le Toeng? For a lift to Sa Kae, we might have to wait three or four days, while trekking would take only two, or so they said. A prolonged wait in such an impoverished place was out of the question, but equally we could not go back to Lae Tong Ku because of the BPP. The only realistic option, therefore, seemed to be to start walking for Sa Kae and hope that the truck might catch us up.

Transplanting ourselves to the back of the compound, where the 4WD track passed through, we looked folornly up and down the dusty way – nothing, just silent withered countryside sizzling in the midday heat. It was like waiting for a train on a disused railway line in a heatwave. We settled on a compromise. We would wait for an hour, have some lunch and then start walking. By the side of the track, at the southern edge of the village, we found a house with a shop rather better stocked than the two others. We stationed ourselves there, ready to leap out and intercept any vehicle that might pass. From the lady owner of the shop, we bought two packets of Ma-maa, and asked her to cook the instant noodles for us. Then we sat down to wait. Our concern was infectious because soon everybody was straining their ears for the sound of a distant motor. A false alarm had us all unnecessarily excited when someone in the village started up the engine of a rice-dehusking machine. But otherwise there was nothing.

When it was clear that no truck was going to come, we started walking. No one seemed concerned, but no one seemed much interested either. We were very concerned. We had no guide. Communication with the locals was problematic. We were illegally out of Thailand and illegally in someone else's country – and not just in any other country, but in a country whose authorities were murderously xenophobic. Further, we had entered an area where a Four Cuts offensive was in progress, yet we did not know where the nearest *tatmadaw* LID might be. But the worst thing was that, where before we had trekked towards some BPP camp, which had been forewarned of our arrival, now there was no *dorchodor* base ahead, and no liaison had been made, either with a BPP chief or with some KNLA commander. Wild-looking Mor Thaing Chor had radioed back to Mae Ta Ro Ta, but not further down the line. Nevertheless, the mystical lure of the Three Pagodas drew us on, and we figured that somehow the find of the ivory was auspicious and that the pendant would protect us.

We walked alone down the track, wondering what lay around every corner. It was flattish country with mixed cover. The powdery laterite track was scarcely wider than a vehicle and lined with dense head-height bamboos. Any spot would have been perfect for an ambush. We were trudging down this way, searching ahead and glancing nervously over our shoulders, when suddenly we heard something remarkable – the sound of an engine. Behind us, a white Toyota Hilux Hero pick-up swung into view. Not caring if it belonged to the Burma army, bandits or the KNLA, we flagged it down. It drew up, enveloping us and its occupants in a cloud of russet dust. It was a high-ride 4WD job, and looked fairly new. As it had no number plates, only a rather sinister sign like a red hand, we could not tell who it belonged to. Probably it was a KNLA general-purpose truck. In the cab was an older man, a youth and a boy. All had jet-black hair and Burmese-style *longyis*. In the back were three dubious-looking youths in tattered T-shirts, slashed jeans, sunglasses and military caps. One fancied himself and sported earrings. Each carried a small backpack. In Thai, we asked the driver where he was going, and the answer back came: Sa Kae. We could not believe our ears. We asked if we could travel with them, and the swarthy unsmiling driver motioned us to climb aboard at the rear.

After the discouraging wait in Kui Le Toeng and the trudge along the track, our spirits soared again. We could be in Sa Kae by nightfall. The truck set off hell for leather, making the ride dreadfully bumpy. The Karen evidently drove at the same lick as they walked. On the floor of the open-backed Hilux was some knobbly cargo, covered with a blanket. The boys, not wanting to sit on this, perched with amazing ease on the tailgate. We took up position behind the roll bar, just behind the cab. Standing there, with legs slightly flexed to absorb the shattering blows as the truck rattled along, we had a commanding view, although repeatedly it was necessary to duck overhanging bamboos to avoid being slashed across the face. The bumping of the truck caused some of the cargo to slither out from under the blanket. It was a cache of semi-automatic weapons and older rifles.

Presently, the truck stopped for no apparent reason in the middle of nowhere. The driver got out and went off into the jungle. The boys fidgeted at the back. They looked at us all the time, seeming to allude alternately in a language we could not understand to our backpacks and to us. Nobody smiled. We began to regret the alacrity with which we had accepted a lift with this dubious outfit on their questionable errand. But after a while, the driver returned with some other men, bearing roofing panels of *jaak* leaves. It transpired that in the bushes there was a settlement. We all got down from the truck and the men piled the panels high in the back. The new load made the ride even more uncomfortable. The *jaak* leaves had long spiny ends and, as we bounced around on top of the panels, their treacherous points speared our legs and bottoms. It was one more complaint to add to the bruised shin bone, the elephant rash, bedbug bites, sunburn, prickly heat, deficient diet, diarrhoea, inexplicable fevers and whatever else had assailed us since Um Pang.

The Hilux ploughed on a good way, the countryside changing from more open, wooded land to denser jungle. We passed the small Karen villages of **Jor Kwa, Ti Mong Koe, Lai Wa Choe**, a nameless settlement and **Ti Lo Na**. At one point, our vehicle took a turn east, alarming us because we seemed to be heading ever deeper into Burma. But there was little we could do. Delivered into the hands of inscrutable people, we could only trust them blindly. At Ti Lo Na, our lift stopped for a while. We had been told that the village was three hours' walk from Kui Le Toeng, and, if we had been on foot, we would probably have spent the night here. It was strange to view the place hypothetically as a point we might have stopped in. A relatively large Karen settlement with fine houses and a school, Ti Lo Na was set against a backdrop of craggy mountains to the east, the continuation of the Dawna Range. We got down to stretch our legs in the dusty central compound. Some urchins kicked a football around us and over our heads.

ELEVEN TIGERS

Following the halt, the truck continued a fair distance through mixed countryside. Isolated dwellings punctuated the route, and at one of them we were held up by a gate built across the 'road'. At a fork, the main track veered off east, but fortunately we went west down a narrower, less promising way, indicating that we were at least heading back towards the border. Before too long, at a place called **Muang Rae** (= mine), we came upon a river. The water was knee-deep, and people were bathing and washing clothes in it. The place was a ford, because we could see the track continuing on the far bank. Our driver plunged the Hilux straight into the middle of the river, stopped and switched the engine off. He motioned everybody to get out. We all jumped down into the water and tried to find out what was happening. We thought that perhaps the truck was stuck. One of the three boys who had sat with us in the back spoke a few words of Thai, and he conveyed to us that the driver was going no further. We tried to remonstrate that the man had said that he was going to Sa Kae. We tried to cajole and even to bribe him to complete the trip, but it was hopeless. He ignored us and with his two mates began washing the Hilux. So this was the new pretty pass. After a 2½-hour ride from Kui Le Toeng, we were abandoned in Burma in the middle of nowhere. What was more, the afternoon was well advanced.

We had no idea where we were, how much further it was to Sa Kae, or what lay ahead. Our greatest fear was that the three boys might now also separate from us. But it turned out that, like us, they were heading for Sa Kae and were as disconcerted as we were at being let down by the lift. So, far from eyeing the boys warily, we now sought to make common cause with them. They enquired of the washerwomen in the river which way went to Sa Kae, and we all set off together. We soon discovered why the truck driver had been unwilling to go further. In places, the track was so rugged that even a high-ride 4WD vehicle would have had difficulty clambering over it. The three boys continued to behave oddly, making us feel uneasy. They did not walk with us, as one might have expected, but lagged far behind, or disappeared altogether, or suddenly reappeared ahead of us, apparently having taken some secret short cut. Evidently, they knew the lie of the land better than we thought or were having little conversations with locals as they went along. Often, it seemed to us that we were guiding them, and we could not understand why they did not take up the lead. The thought was never far from our minds that the shifty threesome might try to ambush us. They had looked once too often at our cameras.

We pressed on as fast as we could, trying to put some distance between the boys and us. The sweat began to pour from our faces, and the shoulder straps of our backpacks cut into our shoulders. We had hardly eaten all day, and hunger pangs were starting to gnaw in our stomachs. The track followed a spectacular series of limestone needles, to the sides and tops of which clung small trees, like hair. The outcrops glowed in the teatime sun. Presently, we passed a small village, followed by two even smaller villages under construction. The people and their mode of housebuilding were unfamiliar to us, and yet they looked Karen. We waited for our laggard companions and asked the boy with earrings, the one who had a smattering of Thai, who these

367

people were. They were "just a kind of Karen", came back the unsatisfactory answer. Then, in the company of the three ne'er-do-wells, we trekked into **Titabong** (Htitaban).

This large ramshackle poverty-stricken village was inhabited by the same strange people as we had seen earlier. They looked in some ways like Karen, and yet there was no trace of pink or red. In fact, mostly they wore no costume at all, except for a few, who were dressed in a kind of brown costume. We knew that we were approaching Mon territory, and at first we took the villagers for Mon folk. But discreet enquiries brought back the firm answer that they were not Mon. Which led us to suppose that the people of Titabong and of the nearby settlements were refugee Burmese Karen in ordinary clothes, perhaps non-costumed plains-dwelling *Yang* rather than traditional costume-wearing hill Karen. That they were refugees was borne out by the newness, meanness and incompleteness of their dwellings. And indeed, near Titabong we found a whole village newly wrecked and deserted. We were told that the villagers had abandoned the old place "to be nearer the road" at Titabong, but it seemed to us that once again SLORC troops had just swept through here, causing the inhabitants to flee and then return to rebuild their village on a new site. Evidently, Titabong lay on the border, and it looked as if the people had simply moved their village from inside Burma to the relative safety of the frontier. Or perhaps the old village was mined and booby-trapped.

We were so hungry and tired that we held up our little party in Titabong to brew up more instant noodles. The boys proved their worth here, for with that easy familiarity which all Karen seem to have in each other's villages, they commandeered someone's house and set the inhabitants to work. Water was boiled over a wood fire, and bowls and spoons appeared. We decided to break once more into our emergency rations, nursed all the way from Mae Sot, and levered open a tin of tuna in masman curry sauce. The consumption of this rare luxury was watched by a circle of awe-struck Titabongers, who had probably never seen a *farang* before, let alone a *farang* scoffing tinned tuna.

Like ourselves, the boys were getting concerned about whether we would ever reach Sa Kae by nightfall. Everyone seemed vague about how far it was. We set off again at a cracking pace, with the three Karen youths in front for a change. As we left Titabong, we struck out once more into Burma. It quickly became clear why the boys had taken up the lead. They had been instructed about another short cut. Leaving the 4WD track, they guided us down a jungle path. After a while, we filed in silence through the spooky village so recently deserted. Rejoining the track, we entered more open country. There were no villages here, but isolated dwellings – some deserted – lined the way. As the sun lowered and our shadows lengthened, we consoled ourselves that in an emergency we could pass the night in one of these rural shacks. We at least had our mosquito net with us. People passed us coming home from working in the fields. They were astonished to see us, but very friendly, and all confirmed that we were heading for Sa Kae.

A long hour later, we chanced upon something strange. At a fork in the route, we saw imprinted on one of the two ways the unmistakable marks of a tracked vehicle. Either a tank had passed down here or a bulldozer. We had visions of another driverless Komatsu in the middle of nowhere. We all followed the caterpillar tracks, thinking that, even if they did not lead to Sa Kae, then they must at least go somewhere, to some form of civilization. How wrong we were. Soon we caught the sound of distant engines and, climbing over the brow of a hill, came upon a mine in the middle of the jungle. It was only a small affair, with some rock-crushing and processing machinery. The plant was stepped in sheds down a hillside. Below it were three or four tipper trucks, noisily making their final manoeuvres for the day. The scene was surprising enough, but the weird thing was that the tippers were being conducted like an orchestra by a fine Indian-looking gentleman in a suit and yellow hard hat. The trucks bore on their sides the words BHOL & SONS CO. LTD - LEAD CONCENTRATES. We picked our way through them and approached the Indian man. He was taken aback to see a *farang* and four others wandering in from Burma, and even looked perturbed, as if I might be a snooping journalist who could discover here some dark secret. Above the deafening roar of the trucks I shouted: "Are we still in Burma here?" "No, Sir", he replied in supercorrect English, "you are back in Thailand now. The men are just finishing work for the day. If you go over there and wait by the office, I will be with you in a minute." As we turned to go, we noticed a nameplate pinned to the breast of this black-faced upright Indian. It announced: MR JOHN SAVARIES, MANAGER – more and more bizarre!

In front of the office, we threw ourselves down on a bench, exhausted. It was gone five o'clock, and the light was beginning to fade. But at least we had arrived somewhere. We contemplated the prospect of staying the night at the mine. It was not appealing. Around the office, there was a small shanty settlement, consisting of squalid workers' huts and oily repair bays for the vehicles and machines. Like us, the three boys were disconsolate. Now that we had a good source of intelligence of our own, they knew that they were marginalized, and they shifted uneasily in the background. For once, we thought, the boot was on the other foot.

Mr Savaries strode over to us. On the one hand, he seemed like some colonial ex-army officer, transposed in place and time, and given a new name; and on the other, he was reminiscent of some Mr Kurtz at the heart of a new heart of darkness. "You come from England?" he enquired, extending a hand and fixing me with glittering eyes. "Yes." That seemed to reassure him slightly, as if 'German' or 'American' would not have been satisfactory. "Where have you come from?" "From Lae Tong Ku." He did not know where that was, so we explained that we had stayed there after trekking south from Um Pang. Our story surprised him, and now that we came to think of it, it surprised us too. How faraway Um Pang seemed, while Mae Sot was some mecca over the horizon. We mentioned that we, for our part, were surprised to find him, Mr Savaries, here. He explained that he had been born in Burma of Indian parents and now managed the mine here. Here, it transpired, was the Karen village of **Ti Po Choe**. We told the manager that our ultimate goal was the Three Pagodas Pass, but that we thought that initially we had to get to Sa Kae. However, as it was getting dark, could we not stay the night here at the mine?

369

THREE PAGODAS

That was not possible, Mr Savaries replied, without elaborating. What we should do was walk to the next village, Ti Po Mo, and stay with a man called Mr Joi-ih. He was a Karen Baptist and would look after us. Then, the next day, we could return and move on to Sa Kae. Or, if we really wanted to get on to Sa Kae today, we could wait and get a lift with a mine lorry later. The only trouble was, the Indian manager continued, he did not know when one might be going, perhaps at ten o'clock. We asked how far it was to Sa Kae. About ten kms, too far to walk now. And to Mr Joi-ih's village? About 20 minutes on foot. And how was the way to Ti Po Mo? That was easy. All we had to do was follow the track! The whole situation was confusing, made more impenetrable by the fact that we had to try to fathom it and make a decision with tired minds and with the pressure of night falling fast. One thing was clear, however. We could not stay at the mine, but had to go on to either Sa Kae or Mr Joi-ih's village of Ti Po Mo.

As Sa Kae was our immediate goal and lay on our route, we decided to go there. We did not know about accommodation there, but at least a truck would carry us there. We told Mr Savaries of our decision. That was good, he said, because next day, or even the same night, a lorry could take us much further along the same route, bringing us nearer our destination. The lorries hauled their lead concentrate from Ti Po Choe to Sa Kae, and then 110 kms through the jungle to a place called Kliti. After that they continued for a further 65 kms, before hitting Highway 323 for Kanchanaburi near Tong Pa Poom (Map 30).

Hearing this last detail, we immediately changed our minds. Tong Pa Poom was going in quite the wrong direction, leading us away from the Three Pagodas. Also, we were not taken with riding on a lead concentrate lorry, whether off or on the highway. So our last question to the Indian manager was which direction Ti Po Mo lay in and what he thought was beyond the village. Ti Po Mo was south of Ti Po Choe (Map 29), but he did not know what lay beyond. No one went that way. Mr Savaries thought that there was a path for about 60 kms through some Karen villages towards the pass. That clinched the matter. We stood up, thanked the mine manager and wearily set off again. And so it was that, after all the brouhaha about Sa Kae, the village did not lie on our route, nor did we ever go there. We heard reports, though, that it had a BPP camp, but was in other respects a small place like Ti Po Choe or Ti Po Mo. As the shifty trio of Karen boys were going to Sa Kae, we now abandoned them at the mine. Judging by their faces, it looked as if they feared that they were going to be eaten by Mr John Savaries for supper.

The way to Ti Po Mo (Map 29) was a track which had been pounded to six inches of ultrafine orange bulldust by vehicles. We found out why. Near Ti Po Mo, there was another mine. The track immediately plunged into the most spectacular virgin jungle we had seen anywhere. The primary canopy was still intact, and gigantic trees soared hundreds of feet into the air. In the twilight, monkeys whooped and birds called. We were filled with consternation at embarking on another trek at nightfall, and only prayed that the Indian man was right. After 20 minutes, there was still no village. After 30 minutes, just when we were getting ready to turn back, we emerged from the forest. The last thing we saw before darkness came promptly at 6pm was a massive monolith immediately to the west. Chao Tao (= rocky hill) dominated the small Karen village of **Tí Po Mo** and was peculiar in that a chunk of its southern edge had fallen away, leaving a cavity beneath an overhanging section – like a mouth and nose. This gave the outcrop an anthropomorphic quality. Silhouetted against the brown of the dying western sky, the face of this monolith looked sinister. We stumbled into Ti Po Mo in darkness, there to be greeted at the office of the second mine by the fabled Mr Joi-ih. Evidently, he had been tipped off by Mr Savaries by radio that we were coming.

✻

Ti Po Mo

Joi-ih, a Karen man in his late forties with a round face, receding hair and scrubby greying chintuft beard and moustache, led us to his house. His good nature, ready smile and unshakable composure made him instantly and lastingly likeable. His dwelling was not the usual simple Karen affair of wood, bamboo and leaf, but a well-constructed wooden house with an upstairs. There was the customary open but covered platform, where anyone could linger or sleep, and in front an open-air dining area. Joi-ih said we could use the platform and also sleep there. We had hardly unpacked when a thermos of boiling water appeared, together with pint-sized mugs, Ovaltine, tea, condensed milk and biscuits. After an arduous day and in the middle of the jungle, this was luxury indeed. We each drank off about three pints of Ovaltine and tea.

Our clothes and bodies were filthy from fording rivers and kicking through bulldust. We asked Joi-ih to take us to the washroom. At that moment, his son-in-law Edu appeared. This brusquer, less mellow man in his twenties was detailed to show us the way. He led us across the village with a torch. On the far side of the dusty village street, behind a vegetable garden, he pointed the torch at the black waters of a small river. There he left us. It was pitch dark, the bank of the river was four feet high, there was a slimy gangplank descending to the water, and the river bed was squelchy mud. In our dispirited state, the difficulties of trying to wash almost made us want to cry. The shampoo got lost in the grass of the river bank, the soap dropped into the water, and we, far from getting cleaner, got steadily dirtier. But the worst thing was that, standing naked in the river in the blackness, we were savaged by mosquitoes. How it was that we did not get malaria we never were able to explain.

Picking our way back to Joi-ih's, we were surprised to see electric lights burning. It turned out that there was a generator in the village, which provided wobbly power every day from 6-9pm. But what astonished us more was the spread of supper which had been put out for us on the long table. When Mr Savaries had said we could stay with the Baptist Mr Joi-ih, we had pictured a frugal repast with austere religious people. But here was stir-fried cabbage, potato curry, omelette, fried salted dried fish, barking deer curry, chilli dip, fresh pineapple, papaya, and *lao kao*. In our experience, the Karen were unsurpassed among 'hill-tribe' peoples for their hospitality, but the food and attention we enjoyed with Joi-ih's family over the next three days was outstanding even by these standards.

THREE PAGODAS

While we ate, most of Joi-ih's extended household came to join us. There was the master and his wife, his daughter and son-in-law Edu, their baby, a brother of Joi-ih's, a grandmother-in-law, and others we never identified. Granny was a phenomenon. She claimed to be 80 and had apparently taught English in Burma when she was young. This sprightly and remarkably well-preserved lady said she owed her longevity to alcohol. She had a few nips every night and periodically let go with more expansive drinking sessions. It seemed that today was the occasion of one of these binges, for according to Joi-ih she had been at the bottle since early morning. Our arrival merely confirmed to her that she had chosen the right day to have her "little medicine" and "look after my health". She drank more and more, grew steadily louder, put her arm around me, cooed in my ear, and began telling tall stories in a mixture of Karen, Thai and incomprehensible English. She also introduced us to some of the arcane practices of her tippling. Besides the rice spirit, she had a bottle of runny wild honey and also a tin of 'Eleven Tigers Ruby Blood Tonic'. This latter red medicinal powder was supposed to "clean ladies' blood". Granny mixed the Eleven Tigers and *lao kao* together, adding a dose of honey. The resulting dark red, savoury, sweet, biting concoction was not at all unpleasant, and it was easy to see how, if one lived in a mining outpost in the jungle, one could become quite attached to it.

In the pauses between the old lady's expatiations, we quizzed Joi-ih about Ti Po Mo and our onward route. Apparently, the village was only about ten years old, although Joi-ih himself had been living in the area for twice as long (he had grown up in Moulmein, a port on the Gulf of Martaban, by the Andaman Sea). There had once been a BPP camp in Ti Po Mo, but it had moved to Sa Kae. Chao Tao was the border with Burma, and it was possible to climb to the top of this enormous precipitous rock. We asked Joi-ih how he liked living in such a remote place. He said he had been to Sangklaburi, the nearest 'town', only four times in 18 years and preferred hunting in the jungle to town life. While we were talking and eating under the single naked light bulb, a succession of people either looked by or reported to the house. They came from the village, the mines, from Kliti, from Sangklaburi, from as far away as Boeng Kloeng, and from Burma. This happened all the time we were there, and we soon realized that the Baptist Karen's house was the nerve centre of Ti Po Mo, indeed of the entire area, while Joi-ih himself was the well-known kingpin.

On the subject of our onward journey, Joi-ih said our best bet was to ride in the cab of a lorry from Ti Po Choe down to the main road and Tong Pa Poom, and then take public transport up to Sangklaburi. When we said that we were unhappy to do this because it was out of our direction and was not in the spirit of our adventure, he replied that the alternative was not good. There was a way through from Ti Po Mo to the area of the Three Pagodas Pass, but it was rarely used. The 60-km-long way was a poor track and passed through four Karen villages: Ti Lai Pa, Ko Ta Doe, Doe Nae Po and Sa Nae Pong (Map 29). The problem was that the first stretch to Ti Lai Pa was 24 kms long, went down the Burmese side of the border through pure jungle, and passed absolutely nothing on the way. It was too far to walk in one day, and nobody would go with us. Beyond Ti Lai Pa, it was a further eight hours on foot to Ko Ta Doe and then another three hours to Doe Nae Po. On the other hand, 4WD trucks passed from time to time down that way in about four hours, on average one every three or four days. But, unfortunately, one had gone today. Not only that, a mini convoy had gone with it, meaning that the potential supply of lifts would have been exhausted not just for three days, but possibly for a week. It was always the same two or three vehicles which plied the route, and before they could set out again, they would all have to come back.

It was bad news. However, Joi-ih promised to ask in the mine office the next morning and suggested we walk down to the mine itself – about ten minutes away – to check the latest vehicle situation. Beyond that, we could only trust to luck. Promptly at 9pm, the light bulb gave two warning flickers, and the power was finished for the night. Granny was quite far gone and wanted to continue the conviviality, but the others got up to retire and dragged her away remonstrating. She grumbled for a long time in a back room, knocking bottles over and repeatedly lighting a pipe. We strung up our net on the public platform and arranged ourselves for sleep. By 9.30, Ti Po Mo was extinct. But these *Yang* villages were never really quiet in the night. Soon we realized that others had come to sleep on the veranda, and there was the usual shuffling and spitting. Occasionally, a lorryload of lead concentrate rumbled through the outpost, and upstairs Edu's baby cried. We reviewed our day's progress. It seemed remarkable, even epic, knocking something like another 40 kms off our journey. We had breakfasted in Lae Tong Ku, met commander Mor Thaing Chor, despaired in Kui Le Toeng, ridden wild with gun-runners through Burma to Muang Rae and the river, trekked with the shifty trio past Titabong to Ti Po Choe, interviewed Mr John Savaries, and blundered into Ti Po Mo to the unexpected welcome of Joi-ih's extended family...

The following morning, while we were breakfasting on Ovaltine and biscuits, we saw the old lady leave the house on some mission. She greeted us as if the previous evening had been as nothing. It transpired that granny was going fishing, and by all accounts she was a champion fisherwoman. Joi-ih returned from the mine office in the village with the news that no truck would be going to Ti Lai Pa either that day or the next. We voiced our concern about outstaying our welcome at his house. "Never mind", he said in Thai, "you can stay as long as you like." However, he did mention that there was a man in Ti Po Mo who might be persuaded to take us in his pick-up down the way we wanted to go. We would have to negotiate a price with him.

Presently, this selfsame wily truck owner arrived at our table. We haggled with him until he would lower his price no further. He was prepared to take us down to Sangklaburi for 900 baht. Although by Western standards this was not so much for two people down a jungle track (£25 at the time, and about £15 at the time of rewriting), it still seemed too much for a four-hour 60-km ride. We had hardly spent much more since leaving Mae Sot. So we rejected the man's offer. We figured that he would return later with a more reasonable price. But he did not. Actually, after we had been holed up in Ti Po Mo for two long days, it was we who returned to the man. But the man simply upped his price to

1,500 baht, causing us to reject his offer once and for all. Our not accepting the man's original proposition was possibly the biggest mistake we made on this last leg of our adventure. For, as things turned out, his offer proved to be a very favourable one. In the end, the track was so atrocious that he would surely have done at least 900 bahts' worth of damage to his vehicle. Moreover, if we had gone with him, we would have had our 'own' transport and driver, enabling us to stop where we wanted and proceed at our own pace. In the event, we were hustled down that nightmare stretch at breakneck speed, half the way in darkness.

Our morning's occupation was to visit the Ti Po Mo mine. We followed an orange bulldust track south of the village for about one km until it divided. The principal way continued to – we never found out, probably a mine. A turn west went to a place with a sign announcing 'Moniko & Korea Mining Company'. Near the entrance to the site was an office. Its wooden buildings were deserted, almost abandoned. However, the door to the bookkeeping office was unlocked, and we looked inside. The wages and employment records for each worker lay in dusty pigeon-holes. The information was an eye-opener. For an eight-hour shift, the most junior worker received 40 baht a day (£1 in 1993, £0.66 in 2001), while the most senior took home a princely 50-60 baht. Opposite the site office, there was a kind of vehicle repair station. The grease and disorder here was considerable. Various ancient lorries lay around in different stages of cannibalization. It looked as if the two mechanics were trying to make one viable vehicle out of the others. We asked the men if any truck would be going down to Ti Lai Pa that day, but they could not say. We further asked a more senior-looking supervisor at the mine itself, but he did not know either. All that anybody could say was that if a vehicle was going, someone would come up to Joi-ih's to tell us.

Between the site office and the mine lay a squalid shanty settlement. The huts were of split bamboo and grass or *jaak*. There were a couple of primitive shops, and people eyed us doubtfully. These impoverished Karen enjoyed one thing – an impressive view from their back doors of the monumental Chao Tao. Behind the huts, we came across an interesting scene. Some men were making sugar. Harvested sugar canes lay piled up, and armfuls of them were being introduced into a press. The press was driven by a poor buffalo, which walked endlessly in a circle with a black blindfold over its eyes. When it stopped to rest in the heat, a boy beat it with a stick. The sap dribbling out of the press was gathered and put into four steel pans, like giant woks. These were boiled over a fire until the sticky juice was reduced to a thick brown liquor. From time to time, the men skimmed off a white froth. The fire was ingenious in its simplicity. It consisted of an underground tunnel beneath the four pans. Long sections of bamboo flamed in the tunnel, and as they burnt down towards the entrance, they were simply kicked further in. The heat, added to the blazing morning sun, was withering. Finally, the molasses was decanted into trays, where it set into slabs of toffee-like cane sugar. We were given a shard to try. It tasted very good.

At the back of the shanty camp was the mine, stepped down a hillside and surrounded by jungle. To be accurate, the Korean mine at Ti Po Mo, like the

ELEVEN TIGERS

Bhol mine at Ti Po Choe, was actually a processing plant. The raw rock was quarried somewhere nearby in real mines and brought by tipper truck to these plants. In aech case, the rock was dumped at the top of a hill and then descended down the hillside through various machines as it was processed. The end-product was a grey metallic sludge containing antimony. It was dried out and taken away in bags, presumably for refinement.

An inspection of the Ti Po Mo plant was a depressing experience. We climbed from the bottom of it to the top. At the bottom end, the Sb sludge dribbled out like slurry from a pig farm. Above it, machines were activating the pulverized ore, spraying it with what looked like oil or solvent. In this reeking treatment shed, a man sat by the hour, tending the machines and breathing in air laden with suspended particles of antimony and spray. In two minutes, my spectacles were covered with fine droplets, yet he wore no protective mask over his mouth. Higher than the shed was a series of crushing drums. They reduced the ore to a powder with a deafening roar. Above the crushing machine, a chute funnelled the rock into the mouth of the first and largest drum. Underneath the end of the chute, two Karen girls squatted on the hillside. In an endless cloud of toxic dust, and amid the frightening thunder of the crushers, they were employed to encourage the chunks of ore down the hopper and into the machine. Their only tools were a wooden spoon and their fingers, and of course they had no mouth masks or earplugs. We infinitely pitied these poor children, exchanging their health and young lives for 30 or 40 baht a day. In the middle of this jungle wilderness, this was the real heart of darkness.

Ti Po Mo itself was understandably not the most beautiful of Karen villages. There were too many oil and diesel drums lying around, as well as broken vehicles and bits of vehicle. But there was an interesting makeshift *wat* on a knoll just outside the village. It was run by two monks, one an older Mon man, and the other a younger fellow of the enigmatic Tuwai group, from southern Burma. The tall striking Mon spoke some English, while the Tuwai knew Thai. They invited us in for refreshments, and we were treated to pint mugs of Ovaltine or tea or coffee, which seemed to be standard in this region. School began presently, and the one multi-purpose class was held in the *wat*. But before the class could begin, the *Yang* infants had to endure a prayer session. In unison, they chanted an interminable Pali rigmarole, doing their best not to laugh at our smiles. Finally, the lesson began, with the shorn Mon bonze trying to teach some Burmese to the children, many with gold *tanaka* discs on their cheeks.

Back at Joi-ih's, we got excited because a KNLA driver arrived in a battered Toyota pick-up (photo of him with Joi-ih in photo section). We asked Joi-ih to find out from this rugged man in a peaked military cap if he was going further. But it was a false alarm. The dust-covered driver was going only as far as Ti Po Mo. He was a jovial fellow and helped himself to the *lao kao*.

The evening of that second day was enlivened by a special prayer ceremony in Joi-ih's house. After another feast, which featured granny's catch of fish with extra helpings of potato curry, we were invited upstairs onto a central landing. Some 20 people were sitting on the wooden floor with their backs to the walls. We learned that Joi-ih's eldest son was setting off into Burma the next day, and they wanted to pray for his safety. Some hymns were sung, and passages were read from a Karen Baptist version of the Bible. Then a young man made a kind of sermon. As this was in Karen, we could not understand what it was about, but it became intriguing and memorable because the text was frequently interspersed with the words 'Stonewall Jackson' and 'Ti Lo Su' (= waterfall). The sermon went on for some time, and we were able to study the posters on the walls. They were a strange collection of icons: a picture of the Thai King and Queen, a KNU calendar, a photo of some eminent Baptist, and a few pin-ups. After the little ceremony, everyone partook of tankards of ultrasweet tea with cream biscuits.

On our third day in Ti Po Mo, we were largely left to our own devices. The novelty of our arrival had worn off, and people just got on with their business. As usual, after breakfast, Joi-ih reported back that no trucks were going to Ti Lai Pa that day. A trip to the Korean mine drew a similar blank. We were beginning to fear that we might be holed up in this unprepossessing village for a long time, caught up in a disheartening waiting game. But we could not walk on and did not want to go backwards to Ti Po Choe and Sa Kae. We moped around the houses for a while, hoping against hope that something might happen. But nothing did.

Two tracks skirted Ti Po Mo, enclosing the village like an envelope. At each end they met. It seemed a good idea to station ourselves at the place where they merged on the southern edge of the village. We figured that if any vehicle did happen to pass, we could not miss it there. So we took up position in the shade of a stand of bamboos, prepared a mat of banana palm leaves, and settled down to wait. The heat was stifling and the waiting boring. To pass the time, we smoked some of the 'Best Thukhita Cheroots' we had acquired in Sa Kaang Thit black market. We reflected on how since Um Pang our journey had proceeded in fits and starts. A day of intensive progress was followed by several of time-biding. Apart from smoking and reminiscing, the only other thing to do was study the monolithic Chao Tao. Depending on one's viewing position and also on the time of day, it changed its aspect. On the evening of our arrival, it had seemed like a sinister human head. But now, from our forsaken mid-morning post by the bamboo clump, it looked more like the mocking head of a parrot or the uplifted snarling head of a tiger. As long as we waited, nothing came, and after two or three hours we gave up the waiting game as ridiculous.

❊ ❊

Postscript 2002

Consideration of the feasibility and modalities of nowadays implementing the end of the journey in this book, the expedition from Boeng Kloeng to the Three Pagodas, was given in the Postscripts to Chapters 13 and 14. A review of the options for proceeding

ELEVEN TIGERS

these days from Lae Tong Ku to Sa Kae and Ti Po Mo was made in the Postscript to
the latter chapter. If, attempting to repeat the expedition, you managed to reach Sa Kae
and then Ti Po Choe as well as Ti Po Mo, you would undoubtedly find a situation very
different from what we encountered back in early 1993. Your options in respect of
how to continue from Ti Po Mo would also be far fewer than were presented to us at
that time. Because, for reasons given earlier, I was unable to revisit Lae Tong Ku and
hence redo the expedition from Boeng Kloeng to the Three Pagodas in 2001, I have
not been able to look again at Ti Po Choe and Ti Po Mo, and so cannot provide any
updated account of them. But I am sure that everything has changed drastically down
there. What do we know? Let us look at things and update them in order.

In Boeng Kloeng, in February 2001, Sooksi said that the wild-looking KNLA
commander of Kui Le Toeng in Burma, Mor Thaing Chor, was dead. At first we
feared that he had been killed by the Burma army or by the DKBA, but it transpired
that he had died a natural death, simply from old age. As already pointed out, you
would not now be able to visit Kui Le Toeng or proceed from the village via Muang
Rae and Titabong down the 4WD track to Ti Po Choe. Since February 1997, the
territory on the Burmese side of the border between Kui Le Toeng and Ti Po Choe
(and beyond both those places) has been held by the Burma army and the DKBA, with
the track interdicted. Not long after we stayed in Joi-ih's home in Ti Po Mo in 1993, we
learned from an aid worker that his big wooden house had burnt down. We never
discovered the reason why, whether perhaps because it got mixed up in fighting during
a SLORC offensive or because the granny inadvertently set fire to it, but hopefully Joi-
ih did not associate the calamity with our recent stay. I am not at all sure that Joi-ih and
people like Mr Savaries live any more in Ti Po Mo and Ti Po Choe. Being mining
people, they may well now live in the mining villages of Kliti or Song Tor (Map 30) or
even in some quite other place, such as Sangklaburi.

This seems likely because the mines and processing facilities at Ti Po Choe and Ti
Po Mo must have closed down sometime between 1993 and 2001, in which case the
two villages would hardly have a *raison d'être* any more. I know this because when in
2000 and 2001, during visits to the Tung Yai Naresuan Wildlife Sanctuary HQ near
Kliti, I asked about the mine lorries still coming from Ti Po Mo and Ti Po Choe via Sa
Kae to Kliti and on out to Song Tor and Tong Pa Poom (Map 30), officials told me
that they no longer came. Nor did the lorries exit via Ti Lai Pa to Sangklaburi, which
they never used to do or, indeed, ever could do because the way is too rough. The
mines and plants must have closed down either because their licences expired or, more
likely, because a vast chunk of Tung Yai was established between Kliti and Sa Kae, or,
rather, because it already existed, but its integrity was more stoutly defended. The Thai
authorities take the countries' wildlife sanctuaries very seriously, and in general no
traffic and especially commercial or heavy industrial traffic is permitted to pass through
them. Tung Yai is a prestige project and so is taken particularly seriously. In 2001, at
the sanctuary HQ near Kliti, I could see that the 100-km-long dirt trail to Sa Kae and
then on to Ti Po Choe and Ti Po Mo through Tung Yai had been allowed to
deteriorate to become nothing but a poor and difficult forestry track. Clearly, no ten-
wheeler lead-concentrate lorries came along it any more or had done so for quite some
time. In fact, no vehicles of any kind used it now. Someone said that at most one pick-
up went from Kliti to Sa Kae every four days or so.

The implication of this is that if you, retracing this final expedition, were to arrive
at Sa Kae, having walked down from Mae Chan Ta or Lae Tong Ku, you would not be
able to exit to Kliti, Song Tor and the H323 north of Tong Pa Poom (Map 30), riding a
mine lorry or other vehicle going that way, an option that was open to us, even if we
did not take it. You could only exit via Ti Lai Pa and Sangklaburi (Maps 30 & 29),
continuing SSW and following the route that we took back in 1993. But here, too,

things have changed, and the options that would be open to you would be more restricted than those that were open to us. You would be able neither to cut through Burma between Ti Po Mo and Ti Lai Pa, nor to travel by truck, both of which we did. The reasons for this are the same as before. No one can cut through Burma any more because the Burma army and the DKBA now control the Burmese side of the border, and no vehicles any longer ply the route between Ti Po Mo and Doe Nae Po, although I believe they travel from Doe Nae Po out to the H323 (Map 29). They do not do so because (1) the way is so awful; (2) the mines at Ti Po Mo and Ti Po Choe have closed down, and there is hardly any reason for vehicles to go that way; and (3) the way passes through another, south-westerly chunk of Tung Yai, whose sacrosanctity has likewise been reasserted, with a prohibition of vehicular travel through it. As can be seen, the villages of Ti Po Mo, Ti Po Choe and Sa Kae are now held virtually in a stranglehold, with no vehicle access, which is why they must be largely defunct. Thus, from Ti Po Mo, to conclude the expedition, if you ever got this far, you would have to walk on out via Ti Lai Pa, Ko Ta Doe, Doe Nae Po and Sa Nae Pong, remaining always in Thailand. It would be a magnificent jungle trek about 60 kms long!

16

THREE PAGODAS

THE MON

Ti Po Mo – Ti Lai Pa – Ko Ta Doe – Doe Nae Po – Sa Nae Pong – Pra Chedi Saam Ong (Three Pagodas)

Deliverance came on the fourth day. A truck was going from Ti Po Mo to Ti Lai Pa, but no further. We figured that we should take the lift because, even if the vehicle was going only to this first village, it would take us across the long difficult section through Burma, and after that we might be able to walk the rest of the way. Very likely the pick-up was Joi-ih's own, or at least on loan from the Korean mine. The master was no doubt getting tired of seeing our long faces and wanted to send us packing before we either became too morose or ate him out of house and home. But we did not feel too guilty about the arrangement because, as we stowed our backpacks and ourselves in the back of the truck, many other people materialized, climbing in too. In the end, there were ten of us aft and three, including Joi-ih and Edu, in the cab. The vehicle was another white Toyota Hilux Hero (4WD, 2.4 litre diesel engine, kicked-out suspension), which seemed to be the standard means of transportation in these parts.

It was a great relief to be on the move again. After three days of enforced confinement in hot dusty Ti Po Mo, it was exhilirating to have the morning air blowing into our faces. Um Pang and our forgotten Honda seemed like ancient history, and we were more than ever anxious to complete our journey and embrace the triple pagodas. A sign of our battle-weariness was that I was now sporting nearly a fortnight's beard growth. Almost immediately, we had a little surprise. One km out from Ti Po Mo, instead of following the main track, the pick-up forked right into the Korean mine (Map 29). It stopped there while some consultations were made. To our delight, we spotted Mr John Savaries, sitting in front of one of the 'shops'. It looked as if it was his day off and he had decided to spend his free time by making an outing from one mine to the other, for he was wearing not the corporate clothing we had once seen him in, but holiday dress. A Burmese *longyi* was complemented by a Thai T-shirt, a Karen shoulder bag, and flip-flops. But best of all, his coal-black face was surmounted by a dapper azure pith helmet. This colourful character, part Indian, part Burmese, part Karen, part British colonial military man, was cleaving forcefully into a coconut with a machete.

We left the mine area by a track we had not previously noticed. It was the way down to Ti Lai Pa. Crossing over the border once again, we straightway plunged into primary jungle. Joi-ih drove steadily but carefully. Nevertheless, it was a bumpy laboured ride, with the 4WD truck grinding over rocks and tree roots. Skirting mountainsides, we climbed over a ridge. The whole of the 24-km journey ran through Burma, and all of it cut through dense jungle. We saw at once the problem of walking through here. There was not a single dwelling on the way, and we passed not a single person on foot.

The only event of the ride was an encounter halfway with another truck. This almost led to an accident. The vehicles met coming round a corner, and as there was nowhere for Joi-ih to go, the other truck ploughed up into the foliage. It was an antiquated affair, with battered, riveted, dark green bodywork, an upright cab and wooden sides at the back. It looked like one of those Dinky toys children used to play with years ago and may have been Burmese or Chinese. Otherwise, the vehicle was equipped with an array of searchlights and a winch. There were ten men aboard, but quite what they were doing was unclear. They had some drums of diesel in the back and had possibly been to collect fuel from Sangklaburi. The two vehicles drew up alongside, and the drivers conferred loudly through their cab windows. Some critical situation had arisen which necessitated Edu transferring from our truck to theirs and returning immediately to Ti Po Mo. The lonely meeting of the vehicles with their small bands of occupants was one of those Stanley-meets-Livingstone situations. But we were struck by another thought which we had often had as we crept through the jungle, that the jungle was a place which could inspire fear, but also a certain profound contentment. The reasons for the fear were obvious, but the reasons for the contentment might be that in the jungle human beings had an obscure feeling of returning 'home'. After all, a theory ran that we all originated there, in a bountiful environment which even today supplied all the needs of, say, the 'Stone Age', hunter-gatherer, 'Yellow Leaf' (Mrabri) people. Maybe when modern humans visited the jungle, some deep-seated sympathy for that long-lost primordial habitat resonated within them.

After a long hour of jolting and shaking, Joi-ih pulled up in the middle of nowhere by a wooden sign. It pointed one way to Huai Mae Ka Sa refugee camp and the other to Ti Lai Pa. He explained to us that if we continued down the track for a while on foot, we would come to the village of Ti Lai Pa. It was the parting of the ways. We thanked Joi-ih for his incomparable hospitality and helpfulness, and watched him disappear towards the camp. One km on, we came to the River Mae Ka Sa. A fair-sized flow, it formed the Thai-Burmese border at that point, and for the umpteenth time we crossed back into the kingdom. The track led straight through the thigh-deep waters, up a precipitous river bank on the far side, up a rise, and to a checkpoint and barrier of Tung Yai Naresuan Wildlife Sanctuary and Forest Protection Zone (southern sector). Near it was a makeshift notice nailed to a tree, saying in Thai, English, Burmese, Karen and another language we could not identify, possibly Mon, WELCOME TO TEA LYE BAA – OUR WORLD HERITAGE.

Ti Lai Pa

Such a portentous notice led us to have high hopes of the checkpoint and Ti Lai Pa village in terms of facilities and the possibility of getting on. We were quickly disillusioned. The barrier was manned by a short Karen youth, Tirapon, who lived in a shack to one side. A couple of other Karen youths also loafed around at the little outpost. It was a beautiful peaceful spot. Trees grew all around, and the boys had laid out well-kept flower beds. Outsize butterflies drifted by on the warm air. We asked the youths about the chances of onward transport. They were not at all hopeful. They produced a logbook of all the traffic movements in both directions. Most of the days were blank. Just as Joi-ih had said, there was on average one vehicle every three days. Entered for three days ago, for our first morning in Ti Po Mo, was the convoy of four trucks we had heard about. As the minutes ticked by, the peacefulness of that isolated spot began to grow rather too quiet for our liking. We contemplated the distinct possibility that we had escaped one place, only to become holed up in a worse one, for there were not even the facilities of Ti Po Mo here.

Opposite the guardbox, by the barrier, was an outdoor canteen area, backed by a row of dilapidated huts. We retired to the mess table to have a mid-morning snack and review our position. Here, we broached our last-but-one tin of food, consumed with cold rice begged from the Karen boys. We could either walk on, or wait in the hope that a truck might come that day, or stay the night and start again the next morning. With the last option in mind, we inspected the huts, where the youths had said we could sleep, although there were no blankets. Two of the rooms were locked up, evidently in use, one was a store, and the remaining free one was so filthy that we straightway ruled it out. Someone had evidently been using the cubicle for stripping down a motorcycle. While we were making our inspection, our ears suddenly discerned the miraculous sound of an engine. As it drew closer, we realized, however, that it was coming from the wrong direction. And soon a white Hilux drew up at the barrier, signed into the book, crumped down the embankment and breasted the river.

We consulted with Tirapon, the short Karen boy. The white Hilux was a KNLA truck, was stopping at Huai Mae Ka Sa camp, but might go on even as far as Mae Ta Ro Ta. No one knew when it would return. As for walking to Ko Ta Doe, that was an eight-hour trek along a route exactly the same at the one we had just come down, and at 11am it was too late to start out now. It would be better to wait until next morning and set off early in the cool. The one straw of hope that Tirapon could offer us was that when vehicles came, heading south, they usually came around midday. We clutched at that straw and decided to wait until midday. But by midday nothing had come, and by one o'clock still nothing had come. The boys went off to snooze, and we decided to take a look at Ti Lai Pa village. We left our backpacks with Tirapon, saying that if any vehicle came, he should let us know at once. Vaguely, he promised to send word.

Ti Lai Pa was a relatively large *Yang* place. We found the headman and some of his friends shredding tobacco. Judging by bundles of freshly picked, white fleece lying around, they also grew cotton nearby. The village was laid out among a lush mixture of betel, coconut and vivid red-flowering trees. In an open area, there was a fine old Burmese-style *wat*. Raised high off the ground on wooden piles, it consisted of a perfectly square wooden box with a two-tier corrugated iron roof. Another feature of the village were some remarkable swaying bamboo bridges over the Mae Ka Sa river. But the most spectacular thing about Ti Lai Pa was its setting. It lay in a valley sided by steep mountains. In particular, it was dominated by two conjoined outcrops, the Song Pinong. On the summits of these, two flags were flying. But the flags were not the same. One monolith was in Thailand, while its twin was in Burma. The Thai peak, of course, had a Thai flag, but its Burmese counterpart, ironically, was flying KNU colours.

The flags were a reminder of the continuing hostilities between the Karen and Rangoon. But the area had been the scene of other earlier conflicts. An engraved border stone near the barrier told that from 1538-1854, during the Sri Ayuttaya and Rattanakosin periods, the Mae Ka Sa river had been used by both the Siamese and Burmese armies for ferrying supplies in their long-running wars with one another. The headman told us that more recently the Song Pinong had been a CPT hideout. Then, in 1973, the Thai military had set up a camp in Ti Lai Pa. The result had been a battle, which the Thai army had lost. The area had remained under the control of the communists until 1981, when government forces returned, this time defeating the local CPT for good. In a for us tantalizing detail, the headman mentioned that from the top of the Song Pinong it was possible to see the Three Pagodas Pass.

Our problem exploring down among the village houses was that we were away from the track and could not watch out for passing traffic. So, rather than wait in the village, we decided to return to the barrier. Up there, we found an older Thai man, also waiting. He had a knapsack, and his identity and purpose were inscrutable. Quizzing him, we realized that our plight was as nothing compared to his. He had been waiting for a lift for a whole week. When we mentioned the mini convoy, he said that he had missed that because he had been out walking all day over the border. We asked him what he was doing in Burma, but he replied evasively that he was "just looking around". The border areas were full of such oddball characters on unaccountable missions.

The waiting game at the deserted checkpoint area continued through the baking, early afternoon heat. Again, it was borne in on us just how awkward it was journeying down this way. We reflected on how crazy we were spending our holidays holed up, wasting our time. Sometimes, we wondered if we were not demented, our minds turned by the heat. In fact, everyone here seemed off their trolley. When we shifted our waiting station down to the ford in order to be cooler, a man came to the river to wash his dog, yet he did not just toss the dog into the water, but carefully washed it with washing powder. When the dog was perfectly clean, it bounded out of the river and rolled 20 times in the dust of the track. A ten-year-old refugee girl repeatedly appeared sirenlike on a little promontory of river bank just out of reach from where we were sitting. Each time she did a little dance, erotically aware of her body, flirted outrageously with me, and teasingly scampered away. Was this reality or a figment of the imagination conjured up by jungle fever? She seemed to be an embodiment of the spirit of the quest, luring us on, only to frustrate us, taunting us with the promise of a lift, only to leave us waiting.

THREE PAGODAS

At teatime, the villagers came down to the river to bathe. We went up to the barrier to speak again with Tirapon. The friendly Karen had cooked up some food and invited us and the Thai adventurer in. We all sat with long faces, dipping rice balls into a curry made with the tender core of a banana palm stem. We told Tirapon that we had decided to wait until 5.30pm and then go to stay overnight with the *pu yai baan*. It transpired that the short Karen was himself waiting for a lift, in fact had been waiting for two days. He wanted to get down to Sangklaburi for some time off. So now we were a band of four. We were just clearing away the dishes, when we heard the sound of a truck. What was more, it was coming south through the river towards us. We all leapt up in great excitement, scattering the dishes. Fortunately, the barrier was down, so the vehicle was obliged to stop. Clutching our backpacks and knapsacks, the four of us ran out to the truck. It was the same white KNLA Hilux we had seen that morning. It had been up to Huai Mae Ka Sa refugee camp and was returning with some sacks of rice, bought in from Burma. As if by magic, half a dozen other people also materialized out of the trees and descended on the trapped truck. Without even asking, all ten of us scrambled aboard and sat in the back, utterly grateful that the waiting was over.

The barrier went up and the Hilux moved forward. But on the other side of the checkpoint it stopped, and the Karen driver, a young man called Sawoei (= eat) as well as a burly Thai BPP officer in civilian clothes got out of the cab. They said we could all get down because the truck was going no further than Ti Lai Pa, where the two of them were going to spend the night. They seemed to dispense this news with some relish. Cruelly disillusioned, everyone jumped down. We asked the Karen Sawoei if he was driving on the next morning, but he did not know – it depended on the BPP man, who was conducting a census in the vicinity. And sure enough, the truck disappeared down a side track into the village.

The stranded crestfallen hopefuls held a council of war at the barrier. Some people dropped out at once and went off. We decided to try our luck with the headman. The rest, a party of five which included Tirapon and the Thai adventurer, made the singular decision to start walking to Ko Ta Doe, trekking the eight-hour journey through the night. This left us on the horns of a dilemma. On the one hand, we knew that it was senseless and even dangerous to trek through the jungle at night. It would be pitch black, with – as things turned out – not even a moon to light the way. But, on the other, we knew that the party would be guided by Tirapon, who was familiar with the route and had a torch. Further, the little band would be walking when it was pleasantly cool. But the most aggravating thing for us was that the party of five would be getting out of Ti Lai Pa and would be in Ko Ta Doe before dawn, whereas we would be left behind, separated from them, and faced with the prospect of trekking the long distance alone the next morning. However, for us, common sense in such a predicament was paramount. The idea of stumbling blindly over rocks and roots in the blackness of mosquito-infested jungle was foolhardy, and so we let the band, led by the diminutive *Yang* youth, set off, and folornly waved them goodbye. They departed down a short-cut path, which branched off from the 4WD track.

THREE PAGODAS

With heavy hearts, we made our way down to the headman's house. There we found the truck, Sawoei and the *dorchodor* officer. The two men were tippling *lao kao* with the headman. They looked sheepish when they saw us arrive and invited us to drink with them. We asked the headman if we could stay with him overnight so that we could trek the following morning. That was not necessary, he replied. The truck was leaving for Sangklaburi that night and we could ride with it. We could scarcely believe our ears. We verified the news with the BPP man, who said: yes, it was true, although he himself was not going, but we were free to ride with Sawoei. We asked them why they had made everybody get out at the checkpoint and had come into the village. Oh that, they confessed, was a trick. Too many people had climbed into the truck and they had wanted to get rid of some. Besides, they had found it bad manners of everybody simply to jump aboard. We could not help feeling that for once discretion really had proved the better part of valour. By setting off too precipitately down the short cut, the others were going to miss the lift, whereas we, who had played prudently, were going to get the ride. Just as much as our luck had been down, now suddenly it was up.

Sawoei, 'Mr Eat', helped us rearrange the sacks of rice, and we installed ourselves behind the roll bar, seated on a sack each. Finally, when it was absolutely dark, we left Ti Lai Pa and set off into the jungle. It was a pity to complete the last leg of the journey at night, but we were too tired and emotionally drained to care. Besides there was a certain attraction about making at least one jungle trip in the night. We soon changed our minds about that. Sawoei drove the next 30 kms like a bat out of hell. It was more nightmarish and dangerous that the two rides together with Joi-ih and the grumpy gun-runner who had dumped us in the river back at Muang Rae. Quite why these drivers attacked the route so ferociously was a mystery. They perhaps gained 20 minutes, but destroyed their vehicles in the process. Nor was it clear why Mr Eat should want to travel at night, unless it was because there was something dubious about his errand. We later found out that these KNLA trucks liked to flit down the border during the hours of darkness, perhaps to outmanoeuvre the Burma army.

After a while, the headlights of the Hilux picked out the trudging figures of the little band. The driver did not have the heart to pass them by, and gratefully they clambered in. We were surprised that they had got so far. They were surprised to see us and were not a little peeved that we had outwitted them and got the best seats. Meeting again with the five, everything came together. With the shady Thai adventurer and our new friend Tirapon, we were all now in the same truck that we had seen earlier, and we were all finally heading in the direction we wanted to go.

The rest of the journey was not so much a question of when we would get to our goal, but whether we would reach it alive. The Hilux Hero sped through endless jungle tunnels, with bamboos lashing our faces, and thorny branches lacerating our sides. It groaned up steep gradients, scraping its underside on protruding rocks, and lurched alarmingly to left and right, threatening to spill us all out. It tipped over precipitous river banks with a sickening slithering thud, and forded rivers, the water lapping around the bottoms of the cab doors. Then, with the engine screaming, Sawoei smashed the truck up the far river banks, sometimes, from a standing start in the water, having to take a second shot at them.

On several occasions, for no apparent reason, the pick-up stopped in the middle of nowhere and the driver got out to check something. He seemed bothered by one of the wheels or the suspension. Naturally, this did nothing to allay our fears. The truckload of people seemed like a fragile island of humanity in the black threatening immensity of the jungle, and we kept willing Sawoei to get back in and drive on. On one such occasion, we all had a real turn. The Hilux drew up and we searched the track to see what the matter was. At first, nobody could see anything, but then someone noticed in the headlights the body of a man lying right across the path. How it was that the truck had not run him over was amazing. Nagging thoughts of the murderous 'yellowthread' rishi cultists ran through our heads. Also, we knew that ex-communist bandits and fugitive criminals hid out in these jungles of Kanchanaburi province. Even the Karen Tirapon and Sawoei, who were better able to interpret local irregularities, were visibly uneasy. They glanced nervously around into the blackness.

On either side of the man, large bamboo sections had been placed across the track to stop vehicles. Everyone feared an ambush, and the two Karen flashed their torches into the surrounding bamboos. The Thai adventurer produced a gun. The remnants of a smouldering fire were burning near the man. It seemed that he had made a little camp for the night there and had put the bamboos across the path to stop vehicles running over him, but no one was sure and the man could not be roused. Either he was drunk, or half bitten to death by malarial mosquitoes, or dead. The thought occurred to us that, if we had tried to trek to Ko Ta Doe in the night, this could be us lying here. The two Karen moved the body to one side, removed the bamboo obstacles, and cautiously drove around the man. Then we hurried on in silence.

It was a long way to **Ko Ta Doe**, but finally the truck headlights illuminated a checkpoint at the Karen village. Sawoei got out to report to the guard hut, and then we were off again. Between Ko Ta Doe and Doe Nae Po came the famous score of river crossings – we counted 19 of them. It seemed that on this section the track intertwined with and continually reforded the same river. Some of the crossings were up to 100 metres long and one metre deep. Often, the boulders on the river bed were round and slimy, making progress difficult and slow, even with 4WD. As if to annoy us, Sawoei began stopping the truck in the water to shine his torch along the river banks in search of jungle frogs. From everywhere came a chorus of croaking calls in the night. In the end, the driver's desire got the better of him, and on the approach to one ford he drew up the Hilux definitively, switching off the engine and lights. It was so dark that it was impossible to see anything, not even the nearest person in the back of the truck.

Sawoei came round to the back and explained to Tirapon that he wanted to get some frogs "for a garden pond I have built", but that he needed the other's help to find and catch the frogs while he himself held the torch. Tirapon, as a wildlife sanctuary employee, was understandably unhappy about this, but the driver leaned on him, reminding him that he was after all getting a free lift. Perhaps an element of Karen brotherliness came into the equation. And so the two of them went off along the pitch-black river bank, abandoning the rest of us to our fate. Like Tirapon, we also wanted to remonstrate. It was no fun being ditched in the dark in the jungle. But our position was even weaker than the Karen's.

The men were gone a long time. The cool night air was alive with the waak-waak of the big jungle bullfrogs. In the back of the truck, we were constantly pestered by insects. As the moon had not yet risen, it was still incredibly dark. Nothing could be seen of our companions except the tiny glowing cones of their cigarettes. Over and again, the absolute impossibility of trekking down here at night bore in on us. Someone spoke of bears and tigers in the trees (both exist in Tung Yai). Our own thoughts circled around the idea that the unscrupulous Sawoei was making a rendezvous with some accomplices to double back and ambush us. Everybody was distinctly unhappy. Then the Thai swashbuckler suggested making a fire. It would keep us warm, illuminate the immediate area, drive away insects and animals, and just pass the time. Soon, a fire of dry bamboo was crackling merrily. The situation was so hopeless and absurd that it began to seem amusing.

After a good hour, the pinpoint of the torchlight came dancing erratically back towards us. The two Karen arrived clutching by the legs a dozen foot-long frogs. They put them in a sack and then went to get a spear of bamboo. We were afraid they were going to spit the animals and roast them over the fire. But they merely used the bamboo to fasten the sack. At around 10pm, we set off again. The driver seemed in an even greater hurry now, trying to make up for lost time. We trawled through the remaining fords and then passed through what looked more like open country, even elevated ground. Certainly, that latter section was back on bulldust tracks. In our minds, we tried to translate the ghostly scenery outlined by the truck's headlights into the stunning countryside it must have been in daylight.

The sleeping Karen village of **Doe Nae Po** passed by, and then, not far short of the main road, we drew up in front of yet another barrier. This was no lackadaisical post manned by Karen boys, but a serious checkpoint. In fact, it was the southerly **Sa Nae Pong** entrance to and HQ of Tung Yai Naresuan Wildlife Sanctuary and Forest Protection Zone. Something funny happened here. After the paramilitary *anuraak* guards had logged the arrival of our truck and quizzed everybody, especially us, as to their business, they began to search the vehicle. They inspected the sacks of rice, rifled through our backpacks, and then, inevitably, found the bag of frogs. Sawoei, of course, could not come up with any plausible explanation whatsoever for the freight of frogs, and Tirapon kept remarkably quiet. The bullfrogs were confiscated. Sawoei was visibly sore about it. Tirapon whispered in our ears that the frogs would certainly not be returned to the wild, but would be eaten by the forestry officials. Poor Mr Eat could only watch as the treat that he had envisaged for himself passed into the hands of other eaters. The rest of us were just exasperated that the long hour which we had been forced to wait had all been for nothing.

THREE PAGODAS

At the checkpoint, we enquired of the guards about the route ahead. The main road was only eight kms away and the turning for the Three Pagodas just a couple of kms beyond it. But the truck was bound for Sangklaburi, which was in a different direction. Also, midnight was not a good time to arrive at a strange town. So we asked the forest-conservation men if we could spend the night at their Sa Nae Pong office. Without enthusiasm they agreed. They seemed doubtful about a shattered-looking *farang* dropping out of the jungle in the night with a red face and a jawful of stubble. In fact, after the frog episode, they viewed us all with deep suspicion, and rightly so. We thanked the questionable Sawoei for the bone-shaking ride, and bade farewell to both the shady Thai adventurer and our friend for the day, Tirapon, as well as the others. The red tail lights of the Hilux vanished in the dust and gloom.

The reserved *anuraak* led us to an A-frame bungalow nearby and, as it was late, let us get on with things. We strung up our mosquito net and rolled out our sleeping bags on a pallet bed. A late snack consisted of our very last tin of food, lugged from Mae Sot, and the rest of a bottle of lukewarm water, which had a snow of fragments of purifying tablets slushing around in the bottom. Reviewing the confused events of the day, we tried to get some details down in my diary. Could it really be that we had breakfasted with Joi-ih in Ti Po Mo? And were we actually sleeping within striking distance of our final goal? As we drifted off to sleep, it seemed to us that we heard the contented murmurings of the forestry men, turning jungle frogs on a grill over their fire...

※

The next morning, over a breakfast of eggs, rice and coffee, we learned that a Land Rover was going to Sangklaburi. If we wanted, we could travel with it as far as the turn-off for Ban Pra Chedi Saam Ong (= Three Pagodas village). We accepted the lift and bumped along for eight kms. The terrain in these upper reaches of Kanchanaburi province was every bit as rugged as what we had been seeing. The same Dawna Range lay over to the west, separated from us by scrubland. Suddenly we came to a T-junction and the H323 Kanchanaburi/ Sangklaburi highway. It was a shock. It was the first tarmac we had seen since Um Pang, two weeks earlier. And the few cars and trucks swishing by were the first real traffic since Mae Sot, in quite another part of the country. Even though it was still early morning, we noticed that it was significantly hotter and more humid down here. We were almost on the same latitude as Bangkok.

A road sign pointed south-east 70 kms to Tong Pa Poom and 205 kms to Kanchanaburi town, and north-west 6 kms to out-on-a-limb Sangklaburi and 20 kms to the pass and border (Maps 29 & 30). Our Land Rover turned right and drove the two kms up to the turn-off for the Three Pagodas Pass. We alighted there and were made to sign our names and nationalities into a book at a police box on the junction. Then we waited for the first passing *silor* to take us the last 18 kms to the Three Pagodas. Finally an empty one arrived, charging us 25 baht each. It was strange to be handling money again. Except for paying guides and buying the odd packet of Ma-maa instant noodles, we had been given everything free since Um Pang. The Thai authorities were reconstructing the road up to the pass, engineering a highway out of all proportion to both the traffic on it and the meagre village at its end. The first section had already been paved, while the rest was still dirt. In keeping with so much of our journey, we completed the last stretch with a generous coating of yellow powder.

Halfway up the dust highway lay the mixed Mon and Burmese village of **Huai Song Karia** (also Sangkalia, Chong Kalia and variations), named after a nearby river that flowed into Lake Khao Laem (possibly giving Sangklaburi its name). The countryside to the left was desolate scrub, while to the right loomed the same craggy Dawna mountains we had followed down the border, sometimes on the Thai side, sometimes on the Burmese side, all the way from Ban Ta Song Yang. They were the outermost foothills, the dying ripple, of the Himalayas. The *silor* ascended to a low pass (altitude 1,000 ft), crossed over, and dropped down the other side into the large squat community of **Ban Pra Chedi Saam Ong** or **Three Pagodas Village**. Here our transport parked, and it was but a short walk further to the **Three Pagodas**. The Burmese claimed the pagodas, and we could see why. Both they and the village clearly lay west both of the pass and the border mountains. On the other hand, it was understandable why the Thais should also claim (want to keep) the pagodas. They formed one of the most celebrated shrines in South-East Asia.

The Three Pagodas Pass
And so, alighting from a humble public-transport *silor* in the early morning, this was how we came to behold the goal that we had so long journeyed towards. After the anticipation, the reality of the pagodas was inevitably a trifle disappointing. They were not pieces of monumental architecture, but three piles of whitewashed stones (altitude 295 m or 968 ft above sea level). Encircled by a little garden fence, and with flowering bushes growing in among them, the triple *chedi* were swathed Buddhist-style in lengths of red, green and yellow gauze (see colour photo). People had placed offerings before them. Nearby were a couple of feeble stalls. The big dirt road led up to the pagodas and ended by swinging around them. To put it irreverantly, the Three Pagodas looked like pert little oriental breasts sticking up out of a roundabout.

The shrine was marred not just by the road, but by the paraphernalia of an adjacent Burmese border crossing and military checkpoint. For 130 baht (Thais, of course, only 5 baht), visitors could put a smile on the faces of the Rangoon authorities and cross over to see the village of Payatonzu (also Pia Tong Su = 'three pagodas' in Burmese). Beyond the village, the road continued for 172 kms to Moulmein and the Andaman Sea, and 473 kms to Rangoon (Yangon). The crossing point was quiet. Flags were flying, and authoritarian notices abounded, such as WELCOME TO MYANMAR – LOVE YOUR MOTHERLAND, RESPECT THE LAW and WELCOME TO PHAYATONZU – THIS CITY WAS ESTABLISHED BY THE ARMY AND PEOPLE IN 8-2-90. The joint presence at the pass of SLORC troops and the Thai army reflected the current disposition of ownership and control of the pagodas. Judging by the way a Thai highway ran up to the shrine, it looked as if the cairns were firmly part of the kingdom, but actually they sat more in a piece of no man's land or 'extra-territory', ruled by neither power or both.

THREE PAGODAS

The Burmese notices reflected just the latest chapter in the long chequered history of the Three Pagodas. When not in itself a flashpoint, the pass had often been the vehicle of invasions going in both directions. More than a few times, the Burmese and the Siamese, traditional enemies who even today remained mutually suspicious, had crossed the pass to conquer each other's kingdoms, sack each other's towns, and steal each other's most important Buddha figures. The Burmese, for example, had come this way when in 1765 they infamously destroyed Ayuttaya, the wondrous former capital of Siam. In calmer times, the Three Pagodas had been the age-old and principal link between Burma and the fertile plain of the Chao Praya river, channelling traders, pilgrims, diplomats and migrants. These individuals, when leaving their own land and before entering the territory of the 'enemy', used to pause at the pass to make an offering. They found the frontier marked by three little cairns, and in fact the Three Pagodas Pass was originally known as 'the three cairns'. By adding a stone to the cairns, the wayfarers sought to draw down blessing on their journey, and this was how the *chedi* started life. In 1929, Pra Sri Suan Kiri, the governor of Sangklaburi, brought local people up to Pra Chedi Saam Ong to transform the cairns into the pagodas as we now know them.

In more recent times, the Three Pagodas Pass was the conduit of a much larger invasion. During the Second World War, the Japanese used the route to help launch their attack on Burma from occupied Thailand. They invaded also from other points further north, for example Khun Yuam and Wiang Haeng (as we have seen), but the pass was of especial significance because it was the only route for hundreds of miles by which they could forward large quantities of heavy supplies. To enable them to sustain their offensive, the Japanese had the idea of building a 415-km-long railway over the pass, linking the Thai and Burmese railway systems. It was projected that a 304-km Thai stretch and a 111-km section in Burma would meet at Pra Chedi Saam Ong. The idea gave birth to the infamous 'Death Railway', associated with the Three Pagodas.

Work began on the railway in June 1942 at the existing terminals of Nong Pladuk in Thailand and Thanbyuzayat in Burma. It had been estimated that the line would take five years to build, but work was completed in September 1943, in little more than a year. The two railheads met just south of the Three Pagodas. Such an extraordinary feat of engineering through mountainous jungle terrain was only possible due to the forced labour of a huge army of prisoners of war and pressganged coolies. Out of the workforce, which has been estimated to have numbered approximately 200,000 men,[1] some 13,000 POWs (principally Australian, British and Dutch) and perhaps as many as 90,000 coolies (from Thailand, Burma, Malaysia, Indonesia, India and China) perished. They died from malnutrition, disease (notably malaria), exhaustion and accidents, but quite especially from the bestial treatment meted out to them by their Japanese captors. Two celebrated war cemeteries at Kanchanaburi town honour the Allied dead.

The story of the building of 'Death Railway' up to the pass is well-known on account of one of the line's bridges, the one which spans the River Kwae

---

[1] Another estimate puts the number of Thai and other South-East Asian coolies alone at 200,000.

THREE PAGODAS

Yai near Kanchanaburi town. The construction of this bridge was famously documented in Boulle's book *The Bridge over the River Kwai* (should be 'Kwae') and subsequently celebrated in the film of the same name. The bridge was in use for almost two years before it was bombed by the Allies in 1945. After the war, the bridge was rebuilt and is still in use today. You can walk over it, and it has now become a major tourist attraction. Of 'Death Railway' itself, the first 77 kms on the Thai side still exist, running as far as Nam Tok, near the Sai Yok Falls. The rest has been dismantled or reclaimed by the jungle.

Until a short time before our visit at the end of our journey (early 1993), the Three Pagodas Pass had always stood in territory historically Mon, but latterly controlled jointly by the Mon and the Karen. We had come across our first Mon man, the monk, back at Joi-ih's village. Song Karia, just before the Three Pagodas, was full of Mon people, and other villages in the vicinity were also Mon. The nearby district seat of Sangklaburi was in essence a Mon town. With our route ending by brushing the Mon homeland, it is appropriate to say a few words about this last minority people of our border journey.

✤

Mon people, history and culture

The Mon are classified as belonging to the Monic branch of Mon-Khmer group in the Austro-Asiatic family of peoples or linguistic superstock. They go by many alternative names, including Talaing, Taleng, Rmen, Rman, Mun/Man, Mou, Peguan and Takanoon. 'Talaing' is the name that the Burmese use to refer to the Mon and is a name that the Mon used to be called, after a region on the Madras coast of India. 'Rmen', according to Schliesinger (2000), is an archaic name for the Mon, which changed in mediaeval times to 'Rman' and later to 'Mon', which is what these people call themselves today. Historically, the Mon have inhabited the territory that is now Burma and Thailand, and today they continue to live in both countries, but mainly in Burma. These days they are a marginalized and suppressed ethnic minority, but once they were a proud and powerful people with a flourishing, well-developed, and highly civilized independent state, which was subsequently conquered by the stronger Burman and Tai ethnic groups, after which the Mon became poor and politically weak. In Burma, the Mon would seem to be the oldest inhabitants still surviving today, predating the Burman by hundreds of years. In Thailand, they likewise predate the Tai by many centuries, and, if we disregard the even older Lawa, must have been the first people with an advanced civilization to settle in the plains of the Chao Praya river. Certainly, they are one of the oldest settlers in Thailand. Looking at today's backward Mon of, say, the enclave beside Sangklaburi town, it is difficult to imagine that they are the descendants of a race of people who once had a mighty South-East Asian empire.

The origins of the ancient Mon race are uncertain. They are known to have once lived in south-west China, in space south of territory occupied by the Tai peoples. The Tai, perhaps themselves under pressure from other peoples to the north, apparently displaced the Mon into 'Upper Burma'. Then, in the first centuries AD, Tibeto-Burman peoples moving down the valley of

THREE PAGODAS

the Irrawaddy river drove them both south to Pegu and Thaton in 'Lower Burma', and east into 'Thailand', where they settled in the plains of the Chao Praya river to the south and of the Ping river to the north. In the centuries after about the 3rd century AD, the Mon began founding a kingdom or empire called Suvannabhumi (Golden Land), known to modern-day Mon as Hongsawatoi, which was a loose federation of three city states or principalities. These states comprised Dvaravati, which was based on Lopburi in central 'Thailand', Haripoonjaya or Haripoonchai, which was based on Lampoon in northern 'Thailand' (the name of the modern town of Lampoon is derived from Haripoonjaya), and Thaton, based on the town of Thaton in southern or 'Lower Burma' (near Martaban and Moulmein, close to the Gulf of Martaban and the Andaman Sea), which is still important for the Mon in today's Mon State, Burma. As these states were established, a famous overall kingdom or empire with an advanced civilization arose, generally known as the Dvaravati kingdom, empire and civilization, taking its name from the Lopburi city state and culture, perhaps because this was the most important.

From the 'imperial' capital of Lopburi outwards, the Mon went north to found in AD 769 the great city state or principality of Haripoonjaya on the site of present-day Lampoon (a few kms south of Chiang Mai), thus extending their Dvaravati kingdom. Doing so they encountered, as we saw in Chapter 8, the L'wa (ancestors of the Lawa and Wa), who were the predominant group in northern Thailand and the wider region, and who for a considerable period had had their own civilization, even if it was not a high one like the Dvaravati civilization of the Mon. Haripoonjaya came to be ruled, as we recall, by the Mon princess or queen Chaam Taewi, while the Lawa king Wilanka was installed close by (somewhere near the site of Chiang Mai). Undoubtedly, for a period the two races co-existed harmoniously and enjoyed a close relationship, although ultimately the Mon supplanted the Lawa locally. The eclipse of the Lawa came to be symbolically embodied in the legend of the magic contest between Chaam Taewi and Wilanka, which Wilanka and the Lawa lost. Following the defeat, the Lawa withdrew to the hills and remoter areas of the region. After Haripoonjaya, the major Mon city of Pegu, originally known as Hamsavarti, was founded in the 9th century AD.

From the Martaban coast, the Mon made trading and cultural contacts with the civilizations of India and Ceylon, which significantly influenced the Dvaravati kingdom and culture. They were trading with these places very early on, and as early as the 5th century AD are said to have brought both Hinayana-Buddhist doctrine from the Indian sub-continent and Theravada Buddhism from Ceylon to 'Burma' and 'Thailand'. They also introduced writing to this region and are believed to have founded the world-renowned Shwedagon Pagoda in Rangoon, which was originally a Mon settlement. Soon the Mon established themselves as the most cultured people in South-East Asia at the time, as their art and architecture show. They had their own language, writing and masterly sculptural style. In the modern Thai town of Lopburi, stones have been found dating back to the 8th century bearing old Mon script, while in Lampoon (former Haripoonjaya) artefacts have been dug up with Mon inscriptions. Between the 3rd and 10th centuries AD, the Dvaravati kingdom, as

391

one source says, extended from southern Burma to northern Thailand. Or, as another authority puts it, more than a thousand years ago the Mon Dvaravati empire extended from the Indian Ocean in the west, to the Malay peninsula in the south, and to the high plateauland of north-east Thailand. Or, widening the chronological perspective and narrowing the geographical one, we can say that for a thousand years, until Pegu fell in 1757, the Mon ruled much of Lower Burma from their great cities at Thaton, Martaban and Pegu. The Mon themselves believe that, if their forefathers had been a race of warriors rather than of architects, poets and artists, the whole of South-East Asia could have come under their control. By about AD 1250, Haripoonjaya had grown into the cultural and religious centre of 'northern Thailand'. It maintained links with Ceylon, and Theravada Buddhist schools in the Mon city state taught Buddhism to other ethnic groups, such as the Lawa and also the Tai, who were now arriving in the vicinity.

From about the 9th century onwards, the Mon empire was squeezed from the north and then west by the Burman, from the east by the Khmer, and from the north by the Tai peoples. The Burman and Tai were themselves being displaced by other races in Tibetan and Chinese space. The main body of Burman migration south into Upper Burma took place in the 9th and 10th centuries, as a result of which the Burman pushed the Mon into Lower Burma and established their own realm. Later, they migrated further south into Lower Burma, gradually controlling more and more of Burma and pushing the Mon into south-east Burma, especially into what is now the Tenasserim Division, west of the Tenasserim mountain range, where many Mon now live. In the 11th century, the great Burman king Anawrahta launched an attack from Pagan on Thaton, taking the Mon capital.

At the start of the 11th century, the Mon Dvaravati kingdom and civilization at Lopburi in central 'Thailand' became a vassal of the Khmer empire, which also began to campaign against Mon Haripoonjaya further north. Dvaravati Lopburi was phased out when Khmer military power itself waned in central Thailand around the start of the 13th century and the dominion of the Tai in central Thailand began. The end of the Mon kingdom and civilization of Haripoonjaya came immediately after its golden era from about 1160 to 1280, terminating Mon pre-eminence there that had lasted some 500 years. We have already observed the modalities of the arrival of the Tai in northern Thailand and the Shan State in Chapter 8 (under 'Lawa people, history & culture') and so will not repeat them here. But in 1281 (or possibly 1292), after a long siege, the Tai Yuan (Lan-Na Tai) conquered Haripoonjaya, causing the principality's last Mon ruler to flee south. The advent of the Tai in northern and central Thailand spelled the essential demise in Tai space both of the Mon and – we recall – the Lawa.

Back in Burma, the Mon clung on to some kingdoms or principalities here and there, but they finally completely lost their independence in the 1750s, when the great Burman monarch Alaunghpaya first drove the Mon from and captured Ava in 1753, and then in 1757 crushed the uprising of the last Mon ruler, Smin Dhaw, taking the Mon capital of Pegu. Many of the Mon communities in Thailand date back to the time of the fall of Pegu, following which numerous Mon people fled across the border from Burma into Siam. The Burman may have taken control of large parts of present-day Burma and virtually annihilated the Mon, but the Mon left their mark on their Burman conquerors. For the animist Burman took over from their subjects Theravada Buddhism, writing and other aspects of Mon culture.

In the 19th century, the British annexed Burma during three wars between 1825 and 1886, essentially considering it a province of colonial India. They might have been the saviours of the Mon, for at first they sought to check the expansion of the Burman and considered supporting the Mon against the latter. When the Tenasserim Division came under British rule in 1827, many Mon fled Burmese expansion and found refuge in Tenasserim under the British, to whom they perhaps looked. But the Mon were to be disappointed because eventually the British chose Burmese as the official language of government, thus favouring the Burman at the expense of the Mon. The effect of this colonial decision on Mon culture was devastating, for within two generations many areas lost all traces of their Mon history. Altogether, over the past century, Mon culture has been characterized by rapid assimilation into mainstream Burmese culture.

In the mid-20th century, in response to demands from Burma's Mon for a proper homeland of their own, the Mon State was created, which lies in Lower Burma, to the west of part of the Karen State, near the Salween delta, fronting the Gulf of Martaban and the Andaman Sea, and around the major Mon towns of Thaton, Martaban and Moulmein. But the state did little to assuage nationalist dissatisfaction among Mon leaders and intellectuals. Notably, at the Panglong conference of 1947, when it came to settling independent homelands for Burma's ethnic minorities, the Mon got the same raw deal as the Karen. Occupying land that was both contiguous with Karen territory and shared with the Karen, it made sense for the Mon to make common cause with the Karen. Accordingly, in 1948, the year of Burma's independence from Britain, the Mon allied with the KNU. The two peoples agreed to work for a joint Mon-Karen independent state, particularly in territory inhabited by both groups. Bridling with dissatisfaction and smarting from the affront of Panglong, the Mon rose up in 1949, the same year as the outbreak of the Karen insurgency. Like that of many other ethnic groups in Burma, the rebellion of the Mon dragged on for decades. The Mon people suffered all the same calamities – SLORC attacks on and militarization of their homeland, a war of attrition against them, as well as displacement of their villages and people etc. – that other insurgent ethnic minorities suffered, such as the Karen, Karenni, Padaung and Kayaw, leading to the flight of large numbers of Mon into Thailand. Around 2000, the number of Mon refugees and illegal migrants in Thailand was estimated to be over 100,000. In the 1990s, there were several Mon refugee camps in the inaccessible border area between Sangklaburi/the Three Pagodas Pass and Pilok (south-west of Tong Pa Poom), which may (in 2002) still be there. In 1995, a ceasefire was agreed between the New Mon State Party and the SLORC, but, despite this, numerous Mon villagers have continued to leave their homes inside Burma and flee to the border areas or into Thailand. We return to recent events in the Mon rebellion and in particular to events relating to the Karen and the Three Pagodas Pass below.

Today, as indicated, the Mon live in the Mon State in Burma, in part of Burma's Tenasserim Division (especially the coastal part, west of the Tenasserim range), in the border areas opposite Thailand's Kanchanaburi province, and elsewhere in Burma, as well as in Thailand. In the kingdom, where a few indigenous or long-established communities survive, the Mon live mostly in the west of the country, particularly in the border provinces of Kanchanaburi, Ratchaburi and Petchaburi. But they are also to be found in Pra Nakhon Si Ayuttaya, Lopburi and Khorat provinces. As we have seen, centuries ago Mon lived in the Lopburi (Dhavarati) and Lampoon (Haripoonchai) areas, and post-1757, when Pegu fell, many Mon fled to Thailand. Most of the country's Mon communities are peopled with descendants of these fugitives. I am not sure about the age and status of Sangklaburi as a Mon refugee place, but undoubtedly many villages up and down the border, on the Thai side, are refugee or quasi-refugee Mon places relatively recently established, and many Mon have escaped SLORC offensives by fleeing into Thailand in the past few years. Estimates as to the number of Mon in Burma and Thailand vary. The Mon themselves claim that there are 4 million of them in Burma, while the Burmese – following their own political agenda – put the figure at just over 1 million. Large numbers of Mon are to be found in the towns of Martaban and Moulmein. Schliesinger (2000) estimates that there are 120,000 'indigenous' Mon in Thailand, to which can now be added the 100,000 + refugees. Of the 'indigenous' Mon in Thailand, less than 50,000 still speak Mon. The majority have forgotten their own language and speak Thai, just as in Burma most Mon have become partially or completely Burmanized, having assimilated Burman customs and dress. Today, traditional Mon culture and language survive mostly in rural areas of Burma and the south-east borderlands.

The Mon are traditionally lowlanders, who raise cattle and cultivate wet rice as well as vegetables. They live in villages that are typically compact and large (like the one at Sangklaburi), with several hundred houses, built on stilts. The Mon live in patrilineal nuclear families, and their costume is non-traditional and uninteresting. Every Mon village has a *wat*, which also serves as a school for the children, as we saw in Ti Po Mo. The Mon are Buddhists and have been so, as said earlier, since the 5th century AD. Theravada Buddhism is a major element in their culture, just as Buddhist monks, who are highly respected, play a central role in the life of all Mon communities.

Now we return to the Mon rebellion, to relations between the Mon and the insurgent Karen, and to the recent history of the Three Pagodas Pass. The alliance between the Mon and the Karen that was started in 1948 held in one form or another until the 1980s, when simmering discontents over land and taxation in the region of the Three Pagodas began to boil over. Back in the mid-1960s, KNU 6th Brigade district had opened a new trading post/customs gate at the pass. Controlled jointly by the Karen and the Mon, it rapidly grew – like Palu and Kawmoorah further north – into one of the most important of all Kawthoolei's (the Karen State's) frontier outposts, boasting a population of some 5,000 Karen, Mon, Indo-Burmese, Burmese and others. Travellers to the Three Pagodas 'black market' reported seeing temples, churches, a mosque, and even a cinema hall. With the revenue from taxation booming, each side must have secretly considered how much it would have liked to have all the income for its own purposes.

At the beginning of the 1980s, the Mon insurgent movement fissured into two rival factions. The split, which lasted six years, seriously compromised the Mon cause. It also weakened the Mon vis-à-vis their allies, in spite of the fact that one faction, the 1,000-strong New Mon State Party/Army, stayed with the KNU. In the matter of control of the Three Pagodas, the Karen, who at that time were anyway gaining in absolute strength, were in the ascendant. In 1987, however, the two rival Mon factions reunited, restoring Mon military clout. Overnight, the Mon felt confident enough again to challenge the Karen for overall control of the pass. There was a new twist in the spiral of tension between the two ethnic rebel armies. The resulting skirmishing between old allies was senseless enough, but it was utterly absurd in view of the offensives against both of them by a common foe, Rangoon. In 1977, 1980 and 1986/87 the Burma army, pursuing its Four Cuts campaign, repeatedly attacked Karen/Mon bases at and around the Three Pagodas. Finally, the allies themselves achieved – incredibly – what the Burmese had for so long failed to do. In a major battle in July 1988 between the KNLA and the NMSA, the Three Pagodas village and base was virtually razed to the ground.

But that fatal and tragic mistake, which cost the lives of more than 100 Karen and Mon, was as nothing compared to what was about to happen. In early 1990, the Three Pagodas became the scene of the last in the long line of invasions through the pass. This time it was a cross-border incursion by SLORC troops into Thailand. But the Burmese were not, as so often in history, after the Siamese, but the insurgents. On Friday 9 February, Rangoon forces captured and destroyed what was left of the black market immediately behind the pagodas, paving the way for a larger offensive. Then, at midnight Saturday 10 February, they launched a major attack on the NMSA HQ at Nam Koek, a few kms north of the pass. However, the 'Myanmar' troops did not make a frontal assault on the rebel stronghold, but used Thailand as a springboard from which to attack it unexpectedly from the rear. It was the same tactic as they had used almost contemporaneously up at Kawmoorah. The Mon were furious that the Thais had 'allowed' the Burmese to use their territory. But for the moment they, like the Karen, were a casualty of thawing relations between Bangkok and Rangoon. *Tatmadaw* troops manoeuvred on Thai soil with the infamous tacit support of the Thai military, as directed by army supremo Gen. 'logger' Chaovalit.

1,000 SLORC soldiers, led by Col. Chit Maung, poured through a corner of the kingdom to capture Nam Koek village and base on the morning of Sunday 11 February. There were heavy casualties on both sides. All Sunday 11 and Monday 12, the junta forces made helicopter drops of supplies, transporting these and marching across Siamese soil south-east of the Three Pagodas. They even passed a tellingly empty Thai army 9th Division outpost. The upshot of the fighting was that between 4,000 and 7,000 Mon civilians fled to Song Karia (Sangkalia), while 200 or more Thais sought refuge in Sangklaburi. Numerous Burmese people also fled to the Thai side to escape the fighting and avoid being pressganged into portering. The Mon insurgents retreated from Nam Koek to regroup. With a view to 'stretching' their assailants and counter-attacking, they buried their differences with the Karen and linked up with KNLA troops operating nearby. However, the Burma army, far from crumbling, held on to the pass area. It did not even completely withdraw from 'Thai' territory, but held onto the Three Pagodas, claiming that they belonged to 'Myanmar'. To back up their claim, the Burmese produced an old British colonial map showing the pagodas inside their country. While they were there, they gave the three ancient venerated *chedi* a coat of white paint, ironically using Thai paint to do the job. The following day an incensed Thai nation awoke to see pictures of marauding gun-toting bandanna-clad Burmese infantrymen roaming around the freshly whitewashed pagodas. Needless to say, the Burmese were soon dispatched from regular Thai soil, but they were not entirely removed from the pass – witness their presence now (in 1995, and still in 2002) immediately beside the Three Pagodas.

✳

The Three Pagodas made a fitting end to our journey. Purely on their own account, these ancient, famous, revered and remote *chedi* would have been an appropriate enough destination. But, marking a frontier pass, they formed an especially apt conclusion to a journey which had passed down the border, zigzagging across it. The three cairns which had guided generations of wayfarers going east and west now greeted new travellers coming from the north. Travelling is in some respects a quasi-religious quest, and what better goal could there have been for such a pilgrimage than this shrine? In the early morning sun, untroubled by anyone except for a man making a votive offering, we sat in a crude shelter, savouring undisturbed both the magic of arrival and the mystical presence of the pagodas. The three wild piles of stones stood silent and gleaming in a desolate forbidding arena. Behind them squatted the shacks of Pra Chedi Saam Ong village, in the middle distance lay what looked like some abandoned *wat* construction, and in the background towered the precipitous tree-covered Dawna mountains of the border ridge. We were tired, dirty and very hungry. Our clothes were grimy and our faces burnt red by the sun. My ankle was as painful and swollen as ever, and the red spots of the elephant rash had still not gone. A fortnight out from Um Pang, a good centimetre of traveller's stubble had grown. But all these discomforts were as nothing now that we were finally able to joyfully embrace the Three Pagodas.

The latest Burmese incursion at Pra Chedi Saam Ong was still a fresh event. The praying man, when he had finished his offering, came over to us and pointed out holes in the tin roof of our shelter. They were bullet holes from that assault. This reminded us of the other darker side of the Three Pagodas. Their chequered history and the conflicting claims to them reflected the continuing sporadic warfare all up and down the disputed territory of this western border, not least at the pass itself. Even if for the moment the traditional enemies, Thai and Burman, were sharing the spot in an uneasy stand-off, it was a place where Mon had fought Karen, and Burman had fought both – just as further up the border other ethnic minorities continued to fight each other, with the Burman fighting everyone.

Finally, the pagodas were symbolic in a more abstract way. Their ambivalence reflected not just the deadly freedom fighting up and down the border, but dubious developments in the countries on either side. In the name of 'Burmanization', Burma had been economically, politically and militarily wrecked by the long-standing Ne Win military dictatorship and latterly its SLORC/SPDC replacements. Now, too, the country was a source to be plundered of hardwood, opium and young girls. We only trusted that Thailand would not suffer a similar fate, but from more insidious causes. We hoped that the kingdom, as it changed from being a traditional Buddhist third-world country to a developed nation, would not destroy itself in a riot of headlong modernization, mechanization, roadbuilding, exploitation, tourism, greed and hedonism – that Mr Donut would delay his coming for a while longer, that Shangri-La would persist in spite of the *tuk-tuks*, and that the driverless Komatsu would thrust only so far into the virgin jungle. In his book *Golden Earth*, Norman Lewis wrote that during crucial moments in Burma's history a prophecy had often become current. It had been heard again during the pagoda-building mania which had preceded the Mongol invasion. People had said: "The great pagoda is finished, and the country is ruined." As we rested at our journey's end, contemplating the celebrated Three Pagodas, we hoped that Burma's Siamese neighbour would not be ruined by a modern-day invasion.

✳ ✳

Postscript 2002

As said at the end of the Postscript to Chapter 15, if, repeating the expedition through Um Pang and Tung Yai Wildlife Sanctuaries from Um Pang via Boeng Kloeng and Lae Tong Ku to the Three Pagodas, you have somehow managed to reach Ti Po Mo, you can now almost certainly no longer exit via Sa Kae and Kliti, but will have to exit SSW via Ti Lai Pa and Sa Nae Pong (Maps 29 & 30). However, because the Burma army and DKBA now control the Burmese side of the border opposite Um Pang and Sangklaburi districts, and have interdicted the 4WD track down their side of the frontier, including the stretch between Ti Po Mo and Ti Lai Pa, you cannot any more travel this crucial piece of track either by truck or on foot. In fact, for reasons given earlier, you cannot ride out from Ti Po Mo and Ti Lai Pa to the H323 at all, or only possibly from Doe Nae Po. So you must walk out. But I have heard that, because the Ti Po Mo/Ti Lai Pa leg through Burma is out of commission, the Karen, who have to walk up and down between the villages in this southern chunk of Tung Yai, have forged or re-established a footpath between Ti Po Mo and Ti Lai Pa on the Thai side. This path is probably more direct than the 4WD track through Burma and hence shorter than the 24 kms of the latter, but I imagine that it would take you all day to trek it on foot. Having reached Ti Lai Pa, you would then have to walk on some 8 hours to Ko Ta Doe, after which you would need to hike roughly 3 further hours to Doe Nae Po, wading through the 20 river crossings. I do not know how long it might

THREE PAGODAS

then take you to trek on out through Sa Nae Pong to the H323, perhaps another day, but you might be able to get a lift in a vehicle from Doe Nae Po. The Karen village of Sa Nae Pong lies 9 kms from the main road, and the Tung Yai HQ/checkpoint 8 kms from the highway.

From where you hit the H323, it is 20.8 kms to the Three Pagodas and 6 kms to Sangklaburi. You turn R/NW and proceed 2 kms to a large junction, either catching a bus/*silor* or hitch-hiking or even walking. At the big junction, marked by a police box, go R 18.8 kms for the Three Pagodas Pass, and L/straight 4 kms for Sangklaburi. The road for the Three Pagodas has long since been paved all the way to the pass, and Ban Pra Chedi Saam Ong just before the pass has meanwhile grown considerably and developed. There are hotels, restaurants, shops, street lights and all sorts there now. In late 1999, the border was closed because of problems between Thailand and Burma, and in December 2000 I found at the Three Pagodas 'roundabout' a market, which was doing a brisk trade in orchids and teak furniture, being bought up by Thais by the truckload. I fancy that Huai Mae Ka Sa refugee camp (near Ti Lai Pa), which we passed in 1993 and which no doubt housed Karen and probably Mon people from Burma, has since closed because there is apparently no longer any vehicle access route to it and Ti Lai Pa through Tung Yai.

Back at the large junction down on the H323, you continue 4 kms up the H323 to **Sangklaburi**. You know you have reached the little town because you come to a large permanent market on the left side of the road. The rest of the townlet lies behind the market, including two guest houses you might want to stay in. Sangklaburi is a weird, laid-back, somewhat wild, spread-out place that undoubtedly grows on you. It has good places to stay, decent food, an interesting market with frontier characters and atmosphere, an impressive *wat*, scenic location beside the vast Khao Laem lake, great views over the lake, and a huge enclave of Mon people also by the lake.

If you go down the road that heads S from the H323, on the far western side of the market, you come after almost one km to *Burmese Inn*, a guest house in a side alley just off the road (R side). It is run by the Austrian Armin Hermann and his Thai wife, is built on a steep slope overlooking an arm or inlet of the lake, and has an attractive, peaceful, nicely furnished balcony and restaurant. When I stayed here in the winter of 2000/01, a simple room with own bathroom was 120 baht/night (shared bathroom 80 baht), and a bungalow was 300 baht. Further down than *Burmese Inn*, is *P. Guest House*, also on the right side. I have never stayed here, finding it overpopular and somewhat travellerish, but it is undeniably nice, scenically overlooks the lake, and has a good restaurant and food. In 2000, rooms with a shared bathroom were 150 baht. Sangklaburi's only hotel, the *Phornpailin*, is also worth considering. Located in the market (eastern side, if I remember correctly), it is a big nice place with a vast number of clean teak-floored rooms. You can get a fan room with own cold-water bathroom for 200 baht or so.

Also in the market are a couple of good breakfast places. They lie opposite each other in the uppermost street, the one nearest to and parallel with the H323 highway. Both serve *gaffae tammada* (good ordinary strong Thai coffee), and the one on the northern side of the street is also a bakery, while the one on the southern side is also a big food place. If you go down to the lake near *Burmese Inn*, you come to a quaint long wooden bridge across part of the lake. You used to be able to ride across it, but I think that it is closed now to all except pedestrian traffic. The bridge brings you to an extensive Mon village, which may well have grown out of a refugee camp. A grid of dirt streets runs through scores of thatched wooden huts and little stores. If you want to get a glimpse of Mon life, this is the place to look. Beyond the village lies Wat Wang Wiwekaram, also known as Wat Mon because many Mon monks live there. Although in part vulgar and pretentious, it is nevertheless interesting and repays a visit.

THE MAPS

The maps are diagrammatic only and not to scale

<u>Key to symbols used in the maps:</u>

——	paved road
- - - ·	dirt road
- · - ··	poor dirt road/motorcycle trail/4WD track
··········	footpath
■	village/town
•	feature (e.g. cave/police box/school)
Δ	mountain/ peak
CP	checkpoint
NP	national park
WS	wildlife sanctuary
HQ	headquarters
GH	guest house
w/f	waterfall
mkt	market
m/c	motorcycle
⊞	health centre/hospital
PO	post office
~ ~	river/stream/ford
][	bridge
H	road/highway + number (e.g. H1178)
///	mountain ridge
⊓⊓⊓⊓	cliff(s)
+ + +	border
☀	viewpoint

399

MAP 2

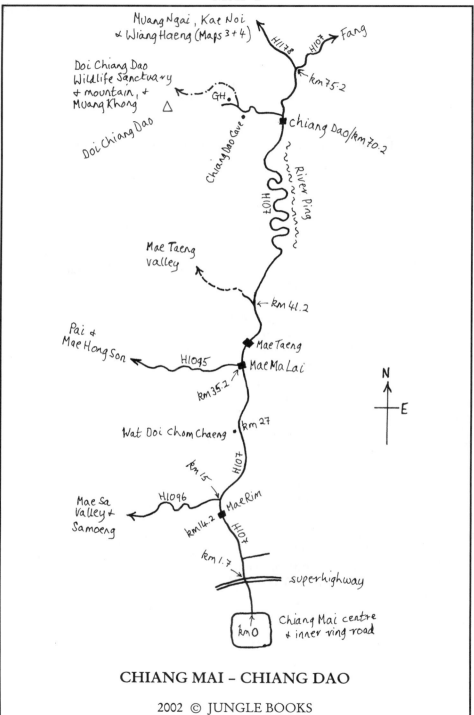

Muang Ngai, Kae Noi
& Wiang Haeng (Maps 3 + 4)

Fang

H1178   H107

km 75.2

Doi Chiang Dao
Wildlife Sanctuary
& mountain, &
Muang Khong

GH.

△

Chiang Dao/km 70.2

Doi Chiang Dao

Chiang Dao Cave

H107

River Ping

Mae Taeng
valley

← km 41.2

Pai &
Mae Hong Son

H1095   Mae Taeng

Mae Ma Lai

km 35.2

Wat Doi Chom Chaeng   • km 27

H107

N

E

Mae Sa
Valley &
Samoeng

km 15

H1096

Mae Rim

km 14.2

H107

km 1.7

superhighway

km 0

Chiang Mai centre
& inner ring road

CHIANG MAI – CHIANG DAO

2002 © JUNGLE BOOKS

MAP 3

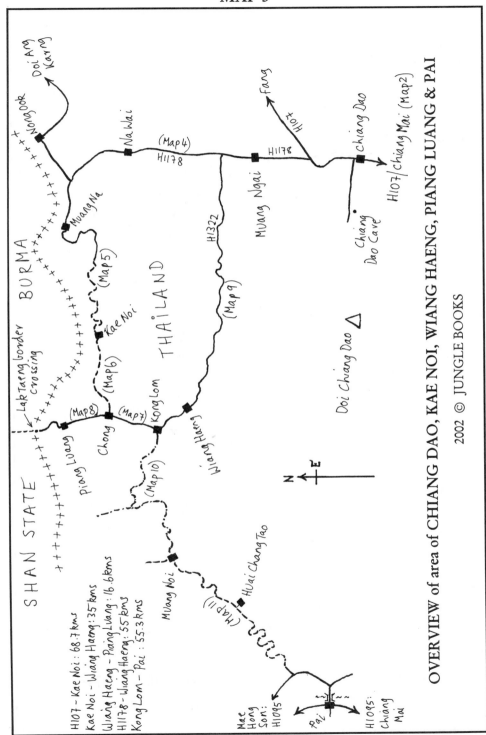

OVERVIEW of area of CHIANG DAO, KAE NOI, WIANG HAENG, PIANG LUANG & PAI

2002 © JUNGLE BOOKS

H107 - Kae Noi : 68.7 kms
Kae Noi - Wiang Haeng : 35 kms
Wiang Haeng - Piang Luang : 16.6 kms
H1178 - Wiang Haeng : 55 kms
Kong Lom - Pai : 55.3 kms

MAP 4

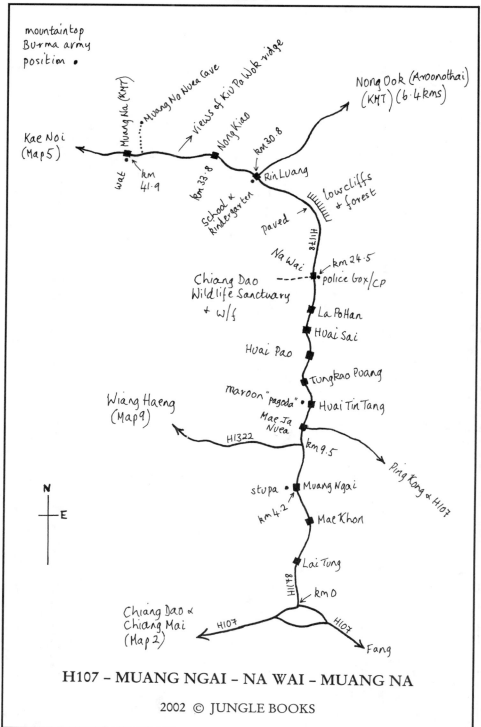

mountaintop
Burma army
position •

Muang Na (KMT)

Muang Na Nuea Cave

views of Kiu Pa Wok ridge

Nong Ook (Aroonothai)
(KMT) (6.4kms)

Kae Noi
(Map 5)

Nongkiao

km 30.8

km 33.8

Rin Luang

wat

km 41.9

School & kindergarten

low cliffs + forest

Paved

H1178

Na Wai

km 24.5

police box/CP

Chiang Dao
Wildlife Sanctuary
+ w/f

La Po Han

Huai Sai

Huai Pao

Tungkao Puang

maroon "pagoda" •

Huai Tin Tang

Wiang Haeng
(Map 9)

Mae Ja Nuea

H1322

km 9.5

Ping Kong & H107

stupa •

Muang Ngai

km 4.2

Mae Khon

Lai Tung

H1178

km 0

Chiang Dao &
Chiang Mai
(Map 2)

H107

H107

Fang

N
E

H107 – MUANG NGAI – NA WAI – MUANG NA

2002 © JUNGLE BOOKS

402

MAP 5

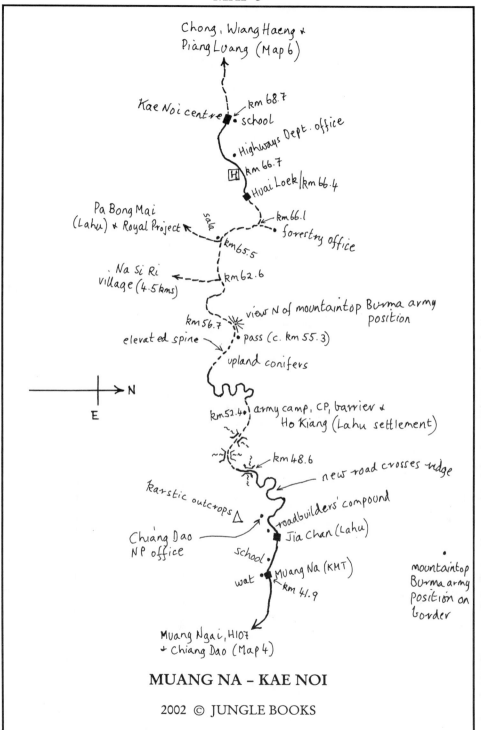

Chong, Wiang Haeng &
Piang Luang (Map 6)

km 68.7
Kae Noi centre
• school

• Highways Dept. office

km 66.7
H
Huai Loek / km 66.4

Pa Bong Mai
(Lahu) & Royal Project
sala
km 66.1
• Forestry office
km 65.5

Na Si Ri
village (4.5 kms)
km 62.6

view N of mountaintop Burma army
position
km 56.7

elevated spine
• pass (c. km 55.3)

upland conifers

N
E

km 52.4 • army camp, CP, barrier &
Ho Kiang (Lahu settlement)

~ km 48.6

new road crosses ridge

karstic outcrops △
roadbuilders' compound
Jia Chan (Lahu)

Chiang Dao
NP office
school •
Muang Na (KMT)

wat •
km 41.9

mountaintop
Burma army
position on
border

Muang Ngai, H107
& Chiang Dao (Map 4)

MUANG NA – KAE NOI

2002 © JUNGLE BOOKS

MAP 6

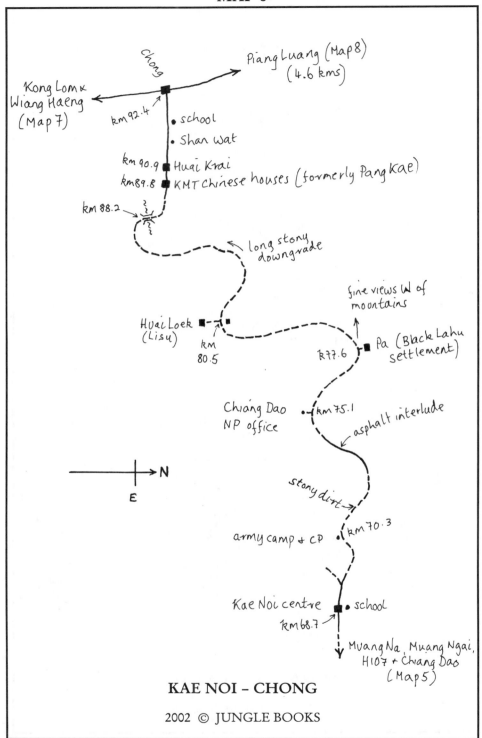

Chong

Piang Luang (Map 8)
(4.6 kms)

Kong Lom &
Wiang Haeng
(Map 7)

km 92.4

• school

• Shan Wat

km 90.9 ■ Huai Krai

km 89.8 ■ KMT Chinese houses (formerly Pang Kae)

km 88.2

long stony downgrade

fine views W of mountains

Huai Loek
(Lisu)

km 80.5

km 77.6

Pa (Black Lahu settlement)

Chiang Dao
NP office

• km 75.1

asphalt interlude

→N

E

stony dirt

km 70.3

army camp & CP

Kae Noi centre
km 68.7

• school

Muang Na, Muang Ngai,
H107 & Chiang Dao
(Map 5)

KAE NOI – CHONG

2002 © JUNGLE BOOKS

MAP 7

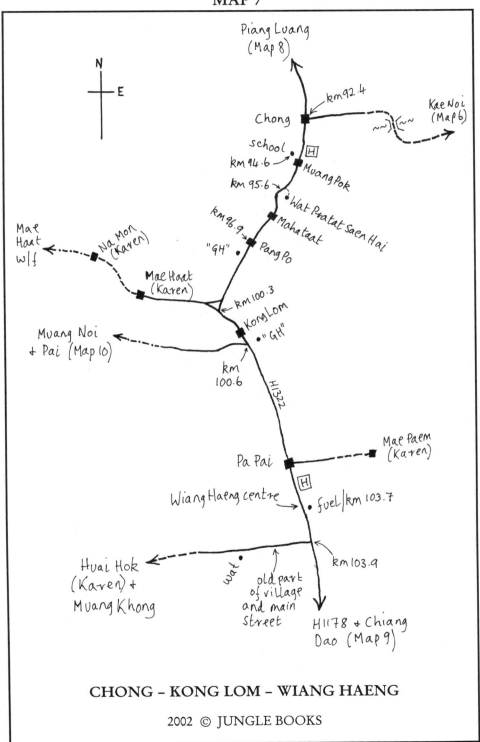

Piang Luang
(Map 8)

N
E

km 92.4

Chong

Kae Noi
(Map 6)

school
km 94.6
[H]
Muang Pok

km 95.6

Wat Pratat Saen Hai

km 96.9

Mahataat

"GH"

Pang Po

Mae
Haat
w/f

Na Mon
(Karen)

Mae Haat
(Karen)

km 100.3

Kong Lom

"GH"

Muang Noi
+ Pai (Map 10)

km
100.6

H 1322

Mae Paem
(Karen)

Pa Pai

[H]

Wiang Haeng centre

• fuel/km 103.7

Huai Hok
(Karen) +
Muang Khong

wat •

old part
of village
and main
street

km 103.9

H 1178 + Chiang
Dao (Map 9)

CHONG – KONG LOM – WIANG HAENG

2002 © JUNGLE BOOKS

MAP 8

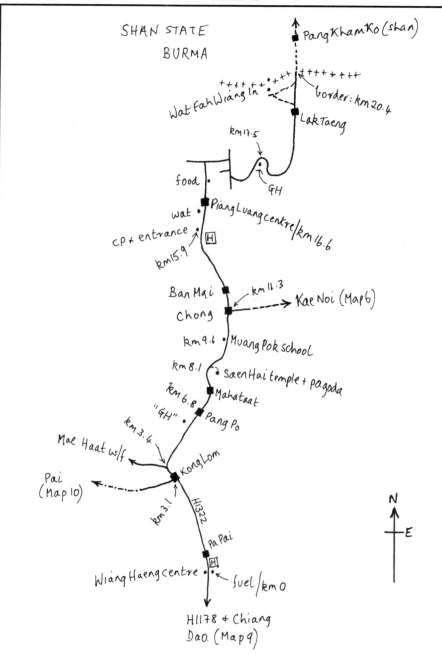

SHAN STATE
BURMA

Pang Kham Ko (shan)

border: km 20.4

Wat Fah Wiang In

Lak Taeng

km 17.5

food

GH

wat

Piang Luang centre / km 16.6

cp + entrance

km 15.9

Ban Mai

Chong

km 11.3

Kae Noi (Map 6)

km 9.6   Muang Pok school

km 8.1   Saen Hai temple + pagoda

km 6.8   Mahataat

"GH"   Pang Po

km 3.4

Mae Haat w/f

Pai
(Map 10)

Kong Lom

km 3.1   H1322

Pa Pai

N

E

Wiang Haeng centre

fuel / km 0

H1178 + Chiang
Dao (Map 9)

WIANG HAENG – CHONG – PIANG LUANG / border

2002 © JUNGLE BOOKS

406

MAP 9

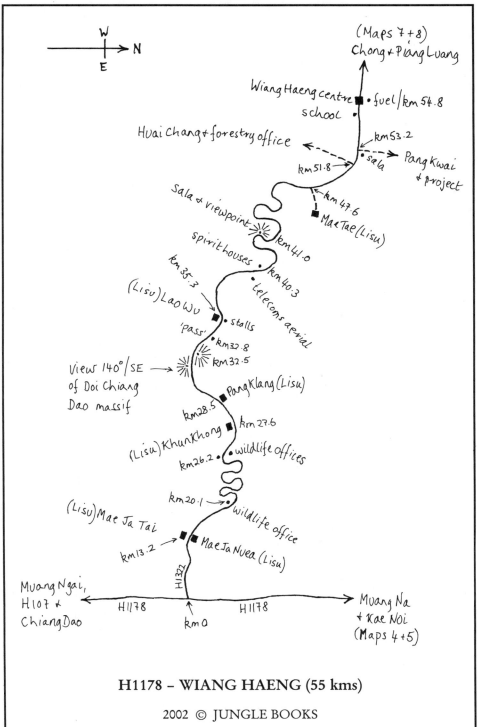

(Maps 7 + 8)
Chong + Piang Luang

Wiang Haeng centre ■ • fuel / km 54.8
school •

Huai Chang + forestry office ←- - - km 53.2
                                        • sala -→ Pang Kwai
km 51.8 -→   + project

Sala + viewpoint ⟵- - - km 47.6
                      ■ Mae Tae (Lisu)

spirit houses • km 41.0
              • km 40.3
              • telecoms aerial

km 35.3
(Lisu) Lao Wu ■ • stalls
'pass' • km 32.8
          ☀ • km 32.5

View 140°/SE -→ ☀
of Doi Chiang
Dao massif   ■ Pang Klang (Lisu)

km 28.5
(Lisu) Khunkhong ■ • km 27.6
km 26.2 • • wildlife offices

km 20.1 •
          • wildlife office

(Lisu) Mae Ja Tai
                ■ ■ Mae Ja Nuea (Lisu)
km 13.2 -→

                    H1322

Muang Ngai,
H107 +   ⟵ H1178   H1178 -→   Muang Na
Chiang Dao   ↑   + Kae Noi
                     km 0   (Maps 4 + 5)

H1178 – WIANG HAENG (55 kms)

2002 © JUNGLE BOOKS

MAP 10

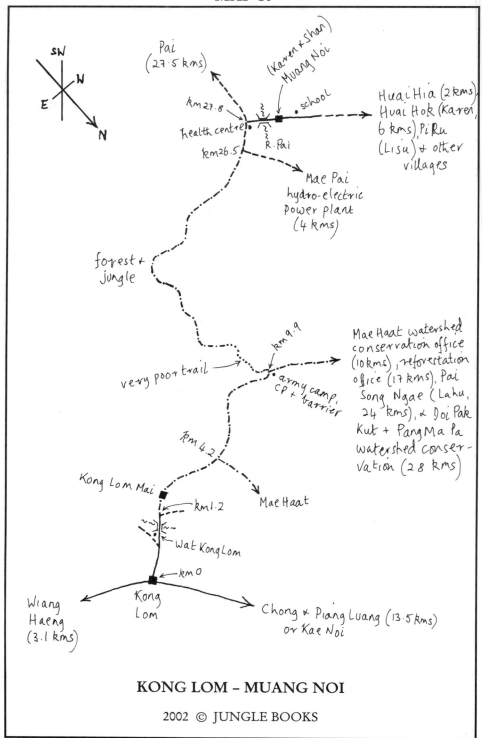

KONG LOM – MUANG NOI

2002 © JUNGLE BOOKS

MAP 11

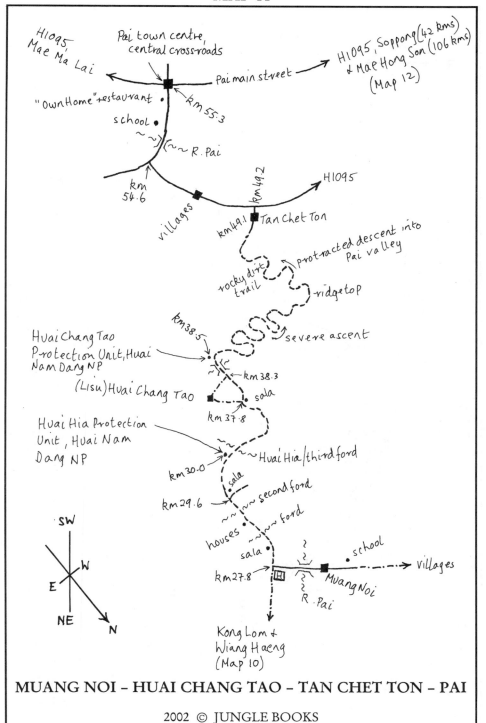

H1095, Mae Ma Lai

Pai town centre, central crossroads

Pai main street →

H1095, Soppong (42 kms) & Mae Hong Son (106 kms) (Map 12)

"Own Home" restaurant

school

~ ~ ~ R. Pai

km 55.3

km 54.6

villages

km 49.1

Tan Chet Ton

km 49.2

H1095

rocky dirt trail

protracted descent into Pai valley

ridgetop

severe ascent

km 38.5

Huai Chang Tao Protection Unit, Huai Nam Dang NP

km 38.3

(Lisu) Huai Chang Tao

sala

km 37.8

Huai Hia Protection Unit, Huai Nam Dang NP

km 30.0

~ Huai Hia / third ford

sala

km 29.6

~~ second ford

~~ ford

houses

sala

school

km 27.8

Muang Noi

→ villages

R. Pai

SW

W

E

NE

N

Kong Lom & Wiang Haeng (Map 10)

MUANG NOI – HUAI CHANG TAO – TAN CHET TON – PAI

2002 © JUNGLE BOOKS

MAP 12

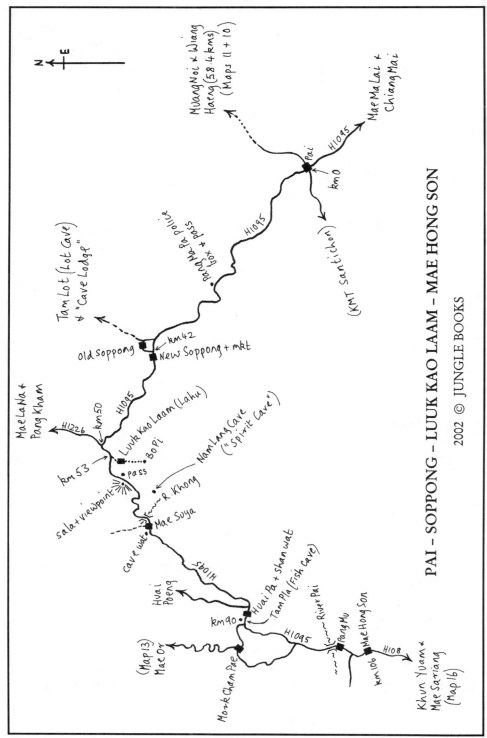

N ← E

MuangNoi & Wiang Haeng (58.4 kms) (Maps 11 + 10)

MaeMaLai + ChiangMai

H1095

Pai

km 0

(KMT Santichon)

H1095

Tam Lot (Lot Cave) + "Cave Lodge"

Pang Ma Pha police + box + pass

H1095

km 42

old Soppong

New Soppong + mkt

H1095

km 50

MaeLaNa + Pang Kham

H1226

km 53

Luuk Kao Laam (Lahu)

Bo Pi

pass

sala + viewpoint

Nam Lang Cave ("Spirit Cave")

R. Khong

Cave wat

Mae Suya

H1095

Huai Pa + Shan wat

Tam Pla (Fish Cave)

Huai Pheng

km 90

River Pai

Pang Mu

Mae Hong Son

H1095

H108

Mok Cham Pae

(Map 13) Mae Or

km 106

Khun Yuam & Mae Sariang (Map 16)

PAI – SOPPONG – LUUK KAO LAAM – MAE HONG SON

2002 © JUNGLE BOOKS

MAP 13

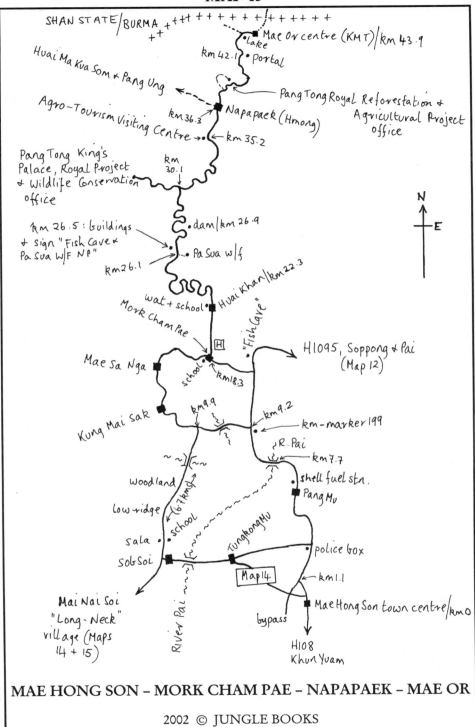

SHAN STATE/BURMA + + + + + + + + + + + +
+ +
Mae Or centre (KMT)/km 43.9
• lake
km 42.1 • portal

Huai Ma Kua Som & Pang Ung

Pang Tong Royal Reforestation &
Agricultural Project
office

Agro-Tourism Visiting Centre →•

km 36.3 Napapaek (Hmong)

← km 35.2

Pang Tong King's
Palace, Royal Project
& Wildlife Conservation
office

km 30.1

km 26.5 : buildings
+ sign "Fish Cave &
Pa Sua W/F NP"

• dam/km 26.9

• Pa Sua w/f

km 26.1

N
E

wat + school •|Huai khan/km 22.3
Mork Cham Pae

"Fish Cave"

H

H1095, Soppong & Pai
(Map 12)

Mae Sa Nga

school km18.3

Kung Mai Sak

km 9.9

km 9.2

• km-marker 199

R. Pai

km 7.7

woodland

(6.7 kms)

shell fuel stn.
Pang Mu

low ridge

school

sala •

Tungkong Mu

Sob Soi

Map 14

police box

km 1.1

Mae Hong Son town centre/km 0

Mai Nai Soi
"Long-Neck"
village (Maps
14 + 15)

River Pai

bypass

H108
Khun Yuam

MAE HONG SON – MORK CHAM PAE – NAPAPAEK – MAE OR

2002 © JUNGLE BOOKS

MAP 14

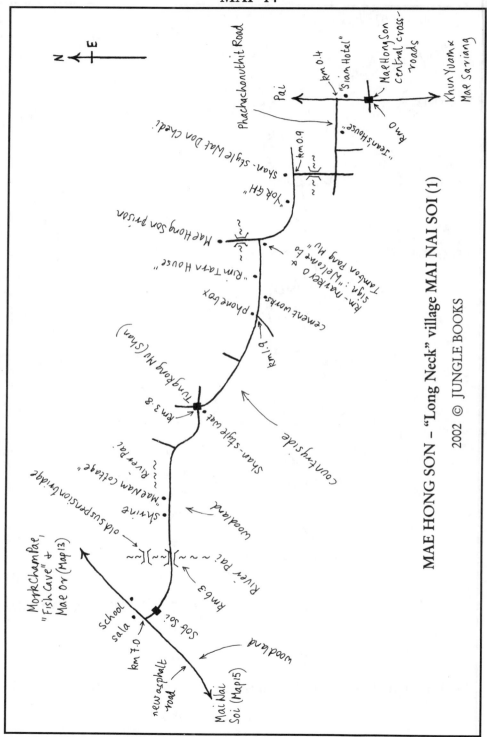

MAE HONG SON – "Long Neck" village MAI NAI SOI (1)

2002 © JUNGLE BOOKS

MAP 15

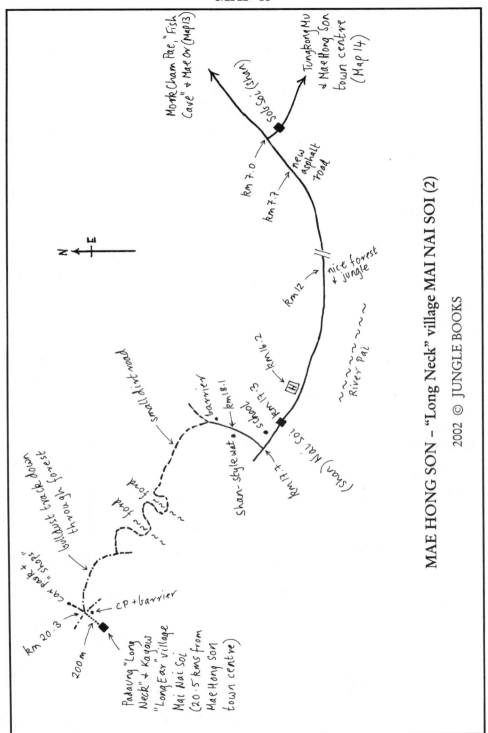

MAE HONG SON – "Long Neck" village MAI NAI SOI (2)

2002 © JUNGLE BOOKS

Mork Cham Pae "Fish Cave" + Mae Or (Map 13)

Soppong (Shan)

Tung Kong Mu + Mae Hong Son town centre (Map 14)

new asphalt road

km 7.0

km 7.7

nice forest + jungle

km 12

km 2.6

River Pai

km 1.3

school

Shan-style wat

km 1.1

Mai Nai Soi (Shan)

km 18.1

barrier

small dirt road

ford

ford

bumpy first track down through forest

car park + shops

CP + barrier

200 m

km 20.3

Padaung "Long Neck" + Kayaw "Long Ear" village Mai Nai Soi (20.5 kms from Mae Hong Son town centre)

N E

MAP 16

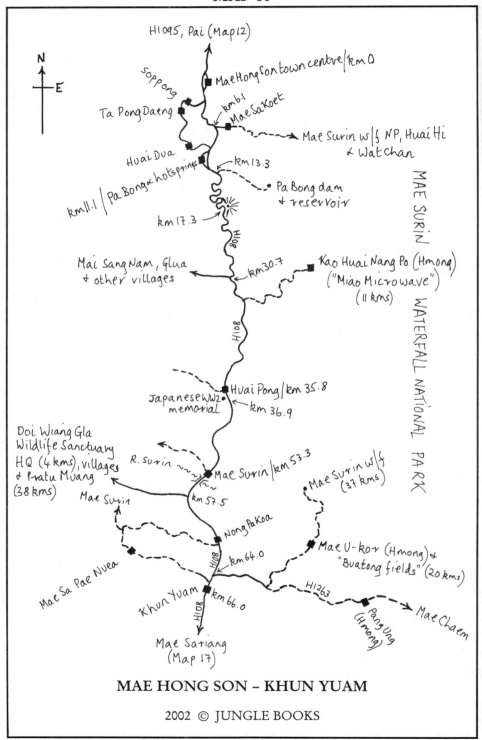

H1095, Pai (Map 12)

N
E

Soppong

Mae Hong Son town centre / km 0

Ta Pong Daeng

km 6.1
Mae Sa Koet

Mae Surin w/f NP, Huai Hi & Wat Chan

Huai Dua

km 11.1 | Pa Bong & hotsprings

km 13.3

Pa Bong dam & reservoir

km 17.3

H108

Mai Sang Nam, Glua & other villages

km 30.7

Kao Huai Nang Po (Hmong) ("Miao Microwave") (11 kms)

H108

Huai Pong / km 35.8

Japanese WW2 memorial

km 36.9

Doi Wiang Gla Wildlife Sanctuary HQ (4 kms), villages & Pratu Muang (38 kms)

R. Surin

Mae Surin | km 53.3

Mae Surin w/f (37 kms)

Mae Surin

km 57.5

Nong Pa Koa

H108

km 64.0

Mae U-kor (Hmong) & "Buatong fields" (20 kms)

Mae Sa Pae Nuea

Khun Yuam | km 66.0

H108

H1263

Pang Ung (Hmong)

Mae Chaem

Mae Sariang (Map 17)

MAE SURIN WATERFALL NATIONAL PARK

MAE HONG SON – KHUN YUAM

2002 © JUNGLE BOOKS

MAP 17

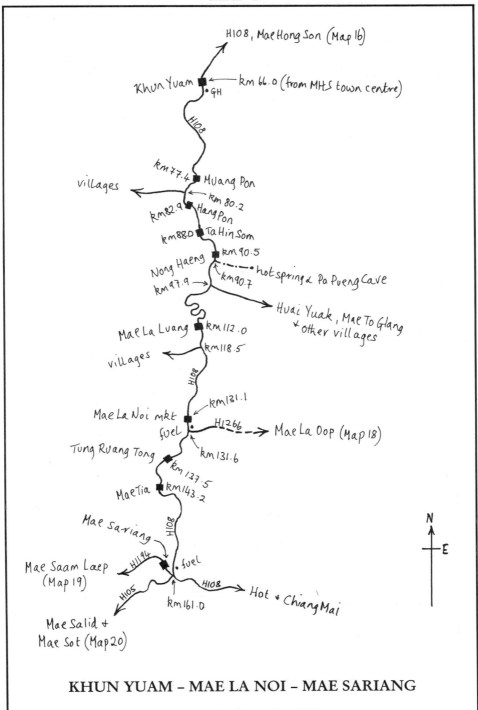

H108, Mae Hong Son (Map 16)

Khun Yuam
• GH
← km 66.0 (from MHS town centre)

H108

km 77.4
Muang Pon

villages ←
← km 80.2
km 82.9
Hang Pon
km 88.0
Ta Hin Som
km 90.5

Nong Haeng
•–•–• hot spring & Pa Pueng Cave
km 97.9 →
km 90.7
→ Huai Yuak, Mae To Glang
& other villages

Mae La Luang
km 112.0
villages ←
km 118.5

H108

km 131.1
Mae La Noi mkt
fuel
H1266 ––→ Mae La Oop (Map 18)
Tung Ruang Tong
km 131.6
km 137.5
Mae Tia
km 143.2

H108

Mae Sariang
H1194
Mae Saam Laep ←
(Map 19)
• fuel

H105
km 161.0
H108 → Hot & Chiang Mai

Mae Salid &
Mae Sot (Map 20)

N
├ E

KHUN YUAM – MAE LA NOI – MAE SARIANG

2002 © JUNGLE BOOKS

MAP 18

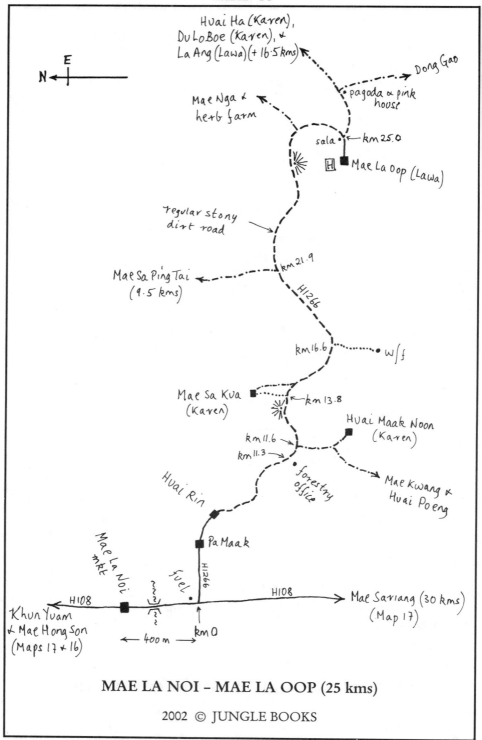

Huai Ha (Karen),
DuLoBoe (Karen), &
La Ang (Lawa) (+ 16.5 kms)

Dong Gao

pagoda & pink house

N ← E

Mae Nga & herb farm

sala ← km 25.0

H   Mae La Oop (Lawa)

regular stony dirt road

km 21.9

Mae Sa Ping Tai
(9.5 kms)

H1266

km 16.6   w/f

Mae Sa Kua
(Karen)   ← km 13.8

Huai Maak Noon
(Karen)

km 11.6
km 11.3

Huai Rin

forestry office

Mae Kwang &
Huai Po eng

Mae La Noi mkt

fuel

Pa Maak

H1266

H108   H108   Mae Sariang (30 kms)
                                                (Map 17)

Khun Yuam
& Mae Hong Son
(Maps 17 & 16)

← 400 m →   km 0

MAE LA NOI – MAE LA OOP (25 kms)

2002 © JUNGLE BOOKS

MAP 19

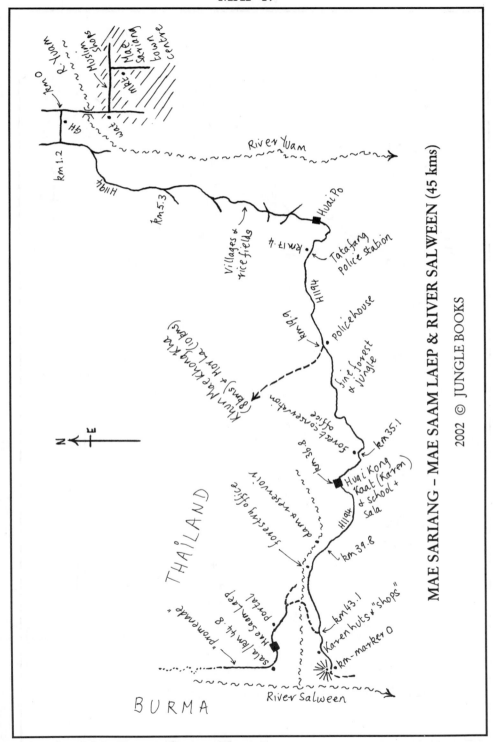

MAE SARIANG – MAE SAAM LAEP & RIVER SALWEEN (45 kms)

2002 © JUNGLE BOOKS

MAP 20

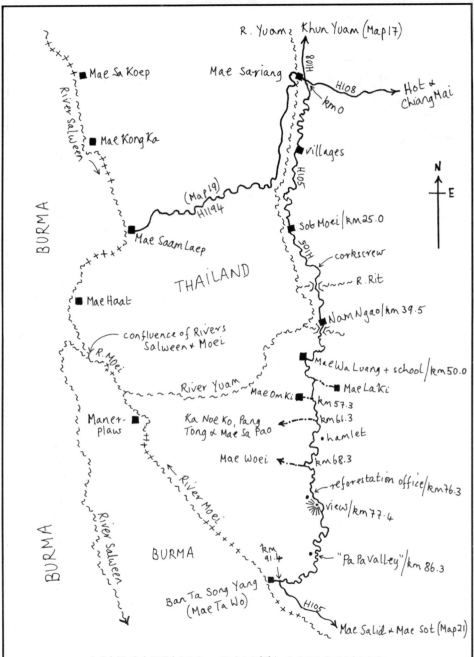

R. Yuam Khun Yuam (Map 17)

Mae Sa Koep

Mae Sariang

River Salween

H108 → Hot & Chiang Mai

km 0

Mae Kong Ka

villages

BURMA

(Map 19)

H1194

Mae Saam Laep

Sob Moei / km 25.0

THAILAND

corkscrew

R. Rit

Mae Haat

Nam Ngao / km 39.5

confluence of Rivers
Salween + Moei

R. Moei

Mae Wa Luang + school / km 50.0

Mae La Ki

River Yuam

Mae Om Ki

km 57.3

Maner-
plaw

Ka Noe Ko, Pang
Tong & Mae Sa Pao

km 61.3

hamlet

Mae Woei

km 68.3

River Moei

reforestation office / km 76.3

view / km 77.4

BURMA

River Salween

BURMA

km
91.4

"Pa Pa Valley" / km 86.3

Ban Ta Song Yang
(Mae Ta Wo)

H105

Mae Salid & Mae Sot (Map 21)

MAE SARIANG – BAN TA SONG YANG

via Mae Saam Laep & Manerplaw or via H105 & Nam Ngao

2002 © JUNGLE BOOKS

MAP 21

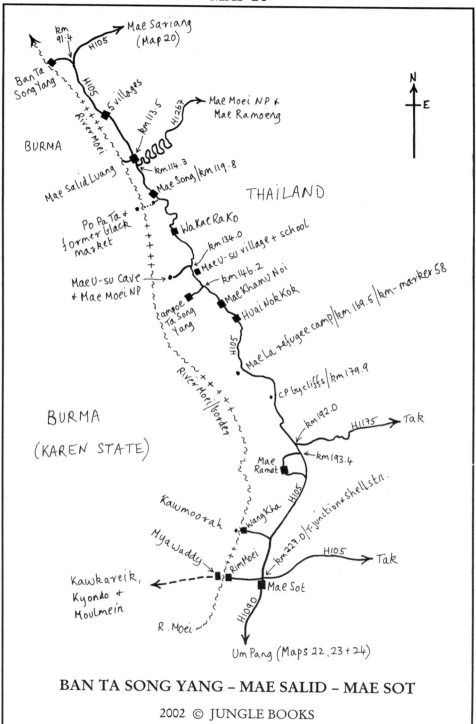

km 91.4
H105
Mae Sariang
(Map 20)
Ban Ta
Song Yang
H105
5 villages
km 113.5
H1267
Mae Moei NP &
Mae Ramoeng
River Moei
BURMA
km 114.3
Mae Salid Luang
Mae Song / km 119.8
THAILAND
Po Pa Ta &
former black
market
Wa Kae Ra Ko
km 134.0
Mae U-su village + school
Mae U-su Cave
+ Mae Moei NP
km 146.2
Mae Khamu Noi
Ampoe
Ta Song
Yang
Huai Nok Kok
Mae La refugee camp / km 169.5 / km-marker 58
H105
River Moei / border
CP by cliffs / km 179.9
BURMA
(KAREN STATE)
km 192.0
H1175
Tak
km 193.4
Mae
Ramat
H105
Kawmoorah
Wang Kha
km 227.0 / T-junction + shell stn.
Myawaddy
Rim Moei
H105
Tak
Kawkareik,
Kyondo +
Moulmein
Mae Sot
H1090
R. Moei
Um Pang (Maps 22, 23 + 24)

BAN TA SONG YANG – MAE SALID – MAE SOT

2002 © JUNGLE BOOKS

MAP 22

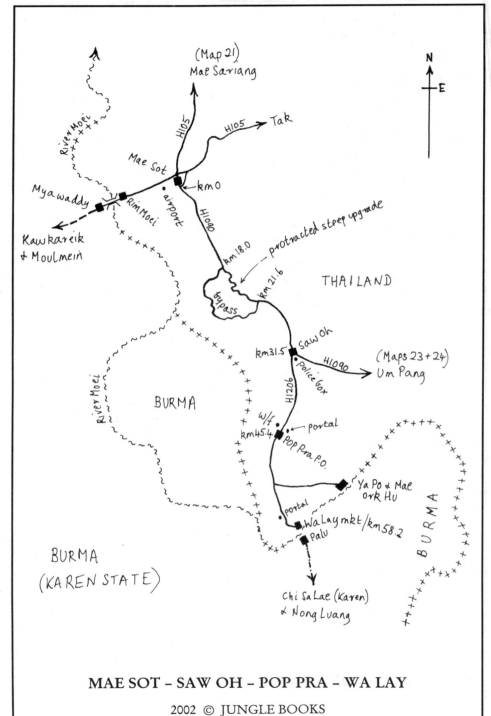

MAE SOT – SAW OH – POP PRA – WA LAY

2002 © JUNGLE BOOKS

MAP 23

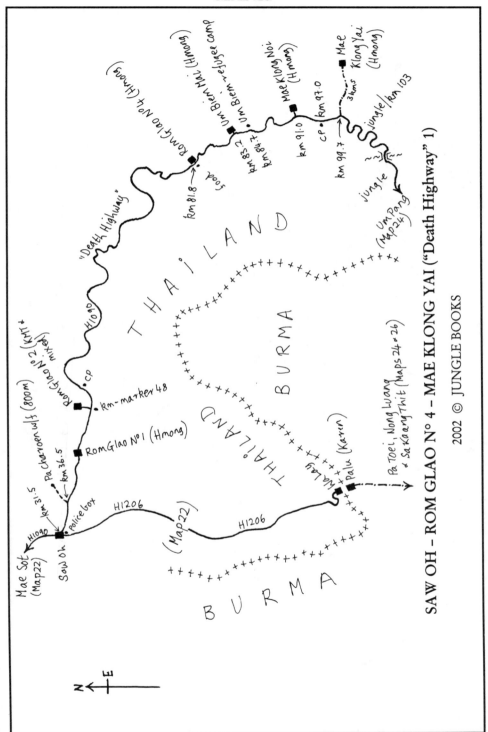

SAW OH – ROM GLAO N° 4 – MAE KLONG YAI ("Death Highway" 1)

2002 © JUNGLE BOOKS

MAP 24

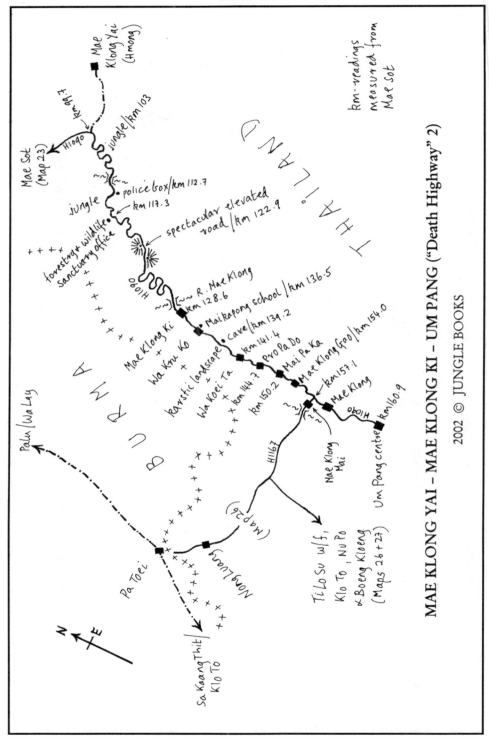

MAE KLONG YAI – MAE KLONG KI – UM PANG ("Death Highway" 2)

2002 © JUNGLE BOOKS

MAP 25

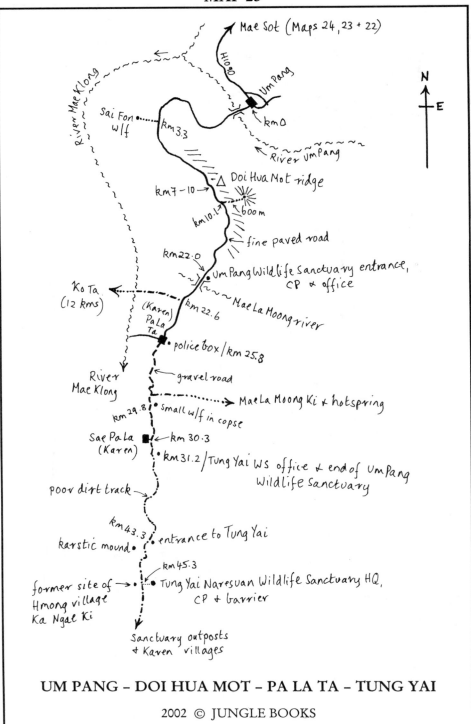

UM PANG – DOI HUA MOT – PA LA TA – TUNG YAI

2002 © JUNGLE BOOKS

MAP 26

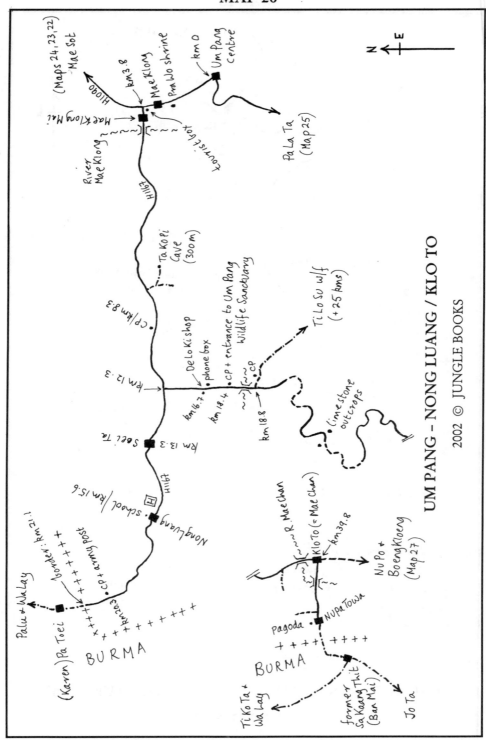

UM PANG – NONG LUANG / KLO TO

2002 © JUNGLE BOOKS

MAP 27

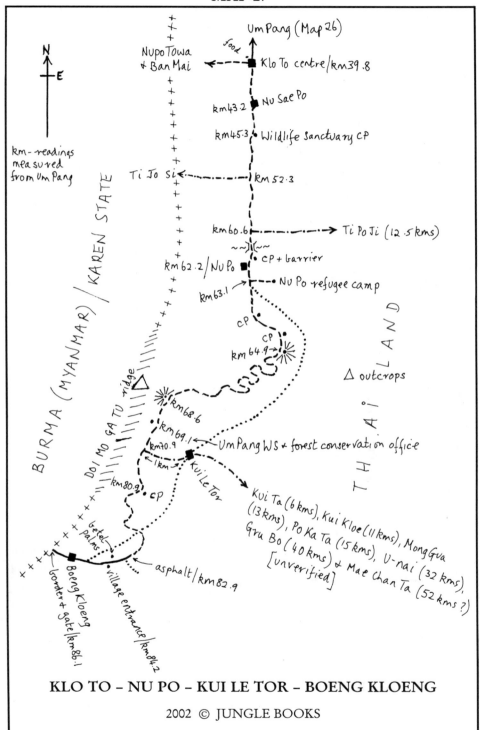

N
E

Um Pang (Map 26)

NupoTowa
& Ban Mai

food

Klo To centre/km 39.8

km 43.2 Nu Sae Po

km 45.3 Wildlife Sanctuary CP

km-readings
measured
from Um Pang

Ti Jo Si ← km 52.3

km 60.6 Ti Po Ji (12.5 kms)

CP + barrier

km 62.2/Nu Po

km 63.1 Nu Po refugee camp

CP

CP

km 64.9

△ outcrops

km 68.6

km 69.1

km 70.9 Um Pang WS & forest conservation office

1 km

km 80.9 CP

Kui Le Tor

Kui Ta (6 kms), Kui Kloe (11 kms), Mong Gua
(13 kms), Po Ka Ta (15 kms), U-nai (32 kms),
Gru Bo (40 kms) & Mae Chan Ta (52 kms?)
[unverified]

betel
palms

asphalt/km 82.9

village entrance/km 84.2

Boeng Kloeng
border & gate/km 86.1

BURMA (MYANMAR) / KAREN STATE

DOI MO GA TU ridge

T H A I L A N D

KLO TO – NU PO – KUI LE TOR – BOENG KLOENG

2002 © JUNGLE BOOKS

MAP 28

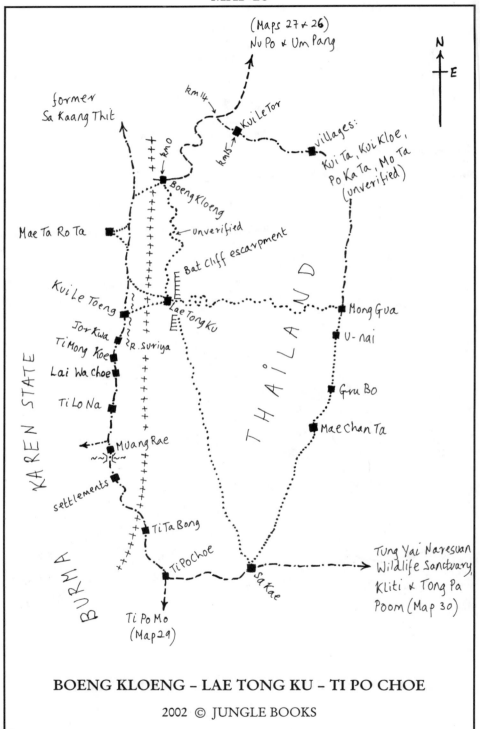

(Maps 27 & 26)
Nu Po & Um Pang

N
E

former
Sa Kaang Thit

km 14

Kui Le Tor

km 0

km 15

villages:
Kui Ta, Kui Kloe,
Po Ka Ta, Mo Ta
(unverified)

Boeng Kloeng

unverified

Mae Ta Ro Ta

Bat cliff escarpment

Kui Le Toeng

Lae Tong Ku

Mong Gua

Jor Kwa

R. Suriya

U-nai

Ti Mong Koe

Lai Wa Choe

Gru Bo

Ti Lo Na

Mae Chan Ta

THAILAND

Muang Rae

KAREN STATE

settlements

Ti Ta Bong

Ti Po Choe

Tung Yai Naresuan
Wildlife Sanctuary,
Kliti & Tong Pa
Poom (Map 30)

Sa Kae

BURMA

Ti Po Mo
(Map 29)

BOENG KLOENG – LAE TONG KU – TI PO CHOE

2002 © JUNGLE BOOKS

MAP 29

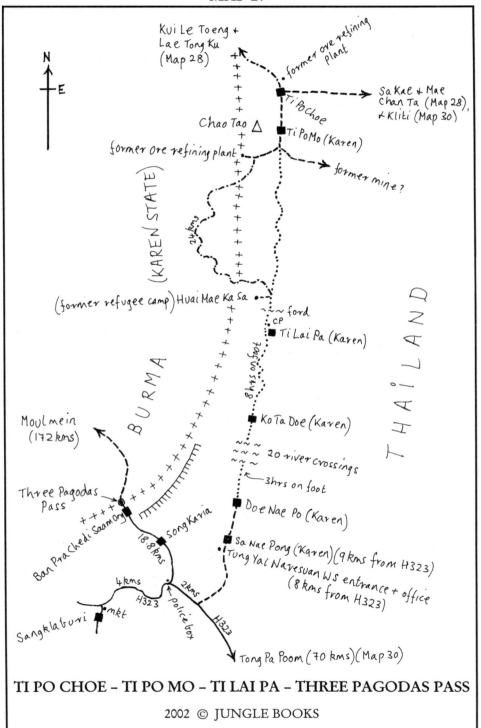

Kui Le Toeng +
Lae Tong Ku
(Map 28)

former ore refining plant

N
E

Sa Kae + Mae
Chan Ta (Map 28),
+ Kliti (Map 30)

Ti Po Choe

Chao Tao △

Ti Po Mo (Karen)

former ore refining plant

former mine?

(KAREN STATE)

24 kms

(former refugee camp) Huai Mae Ka Sa

ford
CP
Ti Lai Pa (Karen)

BURMA

8 hrs on foot

THAILAND

Ko Ta Doe (Karen)

Moulmein
(172 kms)

20 river crossings

3 hrs on foot

Three Pagodas
Pass

Doe Nae Po (Karen)

Ban Pra Chedi Saam Ong

Song Karia

Sa Nae Pong (Karen)(9 kms from H323)
Tung Yai Navesuan WS entrance + office
(8 kms from H323)

18.8 kms

4 kms

2 kms

H323

police box

H323

Sangklaburi ▪ mkt

Tong Pa Poom (70 kms)(Map 30)

TI PO CHOE – TI PO MO – TI LAI PA – THREE PAGODAS PASS

2002 © JUNGLE BOOKS

MAP 30

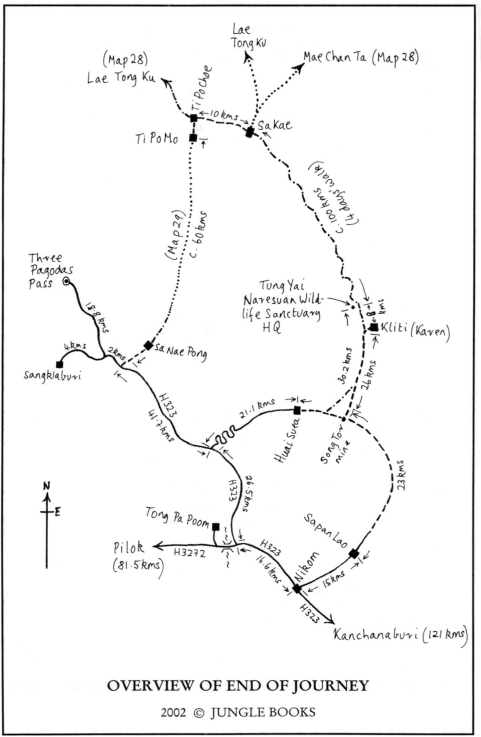

Lae Tong Ku

Mae Chan Ta (Map 28)

(Map 28)
Lae Tong Ku

Ti Pochoe

← 10 kms →

Sakae

Ti Po Mo

(Map 29) c. 60 kms

c. 100 kms (4 days' walk)

Three Pagodas Pass

18.8 kms

Tung Yai Naresuan Wild-life Sanctuary HQ

8 kms

Kliti (Karen)

4 kms

2 kms

Sa Nae Pong

30.2 kms

26 kms

Sangklaburi

H323

41.7 kms

21.1 kms

Huai Suea

Song Tor mine

23 kms

N
E

H323

26.5 kms

Tong Pa Poom

Pilok
(81.5 kms)

H3272

H323

Sapan Lao

16.6 kms

Nikom

15 kms

H323

Kanchanaburi (121 kms)

OVERVIEW OF END OF JOURNEY

2002 © JUNGLE BOOKS

GLOSSARY

This is a glossary of Thai and other non-English words
as well as acronyms and abbreviations relevant to this book

4WD: four-wheel drive
ABSDF: All Burma Students Democratic Front
ampoe (also amphoer, ampher, amphur): district, district office
anamai: health centre/personnel
anuraak: forest and wildlife conservation office/personnel
ban: (= muban) (pronounced 'barn' or 'baan') village
BPP: (= Border Patrol Police) Thai paramilitary force operating in the border areas,
    popularly known in Thai as *dorchodor*
changwat: province
chao fah: title meaning prince(ling), akin to or same as the *sawbwa* of the old Shan and
    Wa 'states' or sub-states or principalities
chao paya: title roughly equivalent to chieftain or feudal lord, the highest rank of Thai
    ancient, civil, non-royal nobility, akin to the *sawbwa* of the old Shan states
chao pra ya/praya: title of high-ranking nobleman
chao pu: a kind of title meaning 'venerated old man'
chedi: pagoda or *pratat* or stupa, a monument with a thin pointed spire, containing a
    relic of the Buddha (allegedly) or the ashes of some prominent person
chiang/chieng: city, formerly a *wiang* inhabited by senior royalty, e.g. Chiang Mai
cho fah: the projecting sculpted piece of wood at the top of a gable, often reminiscent
    of the head and part of the body of a large bird; not to be confused with *galae*
CPB: Communist Party of Burma (also BCP)
CPT: Communist Party of Thailand
DAB: Democratic Alliance of Burma, major rebel alliance
DEA: (United States) Drug Enforcement Administration, American anti-narcotics
    agency
DKBO/DKBA: Democratic Kayin (Karen) Buddhist Organization/Army
doi: mountain, Mount
dorchodor: Border Patrol Police, see BPP
farang: Caucasian foreigner, especially European, American or Australian (derived from
    farangset, a Thai attempt at 'français')
gaffae tammada: strong ordinary Thai coffee (as opposed to imported instant coffee,
    Nescafé etc.)
gai yang: grilled chicken, spatchcock
galae/galare: an ornamented V-shaped wooden decorative gable-end, mounted like
    'horns' on the peak of the roof of a building and being a typical feature of a
    northern Thai house; may have been taken over from Lawa housebuilding
grom pamai: forest protection office/personnel
hongnam: typical Thai ablution cubicle combining washing and toilet facilities, the
    water coming from a big earthenware pot or cement tank to be scooped up
    with a plastic dipper
huai: stream

Isaan (also Esarn, Isan): large area in NE Thailand, marked by Lao influence
jiin/Jiin: chin/Chin (Chinese)
Job's tear seeds: inedible small white seeds grown locally in northern Thailand, easily
     strung and used in hill-tribe costume decoration
ka kwae yae (KKY): local militias set up by the Burmese authorities around 1963-73
     with a view to bringing rebel/private militias over to government side
kamnaan: village 'mayor', but not quite the same as headman
kao soi: tasty dish of yellow noodles served in curry soup, accompanied by a side salad
     of pickled cabbage and chopped raw shallots
kateuy: ladyboy
king ampoe: sub-district
KKY: see *ka kwe yae*
KMT: (= Kuomintang) Chinese Nationalist refugees loyal to Chiang Kai-shek, ousted
     by Mao Tse-tung's Communist revolutionaries in 1949 and forced to flee
     mainland China to Taiwan (Formosa) and also to Burma, Laos and Thailand
KNLA: Karen National Liberation Army, military arm of KNU
KNLP: Kayan New Land Party, a small but resilient armed force, founded in 1964,
     that operates along the Karenni/Shan State borders, and which has resisted
     fusion with its cousin Karen and other Karenni organizations, e.g. KNPP
KSNLF: Karenni State Nationalities Liberation Front
KNPP: Karenni National Progressive Party, founded in July 1957 and led for a long
     period by veteran Baptist Karenni Saw Maw Reh
KNU: Karen National Union, political arm of KNLA
kru (yai): (head)teacher
kwan: circle, administrative region (same as *mon ton*)
lak muang: town pillar or phallus
Lan-Na: area associated with northern Thailand. Once an autonomous Tai kingdom
     (founded 1296), it was assimilated into Thailand (Siam) in the late 19th
     century. The kingdom (actually a conglomerate of semi-autonomous mini-
     kingdoms or principalities) used to include Chiang Mai, Chiang Rai, Chiang
     Saen, Lampoon and Lampang, was allied with Payao, and during Lan-Na's
     'Golden Age' (1400-1525 and especially in the second half of 15th century)
     expanded to incorporate Nan and Prae, later also including Mae Hong Son.
     At times it spilled out to incorporate territories in present-day Laos and
     Burma. Comparable kingdoms surrounding Lan-Na have been Ayuttaya,
     Sukothai, Lan Chang, Nan Chao and Sipsong Pan-Na
Lao: adjectival form of Laos (in preference to Laotian, which is derived from French),
     pertaining to Laos or to a person from Laos, e.g. the Thai-*Lao* border, the *Lao*
     army etc.; this term, not Laotian, is used by Thais and people from Laos
Lao: used sometimes loosely to describe someone from or the dialect of northern
     Thailand. The various Tai groups who have resettled in northern Thailand
     (Lan-Na) from Laos and who are collectively referred to as 'Lao' are more
     properly Tai Puan and Tai Nuea
lao: spirit, alcohol or 'whisky'
lao kao (= white spirit): rice whisky, schnapps, made from rice and palm sugar
LID: Light Infantry Division
li kae: traditional Thai costumed burlesque theatrical performance, folk dance-drama
loe-si (lü-si, lur-si, lercy): the leader of the Karen Telakhon cult in Lae Tong Ku village.
     Thai vernacular word derived from the Sanskrit *rishi* and used to refer to the
     rishi of Lae Tong Ku; see *rishi*
longyi (soft 'g'): Burmese wrap-around skirt (not joined into a tube) worn by men and
     women, sarong

Lua: an ancient Mon-Khmer people of Austro-Asiatic stock, called by Thais 'Htin'. In Thailand resident in Nan province near Lao border. More or less closely related to the Lawa and the Wa. Thais sometimes loosely refer to all the ancient Mon-Khmer peoples of Thailand and the wider region as 'Lua', especially to the Lua/Htin, Lawa and Wa

mae: (short for *maenam*) river

mai dai: can't, not possible

mai mi: don't have

mai ru: don't know

miang: tree perhaps related to the coca tree, with leaves producing a species of wild tea leaf, chewed by peasants often in small balls rather as sailors chew their quids of tobacco; wild tea or the tea-leaf mixture made from these leaves

moeng: a wide flat valley up on the Shan plateau

mon ton: 'circle', an administrative entity in old Siam higher than a province (see Chapter 5, Footnote 1 for more information)

Mrabri/Mlabri: nomadic 'Stone Age' hunter-gatherer tribe belonging to Mon-Khmer group of peoples, which lives in tiny numbers in Nan province, called by Thais *pi tong luang* (= spirits of the yellow leaves)

MTA: Mong Tai Army (= Army of the Tai [Shan] Land), private army of former warlord and opium baron Khun Sa

mu/moo: section of a village, ward

muang/meuang: Lao-Thai city state, principality, district, fiefdom; several villages with a *wiang* or *chiang*, bordered by hills and beyond which is another *muang*

naga (*naak* in modern Thai): snakelike river dragon

nakrong ying: restaurant singing girl, quasi prostitute (*nakrong chai*: male singer)

nam: river, also water

nam tok: waterfall

NCGUB: National Coalition Government of the Union of Burma, Washington-based Burmese government in exile

NDF: National Democratic Front, major alliance of a dozen ethnic insurgent groups in Burma, formerly based in KNLA GHQ, Manerplaw

ngaan ledu nao: winter fair

NLD: National League for Democracy, Suu Kyi's democratic opposition movement in Burma

NMSP/NMSA: New Mon State Party/Army

oliang: traditional cold or iced Thai drink made with ordinary coffee

pak dong/pakkad dong: spicy pickled cabbage condiment, as often found in KMT Chinese villages (in Chinese something like *yeng chi* or *yen tsai*)

Pali: the ancient sacred language of Theravada Buddhism, understood today mostly only by monks

pamai: (= *grom pamai*) forestry office/personnel

pa sin: wrap-around skirt similar to Malaysian sarong or Burmese *longyi*, but always joined at the ends into a tube, tube skirt

pat thai: meal/snack of rice noodle fried with beansprouts, egg, diced tofu, preserved shredded turnip, dried shrimps, crumbled peanuts etc., and served with raw green side salad

paya: king, lord, leader, chief

Payap/Payab: one of the two *mon ton* or 'circles' into which Lan-Na (northern Thailand) used to be divided (more details at Chapter 5, Footnote 1)

pi tong luang: Spirits of the Yellow Leaves – 'Stone Age' hunter-gatherer Mrabri people from Nan province, NNE Thailand

PLAT: People's Liberation Army of Thailand, military arm of CPT poi sang long: Shan name (in Thai *buat naak* or *buat luuk kaew*) for festival during which boys are ordained to become novice monks. *Poi sang long* is celebrated particularly dramatically and colourfully at Mae Hong Son town and at Wat Wiang Fah In near Piang Luang

po luang: dialect word for *pu yai*, headman

prasat/prasart: monument

pratat/phrathat: grand pagoda or *chedi*

pra ya/praya: title of nobility between lower-ranking *pra* and higher-ranking *chao pra ya*

pu chaik: a title for the rishi or *loe-si* of the Telakhon cultist village of Lae Tong Ku

pu yai (baan): (village) headman

raat na/laat na: dish of fried meat, greens and wide noodles in 'gravy'

rai: area of land comprising approximately 1600 sq metres (40 x 40 m)

rishi: Indian hermit-ascetic sage of early Vedic times. In this book refers to the spiritual leader or *pu chaik*, meanwhile endowed with magical knowledge and supernatural powers, of the Telakhon (Talarku, Lagu) Karen sect, found in Lae Tong Ku and associated villages. 'Rishi', originally a Sanskrit word, has been corrupted by Thais and others via the intermediate stages of *roe-si* or *rü-si* into the vernacular *loe-si* or *lü-si*

sala: open-sided waiting hut, shelter or pavilion usually at roadside, typically on a junction; formerly a kind of lodging or rest house where journeying officials, travellers etc. could stay

samlor: (= three wheels) a three wheeler or tricycle, either pedal-powered (pedicab or trishaw) or motorized (*tuk-tuk*)

sanuk (sanook): fun

sawbwa (*chao fah*): traditional feudal lord or princeling in former Shan states

silor: (= four wheels) four-wheeler, open-sided public-transport pick-up, share-taxi

Sipsong Pan-Na: (= twelve thousand paddy fields) former kingdom of Tai peoples at the source of the Mae Khong river in southern China, Yunnan province

SLORC: State Law and Order Restoration Council, replaced November 1997 by another illegal Burmese governing military body, equally euphemistically named the SPDC or State Peace and Development Council

sob/sop: (= meet, come upon) confluence (in context of rivers)

soi: side road, lane, alleyway

somtam: spicy salad (also popularly known as *papaya pok-pok*) of grated green papaya, tomato, raw green beans, lemon juice, dried shrimps and sometimes little crabs, peanuts, fish sauce, shrimp paste, palm sugar, chilli peppers and other ingredients, stamped together ('pok-pok') in a mortar

songkraan: religious festival to mark the Thai new year, held in the hot season and now associated with a lot of gratuitous water-throwing

songtaew: (= two benches) a small public means of transport with two rows of seats in the back, also known as a *silor*

SPDC: State Peace and Development Council (since November 1997 successor to the SLORC), new name for the Burmese junta in Rangoon

SSA: Shan State Army

stupa: *chedi*, shrine

SUA: Shan United Army, former name of warlord Khun Sa's MTA

SURA: Shan United Revolutionary Army, name of warlord Mo Heng's force before it became TRC, later MTA

tahaan praan: crack Thai military force, the rangers who wear the black uniform

tai/Tai: pertaining to/someone belonging to one of the many sub-groups of the ethnic Tai family of peoples. Today the Tai linguistic group can be found spread throughout the South-East Asian mainland from as far west as Assam in India to as far south as the Malay peninsula. The group is marked by a strong overall cultural identity, shown e.g. in its housebuilding style or in its textiles, and includes among other sub-groups: the Tai Siam (Noi), Tai Yuan (Lan-Na Tai), Tai Yai (Shan), Tai Lao, Tai Lue, Tai Daeng, Tai Dam, Tai Nuea, Tai Puan, Tai Kao, Tai Chuang, Tai Toh, Tai Nung, Tai Muai, Tai Muong and Pu Tai

Tai Noi: (= little Tai in contrast to the Shan Tai Yai) the Siamese Thais of modern Thailand

Tai Siam: Siamese Tai of central Thailand, sometimes also called Tai Noi or 'little Tai' in contrast to the Tai Yai (Shan) or 'big Tai'

Tai Yai: (= big Tai) Shan, also known as Tai Ngieo

Tai Yuan: the ethnic Tai sub-group now living especially in northern Thailand or Lan-Na, also known as Lan-Na Tai or Lannatai

tam (tham): cave

tambon: administrative sub-division below *ampoe*, precinct

tanaka/thanaka: a paste made from the bark of the *tanaka* tree, which is ground and mixed with water. Especially Shan, Karen and Burmese women and children smear the paste on their faces to condition their skins, enhance their complexions, block out the sun, and generally cosmeticize themselves. They often apply *tanaka* to form white or gold discs, one on each cheek, or smear the paste all over their faces, etching a design with a comb or the fingernails

tanon/thanon: road, street

tatmadaw: name commonly given to the Burma army, dates back to 1964

Thai: citizen of modern Thailand

tom yam goong/gai: fiery sour soup made with mushrooms, lemongrass, kaffir lime leaves, chillies and variously prawns/chicken

TRA: Tailand Revolutionary Army, formerly SURA and later MTA, Mo Heng's force, which amalgamated with Khun Sa's SUA

TRC: Tailand Revolutionary Council, political wing of TRA

tuk-tuk: motorized *samlor* or tricycle, half-car half-motorcycle, so called because of the sound of its engine

tung/toong: long thin banner of woven material presented to a *wat* for votive purposes

UWSA: United Wa State Army of the Wa Daeng ('Red' Wa)

viharn: see *wihaan*

wai: traditional Buddhist greeting, palms of hands pressed together below the chin

wat: monastery-temple

wat pratat: monastery-temple with a grand pagoda or *chedi*

wiang/wieng: 'town' or important village once fortified with ramparts and a moat, e.g. Wiang Haeng

wihaan/wiharn/viharn: the building in a temple complex housing the Buddha figures

WNA: Wa National Army, Maha San's force

WNC: Wa National Council, a Wa faction formerly under Ai Siao-su (and also his wife Li Ching), predecessor of the UWSA

WNO: Wa National Organization, political wing of WNA, affiliated to NDF

yaam: smallish, thin, square, shoulder bag or sling-bag, made of handwoven cloth and hung from the shoulder, used by the hill tribes, especially the Karen

yaku: Shan sweetmeat made of sticky rice, sugar cane, coconut and peanut

Yang: Thai name for the Karen people, also Kaliang/Kariang

Yellow Leaves = *pi tong luang* or Mrabri people

ying tong: bamboo water pipe, also called a *bong*

SELECT BIBLIOGRAPHY

Amnesty International: *Myanmar: 'No Law at All': Human Rights Violations Under Military Rule*, London, 1992

Asiaweek: "Myanmar. The Fall of Manerplaw: The Karens Are in Disarray as SLORC Scores Big" in *Asiaweek*, 17 February 1995, pp. 31-32

"The Fall of Manerplaw" in *Asiaweek*, 17 February 1995, p. 81

Ball, Desmond: *Burma's Military Secrets. Signals Intelligence (SIGINT) from 1941 to Cyber Warfare*, Bangkok (White Lotus Press), 1998

Belanger, Francis W.: *Drugs, the US and Khun Sa*, Bangkok (DK Books), 1989

Border, Jake: "Battle at Three Pagodas Pass: Burmese Attack Mon Army" in *Soldier of Fortune*, August 1987, pp. 38-45, 77-78

Boucaud, André & Louis: *Burma's Golden Triangle. On the Trail of the Opium Warlords*, Bangkok (Asia Books), 1992

Chaturabhand, Preecha: *People of the Hills*, Bangkok (DK), 1987

Condominas, Georges: "Notes sur l'histoire Lawa. A propos d'un lieu-dit Lua' (lawa) en pays Karen (Amphoe Chom Thong, Changwat Chiang Mai)" in *Art and Archaeology in Thailand*, Bangkok (Fine Arts Department), 1974, pp. 46-64

Davies, John R.: *A Trekker's Guide to the Hill Tribes of Northern Thailand*, Salisbury (Footloose Books), 2nd edition, 1990

Dickinson, Don: "Burma. Betrayed and Beaten in Battle: Karens on the Ropes after Fall of Manerplaw" in *Soldier of Fortune*, July 1995, pp. 48-51, 73-75

Diran, Richard K.: *The Vanishing Tribes of Burma*, London (Weidenfeld & Nicolson), 1997 [magnificent book, useful bibliography]

Enriques, Major C.M.: *Races of Burma* (Handbook for the Indian Army), Delhi, 2nd edition, 1933

Evers, Cornelis B.: *Death Railway*, Bangkok (Craftsman Press), 1993

Falla, Jonathan: *True Love and Bartholomew. Rebels on the Burmese Border*, Cambridge (Cambridge University Press), 1991 [bibliography has many entries for the Karen]

Forbes, Andrew & Henley, David: *The Haw: Traders of the Golden Triangle*, Bangkok (Teak House Books), 1997

Forsyth, Tim: "Refugees and Freaks: Plight of the Long Neck People" in *Bangkok Post*, 9 November 1991 (Vol. XLVI, No. 313), Section 3, pp. 21 & 23

Fredholm, Michael: *Burma: Ethnicity and Insurgency*, Westport, Connecticut (Praeger Publishers), 1993

Golish, Vitold de: *Au pays des femmes girafes*, Grenoble (Arthaud), 1958

Guillon, Emmanuel (translated & edited by James V. Di Crocco): *The Mons: A Civilization of Southeast Asia*, Bangkok (White Lotus Press), 1999

Hallett, Holt S.: *A Thousand Miles on an Elephant in the Shan States*, Edinburgh and London, 1890 (reprinted White Lotus Press, Bangkok, 1988 and more recently)

Halliday, Robert: *The Mons of Burma and Thailand*, two vols, Bangkok, 2000. Vol. 1: "The Talaings" (White Lotus Press reprint of 1917 monograph); Vol. 2 (ed. Christian Bauer): "Selected Articles" (White Lotus Press reprint of articles from 1923)

Halliday, Robert: "Immigration of the Mons into Siam" in *Journal of the Siam Society*, Vol. 10, Part 3 (1913), pp. 1-15

"The Mons in Siam" in *Journal of the Burma Research Society*, Vol. 12 (1922), pp. 69-79

Hamilton, J.W.: *Pwo Karen: At the Edge of Mountain and Plain*, St Paul, Minnesota (West Publications), 1976

Hanson, Kurt: "Calamity at Kawmura: Last Karen Stronghold Slashed by SLORC" in *Soldier of Fortune*, September 1995 (Vol. 20, No. 9), pp. 36-37, 70-73

Holloday, J.S. & Bevan, T.W.: "The Lawa of Umphai and Middle Mae Ping" in *Journal of the Siam Society*, Vol. 32, Part 1 (1940)

Howard, Michael C.: *Textiles of the Hill Tribes of Burma*, Bangkok (White Lotus Press), 1999

Hutchison, E.W. & Seidenfaden, E.: "The Lawa in Northern Siam" in *Journal of the Siam Society*, Vol. 27, Part 2 (1935), pp. 153-182

Kaplan, David E.: *Fires of the Dragon: Politics, Murder and the Kuomintang*, New York (Atheneum), 1992

Karen Human Rights Group: *Inside the DKBA*, KHRG (Karen Human Rights Group) No. 96/14, 31 March 1996

DKBA/SLORC Cross-Border Attacks, KHRG No. 96/31, 1 August 1996

Attacks on Karen Refugee Camps, KHRG No. 97/05, 18 March 1997

Kaufmann, H.E.: "Some Social and Religious Institutions of the Lawa (NW Thailand)" in *Journal of the Siam Society*, Vol. 60, Part 2 (1972), pp. 237-306

Keyes, Charles F. (ed.): *Ethnic Adaptation and Identity: The Karens on the Thai Frontier with Burma*, Philadelphia (Institute for the Study of Human Issues), 1979

Khun Sa, *His Own Story and His Thoughts* (undated MTA propaganda)

Kuhn, Isobel: *Ascent to the Tribes: Pioneering in Northern Thailand*, London (Overseas Missionary Fellowship), 1958

Kunstadter, Peter: *Research on the Lua and Skaw Karen Hill People of Northern Thailand, With Some Practical Implications*, Bangkok, 1964

　　The Lua (Lawa) of Northern Thailand: Aspects of Social Structure, Agriculture and Religion, Center of International Studies Research Monograph No. 21, Princeton University, 1965

　　"Living with the Gentle Lua" in *National Geographic Magazine*, 130, No. 1 (1966), pp. 122-152

　　"Animism, Buddhism and Christianity: Religion in the Life of Lua People of Pa Pae, North-Western Thailand" in *Highlanders of Thailand*, ed. John McKinnon & Wanat Bhruksasri, Kuala Lumpur (Oxford University Press), 1983

Lebar, F. M. et al.: *Ethnic Groups of Mainland South-East Asia*, Human Relations Files Inc., New Haven, 1964

LeMay, Reginald: *An Asian Arcady – The Land and Peoples of Northern Siam*, Cambridge, 1926 (reprinted White Lotus Press, Bangkok, 1999)

Lewis, Norman: *A Dragon Apparent: Travels in Cambodia, Laos and Vietnam*, London (Eland Books reprint), 1987

　　Golden Earth: Travels in Burma, London (Eland Books reprint), 1991

Lewis, Paul & Elaine: *Peoples of the Golden Triangle*, London (Thames & Hudson), 1984

Lintner, Bertil: *Outrage*, Hong Kong (Review Publishing), 1989

　　Land of Jade. A Journey Through Insurgent Burma, Edinburgh & Bangkok (Kiscadale & White Lotus Press), 1990

　　Aung San Suu Kyi and Burma's Unfinished Renaissance, Bangkok (White Lotus Press), 1991

　　Burma in Revolt, Opium and Insurgency Since 1948, Westview Press, 1994

　　"Burma. Loss and Exile: Manerplaw's Fall Could End Karen Rebellion" in *Far Eastern Economic Review*, 16 February 1995, p. 23

Lowis, C.C.: *The Tribes of Burma*, Rangoon (Superintendent of Government Printing), 1919

MacDonald, Martin: *Kawthoolei Dreams, Malaria Nights. Burma's Civil War*, Bangkok (White Lotus Press), 1999

Marshall, Rev. Harry Ignatius: *The Karen Peoples of Burma. A Study in Anthropology and Ethnology*, Columbus (Ohio University Press), 1922 (reprinted by White Lotus Press, Bangkok, 1997)

McCarthy, James: *Surveying and Exploring in Siam*, London (John Murray), 1900 (reprinted White Lotus Press, Bangkok, 1994)

McCoy, Alfred: *The Politics of Heroin in South-East Asia*, New York (Harper & Row), 1972

McGilvary, D.: *A Half-Century Among the Siamese and the Lao*, New York, 1912

McKinnon, John & Bhruksasri, W. (eds.): *Highlanders of Thailand*, Kuala Lumpur (Oxford University Press), 1986

McKinnon, J. & Vienne, B.: *Hill Tribes Today*, Bangkok (White Lotus Press), 1989

Mirante, Edith T.: *Burmese Looking Glass: A Human Rights Adventure and a Jungle Revolution*, New York (Grove Press), 1993

Naing, U. Min (transl. Thant, Hpone): *National Ethnic Groups of Myanmar*, Rangoon, 2000 [purportedly covers 129 out of 135 tribes]

Nimmanhaeminda, Kraisri: "The Lawa Guardian Spirits of Chiang Mai" in *Journal of the Siam Society*, Vol. 55, Part 2 (1967)

Penth, Hans: *A Brief History of Lan Na. Civilizations of North Thailand*, Chiang Mai, 1994

Pragadwootisan, Kanchana: *History of Doi Mae Salong – Ban Santikiri*, Chiang Mai (Siamrat), 1992 [in Thai]

The 93rd Regiment of the Former Nationalist Army in Doi Pa Taang, Chiang Mai (Siamrat), 1994 [in Thai]

Renard, Ronald D.: *The Burmese Connection: Illegal Drugs and the Making of the Golden Triangle*, Boulder & London (Lynne Rienner Publishers), 1996

Schliesinger, Joachim: *Ethnic Groups of Thailand: Non-Tai-Speaking Peoples*, Bangkok (White Lotus Press), 2000 [describes 38 non-Tai peoples resident in Thailand, including the Padaung, Kayaw, Mon, Lawa, Palaung, Pa-O, Kachin, Lamet, Pwo Karen, Bru etc.; contains an extensive bibliography]

Scott, James George & Hardiman, J.P.: *Gazetteer of Upper Burma and the Shan States*, Rangoon (Superintendent of Government Printing and Stationery), 5 vols., 1900-01 [delineates the different ethnolinguistic groups in the area covered, including brief descriptions of the costumes of many of the groups. It was the basic ethnic/geo-

graphical handbook for government officers posted to Burma, and is still a
starting point for ethnic studies today]

Scott, James George: *Burma: A Handbook of Practical Information*, London (Alexander
Moring), 1911 [= revised version of the *Gazetteer* and once the standard reference
work on Burma]

"The Wa or Lawa: Head-Hunters" in *Burma and Beyond*, London (Grayson &
Grayson), 1935

Smith, Martin: *Burma. Insurgency and the Politics of Ethnicity*, London & New Jersey (Zed
Books), 2nd impression, 1993

Smithies, M. (ed.): *The Mons*, Bangkok (The Siam Society), 1986

Smyth, H. Warington: *Five Years in Siam. From 1891 to 1896*, London, 1897 (2 vols)
(reprinted 1994, White Lotus Press, Bangkok)

Spies, John: "Piecing Together the Past", article in *Sawasdee* Thai Air magazine, January
issue, 2001, p. 44f

Stern, Theodore: "Ariya and the Golden Book: A Millenarian Buddhist Sect Among the
Karen" in *Journal of Asian Studies*, 27 (2), 1968, pp. 297-328

Tettoni, Luca I.: *Introduction to Chiang Mai and Northern Thailand*, Hong Kong (The Guidebook Company Limited), 1992

Tribal Research Institute: *The Hill Tribes of Thailand*, Technical Service Club, Chiang Mai
University, 4th edition, 1995

Tucker, Shelby: *Among Insurgents: Walking Through Burma*, London (Radcliffe Press), 2000

Burma: The Curse of Independence, London (Pluto Press), 2001

Unkovich, David: *The Mae Hong Son Loop. Northern Thailand*, Grafton (Compustyle Publications), 1991

A Pocket Guide for Motorcycle Touring in Northern Thailand, Chiang Mai (Jareuk Publications), 1988

Wyatt, David K.: *Thailand: A Short History*, London (Watana Panich & Yale University
Press), 1984

Yang, Bo: *Golden Triangle: Frontier and Wilderness*, Hong Kong (Joint Publishing Co.), 1987

Young, Oliver Gordon: *The Hill Tribes of Northern Thailand*, Journal of the Siam Society
Monograph No. 1, Bangkok, May 1961 (5th edition, 1974)

Tracks of an Intruder, London (Souvenir Press), 1967

INDEX

Bold page numbers indicate main entry or entries

Some entries (e.g. Karen, KNU, KNLA, KMT, SLORC, *Tatmadaw* & Burma army) appear so frequently throughout the book that they have not been completely indexed, in which case some of the key instances are given

439

BY THE SAME AUTHOR

HINTERLANDS

SIXTEEN NEW DO-IT-YOURSELF

JUNGLE TREKS IN THAILAND'S

NAN & MAE HONG SON PROVINCES

Hard on the heels of the author's path-breaking *Trek It Yourself in Northern Thailand*, this follow-up guide profiles 16 exciting new do-it-yourself treks that independent travellers can launch in the mountains, jungle and forests of Thailand's north. The majority of the trips, which range from short easy rambles to challenging 3-day adventures, are done on foot, but many can be carried out by motorbike or bicycle, or by a combination of walking and riding.

The book focusses on two areas in northern Thailand: the undiscovered hinterlands of Nan and Mae Hong Son towns. Here, the expeditions almost all take place in the beautiful and impressive conservation zones of Nan's Doi Pu Kha National Park and Mae Hong Son's Mae Surin Waterfall National Park. The trips provide ample scope for 'Rambo' adventuring, dirt riding, camping wild in exemplary jungle, marching over remote mountain ridges, and experiencing the local hill-tribe peoples and their culture. Some hikes are suitable for more modest travellers new to trekking in Thailand.

In Nan readers can climb Doi Pu Kha, the province's highest mountain, also ascend imposing Mount Pu Wae, ride the long exhilirating northern and southern national park loops, stay at Doi Pu Kha National Park HQ, penetrate to jungle-bound River Pua Waterfall, and hike down the Thai-Lao border ridge through elevated Lua (Htin) settlements. In Mae Hong Son they can scale Doi Pui, the province's highest peak, admire Piang Fah Cliff, stay in isolated Karen settlements, and hear the cries of gibbons and great hornbills.

Hinterlands features explicit route data, 36 detailed maps, 32 pages of photos, including shots of all the guides that readers might need, an introduction reviewing equipment, food, health and security issues, accommodation, guides, transport and bike hire, and background cultural information.

JUNGLE BOOKS

"BY TRAVELLERS FOR TRAVELLERS"

ISBN 0-9527383-3-3

UK price £14.95

BY THE SAME AUTHOR

TREK IT YOURSELF
IN NORTHERN THAILAND
TWENTY-FIVE SOLO JUNGLE TREKS
ON FOOT & BY MOTORCYCLE

Want to strike out into the jungle on your own? Don't want to be taken for a costly ride by the trekking agencies shunting novice 'trekkies' around 'new', 'non-tourist', 'unvisited' areas, routes and villages, where hill-tribe women come running to sell you souvenirs? Feel yourself to be an aspiring Rambo or Tarzan with a thirst for real adventure in genuinely untrekked outreaches? Sympathetic to the ideals of solo, low-impact tourism, sensitive to the needs and feelings of tribal highlanders? Then this is the book for you – the first ever thoroughgoing guide to do-it-yourself trekking in northern Thailand.

Not for wimps or whingers, *Trek It Yourself* provides detailed accounts and 50 maps, researched over five years, of 25 treks in the provinces of Chiang Mai, Chiang Rai, Nan and Mae Hong Son that travellers can undertake themselves on foot and – where more appropriate – by motorcycle or even mountain bike. Further, it suggests how the expeditions could be shortened or lengthened, altered or combined. In fact, if all the possible variations on the two dozen featured treks are included, the book outlines up to a hundred trips. The treks are generously illustrated with 36 pages of colour and black-and-white photos.

Find out how to access and bust through dense jungle, pitch tent in cloud forest, scale Doi Pahom Pok and Doi Chiang Dao (Thailand's second- and third-highest mountains), stay in remote Lua, Pwo Karen and Lawa villages, hoof it over successive ridges in Nan's Doi Pu Kha National Park, and marvel at the upland scenery along the 'Old Elephant Trail' between Mae Hong Son and Chiang Mai. See how to hire Lua, Karen and Wa guides, and discover what equipment and food to take. It's all in this unique book, an invaluable key to tough and sweaty, but exhilirating and unforgettable adventure.

JUNGLE BOOKS
"BY TRAVELLERS FOR TRAVELLERS"

ISBN 0-9527383-2-5   UK price £14.95

BY THE SAME AUTHOR

AROUND LAN-NA

A GUIDE TO THAILAND'S NORTHERN BORDER REGION FROM CHIANG MAI TO NAN

Around Lan-Na is a narrative and cultural guide describing an arc around Thailand's north-western and north-eastern borders with Burma and Laos. Ten years in the making, the book masterfully presents the same blend of adventure travel, anecdote, personally researched route detail, and cultural-historical information that the author deployed in his acclaimed *Three Pagodas – A Journey down the Thai-Burmese Border*. Aimed at travellers graduating from the conventional guidebooks, *Around Lan-Na* maps out an exciting off-the-beaten-track border journey by public transport, by motorcycle and on foot from Chiang Mai to Nan, taking in the KMT Chinese outposts of Nong Ook and Mae Salong, the recently vacated opium warlord territories of Hin Taek and Doi Larng, Mae Sai and the "Golden Triangle", the ancient Mekong riverfront towns of Chiang Saen and Chiang Khong, the Tai Lue weaving village of Huai Khon, and a swathe of remote mountainous jungle extending down the Lao border as far as Bo Bia.

The book includes details of treks in unfrequented areas that travellers can make themselves: climbing poppy-covered Doi Chiang Dao (Thailand's third-highest mountain), in Doi Pu Kha National Park, and east of Nan town in the jungles of the Lao frontier. It contains practical tips on how to get by in difficult situations in isolated places. The second half of the book provides the first thoroughgoing exploration of the kingdom's least-known province and best-kept secret: Nan.

In this guide the culturally-minded reader can learn about the exquisite weaving of the Tai Lue people, Nan's temple murals, and the salt wells of Bo Glua. The armchair traveller can join a trailblazing jungle trek through the "Empty Quarter" guided by ex-communist guerrillas. And the student of northern Thailand can read about the history of Lan-Na, of Chiang Mai, of Chiang Saen, of the KMT and of the CPT insurgency. There are separate accounts of several minority peoples, including the KMT, Wa, Akha, Hmong, Yao, Khmu, Tai Lue, Palaung, the entropic Lua (Htin) and the vanishing "Stone Age" Mrabri ("Spirits of the Yellow Leaves"). Four hundred pages of text are complemented by 36 pages of arresting photographs and 32 maps. Together *Three Pagodas* and *Around Lan-Na* provide the independent traveller with the most comprehensive account available of Thailand's entire northern border region from the Three Pagodas Pass to Nan.

JUNGLE BOOKS

ISBN 0-9527383-1-7   UK price £14.95

NOTES

NOTES

In Thailand:
Asia Books Co. Ltd, 5, Soi 61, Sukhumvit Road, Bangkok 10110, Thailand
purchase@asiabooks-thailand.com   purchase@asiabooks.co.th
www.asiabooks.co.th

**In USA, Australia, New Zealand, Canada, South Africa
& rest of world except Thailand & UK:**
White Lotus Co. Ltd, 11/2, Soi 58, Sukhumvit Road, Bangkok 10250, Thailand
ande@loxinfo.co.th   http://thailine.com/lotus

In UK:
Jungle Books
junglebooks2000@hotmail.com   junglebooks@compuserve.com

Books by Christian Goodden are also available from:
amazon.com   and   amazon.co.uk